BROWNING: THE CRITICAL HERITAGE

THE CRITICAL HERITAGE SERIES

GENERAL EDITOR: B. C. SOUTHAM, M.A., B.LITT. (OXON.)
Formerly Department of English, Westfield College, University of London

---

Volumes in the series include

JANE AUSTEN	B. C. Southam
BROWNING	Boyd Litzinger, *St. Bonaventure University* and Donald Smalley, *University of Illinois*
BYRON	Andrew Rutherford, *University of Aberdeen*
COLERIDGE	J. R. de J. Jackson, *Victoria College, Toronto*
DICKENS	Philip Collins, *University of Leicester*
HENRY FIELDING	Ronald Paulson, *The Johns Hopkins University, Baltimore* and Thomas Lockwood, *University of Washington*
THOMAS HARDY	R. G. Cox, *University of Manchester*
HENRY JAMES	Roger Gard, *Queen Mary College, London*
JAMES JOYCE (2 vols)	Robert H. Deming, *University of Miami*
D. H. LAWRENCE	R. P. Draper, *University of Leicester*
MILTON	John T. Shawcross, *University of Wisconsin*
SCOTT	John O. Hayden, *University of California, Davis*
SWIFT	Kathleen Williams, *Rice University, Houston*
SWINBURNE	Clyde K. Hyder
TENNYSON	J. D. Jump, *University of Manchester*
THACKERAY	Geoffrey Tillotson and Donald Hawes, *Birkbeck College, London*
TROLLOPE	Donald Smalley, *University of Illinois*

BROWNING

THE CRITICAL HERITAGE

Edited by

BOYD LITZINGER

Professor of English, St. Bonaventure University

and

DONALD SMALLEY

Professor of English, University of Illinois

NEW YORK

BARNES & NOBLE, INC.

First published in Great Britain 1970
Published in the United States of America 1970
by Barnes & Noble, Inc., New York, N.Y.

© *Boyd Litzinger and Donald Smalley 1970*

SBN 389 01024 3

1. Browning, Robert - Criticism

SHP8
do.ty

Printed in Great Britain

General Editor's Preface

The reception given to a writer by his contemporaries and near-contemporaries is evidence of considerable value to the student of literature. On one side we learn a great deal about the state of criticism at large and in particular about the development of critical attitudes towards a single writer; at the same time, through private comments in letters, journals or marginalia, we gain an insight upon the tastes and literary thought of individual readers of the period. Evidence of this kind helps us to understand the writer's historical situation, the nature of his immediate reading-public, and his response to these pressures.

The separate volumes in the *Critical Heritage Series* present a record of this early criticism. Clearly, for many of the highly productive and lengthily reviewed nineteenth- and twentieth-century writers, there exists an enormous body of material; and in these cases the volume editors have made a selection of the most important views, significant for their intrinsic critical worth or for their representative quality— perhaps even registering incomprehension!

For earlier writers, notably pre-eighteenth century, the materials are much scarcer and the historical period has been extended, sometimes far beyond the writer's lifetime, in order to show the inception and growth of critical views that were initially slow to appear.

In each volume the documents are headed by an Introduction, discussing the material assembled and relating the early stages of the author's reception to what we have come to identify as the critical tradition. The volumes will make available much material which would otherwise be difficult of access, and it is hoped that the modern reader will be thereby helped towards an informed understanding of the ways in which literature has been read and judged.

B.C.S.

Contents

CONTENTS

Sordello (1840)

Pippa Passes (1841)

King Victor and King Charles (1842)

Dramatic Lyrics (1842)

The Return of the Druses (1843)

A Blot in the 'Scutcheon (1843)

CONTENTS

Dramatis Personae (1864)

The Ring and the Book (1868–9)

CONTENTS

Dramatic Idyls (1879 and 1880)

Selections from the Poetical Works of Robert Browning (1880)

Jocoseria (1883)

Ferishtah's Fancies (1884)

A Blot, Revived (1885)

Parleyings with Certain People of Importance in Their Day (1887)

Acknowledgments

It is a pleasure to acknowledge our indebtedness to those who have helped us in the preparation of this book. We are especially grateful to Mrs. Julia Demmin for her good work as our research assistant, to the University of Illinois Research Board for its generosity in granting funds to support this project, to the librarians of the University of Illinois for making fully available the remarkable resources of the Library in Victorian periodicals and in other aids for research, with particular mention of the reference librarians for their patience and skill in procuring additional materials through interlibrary loan services. Professor Walter E. Houghton, editor of *The Wellesley Index*, helped us by identifying the authors of some of the unsigned reviews and notices. Miss Mary Lou Campbell worked hard and long at preparing the typescript in its various stages.

Grateful acknowledgment is due to those who have permitted us to reprint copyrighted material: to Professor Cecil Y. Lang and the Syracuse University Press for passages from 'The Chaotic School', in *New Writings by Swinburne* (1964); to Professor Lang and the Yale University Press for a passage from *The Swinburne Letters* (1954–1962); to John Murray Publishers for the essay by Rowland Edward Prothero in the *Quarterly Review* (April 1890); to the Oxford University Press for a passage from *The Correspondence of Gerard Manley Hopkins and Richard Watson Dixon* (1955); and to Dr. Gordon N. Ray for an excerpt from Joseph Arnould's verse-epistle to Robert Browning.

Finally, we have incurred a special debt to our wives, who have shown that forbearance which authors and editors invariably require.

Preface

Browning criticism is an extremely full and fertile field. As a leading figure in Victorian literature, and as one of the most prolific poets of his time, Browning inspired a massive amount of critical commentary—much of it knowledgeable, some of it obtuse, almost all of it interesting to scholars and to students of the poet. The purpose of this book is to give the reader a clear picture of how Browning's poetry looked to his contemporaries. The selections which make up the body of this book begin with printed notices Browning received when he published his first poem, *Pauline*, in 1833; they end with a summary essay written by the novelist, Henry James, a year after Browning's death in 1889. Between the two are more than two hundred and forty samplings of critical opinion, reflecting the fluctuations of the poet's reputation. A representative selection of contemporary critical comment drawn from many sources—periodicals, newspapers, diaries, journals, letters, and biographies among them—has been compiled to achieve that purpose.

Reviewers in the nineteenth century were a leisurely lot, and the editors of most periodicals were quite generous in granting space to their contributors. A major review, as a result, might easily run to five or ten thousand words (and a surprising number ranged well beyond those limits), a good part of which might be devoted to a general survey of contemporary poetry or to the elaboration of a pet critical theory. Browning himself, indeed, once turned the assigned review of a book on Tasso into a lengthy defence of Thomas Chatterton, the eighteenth-century poet and forger. The upshot of the matter is that we have been most selective, often excerpting relatively short passages from very long articles in order to get at the heart of Browning criticism. Further, as Browning's fame grew, so multiplied the number of reviews of his work, and the need for selection intensifies after the publication of *The Ring and the Book* in 1869.

To increase the usefulness of this book, a number of editorial devices have been employed. The materials themselves have been arranged chronologically and numbered for easy cross-reference. Each item begins with a bibliographical reference which includes the critic's name (when known), the title and the date of the publication in which the criticism is to be found, and the appropriate page numbers. Headnotes are employed to provide information about the reviewer or about Browning's reaction to a particular review, when these are pertinent, and to cross-reference certain items. Footnotes are used sparingly, and then only to identify matters with which a reader might not be fully acquainted. A chronology of important dates in Browning's life and a note on the sales of Browning's poems and their introduction into the French and American markets are appended for easy reference. The Introduction shows how Browning's reputation grew and how he reacted to the critical and public reception of his poetry. Finally, for the reader who might wish to pursue these subjects further, we have selected a bibliography of the published works most useful for such a study. The following abbreviations have been used in the notes which accompany the Introduction and the texts:

DI *Dearest Isa: Robert Browning's Letters to Isabella Blagden,* ed. by Edward C. McAleer, Nelson, 1952.

LEBB *Letters of Elizabeth Barrett Browning,* ed. by F. G. Kenyon, 2 vols., Macmillan & Co., Ltd., 1897.

LRB *Letters of Robert Browning, Collected by Thomas J. Wise,* ed. by Thurman L. Hood, Murray, 1933.

NL *New Letters of Robert Browning,* ed. by William C. DeVane and Kenneth L. Knickerbocker, Murray, 1950.

RB-AD *Robert Browning and Alfred Domett,* ed. by F. G. Kenyon, Smith, Elder & Co., 1906.

RB-EBB *The Letters of Robert Browning and Elizabeth Barrett Barrett 1845–1846,* 2 vols., Smith, Elder & Co., 1899.

Introduction

APPRENTICESHIP AND OBSCURITY

'Then you inquire about my "sensitiveness to criticism",' Browning
wrote Elizabeth Barrett within the first weeks of the famous courtship,
'and I shall be glad to tell you exactly, because I have, more than once,
taken a course you might else not understand.'[1] There follows a desperately earnest and—perhaps for that reason—a fantastically contorted
paragraph in which the poet attempts to define his relationship to his
critics so far as he was able to define it on 11 February 1845. He is, he
insists, and intends to remain, quite independent of his critics, and of the
public as well. He writes his poems because it is his duty to struggle,
however ineffectually, to express the perceptions that well up inside
him. He is experiencing much trouble getting any part of his real
thought and feeling down on paper. But once he has done his best to do
so and offered his poetry to the outside world, 'the not being listened to
by one human creature would I hope, in nowise affect me'. ('A poet's
affair is with God', he was to write Ruskin ten years later in another
earnest attempt to define his position [see pp. 14ff.], 'to whom he is
accountable, and of whom is his reward; look elsewhere, and you find
misery enough.') Browning grants in his letters to Elizabeth that it
would be pleasant to be lauded by the critics as he sees some other
writers lauded from time to time. His father and his mother would then
be proud of 'this and the other "favourable critique",' and Moxon, his
publisher, might then be paying for the privilege of bringing out his
poems instead of requiring to be subsidized for printing them at all. But
Browning is determined to alter nothing to suit the critics. He can live
and write and enjoy the pleasures of his private world without their
applause or that of society. ' "It's nothing to *you*, critics, hucksters all of
you",' Browning imagines himself saying to them, ' "if I *have* this
garden and this conscience. . . ." ' He cannot understand how Keats
and Tennyson could be made to ' "go softly all their days" for a gruff
word or two' from the critics. 'Tennyson reads the *Quarterly* and does

as they bid him, with the most solemn face in the world—out goes this, in goes that, all is changed and ranged. Oh me!' 'But it does so happen', Browning asserts in this curious and tangled paragraph, 'that I have met with much more than I could have expected in this matter of kindly and prompt recognition. I never wanted a real set of good hearty praisers—and no bad reviewers—I am quite content with my share.'

It is a remarkable statement to come from a poet whose works had still, after a dozen years, to be published at his family's expense. He had defined his relation to the critics somewhat differently two years earlier in writing his friend Alfred Domett, who had by that time migrated to New Zealand: 'They take to criticising me a little more, in the Reviews —and God send I be not too proud of their abuse! For there is no hiding the fact that it is of the proper old drivelling virulence with which God's Elect have in all ages been regaled.'[2] One critic had assured a friend of Browning's that he in reality admired the poet but could not find saying so expedient in his review. 'This abhorson', Browning adds, 'boasted that he got £400 a year by his practices!' 'But', Browning writes ominously in conclusion, 'New Zealand [that is, emigration to New Zealand] is still left me!' It is unlikely that in the twenty months that had passed between his letter to Domett and his letter to Miss Barrett, Browning had learned to look upon critics unsympathetic to his work with as much equanimity as he himself wished to believe; but it is also true that from the very beginning of his career, in 1833, he had indeed received, and accepted with much gratitude, an amount of discerning approval. More than one of his friends in 1845 (including R. H. Horne, Leigh Hunt, H. F. Chorley, and Joseph Arnould) often wrote reviews; and a list of critics for the periodicals who played significant parts in Browning's life would, as will be seen in the body of this book, need to run to a considerable length. John Forster, literary critic for the *Examiner*, had had a great deal to do with Browning's experiences as a dramatist (though by 1845 Forster and Browning were, indeed, in a period of mutual hostility). Joseph Milsand, the French critic, was in the eighteen-fifties to become one of Browning's closest friends and in the sixties and beyond a frequent adviser and companion.[3] But it was still another critic, one for whom Browning continued to hold high esteem and gratitude even in the years of his late-arriving success, that had welcomed Browning's first published poem.

Well before his twentieth birthday, Browning had conceived a plan for startling the world: anonymously he would produce a play, an opera, a novel, and a poem and, when all had succeeded, disclose his authorship to an astonished world. The first and only fruit of this ambitious plan was *Pauline*, a 'confessional' poem published by Saunders and Otley in 1833. With a dozen copies of the poem, Browning sent a thinly veiled request for a favourable review to the Rev. William Johnson Fox, a family friend, whose influence extended beyond the pulpit and liberal politics into the reviews. At the time, Fox was editing the *Monthly Repository* and, within a month of the publication of *Pauline*, gave the poem the warmest praise it was to receive (No. 3). In return, a grateful Browning wrote, 'I shall never write a line without thinking of the source of my first praise.'[4] Nor did he forget, for Browning referred throughout his life to Fox as his literary god-father.

But Fox did more than give the aspiring poet a favourable review: it was he who encouraged Effingham Wilson to publish *Paracelsus*; who brought Browning to the attention of Edward Moxon, his future publisher; who brought the young poet into a larger literary circle, including the influential John Forster, who in turn helped Browning to a large and important acquaintance; who introduced Browning in the pages of the *Monthly Repository*, to which the poet contributed five poems[5] over the course of eighteen months.

The published reviews of *Pauline* (see Nos. 1–6) were, as one might have expected, mixed, but they can hardly be thought to have discouraged Browning. More influential were the unpublished comments of John Stuart Mill. Mill's copy of *Pauline*, with marginal notes for a review which was never written, was returned to Browning, who found his fictional hero-narrator of *Pauline* (and, implicitly, the poet himself) described as 'endowed with a more intense and morbid self-consciousness than I ever knew in any sane human being'. There is no evidence that Browning was crushed by the charges of self-conceit and self-consciousness, as some scholars believe,[6] but there is little question that for years to come Browning was to eschew the writing of poetry in which the voices of the *persona* and the author might readily be equated. In fact, when in 1867 Browning decided to acknowledge publicly his authorship of *Pauline*,[7] he prefaced the poem with a statement insisting that the poem had been his 'earliest attempt at "poetry always dramatic in principle, and so many utterances of so many imaginary persons, not mine"'.

In 1833, however, there was no need for public embarrassment or acknowledgment. The poem did not sell, and Browning simply withdrew the book from circulation and set about the serious work of composing *Paracelsus*, published in 1835. For the first time, Browning affixed his name to a poem, a measure of his growing confidence. *Paracelsus* was longer, more varied, yet more tightly structured than *Pauline*. It offered scope to his dramatic, narrative, and lyric powers, and, when he wrote again to Fox ('I really shall *need* your notice'),[8] it was with the hope that *Paracelsus* would establish his reputation.

The reviews of *Paracelsus* were both more numerous and more favourable than those of *Pauline*. Fox's review (No. 10) was all that Browning could wish for, and John Forster did double duty, reviewing the poem favourably in the *Examiner* (No. 9) and seven months later (after his personal acquaintance with Browning had deepened). in a lengthy article in the *New Monthly Magazine and Literary Journal* (No. 13), placing Browning among the leading young poets of the day. If *Fraser's* maintained its supercilious tone (No. 14), Browning could take real pride in a generous review by Leigh Hunt in the *London Journal* (No. 11). A pair of undistinguished sonnets (probably written by Browning's good friend Euphrasia Fanny Haworth) addressed 'To the Author of "Paracelsus"' appeared in the *New Monthly Magazine and Literary Journal*, likening his poetry to the 'green fruits of Spring Telling rich Autumn's promise';[9] and Walter Savage Landor wrote to Forster, 'When you told us that the author of Paracelsus would be a great poet, you came rather too late in the exercise of prophecy—he was one already, and will be among the greatest.' But Landor added, characteristically, 'I hope he does not relax in that sirocco of faint praise which brother poets are fond of giving.'[10] Harriet Martineau made her acquaintance with Browning's poetry in *Paracelsus*. 'It was a wonderful event to me,—my first acquaintance with his poetry.—Mr. Macready put "Paracelsus" into my hand, when I was staying at his house; and I read a canto before going to bed. For the first time in my life, I passed a whole night without sleeping a wink.' [*Harriet Martineau's Autobiography*, ed. Maria Weston Chapman (1877), I, 314.] *Paracelsus* had given her an 'unbounded expectation' for Browning's future which was later to be disappointed by *Sordello*. It was a most auspicious entry upon the public stage, and for the next ten years the title pages of his publications would read, 'By Robert Browning, Author of "Paracelsus"'. Browning's public fame had at least begun.

With the general reception of *Paracelsus*, Browning's hopes seemed on the way to fulfilment. He was already deep in the composition of *Sordello*, a poem more ambitious than anything he had yet attempted, and other avenues to fame were opening before him. On 26 May 1836, Browning made one of a party that included William Charles Macready,[11] the famous actor and stage manager, who casually suggested that Browning write him a tragedy. Within a few days Browning had put aside *Sordello* and was at work on *Strafford*, an English historical tragedy. The 'stage-bug' had bitten the poet; it was to give Browning much discomfort and no great amount of satisfaction during the next ten years.

Strafford opened at Covent Garden 1 May 1837, and was acted a total of five times. As Macready approached opening night, his faith in the play had failed utterly; the revisions he had suggested to Browning were not done to his satisfaction ('quite bad—mere feeble rant—neither power, nor nature, nor healthy fancy—very unworthy of Browning'),[12] and on 28 April he confided to his diary, 'Would it were over! It must fail—and it grieves me to think that *I am so placed.*'[13] Browning's hopes were not much higher, for he could sense that Macready's heart was not in the play. It came, therefore, as something of a surprise when the reviews proved to be generally favourable and of such a nature that Browning could blame the failure of the play upon Macready rather than upon himself. Actor-managers might be difficult to deal with, but a part of the drama-critics plainly were ready to welcome new blood to the theatre. In the heat of his anger with Macready, Browning declared that he would never write another play, and he returned to the oft-delayed composition of *Sordello*. The unexpectedly favourable reception of *Strafford*, however, encouraged Browning to try his hand further in drama. On the other side, the critical treatment of *Strafford* was not entirely pleasing to Macready, who felt strongly that Browning's self-confidence was misplaced. 'Now really', he wrote, 'this is too bad—without *great assistance* his tragedy could never have been put in a condition to be proposed for representation—without great assistance it could never have been put upon the stage.'[14]

Browning was back at the craft of playwright within a few months. He wrote *King Victor and King Charles* and *The Return of the Druses* for Macready, who turned both down and noted in his diary, '. . . with the deepest concern I yield to the belief that he will *never write again*—to any purpose. I fear', he added ominously, 'his intellect is not quite clear.'[15]

Browning's natural annoyance with Macready was tempered by his hopes for *Sordello*. He had been working at the poem off and on for seven years and, as DeVane remarked, *Sordello* probably cost Browning more time and energy than any other work he was to write, with the possible exception of *The Ring and the Book*.[16] The poem, which was published in March 1840, was the result of years of research, study, and re-writing. Browning knew that some readers would find the poem difficult, and he toyed with the idea of adding a preface and explanatory notes.[17] To Eliza Flower he wrote, 'Do me all the good you can, you and Mr. Fox',[18] and he awaited the judgment of the critics.

They responded as with one voice, burying *Sordello* under a heap of epithets—'obscure', 'trash, of the worst description', 'unreadable', and the like. The poem brought notoriety, not fame, to Browning, and it became the butt of many jokes. Nor were private judgments much more kind. On 17 June 1840, Macready recorded in his diary: 'After dinner tried—another attempt—utterly desperate—on *Sordello*; it is *not* readable.'[19] Both Douglas Jerrold and Harriet Martineau wondered, upon reading the poem, whether they had taken leave of their senses.[20] Tennyson found only the first and last lines understandable ('Whoever wills may hear Sordello's story told' and 'Whoever would has heard Sordello's story told') but added, 'And both of them are damned lies.'[21] John Sterling wrote to a friend, 'Browning requires at least some hundred years of culture to be anything but unbaked dough.'[22] Even Landor was worried, wishing Browning 'would atticize a little'. 'Few of the Athenians', he remarked, 'had such a quarry on their property, but they constructed better roads for the conveyance of the material.'[23] Years in the future, Swinburne would refer to *Sordello* as 'one of my canonical scriptures',[24] and in our century Pound would open the second of his *Cantos* with a tribute to Browning's poem, but there was little encouragement for the poet in 1840. To Fanny Haworth, Browning wrote ruefully, 'You say roses and lilies and lilac-bunches and lemon-flowers about it while everybody else pelts cabbage stump after potato-paring.'[25] To Macready, he complained in a more bitter vein: 'Tomorrow will I betimes break new ground with So and So—an epic in so many books . . . let it but do me half the good "Sordello" has done—be praised by the units, cursed by the tens, and unmeddled with by the hundreds.'[26] Browning's faith in the poem was not utterly destroyed[27] but it was indeed clear that his volume had not reached the hundreds: of the 500 copies printed, more than half still remained in the hands of the publisher in 1855. Browning did not reprint the poem until 1863 and then only after extensive revisions which show that he recognized the charge of obscurity as partly valid.

Browning returned vigorously to work. At the suggestion of Moxon, he decided to approach the public in a different way, publishing his poems and plays not in boards but in a series of inexpensive pamphlets. Extending from April 1841 to April 1846, the eight pamphlets included *Pippa Passes, King Victor and King Charles, Dramatic Lyrics, The Return of* the Druses, A Blot in the 'Scutcheon, Colombe's Birthday, Dramatic Romances and Lyrics, and Luria; and A Soul's Tragedy; the series went under the general title of Bells and Pomegranates.[28] It was, as DeVane observes, an attempt to recoup his reputation after the disaster of Sordello,[29] an attempt which met with a measure of success.

In the meantime, Browning's friends and literary supporters had not deserted him, and his first champions—Fox and Forster—did what they could in his behalf. Forster, in his review of Dramatic Lyrics (No. 41) for the Examiner, simply treated Sordello as a wrong turning in Browning's career and reaffirmed his belief that 'we shall see him reach the goal'. Landor, Leigh Hunt, Talfourd, and Carlyle all continued their private encouragement (even though Carlyle felt that Browning should give up poetry for prose, an attitude he took towards most poets). Richard Hengist Horne and John Kenyon served more practically, the former by defending even Sordello in his A New Spirit of the Age (No. 46), the latter by introducing Browning to a fellow poet, an invalid cousin named Elizabeth Barrett. Alfred Domett and Joseph Arnould, steadfast friends, expressed their support in verse. Among the satiric lines penned by Domett, we find an obtuse critic described as a 'black squat beetle' who 'Has knocked himself full-butt with blundering trouble/. Against a mountain he can neither double/Nor ever hope to scale', with the result that he must 'swear/There's no such thing as any mountain there'. Browning, in short, was not without his resources.

During the early forties Browning's letters to Domett are an index of the poet's mental state, and this index shows us a man working strenuously to restore his confidence in himself. In March 1840 he thanks Domett for his constructive criticism;[30] two years later he can insist that 'The true best of me is to come';[31] in December 1842 he remarks gratefully on Horne's 'generous' review in the Church of England Quarterly (see No. 34) and tells of receiving Arnould's verse-epistle (see No. 43).[32] The next March he reports the Arnoulds 'have been zealous as Chris. himself on my side'.[33] By 31 July 1844, he can confide to Domett, to whom he has sent Colombe's Birthday, 'I feel myself so much stronger, if flattery not deceive, that I shall stop some things that were meant to follow, and begin again. I really seem to have something fresh to say. . . . I never took so earnestly to the craft as I think I shall—or may, for these things are with God.'[34] On 23 February 1845, he offers to help Domett place articles and poetry in the reviews, 'knowing more editors, &c. than I did'.[35]

A survey of the reviews of Bells and Pomegranates shows that

Browning had good reason for his revived hopes. There was a widening appreciation of his recent poetry. Few reviewers resisted the temptation to refer to the poet's obscurity—and many persisted in commenting anew upon *Sordello*—but more and more frequently there appear references to the poet's originality, his bold imagery, and his resourceful imagination. The reviews frequently quote his poems at generous length, and the impression one brings away is of a general consensus that if Browning can manage to purge himself of 'muddiness' and 'eccentricity', he will become a poet to be reckoned with.

In sum, the few years following the disaster of *Sordello* were active ones during which Browning's confidence rose as his poetic powers continued to grow and as *Bells and Pomegranates* extended his reputation. He once more attempted stagecraft, offering *A Blot in the 'Scutcheon* to Macready and *Colombe's Birthday* to Charles Kean—but with discouraging results. *Colombe's Birthday* never reached the boards, and *A Blot in the 'Scutcheon*, presented briefly under adverse conditions, led to an open break with Macready and with Forster. The poet was cured of stage-sickness. 'The poorest Man of letters', he wrote to Christopher Dowson, '(if *really* of letters) I ever knew is of far higher talent than the best actor I ever expect to know.'[36]

In the autumn of 1844 Browning made his second trip to Italy, a leisurely one during which he stored up impressions for future poems, the results of which are apparent in some of the pieces which appeared the next year in *Dramatic Romances and Lyrics*—'Pictor Ignotus', 'The Tomb at St. Praxed's', and the two 'Home-Thoughts' lyrics among them. With his second visit to Italy, Browning's youth may be said to have come to an end and the period of his maturity to have begun; for upon his return to England, he read the newly published *Poems* of Elizabeth Barrett and, with the encouragement of her relative and his friend John Kenyon, Browning on 10 January 1845, opened the correspondence which was to change his life.

II

MATURITY AND ACHIEVEMENT

Their value as the chronicle of a famous love affair aside, the Browning-Barrett letters are a treasure of information regarding Browning's literary hopes and a record of his poetic fortunes to mid-September 1846. Herself a poet and an admirer of Browning's poetry, Elizabeth Barrett became the confidante and he the confessor. Making due allowance for the fact that Browning wanted to impress her favourably, the letters still portray an enthusiastic young man—beyond the first flush of boyish optimism, sobered by the knowledge that his attempts to win the public favour have not met with unqualified success, humble enough to accept criticism from a fellow poet (who, from a point early in the exchange of letters becomes the avowed object of his love), but still confident in his developing power and hopeful of his ultimate achievement.

One pleasant aspect of Browning's letters is the frequent expression of the gratitude he feels for his literary patrons. 'I never was', he writes, 'without good, kind, generous friends and lovers.'[37] Of Richard Hengist Horne's review (No. 34) he says, '*I* feel grateful to him . . . for his generous criticism, and glad and proud of in any way approaching such a man's standard of poetical height.'[38] John Forster, with whom by this time Browning had quarrelled, is credited with having 'rescued' *Paracelsus*: '. . . until Forster's notice in the *Examiner* appeared (No. 9) *every* journal that thought worth while to allude to the poem at all, treated it with contempt . . . beginning, I think, with the *Athenæum* (No. 7).'[39] On 21 November 1845, Browning sends Elizabeth a copy of Walter Savage Landor's now-famous sonnet, 'To R. B.' (No. 59), the highest praise the young poet had yet received, and Browning's gratitude shines through the next several letters: It is 'a gold vase from King Hiram',[40] and Browning is elated that Landor has sent the poem to Forster.[41] A review of *Luria* in the *Athenæum* 'By Chorley surely', he calls 'kind and satisfactory',[42] and he can report with pride that Carlyle has 'said wonderfully kind things'.[43]

There is evidence, however, that, fully as they discuss that subject, the love letters do not tell the whole story of Browning's attitude towards the critics in 1845–6. As the lovers move towards marriage, Browning's letters are filled more and more with tender expressions, less and less with poetic and critical matters. His letters to other correspondents at this time—those to Moxon, his publisher, most notably—are more business-like. In November 1845 Browning writes of one William James Harness[44] who has snubbed him and who threatens to write an article quizzing the poet. If the threat is carried out, Browning swears to 'rhyme him to death like an Irish rat!'[45] It would not be until 1876, and *Pacchiarotto*, that Browning would take his critics publicly to the pillory, but here as early as 1845 is evident Browning's desire to emulate Byron and excoriate his critics in a new *English Bards and Scotch Reviewers*. Finally, on the threshold of marriage, Browning writes to his friend Alfred Domett, apologizing for the obscurity of his poetry, but defending himself as well:

I felt so instinctively from the beginning [he writes] that unless I tumbled out the dozen more or less of conceptions, I should bear them about forever . . . and at last parturition would be the curse indeed. Mine was the better way, I do calmly believe, for at this moment I feel as everybody does who has *worked*—'in vain'? no matter, if the work was real . . . . I stand at present and wait . . . if the real work should present itself to be done, I shall begin at once and in earnest.[46]

During the years of his marriage (1846–61) Robert Browning left most casual correspondence to his wife, while he attended to the business affairs of the family—negotiating the agreements with publishers, asking for their semi-annual accountings, prodding the publishers to advertise their books properly. The marriage years were not prolific ones for the poet (from 1846 to 1861 Browning published only two new titles, the slender *Christmas-Eve and Easter-Day* and *Men and Women*), but the monologues of *Men and Women* were among the best poems he ever wrote and show an amazing growth of the man and the artist. What was lost in quantity was more than balanced by what was gained in artistry. But the experience of marriage cut into the time Browning had, as a bachelor, been able to devote to poetry.[47] In the first place, the Brownings lived in Italy during their marriage, away from the literary stimulus of his earlier London environment. Second, the responsibility of caring for an invalid wife—of nursing her during frequent periods of serious decline, of travelling with the changing Italian seasons in search of a salubrious climate—was heavy, and it became still heavier with the birth of a son, their only child, in 1849. Next, there is little question that in his new role as husband and father Browning found an emotional release and satisfaction that he had, in earlier years, been striving for in the vigorous pursuit of literary activity. Finally, although he had travelled somewhat during the years of his bachelorhood, he now for the first time could savour at his leisure the experience of living in a country rich with art, architecture, and culture different from, and centuries older than, those of his native England. It was, really, these years of which Browning could write that 'Italy was my university'.

In 1848, Browning changed publishers, taking his poems to Chapman and Hall, who were also the publishers of Elizabeth's poetry. In

1849, Browning's collected poems were printed in two volumes. The collection had been on Browning's mind as early as December 1846, when Elizabeth wrote of it to her old friend Hugh Boyd, confiding proudly, 'I heard of Carlyle's saying the other day "that he hoped for more from Robert Browning, for the people of England, than from any other living English writer".'[48] From this collection Browning omitted *Sordello*, a handful of lesser poems, and, of course, *Pauline*; but he revised *Paracelsus* substantially and made a number of changes in the pieces that had appeared in *Bells and Pomegranates*, nearly always with a view to rendering the lines clearer, smoother, and more musical. Whether the strictures of his early critics or the advice of his wife bore the greater weight, it is difficult to tell. It is also difficult to know how Browning reacted to the critical reception of the collected poems, for letters written by him in 1849 and 1850 are few, and only a letter to John Kenyon, complaining mildly of straitened finances, lets us know that the poet had settled into an attitude of equanimity at the prospect of continued financial unsuccess.[49] Elizabeth's letters, much more frequent and voluminous, contain a great deal of literary talk and show that, even in Italy, the couple had regular access to English books and reviews, both in their original forms and in the selected reprints published in *Galignani's*. And in Galignani's reading room, writes Elizabeth, Robert 'has sight of nearly every newspaper printed in Europe'.[50]

In January of 1850, Elizabeth wrote to Miss Mitford, 'Robert is engaged on a poem'.[51] *Christmas-Eve and Easter-Day*, although dramatic in principle, contains more of Robert Browning's personal views upon religion than anything he had hitherto written. It is deeply English in spirit, strongly Evangelical in its attitudes, and graphically Hogarthian in the sketches of the devotees of Mount Zion Chapel that open *Christmas-Eve*. It was altogether *apropos* of the religious ferment in England at the time. 'Whether you will like Robert's new book I don't know', Elizabeth wrote to Mrs. Jameson, 'but I am sure you will admit the originality and power in it. . . . There is nothing *Italian* in the book.'[52] But a month later, Elizabeth also confessed to the same correspondent one of her doubts about the new work: 'I have complained of the *asceticism* in the second part (*Easter-Day*), but he said it was "one side of the question".'[53]

For a time after the volume went on sale on 1 April it moved briskly; within two weeks 200 copies were sold. But then 'the sale drew to a virtual stop'.[54] With notable exceptions—for example the *Athenæum* (No. 77)—the reviews were friendly, if not always astute. The *Examiner*

(No. 81), among others, found traces of bigotry in *Christmas-Eve*; and commonly, the reviewers objected to the almost Hudibrastic rhymes with which the opening poem is liberally sprinkled. On balance Browning was praised for his spiritual bent and for his intellectual force, but the stark realism of *Christmas-Eve* was not appreciated. Joseph Arnould wrote Browning on 25 April 1850 that he found many of his acquaintance praising the new poem, with Chorley 'pre-eminent among the number' and Arnould's own wife among the enthusiasts. For himself, Arnould deplored Browning's shift into the grotesque, grand as he considered some of the scenes to be in their colour and vividness, but 'As to the superb magnificences of your poem—your moonrise, your night-rainbow, your St. Peter's, your visioned Form, your theory of Christian Art—they are in the memories and filling the hearts of hundreds of your true admirers.'[55] The strongest public praise—aside from William Michael Rossetti's notable defence of Browning's art in the *Germ* (No. 80)—came from outside England: in America, John Weiss hailed Browning as a poet with 'all the gifts and the exuberant life needed by a great artist';[56] and in France, Joseph Milsand boldly placed Browning in the front rank of all English poets.[57] Though the poem may have helped Browning's reputation, it apparently yielded nothing in more tangible rewards. In December 1850 Elizabeth could write that neither she nor Robert had 'had a sou from our books for a year past, the booksellers being bound of course to cover their own expenses first'.[58]

With the death of Wordsworth on 23 April 1850, the Poet Laureateship fell vacant. Elizabeth Barrett Browning's name was mentioned in various journals as an appropriate successor;[59] but Robert Browning, whose poems had at no time approached Elizabeth's in popularity, was never a serious contender. Although *Christmas-Eve and Easter-Day* and *In Memoriam* both treated of faith and doubt in nineteenth-century England, the mid-Victorian public (like Queen Victoria herself) took *In Memoriam* to their hearts but, with few exceptions, ignored Browning's poem. The Laureateship, together with a consequent increase of fame, went to Alfred Tennyson. Having entertained no hopes, Browning suffered no depression over the affair of the Laureateship. Family matters took up much of his time for the next two years—Elizabeth's recurring illnesses, trips to Siena, Paris, and England, an unhappy episode in which Browning's father was successfully sued for breach of promise—and the poet's writing seemed for a time to have suffered.

In 1852 Browning prepared an appreciative essay on Shelley to preface an edition of Shelley's letters. The letters were shown to be spurious, however, and the book was withdrawn.[60] On 25 April 1853 *Colombe's Birthday* (published in 1844) was produced at the Haymarket Theatre, with Helen Faucit in the title role. The play enjoyed a modest success, both with the patrons and with the critics (See No. 86). By this time, however, Browning was working at something more important —the poems which were to make up the two volumes of *Men and Women*. 'I am writing', he wrote to Milsand (24 February 1853) '—a first step towards popularity for me—lyrics with more music and painting than before, so as to get people to hear and see.'[61] No doubt the repeated criticisms of unmusicality and obscurity had had their effect, but the influence of Mrs. Browning can be seen as well, as is shown by a letter Browning wrote to a friend in July 1853: 'I shall mend my warp, I assure you, get as smooth as I can, and as plain as I can, and you shall re-criticize, if you will be so good, and take due credit to yourself for my improvement—which Ba (my wife) declares is manifest already.'[62] Elizabeth, who had criticized the poems in manuscript, wrote enthusiastically to her sister that *Men and Women* would be 'magnificent'[63] and, the week after publication (November 1855), reaffirmed her faith:

Robert will stand higher than ever through these poems—I am ready to die for them, at the stake, that they are his ablest works. They are making translations of nearly half of them for the 'Revue des deux Mondes' and Mr. Milsand told me quietly the other day, that he considered the poems 'superhuman'. Mark that! Only superhuman.[64]

The result—the fifty-one poems which comprise *Men and Women*— fully justified her enthusiasm. Many of the poems—'Love Among the Ruins', 'Fra Lippo Lippi', 'Andrea del Sarto', 'The Guardian-Angel', 'Childe Roland' among them—would mark the high point of Browning's art and would serve as the true foundation for his fame. Browning sealed his confidence publicly by writing 'One Word More', the fifty-first poem, with which he dedicated the volumes to his wife.

To look over the reviews of *Men and Women* is even for the modern reader something of a shock. For Browning, they were a most bitter disappointment. 'Energy wasted and power misspent . . .', 'It is really high time that this sort of thing should, if possible, be stopped . . .', 'Perversity, carelessness, and bad taste . . .'—such was the critical reception of Browning's finest poems (Nos. 89ff.). The major reviews were uniformly unfavourable, and the poet had to take cold comfort from John Ruskin's well-known praise of 'The Bishop Orders His Tomb', a poem first published in 1845. Writing in the *Oxford and Cambridge Magazine* (No. 104), the young William Morris defended the poet and raised the only intelligent question of the time: 'I wonder what the critics would have said to "Hamlet, Prince of Denmark", if it had been first published by Messrs. Chapman and Hall in the year 1855.'

Browning's patience was nearly at an end. He was no longer a *tyro*, but a mature poet, a man who knew his own worth and saw mediocrities winning public acclaim. His publishers were naturally concerned, but Browning advised Chapman not to 'take to heart the zoological utterances I have stopped my ears against at Galignani's of late', adding with a significant foretaste of the language he would employ years later in a public chastisement of his critics, ' "Whoo-oo-oo-oo" mouths the big monkey—"Whee-ee-ee-ee" squeaks the little monkey and such a dig with the end of my umbrella I should give the brutes if I couldn't keep my temper, and consider how they miss their nut[s] and gingerbread!'[65] 'I have read heaps of critiques at Galignani's', he wrote a month later, 'mostly stupid and spiteful, self-contradicting and contradictory of each other.'[66]

Once again, the most sympathetic review would come from abroad. Milsand admired the poems almost inordinately and translated a good number of them for the *Revue des deux mondes*.[67] Privately, Carlyle wrote his encouragement, praising in particular 'How It Strikes a Contemporary', and adding, 'Courage ever, and stand to your arms!'[68] To his friend and correspondent Emerson, Carlyle wrote, 'Do you know Browning at all? He is abstruse; but worth knowing.'[69] And a kind word from Leigh Hunt drew a grateful letter from the poet.[70]

The most revealing document of this time is a letter Browning wrote on 10 December 1855 to John Ruskin, who had sent his personal advice to Browning. It is well worth quoting at length:

You never were more in the wrong [Browning writes] than when you professed to say 'your unpleasant things' to me. This is pleasant and proper at all points, over-liberal of praise here and there, kindly and sympathetic everywhere, and with enough of yourself in even—what I fancy—the misjudging, to make the whole letter precious indeed. . . . For the deepnesses you think you discern, —may they be more than mere blacknesses! For the hopes you entertain of what may come of subsequent readings,—all success to them! For your bewilderment more especially noted—how shall I help *that*? We don't read poetry the same way, by the same law; it is too clear. I cannot begin writing poetry till my imaginary reader has conceded licences to me which you demur at altogether. I *know* that I don't make out my conception by my language, all poetry being a putting in infinite within the finite. You would have me paint it all plain out, which can't be; but by various artifices I try to make shift with touches and bits of outlines which *succeed* if they bear the conception from me to you. You ought, I think, to keep pace with the thought tripping from ledge to ledge of my 'glaciers', as you call them; not stand poking your alpenstock into the holes, and demonstrating that no foot could have stood there;—suppose it sprang over there? In *prose* you may criticise so—because that is the absolute representation of portions of truth, what chronicling is to history—but in asking for more *ultimates* you must accept less *mediates*, nor expect that a Druid stone-circle will be traced for you with as few breaks to the eye as the North Crescent and South Crescent that go together so cleverly in many a suburb. . . .

Do you think poetry was ever generally understood—or can be? Is the business of it to tell people what they know already, as they know it, and so precisely that they shall be able to cry out—'Here you should supply *this*—*that*, you evidently pass over, and I'll help you from my own stock'? It is all teaching, on the contrary, and the people hate to be taught. They say otherwise,—make foolish fables about Orpheus enchanting stocks and stones, poets standing up and being worshipped,—all nonsense and impossible dreaming. A poet's affair is with God,—to whom he is accountable, and of whom is his reward; look elsewhere, and you find misery enough. Do you believe people understand 'Hamlet'? The last time I saw it acted, the heartiest applause of the night went to a little by-play of the actor's own—who, to simulate madness in a hurry, plucked forth his handkerchief and flourished it hither and thither: certainly a third of the play, with no end of noble things, had been (as from time immemorial) suppressed, with the auditory's amplest acquiescence and benediction. Are these wasted, therefore? No—they act upon a very few, who react upon the rest: as Goldsmith says, 'some lords, my acquaintance, that settle the nation, are pleased to be kind'. Don't let me lose *my* lord by any seeming self-sufficiency or petulance: I look on my own shortcomings too sorrowfully, try to remedy them too earnestly: but I shall never change my point of sight, or feel other than disconcerted and apprehensive when the public, critics and all, begin to understand and approve me. But what right have *you* to disconcert me in the other way?[71]

Browning's bitterness encompassed the critics and the public alike. To his publisher he wrote:

As to my own Poems—they must be left to Providence and that fine sense of discrimination which I never cease to meditate upon and admire in the public: they cry out for new things and when you furnish them with what they cried for, 'it's *so* new', they grunt. The half-dozen people who know and could impose their opinions on the whole sty say nothing to *them* (I don't wonder) and speak so low in my own ear that it's lost to all intents and purposes.[72]

A note written some months later, again to Chapman, raises anew the promise of retaliation: 'Don't you mind them [the critics], and leave me to rub their noses in their own filth some fine day.'[73]

The reception of *Men and Women* was probably the deepest literary disappointment Browning ever experienced, but forces were already at work which would raise him to popularity and general fame. In America, his books were selling well, and he had admirers in such cultivated and influential men as John Weiss and James T. Fields.[74] More important, at Oxford and Cambridge young men were beginning to 'discover' him. The Pre-Raphaelites, spurred by the exuberance of Dante Gabriel Rossetti, had been Browning devotees since 1847, and his poetry—not excluding the 'incomprehensible' *Sordello*—was read, argued over, and enthusiastically pressed on the attention of anyone who would listen. They gave copies of Browning to their friends,[75] maintained against Coventry Patmore that 'Browning would be *the* man some twenty years hence',[76] competed for the first reading of *Christmas-Eve and Easter-Day*,[77] and recited Browning's poems to their friends.[78] For them, the publication of *Men and Women* was a fulfilment of their expectations, and the angry tone of Morris's review (No. 104) simply reflected their commonly felt indignation at the ignorance of the critics. Edward Burne-Jones records an occasion when 'someone speaking disrespectfully of . . . [*Men and Women*] was rent in pieces at once [by Dante Rossetti] for his pains, and was dumb for the rest of the evening.'[79] William Allingham complained of the '*semi*-sensible and wholly idiotic notice' in the *Athenæum* (No. 89), and Thomas Woolner wrote to Allingham, 'I rejoice to hear the great Robert praised, for he deserves the best that can be bestowed.'[80] Outside the Pre-Raphaelite circle, among other young intellectuals, Browning's *Men and Women* was under discussion. Not every young man was captivated, of course. Matthew Arnold never became a warm admirer of Browning the poet (even though he much liked Browning the man), and Arthur H. Clough, characteristically, had his doubts: ' "Fra Lippo" I liked; but some of the passages seemed to be in his most reckless, de-composite manner—dashing at anything and insisting that it would do.'[81] Nevertheless, the young intellectuals—the taste-makers of the next generation—had taken Browning to their bosoms, and the groundwork for his future fame was being laid.

In the meantime, a disappointed Browning re-absorbed himself into the life of his family and friends. In Florence, his circle of acquaintances, though not large, was in many ways a colourful one: the ageing Walter

Savage Landor lived nearby, and Browning in 1859 assumed the difficult chore of looking after that irascible genius's affairs; William Wetmore Story, the American sculptor, had established a studio in Florence, and there Browning tried his hand at another art—and through Story saw a number of the visiting American *literati*. Among these, one—Hawthorne—was surprised to find Browning so lucid in conversation 'since his poetry can seldom proceed far without running into the high grass of latent meanings and obscure allusions.'[82] The Brownings' closest friend, Isabella Blagden, entertained guests frequently at her villa on Bellosguardo, and there Browning could converse with such literary figures as the Trollopes, Robert Lytton, and Tennyson's brother Frederick. Careful measures for the guarding of Elizabeth's health and for Pen's development in music, language, and other studies took up much of the remaining time and energy, with the result that Browning apparently wrote little, and published still less—little more than 'May and Death' and 'Ben Karshook's Wisdom', both in a literary annual—in the six years between the publication of *Men and Women* and Elizabeth's death in 1861.

With Elizabeth's death Browning brought to an end his long period of residence in Italy. Once settled in London, he gradually returned to literary composition. While completing the poems which were to make up *Dramatis Personae*, he edited one volume of his *Poetical Works* and his friends John Forster and B. W. Procter (Barry Cornwall) edited *Selections from the Poetical Works of Robert Browning*. As the books were going through the press, Browning had occasion to remark upon the vagaries of the critics: '. . . so and so means to review it, and somebody or [other] always was looking out for such an occasion, and what's his name always said he admired me, only he didn't say it, though he said something else every week of his life in some Journal. The breath of man!'[83] Both volumes were published in 1863 and sold so well that the publication of *Dramatis Personae* was deliberately postponed for a year. Browning's public fame, long delayed, was beginning in earnest. He was still not happy with the critics and complained of their obtuseness,[84] but he was pleased at gaining a wider audience.

Dramatis Personae turned out to be a critical and popular success. A second printing was called for within a year, the poet was lionized, and, to Browning's deep satisfaction, his publisher reported that a large proportion of orders for the two volumes were coming from Oxford and Cambridge.[85] Retrospective estimates, most of them favourable, now began to appear; and at the hands of Edward Dowden even *Sordello* came in for a generous reassessment (No. 127). In 1868, the first book devoted entirely to Browning's works—John T. Nettleship's *Essays on Robert Browning's Poetry*—was widely and favourably received. The beginnings of a Browning cult were growing in evidence. Another sort of honour, one which Browning prized very highly, came in October 1867, when Balliol College elected him Honorary Fellow and Oxford bestowed an honorary M.A. upon him. Exercising his right to keep rooms at Balliol, he chose them side by side with those of Benjamin Jowett, the famous classicist and the Master of the College.[86] But despite his rising popularity with the press and in the universities, Browning could reaffirm his long-standing resolve to follow his own path regardless of the critics and the public—a resolve he had kept with a remarkable singleness of purpose ever since he had earnestly attempted to define it for Miss Barrett in his letter of 1845. 'As I began, so I shall end', he wrote to Isa Blagden, 'taking my own course, pleasing myself, or aiming at doing so, and thereby, I hope, pleasing God.'[87]

III

THE PINNACLE OF FAME

His faith in himself reassured, Browning turned to serious work on what he trusted would be his *magnum opus*, *The Ring and the Book*. With *The Ring and the Book* Browning began his long association with the publishing firm of Smith, Elder, and Company, having dropped Chapman and Hall for, among other reasons, Chapman's lack of confidence in his drawing-power.[88] The new publishers treated Browning royally; they advanced £1,250 against the sale of his poems for five years and acquiesced in his plan to issue *The Ring and the Book* in four volumes, to be published successively in November and December of 1868 and January and February of 1869.

The Ring and the Book was a resounding success, both with the critics and with the reading public. Praise reached a pitch of adulation. Even the *Athenæum*—traditionally no friend of Browning's—hailed his poem in extravagant terms: 'We must record at once our conviction, not merely that *The Ring and the Book* is beyond all parallel the supremest poetical achievement of our time, but that it is the most precious and profound spiritual treasure that England has produced since the days of

Shakespeare' (No. 133). Thereafter Browning and Tennyson would share the limelight; and, if their relative merits were often debated, there was little debate over accepting them taken together as the twin glories of the poetry of the age. Ironically the critic of *The Ring and the Book* who most irritated Browning was a personal friend. Julia Wedgwood, an authentic Victorian bluestocking, read the poem volume by volume as Browning sent it to her (in line with an earlier promise he had made her). From the start she objected pointedly to the quantity of evil Browning was portraying. Admitting that he believed he did 'unduly like the study of morbid cases of the soul', Browning rejoined that he had nevertheless worked with this particular subject in the right way. He had endeavoured to paint the exact truths of the case as he saw them, neither whiter nor blacker than they existed in the actual records of this Roman murder case in the Old Yellow Book, the collection of late seventeenth-century documents 'part print, part manuscript', on which he based his poem.[89] But Miss Wedgwood, as she read the successive volumes, would not let the matter drop, and for several months the correspondence continued, Miss Wedgwood objecting to and Browning defending his view of life until the two decided to let the correspondence—and the friendship—drop. But not before Browning could underscore his defence with evidence of his growing popularity. 'Yes', he writes, 'the British Public like, and more than like me, this week, they let their admiration ray out on me . . . which all comes of the Queen's having desired to see me . . . last Thursday.'[90] This audience—Thomas Carlyle, George Grote, and Sir Charles Lyell were also invited—was a high point in Browning's literary life, and the *Court Circular* described Carlyle and Browning as 'eminent men—who so far as intellect is concerned, stand head and shoulders above their contemporaries.'[91] Further honours came unbidden. Browning was offered and declined the Lord Rectorship of St. Andrews, a purely honorary post, which then went to the historian James Anthony Froude. It was only the first of a number of such offers. His fame made him, of course, a favourite dinner and house guest throughout the London season. In short, all the resources that are thought to accompany literary fame were his.

In every Eden, however, there lurks a serpent—and in this instance the role fell to one Alfred Austin, a critic and minor poet who, dissenting from the popular view, held neither Browning nor Tennyson in esteem. In a heavy-handed article in *Temple Bar* (No. 151) Austin attacked Browning as both unmusical and unintelligible. Worst of all,

Austin ended his critique with a paragraph *ad hominem*, accusing the poet of 'looking for fame' and having sought it in 'small London literary coteries, and large fashionable London salons'.[92] Browning was furious. On the head of Alfred Austin fell the accumulated wrath of nearly forty years. To Isa Blagden he referred to Austin as a 'filthy little snob' and recounted a story of how Thackeray had unintentionally insulted the critic.[93] Three years later, Austin is one of 'your more lively article-mongers, who tell these lies . . . for the malice rather than the fun of the thing'.[94] Two years later still, Browning could complain to his brother-in-law, 'Whenever there is a funny piece of raving against me in a newspaper, you may be sure my little bug of an Austin is biting his best. . . .'[95] But by this time (May 1875), Browning's plan for revenge was settled upon, with results to be discussed later in this essay.

Aside from the annoyance caused by Austin, Browning had every reason to be satisfied with his position, and the years 1870–5 were exceptionally prolific ones, even for Browning. He published six new titles—in 1871, *Balaustion's Adventure*, a graceful adaptation of the Alcestis legend, and *Prince Hohenstiel-Schwangau*, a satirical portrait of Napoleon III in the form of a dramatic monologue; in 1872, *Fifine at the Fair*, a monologue in which Don Juan builds intricate fugues of casuistry to justify his infidelities; in 1873, *Red Cotton Night-Cap Country*, a remarkably graphic and grotesque narrative based on accounts of a sordid case involving madness and suicide in Normandy; in 1875, *The Inn Album*, another narrative of sordid events drawn from contemporary life. In 1875 also, Browning brought out *Aristophanes' Apology*, a lengthy sequel to *Balaustion's Adventure*, lacking the relative clarity and grace of its predecessor. In the latter work, Browning is much preoccupied with his own relation to his critics, and especially Alfred Austin. Austin, who was soon to become the 'homunculus', the 'thing so very small', the 'Quilp-Hop-o'-my-thumb' of *Pacchiarotto*, had been made to figure in thinly veiled allusions as a critic of Euripides in *Balaustion's Adventure*—'a brisk little somebody, Critic and whipper-snapper. . . .' In *Aristophanes' Apology* Browning makes his own defence through defending Euripides in still more patent terms, placing in the mouth of the chief defender of Euripides the aspersions that Austin had made against Browning's own poetry. The allusions to Austin as 'Dogface Eruxis, the small satirist . . . the manikin' and his particular charges brought against Browning are scarcely mistakable. *Aristophanes' Apology* represents in good part an ambitious though intricate and veiled defence of Browning's own theory and practice as poet against the allegations of his critics.[96] The period 1870–5 was also notable for the increase in reprintings of Browning's work that by now came into demand. In 1872 both Smith, Elder and Company and Bernhard Tauchnitz brought out new volumes of selections from Browning's poetry, and—in a rare combination of verse with the prose of daily transportation—the Chicago and Alton Railroad began to reprint 'everything of Mr. Browning's which had been published in England' in the monthly issues of its time tables.[97] Reprints and selections too numerous to describe came from a variety of presses from this time on, both in England and in the United States.

Except for *Balaustion's Adventure*, which was received well by the critics and the public, none of the works Browning brought out in the six years following *The Ring and the Book* added greatly to his fame. Carlyle did not like any of them; in fact, Carlyle seems to have liked almost nothing Browning had done since *Men and Women*. Of *Balaustion* Carlyle complained that Browning had with much ingenuity twisted the English language 'into riddles',[98] and of *Red Cotton Night-Cap Country* that no one out of Bedlam had ever thought of working such material into a poem.[99] Tennyson found that he could not enjoy or even understand *Fifine*, though he had carried it along on a walk in the hope of making sense of it.[100] Swinburne admired *The Inn Album* as an exemplar of a realistic study in the 'later manner of Balzac',[101] but he could not countenance Browning's crabbed excursions into the Greek dramatists, especially his 'libel on Aristophanes'. He seems half-seriously to have contemplated writing a parody of it.[102] In short, although Browning had overcome the indifference of the public and had become famous after *The Ring and the Book*, his next productions did not increase his favour with the public or with leading critics of the day.

In 1876 Browning was no longer content with veiled allusions to Austin and other detractors. With *Pacchiarotto and How He Worked in Distemper* Browning trained his heavy artillery directly upon the critic who had annoyed him beyond forbearance and poured upon him ridicule that was heavily Rabelaisian in manner and frequently in its detail as well. If Browning was aspiring to emulate Byron, he failed of his purpose; for personalities bestowed on Austin and his diminutive stature are often simply ill-natured and more diatribe than poetry.[103] Despite this failing, the *Pacchiarotto* volume offers an intimate view of Browning's attitudes in the mid-seventies toward his critics and his public. In 'At the "Mermaid"' Browning answers his own rhetorical question, 'I—"Next Poet?"' with a firm 'No my hearties,/I nor am

nor fain would be!' In 'House' he denies to his reading public the right
to pry into his private life, and in the 'Epilogue' he chides those critics
who want the wine of his poetry to have both 'body and bouquet',
strength as well as sweetness, but who do not appreciate that 'Mighty
and mellow are never mixed'.

But it is in the title-poem that Browning most reveals himself.
Giving a one-sided history of Browning criticism, he accuses the reviewers of ignorance, obtuseness, and sheer malignity. As for their
influence upon the poet himself, it is nil, for the poet, as he had asserted
to Elizabeth Barrett in 1845 and to Ruskin a decade later, writes out of
duty to God, not to the reviewers and the public:

> Mine's freehold, by grace of the grand Lord
> Who lets out the ground here,—my landlord:
> Nor hence shall I budge, I've a notion,
> Nay, here shall my whistling and singing
> Set all his street's echoes a-ringing
> Long after the last of your number
> Has ceased my front-court to encumber . . .

Pacchiarotto discomforted friends and reviewers alike. The *Examiner*,
taking a holier-than-thou attitude, was typical of the one class,[104] while
Edmund Gosse wrote Browning to disclaim authorship of any of the
reviews which had irritated the poet.[105] In his turn, Browning denied
having known that Austin was a near-dwarf, but added—with evident
satisfaction—'it seems that one fillip more than avenges fifty flea-bites'.[106]
Once he had settled with Austin and the critical malignity Austin had
come to represent for him, the poet went back to a more profitable
line of work. In the dozen years remaining to him, he published eight
new volumes. He continued, of course, as he had vowed he would, to
consult his own tastes rather than those of his critics. The resultant
variety of manner and matter is quite astonishing. With notable exceptions, philosophical topics—'mere grey argument'—begin to displace
purely dramatic work; and the form of the dramatic monologue more
and more gives way to the argumentative style in which Browning
speaks in his own voice.

One of the exceptions was Browning's final—and probably least
successful—incursion into Greek drama, a translation of *The Agamemnon
of Aeschylus* (1877), a task, it has been conjectured, that he took on himself at the mild urging of Carlyle. Unfortunately, Browning attempted
a literal translation and incorporated a system of spelling which he

thought would approximate in English the proper pronunciation of the difficult Greek. The results were awkward. Clytemnestra, for example, became *Klutaimnestra*; Aegisthus came out *Aigisthos*; and in achieving (not without lapses) a certain literalness, Browning missed many of the other qualities that can grace a translation.

Although Browning defended his method, the public, the scholars, and the critics—J. A. Symonds excepted (see No. 202)—did not like the work. The general critical attitude toward Browning's *Agamemnon* is pretty well summed up in a sentence attributed to an anonymous 'young Oxford B.A.': 'At almost every page I had to turn to the Greek to see what the English meant.' The *London Quarterly Review* found this judgment 'severe, but . . . not unmerited'.[107] Swinburne, forced to write a polite note upon receipt of a complimentary copy, was puzzled as to what he could say without hypocrisy and 'went straight to bed';[108] Arnold accepted a copy with decent gravity, but added that he preferred Browning's manner elsewhere;[109] Carlyle, who had possibly started the whole matter, was aghast and found the piece incomprehensible. 'O dear! he's a very foolish fellow', the Sage of Chelsea exclaimed. 'He picks you out the English for the Greek word by word, and now and again sticks two or three words together with hyphens; then again he snips up the sense and jingles it into rhyme!'[110]

The next of Browning's productions, *La Saisiaz* (1878), is also the most directly personal. In it Browning, spurred by the unexpected death of Mrs. Anne Egerton Smith, a close friend and travelling companion, debated the possibility of personal immortality after death. *La Saisiaz* is a sober poem, one in which Browning concludes, surprisingly, that this life, taken alone, produces more sorrow than joy and requires an afterlife to redress the balance. Modestly, he insists that this answer is a personal one, and that what suited Robert Browning was in no way intended to solve the problem for all men. The poem received wide attention and much favourable comment. In an age of shifting religious values, of hot theological debate, and of rising scientific scepticism, the immortality of the soul was an important question. In one sense, *La Saisiaz* was Browning's *In Memoriam*—for it advances the same basic problem and reaches a not dissimilar personal conclusion—but Browning's poem, written in the decline of his powers rather than at the apex, is decidedly less than a masterpiece of technique, thought, or feeling. The general temper of the reviews was favourable, nonetheless, with the *Athenæum* loudest in praise (No. 207).

As he entered the last decade of his life, Browning was not, as many other poets had been, content to rest on his honours. Instead, he continued to pour out verse copious in quantity and astonishing in its variety: in 1879 and 1880 *Dramatic Idyls*, two volumes of poetry mainly narrative; in 1883 *Jocoseria*, a curious mixture of lyric, dramatic, and narrative poems; in 1884 *Ferishtah's Fancies*, an examination of philosophic problems cast in the form questions set before and answered by a Persian sage, with a reinforcement of each answer by a lyric verse; in 1887, *Parleyings with Certain People of Importance in Their Day*, in which Browning speaks in his own person and says 'a thing or two that I "fancied" I should like to say';[111] and finally, in 1889—published on the very day of his death—*Asolando: Fancies and Facts*, a volume of lyric poetry on the subject of love, inspired both by mellowed memories of his own life and by the recent marriage of his son.

With the exception of the *Parleyings*, which most of the reviewers (and, presumably, the reading public also) misinterpreted, all of the volumes in this last decade were received well enough so that reprintings were demanded. The best of the *Idyls*, 'Clive', was pronounced worthy of a place in *Men and Women* (although Tennyson missed the point until it was explained to him),[112] and the *Idyls* as a whole were welcomed by the reviewers as proper additions to the literature of the dramatic monologue. Both *Jocoseria* and *Ferishtah's Fancies* struck the reviewers by their originality and variety; and, if there were still occasional complaints of wilfulness and obscurity, they were mild and Browning had little reason to complain.

In 1881, a group of Browning devotees, under the leadership of F. J. Furnival and Emily Hickey, announced the founding of a Browning Society 'for the study and discussion of the works of the poet Browning, and the publication of essays on them, and extracts from works illustrating them'. The Society fulfilled its stated purposes zealously and, if Browning was occasionally embarrassed to see his poetry treated as prophecy or as a riddle to be solved by dedicated students of the arcane, he was also pleased by the evidence of the manifest good will and grateful for the increased popularity of his work. Essays, a bibliography, annotated and improved texts, and productions of the plays came into being as a result of the Browning Society, and its counterparts spread to many corners of the English-speaking world.[113] Nor was membership confined to enthusiasts and knitting-circle ladies. The Society numbered among its members such diverse types as George Bernard Shaw,[114] Augustine Birrell, James Lecky, John Bury, James (B.V.) Thomson, and Karl Marx's daughter Eleanor. Although he did not participate actively in the work of the Society—his sense of propriety was too strong for that—Browning did assist the officers by providing information about his poems, sometimes clarifying a vague passage, sometimes recounting the circumstances of composition, and occasionally reading manuscripts of essays before they were sent to the printer. To Furnival, who had undertaken the compilation of a bibliography of Browning's poetry and Browning criticism from *Pauline* onward, Browning wrote that he preferred in the main simply to forget forever the mass of early strictures on his poetry—the 'misconception at best, ignorance at middling, and malice at worst' that had been expended on him. He would remember the conscientious criticism he had received, but he wished to leave to oblivion the amount of 'mere mopping and mowing and such monkey-tricks'.[115] The monkey-image for the critics who had plagued him through the years seems to have been a recurrent one in his intimate thoughts. As we have seen, he had used it often since applying it to the critics of *Men and Women* in his letter to Chapman in December 1855 [see above, p. 14], and always with feeling.

The activities of the Society were widely reported in the periodicals and at first found a favourable reception. A curiously ambivalent comment appeared in *Notes and Queries* in 1882:

This society is thoroughly justifying its existence. It will be impossible for any future writer upon Browning to neglect its labours—if, indeed, it does not make any further writing upon the subject entirely superfluous.[116]

The second possibility feared (or is it hoped for?) by the writers in *Notes and Queries* lost its threat with the passage of time. As the influence of the societies spread, an inevitable reaction set in (see Nos. 225 and 235). The poet was amused. 'That there is a grotesque side to the thing is certain', he wrote, 'but . . . as I never felt inconvenienced by hard words, you will not expect me to wax bumptious because of undue compliment.'[117] Undue or not, the 'compliments' of the societies spurred the sale of Browning's poetry and gave him, in the minds of many, an ascendancy over all his contemporaries, Tennyson included.[118] Books of exegesis multiplied, preachers used the poems for moral exemplars, and public readings, especially readings featuring such inspirational favourites as 'Saul' and 'Abt Vogler', were frequent and widespread. In America, even the celebrated author and humorist Mark Twain gave regular readings. To a friend, Twain wrote:

I am pretty proud of my Browning class. . . . I prepare 30 or 40 pages of new matter for each setting—along with a modest small lecture, usually—I then re-

read poems called for by the class. I suppose I have read 'Rabbi Ben Ezra' and 'Up at a Villa' a couple of dozen times. . . . Folks ask permission to come, as if it were a privilege . . . it is no nickle-plated compliment for the poet.[119]

Twain came to pride himself greatly on the quality of such readings. 'Put me in the right condition', he said, 'and give me room according to my strength and I can read Browning so Browning himself can understand it.'[120] Browning had, in short, become a literary commodity and an institution.

As the poet entered the seventy-eighth (and last) year of his life, he could have found many reasons to congratulate himself. Honours had been heaped upon him, the last of his family problems had dissolved when his son had made what promised to be an eminently suitable marriage to a wealthy young American girl, the final sixteen-volume collection of his works was completed, and *Asolando*—with its famous 'Epilogue' a reaffirmation of his faith—was in the hands of his publisher. It was on the day of publication of this last volume of his poetry, 12 December 1889, that Browning, following a brief illness, died at his son's home in Venice. News had already reached him by telegraph that afternoon of the enthusiastic critical reception of *Asolando*. Browning's death occasioned a flood of tributes *in memoriam*, and interment in the Poet's Corner of Westminster Abbey appropriately sealed a career which had spanned nearly six decades and climaxed a poetic reputation which had grown from obscurity through misunderstanding and much cavil to mild acceptance, enthusiasm, and finally adulation. Browning's deathbed comment when he heard the good news of the critical reception of *Asolando* was 'How gratifying.' The words might well have been applied, looking backward, to the course of his long career.

IV

THE AFTERMATH

Browning's death in 1889 produced such a flood of encomiums that no bibliographer has been able to catalogue it fully. Obituaries, memorabilia, and retrospective essays dominated Browning criticism and pretty well silenced adverse comment for nearly a decade. The 'Browningites' flourished and, unfortunately, the emphasis was laid upon Browning as philosopher, as teacher, as religious thinker, rather than upon Browning as poet.[121] The result of such uncritical adulation was to lay the ground-work for an inevitable reaction, begun by Henry Jones, George Santayana, and John Robertson,[122] and culminating in the rejection of Browning (together with most of the other Victorian poets, it must be admitted) around the time of World War I, when a 'modern' literary world, having destroyed the old, was seeking after new idols.

Serious revaluation of Browning's poetry would not begin again until the 1930s and 1940s, with the work of such scholars as W. O. Raymond and William C. DeVane.[123] Since their pioneer work, and partially as a result of it, the study and criticism of Browning the man and the poet has set the poet's reputation upon firmer ground. No longer is it fashionable to portray Browning as a deep philosopher-psychologist and a careless technician. Contemporary critics are less likely than their predecessors to study Browning for 'meaning' and more likely to find in his poetry the marks of an artistry his own contemporaries never noticed. The debt modern poetry owes to Browning—a debt which was never denied by such luminaries as Pound, Eliot, and Yeats—is being explored by a generation of critics who have achieved a respectable aesthetic distance from the Victorians.

Seminal re-examinations of individual poems and of Browning's total work have opened new avenues of understanding. The scholarly editing of new letters and the proper re-editing of others[124] will prepare the way for an as yet unwritten definitive biography. And, finally, a modern, complete edition of Browning's poetry, prose, and drama—announced by the Ohio University Press and already underway—should provide future critics with a sound and readily available text.

As a result of these endeavours, the present view of Browning's poetry is being set upon somewhat firmer ground. And, if Browning will never regain the place the Browning Society wrongly assigned to him in the 1880s and 1890s, neither will he sink again into the near oblivion against which he had to struggle for the thirty years between the rejection of *Pauline* and the acceptance of *Dramatis Personae*. And if (as is very likely) more copies of his poems are sold each year now than were sold in any year during his lifetime—and those, mainly, in the colleges and universities—it is a fate shared by many another poet, and one with which Robert Browning would probably be content.

NOTES

1. *RB-EBB*, I, 17. The last part of the paragraph preceding this one in the letter is also relevant, dealing as it does with Browning's struggles to get his inner light outside him—'if I might only knock the whole clumsy top off my tower!'
2. *RB-AD*, p. 56 (15 May 1843).
3. See Th. Bentzon (Mme Blanc), 'A French Friend of Browning—Joseph Milsand', *Scribner's Magazine*, XX (1896), 108–20. See also Mrs Sutherland Orr, *Life and Letters of Robert Browning*, ed. Frederic G. Kenyon (1908), pp. 176, 275ff.
4. Quoted in Orr, p. 54.
5. See *Robert Browning: A Bibliography, 1830–1950,* compiled by L. N. Broughton, C. S. Northup, and Robert Pearsall (1953), p. 24, for details of their publication.
6. For an interesting analysis of the influence of Mill's remarks upon Browning, see Masao Miyoshi, 'Mill and *Pauline:* The Myth and Some Facts', *Victorian Studies,* IX (1965), 154–63.
7. Browning decided ('with extreme repugnance') to include *Pauline* in the 1868 edition of his poems partly because his authorship had become an open secret (Dante Rossetti, indeed, had in 1847 recognized Browning's characteristic voice in the British Museum's copy), but also because he wanted to forestall pirated editions.
8. Orr, p. 66.
9. In return, Browning complimented Miss Haworth with the graceful lines in *Sordello* addressed to 'English Eye-bright'.
10. Walter Savage Landor, *Letters and Conversations,* ed. by H. C. Minchin (1934), p. 16.
11. A brief account of this famous affair at the home of T. N. Talfourd, the success of whose play *Ion* was the reason for the celebration, has been left by another of the guests, Mary Russell Mitford, in *Harper's Magazine,* IV, (March 1852), 507.
12. *The Diaries of William Charles Macready, 1833–1851,* ed. by William Toynbee (1912), I, 389. Hereafter referred to as *Diaries.*
13. *Diaries,* I, 390.
14. *Diaries,* I, 393.
15. *Diaries,* II, 72.
16. William C. DeVane, *A Browning Handbook,* 2nd ed. (1955), p. 72.
17. When Browning demanded an opinion of her, Harriet Martineau confirmed his own inclination to dispense with any special aids for the reader. *Harriet Martineau's Autobiography,* ed. Maria Weston Chapman (1877), II, 325.

18. *LRB*, p. 4.
19. *Diaries*, II, 64.
20. There are many variants of this story.
21. And of this one as well.
22. Anne Kimball Tuell, *John Sterling: A Representative Victorian* (1941), p. 145.
23. Quoted in John Forster, *The Works and Life of Walter Savage Landor* (1876), I, 428.
24. *The Swinburne Letters*, ed. by Cecil Y. Lang (1954–62), I, 16.
25. *NL*, p. 18.
26. *NL*, p. 23.
27. On 27 August 1840 Macready recorded, 'Browning came before I had finished my bath, and really *wearied* me with his obstinate faith in his poem of *Sordello.* . . .' *Diaries*, II, 76.
28. As Browning explained to Miss Barrett, and later to the public, he meant his general title to signify 'an alternation, or mixture, of music with discoursing, sound with sense, poetry with thought'.
29. DeVane, p. 90.
30. *RB-AD*, p. 28.
31. *RB-AD*, p. 37.
32. *RB-AD*, pp. 49–50.
33. *RB-AD*, p. 52. 'Chris.' is, no doubt, Christopher Dowson, a close mutual friend.
34. *RB-AD*, p. 106.
35. *RB-AD*, p. 113.
36. *LRB*, p. 10.
37. *RB-EBB*, I, 28.
38. *RB-EBB*, I, 65.
39. *RB-EBB*, I, 322.
40. *RB-EBB*, I, 286.
41. *RB-EBB*, I, 292.
42. *RB-EBB*, I, 410.
43. *RB-EBB*, II, 90.
44. A reviewer for the *Quarterly* and author of a *Life of William Shakespeare*.
45. *NL*, 37–8.
46. *RB-AD*, 127–8.
47. Elizabeth was somewhat worried by it. 'What am I to say', she wrote to Mrs. Jameson in 1849, 'about Robert's idleness and mine? I scold him about it in a most anti-conjugal manner, but, you know, his spirits and nerves have been shaken of late; we must have patience.' *LEBB*, I, 422. It was the death of Browning's mother, earlier in the year, which had 'shaken' the poet.
48. *Elizabeth Barrett to Mr. Boyd*, ed. by Barbara P. McCarthy (1955), p. 283.
49. *LRB*, pp. 28–9.

50. *Elizabeth Barrett Browning: Letters to Her Sister, 1846–1859,* ed. by Leonard Huxley (1929), 186.

51. *LEBB,* I, 432.

52. *LEBB,* I, 441.

53. *LEBB,* I, 449.

54. Broughton, p. 11.

55. See Donald Smalley, 'Joseph Arnould and Robert Browning: New Letters (1842–50) and A Verse Epistle', *PMLA,* LXXX (March 1965), 90–101.

56. Weiss's long and enthusiastic review appeared in *Massachusetts Quarterly Review,* III (June 1850), 347–85.

57. 'La Poésie anglais depuis Byron, II—Robert Browning', *Revue des deux mondes,* NS XI (15 August 1851), 661–89. This perceptive and sympathetic article preluded a close friendship which ended only with Milsand's death in 1886.

58. *LEBB,* I, 471.

59. A fact which she took lightly, suggesting to Miss Mitford that Leigh Hunt ought to have it. Ironically, the *Athenæum* was foremost among the journals which proposed Elizabeth, and she did not miss the cream of the jest. 'Shall I ask the "Note and Query" [*sic*] magazine why the *Athenæum* does show me so much favour, while, as in a late instance, so little justice is shown to my husband?' *LEBB,* I, 469.

60. The essay brought a bracing letter from Carlyle, ending with a typical exhortation: 'Seriously, dear Browning, you must at least gird up your loins again; and give us a right stroke of work . . . Prose or Poetry . . . in whatever form your own Daimon bids.' *Letters of Thomas Carlyle to John Stuart Mill, John Sterling, and Robert Browning,* ed. by Alexander Carlyle (1923), p. 293.

61. Quoted in DeVane, p. 207.

62. *LRB,* p. 40.

63. *Elizabeth . . . to Her Sister,* p. 216.

64. *Elizabeth . . . to Her Sister,* p. 233.

65. *NL,* p. 85.

66. *NL,* p. 87.

67. See above, p. 13.

68. *Letters of Thomas Carlyle . . . Robert Browning,* p. 296.

69. *The Correspondence of Emerson and Carlyle,* ed. by Joseph Slater (1965), p. 512.

70. *NL,* p. 93.

71. Quoted in W. G. Collingwood, *The Life and Work of John Ruskin* (1893), pp. 232–5.

72. *NL,* pp. 92–3.

73. *NL,* p. 97.

74. The latter was junior partner in the firm of Ticknor and Fields, which

actually paid Browning for the right to print *Men and Women*, when in fact, it could as easily have pirated the poems. Browning was duly grateful. The course of Browning's reputation in America has been treated fully in Louise Greer's *Browning and America* (1952).

75. William Michael Rossetti, *The Praeraphaelite Brotherhood Journal* (1900), p. 211.

76. Rossetti, pp. 226-7.

77. Rossetti, p. 271.

78. Rossetti, *passim*.

79. Georgiana Burne-Jones, *Memorial of Edward Burne-Jones* (1904), I, 128-9. Cf. the excellent article by M. B. Cramer, 'What Browning's Literary Reputation Owed to the Pre-Raphaelites, 1847-1856', *English Literary History*, VIII (December 1941), p. 305-21.

80. *Letters to William Allingham*, ed. by H. Allingham and E. B. Williams (1911), pp. 64 and 290.

81. *Letters to William Allingham*, p. 160.

82. Nathaniel Hawthorne, *French and Italian Notebooks* (1871), p. 293.

83. *Browning to His American Friends*, ed. by Gertrude Reese Hudson (1965), p. 101. At the same time, Browning admitted that the ordinary critic would have some difficulty, for 'there is more in my works than a newcomer can take in at once. . . .' *DI*, p. 181.

84. See for example *Robert Browning and Julia Wedgwood*, ed. by Richard Curle (1937), pp. 87, 93; and *DI*, pp. 180-1.

85. *DI*, p. 220.

86. Browning's acquaintance with Jowett began in 1865, when the poet was hoping to have his son, Pen, enrolled in Balliol. The attempt was unsuccessful, for Pen was by no means a diligent student, but Browning and the Master struck it off well. In June 1865, Jowett could record, 'I thought I was getting too old to make new friends. But I believe that I have made one—Mr. Browning, the poet, . . . I had no idea that there was a perfectly sensible poet in the world, entirely free from vanity, jealousy, or any other littleness, and thinking no more of himself than if he were an ordinary man.' *Life and Letters of Benjamin Jowett*, ed. by Evelyn Abbott and Lewis Campbell (1897), I, 400. Jowett admired the man more than the poet; the friendship deepened through the years in which Browning visited Oxford as often as he could and lasted until the poet's death. Jowett was delighted by, and probably influential in procuring, the honorary fellowship which Browning received from Balliol in 1867.

87. *DI*, p. 220.

88. See Kenneth L. Knickerbocker, 'Why Browning Severed Relations with Chapman and Hall', *NL*, pp. 393-400, for a detailed account of this complex affair.

89. *Robert Browning and Julia Wedgwood*, pp. 143-4.

90. *Robert Browning and Julia Wedgwood*, p. 182.

91. In a letter to Jean Aitken, Carlyle recorded an amusing sidelight. The Queen, he wrote, asked Browning, 'Are you writing anything?' But Carlyle, thinking of *The Ring and the Book*, added to Mrs. Aitken, 'He has just been publishing the absurdest of things!' *New Letters of Thomas Carlyle*, ed. by Alexander Carlyle (1904), p. 252.

92. Matthew Arnold, writing to his mother, took a different view of Austin's article, holding it up as an example of 'ability, and . . . showing with what much greater independence . . . poets are now judged.' *Letters of Matthew Arnold, 1848–1888,* ed. by George Russell (1895), II, pp. 10–11.

93. *DI*, p. 332.

94. *LRB*, p. 159.

95. *Letters of the Brownings to George Barrett*, ed. by Paul Landis with the assistance of Ronald E. Freeman (1958), p. 300.

96. See Donald Smalley, 'A Parleying with Aristophanes', *PMLA*, LV (September 1940), 823–38, for an analysis of the matter.

97. The edition ran to nineteen issues, at which point the project was abandoned for 'views of scenery and Summer Resorts in Wisconsin and Minnesota'. See Broughton, pp. 32–33.

98. *William Allingham: A Diary*, ed. by Helen Allingham and D. Radford (1907), p. 205.

99. *Allingham Diary*, p. 225.

100. Sir Charles Tennyson, *Alfred Tennyson* (1949), p. 452.

101. *The Letters of Algernon Charles Swinburne*, ed. by Edmund Gosse and T. J. Wise (1919), I, pp. 222–3.

102. *The Swinburne Letters*, III, p. 628.

103. Among the lines which seem most personal are the following:

'Dwarfs are saucy,' says Dickens: so, sauced in
Your own sauce, . . .

Browning ended the sentence thus, with three periods, but at the bottom of the page added a footnote:

'No, please! For
'Who would be satirical
On a thing so very small?'

104. The controversy stirred up over the attack on Austin, together with some of the pertinent documents, is treated in *LRB*, pp. 358–63. See also No. 196.

105. See *LRB*, p. 175.

106. *LRB*, p. 175.

107. Quoted in Broughton, p. 126.

108. *The Swinburne Letters,* III, 31.

109. John Drinkwater, 'New Letters of Matthew Arnold to Robert Browning', *Cornhill Magazine*, CXXVIII (1923), pp. 663–4.

110. *Allingham Diary*, pp. 258–60.
111. *LRB*, p. 231.
112. *Allingham Diary*, p. 291.
113 Browning societies, some quite active, still exist in a variety of places, including New York; Independence, Missouri; and Hollywood, California.
114. See Donald Smalley, 'Mephistopheles at the Conventicle: G. B. S. amid the Browningites', *Saturday Review of Literature*, XXVII (22 July 1944), 13–15, for a full account of Shavian participation in the society.
115. *LRB*, p. 205.
116. 6th ser. V (6 May 1882), p. 360.
117. *LRB*, p. 212.
118. Gerard Manley Hopkins, who never admired Browning's artistry, noted in 1884 that Browning had won a popularity poll reported in *The Spectator*. *Further Letters of Gerard Manley Hopkins*, ed. by C. C. Abbott (1956), p. 349.
119. *Letters to Mrs. Fairbanks*, ed. by Dixon Wecter (1949), pp. 260–1.
120. Quoted in DeLancey Ferguson, *Mark Twain—Man and Legend* (1943), p. 207.
121. See Boyd Litzinger, *Time's Revenges: Browning's Reputation as a Thinker, 1889–1962* (1964), *passim*, for evidence of this melancholy fact.
122. See Henry Jones, *Browning as a Philosophical and Religious Teacher* (1891); George Santayana, 'The Poetry of Barbarism', *Interpretations of Poetry and Religion* (1900); and John Robertson, *Browning and Tennyson as Teachers: Two Studies* (1903).
123. In addition to DeVane's *Handbook*, see also his *Browning's Parleyings: The Autobiography of a Mind* (1927), an excellent early study. Some of Professor Raymond's best work has been reprinted in *The Infinite Moment and Other Essays in Robert Browning* (1950).
124. The DeVane and Knickerbocker edition of *New Letters of Robert Browning* and the McAleer edition of *Dearest Isa*, both referred to often in this introduction, set a standard for later editions to meet.

PAULINE

January 1833

---

1. Unsigned notice, *The Literary Gazette*

23 March 1833, p. 183

Somewhat mystical, somewhat poetical, somewhat sensual, and not a little unintelligible,—this is a dreamy volume, without an object, and unfit for publication.

2. Allan Cunningham, *The Athenæum*

6 April 1833, p. 216

From his unsigned review.

There is not a little true poetry in this very little book: here and there we have a touch of the mysterious, which we cannot admire; and now and then a want of true melody, which we can forgive; with perhaps more abruptness than what is necessary: all that, however, is as a grain of sand in a cup of pure water, compared to the nature, and passion, and fancy of the poem. We open the book at random; but fine things abound; there is no difficulty in finding passages to vindicate our praise:

[Quotes ll. 230–59; 732–80]

The poem is dated Richmond, Oct. 22, 1832; it bears no name, and carries the stamp of no poet with whose works we are intimate. We hope the author's next strains will be more cheerful, and as original as these; the day is past, we fear, for either fee or fame in the service of the muse; but to one who sings so naturally, poetry must be as easy as music is to a bird, and no doubt it has a solace all its own.

3. W. J. Fox, *The Monthly Repository*

April 1833, N.S. vii. 252–62

With this unsigned review, Fox—who knew, of course, that Browning was the author of *Pauline*—put Browning for ever in his debt and made himself the poet's literary godfather. See Introduction, p. 3.

These thoughts have been suggested by the work before us, which, though evidently a hasty and imperfect sketch, has truth and life in it, which gave us the thrill, and laid hold of us with the power, the sensation of which has never yet failed us as a test of genius. Whoever the anonymous author may be, he is a poet. A pretender to science cannot always be safely judged of by a brief publication, for the knowledge of some facts does not imply the knowledge of other facts; but the claimant of poetic honours may generally be appreciated by a few pages, often by a few lines, for if they be poetry, he is a poet. We cannot judge of the house by the brick, but we can judge of the statue of Hercules by its foot. We felt certain of Tennyson, before we saw the book, by a few verses which had straggled into a newspaper; we are not less certain of the author of *Pauline*. . . .

The author cannot expect such a poem as this to be popular, to make 'a hit', to produce a 'sensation.' The public are but slow in recognizing the claims of Tennyson, whom in some respects he resembles; and the common eye scarcely yet discerns among the laurel-crowned, the form of Shelley, who seems (how justly, we stop not now to discuss), to have been the god of his early idolatry. Whatever inspiration may have been upon him from that deity, the mysticism of the original oracles has been happily avoided. And whatever resemblance he may bear to Tennyson (a fellow worshipper probably at the same shrine), he owes nothing of the perhaps inferior melody of his verse to an employment of archaisms which it is difficult to defend from the charge of affectation. But he has not given himself the chance for popularity which Tennyson did, and which it is evident that he easily might have done. . . .

Our limit compels us to pause. Our opinion will be readily inferred from the quantity which we have quoted from a publication of only seventy pages. The chief blemish is a note ascribed to Pauline, p. 55; and there are a few passages rather obscure, 'but that's not much.' In recognising a poet we cannot stand upon trifles, nor fret ourselves about such matters. Time enough for that afterwards, when larger works come before us. Archimedes in the bath had many particulars to settle about specific gravities, and Hiero's crown, but he first gave a glorious leap and shouted *Eureka!*

4. From an unsigned review, *The Atlas*

14 April 1833, p. 228

Consisting as it does of only two critical paragraphs, this extract from an unsigned review must still be considered a not-inauspicious one, for the reviewer thought well enough of the poem to excerpt some fifty lines for his readers.

In this little poem, a poetical spirit struggles against some mechanical difficulties that often give to the lines a prosaic character. The metrical construction is occasionally faulty, and the language is often plain where the image with which the poet is labouring is mystical.

Pauline is metaphysical throughout, or is intended to be so. The author is in the confessional, and acknowledges to his mistress the strange thoughts and fancies with which his past life has been crowded. This is not always accomplished with becoming dignity. He does not always speak of his agonies in language worthy of one who evidently understood them so well; he sometimes runs slip-shod through his afflictions. But there are many passages in the piece of considerable beauty, and a few of such positive excellence that we augur very favorably of the genius that produced them.

5. From an unsigned notice, *Tait's Edinburgh Magazine*

August 1833, iii. 668

John Stuart Mill was preparing a careful review of *Pauline* for *Tait's* when this contemptuous notice appeared. Mill thereupon returned his annotated copy of the poem to the sender, and the review was never written.

. . . we have *Paulina* [*sic*], *a Fragment of a Confession;* a piece of pure bewilderment.

6. William Maginn, *Fraser's Magazine*

December 1833, xlii. 699–70

From an unsigned review entitled 'The Poets of the Day: Batch the Third'.

In the course of a condescending notice of newly published poetry, the reviewer turns to *Pauline*. The notice ends with a column and a half of heavy-handed humour (omitted here), consisting of lines taken from the poem and put into the mouths of Lord Grey, his ministers, and friends.

M. M. H. Thrall suggests that Thackeray may have collaborated with Maginn in this review (*Rebellious Fraser's*, 1934, p. 297); but Edward M. White, in 'Thackeray's Contributions to *Fraser's Magazine*', *Studies in Bibliography*, ed. by Fredson Bowers, 19 (1966), 74, rejects the notion that Thackeray had any share in it.

'*Non dubito quin titulus*,' &c., quotes the author of *Pauline*, our next poem, from Cornelius Agrippa; which we, shearing the sentence of its lengthy continuation, translate thus: 'We are under no kind of doubt about the title to be given to you, my poet;' you being, beyond all question, as mad as Cassandra, without any of the power to prophesy like her, or to construct a connected sentence like any body else . . . we designate you 'The Mad Poet of the Batch;' as being mad not in one direction only, but in all. A little lunacy, like a little knowledge, would be a dangerous thing.

We have weighty reasons for believing that *Pauline* is the production of one or all of the Whig ministers. The same folly, incoherence, and reckless assertion, which distinguish their pamphlet on the *Reform Ministry and Parliament,* is visible in each page of the book . . .

PARACELSUS

August 1835

7. Unsigned notice, *The Athenæum*

2 August 1835, p. 640

There is talent in this dramatic poem, (in which is attempted a picture of the mind of this celebrated character,) but it is dreamy and obscure. Writers would do well to remember (by way of example,) that though it is not difficult to imitate the mysticism and vagueness of Shelley, we love him and have taken him to our hearts as a poet, not *because* of these characteristics—but *in spite* of them.

8. Unsigned review, *The Spectator*

15 August 1835, viii. 780–1

A 400-word summary of the plot of *Paracelsus* has been omitted.

The defect in the structure of this poem is palpable: there is neither action nor incident, scarcely even a story to excite the attention of the reader. Of this the author seems to be in some sort conscious; stating that he has endeavoured to write a poem, not a drama, and to reverse the method usually adopted by writers whose aim it is to set forth any phœnomenon of the mind or of the passions by the operations of persons and events; and that instead of having recourse to an external machinery of incidents to create and evolve the crisis he desired to produce, he has ventured to display somewhat minutely the mood itself in its rise and progress, and has suffered the agency by which it is influenced and determined to be generally discernible in its effects alone. But admitting all this to have been designed, the design may still be very injudicious: for the form of dialogue precludes those descriptions and digressions by which the author in a narrative poem can vary his subjects and 'interchange delights'; whilst the fundamental plan renders the whole piece a virtual soliloquy, each person of the drama *speaking up* to Paracelsus, in order to elicit his feelings, thoughts, or opinions. For these reasons, we conceive that such a poem contains in its structure the elements of tediousness, which no execution could obviate; and, unfortunately, the execution of *Paracelsus* is not of a nature to overcome difficulties. Evidences of mental power, perhaps of poetical talent, are visible throughout; but there is no nice conception and development of character, nothing peculiar or striking in the thoughts, whilst the language in which they are clothed gives them an air of mystical or dreamy vagueness.

9. John Forster, *The Examiner*

6 September 1835, pp. 563–5

From his unsigned review.

On 31 December 1835, at the home of William Macready, the actor and stage-manager, Browning was introduced to Forster, who identified himself as the author of this review. The acquaintance deepened, and Forster's growing appreciation of Browning resulted in a second, more favourable, review of *Paracelsus* (No. 13). Browning thought that this review turned the tide of adverse criticism which had been running against his poem. *RB-EBB,*I, 322.

Since the publication of *Philip Van Artevelde*,[1] we have met with no such evidences of poetical genius, and of general intellectual power, as are contained in this volume. It is a philosophical view of incident, to create and evolve the crisis he desires to produce, prefers to display somewhat minutely the mood itself in its rise and progress, and to suffer the agency by which it is influenced and determined, to be generally discernible in its effects alone, and subordinate, if not altogether excluded. The effect of this mode of treatment is necessarily severe, and the reader who takes up the volume must be prepared accordingly. He will find enough of beauty to compensate him for the tedious passages, were they ten times as obscure and tedious. A rich vein of internal sentiment, a deep knowledge of humanity, an intellect subtle and inquisitive, will soon fix his interest, and call forth his warmest admiration. He will probably read the book twice—as we have done . . .

It is some time since we read a work of more unequivocal power than this. We conclude that its author is a young man, as we do not recollect his having published before. If so, we may safely predict for him a brilliant career, if he continues true to the present promise of his genius. He possesses all the elements of a fine poet.

[1] Published in 1834, Henry Taylor's *Philip Van Artevelde: a Dramatic Romance, in Two Parts* retained a certain readership into the 1870s, by which time it had run to a seventh edition.

41

10. W. J. Fox, *The Monthly Repository*

November 1835, N.S. ix. 716–27

From his unsigned review.

This poem is what few modern publications either are, or affect to be; it is a work. It is the result of thought, skill, and toil. Defects and irregularities there may be, but they are those of a building which the architect has erected for posterity, and not the capricious anomalies of the wattled pleasure house, which has served its turn when the summer-day's amusement is over, and may be blown about by the next breeze, or washed away by the next torrent, to be replaced by another as fantastic and as transient . . . —One beauty, of which there are many instances, cannot be exhibited in extract; it is, the touching allusiveness, towards the close of the poem, to the scenery and circumstances of the early life of Paracelsus, as indicated at the commencement. In many instances, too, there is an exquisite adaptation of metaphorical illustration to sentiment and character; so exquisite, that we cannot imagine how a few violations of this harmony which occur, should have escaped the author's correction, or ever have flowed from his pen at all. The argument in the first part of the poem, and some subsequent passages, would bear condensation; and be improved, even in clearness, by the avoidance of an amplification and repetition, which is rhetorical rather than poetical.

11. Leigh Hunt, *The London Journal*

21 November 1835, ii. 405–8

From a full and favourable review, concluding with a lengthy summary of the plot and generous quotations from every part of the poem.

Some questions may be raised as to points in the execution of Mr Browning's poem, but there can be none as to the high poetic power displayed in it. There are, as it appears to us, some marks of haste in the composition, and we should have been better pleased with the absence both of the statement in the preface, that the poem had not been imagined six months before its publication, and of any ground for making such a statement; for we cannot doubt that the same genius which, in the space of time mentioned, produced the work as it now appears, would not have spent six months longer in brooding over its conceptions and their first rapid embodiment, without making the finished whole something still finer than it is. . . .

In its chief constituent qualities Mr Browning's style and manner of writing is, like that of every man of cultivated powers, a sufficiently true representative of his manner of thinking; even its peculiarities, whether they might, in the abstract, be accounted commendable, or the reverse, must be held to be indispensable to its perfection, because they are a reflection of mental habits which have contributed to make his poetry what it is. We do not therefore object generally to his long and often somewhat intricately involved sentences, or to forms of phraseology and construction, of occasional occurrence, which are apt for a moment to perplex or startle on the first reading, or to any other deviations of a similar kind from ordinary usage or the beaten highway prescribed by our books of authority in grammar, rhetoric, and prosody, in so far as such unusual forms are the natural and unaffected product of the writer's genius, working its purposes in its own way. Such distinctive characteristics, when we have become familiar with them, and they have lost any slight repulsiveness with which they may have at first acted upon us, even acquire a power of enhancing the pleasure we

43

receive from a composition otherwise eminently beautiful, and of rivetting our love for it. We do not doubt that there are, in *Paradise Lost* for instance, many peculiar forms of phraseology which the national ear has now learned not only to tolerate but to admire, but which must have surprised more than they pleased the first readers of the poem; and even some cadences of the divine verse which now linger in all memories and all hearts, but which those who first endeavoured to catch their music probably deemed forced and dissonant. But in these cases we must suppose that true art has really been present and at work, although (nothing uncommon or wonderful) the effect may have been too new and too exquisite to be all at once understood and appreciated. The result will be very different where the peculiarity is not a real excellence, but a mere trick or whim. Then the disapproval which it may expect to meet with when the blinding influences of novelty operate no longer,—the condemnatory and decisive verdict of posterity—will be still more severe than that which may have been at first passed upon it. It may then operate as powerfully to scare away the regards of men from the genuine beauties with which it may happen to be associated, as it would help in the other case to attract and fix their admiration.

Mr Browning, like every writer who aims at an original style, would do well to keep these considerations in mind, and to beware of being seduced, while seeking to produce new and bold effects, into either slovenliness or affectation. We think there is in the present poem a slight degree occasionally of both the one and the other; and to many readers it will probably appear that there is a great deal of both. There is much both in the diction and the versification which has a harsh, awkward, and disappointing effect at first; but this, in by far the greater part, arises merely from the poem not being cast in a common mould, or formed so much as most new poems are upon the ordinary models. It is not a mere additional variation of the old air; and it cannot therefore be read off-hand so readily and smoothly as the generality of the poetical productions of the day. There is a hidden soul in its harmony which must be first unwound—a retiring grace in its unwonted forms of phraseology which must be won before the poetry can be rightly enjoyed or understood. The reader of such a work has his effort to make, as well as the writer has had his—his powers of apprehension, as the other has had his powers of production, to keep on the stretch.

12. Unsigned notice, *Tait's Edinburgh Magazine*

November 1835, N.S. ii. 765

It is a dramatic poem, constructed upon the model of *Philip Van Artevelde*; but the author says no. His composition is a *poem*, not a *drama*. Yet what we consider the finest passages in the poem are decidedly dramatic. We have not space to vindicate this dissenting opinion, but refer to the very beautiful and effective opening of a scene—*A chamber in the house of Paracelsus at Basil. Time, 1526.*

13. John Forster, *The New Monthly Magazine and Literary Journal*

March 1836, xlvi. 289–308

From his unsigned article, entitled 'Evidences of a New Genius for Dramatic Poetry'.

This is the simple and unaffected title of a small volume which was published some half-dozen months ago, and which opens a deeper vein of thought, of feeling, and of passion, than any poet has attempted for years. Without the slightest hesitation we name Mr. Robert Browning at once with Shelley, Coleridge, Wordsworth. He has entitled himself to a place among the acknowledged poets of the age. This opinion will possibly startle many persons; but it is most sincere. It is no practice of ours to think nothing of an author because all the world have not pronounced in his favour, any more than we would care to offer him our sympathy and concern on the score of the world's indifference. A man of genius, we have already intimated, needs neither the one nor the other. He who is conscious of great powers can satisfy himself by their unwearied exercise alone. His day will come. He need never be afraid that truth and nature will wear out, or that Time will not eventually claim for its own all that is the handywork of Nature. Mr. Browning is a man of genius, he has in himself all the elements of a great poet, philosophical as well dramatic,—

> The youngest he
> That sits in shadow of Apollo's tree

—but he sits there, and with as much right to his place as the greatest of the men that are around him have to theirs. For the reception that his book has met with he was doubtless already well prepared,—as well for the wondering ignorance that has scouted it, as for the condescending patronage which has sought to bring it forward, as one brings forward a bashful child to make a doubtful display of its wit and learning. 'We hope the best; put a good face on the matter; but are sadly afraid the thing cannot answer.' We tell Mr. Browning, on the other hand, what we do not think *he* needs to be told, that the thing WILL answer. He has written a book that will live—he has scattered the seeds of much thought among his countrymen—he has communicated an impulse and increased activity to reason and inquiry, as well as a pure and high delight to every cultivated mind;—and this in the little and scantily-noticed volume of *Paracelsus*!

Before going farther, it may be as well to come to some understanding with the reader respecting the course of this article. In sitting down to write, we confess we had intended to limit ourselves to the matters strictly embraced in our title, and we took up Mr. Browning's volume with the intention of waiving many new and striking points of philosophical suggestion contained in it, for the purpose of considering more emphatically the evidences it abundantly presents of a new genius for dramatic poetry. We find, however, on examination, that we cannot restrict ourselves to so narrow a view of the poem. Its subject-matter and treatment are both so startlingly original, and both so likely to be altogether misunderstood; it embraces in its development so many of the highest questions, and glances with such a masterly perception at some of the deepest problems, of man's existence; that we feel, while to touch upon these various topics will not interfere with the object we first proposed, it is only in this way that a proper and just appreciation of the singular power and beauty, even of the dramatic portions of this poem, can be conveyed to the reader. We promise him, in accompanying us through our criticism, that if, in its course, we do not break even a wholly new ground of philosophical inquiry into character, we shall at least suggest to him some valuable and very interesting trains of thought. It is the greatest glory of such labours as those of Mr. Browning, that they open up, on every side of us in the actual world, new sources of understanding and sympathy. . . .

. . . Passion is invariably displayed, and never merely analysed. Even at those moments when we seem most of all to be listening to its results alone, we are made most vividly sensible of the presence of the very agents by which the results have been determined. Mr. Browning has the power of a great dramatic poet; we never think of Mr. Browning while we read his poem; we are not identified with him, but with the persons into whom he has flung his genius. The objections to a dialogue of the French school do not apply. We get beyond conjecture and reasoning, beyond a general impression of the situation of the speakers, beyond general reflections on their passions, and hints as to their rise, continuance, and fall. We are upon the scene ourselves,—we hear, feel, and see,—we are face to face with the actors,—we are a party to the tears that are shed, to the feelings and passions that are undergone, to the 'flushed cheek and intensely sparkling eye.' The same unrelaxing activity of thought and of emotion, by which the results of the poem are meant to be produced, is made to affect the reader in its progress; and he is as certain of the immediate presence of all that is going on, as in life he would be certain of any thing that made him laugh or weep. *In the agitation of the feelings, sight is given to the imagination.* This is an essential dramatic test, in which Mr. Browning is never found wanting.

14. J. Heraud, *Fraser's Magazine*

March 1836, xiii. 362–74

From his unsigned review, entitled 'A Premature Infant'.

Paracelsus took six months to write; we wish the poet had spent six years upon it. *Artevelde* took six years; we wish the author had admitted us to its perusal when only six months old. The one period, however, is as much too short as is the other too long, for a perfectly healthy gestation. In the one, the soul has not been suffered to mature life; in the other, the body has had a chance of outlasting it. Nevertheless, give us life, passion, motion, growth. The premature infant is yet lovely; the posthumous carcass is only proper for the dissecting-room.

15. An Early American View

1843

An unsigned review by Ralph Waldo Emerson or Margaret Fuller, *The Dial*, April 1843, iii. 535.

This review is generally attributed to Emerson, but Louise Greer has made a case for Margaret Fuller, in her *Browning and America* (1952), pp. 218–23. *The Dial* was the organ of the Transcendentalists, a small but influential group of poets, critics, philosophers and *litterateurs* living in and near Boston.

Mr. Browning was known to us before, by a little book called *Pippa Passes*, full of bold openings, motley with talent like this, and rich in touches of personal experience. A version of the thought of the day so much less penetrating than Faust and Festus cannot detain us long; yet we are pleased to see each man in his kind bearing witness, that neither sight nor thought will enable to attain that golden crown which is the reward of life, of profound experiences and gradual processes, the golden crown of wisdom. The artist nature is painted with great vigour in Aprile. The author has come nearer that, than to the philosophic nature. There is music in the love of Festus for his friend, especially in the last scene, the thought of his taking sides with him against the divine judgment is true as poesy.

STRAFFORD

1837

---

16. From an unsigned review, *The Morning Chronicle*

2 May 1837, p. 3

For Macready's association with Browning, see Introduction, pp. 4–6.

Mr. Macready took his benefit last night, on which occasion a new historical tragedy, entitled *Strafford*, was successfully produced. It is from the pen of Mr. Browning, the author of *Paracelsus*, a play, or rather poem, which, at the time of its appearance, gave promise that if the author assiduously cultivated his powers he might one day be able to produce a good acting tragedy. Those who formed that estimate of his powers will probably not be disappointed by his present effort. We, who formed no anticipations upon the subject, and who thought that praise was too extravagantly showered upon his former production, must own, nevertheless, that Mr. Browning has written a tragedy which does great credit to his judgment, and shows that a little more study will enable him to take a very high rank among modern dramatic poets. It has been said that a good reading play is seldom a good acting play; and some have carried out this assertion still further, and affirmed that a good acting play ought not to read well. We do not profess to go to this length in all cases, but must admit that the mere perusal of Mr. Browning's *Strafford* produced an unfavourable impression upon us. We could find no new thoughts—no bursts of impassioned eloquence —no inspiration, no choice sentences full of truth and poetry, which the mind, if it once receives, retains forever—nothing, in fine that could induce us to pause over the page and say to ourselves, 'This man is a poet.' We entered the theatre with this unfavourable impression, but as the play proceeded it wore gradually away, and when the curtain fell were convinced that we had done the author injustice. We found that it was part of his plan to avoid those sparkling poetic passages which may charm in the closet, but which fall monotonously upon the ear when drawled forth by a second-rate actor, and distract the attention which longs to fix itself upon the incidents of the play. Mr. Browning is, to a certain degree, right, and seems to have formed a tolerably correct estimate of the real difference between a dramatic poem and a play, and it was this, and not a want of inspiration, which made the tragedy so dry in the perusal.

17. From an unsigned review, *The Sun*

2 May 1837, p. 4

It acts even better than it reads, for this reason, that action is substituted for description, and mere poetry made subservient to the sterner business of the drama. Still it is by no means the highest effort of which Mr. Browning is capable. We are convinced he can do better—work out his ideas more fully—develope his characters in a more subtle, analytical spirit. The good stuff is in him, but patience and diligent habits of thought are requisite, to enable him to work out the conceptions with which it is evident his imagination teems, even to overflowing. The leading defect of *Strafford* is that it is, in a great degree, obscure, we might almost say, unintelligible to those who are not well acquainted with the stirring period of which it treats. . . . The language throughout is spirited, sententious, and dramatic; never inflated—never tame—never sinking below the level of mediocrity. Above all, mere poetry—poetry we mean that encumbers dialogue, and bids action halt—is carefully avoided. Mr. Browning has also been scrupulously correct in his adherence to the truth of character. . . . Mr. Browning therefore must set to work again, for if any one can revive the half-extinct taste for the drama, he can.

18. Unsigned review, *The Times*

2 May 1837, p. 5

The tragedy is *very* historical; it would be almost unintelligible to one who had not made himself acquainted with the *minutiae* of the eventful period to which it relates, and hence we almost fear its not becoming so popular as its intrinsic merits deserve. One great secret Mr. Browning has discovered, which is, that the language of the drama should be concise and pointed, instead of being diffuse and florid. There is not through the whole piece an useless declamation introduced for the sake of displaying poetical beauties; each character says what he has to say exactly, and no more. This love of closeness has even in some instances carried the author too far—he has here and there introduced such a number of broken sentences that it is hard to understand him. To Mr. Macready, who played Strafford, was left the task of rendering these obscurities at least comparatively plain, and he acquitted himself exceedingly well. The character of Pym is a bold sketch; he is represented as one who loves Strafford more than any other man, and yet feels himself bound to sacrifice him for his country's sake. The contentions in the daring Republican's spirit pursue him throughout the piece, but he is not brought forward enough to be more than an outline portrait, and Vandenhoff rendered him a much duller gentleman that the author could have desired. The Countess of Carlisle was evidently intended as the ray which should throw a soft light over the piece, but her character wants fullness, and never lays strong hold on the interest. Miss Faucit[1] played the part judiciously. The Earl of Strafford was *the* character; the picture of a man ever falling and ever retaining his loyalty is admirably drawn. His position is made what the German critics call truly 'tragic', that is to say, he does not fall so much on account of the fault of any individual, but on account of the natural chain of events against which he is compelled to struggle. This is Mr. Browning's first dramatic effort, and it is one of no little promise.

[1] Helen Faucit (1817–98) also played leading parts in *A Blot in the 'Scutcheon* and *Colombe's Birthday*. She and her husband (she married Theodore Martin, later Sir Theodore, in 1851) were close friends of Browning until his death, at which time she placed a plaque honouring him in a church in Wales, where he had once worshipped. *Baylor Browning Interests,* Second Series (1931), pp. 7ff.

19. Unsigned review, *The Athenæum*

6 May 1837, p. 331

That there must be much cleverness in anyone who can construct and write a five act tragedy, to which an audience will patiently listen, is beyond a doubt; but we do not think that *Strafford* has interest enough about it, either of plot or dialogue, to give it more than a temporary existence. The personal politics of the individuals brought on the scene, are entered into far too minutely; and the speeches generally contain so many broken sentences, that they become quite unintelligible; indeed, to so extraordinary and unusual an extent was this last fault carried, that we at last discovered that the best way of obtaining an impression of what was going on was, to take care not to follow the speaker too closely, but to hear the opening of a sentence, and supply the remainder by imagination. This style of writing might answer very well, if an author could be sure that the whole audience would be of one mind; but as that is not very probable, we prefer the old-fashioned way of addressing yourself direct to the understanding. Mr. Macready played Strafford with very great ability, and with almost more than even his wonted energy. Mr. Vandenhoff was sadly prosy in Pym; and Mr. Dale, in Charles the First, was nothing short of execrable. Miss Vincent was quite out of place in Henrietta-Maria; and Miss Helen Faucit, in the Countess of Carlisle, contrived, with much feeling, much delicacy, and great skill, to fill up the outline of a very charming character, which the author had rather indicated than drawn, and to make intelligible that which he had left very indistinct.[1]

[1] Of these minor actors mentioned—Vandenhoff, Dale, and Miss Vincent—none reached the pinnacle of success. John Vandenhoff (1790–1861) was admired for his portrayals of Lear and Iago at Covent Gardens, and Mary Ann Vincent (1818–87), an American born in England, played various comic and character roles in both countries. Mr. Dale seems not to have distinguished himself.

20. John Forster, *The Examiner*

7 May 1837, pp. 294–5, 310

From his unsigned review.

This is the work of a writer who is capable of achieving the highest objects and triumphs of dramatic literature. They are not achieved here, but here they lie, 'in the rough', before every reader. . . . We will at once say in what we think the error of the tragedy of *Strafford* consists. The author has suffered himself to yield too much to the impulses of the pure poetical temperament in delineating the character of Strafford. . . .

Strafford was winning its way into even greater success than we had ventured to hope for it, but Mr. Vandenhoff's secession from the theatre has caused its temporary withdrawal.[1] It will be only temporary, we trust; no less in justice to the great genius of the author, than to the fervid applause with which its last performance was received by an admirably filled house.

21. From an unsigned review, *John Bull*

7 May 1837, xvii. 225

Now, unfavourable as is our judgment on this tragedy, it has been given in no intolerant spirit. We would hardly have been so minute, or so diffuse, on an unworthy subject. It is for the promise which the effort betokens that we speak. There is evidence of power in it, from which failure cannot detract. The very faults of the drama are proofs of talent.

---

[1] *Strafford* was acted once more—as a benefit performance, 30 May 1837—and was withdrawn permanently.

The author has aimed at the Greek model in its construction, and successfully. He has shown, and well, the powerlessness of man's will against destiny. The failure here has been the fault of his choice of a hero; for Strafford was not 'a *great* man struggling with the storms of fate.' Nor, as we previously observed, has he made him such. The very plainness of the language, too, evinces strength, and is good augury for the future. In his scorn for what are y'clept *poetic* plays, in other words, for dramas made the vehicle of a puling poetry, he has rushed into the opposite extreme, and rudely discarded the grace of diction. But in this, there is a self-reliance, and a knowledge of the true ends of theatric representation which we honour. In his next attempt, let him bring on the scene Character in Action, and we will answer for it that he triumphs.

22. Thomas Lovell Beddoes, letter

May 1837

From a letter to Thomas Kelsall, *Poems, Posthumous and Collected* (1851), pp. ciii–civ.

Beddoes (1803–49) is best remembered for his *Death's Jest Book,* or *The Fool's Tragedy* (printed in 1850, but begun in 1825), a horror play in the manner of Webster and certain other Elizabethans. Kelsall became his literary executor.

. . . the *Examiner* is quite rapturous about *Strafford*;[1] although I confess that the extracts, he chooses and praises, appear to me not exactly dramatic. One is a dialogue between two people describing Pym's appearance, action &c. in a style, which has been approved by critics of late, and considered highly graphic. But is it not very artificial? In Shakespeare such passages are rare, and only in scenes, where the person, whose actions are described, must necessarily be laconic if not entirely

[1] See No. 20.

speechless, and where the spectators, in their doubt, fear, and wonder, naturally communicate to each other their interpretations of the dumb show before them.

23. From an unsigned review, *La Belle Assemblée*

May 1837, vi. 324–5

Not only does the principal part seem to have been written to suit Mr. Macready's style of acting, but the whole play is penned in a series of abrupt, broken sentences, expressly suited to that style of delivery for which our eminent tragedian is so famous. Too much is left for the performers to fill up by their action and expression; and, of course, except in the character of *Wentworth*, embodied by the superior talents of Macready, the other parts were heavy and purposeless. The frequent interruptions and breaks in the speeches gave them a degree of mystery that the most vivid imagination could not clear up, or the quickest apprehension understand. The plot is by no means coherent, and consequently most of the characters become heavy.

24. From an unsigned review, *The Metropolitan Magazine*

May 1837, xix. 50–1

As an acting play, *Strafford* will undoubtedly hereafter occupy a prominent place on the British stage, but will never, we think, be a favourite in the closet. *Strafford* is as devoid of any effusion of fancy, or flight of imagination, as any play can well be; it is unadorned by poetry, the blank verse is occasionally rough and halting, the sentiments and opinions are few and common-place [*sic*], and, above all, the plot is somewhat obscurely developed to those unread in English history; and yet it was eminently successful. Its success was chiefly owing to the admirable conception, and, what is of more importance in an historical play, the faithful delineation of the characters, and the stirring action of the incidents.

25. Herman Merivale, *The Edinburgh Review*

July 1837, lxv. 132–51

From his unsigned review.

Merivale (1806–74) was a historian who wrote occasional reviews for the *Edinburgh*.

In the general phraseology of the play,—even in the manner in which the rough old Puritans address each other,—there is a sort of affected, fondling tone, which perfectly disconcerts us. As for poor Lady Carlisle, seeing that she is desperately in love with Strafford from the beginning of the play, we can perhaps excuse his calling her 'girl', and 'Lucy', in every line; but really we do not think there was any thing in the character of the lady to justify him in supposing that Denzil Hollis would have taken the liberty of addressing her as 'girl' too.

All these, we must once more repeat it, are, chiefly, defects of taste. They are peculiarities belonging to that which (by the leave of Mr Landor)[1] we must still take the liberty of calling, for want of a better name, the 'Cockney school' of dramatic authorship. And we have not been thus severe in our observations on the bad taste and affectation with which this play abounds, from any malice of criticism. But the author is a young man, and this essay exhibits powers which we can ill afford to see thrown away in the pursuit of false reputation. Had it been otherwise, we should not have taken the trouble to examine his claims to the distinction which he has earned. His defects are fostered by a corrupt taste in theatrical matters; and those defects in turn, meeting with applause instead of correction, tend to increase and perpetuate the evil. For the rest, his success is a proof that his work affords striking situations and dramatic interest. He has developed his matter with breadth and simplicity of purpose, instead of breaking it up into highly-wrought details and insulated scenes; and this is the first great requisite in order to produce effect on miscellaneous readers and spectators. Even his

---

[1] Walter Savage Landor, poet and author of the famous *Imaginary Conversations*. He had been an enthusiastic admirer of Keats, against whom the 'Cockney' epithet had been employed.

style, of which we have thought it our duty to present a few singular specimens, is, on other occasions, wanting neither in power nor richness. When he lays aside affectation, and condescends to employ continuous dramatic dialogue, there is an energy about him not unworthy of the scenes and epochs which he has chosen to represent.

SORDELLO

March 1840

26. Unsigned review, *The Spectator*

14 March 1840, xiii. 257

What this poem may be in its extent we are unable to say, for we *cannot* read it. Whatever may be the poetical spirit of Mr. Browning, it is so overlaid in *Sordello* by digression, affectation, obscurity, and all the faults that spring, it would seem, from crudity of plan and a self opinion which will neither cull thoughts nor revise composition, that the reader—at least a reader of our stamp—turns away.

27. From an unsigned review, *The Atlas: A General Newspaper and Journal of Literature*

28 March 1840, No. 724, xv

We are disappointed in this poem, and have no inclination to dwell at length upon the causes of what we must consider a descent from the high promise of *Paracelsus*. The faults of that production were obvious —rugged and abrupt lines—strange turns of expression—want of fullness and completeness. Its merits were equally striking—intense enthusiasm—rich imagery—profound feeling—strong delineation. In the poem of *Sordello,* all the faults recur in exaggerated shapes, without being relieved or compensated for by an equal amount of excellence in any single point of view.

The subject is one of deep and extraordinary interest. The readers of Dante need not be reminded of it, nor need it be suggested to them as a theme pregnant with capabilities. Mr. Browning has treated it in the narrative form; and an odd, fantastic narrative he has made of it—something starting off into a mood of scoffing humour, anon melting into pathos, and then bursting out into passion, but fulfilling none of the conditions of any of these fits, and producing a mosaic of bits and tints which it is difficult to trace with satisfaction or coherency. Nor does he make amends to us even by occasional fragments of the beautiful, such as we believe his genius to be able to accomplish. The whole structure is faulty, not only in its entire outline, but in its minutest details. One example, long enough to include samples of most of the peculiarities of the writer, will suffice as an illustration:

[Quotes V. 1–47.]

Here we have the same pitching, hysterical, and broken sobs of sentences —the same excisions of words—the same *indications* of power—imperfect grouping of thoughts and images—and hurried, exclamatory, and obscure utterance of things that would, probably, be very fine if we could get them in their full meaning, but which, in this bubbling and tumult of the verse, are hardly intelligible—the same idiosyncrasy of mind and manner that was first exhibited in *Paracelsus*, and that was afterwards carried to still greater excess in *Strafford*. We looked for an improvement upon all this in *Sordello*. We expected that the poet would have shaken off these crudities, and emerged a natural and free man, disenchanted out of his youthful heresies, and prepared to exhibit a sound and vigorous maturity. But we are disappointed. *Sordello* is worse than *Strafford,* with less excuse, for what might be tolerated in the clamour and heat of action in a drama, is intolerable in a narrative; and it is further chargeable with betraying the disagreeable truth that the author has not only benefited nothing from experience, but that the sins of his verse are premeditated, wilful, and incurable.

28. From an unsigned review, *The Athenæum*

30 May 1840, pp. 431–2

If it were Mr. Browning's desire to withdraw himself from the inquest of criticism, he could scarcely have affected that purpose better than by the impenetrable veil, both of manner and language, in which he has contrived to wrap up whatever truths or beauties this volume may contain. Into his peculiarities of language—his quarrels with the prepositions, and other puerilities and affectations, it is scarcely worth while to enter, further than to hint to the author, that even if his truths and beauties lay nearer the surface than they do, they would recommend themselves far more agreeably in the accepted grammatical forms; and that euphony is one of the conditions of poetry, which, as a sort of usher to the rest, is less safely neglected than some of its higher and more essential qualities. The reader's attention, during the first half of this volume, is necessarily occupied in mastering those novelties of mere construction, the perfect understanding of which is necessary to qualify him for grappling with the far more impracticable peculiarities of expression that lie below:—and the second half is exhausted in the attempt to acquire such a familiarity with the author's manner, as may enable him to get at the meanings concealed in the oracles themselves. The first of these difficulties may, of course, be overcome. Like any system of short-hand, the author's scheme of syntax may, with some trouble, be acquired. The second carries us too far into the regions of transcendentalism to offer any certainty of a satisfactory solution. The song of the bard falls dull and muffled on the ear, as from a fog; and if, at times, a breath of purer inspiration sweeps off the vapours, letting his voice come articulately to the understanding, it is but for a moment. Fold upon misty fold has stolen up, while we were yet rejoicing over our premature ευρηκα,[1] and the singer is again lost to our apprehension in cloudy depths, whither it must be a long labour to learn to follow him. It is, nevertheless, these occasional outbreaks of light, giving assurance of a spiritual presence, that win the reader onward,—tempted, as he is, again and again, to throw down the book in despair. The dust and cobwebs of Time, the student is willing to remove, for the purpose of

[1] Eureka.

getting at the old spiritualities that lie beneath a covering, spread over them by the hand of Nature; but the author who chooses deliberately to put 'his light under a bushel' of affectations, must not be surprised if men refuse the labour of searching it out, and leave him to the peaceable enjoyment of that obscurity which he has courted.

29. From an unsigned review, *The Dublin Review*

May 1840, viii. 551-3

This is a work by the author of *Paracelsus*, and one not likely to exalt his reputation, or to produce any adipose tendency in the exchequer of his respectable publisher. The title page is brief, not defining its character. This brevity may be studied, to enhance curiosity, or forced, from the difficulty of selecting the most appropriate description of the production issued. We have noted down several definitions, out of many that have struck us in the perusal, as being fitted to characterise it; such as 'Sordello a conundrum,' from the difficulty of making out the meaning or object of the author. 'Sordello, couplets illustrative of the interrogative system;' from the profuse use made of the contorted marks of interrogation, which are spread in great numbers through the pages, standing like so many Scarrons,[1] Popes and Æsops, but not contributing their wit, melody or wisdom. 'Sordello, or exercises for the asthmatics,' from the wheezy, spasmodic, sobbing nature of the verse. These are but a few specimens which the perusal has suggested to us; but as the determination, seeing their conflicting pretensions, is difficult, we must imitate a late chancellor, and postpone our final judgment.

We remember perusing the *Paracelsus* with some gratification, as a work of promise, which, despite its many defects, led us to hope that ultimately, we should be able to hail the author as one deserving of

[1] Paul Scarron (1610–60), French wit and writer whose burlesques helped to discredit the 'grand' style.

taking his seat among the crowned poets of the age, and whose productions would hereafter contribute fresh stores of beauty, strength, philosophic insight, and harmonious thought, apparelled in majestic and melodious numbers, to the literature of our country. The play of *Strafford* somewhat checked that expectation. Although in it there was no insignificant dexterity in the construction, the language occasionally exhibited power and richness, and somewhat of an artistic eye, there was a meanness in the working out of his conceptions, a want of dignity and appropriateness in the dialogue, and an offensive and vicious style, apparently grounded on some conceited theory, at utter variance with all the canons of taste and propriety.

Our perusal of *Sordello* has not renewed our early anticipation. The faults of Mr. Browning are here exaggerated and profusely displayed, to the destruction of all interest, comprehension of the narrative, sympathy with the author, or approbation of his intellectual pretensions. The story is most elliptically constructed, full of breaks and leaps; the syntax of quite an unusual character, a mass of perplexity and obscurity; the versification is harsh and knotty; the language, instead of being throughout 'English undefiled,' is larded with many fantastic and arbitrary invertions, and the whole set together in a ricketty, hysterical, capricious style, producing the most startling and repulsive effect. All this makes us fear that the defects, which we had previously fancied were ascribable to immaturity, are the result of some obstinate system which has now obtained too strong a control over the writer, ever to let him stand up a free man, to discourse of noble and regenerating themes in a mode worthy of such, or of the sublime and responsible avocation of a poet. If the critical aphorism of Coleridge be true, that the poem to which we *return* with the greatest pleasure, possesses the genuine power and claims the name of *true poetry*, then is *Sordello* certainly condemned; for it is as impossible to *return* to, as to read it for the first time even with pleasure.

We regret that we have not been able to give a more recommendatory notice of Mr. Browning's work; but we have a high estimate of the aim and functions of a poet, and are jealous guardians of our country's literature. We cannot, therefore, to gratify a clever man, or to win a false character for liberality among publishers, compromise our duty and mislead our readers. He has given indication of powers, that if faithfully, diligently, and loftily cultivated, might place him in an honourable and benificent position. The world of the beautiful is not exhausted, the number of the poets is not yet made up; there are thousands of manifestations of the good, the true, the lovely, the eternal in man, yet to be revealed. He may yet give the world assurance that he is one who has been appointed to this high calling which he aims at; If he *aspire rightly*, he will *attain*. We hope that he will do so; but let him take this warning from us, in the only quotation we shall make from his *Sordello*,—

> Change no old standards of perfection; vex
> With no strange forms *created to perplex*.

30. From an unsigned review, *The Monthly Chronicle*

May 1840, v. 476–8

Mr. Browning seems to have forgotten that the medium of art must ever be the *beautiful*; he seems to be totally indifferent to pleasing our imagination and fancy by the music of verse and of thought, by the grace of his diction as well as of his imagery; and when this want of a sweet flowing beauty both in thought and versification . . . is coupled with a positive want of dramatic or speculative interest in the story, and a by no means new or newly put moral, we may be pardoned if we regard *Sordello* as a failure *in toto*.

31. Unsigned review, *The Monthly Review*

May 1840, ii. 149

The scene of this poem is laid in Italy, when the Ghibelline and Guelph factions were in hottest contest. The author's style is rather peculiar, their being affectations of language and invertions of thought, and other causes of obscurity in the course of the story which detract from the pleasure of perusing it. But after all, we are much mistaken if Mr. Browning does not yet prove himself a poet of a right stamp,—original, vigorous, and finely inspired. He appears to us to possess a true sense of the dignity and sacredness of the poet's kingdom; and his imagination wings its way with a boldness, freedom and scope, as if he felt himself at home in that sphere, and was resolved to put his allegiance to the test.

32. Unsigned review, *The Metropolitan Magazine*

1840, xxvii. 108–9

If it were possible to understand the meaning of the writer of this poem, we should be delighted to impart the information to our readers. It is full of hard words and mysterious sentences, but what they allude to, it would puzzle a conjuror to tell. In this dilemma, what can we do better than let Mr. Browning speak for himself?

[Quotes III. 814–30]

This is a fair specimen of the poem throughout. We had rather write sonnets on the *latest*, as well as the earliest *speaking ass,* than be doomed ro read such unintelligible oozings of nonsense.

33. Unsigned review, *The New Monthly, Belle Assemblée*

1840, xii. 214

Sordello, by Robert Browning.—If Mr. Browning will write, we wish he would write something comprehensible. *Sordello* is full of hard names, and nonsense. He calls it poetry, we term it trash of the very worst description.

34. Richard Hengist Horne, 'Robert Browning's Poems', *The Church of England Quarterly*

October 1842, pp. 464–83

In a letter of 13 December 1842 to his close friend Alfred Domett, Browning identified Horne as the author of this unsigned article, adding '. . . was it not generous of an unappreciated man, so to write?' *Robert Browning and Alfred Domett*, ed. F. G. Kenyon (1906), p. 50.

Containing, as it does, so many passages of the finest poetry, no manner of doubt can exist but that *Sordello* has been hitherto treated with great injustice. It has been condemned in terms that would lead any one to suppose there was nothing intelligible throughout the whole poem. We have shown its defects in detail, and we have also shown that it has some of the highest beauties. The style, the manner, the broken measure, the recondite form; these have constituted still greater difficulties than even the recondite matter of which it treats—though the latter only were quite enough to 'settle' or 'unsettle' an ordinary reader.

The poem of *Sordello* is a beautiful globe, which, rolling on its way to its fit place among the sister spheres, met with some accident which gave it such a jar that a multitude of things half slipt into each other's places. It is a modern hieroglyphic, and should be carved on stone for the use of schools and colleges. Professors of poetry should decypher and comment upon a few lines every morning before breakfast, and young students should be *ground* upon it. It is a fine mental exercise, whatever may be said or thought to the contrary. The flowing familiar style sometimes reminds us of Shelley's *Julian and Maddalo* with a touch of Keat's *Endymion*, broken up into numerous pit-falls, whether mines of thought or quirks of fancy; but there are also other occasions when it becomes spiral, and of sustained inspiration, not unlike certain parts of the *Prometheus Unbound* put into rhyme; yet is it no imitation of any other poet. Certain portions also remind us of the suggestive, voluble, disconnected, philosophical jargon of Shakespeare's fools, and with all the meaning which they often have for those who can find it. The poem is thick-sown throughout with suggestions and glances of history, biography, of dark plots, tapestried chambers, eyes behind the arras, clapping doors, dreadful galleries, and deeds in the dark, over which there suddenly bursts a light from on high, and looking up you find a starry shower, as from some remote rocket, descending in silent brilliancy upon the dazzled page. Each book is full of gems set in puzzles. It is like what the most romantic admirers of Goethe insist upon 'making out' that he intended in his simplest fables. It is the poetical portion of three epics, shaken together in a sack and emptied over the hand of the intoxicated reader. It is a perfect storehouse of Italian scenery and exotic fruits, plants, and flowers; so much so, that by the force of contrast it brings to mind the half-dozen flowers and pastoral common-places of nearly all our other modern English poets, till the recollection of the sing-song repetitions makes one almost shout with laughter. It is pure Italian in all its materials. There is not one drop of British ink in the the whole composition. Nay, there is no ink in it, for it is all written in Tuscan grape juice, embrowned by the sun. It abounds in things addressed to a second sight, and we are often required to *see double* in order to apprehend its meaning. The poet may be considered the Columbus of an impossible discovery, as a worthy divine pleasantly observed to us. It is a promised land, spotted all over with disappointments, and yet most truly a land of promise, if ever so rich and rare a chaos can be developed into form and order by revision, and its southern fulness of tumultuous heart and scattered vineyards be ever reduced to given proportion, and wrought into a shape that will fit the average mental vision and harmonize with the more equable pulsations of mankind.

PIPPA PASSES

April 1841

---

35. Unsigned review, *The Spectator*

17 April 1841, xiv. 379

This reviewer's confusion is charming: he does not realize that the poem is complete in itself, and he assumes that Browning hopes to have it staged. Unfortunately, we have no record of Browning's reaction.

This is a publication intended to comprise a series of 'dramatical pieces' by the author of *Paracelsus*, and to appear at intervals; the object of the writer being to procure by such means their introduction to the stage. Allowance is to be made for every first number; especially when it exhibits only part of a play, and that part of necessity the least stirring in its action and the least interesting from its passion. But, judging with this qualification, the scheme of Mr. Browning is not likely to conduct to the wished-for end, unless he greatly change his mode of execution. In *Pippa Passes* (which title apparently means that Pippa, the heroine, only *passes* over the stage, talking to herself, and stimulating the conduct of others by her appearance,) though there is nearly enough letterpress for a short tragedy, we are merely introduced to the actors, and apparently not to all. So far as we have yet the means of judging, *Pippa Passes* is not a drama, but scenes in dialogue, without coherence or action; not devoid of good thoughts poetically expressed, but perfectly ineffective from being in a wrong place. Nor does the moral tone appear to be of the kind likely to be tolerated on the stage, or approved of anywhere. In one scene, a young wife and her paramour discuss their loves and the murder of the 'old husband,' needlessly, openly, wantonly, tediously, and without a touch of compunction, sentiment, or true passion. In another scene, common courtezans of the poorest class are introduced;

70

one gloating, naturally enough perhaps, over what such people in England call a 'blow-out,' to which an admirer had lately treated her, and giving the recipe by which she wheedles her dupes. The story itself, as we gather from the last pages, will probably turn upon the endeavours of an uncle to get his niece, brought up as a peasant, (*novel* incident!) inveigled to Rome as a prostitute, in order that he may get possession of her property—*novelty* again!

36. From an unsigned review, *The Examiner*

2 October 1841, pp. 628–9

Paracelsus announced a new and original poet—one of the rarest things met with in these days: much cried out for, much sought after, and, when found, much objected to. We dare say that *Paracelsus* did not succeed: we never heard of a second edition: but we find it an agreeable circumstance to remember, that from this journal it had its first and heartiest acknowledgment.

Mr. Browning has published since then: in our opinion, not so well. But yet not so, as to falsify any anticipation formed of the character of his genius. To write a bad poem is one thing: to write a poem on a bad system is another, and very different. When a greater curiosity about the writer shall hereafter disentomb *Sordello*, it will not be admired for its faults, but, in spite of them, its power and its beauty will be perceived. It had a magnificent aim, and a great many passages in which justice was done to that, and to the genius of the designer. The temptations which too easily beset a man's pride in his own originality; the enticing and most dangerous depths of metaphysics, which are, to the young and genuine thinker, as the large black eyes of Charlotte were to Werter,[1] [*sic*] a sea, a *precipice*; into these the poet fell. But to rise again. The misfortunes which are apt to occur in this literal world of ours, the seas

---

[1] In Goethe's *The Sorrows of Young Werther,* the hero, realizing the hopelessness of his love for Charlotte, commits suicide.

and precipices that receive one here, the bogs and pitfalls, are seldom recoverable: but he that

has been led astray

Through the HEAVEN'S wide pathless way finds, soon or late, the guide that brings his footsteps home.

This *Pippa Passes* is worthy of the writer of *Paracelsus*. We call it, without doubt, a piece of right inspiration. It is in a dramatic form, and has fine dramatic transitions, but its highest beauty is lyrical. It gushes forth, an irrepressible song. Its rich variety of verse, embodying the nicest shades of poetical and musical rhythm, flows in a full tide of harmony with each lightest change of sentiment. We want no better assurance of entire sincerity, for the Idea presented in the poem. No one ever yet managed to get utterances of this kind, out of what Mr. Carlyle calls the region of *Sham*. . . .

We are told no more, but can guess what the morning brings. This good Pippa is no longer the ragged little silk-winding girl; but Felippa, the rich and wealthy niece of Monsignor; the daughter of his elder brother, whom the wicked second brother had removed for seizure of her inheritance.

The defect in the execution of the work—the whole conception seems to us to have extraordinary beauty—lies in the scene with the young sculptor and his bride. Here, with some few exquisite exceptions, the language is so fitful and obscure, the thoughts themselves so wild and whirling, the whole air of the scene so shadowy and remote, that, with its great blots of gorgeous colour too, we are reminded of nothing so much as of one of Turner's canvasses—pictures *of* Nothing, as some one has called them, and remarkably like. But the very reverse of this, is the general style of the poem: suited to what it has to express; now crisply cutting out the thought, now softly refining or enlarging it; swelling or subsiding at the poet's will; and never at any time failing of originality. . . .

Let us conclude with a hope that she [Pippa] may get the welcome she deserves. Whomever she passes, she cannot but do good to—opening generous hopes, suggesting cheerful thoughts, awakening virtuous impulses.

37. From an unsigned review, *The Athenæum*

11 December 1841, p. 952

. . . Mr. Browning is one of those authors, whom, for the sake of an air of originality, and an apparent disposition to *think,* as a motive for writing,—we have taken more than common pains to understand, or than it may perhaps turn out that he is worth. Our faith in him, however, is not yet extinct,—but our patience *is.* More familiarized as we are, now, with his manner—having conquered that rudiment to the right reading of his productions—we yet find his texts nearly obscure as ever—getting, nevertheless, a glimpse, every now and then, at meanings which it might have been well worth his while to put into English. We have already warned Mr. Browning, that no amount of genius can fling any lights from under the bushel of his affectations. Shakspere himself would, in all probability, have been lost to the world, if he had written in the dead languages. On the present occasion, Mr. Browning's conundrums begin with his very title-page. *Bells and Pomegranates* is the general title given (it is reasonable to suppose Mr. Browning knows why, but certainly we have not yet found out—indeed we 'give it up') to an intended 'Series of Dramatical Pieces,' of which this is the first; and *Pippa Passes* is a very pretty exercise of the reader's ingenuity, which we believe, however, on reading the poem, we may venture to say we have succeeded in solving. A curious part of the matter is, that these 'Dramatical Pieces' are produced in a cheap form (neatly printed in double columns, price sixpence,) to meet and help the large demand—the 'sort of pit-audience'—which Mr. Browning anticipates for them! How many men does Mr. Browning think there are in the world who have time to read this little poem of his? and of these, what proportion does he suppose will waste it, in searching after treasures that he thus unnecessarily and deliberately conceals? 'Of course,' he says, 'such a work as this must go on no longer than it is liked;'—and, therefore, we are speaking of it, now, with that reverence and forbearance which one is accustomed to exercise towards the dead. Still-born, itself, it is also, no doubt, the last of its race—that is, if their being maintained by the public is a positive condition of their being begotten. Yet it has its limbs and lineaments of beauty, and exhibits the traces of an immortal spirit.

The idea of this little drama is, in itself, we think, remarkably beautiful, and well worth working out in language suited to its own simple and healthy moral. One of the daughters of labour, Pippa, a young girl employed in the silk-mills of Asolo, in the Trevisan, rises from her bed, on new-year's morning,—her single holiday of all the year: and, as she pursues the long, but willing, labours of her toilet, the map of its boundless enjoyments unfolds before her imagination. Then, among the light-hearted girl's thoughts, come those which *must* intrude upon the speculations of the poor—the contrasts with her own lowly lot presented by the more fortunate forms of life which she sees everywhere around her. Her neighbours of the little town of Asolo pass in review before her, with their several circumstances of what, to the outward eye, is advantage; and a touch of the envy and ill will, from which even the humble cannot be wholly exempt, mingles with her purer fancies, and dims the brightness of her holiday morning. But, in the breast of this joyous-hearted girl, these feelings soon take a healthier tone,—resolving themselves into reliance upon providence, contentment with her lot, which has in it this *one* chartered day—now only beginning—and a sense that she is a child of God as well as all the others, and has a certain value in the sum of creation, like the rest:— and so, she breaks away out into the sunshine, merry as a May-day queen,—

> Down the grass-path grey with dew,
> Neath the pine-wood blind with boughs,
> Where the swallow never flew
> As yet, nor cicale dared carouse,

with a song expressing such sentiments, and her own joy:

> The year's at the spring,
> And day's at the morn:
> Morning's at seven;
> The hill-side's dew pearled;
> The lark's on the wing,
> The snail's on the thorn;
> God's in his heaven—
> All's right with the world!

And then, the poem, which has no unity of action,—is held together by the single unity of its moral, and is dramatic only because it is written in dialogue-form—introduces us, by a series of changes, into the interiors of certain of those dwellings which the envious thoughts of

Pippa had failed to pierce: and we are present at scenes of passion or intrigue, which the trappings, that had dazzled her eye, serve to hide. One of these, between the wife of a rich miser and her paramour,—on the night which conceals the murder of the husband, by the guilty pair, but just as the day is about to dawn upon it—is written with such power of passion and of painting (with a voluptuousness of colour and incident, however, which Mr. Browning may find it convenient to subdue, for an English public) as marks a master-hand,—and makes it really a matter of lamentation, that he should persist in thinking it necessary for a poet to adopt the tricks of a conjuror, or fancy that among the true spells of the former are the mock ones of the latter's mystical words. Into this scene of guilt and passion,—as into all the others to which we are introduced,—breaks the clear voice of a girl, singing in the young sunshine. By each and all of them, 'Pippa passes,'—carolling away her one untiring burthen of gladness,—carrying everywhere her moral that 'God's in his heaven,' and the world beneath his eye—scattering sophisms and startling crime. Before this one natural and important truth, taught to a cheerful and lowly heart, the artificialities of life severally dissolve, and its criminals grow pale. Surely, there is something very fine in this! Not only have we the trite, but valuable, moral that happiness is more evenly distributed than it seems, enforced in a new form,—but also that other and less popularly understood one, which it were well the poor should learn,—and still better that the rich should ponder,—that the meanest of them all has his appointed value in God's scheme,—and a higher part may be cast to him who has to play it in rags, than to the puppet of the drama who enacts king, and walks the stage in purple. This despised little silk-weaver, like a messenger from God, knocks at the hearts of all these persons who seem to her so privileged,—and the proudest of them all opens to her. Again, we say, this is very fine;—and Mr. Browning is unjust both to himself and others, when he subjects it to the almost certainty of being lost. Why should an author, who can think such living thoughts as these, persist in making mummies of them?—and why should we, ere we could disengage this high and beautiful truth, have had to go through the tedious and diagreeable process of unwrapping?

38. Thomas Carlyle, letter

21 June 1841

From a letter to Robert Browning, *New Letters of Thomas Carlyle*, ed. Alexander Carlyle (1904), i. 233–4.

Acknowledging the receipt of complimentary copies of *Sordello* and *Pippa Passes*, Carlyle here opens a correspondence which led to a friendship which terminated only with Carlyle's death in 1881.

If I have made no answer hitherto, it was surely not for want of interest in you, for want of estimation of you: both Pieces have given rise to many reflexions in me, not without friendly hopes and anxieties in due measure. Alas, it is so seldom that any word one can speak is not worse than a word still unspoken;—seldom that one man, by his speaking or his silence, can, in great vital interests, help another at all!—

Unless I very greatly mistake, judging from these two works, you seem to possess a rare spiritual gift, poetical, pictorial, intellectual, by whatever name we may prefer calling it; to unfold which into articulate clearness is naturally the problem of all problems for you. This noble endowment, it seems to me farther, you are *not* at present on the best way for unfolding;—and if the world had loudly called itself content with these two Poems, my surmise is, the world could have rendered you no fataller disservice than that same! Believe me I speak with sincerity; and if I had not loved you well, I would not have spoken at all.

A long battle, I could guess, lies before you, full of toil and pain, and all sorts of real *fighting*: a man attains to nothing here below without that. Is it not verily the highest prize you fight for? Fight on; that is to say, follow truly, with steadfast singleness of purpose, with valiant humbleness and openness of heart, what best light you can attain to; following truly so, better and ever better light will rise on you. The light we ourselves gain, by our very errors if not otherwise, is the only precious light. Victory, what I call victory, if well fought for, is sure to you.

If your own choice happened to point that way, I for one should hail it as a good omen that your next work were written in prose! Not that I deny you poetic faculty; far, very far from that. But unless poetic faculty mean a higher power of common understanding, I know not what it means. One must first make a true intellectual representation of a thing, before any poetic interest that is true will supervene.

KING VICTOR AND KING CHARLES

March 1842

39. John Forster, *The Examiner*

2 April 1842, pp. 232–4

Forster devotes a good deal of space in this unsigned review to comparing Browning's portrayal of the drama's chief characters with his own interpretation of the historical Victor, Charles, Polyxena and D'Ormea.

. . . Be this as it may—and whether *to return* was a part of the original design, as Mr Browning would make it; or, as we think more likely, a part of the original weakness of the old man's subjection to an infamous woman, for whom he had resigned his crown, and impelled by whom he came to ask for it again—Victor, within a year of his abdication, *did return*. But he found his son less docile and pliant than he had left him. And here equal doubts as with the motives of the father, occur respecting the conduct adopted by the son. It seems questionable whether there were needless cruelty and harshness in what he did, or whether he was urged and sustained through it all by a noble sense of duty. Mr Browning uses the poetic privilege admirably, in reconciling the external facts on which these questions arise; and the decisive measures which are said to have broken the heart of Victor, are with great beauty and masterly skill made quite compatible with the generous character which history gives to Charles. But the mere facts as they stand on record in relation to Victor's return, we take to be these. At first, his son would not believe that his father seriously entertained the intention attributed to him; but on receiving serious proofs to that effect, took council with his nobles, and had him at once arrested. Victor then passed twelve wretched months in solitary detention at Rivoli, and miserably died. The old man's heart was broken, but his passionate temper stayed to the last. It is even said, in some of the more private details of this unhappy time, that from his death bed he drove away the priests of the church, to which he had theretofore never failed in duty, appalled by the nature of his denunciations against King Charles. 'Bring no consolation to me,' he said, when they reminded him of the Great Sacrifice for the remission of suffering and of sin: 'He of whom you speak, had a son to die for Him: *I die for my son.*'

The characters in Mr Browning's tragedy are four: Victor and Charles; Polyxena, the wife of Charles; and D'Ormea, the minister of both kings. Of these, we like Victor the most; and, notwithstanding some exquisite management in relation to him, Charles the least. Until near the close indeed, he is in such a continual and most painful fret and worry that we long for all our sakes to have him any way out of it. The secret of Mr Browning's error in this, we suspect to be one very common with the best young poets: the love of a too decisive contrast. But it needed no such artifice to recommend the more strikingly, the calm and quiet figure by Charles's side. Polyxena is a charming conception, adequately sustained: a delightful picture of the high-toned Love in woman, which without other aid gives brightness to the intellect and irresistible moral strength to the soul. We like D'Ormea too: the rascally, conscience-scared [*sic*] old minister, who suddenly finds himself infected with virtue as with an influenza, and is very nigh falling a martyr to it.

The general fault of the tragedy, as a poem, is in its defects of versification; and, as a dramatic work, in its substitution of the metaphysics of character and passion for their broad and practical results. These mistakes, which have a wilful and deliberate air, are easily pointed and much effective abuse vented upon them without much trouble. But it is worth more trouble to be able to discover, even in these, the wayward perverseness of a man of true genius. Such is Mr. Browning. We ought not to extenuate what we hold to be a grave error; but we think it not difficult to see that, by the very passion for his art, such a man may be so betrayed. Time is the great corrector: as Time is the disinterested, the immortal witness on Poetry's behalf, that her ways are very old and very settled ways, not admitting, like those of steam and other wonderful inventions, of many novel or useful improvements. She had now been current in the world for some thousands of years, and it is generally admitted, we believe, that the first effort she made—the first at any rate of which there is written record—*continues to be the best.*

We cannot subjoin all we could have wished, from the tragedy itself:

but the reader who is wise enough to take our word, and act on it, will find his reward in many beautiful, powerful, and pathetic passages. . . .

[The review ends with a column of quotation from the play.]

40. From an unsigned review, *The Athenæum*

30 April 1842, pp. 376–8

This is the second of a series of poems which, under the whimsical title of *Bells and Pomegranates*, Mr. Browning promises to the world. We have before predicted that Mr. Browning's audience would be limited, and, inasmuch as he has doubled the price of admission, we are led to conclude that our prediction has been fulfilled. If such be the case, even in the teeth of our infallibility, we regret it, for we have faith in Mr. Browning, and trust to see him realize a higher destiny than that of the thousand and one claimants to the laurel crown. . . .

This plot, it will be seen at a glance, is highly dramatic; and Mr. Browning has worked it out with skill. His characters are drawn with breadth and great distinctness of colouring. The sensibility, the true-heart, the vacillating will of Charles at the commencement of the drama, his subsequent energy and developed talents, when the crown is placed on his head, and the noble aim of a nation's welfare, which gives concentration to his powers, are finely conceived. The restless ambition and selfishness of Victor, the bold dishonesty and sarcastic deceit of D'Ormea (the Prime Minister), and the calm, lofty, pure-mindedness of Polyxena, are pictured with unity and vigour. But in giving an extract, or two, we must once again, and emphatically, express our regret, at the extent to which Mr. Browning allows his manner to interpose between his own fine conceptions and the public. Full of thought, full of learning, full of fancy as his poems show him to be, they also exhibit him as cumbered, rather than strengthened by the number of his possessions, and neither few nor far between are the portions where this inability to do justice to his own meanings, takes forms, which might

be confounded by the superficial observer with commonplace. . . .
Of a like quality is the closing scene of the chronicle. It may give our author little popularity among the many: but it must confirm the few in their anxiety to see him take 'the one step more' out of the labyrinth in which he lingers too fondly. . . .

DRAMATIC LYRICS

November 1842

41. John Forster, *The Examiner*

26 November 1842, pp. 756-7

From his unsigned review.

There was an extremely clever dissertation on Mr Browning's poems in one of the quarterly reviews the other day, in which *Sordello* was recommended as 'a fine mental exercise.' Something of the sort we had said ourselves, and if poetry were exactly the thing to grind professors of metaphysics on, we should pray to Mr Browning for perpetual *Sordellos*. As it is, we are humble enough and modest enough to be more thankful for *Dramatic Lyrics*. The collection before us is welcome for its own sake, and more welcome for its indication of the poet's continued advance in a right direction. Some of this we saw and thanked him for in his *Victor and Charles,* much more in his delightful *Pippa Passes,* and in the simple and manly strain of some of these *Dramatic Lyrics,* we find proof of the firmer march and steadier control. Mr Browning will win his laurel. We were the first to hail his noble start in *Paracelsus;* the *Straffords* and *Sordellos* did not shake our faith in him; and we shall see him reach the goal.

And is there nothing to object to, then, in the *Dramatic Lyrics*? Oh, plenty—but so much more to *praise*! Readers as well as critics should oftener *remember* Rochester's couplet, which, not having *quoted* this many a day, we will once again repeat.

> It is a meaner part of sense
> To find a fault than taste an excellence!

—and there being many more excellences to be tasted in Mr Browning than faults to be found, we propose just now to follow the advice of Lord Rochester.

It is an honourable distinction of Mr Browning that in whatever he writes, you discover *an idea* of some sort or other. You shall have great difficulty in finding it, when he happens to have the humour of obscurity upon him; and there are many of his wilful humours, in which it shall not be worth the search: but any how there it is. He is never a tagger of verses. There is purpose in all he does. Often there is thought of the profoundest kind, often the most exquisite tenderness, his best passages are full of the best Saxon words, and in the art of versification he must be called a master. It is his surpassing facility in this particular, that now and then plays bewildering pranks with his reader's ear—distracting, dazing, and confusing it, in mazes of complicated harmony. On more happy occasions, the flow with which his lines gush forth into the kind of music most appropriate to the thoughts that prompt them, is to us extremely charming; and for the neatness of his rhymes in his lighter efforts, we think that Butler would have hugged him. In a word, Mr Browning is a genuine poet, and only needs to have less misgiving on the subject himself, to win his readers to as perfect a trust, and an admiration with as little alloy in it, as any of his living brethren of the laurel are able to lay claim to.

The *Lyrics*, as their title imports, are for the most part dramatic: full of the quick turns of feeling, the local truth, and the picturesque force of expression, which the stage so much delights in. The three that open the collection are *Cavalier Tunes;* two follow called *Italy and France*, apparently designed to show the different estimation of Woman in these different countries: *Camp and Cloister* is the title of the next two, the purpose being to illustrate, in the carking monk and careless generous soldier, effects of either training. We have afterwards two on the subject of *Queen-worship*, and two of *Madhouse Cells;* the rest being matters detached, with stories of their own to tell. *Artemis Prologuises* in the stately and sonorous march of the Greek drama: two watched and fated lovers rehearse, *In a Gondola*, their love and their voluptuous fancies, with contrasts of dread and pleasure, till the sudden dagger ends the passionate interchange: and in the piece called *Waring*, the writer, dramatically assuming the garb of a very commonplace person, seems to regret hugely one of those wonderful friends who are supposed to be able to do everything because they never attempt to do anything. Various is the merit of these various poems: sometimes very grave the faults. But on the whole they confirm what we have said of Mr

Browning's genius, and prove that he is fast reclaiming it from the 'vague and formless infinite' of mere metaphysical abstraction. . . .

[Forster then quotes at length, with brief comments interspersed, 'Give a Rouse', 'Incident of the French Camp', and about 130 lines of 'The Pied Piper of Hamelin'.]

42. Unsigned review, *The Athenæum*

22 April 1843, p. 385

That it is Mr. Browning's pleasure to be enigmatical, may now, we suppose, be considered as an accepted condition of his literary dealings with the public; and any further attempt on the critic's part to obtain better terms, would seem to be a waste of time and argument. The subject of his mannerisms we shall, therefore, abandon, as one on which we have no motive to dwell further—taking leave of it, however, with this final hint:—that what Mr. Browning may, perhaps, consider as an evidence of strength is a sign of weakness—what he may regard as a portion of his wealth, is a witness of its limitation. The inaptitude for giving intelligible expression to his meanings, whether unconscious or artificial, whether its cause be affectation or incapacity, is a defect, lessening the value, in any available sense, of the meanings themselves; and the riches which can be turned to no account lose their character of riches. Golden thoughts affect simple forms; and where the precious metal is most abundant, men have least time and temptation to work it into strange and fantastic characters. Mr. Browning's style is, therefore, *primâ facie* evidence against his muse; and, for his own sake—and something for the public's—we wish it were not so; because they who will take the trouble to question further, will find that its implied testimony does not report quite truly.

The titles that head this article are those of small volumes forming Nos. III. and IV. of the series whose general designation, *Bells and Pomegranates*, as yet remains a mystery. Which of these poems are Bells,

and which Pomegrantes—or why any one of them is either—is one of
those secrets which we may suppose 'shall be unriddled by and bye.' In
the meantime, it is equally difficult to understand how the *disjecta
membra* which compose No. III. should have found their way into a
professed collection of 'Dramatical Pieces.' Mr. Browning, who has a
regal way of disposing of all such trifling difficulties, and considers his
author's *'stet pro ratione voluntas!'* binding on the reader, summarily
observes that he 'supposes they come properly enough under that head,
—being, though for the most part lyric in expression, always dramatic
in principle, and so many utterances of so many imaginary persons, not
his.' For ourselves, in considerably more than one half of them, we
have not been able to discover any dramatic quality whatever. In any
case, however, they are mere fragments, varying in length from half a
dozen lines upwards—apparently thoughts jotted down for after use—
or rejected from their places in longer pieces, and denoting foregone
conclusions—but scarcely important enough to have formed the
materials of an independent publication. Out of the collection, such
as it is, we would gladly have selected the ballad of Count Gismond;
but its length compels us to a shorter and less interesting specimen of
the author's ballad-style—spirited and characteristic, notwithstanding:—. . . .

[The reviewer quotes, in their entirety, 'Incident of the French Camp',
'Soliloquy of the Spanish Cloister', and 'Marching Along'.]

43. From a verse-epistle by Arnould addressed to Browning

27 November 1842

To be found in Donald Smalley, 'Joseph Arnould and Robert Browning: New Letters (1842–50) and a Verse Epistle', *PMLA* (March 1965), lxxx. 90–101.

During the early 1840s Joseph Arnould was one of Browning's closest friends and warmest admirers, though by no means a blind one. A minor poet himself (as an Oxford student he won the Newdigate prize in 1834), Arnould defended Browning's plays, deplored the obscurity of *Sordello*. Arnould's practice at law and Browning's removal to Italy did not end the friendship. Arnould acted as one of the trustees of the Browning marriage settlement, and even long after he became Judge of the Supreme Court in Bombay he retained a warm opinion of his friend. Mr. Smalley, whose edition of the poem is used, has traced the Arnould-Browning relationship fully in his article. The 'Three giant strides' in the epistle probably refer to the first three numbers of *Bells and Pomegranates* as advances over *Sordello*.

> Friend you have triumphed, with imperious skill,
> And a strong energy of Stoic will,
> Sage Lord of wealth unbounded you have taught
> Language to be the *minister* of thought;
> No harlot handmaid, finically gay
> Who seeks to rival Her she should obey,
> No formal slave, whose niggard speech conceals
> One half her sense, & mars what it reveals,
> No mystic priest whose smoke of rare perfume
> Enwraps his Deity in three-fold gloom,
> But a sublime Interpreter; . . .
> Such was *Sordello's* fault all art, all man
> All nature grasped at in one noble plan—
> All nature there, all man, all art was traced,

The *poet* saw, the *poet* had embraced;
But in his extacy of soft delight
Too steeply soaring in his Godlike fight
He half forgot the multitude he meant
To carry with him in his grand intent,
And left them gazing in bewildered crowds
At gorgeous mists, & skirts of gilded clouds
Which wrapt from them the empyrean blue
In whose pure void his revelling spirit flew—
All praise be his, the Poet's! he has learned
A noble lesson, and to Earth has turned,
Our beautiful, brave Earth, where not a sod
But, touched by Poetry, is quick with God.
Honour to him our Poet! he has broke
From his freed neck the metaphysic yoke. . . .
Three giant strides each firmer, than the last
Have set you free—the peril's overpast; . . .
Yet Browning other strides remain to take:
The thirst you kindle you alone can slake!
Ours is a noble age, an age of faith
A resurrection after years of death.
The men who *are*, the men who are to come
Their hopes, their fears, their aims must not be dumb.
Reawakened Love & Reverence that requires
A Priest to guide it to the Sacred fires,
The boundless hope of something to supply
The want of that, which, while we want we die,
The strong assurance, dashed at times with doubt,
That from our darkness Light must be struck out,
That the dim twilight which now lowers o'er all
Is but a cradle curtain not a pall,
That the great hope, which swells the worlds great soul
Is impulse struggling to a glorious goal—
To teach us this by some undying word
Is your high mission—be it's mandate heard!
Then dash the veils away, the curtain rend
Make plain all riddles, let all mysteries end.
Let the throned Genius with majestic grace
Put by the mists that still obscure his face
Divide the vapours with his parting hand
And full before the world then Seer & Teacher stand!

THE RETURN OF THE DRUSES

January 1843

44. Unsigned notice, *The Spectator*

4 February 1843, xvi. 116

The scene of this 'tragedy' (God wot!) is laid in an island of the Grecian seas, where some Druses have been reduced to bondage by the Knights of Rhodes, and oppressed by their Prefect. The story is not told very intelligibly; but, as near as we can make it out, a Druse professes himself their Khaliff Hakeem, who had been dead some hundred years; gets up a conspiracy against the Knights; and, by expressing himself in a style obscurely mystical, he unintentionally excites his mistress, Anael, to kill the Prefect; when, after a series of dull and puzzling situations, Anael dies, the impostor Khaliff stabs himself, and the Druses are left on the start for Asia Minor. After this, we need not say that the story is improbable, and without interest: but it may be added, that the actors are mere phantasmagoria, *talking Browning*; and that the composition, with the usual faults, displays little of the power of the writer.

45. From an unsigned review, *The Athenæum*

1 July 1843, pp. 608–9

This three-column review is given almost entirely to a sympathetic and, on the whole, an intelligent tracing and analysis
of the plot. The complaint with which the reviewer concludes is
therefore the more interesting.

. . . Our readers will see that these are powerful dramatic elements;
and, in many respects, the author has used them with great poetical
skill. The interest and action are, of course, complicated by the introduction of other characters and episodes,—the principal of which are the
heroine Anael,—and the love betwixt her and Djabal. Anael, who had
been secreted by her brother, Khalil, from the licentious pursuit of the
Knight-Prefect, in the abode where Djabal found them when seeking
partizans amongst the islanders,—had made a vow, in the spirit of a
Grecian maiden, to love 'only one who should revenge the Druses;'
and Djabal, coming to her at once an avenger and almost a god, had
both fulfilled its condition and dazzled her with his assumed glory. Out
of this double character in which he wooed her, the author has extracted
a means of interest finely conceived,—but not quite so finely managed.
In Djabal's heart, a fear springs up, that Anael's love is rather for the
Hakeem than for the wandering sheikh, and that the knowledge of his
imposture would change it to contempt: and his nature is shaken
between the struggle of a generous impulse to confess to her his secret,
and the fear of ruining the conspiracy by its betrayal. On the other
hand, the heart of Anael has had certain revelations, which lead her to
fear that she loves the man more than the Khalif—that the bright trans-
formation to which he is destined before her eyes is a change for the
worse—and hence she is disturbed by an apprehension, that her love is
not such a love as he expects, and she ought to entertain for a prophet.
It must be confessed that the means by which she arrives at this secret of
her nature are of a rather questionable description, and our author has
not been poetically felicitous in their adoption. There is a certain

Christian knight, a model of chivalry, who has fallen in Anael's way; and she, in analyzing her feelings, finds that Loÿs de Dreux makes an impression upon her so nearly similar to that which, barring his spiritual character, Djabal creates, that her mind is reduced to a state of great uncertainty and disturbance. Certainly, although this desecration of his heroine, we believe, is not exactly what the author intends, he has so managed this portion of his scheme, that there is more than one scene in which she seems greatly at a loss to know which of the candidates for her favour she prefers, and so, consequently, is the reader, as to which she is likely finally to choose. The following passage will at once describe, in the author's own language, this rather complicated condition of things, and give a good specimen of the poetry of his drama:—

[Quotes Act II. 177–322]

From this point of the drama, the author's intentions are not quite clear. Impelled, as it would seem, by a wish to prove her faith in Djabal's mission, and do something in testimony of her attachment to his supernatural character, Anael with her own hand stabs the Prefect —a portion of the plot which the pretending Khalif had reserved for himself. Djabal finds her with the blood upon her hand; and then, in the excitement of the moment, comes a confession of his imposture. Then we have Anael's struggle between the sense of his degradation and the joy of his restoration to the level of her woman's heart; and, urging him to make confession to the people on whom he has imposed, she offers to share his shame. Djabal, however, refuses to abandon his deception till its object shall have been achieved; and Anael, therefore, denounces his fraud,—with what object we can only *conjecture* from what follows. Called upon by his own adherents to show his power upon the unknown blasphemer of that power, he is confronted with Anael, who is brought in veiled: and who, on the veil being removed, hails him, before them all, as *Hakeem*, and falls dead! Why, or by what instrument, she dies, is no way explained. The presumption seems to be, that her denunciation had been made with the view of confirming his authority, by seeming, afterwards, to perish before his eyes, the victim of her own sacrilege,—and that she had previously secured the means of her unexplained death. If this be not the author's meaning, we have no clue to what *is*. If it *be*, the catastrophe is managed in a manner bungling and obscure,—and might readily be mended. The end of all is, that Djabal, retaining his character of Hakeem, thus awfully confirmed, but announcing his mission as ended, delegates the 'leading home' to Khalil, under the escort of the good Knight Loys, and the protection of the Venetians; and, advancing at their head a few steps, on the way back to the Cedars, falls dead before their eyes,—supposed, of course, to have fulfilled the tradition, and returned to his slumber of ages!

46. Richard Hengist Horne on Browning, *A New Spirit of the Age*

1844, ii. 153–86

From his 'Robert Browning and J. W. Marston'.[1]

The main requisites for a successful acting tragedy are character and passionate action—and these the *Druses* possesses in the highest degree; the next requisite is the perspicuous distribution of the action—and here this tragedy is deficient, but in a way that might easily be remedied, and with far less trouble than is always taken with the works of Mr. Knowles, or Sir Edward Bulwer, or with any of the 'great discoveries' and failures of Mr. Macready.[2] The character of Djabal is a masterpiece, and of the highest order of dramatic portraiture. It is at once complicated and clear; the motives intervolved and conflicting, yet 'palpable to feeling as to sight'; and all his actions, their results, and his own end, are perfectly in harmony with these premises. Anything in him that puzzles us, is only in the progress of the drama; for eventually he stands out in the finest relief, as though upon 'the mountain', to which his dying steps lead on his emancipated people.

---

[1] John Westland Marston (1819–90) had attempted to adapt the dramatic structure of Elizabethan plays to a modern subject in his *The Patrician's Daughter* (1841).

[2] James Sheridan Knowles (1784–1862), actor and playwright in whose plays Macready sometimes took the lead. Edward Lytton Bulwer (later Bulwer-Lytton and, after 1866, Baron Lytton), novelist and dramatist whose *Richelieu* (1839) was long a popular play. It is ironic that, as a dramatist, Browning was himself one of Macready's 'discoveries'.

A BLOT IN THE 'SCUTCHEON

February 1843

47. Charles Dickens, letter

25 November 1842

From a letter to John Forster, *The Life of Charles Dickens* (1872–4), ii. 24–25.

Browning was deeply disappointed that Dickens' opinion was not made public in 1842, when its effect would have been most welcome to the struggling poet-playwright.

Browning's play has thrown me into a perfect passion of sorrow. To say there is anything in its subject save what is lovely, true, deeply affecting, full of the best emotion, the most earnest feeling, and the most true and tender a source of interest, is to say that there is no light in the sun, and no heat in the blood. It is full of genius, natural and great thoughts, profound and yet simple and beautiful in its vigour. I know of nothing that is so affecting, nothing in any books I have ever read, as Mildred's recurrence to that 'I was so young—I had no mother.' I know no love like it, no passion like it, no moulding of a splendid thing after its conception, like it. And I swear it is a tragedy that *must* be played; and must be played, moreover, by Macready. There are some things I would have changed if I could (they are very slight, mostly broken lines), and I assuredly would have the old servant begin his tale upon the scene; and be taken by the throat, or drawn upon, by his master, in its commencement. But the tragedy I never shall forget, or less vividly remember than I do now. And if you tell Browning that I have seen it, tell him that I believe from my soul there is no man living (and not many dead) who could produce such a work.

48. From an unsigned review, *The Times*

13 February 1843, p. 5, col. 6

The opening plot-summary has been omitted.

. . . In this outline there is nothing objectionable; on the contrary, it does great credit to the man who selected it. But it seems a good tragedy was not to be, and accordingly Mr. Browning, though he went to work with a good fundamental idea, though he has displayed much vigour, and though he has poetical qualifications of no common order, has by a defect in the organ of constructiveness produced one of the most faulty dramas we ever beheld. His whole thoughts seem to have been directed to the production of striking effects, and these, in some instances, he certainly has obtained, but it has been at the expense of nature and probability.

49. John Forster, *The Examiner*

18 February 1843, p. 101

An unsigned review.

Mr Browning—a writer whose career we watch with great interest, because we believe him to be a man of genius and a true poet—is the author of a tragedy in three acts, produced at this theatre, on Saturday last, and entitled *A Blot on the 'Scutcheon*. In performance it was successful: a result which it had been hardly safe to predict of a work of so much rare beauty, and of such decisive originality.

These are qualities that seldom, at first starting, make their way in the world, more especially the world theatrical. And we are not sanguine of the chances of continued patronage to the *Blot in the 'Scutcheon*. People are already finding out, we see, that there is a great deal that is equivocal in its sentiment, a vast quantity of mere artifice in its situations, and in its general composition not much to 'touch humanity.' We do not pretend to know what should touch humanity, beyond that which touches our own hearts, but we would give little for the feelings of the man who could read this tragedy without a deep emotion. It is very sad; painfully and perhaps needlessly so; but it is unutterably tender, passionate, and true. It is not copied from this or that existing notion; it is not moulded on this or the other of the old authors; it is the growth of the writer's heart, and has the distinct truth, the animated pathos, the freshness and unexaggerated strength, which spring in that soil alone.

We seldom describe the plots of plays. The interest here turns on the shame which is brought upon an old English family, and the vengeance it provokes; upon the suffering which sin engenders, and which death only ends. There is a deeper moral for those who can see deeper truths than the conventional ones. At the opening of the first act, the hand of Mildred Tresham is sought by Henry Earl of Mertoun, but before the act closes, the honour of Mildred has been brought into question in the presence of her proud and sensitive brother, the Lord of Tresham, the passionate, impetuous, high-hearted, self-willed Thorold. In the second act Mildred's shame is disclosed, but she dares not couple with it her lover's name. At the opening of the third act, Thorold learns it, but nothing gives pause to his savage instinct of revenge, till he sees bleeding beneath his sword the author of his sister's shame, and the only creature who could have saved, and who had already earnestly striven to save, the house's honour. It is the young Earl of Mertoun. The sister dies of a broken heart, and Thorold takes poison.

To all this it is objected, that, as a matter of course, the lover's name should have been surrendered, and all further evil put an end to on the instant. We know of few tragedies that would stand this sort of criticism. As if it were not at the very root of the feeling on which the whole is based, that the poor shame-crushed girl should be silent with a thousand fears, where the ruder nature wou'd at once have spoken. 'Courtly Mildred dies when country Madge survives.' And did not the issue justify her fears? It is objected, too, that if Thorold repents his rage when his victim has fallen under it, there is no reason that he should not have repented before, and time enough to end matters amicably. A wise and satisfactory suggestion, that proves the needlessness of how much sorrow, real and theatrical. Oh! that both worlds would but take it to heart, and always repent before it is too late!

There are defects in the tragedy, though these are not of them. But we shall not stop to dwell upon them, till we have also space for one or two short extracts from the work itself, which will do better justice to its writer than all that we have said. There is no defect that calls for instant exposure. There is no equivocal morality in it, no false sympathies to set the judgment halting between right and wrong; no good that deters, no bad that encourages. It is full of manly tenderness —of tenderness which remains in the heart when the guilt and sadness are forgotten. And though there are causes in the subject itself—and most of all, 'the pity of it'—which may for the present give it short existence on the stage, it is a work, we are very sure, that will not be willingly let die. Of the performance we have little to say, but that we think it on the whole under-acted. The character best sustained was that of Miss Helen Faucit.[1]

50. Unsigned review, *The Athenæum*

18 February 1843, p. 166

. . . If to pain and perplex were the end and aim of tragedy, Mr. Browning's poetic melodrama, called *A Blot on the 'Scutcheon*, would be worthy of admiration, for it is a very puzzling and unpleasant piece of business. The plot is plain enough, but the acts and feelings of the characters are inscrutable and abhorrent, and their language is as strange as their proceedings. The subject is of Spanish nature in an English guise—revenge for a stain on the honour of an ancient and noble house being the main passion. Lord Tresham is as proud and fierce as a Castilian, and as jealous of 'a blot on the 'scutcheon' of his

---

[1] Miss Faucit played the part of Mildred Tresham. The other members of the cast are mentioned in the reviews which follow this one.

family. In the first scene, Earl Mertoun, a gallant youth, 'noble among the noblest,' appears, a suitor to Lord Tresham for his sister's hand; in the next, he enters her chamber-window at midnight, a cherished lover. The brother learns his sister's shame, and accuses her before her kindred of the double baseness of inveigling an honourable lover while harbouring a paramour: yet she is silent, although a word would have averted the catastrophe that follows. Lord Tresham waylays the nocturnal visitor; they cross swords, and the lover falls mortally wounded, though he had revealed himself as Earl Mertoun. The slayer, who but the moment before spurned his adversary as a 'miscreant,' now repents: he seeks his sister's chamber, to whom he imparts the horrible tidings; she blesses him and dies; and he dies also. A few of the audience laughed, others were shocked, and many applauded; but it is impossible that such a drama should live, even if it were artfully constructed, which this is not. The acting of Mr. Phelps[1] and and Miss Helen Faucit, as the brother and sister, and Mr. Anderson as the lover, though not faultless, was powerful and effective. . . .

51. Unsigned review, *The Literary Gazette, and Journal of the Belles Lettres*

18 February 1843, pp. 107–8

—On Saturday a 'tragic play' in three acts, by Mr. Robert Browning, the author of *Paracelsus*, was produced here, and with doubtful success, though the audience in general certainly went along with the author. And, indeed, it would have been difficult not to do so; for albeit some of the scenes and much of the dialogue are too long, there is a sufficient variety and constant moving in the action, which keeps the mind engaged, and prevents it from detecting and dwelling upon the faultiness of the plot. It requires the pause of reflection to feel the full force

[1] Samuel Phelps (1804–78) later managed Sadlers Wells, to which he brought *A Blot* in 1848.

of the error, and be aware that human nature, physics, and metaphysics, must be outraged, or there would be no play at all. Allowing Mr. Browning his grounds, we are bound to say there are fine marks of genius in the working-out of his conception, and not a few beautiful touches of genuine pathos and poetry—half lines worth a world of declamation. But the grounds slip from under him—there is no critical *locus standi* for the drama of the *Blot on the 'Scutcheon*. It is, besides, a disagreeable subject. Two young people, but old enough to know better,—Lord Mertoun (Anderson), and Mildred (Miss Faucit), sister of Lord Tresham (Phelps),—have formed an illicit amour; for which the lover makes a lame excuse of extreme youth and profound admiration for his mistress's brother, and to which the lady seems not to be reconciled by any likely process. For the piece opens with Lord Mertoun at last summoning up courage to propose himself as husband to his secret love, and being favourably received by her brother. His joy is excessive, and though late, we hardly care to ask why he did not apply before. His midnight visit to Mildred ensues, and he communicates the happy auspices to her; and then comes the unnatural foundation for all that is to follow. Instead of rejoicing, as all females under similarly untoward circumstances do, that she is about to be made, according to the old saying, "an honest woman," she flies off at a tangent, and declares that she is born to misery and tragedy. It is clear that things are likely to take a bad turn, though the easiest and most certain path is straight to the church, the second or public honeymoon, and a tolerably comfortable life even after the indiscretion of its commencement. An old retainer informs Lord Tresham of Mildred's midnight gallantries, her lamp lighting an unknown stranger to her chamber, and he climbing thereto with Capuletish ardour and alacrity. The "blot" is hit, and the earl is thrown into a vortex of passion. He seeks his sister, and she confesses her frailty, but refuses to give the name of her visitor, simply, as it would seem, because that straight-forward and natural course would have obliged the curtain to drop on a wedding most satisfactory to all parties concerned. Lord Tresham, in consequence, rushes out furiously to inform the other lord of Mildred's infamy (for she has *aggravated* him by offering to receive Mertoun's proposals)—wanders about till night; meets the incognito lover, and hastily slays him; then tells the news to his sister, who dies thereon; and, finally, gives himself to imperishable remorse or death. Such is the outline of a play, in poetical composition far above the mediocrity of our ordinary writers. But its inherent faults are fatal. No man or woman that ever existed, if they fell into the base position, so improbable too, of this noble-minded young lord and most admirably virtuous young lady, would conduct themselves in the way Mr. Browning paints. Mildred has no reason on earth, when detected in and confessing her folly, for not telling her doating brother the whole truth, saving him from paroxysms of passion, herself from the bitterest denunciations, and, in short—the tragedy from its catastrophe. Miss H. Faucit performed the part tenderly and sweetly; and the scene when she sinks senseless to the ground on her brother's reproaches, was very effective. Mr. Phelps was unequal. He has too much of violence to deliver, and it occasionally degenerated into rant and hair-tearing. But some portions were excellently done. Anderson was judicious and effective in spite of a dying scene in which his martyrdom of talking, after being mortally hurt, was enough to try the patience of Job. His conversation with his slayer, intermixed with groans and twistings, became almost ludicrous. Two other characters, cousins of Tresham, and his successors in the family *blotted* out by his rashness, are introduced; but they have not much to do; and so Mrs. Stirling and Mr. Hudson did their best. At the end the applause greatly predominated; but still we cannot promise the Blot that it will not soon be wiped off the stage.*

[The asterisk refers to the following note at the bottom of the column:]

* It may be convenient here to notice that Mr. Browning is publishing from time to time a series of poetical and dramatic compositions, under the quaint title of *Bells and Pomegranates* (London, E. Moxon), in which there is much to admire as well as to question;—just as in this play. We observe Nos. III. and IV. on our table (Nos. I. and II. being momentarily mislaid, and V., we believe, the 'Blot on the 'Scutcheon'); and dipping into them, find the same sort of mixture of beauty and extravagance, of true poetry and metaphysical maudlin incomprehensibility which disfigured the volume called *Sordello,* from which our taste was so utterly repelled, that we never could bring our minds to read it through. Yet we have to repeat, if Mr. Browning could and would leave off his dreamy stuff, he has the pith of better things within him.

52. From an unsigned review, *The Spectator*

18 February 1843, xvi. 159–60

The new tragedy produced at Drury Lane on Saturday is in three acts; an innovation that, so far from being objectionable, is a welcome improvement: many recent five-act inflictions might have been advantageously compressed into three: in the present instance, the story would have been better told in one—and best left untold. *A Blot in the 'Scutcheon* is brief, yet tedious: shocking, but unimpressive; and melodramatic, without being effective. The incidents are few, but of a revolting character. Lord Tresham, a man proud of his high and unspotted lineage, discovers that his young sister Mildred, for whose hand he had just sanctioned a noble suitor, receives a gallant in her chamber nightly. The incensed brother taxes his sister with her guilt; which she does not deny; and in the presence of their kindred he denounces her shamelessness. Lord Tresham intercepts the midnight visiter, whom he kills in a duel; notwithstanding he recognizes in him the young Earl of Merton, who had got his consent to wed Mildred. The guilty girl dies broken-hearted, and her brother poisons himself out of remorse. The unchasteness of the heroine, for whose frality no palliation is offered, is fatal to dramatic sympathy: the lover falls a sacrifice to her mysterious silence; while the brother, in his blind fury, slays a wrong-doer willing to make reparation, and thus destroys the only means of wiping off the 'blot of his 'scutcheon.' The subject, in itself, is unfit for tragedy; and Mr. Browning in his endeavours to excite strong emotions by making what is disagreeable horrible, defeats his purpose. Aversion is the predominant feeling created. This was audibly, though not loudly expressed, on two or three occasions during the first representation; but it took a ludicrous turn towards the close, and the catastrophe elicited an involuntary titter. In the construction of the drama, stage-effect has been studied, but so unskilfully, that after a scene is enacted the audience are obliged to listen to an account of what they have witnessed. The motives, situation, and purpose of the characters, are alike unaccountable: neither soliloquy nor dialogue throws much light upon either; the author's ideas being so farfetched, and his phraseology so quaint, that the drift of the speeches is scarcely understood.

The acting was more than adequate to the merits of the drama. Phelps as Lord Tresham, though occasionally too loud and violent, gave vent to the rage and indignation of the proud noble with force and vehemence; tempering his fury with tenderness in the scenes with his sister. Miss H. Faucit depicted the shame and wretchedness of the guilty girl with an intensity that would have been pathetic had there been room for sympathy. Anderson was a seemly gallant; but he breathed both his vows and lamentations monotonously, and his dying groans were much too sonorous. Hudson and Mrs. Sterling were a pair of lively lovers, whose levity was always malapropos; and both these and the old servant who tells of his young mistress's faux pas—well played by G. Bennett—might have been dispensed with.

There was considerable applause on the first night; and the author was called for, as usual—though he very properly kept in the background: but the piece cannot retain possession of the stage. . . .

53. A Partial Survey

August 1843

Unsigned review, *The Gentleman's Magazine* (August 1843), N.S. xx. 168-9.

The reviewer's casual spelling of Ottima and Sebald—two of the strongest characters in *Pippa Passes*—could not have pleased Browning much.

Of Mr. Browning's poetical powers and philosophical knowledge of the mind of man, we have a very high opinion, and on some of the eloquent and powerful passages in his former productions we have been delighted to dwell. His *Paracelsus* was a *noble monster;* but as regards the present work, we take it that Mr. Browning in poetry, as Mr. Turner[1] in the

[1] Joseph Mallord William Turner (1775-1851).

sister art of painting, being self-delighted with the exercise of his acknowledged powers, writes for his own gratification and to his own will, without much regard to the approbation of applause of his readers. His mind is full of imagery, and all fancies quaint and noble; a copious flow of language is at his command; he is master of the passions that sway the human heart; and thus conscious of his powers, he mounts his steed, turns the magic peg in its ear, and instantly shoots aloft, and goes careering along in the high regions of the empyrean, hardly visible to ordinary mortals. Of his four numbers we like best his first, *Pippa Passes*. The scene between the wife Olivia and her paramour Sibald, though wild and fantastic, is very poetically drawn; and so is the sketch of the Poor Girls who sit on the steps near the Duomo of S. Maria. In the second tragedy, *King Victor and King Charles*, we confess the ability, but consider the result inadequate. In *The Return of the Druses*, we did not feel at all interested. The dramatic lyrics are very clever in parts; but the following is perfect as a whole, as an excellent companion to the best of the spirited old political ballads and garlands. . . .

['Marching Along' is quoted in full.]

'The Cloister' (Spanish) is the next best, in our belief, but we have not room to extract it.

COLOMBE'S BIRTHDAY

March 1844

54. From an unsigned review, *The Examiner*

22 June 1844, pp. 388–9

Maurice B. Cramer attributes this review, as well as No. 56, to John Forster. See 'Browning's Friendships and Fame Before Marriage (1833–1846)', *PMLA* (March 1940), lv. 207–30.

This play gives sterling proof of Mr. Browning's genius. There is a want in it: but not of passion, nor of thought. We have had to describe the want so often, that we will spare the reader repetition of it. Mr. Browning exacts some hard conditions for the pleasure of his poetry, and could discourse good reasons for them, doubtless. We must at any rate be content to remember what a high authority has said, that if to do were as easy as to teach what were good to be done, chapels had been churches and poor men's cottages princes' palaces. And this not a poor man's cottage. It is a building of strength and stateliness, notwithstanding its intricate passages, and galleries of too quaint device: raised by a man of rich imagination, and many fine and noble sympathies.

[Approximately 75 lines are quoted here.]

There can be no question of the nerve and vigour of this writing, or of its grasp of thought. Whether the present generation of readers will take note of it, or leave it to the uncertain mercies of the future, still rests with Mr. Browning himself. As far as he has gone, we abominate his tastes as much as we respect his genius.

55. From an unsigned review, *The Athenæum*

19 October 1844, pp. 944-5

The writer—almost certainly the author of No. 45—devotes most of his four-column review to a highly appreciative re-counting of the action of the play, liberally interspersed with quotations.

Fertility of invention is a merit which Mr. Browning may claim, and must have allowed. *Paracelsus, Pippa Passes*, the *Druses*, the *Dramatic Lyrics*, a *Blot in the 'Scutcheon*, whatever may be their relative merits or demerits, have all essential differences; and the dramatic tale before us has its own distinctive character.

Well may the Duchess declare that such a speaker 'has opened a new world to her;'—well may the mean-souled courtiers whisper in corners! We must pass rapidly on: Berthold's proposed compromise is laid before Colombe, by her advocate—who, loyal as he is, and indeed, as yet, hardly owning his secret feelings towards his liege's lady, states it fairly. In the statement, however, one point interests his client, which he dreamed not of—the Duchess toys with the idea of retaining Juliers and Cleves—but the woman spies out his secret: makes him unfold it too clearly for disguise: flatters him with brilliant hopes, and then, like a true daughter of Eve, turns him over to the rack of suspense, unable herself to decide betwixt power and love. A superficial observer would have overlooked this natural struggle, a feeble-handed writer hesitated to show the play of light and shade in the character of his heroine; but Mr. Browning has done it, and skilfully, so that we continue to love and to trust in Colombe; and, none the less, because she vacillates.

[Two passages from Act V—266-83 and 322-55—are quoted.]

So ends this drama: beautiful in the lofty and chivalrous spirit it illustrates, in the noble lesson it teaches, and in which Mr. Browning has advanced many steps nearer to simplicity, without his fancy, or feeling, or stores of imagery showing a trace of impoverishment.

DRAMATIC ROMANCES
AND LYRICS

November 1845

---

56. From an unsigned review, *The Examiner*

15 November 1845, pp. 723-4

We are disposed to admire this little book of Mr. Browning's very much. Our readers know how high we have ranked his muse; and how we have grieved when she lost her way in transcendental or other fogs, and, like poor Origen's fallen star, 'rayed out' only darkness. Here she has found the path again.

Mr. Browning's metaphysics have been too abundant for his poetry. That is the substance of the objection to be urged against him. And it is not a slight one. Poetry is a jealous mistress, and will have undivided homage. The analytic and the imaginative powers never yet worked well together. But it is the fault (not an inglorious one) of youth: the fault of which Shelley became conscious before he died, and from which Mr. Browning is fast freeing himself. Nothing but this retarded his advance.

His writing has always the stamp and freshness of originality. It is in no respect imitative or commonplace. Whatever the verse may be, the man is in it: the music of it echoing to his mood. When he succeeds, there have been few so successful in the melodious transitions of his rhythm. In all its most poetical and most musical varieties, he is a master; and to us it expresses, in a rare and exquisite degree, the delicacy and truth of his genius. Proctor says very happily in the *Life of Ben Johnson,* that the motion of verse corresponds with the power of the poet, as the swell and tumult of the sea answer to the winds that call them up; and this is the safe test of a master in the art.

There are some twenty pieces in the collection; each marked out from its fellow by an idea of its own, to which it moves with corresponding music; from the breathless gallop of 'How they brought the good news from Ghent to Aix' to the calm simplicity of the 'Boy and the Angel.' . . .

[Quotes 'The Boy and the Angel', the last six lines of 'The Italian in England', fifty lines from 'The Flight of the Duchess', and all of 'The Lost Leader'.]

We leave several fine pieces unnamed as well as unquoted. Among them the 'Tomb at St. Praxed's,' a death-bed speech of an old Popish Prelate, which, with a grim and awful kind of humour, mixes up concerns of life and death 'in monumental mockery,'—and 'The Glove,' a French romance, given as from the recitation of Peter Ronsard, wherein the incident of the court dame flinging her glove into the den of a lion, is ingeniously and not unpleasantly turned to the lady's advantage.

These *Romances and Lyrics* form the seventh part of a collection of pieces chiefly dramatic, which Mr Browning has been publishing some years, for odd shillings and sixpences, with the title of *Bells and Pomegranates*. On the whole they are a remarkable collection, and proof of a very affluent as well as original genius. Wonderful is the saving of paper and press-work and price, in their small print and double columns. They look as though already packed up and on their way to posterity; nor are we without a confident expectation that some of them will arrive at that journey's end.

57. From an unsigned review, *The Athenæum*

17 January 1846, pp. 58–9

Browning thought this review 'kind and satisfactory', attributing it to Henry Chorley.
The stricture in the second sentence Browning described as 'politic concession to the Powers that Be'. *RB-EBB*, I, 410.

We have here yet another proof of Mr. Browning's fertility. Though his manner changes less than might be wished—since the mist, if it rises and reveals a clear prospect for half a page, as certainly falls again,—there are few of his contemporaries who embrace so wide a field of subjects; be they of thought, or description, or passion, or character. Sometimes *baroque*, Mr. Browning is never ignoble: pushing versification to the extremity of all rational allowances, and sometimes beyond it, with a hardihood of rhythm and cadence little short of Hudibrastic, —he is rarely careless. His aims are truth and freedom. His art is sometimes consummate—'Wherefore not always?' is a question, the reply to which might lead to threadbare dissertations on taste, self-renunciation, and the like. Instead of these, we shall be more just to our author if we give him room to exhibit himself in his strength, and in his variety.

Let us begin by illustrating Mr. Browning's descriptive powers. The first of these *Dramatic Ballads* tells of a night-ride from Ghent to Aix, and is thrown off with an animation which Bürger himself hardly exceeds. There is a picture in every verse. . . .

[Quotes the first and fourth stanzas of 'How They Brought the Good News from Ghent to Aix'.]

We must leave untouched the study of 'Saul' leaning against his tent-pole,—the love verses, in which the book is rich, and the new version of the well-known story of 'King Francis, the Lady, the Glove, and the Lion,'—in which Mr. Browning most chivalrously defends one who has been be-sung and be-scandalized as the cruellest of her sex.— Enough has been given to prove that these Romances will add to the poet's reputation.

58. From an unsigned review, *The Oxford and Cambridge Review and University Magazine*

January 1846, ii 102

Mr. Browning has many faults which, were we disposed to be severe, might be mentioned with proper censure; but his beauties are exceedingly more numerous, and on these we are better pleased to enlarge. These short poems appear to us to happily combine many of the characteristics of real poetry, and more especially its simplicity. We give one extract, and very cordially recommend this, we suppose we must call it a *Serial*, to our readers.

[Quotes 'How They Brought the Good News from Ghent to Aix', 11. 1–24.]

59. A Tribute from Walter Savage Landor

November 1845

Walter Savage Landor, 'To Robert Browning', *The Morning Chronicle* (22 November 1845), p. 5.

Browning was justifiably proud of this sonnet from the pen of a man he admired both for his poetry and for his famous *Imaginary Conversations*. To Browning, it was 'a gold vase from King Hiram', and the young poet's father had the sonnet privately printed and distributed in a two-page leaflet. See *RB-EBB*, I, 286ff., and Broughton, p. 331.

There is delight in singing, tho' none hear
Beside the singer: and there is delight
In praising, tho' the praiser sit alone
And see the prais'd far off him, far above.
Shakespeare is not our poet, but the world's,
Therefore on him no speech! and brief for thee,
Browning! Since Chaucer was alive and hale,
No man hath walkt along our road with step
So active, so inquiring eye, or tongue
So varied in discourse. But warmer climes
Give brighter plumage, stronger wing: the breeze
Of Alpine highths thou playest with, borne on
Beyond Sorrento and Amalfi, where
The Siren waits thee, singing song for song.

60. The Problem of Obscurity

December 1845

From an unsigned review, *The English Review* (December 1845), iv. 273-7.

Mr. Browning unites within himself more of the elements of a true poet than perhaps any other of those whom we call 'modern' amongst us; yet there are few writers so little read, so partially understood. He came into the literary forum in such a mysterious guise, (that *Paracelsus* of his), and carried his great gifts about him with such a careless air, that men took but little notice of the unostentatious stranger. This first work was by no means adapted to be a 'noisy herald of his fame:' it purports to be a sort of autobiography of the great Alchemist, and is almost as obscure as the subject itself. Yet *Paracelsus* won for its author instant consideration among the few who were capable of appreciating its merits: it exhibits great power and resources; but it is perhaps the most difficult *simple* poetry in the English language. The diction is remarkable for simplicity, even when expressing the most complex thought; and the whole poem has an easy rhythmical flow that almost lulls us into forgetfulness of its deep meanings. This is in itself an evidence of the ease and mastery of his subject possessed by the writer. Moreover, notwithstanding its occasional obscurity, this work possesses rare merit: without pausing to examine our author's philosophy, we are struck by the nobleness, energy, and polish of his style, and still more by his delicate delineation of character.

[Summarizes *Paracelsus* and *Pippa Passes*.]

One word must be said about the lesser poems, however hastily; and yet on second consideration it were better to be silent than to speak lightly of any man's work. And these *are* work, strenuous nervous work, that makes the subject ring to the stroke of the workman. They are vigorous, versatile, original; but the knowledge of nature and truthfulness they display are strangely associated with, and expressed in strange words; ingenuity of rhymes is carried to an extreme; and the author will often persist in supposing that we know what he means so well, that there is no necessity for him to inform us on the matter. . . .

61. A Neglected Poet

1845

From an unsigned review, *The Critic* (27 December 1845), pp. 701–2.

Robert Browning has faults—great and obvious faults, which obscure his many beauties to all eyes, not resolutely bent upon piercing the veil which he has himself thrown over his genius. He is a singularly careless writer; he seems to think that manner is of no consequence, and that, provided a man have ideas, it little matters how he expresses them. Again, he is deficient in the musical ear for metre and rhyme which by so many is mistaken for the essence instead of the mere form of poetry. His lines are often loose; he is careless of cadences; he is not choice in the selection of words, but takes the first that offers itself, regardless of its common-place or vulgarity. Then he *affects* a needless plainness of speech; he aims too obviously at originality, which he seems to suppose to lie in differing from all the rest of the world. He has fallen into the besetting sin of our generation of poets, and *strains* after the simple, which is only pleasing when it is the natural expression of a natural emotion, but becomes almost ludicrous and always offensive when it is the result of art, and produced with effort.

But these are faults which ought not to have militated against his great and many merits to the extent they have done in practice. His works are not read so largely as they should be; his powers are not properly appreciated; his genius is recognized only by a very narrow circle. Even to the literary world he is but partially known. It is the duty of all who have the means to do what in them lies to redress this injustice, to spread his reputation on all fair opportunities, and to give to his productions the welcome to which their intrinsic worth entitles them.

LURIA; AND A SOUL'S TRAGEDY

April 1846

62. Unsigned review, *Douglas Jerrold's Shilling Magazine*

June 1846, iii. 573-4

Mr. Browning is, in our opinion, a great poet, and it is probable he is also a great man. We may say this, because there seems to be in him a thorough hatred and scorn of the *ad captandum* school. He has great perceptions and conceptions, and his delight is in his own might, not in the vain plaudits of those who mistake skill for genius, and smartness for originality. If the comparative neglect of the many is displeasing to him, at all events, Coriolanus-like, he will not show his scars; he cannot

Put on the gown, stand naked and entreat them.

He may perchance have a touch too much, with the proud Roman, of resting on his own powers, and if not despising, disregarding his reader. He understands character and human emotion profoundly, and delineates it powerfully. He never aids the reader by narrative or obtrusion of himself. There are character, passion, and poetry, flung down on the paper, and it is certainly the reader's fault or misfortune if he does not perceive them. The great secret of his strength and of his hardness is his utter want of sentimentality. He pourtrays the characters of men in all the nakedness and hideousness of true passion. He has chosen an age and a country where these kind of developments have been most, or at all events, best recorded, and we are present, by his art, with the real and terrific men that have been the slaves of intense hatred, ambition, lust, and of all the impulses of unrestrained human nature. When goodness does appear amongst such a crew, it is of the genuine and angelic kind, as it must be.

In history one reads of the actions of such men, and with but a half belief in the truth of the narration; but the dramatist proves its existence with appalling force. Mr. Browning is deeply imbued and informed with the spirit of the middle age; and he has a great idea, which, in the play of *Luria*, he nobly realises. It is the conflict of mind and matter, of will and intellect.

> Brute force shall not rule Florence! Intellect
> May rule her, bad or good, as chance supplies;
> But intellect it shall be, pure if bad.

The Soul's Tragedy is one of the most intensely dramatic works ever penned. The deepest emotions and the nicest traits of character are developed by the mere external conduct and expression. The villain of the piece is a thorough human villain, and the unfolding his villany is a masterly exposition of the degradations and weakness of human nature. The truly good and the noble are equally powerfully pourtrayed, and Mr. Browning has fulfilled the mission of the poet and the dramatist by giving new and valuable illustrations of our human nature. The theatre and Mr. Browning's dramas are never likely to come in contact; not at all events until, as in the early days of our true drama, the most refined minds, and therefore the comparatively few, again visit the playhouse as a place to study nature and philosophy. The high drama was always played in its entirety, and always must be, to the reflecting few. When we have another 'Globe' or 'Blackfriars,' containing a few hundred cultivated spectators, Mr. Browning's dramas may be performed.

BELLS AND POMEGRANATES

1841-6

63. From an unsigned review, *The Eclectic Review*

April 1846, 4th Ser. xix. 413, 421-6

Mr. Browning would be a poet of high order, if he could free himself from his affectations, and set before himself a great aim in poetry. . . . As it is, with powers capable of all this, he makes himself merely a puzzle to those that see here and there really brilliant passages in him, and to the general reader—caviare. For a long time we were inclined to believe him really insane. We could not bring ourselves to believe that any man who possessed the power evidenced in his writings would voluntarily assume a form of confused and crazy eccentricity, merely for the poor pleasure of making people wonder. But we came at length to his drama of *The Blot in the 'Scutcheon*, . . . and then the conviction was forced on us. Here all is as clear and rational in language as any plain understanding can desire. Mr. Browning, then *can* be intelligible, if he will. . . . But besides muddiness of style, Mr. Browning, has also much muddiness of matter to get rid of. There is a sensual trait about his writings which will bring him one day a bitterness that no amount of reputation will be found an antidote for. Let him purify his style and his spirit, and we shall hope to meet him again on a future day in a far higher and nobler position.

64. 'Past and Present Condition of British Poetry'

From an unsigned article, *Fraser's Magazine* (May, June 1846), xxxiii. 577–90, 708–18.

Our poetry is in a very sorry kind of plight if it has to depend upon Tennyson and Browning for the hereditary honours of its existence. *The Examiner* will tell us 'No!' *The Athenaeum* will do the same; papers remarkable for the vigour of their articles, the excellence of their occasional criticism, and the general asperity of their manner. A page out of every ten in Herrick's *Hesperides* is more certain of an hereafter than any one dramatic romance or lyric in all the *Bells and Pomegranates* of Mr. Browning. Not but what Mr. Browning is a poet. He is unquestionably a poet; but his subject has not unfrequently to bear the weight of sentiments which spring not naturally from it, and his numbers at times are overlaid with affectation, the common conceit of men who affect to tell common things in an uncommon manner. He clogs his verses, moreover, with too many consonants and too many monosyllables, and carries the sense too frequently in a very ungraceful manner from one line to the other. Here is a passage from the seventh number of his *Bells and Pomegranates*, which really is a torture to read:— . . .

[Quotes 'The Englishman in Italy', ll. 69–128.]

65. H. F. Chorley, *People's Journal*

18 July 1846, ii. 38–40

From his review.

When a Poet—who by the cheapness of the form of his publication
seems to invite the great public, and not the 'fit and few' purchasers of
the luxurious quartos that were—affixes to his series of Dramatic Poems
such a title as *Bells and Pomegranates,* one of two consequences is natural:
either that he shall be disregarded by the people as one speaking in
parables not worth the unriddling, or that he shall be followed by some
Interpreter, who shall invite the distant, and smooth the path for the
timid, by pointing out what there is great, what there is beautiful, in
works veiled—though the veil sparkle with fine gold and rubies—from
the common gaze. To dismiss Mr. Browning as a writer who must
needs be 'put out of court', because of a few strange individualities, is
what, we imagine, no one would now think of doing. The days of
slashing at a free rhyme or a plethoric stanza, of making an end of a
conceit by sarcasm, are over. Perhaps we are grown too blindly loving
and tolerant; not, however, in the present case, when we set about doing
our poor best to display one of our noblest contemporary geniuses in all
its strength of variety and passion. To talk to our friends of Mr.
Browning's Poems is a labour of love:—nor can it be unaccompanied
with profit to all, unless the whole art of song, and the whole train of
generous emotions it can excite, are to become a dead letter; or the
Critic be as far from rightly appreciating his author as was the Edinburgh Reviewer, who thought he had 'snuffed out' Wordsworth, with
a bitterly-brief 'This will never do.'

Mr. Browning is not clear. His obscurities, however, do not arise
from affectation, but from the over-richness of a mind embossed and
encrusted, so to say, with the learning and imagery of all schools, of all
countries, of all periods—reflective rather than impulsive; and working
rather by the accumulation than by the digestion of his materials.
There is no want of originality, no purpose prepense to puzzle or to
teaze, still less to 'come over' the vulgar multitude with the Charlatan's

robe decked with mystical signs, which, in nine cases out of ten, are only made of tawdry tinsel. There is much of the man and his training in the explanation of his symbolical title, prefixed to the last of his series—*The Soul's Tragedy*.

'I only meant,' says he, 'to indicate an endeavour towards something like an alternation, or mixture of music with discoursing, sound with sense, poetry with thought, which looks too ambitious so expressed, so the symbol was preferred. It is little to the purpose that such is actually one of the most familiar of the many Rabbinical (and Patristic) acceptations of the phrase; because I confess that, letting authority alone, I supposed the bare words in such juxtaposition would sufficiently convey the desired meaning.'

How, then, shall we best deal with a writer at once so difficult, so full of meaning, and so sincere? By *translation* rather than criticism; by dilution as well as analysis. This manner of proceeding will make it impossible for us, in any attainable space, to lay before the reader the argument of all these eight pamphlets, every one of which is 'full as an egg.' Nor, let us further premise, is there any family likeness in the class of subject, or scene, or story—however impossible it be (here we come upon a characteristic) for Mr. Browning to deny himself the introduction of some character almost superhuman in its grandeur, or delicacy, or depth. In one tale we are among the silk-winders of Trevisan country; in another with our faces set towards the cedars of Lebanon: here dealing with the ambitions of a maiden sovereign; there with the ancestral pride of an English nobleman. In the Dramatic Romances and Lyrics, to which two numbers of the series are devoted, almost every clime, and country, and emotion, is touched. Now the scene is the Spanish cloister, with its miserable jealousies and rancorous hatreds; now the French tilt-yard, with the struggle betwixt the slanderous Count Gauthier and the loyal Count Gismond; now the quaint German town of Hamelin, with the pie-bald piper who charmed thence the rats; now the cell of the Poisoner of Old Paris, who could deal about sudden death in

A signet, a fan, mount, a filigree-basket;

now the tent of Saul, with the Rebellious Monarch wrapped in the mantle of his darkness, and leaning against the central prop. Enough: we have not indicated half the 'changes of view' which our Magician can call up! Let us contentedly stand by as showman; and, with the best of our poor eloquence, describe one or two. . . .

[Chorley here devotes nearly 1,800 words to recounting the action of the first half of the play, quoting I. 14–25, 58–68, and II. 314–18. Although he intended to complete his presentation of *Pippa*, he does not appear to have done so.]

We must 'bate at noon:' lest in unthreading this somewhat tangled skein of beautiful illustrations, we tire the patience of our friends, thus disobeying the sagacious precept of the good Quaker preacher—'Better lacking than loathing.' Some other week, possibly, we may see Pippa to the end of her holiday; or else turn our reading-glass on some other among Mr. Browning's inventions. One last word in fairness. Let no one look into them who merely cares for easy-going verse, with the sense on the surface; and the rhythm making a music to step or dance to, and the imagery reviving old associations. Here, almost every phrase or figure is suggestive; the metre is full of broken and suspended cadences, and the store of allusions collected from sources remote and recondite. But those who are not deterred from a pleasure by the prospect of some labour cannot study these *Bells and Pomegranates* without being made nobler and better by their lesson. There is a room and a mission for the Mystical, no less than for the Clear, Poets!

66. H. F. Chorley, *People's Journal*

22 August 1846, pp. 104–6

From his review.

Perhaps on returning to the *Bells and Pomegranates* of Mr. Browning, for the purpose of showing to a public, yet insufficiently acquainted with these poems, how rich they are in pictures—it will be best to alight upon some other number than that containing the story of Pippa's mission; for, since her Innocence is set against Crime, to complete the tale of her holiday might lead us through scenes so exclusively gloomy, that our friends might thereby receive a false impression of their friend, the Poet, and imagine him one skilled only in painting sorrow, martyrdoms, wounds, and cruel sacrifices. Not even to teach the lesson of 'overcoming Evil with Good,' ought those who deal in imaginative creation 'to dwell for aye 'mid images of Pain.' Callousness, need of stronger excitement, morbid curiosity, and the like, may be encouraged and increased by such a mistaken course. It is often the refuge and relief of those made selfish by suffering. And the healthy and the hopeful will love to fulfill their duty by exalting yet more than by depressing the spirits of those who trust in them. Let us see if this is not done, and well done, in the dramatised tale of *Colombe's Birthday*.

It is a question whether any creation exists more chivalrous in its tone than this legend; that is, if we somewhat refine the epithet, and (by courtesy of poetical fiction) admit it to include loyalty, delicacy—a recognition that there are few who have not some touches of a higher nature than distinguishes the churl and the worshipper of Mammon. *Colombe's Birthday* is a tale of humanity, and grace, and poetry, vindicating themselves in that place where of all others it has been deemed the least possible to find them—a Court:—of Ambition in the moment of its triumph compelled to confess to itself and to the world its own haggard weariness—its inability to rest, its indifference to attempt new conquests—written with all the noble generosity of youth, and all the ripe experience of middle age. This and 'The Blot on the Scutcheon' are the only two of the dramas in Mr. Browning's *Bells* which could be made available on the stage—as the stage stands. 'The Blot', which was tried, failed, in part, owing to some untoward circumstances attending its production; and the story of Colombe, to *secure* its audience, demands what no longer exists in England—a dramatic company of gentlemen and ladies. But *finely* acted—that is, with an appreciation of the lights and shades of its characters—I have a firm belief that its success would surprise the Author himself—having a no less firm belief that our great Public can hardly be too largely credited with power to enjoy the most highly-toned poetry, or to sympathise with the most delicate and generous emotions. *Colombe's Birthday*, too, needs less *clearing* than any other of this series of dramas. . . .

The closing act of this beautiful drama, rich in the loftiest poetry, could have been dwelt and drawn upon, to the pleasure of every one: most of all my own. But enough has been said to indicate—and that is the purpose of these poor sketches. There is small hope of any one's progress in appreciating poetry, if, after having made the slight effort which Mr. Browning's style demands, he, who has began [*sic*] *Colombe's Birthday*, can lay it down till the play be played out and the curtain has fallen. I repeat, that if it be too fine for the stage, the fault is that our actors are too coarse, not that our audiences are incapable of relishing fancies so 'chaste and noble'.

67. George Henry Lewes, *The British Quarterly Review*

November 1847, vi. 490–509

From his unsigned review.

Later famous for his association with George Eliot, Lewes (1817–78) was a journalist with wide-ranging interests—fiction, poetry, psychology, and philosophy.

Robert Browning has conquered for himself a high rank amongst contemporary poets, and there are few persons, we presume, who pretend to an acquaintance with the literature of the day, to whom his name has an unfamiliar sound. If they have not read his poems, they have heard them praised; the chances are, that among their acquaintance, two or three are warm admirers; and in no scanty number of families may one hear energetic protests against the 'affection' of the title which it has pleased him to adopt as a collective name for the effusions of the last five years. *Bells and Pomegranates!* exclaims the testy objurgator, 'what stuff! What is the sense of such an affected title?' Whereupon some admirer replies: *Bells and Pomegranates*, sir, is a Rabbinical symbol, used by Mr. Browning to indicate an alternation of music with discoursing, sound with sense, poetry with thought.' The testy old gentleman refuses to accept such an explanation, and closes the discussion by observing—'Rabbinical, indeed! we want English, not Hebrew, sir!'

Such an objection, such a discussion proves at least that Robert Browning has a place apart from and above the herd of implacable verse-writers, ambitious of demonstrating that poetry *is* a drug—ambitious of proving the truth of Göthe's sarcasm—

'Wer treibt die Dichtkunst ans der Welt?
Die Poeten!'[1]

The objection proves that he has his place in our literature; otherwise, no one would trouble himself with a mere title. Accordingly, we think our duty as critics is calmly to consider his claims to renown; for whatever may be the opinion formed of his poetical powers, the very fact that such powers have in our day raised a man into reputation in a department where, since the giants who lately trod the stage have passed into silence, so few names have been heard above the crowd—this fact, we say, has a significance in it, which the future historian of literature will have to ponder on.

[The reviewer devotes four pages to the condition of poetry in the age, concluding that the times are not propitious ('It is an age of application rather than invention.') and that Victorian poets must either be musically imitative (Tennyson) or unmusically original (Browning).]

If we descend from these preliminary considerations to the application of them to the subject before us, we shall easily point out how and why Robert Browning has attained his present position. He is assuredly not a great poet; he is not even a distinguished poet, whose works will be gathered into future collections; but he is nevertheless a man who stands out in relief from his contemporaries—he is a writer of whom one must speak with the respect due to originality. In an age more favourable to the production of poetry, he might have been conspicuous; for he is endowed with some portion of the great faculty which we may metaphorically call the 'eye to see'. Deficient in some of the great requisites of his art, he has that one primary requisite: the power of seeing for himself and writing in his own language. Robert Browning is Robert Browning—call him sublime or call him feeble, take any view you will of his poems, you must still admit that he is one standing up to speak to mankind in his speech, not theirs—what he thinks, not what they think. We do not say that there are no traces of other poets in his works: he is of his age, and no man can pretend to escape its influence; he has studied poetry, and no man can at all times separate in his mind

[1] 'Who drives the art of poetry from the world? The poets!'

the acquired from the generated; but we do say emphatically that he is, in our strict and narrow sense of the term, no imitator, but an original thinker and an original writer.

Unfortunately, this high praise demands some qualification, and we are forced to add, that he is neither a deep thinker nor a musical writer. So that, although his originality has created for him an eminent position amongst a race of imitators, he has never yet been able to charm the public—he has never produced anything like 'Mariana at the Moated Grange', 'Locksley Hall', 'Ulysses', 'Œnone', 'Godiva', or the 'Miller's Daughter', (we mention those least resembling each other) with which Tennyson has built himself a name. Nor do we anticipate that he will ever do so. He has now been some years before the public, and in various characters. His first poem, which (unlucky circumstance!) is still regarded as his best, was *Paracelsus*. We well remember its appearance, and the attention it drew on the new poet, who, being young, was held destined to achieve great things. As a first work, it was assuredly remarkable. It had good thoughts, clear imagery, genuine original speech, touches of simple pathos, caprices of fancy, and a power of composition which made one hope that more experience and practice would ripen him into a distinguished poet. There were two objections, which occurred to us at the time. We did not lay much stress upon them, as the author was evidently young. Age and practice, we thought, would certainly remove them. They were the sort of faults most likely to be found in youthful works—viz., a great mistake in the choice of subject, and an abruptness, harshness, and inelegance of versification. It was pardonable in a young man to make a quack his hero; it looked a paradox, tempting to wilful and skilful ingenuity. On the other hand, it also betokened, or seemed to betoken, a want of proper earnestness and rectitude of mind—a love rather of the extraordinary than of the true. Paracelsus was not the hero a young man should have chosen; and yet one felt that he was just the hero a young man would choose. It seems to us that what this betokened has come to pass, and that in his subsequent works we have, if not the *same* fault, yet a fault which springs, we take it, from the same source. His conceptions are either false or feeble. In the work which succeeded *Paracelsus* we noted a repetition of the very error itself—viz., in the attempt to idealize into a hero that great but desperate Strafford, the 'wicked earl', as he was called, and as his actions prove him. Meanwhile the other fault—that, namely, of harshness and abruptness—was carried almost to a ridiculous extent; the language was spasmodic, and tortured almost into the style of Alfred Jingle, Esq., in

Pickwick, as the Edinburgh Reviewer remarked at the time. Next, after an interval of two or three years; if our memory serves us, came *Sordello*. What the merit or demerit of conception in that poem may be, no one can presume to say; for except the author himself and the printer's reader (in the course of duty), no earthly being ever toiled through that work. Walking on a new-ploughed field of damp clayey soil, would be skating compared to it. Even his staunchest admirers could say nothing to *Sordello*. Great as is the relish for the obscure and the involved in some minds, there was no one found to listen to these Sybilline incoherences. Other dealers in the obscure have at least charmed the ear with a drowsy music, but *Sordello*'s music was too grating and cacophonous to admit of the least repose. Whether Browning is to this day convinced of his mistake we know not, but to our ever-renewed surprise we often see *Sordello* advertised. That he has not burnt every copy he could by any means lay hands on, is to be explained only upon the principle which makes a mother cherish more fondly the reprobate or the cripple of her family.

This much, at any rate, is significant; he has ventured on no such experiment on the public patience since *Sordello*. The subsequent poems here collected, as *Bells and Pomegranates*, are always readable, if not often musical, and are not insults to our ears. But, as we hinted, the old objections still remain. He has not yet learned to take due pains with his subject, nor to write clearly and musically. It appears as if he sat down to write poetry without the least preparation; that the first subject which presented itself was accepted, as if any canvass was good enough to be embroidered upon. And respecting his versification, it appears as if he consulted his own ease more than the reader's; and if by any arbitrary distribution of accents he could make the verse satisfy his own ear, it must necessarily satisfy the ear of another. At the same time, he occasionally pours forth a strain of real melody, and always exhibits great powers of rhyming. One of the most evenly written of his pieces happens to be a great favourite of ours, and we quote it here for the sake of its manful, sorrowful reproaches. . . .

[Quotes 'The Lost Leader'.]

68. James Russell Lowell, *North American Review*

April 1848, lxvi. 357–400

From his review of *Paracelsus*, *Sordello*, and *Bells and Pomegranates*.

. . . Let us now turn to *Bells and Pomegranates*. And here we are met on the very threshold by the difficulty of selection. Not only are the lyrics singularly various in tone and character, but, in the dramas, that inter-dependence of the parts, which is one of their most striking and singular merits, makes any passage taken by itself do great injustice to the author. These dramas are not made up of a number of beauties, distinct and isolate as pearls, threaded upon the string of the plot. Each has a permeating life and spirit of its own. When we would break off any fragment, we cannot find one which would by itself approach complete-ness. It is like tearing away a limb from a living body. For these are works of art in the truest sense. They are not aggregations of dissonant beauties, like some modern sculptures, against which the Apollo might bring an action of trover for an arm, and the Antinoüs for a leg, but pure statues, in which every thing superfluous has been sternly chiselled away, and whose wonderful balance might seem tameness to the ordinary observer, who demands *strain* as an evidence of strength. They are not arguments on either side of any of the great questions which divide the world. The characters in them are not bundles of different characteristics, but their gradual development runs through the whole drama and makes the life of it. We do not learn what they are by what they say of themselves, or by what is said of them, so much as by what they do or leave undone. Nor does any drama seem to be written for the display of some one character which the author has conceived and makes a favourite of. No undue emphasis is laid upon any. Each fills his part, and each, in his higher or lower grade, his greater or less prominence, is equally necessary to the rest. Above all, his person-ages are not mere mouthpieces for the author's idiosyncrasies. We take leave of Mr. Browning at the end of *Sordello*, and, except in some shorter lyrics, see no more of him. His men and women *are* men and women, and not Mr. Browning masquerading in different-colored dominos. We implied as much when we said that he was an artist. . . .

69. From an unsigned review, *Sharpe's London Magazine*

December 1848, viii. 122–7

To return to Robert Browning, we recognise in him a genius which soars above all the trammels of conventionalism, and which may even be said to have laid the foundation for a new school. He has none of the faults, and perhaps not all the merits, of the Elizabethan dramatists. He approximates in one respect to the French dramatic bards, namely, in unity both of conception and execution. These are qualities which English critics are least able to appreciate; they hunt for show-passages—passages independent of the context, consequently dramatic blots; and if they do not discover these, they can see little or nothing to admire. Now, in Browning's plays, not a speech, not a line, scarcely a word is introduced, which does not tend to exhibit some phase of character, which has not a direct bearing on the development of the plot, which does not contribute to the unity of the whole creation. This, almost as of course, has not been appreciated (speaking generally), and thus Robert Browning's works have been neglected and slighted by the smaller fry of critics in the literary organs of the day. But, despite this, our author has succeeded in placing a series of plays before us in his so-called *Bells and Pomegranates*, which will live and be honoured as long as our country's tongue endures.

And now, without further preamble, we will proceed to notice the first work in this series, entitled *Pippa passes*, which is couched in a peculiar form and vein, but which, nevertheless, must command the sympathies of all who have once learned to understand it. And here let us confess that a certain needless obscurity is but too characteristic of

Browning's strains, and suffices in some degree to account for the slow progress he has made in popular estimation. He is not only in the habit of omitting all relative pronouns and various other small words as well as stage directions, for brevity's sake, but he also endeavours to concentrate both thought and passion within the narrowest possible space—to express a world of meaning sometimes by a word. Again, he assumes the reader's knowledge of all recondite facts, historical, geographical, philosophical, natural and social, which may be accidentally adverted to in his dramas, and he further does appear (there is no denying it,) to take some slight pleasure in perplexing the said reader's brains. Now these are very serious defects, which make the first perusal of one of Browning's works rather a study than an ordinary reading; and though they justify not the dullness of the critic who should have broken through such barriers, they do account for the absence of just appreciation on the part of the general public. But, *allons! à l'ouvrage!* Let us discharge our duty with the utmost possible celerity. . . .

Browning is, undoubtedly, not a perfect artist: far from it. But a certain exquisite and eminently '*patrician*', let us add Christian, delicacy of sentiment will be found to be the prevailing characteristic of his works, combined with a force and truthfulness which are sometimes surprising. Will he ever be popular, in the widest sense of the term? This is very questionable: for, no doubt, this remarkable poet is obscure. When we first perused one of his dramas (we think, *The Last* [sic] *of the Druses*), we were so annoyed by its seeming confusion and mysticism, that we got through the first scene with difficulty; and though recognising great beauties here and there, made our way but slowly to an accurate appreciation of the play. Indeed, while first studying all these works, we feel as though treading the maze of a dark forest in the starlight night. Awhile all seems obscurity around us; but, by degrees, as our eyes grow accustomed to the forest twilight, they discern a thousand beauties that passed at first unnoticed, in every brake and bower. The dark shadows, that stretched across our path in sullen gloom, seem to add a deeper charm to the scene; while the golden star-beams, shining in betwixt green leaves above, fall on lovely flowers beneath our feet, which we trod o'er unheeded, but which prove the more lovely and fragrant the more we examine into their nature and inhale their sweetness. Then, too, there is a sacred melody breathing through the wood: a low continuous warbling, as from a distant chorus of sweet nightingales. All that seemed confusion is order. The very gnarled forest-trunks, with their wide-spread and interwoven branches, the very clouds that pass above, and momently dim the pure stars—the very midnight breezes that wail from afar—add to the beauty, to the unity, of the scene. And, finally, where we at first drew back with a feeling of dismay, we weep, perchance, from the overflowing of our hearts in love, and recognise the presence of the Divine.

70. From an unsigned review, *The English Review*

June 1849, xi. 354–86

This lengthy review (some 14,000 words) is interesting for its evangelical emphasis and for calling the poet to task for, allegedly, condoning murder and suicide in his poems and plays.

. . . His main error, indeed, is one of a serious nature; but some of our readers may perhaps esteem it a virtue. We know that there are enthusiastic Churchmen and earnest Christians, who applaud the murderous deed of *Tell*, and warmly sympathize with, if they do not sanctify the memory of, *Charlotte Corday*. We do not belong to this class of thinkers: in our eyes, murder is always murder; and political murder is perhaps the most odious of slaughters. Once admit the *possible* right, in such a case as Tell's for instance, and the meanest scoundrel has but to allege conscience, and he is justified in assassinating the best of kings, or the first of heroes, because, forsooth, he regards their existence as fatal to the rights of man. Now, we do not assert that Mr. Browning would seriously advocate political murder; but he certainly alludes to it, and even treats of it, in a most lenient tone. To mention one single instance, in his dramatic poem of *Paracelsus*, a certain poet called Aprile, expressing his desire to be at once sculptor, painter, poet, and musician, and giving a list of those objects he should especially wish to embody, declares he would omit

> no youth who stands,
> Silent and very calm amid the throng;
> His right hand ever hid beneath his robe;
> Until the tyrant pass.

In the poem of *Pippa passes*, we have another offensive instance of the same apparent predilection, against which we must beg to enter our most energetic protest. Another mischievous tendency of this poet's, in our opinion, is towards the exaltation of suicide, as a high and noble act. From time immemorial, poets have availed themselves of this method of disposing of troublesome characters, but we have not the less objection to it on this account. It has indeed been made a question, even among Christian casuists, whether in some instances death might not be preferable to shame. We are of opinion, however, that the Christian's paramount duty must be endurance, even in the most extreme cases. But Mr. Browning's suicides are *not* suicides of this character: that in *Luria*, as well as that in *The Blot on the Scutcheon*, do not pertain to any such category, and, from a Christian point of view, they are certainly indefensible. Nevertheless, we should not be too severe on a blot which Mr. Browning shares in common with so many other writers: we would exhort him indeed to avoid this error for the future; but with this, we rest content. Finally, one other moral objection to certain of Mr. Browning's creations may be advanced with too much truth: though the general spirit of purity breathing from his works be deserving of all praise, he is not sufficiently studious of certain external decencies; he has treated themes, with a moral purpose we admit, and perhaps even with a moral effect,—which had better been left untouched. This remark holds good more particularly of parts of *Pippa passes*, of the general design of *The Blot on the Scutcheon*,—otherwise a truly exquisite work, treated with wonderful pathos, grace, and delicacy,—and of two or three of the short dramatic lyrics,—we will name only 'The Confessional'. We have now said the worst that can be said on the score of morality; and the moral and even religious beauties which counterbalance these errors are so great, as to call for the genial appreciation of all true lovers of poetry or of truth. . . .

On the whole, these Lyrics and Romances are well worthy of their author; and that is saying much. They are unlike any thing else we are acquainted with; for Southey's monodramas, very fine in their way, have another cast; and Tennyson's dramatic lyrics, such as 'Ulysses', are more reflective and contemplative, though very noble also. That passion, that intensity, that power, which is the marked characteristic of

Mr. Browning, is conspicuous throughout them. They are not altogether free from morbid tendencies and exaggerations,—witness 'The Confessional,' and 'The Tomb at St. Praxed's', though both of these have merit: they are sometimes painful; but they are always forcible, and in some instances graceful and pleasant also.—We have noticed the series very cursorily, and Mr. Browning is not a Poet who can be done justice to in a few words. He must be illustrated and elucidated with care. No author more requires interpreters to stand betwixt him and the public: and where, in the present dearth of taste or common sense in the critical world, when the English of a Carlyle is thought sublime, and the artificial and conventional are in almost all cases preferred to the truthful, are we to look for such interpreters? Mr. Browning must bide his time, secure of his own greatness, and of the world's awaking sooner or later to a just appreciation of it. Even now a change is manifest; a new and complete edition of his works is called for, and proof is thereby afforded that the public is beginning to open its eyes. . . .

71. Culling Flowers From Marshes

1846

A brief entry for Robert Browning in *The Poets and Poetry of England in the Nineteenth Century*, ed. Rufus W. Griswold (1846), p. 464.

There are in Mr. Browning's writings vigour, force of character, and passionate strength; but unhappily few of them are adapted to the popular apprehension. They are not easily read in the boudoir, where the perusal of Moore and Rogers is the highest exertion of intellect. Indeed, with some striking merits which will give them influence in the formation of the taste of another generation, they are deformed by so many novelties of construction, and affectations of various kinds, that few will have patience to wade through his marshes to cull the flowers with which they are scattered.

72. Leigh Hunt on Browning

June 1847

From the diary entry of 27 June 1847, *William Allingham: A Diary*, ed. H. Allingham and D. Radford (1907), pp. 36-7.

'Browning—lives at Peckham, because no one else does! a born poet, but loves contradictions. Shakespeare and Milton write plainly, the Sun and the Moon write plainly, and why can't Browning?' I suggested he was the Turner of poetry, to which Leigh Hunt replied, 'Now you've said it! He's a pleasant fellow, has few readers, and will be glad to find you admire him.'

ON THE RE-PRODUCTION OF
A BLOT

1848

73. Unsigned review, *The Athenæum*

27 November 1848, p. 1217

SADLER'S WELLS.—The re-production of Mr. Browning's fine drama *The Blot in the 'Scutcheon* was on Monday an exciting incident to the admirers of this gentleman's genius. The play is an attempt to give a poetic interest to a melo-dramatic subject. The circumstances attending the original production under Mr. Macready's management at Drury Lane were thought, at the time, to be peculiarly illustrative of the relative positions of poet and manager—little to the credit of the latter and not to the profit of the first. Without committing ourselves here to either side of the question, we may be permitted to approve of the act of justice now rendered to the dramatist in thus granting him, though at the distance of many years, a new trial. The experiment perfectly succeeded. The play, as now acted, commanded well deserved applause; though we believe its interest to be of too painful a sort to permit its having a long run. The chief merit of the piece lies in the second act; where Thorold, Lord Tresham (Mr. Phelps) seated in his library listens to the disclosure made by his faithful domestic, old Gerard (Mr. Graham), that his only sister, Mildred Tresham (Miss Cooper), has given access at night to a stranger. Hereupon, the young nobleman sends for his sister; and after impressing her with the sense of a brother's love and the importance of the fact that the honour of the house depends on them, the sole survivors of the family,—he first darkly and hesitatingly hints at, and at last decidedly and plainly accuses her with, her transgression. Great are his wonder and indignation to hear her confess it,—yet declare her willingness to wed his friend, Henry, Earl Mertoun (Mr. Dickinson). Mad with anger, he calls his friends into the chamber, curses Mildred in their presence, and thus leaves her. Her cousin, Guendolin Tresham (Miss Huddart), suspects a mystery; and soon learns, by woman's instinct, that the favoured lover and the expected bridegroom are the same person. Meantime, the wrathful brother has come upon the spot where the Earl had been accustomed to gain furtive entrance to his mistress's apartment; and there finding the betrayer of his sister's honour drags him forward and, without allowing explanation, mortally wounds him. Mildred's death and his own follow, as the culminating sequel of this rash deed. Mr. Phelp's acting in Lord Thorold was of such excellence as to deserve especial analysis. The whole of the library scene in particular was admirable. The uneasy, irritable, suppressed feeling—the doubt—the conviction—the tenderness—the irascibility—the overwhelming wrath—the maddening indignation—the fearful curse,—these altogether composed a situation of rare power and effectiveness. In the parts of the frail boy and girl neither Mr. Dickinson nor Miss Cooper had enough of poetic perception to do justice to the sentiment. The tones of Miss Cooper's voice are singularly discordant with the feeling of the text; and she has besides no notion of the intermediate action by which the points of character are to be brought out. Hers, accordingly, was a literal reading,—not an interpretation of the part. Mr. Dickinson, on the other hand, was frequently too violent, and committed again the indiscretions which we have already charged against him. The vehemence of his attachment excited no little laughter in the pit. With these drawbacks, the piece was both excellently mounted and well acted; giving satisfaction to a numerous though not overflowing audience.

74. Unsigned review, *The Examiner*

9 December 1848, p. 789

We ought not to have passed without mention last week a careful revival of Mr Browning's poetical and passionate play of the *Blot on the 'Scutcheon* at Sadler's Wells Theatre. Mr Phelps played the hero with striking effect. Something too subdued, perhaps, in the early scenes, where passion overmasters reason; but when the tide of remorse flows grandly in, full of dignified pathos and true emotion. Mr Dickenson, whom we formerly mentioned, was the hapless lover in the play, and showed a strong sense of the poetry in his part, as well as much eager fervour and delicacy of elocution, which augured well for the future of so young an actor. The scenery and general appointments were rich and tasteful. We could not desire to see better scenes anywhere than the opening hall of the mansion of the Treshams, with their shielded 'scutcheons 'blushing' through countless quarterings; than the chamber of Mildred, or the study of Thorold; or than those dark old clusters of gloomy forest trees which witness at the last, and do their best to conceal, the family shame. Mr Phelps comprehends the poetry of a play and can seize and reproduce it in the arrangements of the scene.

75. Thomas Powell: An 1849 Survey

From his 'Robert Browning', *The Living Authors of England* (1849), pp. 71–85.

In his twentieth year he published a poem called *Pauline*, which he has never acknowledged, and of which he now appears to be ashamed. It has little merit beyond a certain faint evidence of sensuous feeling running through it; that kind of murmuring music which ever accompanies a poet in his walk through life.

In 1836 his first acknowledged poem appeared, called *Paracelsus*, and it is the opinion of many of the critics of the day that this will be the work by which he will be the most remembered. A critic has remarked, that one of the finest thoughts of modern times is embalmed in three lines in this poem.

> There are two points in the adventure of a diver,
> First when a beggar he prepares to plunge,
> Then when a prince he rises with his pearl.
> Festus, I plunge!

An eminent poet remarked that Mr. Browning had lost the chief force of the thought by the first line, which he maintained was very prosaic; he suggested that it ought to be altered, as

'There are two moments in a diver's life,' &c.

This is a point for the author. We named this to Mr. Browning, who acknowledged his own line was feeble.

Mr. Browning's *Paracelsus* excited little attention. Mr. Forster, of *The Examiner*, praised it, Mr. Fox, of *The Monthly Repository*, and *Heraud's New Monthly Magazine*—and there was an end of the matter. It, however, gave the poet a quiet pedestal for his future station, and he is now so proud of his young creation that he generally places it as his peculiar characteristic, and calls himself author of *Paracelsus*.

To *Paracelsus* succeeded a tragedy, called *Strafford*, which owing to Mr. Forster's influence with Mr. Macready, was performed. The great tragedian acted Strafford—but all his efforts were unavailing. It was the tragedy of spasms: the want of personal interest is too deeply felt to allow of any doubt, and the work of a strong mentality went to the tomb of the Capulets for want of a physical Romeo. We fear it will be found to be the verdict of the public, that the author of *Sordello* is a noble abstraction; a great spirit, but he lacks the flesh and blood of Shakspere, and the milk of human kindness.

Four years afterwards *Sordello* astonished his friends, and amazed the world—of this work we shall speak more anon. . . .

Mr. Browning's next work was *Pippa Passes*, the first of a series which he has called *Bells and Pomegranates*. Here begins the real poetic life of Browning, so far as the public know him, and out of these singular productions we hope to justify our faith to the world. The idea of Pippa, a poor factory girl, purifying human nature as she passes about on her vocation, is a fine conception, and it is to be lamented that it is not made so intelligible to the common mind as to be capable of a wider appreciation. To the poet, however, it remains what Keats said of Beauty, 'a joy for ever'. After a time Mr. Macready produced another play, and the reception which the *Blot in the 'Scutcheon* had at Drury Lane in 1843, and at Sadler's Wells in 1848, seems to justify the current opinion that the author is only a dramatist for the poet and the critic. He cannot touch the hearts of the million. That he abounds in the esthetic, may be presumed, but the world at large care little for the subtler and more minute works of the human heart. They demand a broader, wider range, a rougher 'guess' at their nature; when it is borne in mind how many words are not heard in a large theatre; how few of the actors know how to deliver a speech intelligibly; it is evident that a tortuous, obscure and condensed style must be so much Greek to a mixed audience who hear a drama for the first time; when, however, you add to these disadvantages, a plot not springing from the every day impulses of the heart, but evolved from some peculiar idiosyncracy of the mind, it is evident you make a very fatiguing and ingenious puzzle, and not a drama to move our tears or smiles.

We have heard Mr. Browning frequently reply in answer to some of the critics who have accused him of an impracticable style, that he is as clear as any poet can be, who uses a new set of symbols; he declares that he is weary of phoenixes, roses, lilies, and the old stock in trade, which with the aid of ten fingers, he enabled mere versifiers to inundate the reading world with a deluge of 'verse and water'.

For instance, if Mr. Browning wishes to make a simile, and illustrate redness, he will not take the rose, but select some out of the way flower equally red, but of whose name not one in a thousand has ever heard: this added to a style so condensed and clipt of all aids as to sometimes be unintelligible, has sealed Mr. Browning's works to the many. It is indeed the shorthand of poetry. It requires the author or some duly qualified admirer to interpret it to the world. We feel sure it is a great defect in an author when he requires 'an explanator'. He should be able to converse with his reader without intermediate aid. He should sit face to face, flashing bright thoughts into the gazer's mind.

We must not conclude our notice of Robert Browning without alluding to the exquisite spiritual grace and purity he has thrown around his female characters. We confess that they all seem to belong to one family, although brought up at different colleges (for all his women are great metaphysicians), still there is a purity and unselfishness about them which makes one wish that the world were peopled only with such divine creatures as Shakspere and Browning's heroines are.

Lamb once told a friend that he would any day marry, old as he was, if he could only 'find one of Shakspere's women'. The poet, logician, and metaphysician would, in like manner, look out for some Sordellian creature such as Mildred, Pippa, Anael, or one of her sister heroines. The purity of a poet's heart may frequently be tested by his ideal seraglio. We have only to refer to Byron, Shakspere and Browning, for strong cases in support of our opinion.

It would be unjust to Mr. Browning to give any specimen from his larger works; they should be read by themselves; they do not abound in fine isolated passages, like most poets. All their beauties are so interwoven as to render extracts, to inform the reader, well nigh as absurd as to bring a brick as a specimen of the architecture of any particular building.

In November, 1846, Mr. Browning married Miss Barrett, the celebrated poetess, and shortly after went to Florence, where he now remains. The conjugal union of the first poetess of the age with the author of *Paracelsus* is certainly an unparalleled event in the history of matrimony, and a singular illustration of Shakspere's sonnet.

> Let me not to the marriage of pure minds
> Admit impediments.

We are happy to add, that the first social production of these highly favoured children of Apollo is a fine boy, born in the sunny south. In person Browning is small, but well made and active; very dark, with a Jewish cast of countenance; has large black whiskers, which he cultivates under his chin; his eyes are dark; complexion almost approaching to sallow. However obscure in his writings, he is intelligible in his conversation; and his dislike to brusquerie often borders on affectation and punctiliousness unworthy of so true a poet. His marriage with Miss Barrett was the result of a short courtship; their correspondence commenced in Greek, and doubtless in that language their love longings were expressed.

Mr. Browning is very susceptible of criticism, although pretending to a great contempt of it. He is a strong disbeliever in the genius of his contemporaries, and is as chary of his critical praise as Shakspere himself. The absurdity of some of his dedications is in striking contrast to this hesitation; as those to Talfourd, Barry Cornwall, &c. abundantly testify. This is a contradiction in his nature we cannot easily explain, and most probably proceeds from that false courtesy which is, perhaps, his solitary blemish; in other respects he is a gentleman and an undoubted poet. His political principles are republican. He is in his thirty-seventh year.

Mr. Browning's writings are numerous.

76. C. Edmunds, *Eclectic Review*

August 1849, 4th Ser. xxvi. 203–14

From his unsigned review of *Poems, 1849.*

. . . To the deep thought prevailing throughout Mr. Browning's poetry, we have already sufficiently alluded, in passing. It is to be added, however, that difficulty and apparent obscurity form by no means the universal attendant on this poetic exposition of thought. There are passages and whole poems, of which the meaning and beauty may be transparent to any, and at once. And at least a moiety of his writing, we should judge to be not more distant from the ordinary apprehension than all genuine poetry commonly is.

His mastery over language, and of an essentially poetical language,—condensed and imaginatively breathing life, is complete; and, for the most part, would seem inborn. It is, in *Paracelsus*, as conspicuous—and in almost equal refinement, as in the latest of his lyrics or dramas. Luxuriant, however, in beauty, as in his subordinate expression, it is the expression of any one of his poems, as a whole, which most prominently attracts attention and abides by the memory. For herein is his largeness of imagination most saliently seen; realizing its full effect. His verification, again, is a continuously efficient instrument, a noble servant. It is always,—in whatever measure, strictly individual and characteristic, and of exceeding power and facility—the facility of energy, not of smoothness. It is marked by such license and freedom dangerous only to the poetaster, from merely arbitrary rules, as is proper to the right poet, who is his own lawgiver—following the law of use intelligently, not blindly, only so far as is consistent with the end of this law,—in the first instance proceeding from such as himself. And here, the end of the law is melody, and a meet musical interpretation of the subject-matter of poetic speech. It is this which is to be attained by the versifier, by whatever means. Assuredly, here, the end, when actually attained, does justify the means, whatever they may be. The melody of Browning is seldom or never of so finished and heightened a beauty as that of Tennyson. And so, generally, it may be affirmed, he is far from being so consummate an executive artist as his great Brother-poet.

CHRISTMAS-EVE
AND EASTER-DAY

April 1850

77. From an unsigned review, *The Athenæum*

6 April 1850, pp. 370–1

Elizabeth declared herself 'vexed' by this review. *LEBB*, I, 446–7.

The book before us is the work of a poet; though if this fact should gain but a limited recognition, the writer will have only himself to blame. If the Muses *will* masquerade and don the trappings of gipsies, they must feel no offence if they should forfeit by the grotesqueness of their seeming the respect that is due to their nature. True, the Nine may have their seasons of frolic and pastime,—nor is their sporting to be censured when occasion befits; but the Temple of Apollo and the hour of sacrifice are not the place nor the period suitable to such recreations. In a word, our complaint against Mr. Browning is—that while dealing with the highest themes of imagination and indicating his competency to treat them, he has recklessly impaired the dignity of his purpose by the vehicle chosen for its development. The form of doggrel [*sic*]—carried to excess by strange and offensive oddities of versification—is not that in which the mysteries of faith, doubt, and eternity can be consistently treated.

Examples of such versification are painfully abundant. Seeking here only to illustrate the rhyming eccentricities of the writer, we quote one or two without reference to their sense or context.— . . .

[Quotes a wide variety of lines, with comment interspaced, beginning with I. 31.]

It is well for Mr. Browning's present venture, that poetry, from its elemental nature, may to some extent charm even where the entire work violates the harmonies of relation. Morals and science lose all their value if there be incompleteness or incongruity in their exposition; but the primary influences of beauty and truth, which constitute song are welcome even through partial revelations.

> The one blue break of beauty in the clouds,

or the scattered stars that gaze on us through the rift, are prized though the general sky be overcast.—This qualified recognition the poems before us must claim. From their perusal intelligent minds may rise enriched with new images of beauty and new stimulants to thought. But that higher appreciation which belongs to a perfect and consistent whole—to those works in which the form corresponds to the spirit, and in which thought, passion, and even humour are harmoniously fused by the imagination—must be denied to them. If, in spite of many unquestioned excellencies, we turn from what Mr. Browning *has* done to speculate on what he *might have* done, it is his own genius that provokes the comparison and enhances the regret.

78. From an unsigned review, *The Spectator*

6 April 1850, xxiii. 329

. . . It requires esoteric knowledge to speak of a peculiar faith. We cannot tell what those may think who see originality in strangeness; but it does not strike us that Mr. Browning has at all advanced himself by this new poem. There is not such dreary lengths of obscurity as in some of his former pieces; but the cause of that improvement appears mechanical. It arises from the choice of metre whose nature compels brevity; and brevity avoids the obscurity of length and involution, though there is still the obscurity of hazy thought and indistinct expression. In other respects, it seems to us that Mr. Browning is much the same. His every-day subjects are commonplace in their images; though an affected quaintness may give them an air of novelty. His loftier themes are rather shrouded than presented; they pass for anything to the eye of faith, they are nothing in the eye of reason. Passages of merit, though perhaps scarcely equal to the theme, may be picked out; but the whole is strange as poetry, and mystical as Christianity.

79. From an unsigned review, *The Leader*

27 April 1850, i. 111

On the theology of the poem we should have much to say did time and place serve; meanwhile we need only applaud in passing the sincere and earnest spirit which breathes through it. The sincerity of it will to many look like levity. Already we have heard strange objections to the 'tone', as not elevated enough. Do these critics imagine that an 'elevated' tone is difficult? Do they suppose that Browning could not have adopted it, had he thought fit? But he did *not* think fit. Instead of imitating Milton he spoke as Robert Browning; his keen sense of the ludicrous and grotesque fading into the background whenever the presence of more solemn themes overshadowed it. In the bold and artful mingling of the ludicrous with the intensely serious he reminds us of Carlyle. His style is swayed by the subject. It is a garment, not a mould; it takes the varying shapes of varied movement, and does not force its one monotone on all.

As a page out of the history of a life, the poetic confession of a troubled soul, *Christmas Eve* has a significance and a value peculiarly its own. We have read it three times, and with increasing admiration. What it wants to make it an enduring work of art is that which the author cannot give it, has not to give—the magic and the mystery of Beauty. But of its kind it is really great. The luxury of rhyme—the marvelous facility playing with difficulties as an Indian juggler plays with balls, every one will have noticed. Since Butler no English poet has exhibited the same daring propensity and facility in rhyming. If the verse is sometimes rugged it is but the better exponent of the thought Realism in Art has Truth as an aim, Ugliness as a pitfall.

80. W. M. Rossetti, *The Germ*

May 1850, iv. 187–92

From his review.

For the interest of the Pre-Raphaelites in Browning, see the Introduction, p. 16.

Of all poets, there is none more than Robert Browning, in approaching whom diffidence is necessary. The mere extent of his information cannot pass unobserved, either as a fact, or as a title to respect. No one who has read the body of his works will deny that they are replete with mental and speculative subtlety, with vivid and most diversified conception of character, with dramatic incident and feeling; with that intimate knowledge of outward nature which makes every sentence of description a living truth; replete with a most human tenderness and pathos. Common as is the accusation of 'extravagance', and unhesitatingly as it is applied, in a general off-hand style, to the entire character of Browning's poems, it would require some jesuitism of self-persuasion to induce any to affirm his belief in the existence of such extravagance in the conception of the poems, or in the sentiments expressed; of any want of concentration in thought, of national or historical keeping. Far from this, indeed, a deliberate unity of purpose is strikingly apparent.

81. From an unsigned review, *The Examiner*

May 1850, pp. 211–13

It will not be supposed that in seeking to convey to the reader what we have derived of Mr Browning's meaning in these latter respects from the volume before us, we would imply our own implicit agreement with them. Far from this. We are much more disposed than Mr Browning would now seem to be, to perceive in a mutual reverence for differences of creed one of the most Christian manifestations of the religious spirit, and to recognise in those very differences but a better means of development for that free mental life which must always co-operate with religion to make the latter truly profitable to man. We are by no means sure that we should hesitate to call not a few passages in the poem we have been noticing but another form of a common bigotry—poetry veiling a somewhat narrow and intolerant superstition. But unsatisfactory and imperfect in these respects as the composition is, we think its general teaching, as we have sought to explain it, quite sound, apart from the particular applications now and then indiscreetly given to it.

As an emanation of thought in verse we think it every way a most remarkable production, and not unlikely to have effects much beyond the mere pleasure or entertainment of a great many readers. Mr Browning has been steadily reclaiming his genius, of late years, from the 'vague and formless infinite' into which at one time it seemed to be falling, and in this respect the work before us is full of the richest future promise. He will yet win and wear his laurel, and be admitted for what he truly is, one of the most original poets of our time. He is equally a master of thought and emotion, and joins to a rare power of imaginative creation that which is still more rarely found in union with it—the subtlest power of mental reasoning and analysis. Over the instrument of language he exerts the most facile mastery, and few poets have moved with such free and flowing step through the most complicated word-mazes of music and measure. We would challenge for such a writer the respectful attention of those most opposed to the views he promulgates. The feeling of this poem is true, whatever may be thought of its dogmatism; and its essential teaching is independent of particular forms. It will assuredly waken very many to the 'better part' suggested by its theme, and it will stir and quicken thought in all.

82. From an unsigned review, *The English Review*

September 1850, xiv. 65–92

. . . Of the second part, *Easter-Day*, we can only say that it is wilder again than the first, more poetic it may be, and grander; the description of the final conflagration in the vision of the last day is truly magnificent and awful,—and that it deals with a most difficult subject, the degree to which asceticism should enter into the life of the true Christian. Our poet almost seems to imagine that he should give up the use of this world altogether, and to condemn himself because he cannot consent to do this. He states the ascetic argument derived from the death of Christ our Lord, as strongly as it *can* be stated, in the passage commencing:

> Enough! you know
> The all-stupendous tale,—that birth,
> That life, that death!

and appears to imagine the said argument incontrovertible; on which point we differ from him. We think, and know, that the use of this world *is* permitted to the Christian, yes, even to him who aims at perfection; after which all indeed are bound to strive, and not an isolated class. But, as a whole, this second part is far less satisfactory to us than the first: we think it founded, to a great degree, on a mistake. This is not the place, however, at the fag-end of a long literary article, in which we could enter into such a controversy. Much there is, no doubt, that is very admirable here, too, in this second part of the poems: and powerfully does the poet demonstrate, that earth without the hope of heaven would only be a wilderness.

On the whole, however, this contribution of Browning's to our poetic literature is a great work, and is gladly hailed by us as such. Essentially different as it is in all respects from *In Memoriam*, they are both destined to an earthly immortality.

83. A Perverse Genius

1851

D. M. Moir, from his *Sketches of the Poetical Literature of the Past Half Century* (1851), pp. 320–1.

Robert Browning, as a poet of promise, was regarded by some as equalling Tennyson. In his *Paracelsus*, from out a cloudy tabernacle were darted tongues of flame; but the smoke has never cleared away. In it we had much of mysticism, affectation, obscurity, nay, utter incomprehensibility, mixed up with many fine aspirations, and a variety of magnificent outlines, although no separate scene could be said to satisfy. We had abundance of bold rough draughts, some in the manner of Turner, and others in the manner of Martin,[1] all 'dark with excessive bright;' but no single picture filled up and coloured. *Sordello*, which followed it, was the strangest vagary ever submitted to the world in the shape of verse, and as incomprehensibly mysterious as the riddles of the Sphinx. Some recondite meaning the book probably may have; but I am not aware that any one has ever been able to discover it, although I think Mr. Horne, the author of *Orion*, once made a guess.[2] At all events its intelligibility does not shine on the surface, nor in any twenty consecutive lines.

In the *Bells and Pomegranates*, we have now and then glimpses of poetic sentiment and description, like momentary sunbeams darting out between rifted clouds; but straightway the clouds close, and we are

[1] Joseph Mallord William Turner (1775–1851) and John Martin (1789–1854), English painters.
[2] See No. 34 for Horne's 'guess'.

left to plod on in deeper twilight. The truth is, that with an ill-regulated imagination, Mr Browning has utterly mistaken singularity for originality—the uncommon for the fine. Style and manner he despises; indeed, he may be said to have none—for these are with him like the wind blowing where it listeth; or, as extremes meet, he may be said to have all kinds, from the most composite and arabesque to the most disjointed and Doric. Even in his serious and earnest themes, he thinks nothing of leaping at once from the Miltonic to the Hudibrastic; and to poetry as an art, such as it was in the hands of Pope and Collins, of Gray and Goldsmith, of Coleridge and Campbell, he seems to have utterly blinded himself, assuming for his motto the boastful lines of old Withers.[1]—

> Pedants shall not tie my strains
> To our antique poets' veins;
> Being born as free to these,
> I shall sing as I shall please.

Browning never seems to lack materials; but, huddled together as we find them, they may be denominated cairns—not buildings. The creations of his pen have therefore the same relation to external nature, and the goings-on of actual life, that day-dreams have to realities, or apparitional castles and cataracts in the clouds to their earthly counterparts. Genius of some kind—it may be of a high kind—Browning must have; but, most assuredly, never was genius of any kind or degree more perversely misapplied. A small band of transcendental worshippers may follow him, as they do Emerson; but even these will, I fear, be forced to content themselves with the idea, that surely there must be some thread which might enable them to grope their way through the more than Cretan intricacies of his mystical labyrinth,—if they could only catch hold of it.

---

[1] George Wither (1588–1667), an irrepressible satirist who was twice jailed for his verse, the second time for *Wither's Motto*, a poem of self-praise. He is best known for his famous lyric, 'Shall I, wasting in despair'.

84. Charles Kingsley on the defects
of Browning

From his unsigned article, entitled 'Mr. and Mrs. Browning',
Fraser's Magazine (February 1851), xliii. 170–82.

The complaint that Browning fails to treat 'English' subjects is
significant and, perhaps, helps to explain the slow growth of his
English reputation.

Some ten or twelve years have passed since Mr. Browning's first poetic
attempts appeared, to be followed at intervals by fresh productions, con-
stituting altogether two volumes, more than double the size of those
with which Mr. Tennyson has presented the world, as the outcome of
a much longer poetic life. Such an amount of verse, one would have
expected, must contain materials for a clear and definite judgment on
the writer's powers; Mr. Browning's niche in the Temple of the Muses
should be by now a settled point. On the contrary, his poems are still
caviare to the multitude; those who greedily devour, and indiscrimi-
ately worship, anything in the shape of verse, still differ widely in their
verdicts; even those who possess, or fancy that they possess, canons of
scientific criticism, are very much at a loss how to apply them to his
case. These phœnomena, whether or not they prove genius in an author,
prove at least originality; and all will allow this merit to Mr. Browning.
No one can have perused *Sordello* and *Paracelsus* without acknowledging in them the work of a poet distinguished from the herd of scribblers,
by vigorous and manful, often profound, thoughts, raciness of expression, and an amount of learning on the subjects which he handles, which
is becoming more and more rare in these days.

Of *Sordello*, perhaps, we have hardly a right to speak; for Mr.
Browning has not republished it in the last edition of his Poems. And
certainly, those peculiar defects of his, to which we must be allowed
hereafter to allude, had marred *Sordello* more than any other of his
writings, even so far as to leave the reader in doubt as to both the story
and the moral; as to whether a passage was dialogue or description, jest

or earnest, different speeches, by different characters or one by the same. We should not have said so much, if we had not intended to qualify an accusation to which the poet seems already to have pleaded guilty, by most earnest praise, not of the book as a whole, but of such passages as the two which we shall quote; and there are many such. Even when the full account of their faults has been subtracted from their merit, they still remain, surely, poetry, and that such as not three men in England now can write. . . .

But we will complain no more: though, indeed, our complaints are really compliments; for had we not felt certain that Mr. Browning was worthy of better things, we should have left the matter to clear itself, as all poems do pretty accurately in 'the righteous sieve of Time.' But there are fine ballads in the second volume, healthy and English, clear of all that Italianesque pedantry, that *crambe repetita*[1] of olives and lizards, artists and monks, with which the English public, for its sins, has been spoon-fed for the last half-century, ever since Childe Harold, in a luckless hour, thought a warmer climate might make him a better man, and that the way to raise one's own spirit was to escape to a country where humanity has sunk below the beasts. When will poets, as some of our most promising artists are beginning to do, discover that the Italian mine is well-nigh worked out, and that those who go thither for teaching are likely to find swine bad lecturers on the pearls before them?

[The reviewer expresses a dislike for some of Browning's best short poems—'Porphyria's Lover', 'The Bishop Orders His Tomb', and 'Cavalier Tunes'—but recommends a number of passages of *Paracelsus* and *Sordello* as examples of real poetry.]

'The Lost Leader' is English, and nobly English, to its heart's core; and so are these 'Home Thoughts from the Sea:

> Nobly, nobly Cape St. Vincent to the north-west died away;
> Sunset ran, one glorious blood-red reeking into Cadiz Bay;
> Bluish mid the burning water, full in face Trafalgar lay;
> In the dimmest north-east distance dawned Gibraltar grand and gray;
> 'Here and here did England help me,—how can I help England?' say,
> Whoso turns as I, this evening, turns to God to praise and pray,
> While Jove's planet rises yonder, silent over Africa.

How can Mr. Browning help England? By leaving henceforth 'the dead to bury their dead,' in effete and enervating Italy, and casting all

[1] Literally, 'warmed-over cabbage'.

his rugged genial force into the questions and the struggles of that mother-country to whom, and not to Italy at all, he owes all his most valuable characteristics.

85. Browning's Obscurity

1852

Grace Greenwood from her *Greenwood Leaves, a Collection of Sketches and Letters* (1852), pp. 292–6.

Grace Greenwood was the pseudonym used by Sara Jane (Clarke) Lippincott (1823–1904), popular poet, journalist, and essayist.

This poet is, I believe, a great problem to the critics. One who would receive the high imaginings and divinations of genius by some direct and easy process, and through a clear and pleasant medium, would be perplexed and half-angered by him at the first reading, at least. There is often about his poetry a dimness and a density which result from the depth of his thought and the affluence of his fancy. His darkest places are, after all, 'sun-dropped shades,' where the beauty is deeper and richer for the partial obscurity. His style is often singularly involved, dreamy and mystical; but he is never meaningless. Sometimes, amid his most unformed and mystical language, comes a happy, lucid expression, a bright rift, a sudden revealing of heaven through clouds and shadows— verbal felicities, pleasant surprises of humour, delicious turns of sentiment, and soft yet masterly touches of pathos, which would summon smiles to the sternest lip, or from the coldest and most philosophical heart roll away the stone which shuts down the fountain of tears.

Browning has been called unmusical, and, judged by common rules, I suppose his verse lacks melody; but for me, there is always in it a sort of spiritual harmony, which overrules the mere word-sound, and renders him one of the most musical of poets.

For all Browning's power, and learning, and strongly marked peculiarities, much of his poetry seems to me of a most natural and primitive
kind. It is simply poetic reverie, and given in the dreamy, diffuse, inex-
pressive language of reverie, every word obediently written down as it
slid from the murmuring lips of his muse, without question, and without hesitation. In such, nothing is direct or connected, but all wandering
and distracted, and the reader, to comprehend the poet, must, by some
process, place himself in a similar somnambulatory state—must reverize
with him, and go on weaving almost invisible threads of thought,
through an infinitude of words.

Paracelsus is unreadable to the mass; but the enthusiastic student
receives it almost as a new revelation of poetry. Yet it is not a poem
proper, neither is it a regular drama; but a long, winding, subtle, sweet,
and varied *talk*. It is full of grand conceptions, exquisite fancies—sometimes only given in luminous hints, startling intimations, and sometimes diffused and elaborated almost to weakness and folly. Now comes
a stranger thought of giant proportions, almost undraped and wholly
unadorned, followed by some little old friend of ours, wrapt about
and overloaded by a new and gorgeous dress. Who can doubt but that
this poem, peculiar, and in many passages powerful as it is, would be
greatly bettered if compressed into half its present compass? While our
poet spreads his poetry over so wide an expanse, and while its waters
are often so unfathomable or unclear, we think it will remain a luxury
for the few. This is an age of preoccupation and hurry; and not many
of us can stay to study out the most solemn sounding of oracles, if
given in an unknown tongue, or turn aside from direct and pleasant
paths to explore wild forests, of however magnificent growth, into
which open few clear and inviting vistas. *Paracelsus*, and indeed most
of the poetry of Browning, is to be studied, as we have said. And alas!
the many do not study; thus this poet can hardly be to them priest or
interpreter.

When Browning *is* awake, he is alive all over;—witness some of his
Dramatic Lyrics, such as 'Cavalier Tunes', 'Count Gismond', 'Incident
in the French Camp', 'How they brought the good news from Ghent to
Aix'.

I suppose that *Paracelsus* is esteemed the most powerful work of
Browning's genius, and is certainly very great, for the thought it embodies, and its many magnificent bursts of poetry.

The most remarkable thing in it, in my estimation, is the beautiful
allegorical poem introduced into Part IV.,—

'Over the sea our galleys went.'

But I love most *The Blot in the 'Scutcheon*. This is a beautiful drama—rapid in action, clear and musical in language, and most touching and mournful in its story. It inculcates a heavenly lesson of charity, and displays a wonderful knowledge of the human heart—of woman's heart. I have read it many times, and always with intense admiration, with irrepressible tears.

A PRODUCTION OF *COLOMBE'S BIRTHDAY*

1853

86. From an unsigned review, *The Athenæum*

30 April 1853, p. 537

[A brief plot-summary precedes this passage.]

Such is the refined action of this charming poem, rather than drama. Its movements, for the most part, occur in the chambers of the mind. Such themes are evidently not of the usual stage-sort, and will fail of attraction to all who insist on the ordinary dramatic motion and action. To the worn-out and wearied playgoer, who can turn for a moment out of the beaten path, nothing could well be more delicious. The involuntary tear was often felt upon the cheek. We feared that on performance, this fine poem would scarcely be intelligible to a mixed audience. Miss Faucit, however, by her skill, made them perfectly understand it; and the applause came in the proper places. That the performance will become popular, it is not for the critic to determine,—but we can record its apparent perfect success on the first night. Whether the taste of the public for so refined a creation on the stage is yet formed, remains to be seen.

87. From an unsigned review, *The Examiner*

30 April 1853, p. 278

It appears very strange and unreasonable that a writer so intensely dramatic in the spirit of all his writings as Mr Browning undoubtedly is, should have obtained such moderate success on the stage. There can be no question as to the leading characteristic of his poetry. Whether or not he assumes the form, the dramatic spirit is there. If it be a romance, or a lyric, or a play, the same process is going on. Somebody is talking to himself, or exchanging talk with another, or, in collision with a number of persons, eliciting the workings and counterworkings of individual mind or passion. There is the least possible of the descriptive in Mr Browning's poems. With him, those things are in process of doing, in the heat of vivid creation, in projection as the alchemist would say, which it becomes the task of others to describe. His people never go out of their way to narrate their situation, or their feelings, or to explain themselves, for the benefit of others, the peculiarities of their position or disposition. All this is only to be inferred from what they say to the matter they have more immediately in hand; and whatever breaks or intervals of explanation may thus be left, the intelligence of the reader must supply.

Here we touch perhaps on the source of the difficulty in the way of Mr Browning's stage success. He exacts too much both before and behind the curtain. The actor wants intelligence and skill to put the proper meaning into a felicitous word, he cannot supply the look, the gesture, the rich comment of face or voice, which give ease and strength to abrupt transitions of passion. The audience have come to be amused, and have none of their wits disengaged for any harder employment. Little but obscurity therefore,—jerks and jumps of expression, and subtleties lost in the labour of their delivery,—are the result of a stage performance. Of that subtle essence of the poet's genius to which imagination, fancy, intellect, and passion contribute so largely, and which make the writings of this poet so interesting a study to the most cultivated minds, it is little more than the *caput mortuum* that remains.

88. Not a Member of a Poetic School

1853

From an unsigned article, 'The Poetry of Robert Browning', *Chamber's Edinburgh Journal* (16 July 1853), pp. 39–41.

It has been customary, with what amount of correctness we will not stay to inquire, to speak of the 'schools of the poets.' The expression has, perhaps, been more directly applied to modern English writers than to any others; and if we are to believe that, generally speaking, they can be classed into so many grand divisions, each presided over by a power-ful influential mind, we must of necessity consider somewhat in the light of outlaws those whose works give no indication of submission to such control. One of these is Robert Browning, certainly among the most remarkable of living English poets, and to whom Walter Savage Landor—one whose compliments are rare—has paid the graceful tribute of admiration expressed in these lines:

> Since Chaucer was alive and hale,
> No man hath walked along our roads with step
> More active, more inquiring eye, or tongue
> More varied in discourse.

If Mr Browning is thus appreciated by one of the greatest of his con-temporaries, he does not, however, enjoy the popularity which men of much less genius have acquired; nor is he even known to many of those who are really lovers of poetry.

Were this altogether the fault of the poet himself, we might almost infer that the world was nothing the worse for its ignorance of him. He is only partially to blame, however; for while some of his works are sufficiently obscure to deter even the most refined reader, and far too much so ever to become popular in any sense whatever, the greater part of them are really very beautiful, of a highly original character, and deserving of a very wide circulation. They are simple enough to be understood in everything that constitutes them sources of enjoyment —no ordinary recommendation, when we see how largely some in our day act upon Wordsworth's contentment—'to enjoy the things which *others* understand.' They require no other faculty than that which the most ordinary reader brings to bear upon the perusal of our best known English writers; and if we could forget that Robert Browning had written anything but one or two fine dramatic poems, and a series of still finer lyrical ones, we should be wholly at a loss to understand why he is not as well known as any writer of our times. We cannot, however, shut our eyes to the fact, that he has taken great liberties with the public, and even with that portion of it who readily appreciate the most subtle and refined kind of poetry. The author of *Paracelsus* put forth strong claims on the attention of all who could perceive and enjoy the most delicate and beautiful expressions of poetic genius. That work was eminently calculated to awaken hopes of something very noble and powerful in the future; but when Mr Browning chose to address himself to a small—we should say, a very small circle, in his *Sordello*, rather than to fulfil the promise of his first essay, it was very natural that something like dissatisfaction should have been felt by his admirers. Subsequent writings deepened this dissatisfaction into an impression that the poet had abandoned altogether the intention of writing intelligibly, or of making himself heard, as the poet ought to be; and as the public is little disposed to give itself trouble about understanding poetry which it cannot feel, much that he has since written has been received with a certain degree of jealousy—certainly not with that frank admiration to which a large portion of it is entitled. . . .

We have taken no notice of Mr Browning's latest work, *Christmas-eve and Easter-Day*; for although it contains, in fuller measure, perhaps, than any of his other writings, those evidences of strong originality to which we have already referred, the subject is one of which we cannot properly give an outline. It is a metaphysical and essentially religious poem, though partaking to a very slight degree of the character of religious poetry generally. It is too full of close and subtile reasoning ever to be popular; for while it combines much that is striking in thought and imagery, with a high tone of devotional feeling, it has depths of spiritual experience into which the ordinary reader of poetry will scarcely be inclined to go.

MEN AND WOMEN

November 1855

89. From an unsigned review, *The Athenæum*

17 November 1855, pp. 1327–8

These volumes contain some fifty poems, which will make the least imaginative man think, and the least thoughtful man grieve. Who will not grieve over energy wasted and power misspent,—over fancies chaste and noble, so overhung by the 'seven veils' of obscurity, that we can oftentimes be only sure that fancies exist? What they are meant to typify or illustrate cannot always be detected by the eyes of even kindred dreamers. Again, in the versification of these new poems, there is an amount of extravagant licence, belonging to a superfluity of power, for which only those who have studied versification as an art will be able to account or apologize. That some among the poets having the finest musical sense have written the most irregular verses, is a fact strange and true. They have relied on the sympathy of the interpreter: they have expected him here to lean on a cadence,—there to lend accent to the rhyme, or motion to the languid phrase; in another place, to condense a multitude of syllables, so as to give an effect of concrete strength. Indeed, it may be generally declared, that for those who have not this fine artistic sense, a large proportion of modern verse is not verse at all, by reason of its licence and assumption. The artists show themselves, by their exigencies, to be less masterly than the artists of old, who had their fullest praise from the few, but their full praise also from the many,—who knew that, whereas their thoughts raised them to heights where only a limited number could bear them company, the perfection of form was such that their works, if incompletely apprehended by the ignorant, the timid, and the frivolous, had still a complete charm of their own for these,—a charm of music, a charm of imagery,—a charm which kept the idea of poetry as a separate and refined art select and holy in the popular mind. Our poets now speak in an unknown tongue,—wear whatever unpoetic garniture it pleases their conceit or their idleness to snatch up; and the end too often is, pain to those who love them best, and who most appreciate their high gifts and real nobleness,—and to the vast world, whom they might assist, they bring only a mystery and receive nothing but wonder and scorn.

We fear that no one who goes through these volumes can question the justice of our remarks on their general style; no one, we are sure, can read them with understanding, and not again and again pause over thoughts, verses, pictures,—oases in the wilderness of mist and of sand, —of a bloom and a freshness such as few modern magicians are able to conjure up. What—to give an instance from the second poem in the collection—can be more lyrical than the first verse of 'A Lovers' Quarrel'?—

> Oh, what a dawn of day!
> How the March sun feels like May!
>   All is blue again
>   After last night's rain,
> And the South dries the hawthorn-spray.
>   Only, my Love's away!
> I'd as lief that the blue were grey.

But when the Lover begins to recall the happiness he enjoyed with his Lady-love in the cold winter time, ere they had quarrelled, we imagine that the most tolerant of lovers will find such reminiscences of past happiness as the following somewhat prosaic:—

> What's in the 'Times'?—a scold
> At the emperor deep and cold;
>   He has taken a bride
>   To his gruesome side,
> That's as fair as himself is bold:
>   There they sit ermine stoled,
> And she powders her hair with gold.

Too many of Mr. Browning's fifty poems are flawed by impertinences such as these, borne out by an audacity in Hudibrastic versification in which our author is without a rival. We do not recollect to have ever seen syllables 'tossed about' with such unhesitating legerdemain, as in the lyric called 'Old Pictures in Florence.' But in this poem the ease is too much the ease of the acrobat, who by much practice has learnt how to disjoint his limbs, and fling himself into any conceivable attitude;

and the effect is dislocation—not grace. When, however, Mr. Browning is avowedly humorous, his mastery over diction and language takes forms of a quaintness which will be precious to all who relish humour. We have a great liking for 'Life up at a Villa,' as described by 'An Italian Person of Quality,'—one of those dear, insipid, voluble gentle-folks—poor, but pleasure-loving—whom Goldoni[1] loved to draw; who hate what stands to them for country as devotedly as *Millamant*[2] loathed walking in green fields. Listen only how the Signor or Signora (the latter it must be, we should say, could we forget how Italian men gossip over their cups of water) babbles about town and country: . . .

Those who love old Italian stories will not be long, we imagine, ere they get to the end of the tale so powerfully begun. If its moral be avoided, this legend may almost pair off with its author's 'Laboratory', which, of its order, we have always held to be one of the most com-plete poems existing in any language. The following short lyric is also full of power, picture, and prophecy, though the last verse is clumsier than it needed to have been.— . . .

[Quotes 'The Patriot'.]

Why one who can pour out his thoughts, fancies, stores of learning, and emotions, with an eloquent and direct sincerity such as this, should, so often as Mr. Browning has here done, prefer to rhyme the pleadings of a casuist, or the arguments of a critic, or the ponderous discoursings of some obsolete schoolman—why he should turn away from themes in which every one can answer to his sympathies, and from modes of the lyre which find their echoes wherever hearts and ears know aught of music—is an enigma no less painful than perplexing, the unriddling of which is possibly reserved for no contemporary. We had hoped that 'Men and Women' would enable us to register progress in the poet's mind (always rich to overflowing) and in the artist's hand (always able to draw whatever its owner pleased). The riches and the ability are there, but the employment and the expression of them seem to us, on the whole, more perverse, personal, and incomplete than they were formerly.

---

[1] Carlo Goldoni (1707-93), whose plays helped to free Italian comedy from the monopoly of 'Commedia del Arte'.
[2] The heroine of William Congreve's *The Way of the World*.

90. Joseph [?] Arnould, *The Saturday Review*

24 November 1855, i. 69–70

Merle M. Bevington has identified the author of this unsigned review as someone named Arnould and, lacking any other candidate of the same name, has reluctantly attributed the paternity to Joseph Arnould, Browning's old friend (*The Saturday Review, 1855–1868* [1941], pp. 332–3). The present editors are even more hesitant to make the attribution, for, although Arnould was not an uncritical adulator (See No. 43), there is no evidence of any rift between Arnould and Browning which might have led to this scathing attack. But perhaps stranger things have happened. For an account of the Arnould-Browning relationship, see Donald Smalley, 'Joseph Arnould and Robert Browning: New Letters (1842–50) and a Verse Epistle', *PMLA* (March 1965), lxxx. 90–101.

It is really high time that this sort of thing should, if possible, be stopped. Here is another book of madness and mysticism—another melancholy specimen of power wantonly wasted, and talent deliberately perverted —another act of self-prostration before that demon of bad taste who now seems to hold in absolute possession the fashionable masters of our ideal literature. It is a strong case for the correctional justice of criticism, which has too long abdicated its proper functions. The Della Crusca of Sentimentalism perished under the *Baviad*—is there to be no future Gifford for the Della Crusca of Transcendentalism?[1] The thing has really grown to a lamentable head amongst us. The contagion has affected not only our sciolists and our versifiers, but those whom, in the absence of a mightier race, we must be content to accept as the poets of our age. Here is Robert Browning, for instance—no one can doubt that he is

[1] The Accademia Della Crusca, literally 'The Academy of the Chaff', began in Florence at the end of the sixteenth century with an aim to purify the Italian language; its emblem, appropriately, was a sieve. Towards the end of the eighteenth century, a Della Cruscan school of English poets began. Its pretensions and other weaknesses were satirized by William Gifford (1756–1826) in two mock-heroics, *The Baviad* (1784) and *The Maviad* (1785). Gifford is better remembered now for his bitter and biassed policies as editor (1809–24) of the *Quarterly Review*.

capable of better things—no one, while deploring the obscurities that deface the *Paracelsus* and the *Dramatic Lyrics*, can deny the less questionable qualities which characterized those remarkable poems—but can any of his devotees be found to uphold his present elaborate experiment on the patience of the public? Take any of his worshippers you please—let him be 'well up' in the transcendental poets of the day—take him fresh from Alexander Smith[1] or Alfred Tennyson's *Maud*, or the *Mystic* of Bailey[2]—and we will engage to find him at least ten passages in the first ten pages of *Men and Women*, some of which, even after profound study, he will not be able to construe at all, and not one of which will he be able to read off at sight. Let us take one or two selections at random from the first volume, and try. What, for instance, is the meaning of these four stanzas from the poem, entitled 'By the Fireside'?— . . .

[Quotes lines 101–20]

We really should think highly of the powers of any interpreter who could 'pierce' the obscurity of such 'stuff' as this. One extract more, and we have done. A gold medal in the department of Hermeneutical Science to the ingenious individual who, after any length of study, can succeed in unriddling this tremendous passage from 'Master Hugues of Saxe-Gotha,' the organist:—

[Quotes lines 56–98]

Do our readers exclaim, 'But where's poetry—the dickens!—in all this rigmarole?' We confess we can find none—we can find nothing but a set purpose to be obscure, and an idiot captivity to the jingle of Hudibrastic rhyme. This idle weakness really appears to be at the bottom of half the daring nonsense in this most daringly nonsensical book. Hudibras Butler told us long ago that 'rhyme the rudder is of verses'; and when, as in his case, or in that of Ingoldsby Barham[3] or Whims and-Oddities Hood,[4] the rudder guides the good ship into tracks of fun and fancy she might otherwise have missed, we are grateful to the

---

[1] Alexander Smith (1830–67), one of the 'Spasmodic' poets ridiculed in William Aytoun's 'Firmilian'.

[2] Philip James Bailey (1816–1902), considered the founder of the 'Spasmodics', published *The Mystic* in 1855. Parts of this volume were later absorbed in his turgid, enormous (some 40,000 lines) treatment of the Faust legend, *Festus*. The association of Tennyson's *Maud* with this school was not uncommon at the time.

[3] Richard Harris Barham (1788–1845) published a series of metrical burlesque tales under the pseudonym 'Thomas Ingoldsby'.

[4] Best known as the author of 'The Song of the Shirt', Thomas Hood (1799–1845) published a series of illustrated 'picture-puns' under the title *Whims and Oddities*.

Men and Women

double-endings, not on their own account, but for what they have led us to. But Mr. Browning is the mere thrall of his own rudder, and is constantly being steered by it into whirlpools of the most raging absurdity. This morbid passion for double rhymes, which is observable more or less throughout the book, reaches its climax in a long copy of verses on the 'Old Pictures of Florence,' which, with every disposition to be tolerant of the frailties of genius, we cannot hesitate to pronounce a masterpiece of absurdity. Let the lovers of the Hudibrastic admire these *tours de force:*— . . .

Our main object has been to protest against what we feel to be the false teachings of a perverted school of art; and we have used this book of Mr. Browning's chiefly as a means of showing the extravagant lengths of absurdity to which the tenets of that school can lead a man of admitted powers. We should regret, however, in the pursuit of this object, to inflict injustice on Mr. Browning. This last book of his, like most of its predecessors, contains some undeniable beauties—subtle thoughts, graceful fancies, and occasionally a strain of music, which only makes the chaos of surrounding discords jar more harshly on the ear. The dramatic scenes 'In a Balcony' are finely conceived and vigorously written; 'Bishop Blougram's Apology', and 'Cleon', are well worth reading and thinking over; and there is a certain grace and beauty in several of the minor poems. That which, on the whole, has pleased us most—really, perhaps, because we could read it off-hand—is 'The Statue and the Bust', of which we give the opening stanzas:—. . . .

Why should a man who, with so little apparent labour, can write naturally and well, take so much apparent labour to write affectedly and ill? There can be but one of two solutions. Either he goes wrong from want of knowledge, in which case it is clear that he wants the highest institutions of genius; or he sins against knowledge, in which case he must have been misled by the false promptings of a morbid vanity, eager for that applause of fools which always waits on quackery, and which is never refused to extravagance when tricked out in the guise of originality. It is difficult, from the internal evidence supplied by his works, to know which of these two theories to adopt. Frequently the conclusion is almost irresistible, that Mr. Browning's mysticism must be of *malice prepense:* on the whole, however, we are inclined to clear his honesty at the expense of his powers, and to conclude that he is obscure, not so much because he has the vanity to be thought original, as because he lacks sufficient genius to make himself clear.

91. D. G. Rossetti, letter,

25 November 1855

From a letter to William Allingham, in 'Letters of D. G. Rossetti', *The Atlantic Monthly* (1896), lxxviii. 45–9.

What a magnificent series is *Men and Women*! Of course you have it half by heart ere this. The comparative stagnation, even among those I see, and complete torpor elsewhere, which greet this my Elixir of Life, are awful signs of the times to me—'and I must hold my peace!'— for it isn't fair to Browning (besides, indeed, being too much trouble) to bicker and flicker about it. I fancy we shall agree pretty well on favourites, though one's mind has no right to be quite made up so soon on such a subject. For my own part, I don't reckon I've read them at all yet, as I only got them the day before leaving town, and couldn't possibly read them then,—the best proof to you how hard at work I was for once—so heard them read by William;[1] since then read them on the journey again, and some a third time at intervals; but they'll bear lots of squeezing yet. My prime favourites hitherto (without the book by me) are 'Childe Roland', 'Bishop Blougram', 'Karshish', 'The Contemporary', 'Lippo Lippi', 'Cleon', and 'Popularity'; about the other lyrical ones I can't quite speak yet, and their names don't stick in my head; but I'm afraid 'The Heretic's Tragedy' rather gave me the gripes at first, though I've tried since to think it didn't on finding *The Athenæum* similarly affected. [No. 89]

[1] Rossetti's brother.

92. John Forster, *The Examiner*

1 December 1855, pp. 756–7

A summary of various poems, with generous quotations, precedes this excerpt from his unsigned review.

All through these poems, at the same time, are touches in abundance that save the poet from any charge of a materialist temper in such teaching. In 'Evelyn Hope;' in the address of the dying wife, 'Any Wife to any Husband'; in many another page, and not least in those pages where the poet, speaking in his own person, dedicates his *Men and Women* to his own wife; there is full expression given to the purest spiritual feeling.

But we must quote no more. Only indeed to establish beyond dispute that these volumes are not exclusively 'obscure and mystical' have we been induced to quote so much. No doubt there are too many pieces in the volumes to which the objection of obscurity in the meaning, and of a perverse harshness in the metres, may be justly urged. It is Mr. Browning's old fault. Since his first poem was published twenty years ago, when we were the first to promise him the reputation he has won, this journal has been incessantly objecting to it. But there is some danger at present, we see, of the objection being carried too far. An occasional obscurity of expression which may be the drawback on a full mind, is a very different thing from that constant, obscurity of no expression which is the only claim to admiration in an empty one. Much of the former proceeds in the present case from what we fear is inseparable from a cast of thought imparting nevertheless to the whole its pervading excellence and flavour. The robust intellect works actively; and the perceptions of a poet, when applied to thoughts of more than common subtlety, will often necessarily outrun his reader's. Such obscurity proceeds from fullness, not emptiness; and it is not always that a thought which is hard to follow will be found not worth the exercise of mind required for overtaking it. A distinctive quaintness, a complete absence of diffuseness, and the inborn dramatic feeling which is often apt to suggest breaks of phrase, and striking interruptions to a train of thought, are among the chief causes of what is most complained of in Mr. Browning. They are part of the writer's individuality, and it is by right of his individuality that he will live, if he is to be read by future generations. We do not say this by way of defending unquestionable faults, but to explain why they disfigure the work of a man of true genius. We heartily wish them all away; but they shall not prevent our pronouncing the poems we have quoted or named in this review, and many others which we have not been able either to quote or name (such charming lyrics as 'A Woman's Last Word', 'Love among the Ruins', the stanzas so wonderfully expressive of 'Mesmerism', the 'Last Ride', the 'Patriot', &c.), to be as genuine as poetry any that has been written in our time.

93. From an unsigned review, *The Spectator*

22 December 1855, xxviii. 1346–7

If these volumes, which Mr. Robert Browning offers to the public under the title of *Men and Women*, were the production of a young and unknown poet, no hesitation need be felt in pronouncing the work to be of the highest promise, dashed only by symptoms of perversity, carelessness, and bad taste, which study, matured judgment, and the criticism of kindly warning tempered with genial admiration, might be expected to eradicate or at least materially soften. Unfortunately, Mr. Browning is no untried aspirant for poetical fame, in whose case hopes may be reasonably indulged and warnings be supposed of any avail. His vices of style are stereotyped, and belong to him as inseparably as his powerful imagination and acute intellect. He can hardly be unconscious of the imperfections which continually mar the reader's enjoyment of poems among the most remarkable literary productions of our time; and the only possible conclusion is, now that twenty years have elapsed since his first appearance as a poet, that he either cannot mend or will not. In either case, criticism ceases to be of much avail, as few persons are likely to be seduced into imitation or admiration of his defects from any cause but a perversity of judgment and a silly affectation of originality, upon which the lessons of criticism would be wasted. So, as he is beyond cure, let us leave him alone, regretting in him a fine mind enfeebled by caprice and want of discipline, and a true poet defrauding himself of fame, and the public of pleasure and improvement, by affectations, and puerilities, and awkwardnesses, that too often quite overgrow and hide the genuine power of his natural gifts. Only, that the standard of poetic excellence may not through condonation of his lapse be lowered, we must enter a passing protest against his fashion of presenting incidents so allusively as to baffle ordinary penetration to discover what he means —of printing poems having reference to some facts or conversation not given and needed to explain them—of continually running into absurd phrases and ridiculous rhymes in the midst of serious and impassioned poems, and in poems intentionally grotesque descending to a reckless-ness of expression and meaning, devoid alike of wit, humour, and sense —his fashion of perpetual obscurity where lucid statement is necessary, of oddity where a grave or tender tone befits his subject, of folly and unmeaning gabble where his intention is to be sparkling and clever. All these faults seem to us attributable either to the low vanity of attaining the praise of originality by the cheap method of being different from other people, or the inexcusable laziness of not choosing to take the trouble to correct his first thoughts.

This protest entered, we can honestly say that the two new volumes contain more genuine poetry than ninety-nine out of a hundred volumes pretending to that venerable title. There are, indeed, few of the poems that are altogether contemptible: the majority at once delight us by their evidences of power and distress us by their incompleteness of conception and their faults of execution. Some few are sufficiently perfect to become abiding favourites. The general characteristic which pervades the collection is the large amount and high quality of thought, as distinguished from fancy, painting-power, or even passion; thought, however, not abstract and scientific, but real, embodied in persons and things, learnt from life or from living study of books.

94. G. Brimley-T. C. C., *Fraser's Magazine*

January 1856, liii. 105-16

T. C. C. has not been identified. For an interesting comment by Dante Gabriel Rossetti on Brimley, see No. 97. 'On 22 April 1856, Browning wrote to Rossetti on the subject of critics: some, he says, like Ruskin [No. 105] "pay" the poet generously, whereas "some grimley or whatever is the name is sure to be picking my pocket. . . ." ' *Catalogue of the Browning Collection at the University of Texas,* ed. Warner Barnes (1966), p. 48.

Brimley (1819–57) contributed often to *Fraser's* and *The Spectator*.

Robert Browning is a name which will serve the future historian of the English literature of the nineteenth century to point the moral of of genius unfaithful to its trust. Endowed by nature with those gifts which, duly cultivated, enable a man to become a fine poet, he has chosen to let them run wild; and what might have been a beautiful garden is but a wilderness overgrown with a rank and riotous vegetation. Writer of plays, of philosophical poems, of dramatic lyrics, he has in each class given evidence of strong natural powers weakened by self-indulgence, by caprice, by hankering after originality, by all the mental vices which are but so many names of vanity and self-seeking. Instead of looking on his gifts of imagination and of intellect as entrusted to him for the benefit of others, and as imposing on him the duty of training their rude forces into a perfect faculty of song, he has just got out of them the utmost personal pleasure that they would yield with the least possible trouble. The new thoughts, the passionate emotions, which make life so rich to men of the poetic nature, he has enjoyed keenly, and they have been to him impulses to express himself in various forms of rhythmical art. But art, except as this mere vehicle and vent for his own intellectual energy, he has neglected; its mechanism is troublesome, its processes imply self-restraint, laborious discipline, and patient exercise of judgment; its principle object is to communicate to others what the artist feels and knows. And Mr.

Browning not seeming to care for the enjoyment, or the instruction he could afford his fellow-creatures, but only to ease his own conceiving mind and fervent heart, naturally enough refuses to submit to toil which, after all, would probably lessen the actual pleasure of composition, and by refining his taste, lower his estimate of his own productions. Well, if man was not sent here to help his fellow-man, if men of genius especially were not, by the mere possession of that genius, emphatically singled out to be the helpers of their kind, this wantonness would be quite intelligible.

It may fairly be questioned whether the pains by which such a poet as Mr. Tennyson, for instance, makes his poems as good and perfect as he can, before offering them to the public, ever meets with general appreciation, inasmuch as such painstaking in a writer demands a corresponding painstaking in the reader. And still more may it be questioned whether the fervid fluency of a writer who pours his full stream of words, careless how much mud is held in deposit by the flood, is not accompanied by a larger amount of gross self-satisfaction than the rigid self-restraint of the writer who checks the rapidity of his current, and lets the mud fall to the bottom before he presents the cup—which should be the cup of healing—to the nations. On the Epicurean theory, there is small doubt that Mr. Browning is right; it is far pleasanter, for a time at least, to do one's work in the way that gives one least trouble. And as for fame, or its counterfeit, popularity, there are silly people enough in English society, who look on this carelessness as the fitting and only garb of genius; who, if a poet will but be slovenly, will applaud his graceful audacity, and if obscure, will worship his profundity. And thus laziness and vanity—the two most fatal forms of selfishness—do their worst, and the cliques are in admiration at one of the saddest sights under God's sky, when the light that came from heaven burns murkier and murkier in a poet's soul; and instead of making God's world more intelligible by unfolding the beauty and meaning of its objects and events with loving care and grateful painstaking, he scrawls down the first rough hints that suggest themselves to him, and will not even take the trouble to make them legible. We blame the man who wastes bodily strength and beauty in laziness or aimless feats, while we are far too lenient to men of high mental power who allow their faculties to decay through want of proper training, or to become distorted through false and inferior aims. We condemn the man who hides his one talent in the earth, and refuses to put it to its uses; what shall we say to him who, possessed of ten talents, wants the self-respect which would dictate their perfect development, and the genuine regard for his fellow-creatures, which would enjoin their strenuous employment.

This may be thought a somewhat harsh and rude tone to adopt towards a man for writing poems disfigured by obscurity, and wanting in the graces of a finished art. If poetical genius were showered upon men and women with unsparing hand—if a man with the capacity for becoming a true poet were of every-day occurrence, one more or less would be very little matter, and the due cultivation of his gifts would chiefly concern himself. It is because such poetical faculties as Mr. Browning had given him by nature are not the ordinary endowment of men—because such faculties rightly employed we believe to be a most precious boon to the nation among which they are exercised, that we are inclined to treat him, not as a whimsical person who chooses to be eccentric in a matter indifferent to the world, and defrauds himself alone by his caprice, but as one who, choosing to make himself a law and idol to himself, defrauds the world at large of what they would be the happier and the wiser for possessing. He commits the crime of a man who, entrusted with the germ of a great scientific discovery, and endowed with faculties to work it out to a clear result, refuses to undergo the labour necessary for this purpose. We believe that Mr. Browning might, had he chosen, have become the interpreter of our modern life to us in dramas that would have recalled the force and clearness of the Elizabethan day. We believe that he could have sung the passions and the thoughts of our time with a lyric intensity which would have purified the rough ore of our life of its prosaic dross, and have reacted on that life to make it deeper, truer, and more human. He possesses exactly that combination of curious and extended observation of mankind, with a subtle power of analysing motives and a vivid imagination, which is necessary for the great dramatist. He shrinks from no facts, does not pick his path with delicate step along the world's highway, fearful of dirtying his feet, is startled at nothing, peers with scrutinising glance into byeways, alleys, and noisome dens, and what he sees he can record, not with the cold, natural-history voice of a speculator, but the living tones of a man who enters into the human and passionate element in all the varied world of suffering and enjoyment, of virtue and of crime, of good and evil. To fill his mind with the elements of dramas, to enter by sympathy into the lives, characters and conduct of others, has plainly been the business of his life. What we complain of him for is, that he has been satisfied with this; that the stir, and business, and passion of the scene has been all he cared for;

that what it all meant has seldom seemed to occur to him as worth asking; that even for its mere dramatic interest he has not cared, except as a passing spectacle, keeping his appetite for excitement on the stretch. That what he saw clearly for a moment he was bound to render as clear to others as language could make it, he seems never to have dreamt; the scrawl that served to jot down his memoranda, the few rough notes that his momentary feeling completed for him, seem generally to have exhausted his interest in the revelations made to him. Not only does he not attempt to solve the moral problems which a wide experience of men presents to him; he will not even take the trouble to write the problems out legibly for others to study. His longest poem, *Sordello*, is so unintelligible from beginning to end, that we once heard an ardent admirer of his, and an accomplished man, acknowledge that only at the third careful reading could one begin to see what the peom at all meant; and that to the last only faint glimmerings of light flitted amid the chasms of black darkness. *Paracelsus* is a grand conception, utterly abortive, through hasty execution and slipshod verbiage. *Pippa Passes* is a chaos of fine material, through which a grand purpose begins the creative organising movement, but leaves off with the merest hint of what the work might have become had the natural powers of the writer been effectually disciplined. Even of the short dramatic lyrics, scarce one approaches even completeness of conception, and certainly, with one or two exceptions, they are miserably short of attainable perfection in execution. They are too often mere hints, rough sketches, requiring clearer statement of facts, more careful elaboration of both phrase and rhythm. Everywhere alike one finds evidence of power not half put forth, of first thoughts printed instead of best thoughts, a facility of execution aimed at, the right to and faculty of which have not been earned by previous labour. A genius everywhere profuse, striking, vigorous, but which mixes indiscriminately weeds and flowers, utters itself always at random, and as often misses as hits its mark. Such is, in our opinion, the character of the poems which Mr. Browning has hitherto published. If his aim has been simply to prove himself a clever man, he has succeeded; if he has aimed at making his fellow-creatures wiser and happier through the talents bestowed upon him, his success has fallen miserably short of what might have been attained by the simple resolution to speak as intelligibly as he could what he had to say. His new volumes have precisely the same faults in about the same proportion. We could select scarcely one poem from these two volumes—with the exception of a particular class of poems to be specially mentioned—which was not more or less spoiled by the most obvious and easily removable faults, either of conception or execution, or both. Many of them are, as they stand, utterly unintelligible; the incidents to which they refer being neither stated nor deducible from the comment. Mr. Browning may possibly hold the key to these enigmas; or here and there one of Mr. Browning's intimates may guess at the circumstances to which the poems refer. But this is pure impertinence, to publish poems the interpretation of which is a private occurrence, or a conversation to which the public is not admitted, and of which it hears only so much as has no meaning by itself,—just illustrating the selfish temper and carelessness for the gratification of others which lie at the root of all Mr. Browning's faults. Of course Mr. Browning has a fine reason to give for what we attribute to carelessness and slovenly haste. He tells us that:

> Grand, rough old Martin Luther
> Bloomed fables, flowers on furze,
> *The better the uncouther:*
> *Do roses stick like burrs?*

A question we might answer by another somewhat more to the purpose,—Are burrs loved and prized like roses? If an irritated feeling of having been balked, disappointed, defrauded, be an essential element in the impression poetry should make, Mr. Browning's burrs undoubtedly often attain their success. Only that as the public has the option of submitting to the burr—infliction or not, even this success is partial. We have in these volumes abundant instances of this most provoking of faults in a writer whose fragments are good enough to interest one,—none more striking than a comparatively long and highly-wrought poem, with the title *Childe Roland to the Dark Tower came.* The poem consists of thirty-four stanzas of six lines each, and is, we suppose, allegorical; but from beginning to end we can discover no hint as to what the allegory means, and find only description preparatory to some adventure which is to disclose the symbol of the 'dark tower' and its terrible neighbourhood—but the adventure never comes off in the poem, which thus closes:

> There they stood, ranged along the hillsides—met
> To view the last of me, a living frame
> For one more picture! in a sheet of flame
> I saw them and I knew them all. And yet
> Dauntless the slug-horn to my lips I set
> And blew. *'Childe Roland to the Dark Tower came.'*

This seems to us very much like making a fool of the public, and all the worse for the striking ability lavished upon the fragment, as if a showman should hang round his caravan-front with the most wonderful pictures of the rarities on view inside, and the public after 'walking up, walking up,' should find nothing behind the front, not even four bare walls. We guess what the fate of the showman would be if a pump or a pond were at hand. Such impatience of the labour necessary to work out fine conceptions, such a resting satisfied with the portico to which a temple naturally belongs, is at least as good an instance of 'indolence which aspires to strive' as the story of *The Statue and the Bust*, one of the best poems, undoubtedly, in these volumes, interesting in itself as a history, and well told in a *terza rima* new, if we mistake not, to the English language, but as usual with Browning, marred by a close, in which a fine moral struggles obscurely through slovenly phraseology, and—its counterpart and cause—thought only half elaborated. The story is of a Grand Duke of Florence, who loved and was loved by the bride of one of his ministers, both resolving to act out their love, and both dallying with this purpose till years flew by, and the lady and her lover grew old and died baffled of their 'life's set prize.' Before this, however, the lady has her bust, in scorn of her feebleness of will, executed by Robbia, and set in the cornice over the window at which she used to watch the Grand Duke pass daily; and the duke has himself, from a similar feeling, cast in bronze, by John of Douay, on horseback, in the square, looking up to the window where his lady-love sat. Mr. Browning fancies the two in their tombs pondering what a gift life was, and sensible they had missed its aim, and thus delivers his moral of their story:

[Quotes 11. 226–50.]

Here is the bold morality of a man who refuses to see life through conventional spectacles; but unless one were tolerably familiar with the train of thought that energy of act and force of purpose are the most important elements in character, and that life is given to test these, we should hardly make out Mr. Browning's meaning clearly from the slovenly and careless enunciation of it in these stanzas. Nor ought a poet of Mr. Browning's principles to state thus nakedly what is only a half-truth after all, and which Mr. Browning knows as well as we do to be only a half-truth. But it would have given him some trouble, we suppose, to re-write these concluding stanzas so as to express his meaning less obscurely, and with its proper limitation. So he leaves his word-puzzles to acute people, and his morality to shift for itself: one consequence of which is that he has spoiled the effect of what would otherwise be one of the most complete and striking poems in his collection.

Our main object in this paper is to show how Mr. Browning defrauds himself of sympathy and fame, and his readers of enjoyment, by not doing justice to his own genius,—by wilfulness, caprice, and carelessness. Here is a pair of poems that are short enough to be quoted largely, the first of which is almost perfect—quite perfect but for an occasional awkwardness of phrase, perhaps mainly due to the frequency and doubling of the rhyme. While the second, conceived as tenderly and as truly, is wholly sacrificed to a metre that is but disjointed prose, and an arrangement of rhymes that baffles ordinary ears to catch,— rhymes that are so to the eye merely, like an occasional unintentional jingling of like sounds in careless prose:

[Quotes 'A Woman's Last Word' and 'In a Year'.]

We say that the man who could write the first of these poems, and did write the second, must be utterly reckless in the employment of his faculties, utterly careless whether his art produce beauty or deformity. More often, however, Mr. Browning's caprice mixes in the same poem the best and the worst, and that is to our thinking a still greater offence. The two first poems of the collection are instances. *Love among the Ruins* is really a description of some such place as Old Sarum, vivid with touches of wonderful pictorial power, but which is continually marred by the sacrifice of meaning and appropriate language to a metre quite unadapted for the subject predominant, though, not unadapted for the subject indicated in the title. Talk about the old city and its ruins fills eleven and a half of fourteen stanzas, the love occupies a stanza and a half, and the moral the concluding stanza. How beautiful a poem Browning might have written in this metre had he almost reversed these proportions, and taken the pains such a metre demands, may be judged from this specimen, in which the love is included:

[Quotes 11. 49–84.]
[After quoting 'A Lover's Quarrel', 11. 29–133.]

Perhaps Mr. Browning would justify such writing on the ground of its representing fairly the tone of mind depicted; but art's realism is surely not to be confounded with literalness, the artist's business is not to make people speak and look exactly as they would speak and look, with all the accidents of human weakness about them. It is a large subject to discuss, but surely art is not daguerreotyping, even if the literal truth for which we value the sun-picture were attainable by the artist. Mr. Browning seems to us wholly to forget this distinction, and in forgetting it to abdicate altogether the true function of the poet.

The blemishes we have been noticing are blemishes for the most part upon poems of a serious or impassioned cast, and may be classed as faults of conception arising from impatience and feebleness of purpose, producing fragments instead of wholes; and as faults of execution, where a similar dislike of labour and carelessness of perfection produce doggrel. But Mr. Browning is fond of the grotesque for its own sake. Odd phrases, startling rhymes, strange arrangements, sudden transitions of thought, all kinds of eccentricities of style, have a fascination for him, we imagine, apart from the saving of labour accomplished by their means, and he writes whole poems apparently with little other object than to indulge this taste. It may easily be imagined that the writer who cannot keep himself from doggrel in poems intended to convey grave thoughts and tender sentiments, will play antics sufficiently extravagant when his purpose is to set things in the light of a playful or a tragical humour. But Mr. Browning unfortunately wants both wit to furnish the garb of wisdom in her sportive moods, and taste to warn him where the dangerous edge of sense and nonsense runs. He has not feeling enough of congruity to venture safely on a style in which airy grace and ease of movement are the condition of success. He tumbles, like a man who cannot keep his legs, not like a man who has such perfect command of his muscles that he can balance himself in a position of unstable equilibrium. And when he seeks to exhibit, as he sometimes does, the true grotesque, the blending of the tragic and comic, the terrible and the ridiculous, he seems to us, from a want of earnestness of feeling, or habitual carelessness of execution, to fall short at buffoonery. We have specimens of both classes of poems in these volumes. *Old Pictures at Florence* and *Master Hugues of Saxe Gotha* belong to the former; *The Heretic's Tragedy* and *Holy-Cross Day* to the latter. In not one of these are evidences of Mr. Browning's imagination and intellectual capacity wanting—the power to bring realities before his mind, and the power to think about them to some purpose when they are there; but what he sees he scrawls on his canvas with such a rough and ready hand, and what he thinks he expresses in such broken hints and such strange jargon, that the reader has a task to perform in getting them, quite unnecessary from any profundity natural to the thoughts, or any obscurity to the things themselves, and strikingly illustrating the truth that the labour of a reader is generally in inverse proportion to that of the writer whose works he is studying. Here is a passage in which Mr. Browning is complaining of his ill-luck in finding no buried scrap of any of the early Florentine painters whose praises he is singing, and after a mere tiresome list of names, about as suitable to verse as an auctioneer's catalogue, he goes on:

[Quotes 'Old Pictures in Florence', ll. 249–72.]

And now, in closing Mr. Browning's volumes we hope neither he nor any of our readers will for a moment mistake the tone and intention of our remarks. If we valued Mr. Browning's abilities at a lower rate, we certainly should have treated his faults with more leniency, and should have had no difficulty in filling our pages with admirable passages, and some few almost perfect poems. Compared with ninety-nine of a hundred volumes of contemporary poetry, these of Mr. Browning's are a treasury of beauty, and sense, and feeling; and it is just because we feel how great Mr. Browning's capacity is still—though his vices of style have the strength of indurate habits—that we think criticism worth bestowing opon him. There is not more than one poet of the present day whose genius is superior to his. If Mr. Tennyson is not to be brought into comparison with him, it is, however, mainly because he respects himself and respects the public, and is too grateful to his Master for the gifts he has bestowed upon him to play tricks with himself. He gives the world of his best, and the world honours him increasingly. If Mr. Browning covets his fame and usefulness, he must show the same sensitive artistic conscience, which is after all but acting on the principle that great talents are given men for the glory of God and the good of mankind.

95. George Eliot, *The Westminster Review*

January 1856, lxv. 290–6

From her unsigned review

From 1851 to 1854, George Eliot (Mary Ann Evans Cross) had served as an assistant editor of *The Westminster Review*. She and Browning met for the first time in 1862, Browning recording, 'I liked her much'. *DI*, p. 143.

We never read Heinsius—a great admission for a reviewer—but we learn from M. Arago that that formidably erudite writer pronounces Aristotle's works to be characterized by a *majestic obscurity which repels the ignorant*.[1] We borrow these words to indicate what is likely to be the first impression of a reader who, without any previous familiarity with Browning, glances through his two new volumes of poems. The less acute he is, the more easily will he arrive at the undeniable criticism, that these poems have a 'majestic obscurity', which repels not only the ignorant but the idle. To read poems is often a substitute for thought: fine-sounding conventional phrases and the sing-song of verse demand no co-operation in the reader; they glide over his mind with the agreeable unmeaningness of 'the compliments of the season', or a speaker's exordium on 'feelings too deep for expression'. But let him expect no such drowsy passivity in reading Browning. Here he will find no conventionality, no melodious commonplace, but freshness, originality, sometimes eccentricity of expression; no didactic laying-out of a subject, but dramatic indication, which requires the reader to trace by his own mental activity the underground stream of thought that jets out in elliptical and pithy verse. To read Browning he must exert himself, but he will exert himself to some purpose. If he finds the meaning difficult of access, it is always worth his effort—if he has to dive deep, 'he rises with his pearl'. Indeed, in Browning's best poems he makes us feel that what we took for obscurity in him was superfici-

[1] Daniel Heinsius (Heins), (*c.* 1580–1665), Latin and Greek scholar of the Dutch renaissance, wrote original Latin poetry as well as editing Horace, Seneca, and Aristotle. Arago, no doubt a commentator, has not been identified.

ality in ourselves. We are far from meaning that all his obscurity is like the obscurity of the stars, dependent simply on the feebleness of men's vision. On the contrary, our admiration for his genius only makes us feel the more acutely that its inspirations are too often straitened by the garb of whimsical mannerism with which he clothes them. This mannerism is even irritating sometimes, and should at least be kept under restraint in *printed* poems, where the writer is not merely indulging his own vein, but is avowedly appealing to the mind of his reader.

Turning from the ordinary literature of the day to such a writer as Browning, is like turning from Flotow's music, made up of well-pieced shreds and patches, to the distinct individuality of Chopin's Studies or Schubert's Songs. Here, at least, is a man who has something of his own to tell us, and who can tell it impressively, if not with faultless art. There is nothing sickly or dreamy in him: he has a clear eye, a vigorous grasp, and courage to utter what he sees and handles. His robust energy is informed by a subtle, penetrating spirit, and this blending of opposite qualities gives his mind a rough piquancy that reminds one of a russet apple. His keen glance pierces into all the secrets of human character, but, being as thoroughly alive to the outward as to the inward, he reveals those secrets, not by a process of dissection, but by dramatic painting. We fancy his own description of a poet applies to himself:

> He stood and watched the cobbler at his trade,
> The man who slices lemons into drink,
> The coffee-roaster's brazier, and the boys
> That volunteer to help him at the winch.
> He glanced o'er books on stalls with half an eye,
> And fly-leaf ballads on the vendor's string,
> And broad-edge hold-print posters by the wall
> *He took such cognizance of men and things,*
> *If any beat a horse, you felt he saw;*
> *If any cursed a woman, he took note;*
> *Yet stared at nobody,—they stared at him,*
> *And found, less to their pleasure than surprise,*
> *He seemed to know them and expect as much.*[1]

Browning has no soothing strains, no chants, no lullabys; he rarely gives voice to our melancholy, still less to our gaiety; he sets our thoughts at work rather than our emotions. But though eminently a thinker, he is as far as possible from prosaic; his mode of presentation is always concrete, artistic, and, where it is most felicitous, dramatic. Take, for

---

[1] 'How It Strikes a Contemporary', ll. 23–35.

example, 'Fra Lippo Lippi', a poem at once original and perfect in its kind. The artist-monk, Fra Lippo, is supposed to be detected by the night-watch roaming the streets of Florence, and while sharing the wine with which he makes amends to the Dogberrys for the roughness of his tongue, he pours forth the story of his life and his art with the racy conversational vigour of a brawny genius under the influence of the Care-dispeller. . . .

[Extracts nearly 200 lines of 'Fra Lippo Lippi', beginning with line 81 and ending with line 306.]

Extracts cannot do justice to the fine dramatic touches by which Fra Lippo is made present to us, while he throws out this instinctive Art-criticism. And extracts from 'Bishop Blougram's Apology', an equally remarkable poem of what we may call the dramatic-psychological kind, would be still more ineffective. 'Sylvester Blougram, styled *in partibus Episcopus*', is talking

> Over the glass's edge when dinner's done,
> And body gets its sop and holds its noise
> And leaves soul free a little,

with 'Gigadibs the literary man', to whom he is bent on proving by the most exasperatingly ingenious sophistry, that the theory of life on which he grounds his choice of being a bishop, though a doubting one is wiser in the moderation of its ideal, with the certainty of attainment, than the Gigadibs theory, which aspires after the highest and attains nothing. The way in which Blougram's motives are dug up from below the roots, and laid bare to the very last fibre, not by a process of hostile exposure, not by invective or sarcasm, but by making himself exhibit them with a self-complacent sense of supreme acuteness, and even with a crushing force of worldly common sense, has the effect of masterly satire. But the poem is too strictly consecutive for any fragments of it to be a fair specimen. Belonging to the same order of subtle yet vigorous writing are the 'Epistle of Karshish, the Arab physician', 'Cleon', and 'How it strikes a Contemporary'. 'In a Balcony', is so fine, that we regret it is not a complete drama instead of being merely the suggestion of a drama. One passage especially tempts us to extract.

> All women love great men
> If young or old—it is in all the tales—
> Young beauties love old poets who can love—
> Why should not he the poems in my soul,

> The love, the passionate faith, the sacrifice,
> The constancy? I throw them at his feet.
> Who cares to see the fountain's very shape
> And whether it be a Triton's or a Nymph's
> That pours the foam, makes rainbows all around?
> You could not praise indeed the empty conch;
> *But I'll pour floods of love and hide myself.*

These lines are less rugged than is usual with Browning's blank verse; but generally, the greatest deficiency we feel in his poetry is its want of music. The worst poems in his new volumes are, in our opinion, his lyrical efforts; for in these, where he engrosses us less by his thought, we are more sensible of his obscurity and his want of melody. His lyrics, instead of tripping along with easy grace, or rolling with a torrent-like grandeur, seem to be struggling painfully under a burthen too heavy for them; and many of them have the disagreeable puzzling effect of a charade, rather than the touching or animating influence of song. We have said that he is never prosaic; and it is remarkable that in his blank verse, though it is often colloquial, we are never shocked by the sense of a sudden lapse into prose. Wordsworth is, on the whole, a far more musical poet than Browning, yet we remember no line in Browning so prosaic as many of Wordsworth's, which in some of his finest poems have the effect of bricks built into a rock. But we must also say that though Browning never flounders help-lessly on the plain, he rarely soars above a certain table-land—a footing between the level of prose and the topmost heights of poetry. He does not take possession of our souls and set them aglow, as the greatest poets—the greatest artists do. We admire his power, we are not sub-dued by it. Language with him does not seem spontaneously to link itself into song, as sounds link themselves into melody in the mind of the creative musician; he rather seems by his commanding powers to compel language into verse. He has *chosen* verse as his medium; but of our greatest poets we feel that they had no choice: Verse chose them. Still we are grateful that Browning chose this medium: we would rather have 'Fra Lippo Lippi' than an essay on Realism in Art; we would rather have 'The Statue and the Bust' than a three-volumed novel with the same moral; we would rather have 'Holy Cross-Day' than 'Strictures on the Society for the Emancipation of the Jews'.

96. David Masson, *The British Quarterly Review*

January 1856, xxiii. 151–80

Masson (1822–1907) was to write the magnificent *Life of Milton*.

That, among the English authors of our day, very few, indeed, could be compared with Mr. Browning for power and originality of mind, has long been the settled opinion of all acquainted with his writings, and capable of judging of them. To an intellect of extraordinary natural force and subtlety, it was plain that he added many of those other qualifications not always combined with this, which help to make an author distinguished, and to give body and character to his works—a large store of acquired ideas, the results of his previous thinking on a variety of subjects; no mean amount of learning in tracks not commonly explored, even by scholars; keen powers of observation, wit, and sarcasm, and a shrewd acquaintance with the world and its ways; and yet, with all this, and ruling it all, a certain isolated speciality of purpose, a certain rigid determination of his genius towards the noble and elevated, and towards that only. No competent person, we say, who had read *Paracelsus*, *Pippa Passes*, *Christmas-Eve and Easter-Day*, or any other of Mr. Browning's poems, published before the present work, could doubt his intellectual power, or his firmness in keeping that power free from all the entanglements of mere literary precedent and popularity, and pursuing a path of his own. It was felt, that as the author himself was rarely seen in those circles of our British society where authors most do congregate, so also his genius kept aloof from the beaten ways—snugly ensconced, as it seemed, for the most part, in some Italian or other foreign retreat, whence it could see all that was going on, and yet be at liberty to build up its own fancies with just as much and just as little reference to the contemporary world as it thought proper. . . .

[Reviews Browning's career.]

In the first place, then, all one's previous opinions as to the force, and subtlety, and variety of Mr. Browning's intellectual powers, and as to the extent of his acquirements, are confirmed by this book. Consisting, as it does, of some fifty distinct pieces, some short and some rather long, all gathered together under the somewhat weak and, in this case, really unmeaning title of *Men and Women*, the work does not, indeed, exhibit Mr. Browning's powers at the same continuous stretch of exercise as such previous works as *Paracelsus, Sordello*, or *Christmas-Eve and Easter-Day*. There is no such profound or elaborate exposition of philosophical notions, doubts, and conclusions, for example, as in the last-named poem—a poem which, little as it seems to have impressed either the critics or the public at the time of its publication, and little as it is now talked of, is truly one of the most extraordinary of recent writings. On the other hand, however, the variety of the contents of the present work gives perhaps a better idea of the range of Mr. Browning's tastes and faculties than is obtained from any longer poem. It is difficult, where so many passages might be quoted for the purpose, to select one specially to illustrate Mr. Browning's quickness, originality, and ingenuity as a speculative thinker or reasoner; but perhaps the following, though not the best in other respects, may be chosen with advantage, as being a complete piece in itself, and also as being in reality a discussion by Mr. Browning of this very question of the relations of the pure thinker to the poet. The piece is entitled 'Transcendentalism', and the poet is supposed to be addressing a brother-poet, who has put forth a long didactic poem under that title. . . .

[Quotes the entire 51 lines.]

The man who wrote that is clearly capable of thinking subtly and vigorously on all sorts of subjects—of writing a good essay on the Transcendental Metaphysics, if he chose; or one on Poetry; or even, with time and materials, one on the Decimal Coinage. He is evidently not a man who has betaken himself to verse as younger sons, too stupid for either law or commerce, betake themselves to the church or the army; but a man of general available faculty, of strong, rapid, nimble intellect, that it would be rather perilous to tussle with in a prose encounter about any matter whatever, though, for reasons of its own, it disports itself usually in verse. The allusions, too, to Jacob Boehme and John of Halberstadt, show a man whose knowledge even about tough matters to be got by reading, might prove too much for one, if the trial were but in mere learning. These, of course, are but two allusions by the way, which might be incidental; but there is an abundance of others in the other poems proving a tolerably tenacious memory on

Mr. Browning's part of the kind of facts which one finds accumulated in Bayle's *Dictionary*, Hallam's *Middle Ages*, and the *Penny Cyclopædia*.

As specimens of Mr. Browning's ability in giving poetical shape and expression to simple, transient feelings, whether sweet, gentle, and sprightly, or more grave, passionate, and intense, the reader may take, if he chooses, all the shorter pieces in the volumes. Of this kind are 'Evelyn Hope', 'A Lover's Quarrel', 'Any Wife to Any Husband', 'A Serenade at the Villa', 'Love in a Life', 'Life in a Love', 'Women and Roses', &c. We cannot say, however, that we greatly admire these shorter sentimental pieces of Browning, or think them equal to his genius as shown in others. He does not seem at home in such brief and purely lyrical effusions, requiring, as they do, an instant gush of feeling, a cessation for the time of all merely intellectual activity, and a clear and flowing tune. Other poets greatly excel Mr. Browning in these melodious love-songs and outpourings of immediate emotion. In his case, the head is constantly intruding its suggestions where the heart alone should be speaking; we have strokes of the hard imagination where we expect nothing but unconscious melody and cadence; and hence a roughness and a constraint incompatible with the simple beauty and warmth of the lyric. But for this very reason, when Mr. Browning takes that larger space for his pen which the intellectual nature of his genius requires, when he adopts the narrative or dramatic form in lieu of the lyric, and sets himself to the work of representing feeling or passion expanded and complicated into character and mode of existence, he attains a success which few can rival. In the art of character-painting, as we have said, in the power of throwing himself into states of mind and trains of circumstance the most alien from our present habits, in the intuitive faculty of reconceiving the most peculiar and obsolete modes of thinking, he ranks as a master. Generally, as we have seen, when he exercises his genius in this manner, he works on a basis of history, adopting a story, or appropriating a character, or at least borrowing a hint from the actual records of the past ages of the world; and almost always when he does so we are struck by the strange selection he makes. It is from the bye-laws of history, or, at least, from what are reckoned such, that he derives the hints on which he proceeds; or, if ever he comes upon the great broad track familiar to the traditions of common men, he is seen approaching it by some unexpected bye-path. Thus, if you would meet him in the domain of ancient Roman history, it is in the Byzantine portion of it that you must seek him, and even there it is not before the busts of Diocletian or Constantine that you will find him, but most probably before those of the baby-emperor Protus, and his successor and dethroner John the Blacksmith with the massive jaws. And yet, finding him there and standing beside him, how you see the busts become animated beneath his gaze, and Protus and John, and the decrepit Byzantine empire, with the Huns raging round its borders till John's death shall let them in, all again existing as they were. No reader of the volumes should miss the little sketch entitled *Protus.* . . .

But Mr. Browning, though he usually exercises his imagination in giving body and expansion to some hint furnished by the actual world of history, can yet, when he chooses, fling reality and history aside altogether, and revel, as well as any poet, in a world of shifting allegoric shapes and sounds and phantasies, where nothing is fixed and nothing literal. This is proved by more than one piece in the present volume, but above all by the one entitled 'Childe Roland to the Dark Tower came'. Perhaps, indeed, taking the *kind* of the poetry here attempted into account, as well as the success of the attempt *in* that kind, this poem deserves all in all to be regarded as the greatest thing in the volumes. The notion of the poem, as in Tennyson's *Mariana*, is that of expanding one of those snatches of old ballad and allusion which have such a mystic effect in Shakespeare. 'Childe Roland to the Dark Tower came' is one such snatch of old song quoted by Edgar in *Lear*; and Mr. Browning offers us *his* imaginative rendering of these gloomy hieroglyphic words. The phantasy is one of the most wild and ghastly within the range of our literature, with more of sheer terror in it than in any corresponding phantasy in Spenser. . . .

If this piece be not poetry, we do not know what is. It is poetry of the highest symbolic kind, and we have reserved it to the last among our quotations, as being the farthest removed in its nature of all the pieces in the volumes from the domain of the mere understanding. How it holds the imagination, and is felt to be coherent and significant in meaning, though no one will venture to explain what the meaning is! . . .

Mr. Browning's familiarity with Italian art and painting is something far beyond that of ordinary *connoisseurs*. He has studied painting and art generally with an interest and a minuteness of inquiry which, even in technical disquisition on such subjects, might enable him to co-operate or contest with Mr. Ruskin; and few of his poems are more remarkable than those, in which he displays, at length or incidentally, his acquaintance with the history and principles of art. In the present work, in particular, there are two poems in which he shows the most subtle power of conceiving, by a kind of inference from their works, the modes of thinking and personal characters of two of the most eminent of the Italian artists of the fifteenth and sixteenth centuries. In the piece called 'Fra Lippo Lippi', we have a delineation from the very life of the intellectual and moral habits of one kind of painter; and in the piece entitled 'Andrea Del Sarto', we have a companion-portrait, equally vivid, of a painter of graver and more melancholy nature. These two poems are, in fact, biographies in miniature, and, probably, give a more perfect idea of the two men as they lived, and of the principles on which they painted, than many more extensive accounts of them, accompanied by criticisms of their pictures. They ought to be read entire to be fully appreciated; and extracts may, therefore, be spared. . . .

For ourselves, trying to combine what we think just in all this adverse criticism with our already expressed agreement with Mr. Browning's highest admirers on the ground of his general merits, the final judgment is still immensely more on the side of admiration than on that of dissatisfaction or criticism.

As regards the objections popularly taken to the quality of his thought and to his strange choice of themes and materials, these, it seems to us, are not properly objections at all, but rather indications of his peculiar place and rank among British poets. That, for the reasons so stated, much of Mr. Browning's poetry is and must always remain 'caviare to the general' must of course be admitted; but we have yet to learn that a man may not be a great poet, and yet be 'caviare to the general'. It may be that the greatest poets of all are those whose genius enables them to thrill the most universal human emotions, and so to command the largest constituencies; but surely, if the select and most cultured minds of a time can have a poet all to themselves, or nearly so, handling the questions which they handle, and leading them out in new tracks which have for them all the interest of blended curiosity and familiarity, that is also a great gain to the community.

97. D. G. Rossetti, letter

8 January 1856

From a letter to William Allingham, in 'Letters of D. G. Rossetti', *The Atlantic Monthly* (1896), lxxviii. 45–9.

I broke off at the last sheet in mid-Browning. Of course I've been drenching myself with him at intervals since, only he got carried off by friends, and I have him not always by me. I wish you would let me hear in a speedy answer (there's cheek for you!) all you think about his new work, and it shall nerve me to express my ideas in return; but since I have given up poetry as a pursuit of my own, I really find my thoughts on the subject generally require a starting-point from somebody else to bring them into activity; and as you're the only man I know who'd be really in my mood of receptiveness in regard to Browning, and as I can't get at you, I've been bottled up ever since *Men and Women* came out. By the bye, I don't reckon William, the intensity of fellow-feeling on the subject making the discussion of it between us rather flat. I went the other day to a penny reading-room,—a real blessing, which now occupies the place of Burford's Panorama, and where all papers and reviews whatsoever are taken in. There I saw two articles on Browning: one by Masson—really thoroughly appreciative, but slow—in the *British Quarterly* [No. 96]; and one by a certain Brimley, of Trinity College, Cambridge, in *Fraser* [No. 94],—the cheekiest of human products. This man, less than two years ago, had not read a line of Browning, as I know through my brother, and I have no doubt he has just read him up to write this article; which opens, nevertheless, with accusations against R. B. of nothing less than personal selfishness and vanity, so plumply put as to be justified by nothing less than personal intimacy of many years. When I went to Paris, I took my copy of *Men and Women* (which had been sent me the day before) with me, and got B. to write my name in it. Did you get a copy? We spoke often of you,— he with great personal and poetical regard, I of course with loathing. I enclose herewith a note which reached me before the book, containing emendations; copy them, if you please, and return the note. I spent some most delightful time with Browning at Paris, both in the evenings and at the Louvre, where (and throughout conversation) I found his knowledge of early Italian art beyond that of any one I ever met,—encyclopaedically beyond that of Ruskin himself. What a jolly thing is 'Old Pictures in Florence'! It seems all the pictures desired by the poet are in his possession, in fact. At Paris I met his father, and in London an uncle of his and his sister, who, it appears, performed the singular female feat of copying *Sordello* for him, to which some of its eccentricities may possibly be referred. . . . Ruskin, on reading *Men and Women* (and with it some of the other works which he did not know before), declared them, rebelliously, to be a mass of conundrums, and compelled me to sit down before him and lay siege for one whole night, the result of which was that he sent me next morning a bulky letter to be forwarded to B., in which I trust he told him that he was the greatest man since Shakespeare. . . .

98. Richard Simpson, *The Rambler*

January 1856, v. 54–71

This unsigned review has long been attributed to Cardinal Wiseman, whose 'fancy portrait' Browning had drawn in 'Bishop Blougram's Apology'. Wiseman's authorship was questioned in Boyd Litzinger, 'Did Cardinal Wiseman Review *Men and Women?*', *Victorian Newsletter* (Fall 1960), No. 18, pp. 22–3. Professor and Mrs. Walter E. Houghton, editors of *The Wellesley Index to Victorian Periodicals, 1824–1900*, made the positive identification of Simpson. See Esther Rhoades Houghton, *Victorian Newsletter* (Spring 1968), No. 33, p. 46.

Perhaps one of the first things that strikes a person in turning over the leaves of these volumes is a certain Hudibrastic recklessness of thought and diction; a higgledy-piggledy mixture of the grand rage of Lear, the sly wisdom of the fool, and the maniac ravings of mad Tom. Allied to this, the reader will also discover a keen enjoyment of dirt as such, a poking of the nose into dunghills and the refuse of hospitals, into beggars' wallets and into Jews' 'old-clo' bags' accompanied by the peculiar grunt which expresses not only the pleasure experienced but also the nature of the experience. . . .

[After treating several of the poems, including 'Fra Lippo Lippi' and 'Andrea del Sarto', Simpson takes up 'Bishop Blougram's Apology'.]

. . . It is scandalous in Mr. Browning *first* to show so plainly *whom* he means, when he describes an English Catholic bishop, once bishop *in partibus*, now a member of 'our novel hierarchy', one who 'plays the part of Pandulph', one too, who though an Englishman, was born in foreign lands; and *then* to go on sketching a fancy portrait which is abominably untrue, and to draw this person not only as an archhypocrite, but also as the frankest of fools. . . . [However,] For ourselves, we thank Mr. Browning, sceptical and reckless as he is, for a rare treat in these thoughtful and able volumes. We do not suppose that they will command any extensive popularity, for except the rather select audience to which they are addressed, the rest of the world will probably only use them as a magazine of polemical weapons.

99. From an unsigned review, *Bentley's Miscellany*

January 1856, xxxix. 64–70

The title of these volumes, *Men and Women*, is not much more definitely indicative of their contents than was that of *Bells and Pomegranates*—that chokepear to literal quidnuncs. The titles of the poems themselves are sometimes correspondingly vague, in relation to their subjects: thus we have 'Before', 'After', 'De Gustibus——', 'One Way of Love', 'Another Way of Love', 'In Three Days', 'In a Year', 'Love in a Life', 'Life in a Love', 'Any Wife to Any Husband', and so on. They all are dedicated to Mrs. Browning in a final 'One Word More':

> There they are, my fifty men and women
> Naming me the fifty poems finished!
> Take them, Love, the book and me together.
> Where the heart lies, let the brain lie also.

There is little observable deviation in them from Mr. Browning's characteristic 'points', whether good points or bad; though one may unwillingly fear that of the two classes, positive good and positive bad, it is rather in the latter than the former that advance from the positive to the comparative degree is perceptible. Perhaps closer study, such as this poet requires as a *sine quâ non* to appreciation, will discover beauties that lurk unseen during a too cursory perusal; but the most cursory perusal can hardly escape a conviction that the poet's *penchant* for elliptical diction, interjectional dark sayings, *multum in parvo* (and, sometimes, seemingly *minimum in multo*) 'deliverances', flighty fancies, unkempt similitudes, quaintest conceits, slipshod familiarities, and grotesque exaggerations, is unhealthily on the increase. Greatly they wrong him, nevertheless, who proceed, as some do, to confound these excrescent 'accidents' with the 'essence' of his poetical genius, and to judge him by these, with a radical perversion of inductive method, as though a piled-up *sorites* of these by-way blemishes were identical with a logical conclusion that he is no poet at all. How much greater a poet he might be, would he but anticipate the easy every-day work of fault-finders, by striking out what they so readily find, and by taking upon himself before publication the duty they promptly assume after it, of rooting out the tares from his wheat,—it is pardonably provoking to think. Nobly endowed is Robert Browning with gifts superior not only in degree but in kind to more than two or three, among contemporary poets, who are read and applauded to the echo by thousands, where he is read and musingly beloved by tens. The excellence of his gifts—a rare union of subjective reflectiveness with objective life and vigour, so that he can make his *personæ* speak out his thoughts without prejudice to their own individual being,—a lofty moral earnestness, masked often, and so unrecognised or repudiated ever by the short-sighted—nay, a pervading religious tone, jarred only, not drowned, by mocking-bird discords and 'accidental sharps' (exceptions by which some would triumphantly prove the rule),—subtle intellect, deep searchings of heart, shrewd experience, genial spirits, æsthetic culture, lyrical expression,— what gifts are these, and more besides them, for the *making* of a not-to-be-made Poet (*nascitur non fit*). Yet time as it passes, instead of exalting these gifts to the exclusion of faulty mannerisms, and once easily now hardly eradicable blemishes, seems to confirm the singer in a habit of putting on his singing-robes after so strange a fashion, that one's wonder is the inverse of one's regret that so few should gather round him, with a mind to hear, and the mind to understand. . . .

'Cleon' will repay a reflective and time-taking perusal. So, on a cognate topic, or group of topics, but radically alien in style, will the polemical nondescript yclept 'Bishop Blougram's Apology'—a tissue of violent contrasts and provoking incongruities—fine irony and coarse abuse, subtle reasoning and halting twaddle, the lofty and the low, the refined and the vulgar, earnestness and levity, outpoured pell-mell by the blustering yet 'pawky' bishop over his wine. But what is probably the most perfect specimen of even, sustained, and lofty excellence afforded in this collection, is the dramatic fragment, 'In a Balcony'—than which there are few better things in the best of its author's dramas; and that is saying more, by a great deal, than would be supposed by idle play-goers and railway-bookstall-keepers, whose gauge of excellence is the run of so many nights, and the run on so many copies. Let such as doubt Mr.

Browning's possession of a real dramatic talent, listen to his speakers 'In a Balcony', and note the construction and quietly marked-out action of the piece; and they will surely abate their scepticism, or the avowal of it.

100. Margaret Oliphant, *Blackwood's Edinburgh Magazine*

February 1856, lxxix. 135–7

From her unsigned article, 'Modern Light Literature—Poetry'.

Margaret Wilson Oliphant (1828–97) was a popular novelist and a regular contributor to *Blackwood's*.

. . . And Robert Browning is the wild boy of the household—the boisterous noisy shouting voice which the elder people shake their heads to hear. It is very hard to make out what he would be at with those marvellous convolutions of words; but, after all, he really seems to mean something, which is a comfort in its way. Then there is an unmistakable enjoyment in this wild sport of his—*he* likes it, though we are puzzled; and sometimes he works like the old primitive painters, with little command of his tools, but something genuine in his mind, which comes out in spite of the stubborn brushes and pigments, marvellous ugly, yet somehow true. Only very few of his *Men and Women* is it possible to make out: indeed, we fear that the Andrea and the Bishop Blougram are about the only intelligible sketches, to our poor apprehension, in the volumes; but there is a pleasant glimmer of the author himself through the rent and tortured fabric of his poetry, which commends him to a kindly judgment; and, unlike those brothers of his who use the dramatic form with an entire contravention of its principles, this writer of rugged verses has a dramatic gift, the power of contrasting character, and expressing its distinctions.

101. From an unsigned review, *The Dublin University Magazine*

June 1856, xlvii. 667–81

We took up Mr. Browning's poems not without the recollection of the tone of the criticisms which have issued from the press upon his latest work, *Men and Women*. When we had read it through, we laid it down with a very different appreciation from that which it has received elsewhere; we could not but feel that this man was himself, and no one else. In style, in mode of expression, in an abrupt careless strength of thought, in often times an acute analysis of supposed states of existence, and the action of the mind therein, he stands alone. To be a distinct spoke in the wheel of literature is, at least, something to be praised for. But at times his originality locks its legs around his throat, like the Old Man of the Sea, and chokes his distinct utterance. There is always a pearl in the oyster-poem, but it is so encrusted with barnacle words, and long trails of entangled sea weed sentences, that the reading public would abandon the task of opening the meaning from want of the knife of patience. A little trouble on Mr. Browning's part would, with his strong and acute mind, satisfy both himself and the public better. We are far from imagining that poetry of this class must be understood at once, but there is a needless obscurity and uncouthness in Mr. Browning's modes of expression which might be avoided. The same strength of thought which produced this rough wild etching could, if brought more within the ordinary rules of art, produce more delicate pencilling, without losing a bold reality. To be useful to many is better than to be useful to a few. But this careless strength is Mr. Browning's idiosyncrasy. Well, we only wish Mr. Browning not to be content with himself; let him pass on from Æschylus to Sophocles; we have had the great rough block of pure marble, let us have it carved into the finished statue.

. . . There is one strange poem in his collection, which will give many curious thoughts to any one fond of psychological enquiries. It is a letter from a Syrian physician who has met Lazarus. It would be too long for us to give an analysis of this strange poem, but it is interesting and novel, and treated in a manner which discloses great subtlety of thought and metaphysical imagination.

Mr. Browning is a lover of art. His criticisms are distinguished by the same 'dash', which we half suspect to be affectation. Still, the words of a man who thinks are always worth reading. 'Andrea del Sarto' will well repay a careful perusal. The following lines seem to us so true an analysis between the spiritual and material in painting, and how each should never stand alone, but be always the complement of the other, that we cannot forbear quoting them, and it shall be our last quotation; moreover the quotation will give the reader an idea of Mr. Browning's dashing style:

[Quotes 'Fra Lippo Lippi', ll. 199–220.]

102. T. McNicoll, *London Quarterly Review*

July 1856, vi. 493–501

From his review.

The new poems of Mr. Browning are only so many new examples of his peculiar style,—a style still harsh, in spite of intimations of a hidden music, and still obscure, in spite of occasional gleams of happiest meaning. They show no improvement in the sense of genial growth, but only some advance of technical skill. They are effusions which have hardened in the mould of a definite and curious intellect,—not fruits which have ripened on the living vine of genius. It happens always in such cases that any eccentricity of style becomes more marked, and any defective vision more contracted; and it is strikingly so in the instance now before us, where the author's mannerism is more prominent and gratuitous than ever. And in this respect the poetry of Mr. Browning is actually opposed to that of Mr. Tennyson. While the genius of the latter is mellowing year by year, the muse of the former becomes only more perverse. The spirit of poetry is an eminently plastic power,—the only certain agent of poetical expression; and in fostering this expansive spirit, which is to

works of art what the vital power is in the organic world, Mr. Tennyson
has caused his genius to effloresce so freely and spontaneously, that the
crude husk has fallen more and more away,—his early faults of language
have ceased insensibly, and his verse has gradually become the pure
transparent medium of his thoughts. Mr. Browning has not so rid himself of his besetting faults. We do not forget that the style of art he
practises is wholly different, that his range and object are expressly
limited. Very unequal are these two, in depth and compass, as well as in
tone and colour. The one is daily getting farther out to sea, takes deeper
soundings and fresh observations; while the other rocks idly in the same
Italian bay, and levels his glass at the same few quaint and listless figures
on the beach. But independently of this essential difference, we would
point attention to the fact, that the inferior poet is also the inferior artist;
that, while the expression of the one always finds entrance, and is felt
within the soul, the other not seldom fails in his humble appeal to the
understanding and æsthetic sense. It may be difficult—or, indeed,
impossible—to give the full meaning of Mr. Tennyson's language in
any other terms; but this is only because true poetry has no equivalent;
we are borne along with it notwithstanding,—it does not leave us
where we were, but carries us whithersoever it will. But Mr. Browning
is a lover of the picturesque, a student of men, and a sketcher of character and costume; and it behoves him to be at least so far literal and
intelligible, that we may appreciate the object he draws from the same
position which he occupies. Now, our charge is, that he is not thus
literal and intelligible; and this brings us to the question which so many
ask themselves,—Mr. Browning is acknowledged for so clever a man,
that they are almost ashamed to ask their neighbours,—How is it that
Mr. Browning's poetry is so hard to read, so very difficult to understand?

[Quotes 'The Statue and the Bust']

It must be owned that the poem is sadly wanting in clearness and direct-
ness. Even those who are fain to admire because they are content to
study it, and who fancy they discern and feel something of its fine impressive moral, are not thoroughly assured that they enter into the
author's spirit, or rightly estimate the sentiment and meaning of his
verses. To some—and not a few—the poem will be writ in hieroglyphic
symbols; and the fault is not wholly in themselves,—the poet's style and
language is unwarrantably broken and obscure. The fact is, that Mr.
Browning is too proud for anything. He disdains to take a little pains to

put the reader at a similar advantage with himself,—to give a preparatory statement which may help to make his subsequent effusion plain and logical. He scorns the good old style of beginning at the beginning. He starts from any point and speaks in any tense he pleases; is never simple or literal for a moment; leaves out (or out of sight) a link here and another there of that which forms the inevitable chain of truth, making a hint or a word supply its place; and, if you fail to comprehend the whole, is apparently satisfied that he knows better, and has the advantage of you there. He abandons himself to a train of vivid associations, and brings out some features of them with remarkable effect; but he gives you no clue whereby to follow him throughout. It may seem odd, to compare a man so reticent and clever with the weak and loquacious Mrs. Nickleby;[1] but really his random style of address is not unlike that lady's; and in respect to both, we rather plume ourselves upon the exercise of conjectural skill, than feel indebted to the speaker for a satisfactory and distinct relation. No doubt there is more real coherence in Mr. Browning's language, but it is not apparent,—it is for the student, and not the reader. We suppose, too, that while the one is artlessness itself, the other is supreme and cunning art. No matter, however, if these extremes meet; the effect in either case is impatience and fatigue.

It is this harshness, which of course is real, and this obscurity which is chiefly superficial, that will always render Mr. Browning's poetry unpopular, because they interfere with its easy and complete enjoyment. But we can readily believe that his small circle of admirers are very ardent in their admiration, and almost unmeasured in their praise. In the first place, we value an appreciation arrived at only after some expenditure of time and study. And then the ear, the mind, become gradually attuned to the new modes of thought and speech. But there is something more than this. Both the merits and defects of Mr. Browning's poetry are such as belong to a peculiar school of art; and the masters in every school have the power of rousing the enthusiasm of kindred minds; they gather round them a band of attached disciples, and are followed by the plaudits of delighted connoisseurs. This is more seldom noticed in our poets than in the sister art of painting; and, indeed, the poems of Mr. Browning find an almost perfect analogy in the pictures of a certain modern school. Our author resembles the pre-Raffaelites [*sic*] both in choice of subject and in style of treatment. He has the same vivid and realizing touch, and the same love of exquisite detail. Like them he has a

[1] The talkative mother of the title-character in Dickens' *Nicholas Nickleby*.

strong aversion to all that is conventional in the language of his art, and like them, also, is liable to be misapprehended and decried. His very fidelity to nature, expressed with so much novelty and boldness, incurs the charge of eccentricity and heresy. The traditions of his art are less to him than the impression of his own senses, and the skill of his own right hand. But, as a poet, he must count upon less general admiration than his brother artist. If even truth of colour is not fully estimated by the uneducated sense, and the pre-Raffaelite must first surprise before thoroughly convincing and delighting us, much more the independent use of language. We must know the right force of words before we feel them; and then only are we prepared to recognise the completer measures of poetic truth, which Coleridge has defined to be *the best words in the best order*.[1] We say, then, of Mr. Browning, that although any reader may be warranted in saying what he is not,—a great poet; yet only an accomplished few are able to judge of his peculiar merits, and pronounce him what he is,—an original and graphic artist. He is fairly open to rebuke, and liable, besides, to general neglect; but no thoughtful person will despise either his talents or attainments.

[1] In *Table-Talk*, for 12 July 1827.

103. 'The Editor's Easy Chair',
Harper's Magazine
August 1856, xiii. 428

The anonymous column 'The Editor's Easy Chair', a regular feature of *Harper's*, was written by Donald Mitchell alone from 1851
to 1853, when George William Curtis joined him. It is likely that
Curtis was the author of this item because of his interest in Browning. After 1859, when Curtis alone held the chair, he devoted a
number of 'Easy Chair' essays to the poet, e.g., No. 236. The
anecdote recorded here may well be true (others recorded similar
reactions) but Douglas Jerrold was a noted wit and was not averse
to improving a story.

Sordello is one of the poems by Browning, which answers well to the
definition of metaphysics—when the reader doesn't know what the
writer means, and the writer doesn't know what he means himself, that
is metaphysics. When Browning found that he had missed a figure in
printing such an unintelligible volume of verse, he is said to have said
that he put forth by way of an experiment, having struck out every other
line of it as it stood in the manuscript. This was rather a poor 'get off',
but still it was better than nothing, and that is more than can be said of
the poem. Douglas Jerrold had been ill, and forbidden to read anything.
But one day, seeing a package of new books, he could not resist the
temptation to open it, and, for his sins, he lit upon *Sordello*. On he read,
page after page, without being able to get a distinct impression, or form
a coherent idea, from the types before his eyes. 'My gracious!' exclaimed
Jerrold, 'I must be going mad!' A thought struck him; he summoned
all his relations and friends on the premises, and put them at the book.
All were equally graveled, and the frightened dramatist became reassured
as to his own mental condition!

104. William Morris,
Oxford and Cambridge Magazine

1856, i. 3. 162–72

From his unsigned review.

Pardon me, reader, that I have said little about many of the best poems; that I have said nothing at all about several; nothing about the ecstasy of prayer and love in 'Saul'; nothing about the sacrifice of life and its enjoyments, to knowledge in the 'Grammarian's Funeral'; nothing about the passionate 'Lover's Quarrel', about 'Mesmerism', 'Any Wife to Any Husband' and many others. My consolation is, that we shall have a good deal more to say of Robert Browning in this Magazine and then we can make amends.

Yet a few words, and I have done. For, as I wrote this, many times angry indignant words came to my lips, which stopped my writing till I could be quieter. For I suppose, reader, that you see whereabouts among the poets I place Robert Browning; high among the poets of all time, and I scarce know whether first, or second, in our own: and it is a bitter thing to me to see the way in which he has been received by almost everybody; many, having formed a certain theory of their own about him, from reading, I suppose, some of the least finished poems among the *Dramatic Lyrics*, make all facts bend to this theory, after the fashion of theory-mongers: they think him, or say they think him, a careless man, writing down anyhow anything that comes into his head. Oh truly! 'The Statue and the Bust' shows this! or the soft solemn flow of that poem, 'By the Fireside', *Paracelsus*—that, with its wonderful rhythm, its tender sadness, its noble thoughts, must have been very easy to write, surely!

Then they say, too, that Browning is so obscure as not to be understood by any one. Now, I know well enough what they mean by obscure, and I know also that they use the word wrongly; meaning difficult to understand fully at first reading, or, say at second reading, even: yet, taken so, in what a cloud of obscurity would *Hamlet* be! Do they think this to be the case? they daren't say so at all events, though I suspect some of them of thinking so. Now, I don't say that Robert Browning is not sometimes really obscure. He would be a perfect poet (of some calibre or other) if he were not; I assert, fearlessly, that this obscurity is seldom so prominent as to make his poems hard to understand on this ground: while, as to that which they call obscurity, it results from depth of thought and greatness of subject on the poet's part, and on his readers' part, from their shallower brains and more bounded knowledge; nay, often I fear from mere wanton ignorance and idleness. So I believe that though this obscurity, so called, would indeed be very objectionable if, as some seem to think, poetry is merely a department of 'light literature'; yet, if it is rather one of the very grandest of all God's gifts to men, we must not think it hard if we have sometimes to exercise thought over a great poem, nay, even sometimes the utmost straining of all our thoughts, an agony almost equal to that of the poet who created the poem.

However, this accusation against Browning of carelessness, and consequent roughness in rhythm, and obscurity in language and thought, has come to be pretty generally believed; and people, as a rule, do not read him; this evil spreading so, that many, almost unconsciously, are kept from reading him, who, if they did read, would sympathise with him thoroughly. But it was always so; it was so with Tennyson when he first published his poems; it was so last year with 'Maud'; it is so with Ruskin; they petted him indeed at first, his wonderful eloquence having some effect even upon the critics; but as his circle grew larger and larger, embracing more and more truth, they more and more fell off from him; his firm faith in right they call arrogance and conceit now; his eager fighting with falsehood and wrong they call unfairness. I wonder what they will say to his new volume.

The story of the Pre-Raphaelites, we all know that; only here, thank Heaven! the public has chosen to judge for itself somewhat, though to this day their noblest pictures are the least popular.

Yes, I wonder what the critics would have said to *Hamlet, Prince of Denmark*, if it had been first published by Messrs. Chapman and Hall in the year 1855.

105. John Ruskin, *Modern Painters*

1856, iv. 377–9

But see the Introduction, pp. 14ff.

Robert Browning is unerring in every sentence he writes of the Middle Ages; always vital, right, and profound; so that in the matter of art, with which we have been specially concerned, there is hardly a principle connected with the mediæval temper, that he has not struck upon in those seemingly careless and too rugged rhymes of his. There is a curious instance, by the way, in a short poem referring to this very subject of tomb and image sculpture; and illustrating just one of those phases of local human character which, though belonging to Shakespere's own age, he never noticed, because it was specially Italian and un-English; connected also closely with the influence of mountains on the heart, and therefore with our immediate inquiries. I mean the kind of admiration with which a southern artist regarded the *stone* he worked in; and the pride which populace or priest took in the possession of precious mountain substance, worked into the pavements of their cathedrals, and the shafts of their tombs.

Observe, Shakespere, in the midst of architecture and tombs of wood, or freestone, or brass, naturally thinks of *gold* as the best enriching and ennobling substance for them;—in the midst also of the fever of the Renaissance he writes, as every one else did, in praise of precisely the most vicious master of that school—Giulio Romano; but the modern poet, living much in Italy, and quit of the Renaissance influence, is able fully to enter into the Italian feeling, and to see the evil of the Renaissance tendency, not because he is greater than Shakespere, but because he is in another element, and has *seen* other things. I miss fragments here and there not needed for my purpose in the passage quoted, without putting asterisks, for I weaken the poem enough by the omissions, without spoiling it also by breaks. . . .

[Quotes 'The Bishop Orders His Tomb', ll. 10–81.]

I know no other piece of modern English, prose or poetry, in which there is so much told, as in these lines, of the Renaissance spirit,—its worldliness, inconsistency, pride, hypocrisy, ignorance of itself, love of art, of luxury, and of good Latin. It is nearly all that I said of the central Renaissance in thirty pages of the 'Stones of Venice' put into as many lines, Browning's being also the antecedent work. The worst of it is that this kind of concentrated writing needs so much *solution* before the reader can fairly get the good of it, that people's patience fails them, and they give the thing up as insoluble; though, truly, it ought to be to the current of common thought like Saladin's talisman, dipped in clear water, not soluble altogether, but making the element medicinal.

106. Advice from a Master

1856

Thomas Carlyle, from a letter to Robert Browning of 25 April 1856, in 'Correspondence Between Carlyle and Browning', ed. Alexander Carlyle, *Cornhill Magazine* (May 1915), cxi. 642–69.

It is a long time since I got your book according to programme; a long time since I read it all, many of the pieces again and again: nor was it a difficulty of conscience that has kept me silent; my approval was hearty and spontaneous, able I was and am to give you 'Euge!' far beyond what I reckon you desire; and indeed I believe myself to stand among the first ranks of your readers in that particular. But you asked with so much loyalty, 'What shall I do to be saved, and gain the top of this sore upward course?' and seemed to have such a faith in the older stager and fellow-climber to give you a word of advice,—I really knew not what to say, and hesitated always. . . . Accept a few rough human words, then, such as the day gives; and do not consider them as pretending to be more than honest words, rough and ready, from a fellow-pilgrim well-affected to you.

It is certain there is an excellent opulence of intellect in these two rhymed volumes: intellect in the big ingot shape and down to the smallest current coin;—I shall look far, I believe, to find such a pair of eyes as I see busy there inspecting human life this long while. The keenest just insight into men and things;—and all that goes along with really good insight: a fresh valiant manful character, equipped with rugged humour, with just love, just contempt, well carried and bestowed;—in fine a most extraordinary power of expression; such I must call it, whether it be 'expressive' enough, or not. Rhythm there is too, endless poetic fancy, symbolical help to express; and if not melody always or often (for that would mean finish and perfection), there is what the Germans call *Takt*,—fine dancing, if to the music only of drums.

Such a faculty of talent, 'genius' if you like the name better, seems to me worth cultivating, worth sacrificing oneself to tame and subdue into perfection;—none more so, that I know, of men now alive. Nay, in a private way, I admit to myself that here apparently is the finest poetic genius, finest possibility of such, we have got vouchsafed us in this generation, and that it will be a terrible pity if we spill it in the process of elaboration. Said genius, too, I perceive, has really grown, in all ways, since I saw it last; I hope it will continue growing, tho' the difficulties are neither few nor small!

Well! but what is the shadow side of the picture, then? For in that too I ought to be equally honest. My friends, it is what they call 'unintelligibility!' That is a fact: you are dreadfully difficult to understand; and that is really a sin. Admit the accusation: I testify to it; I found most of your pieces too hard of interpretation, and more than one (chiefly of the short kind) I had to read as a very enigma. I did make them all out,—all with about two insignificant exceptions;—but I do not know if many readers have got so far. Consider that case; it is actually flagrant!

Now I do not mean to say the cure is easy, or the sin a mere perversity. God knows I too understand very well what it is to be 'unintelligible' so-called. It is the effort of a man with very much to say, endeavouring to get it said in a not sordid or unworthy way, to men who are at home chiefly in the sordid, the prosaic, inane and unworthy. I see you pitching big crags into the dirty bottomless morass, trying to found your marble work,—Oh, it is a tragic condition withal!—But yet you must mend it, and alter. A writing man is there to be understood: let him lay that entirely to heart, and conform to it patiently; the sooner the better!

I do not at this point any longer forbid you verse, as probably I once did. I perceive it has grown to be your dialect, it comes more naturally

than prose;—and in prose too a man can be 'unintelligible' if he like!
My private notion of what is Poetry—Oh, I do hope to make you, one
day, understand that: which hitherto no one will do: but it must not
concern us at present. Continue to write in verse, if you find it handier,
And what more? Aye, what, what! Well, the sum of my ideas is: If you
took up some one great subject, and tasked all your powers upon it for a
long while, vowing to Heaven that you would be plain to mean capacities, then—!—But I have done, done. Good be with you always, dear
Browning; and high victory to sore fight!

107. A Mild Debate

1858

William Allingham and William Makepeace Thackeray, from
the diary entry August 1858, *William Allingham: A Diary,* ed. H.
Allingham and D. Radford (1907), pp. 76-7.

Anecdotes like these are what makes Allingham's *Diary* such a
delight. He was almost a Victorian Pepys.

I told him I had been with the Brownings (who were then in Paris,
staying in the Rue Castiglioni, No. 6).

'Browning was here this morning,' Thackeray said, 'what spirits he
has—almost too much for me in my weak state. He almost blew me out
of bed!'

'A wonderful fellow, indeed!'

'Yes, and he doesn't drink wine.'

'He's already screwed up to concert pitch.'

'Far above it. But I can't manage his poetry. What do you say?'
(I spoke highly of it.)

'Well, you see, I want poetry to be musical, to run sweetly.

'So do I——'

'Then that *does for* your friend B.!'

I spoke of Browning's other qualities as so splendid as to make him, as it were, a law in himself. But Thackeray only smiled and declined further discussion.

'He has a good belief, in himself, at all events. I suppose he doesn't care whether people praise him or not.'

'I think he does, very much.'

'O does he? Then I'll say something about him in a number.'

108. Hawthorne's Impression of Browning in 1858

From his *French and Italian Notebooks, The Complete Works of Nathaniel Hawthorne* (1882), x. 296.

This passage, in which the American writer records a visit made in 1858, is of especial interest in that Hawthorne expresses what so many others who knew Browning felt: that the 'private' Browning was so much more simple, straightforward (and, for Henry James, at least, less interesting) than the 'public' Browning of the difficult poetry. Home is, of course, the American 'medium', D. D. Home, whom Browning characterized as 'Mr. Sludge'.

We had some tea and some strawberries, and passed a pleasant evening. There was no very noteworthy conversation; the most interesting topic being that disagreeable and now wearisome one of spiritual communications, as regards which Mrs. Browning is a believer, and her husband an infidel. . . . Browning and his wife had both been present at a spiritual session held by Mr. Home, and had seen and felt the unearthly hands, one of which had placed a laurel wreath on Mrs. Browning's head. Browning, however, avowed his belief that these hands were affixed to the feet of Mr. Home, who lay extended in his chair, with his legs stretched far under the table. The marvellousness of the fact, as I have read of it, and heard it from other eye-witnesses, melted strangely away in his hearty gripe, and at the sharp touch of his logic; while his wife, ever and anon, put in a little gentle word of expostulation.

I am rather surprised that Browning's conversation should be so clear, and so much to the purpose at the moment, since his poetry can seldom proceed far without running into the high grass of latent meanings and obscure allusions.

SELECTIONS FROM
THE POETICAL WORKS OF
ROBERT BROWNING

1863

109. W. B. Donne, *Saturday Review*

7 February 1863, xv. 179–80

From his review of *Selections from the Poetry of Robert Browning*.

A Greek scholar, Donne liked Browning's *Balaustion's Adventures* better, and in a letter of 27 November 1871 asked Browning's permission to extract passages for a book he was writing. *Intimate Glimpses*, p. 55.

The irresistible impression made upon the mind of an unprejudiced reader by these selected poems of Mr. Browning must be, that he is, beyond all question, a man of very remarkable faculties. We perhaps may incline to the belief that his special intellectual province is to be looked for rather in an extraordinary power of psychological analysis than in what is usually regarded as poetical inspiration; but even if this attribute were separated from his other gifts, and not allowed to count at all, there would still remain behind so much real originality and strength that we cannot wonder if the partial friends whom genius such as his is sure to make and to keep are surprised and mortified at his comparative unpopularity. We say comparative unpopularity because we have always understood that among those who are fond enough of poetry not to be repelled by a manner which his friends describe as 'marked and peculiar', but which we should speak of in terms somewhat more unfavourable, he has never wanted an attentive, and seldom an admiring audience. Comparatively unpopular, however, he certainly is. For example, Mr. Longfellow, of whom we wish to speak with the utmost respect as a thoroughly accomplished versifier and something more, has taken the young ladies of England by storm. Now, in our judgment (and we say again, with perfect sincerity, that no sneer is aimed at the American author) Mr. Browning contains within himself a mass of solid metal which might be beaten thin into a couple of Longfellows at least. And yet we apprehend that (on principles somewhat similar to those on which the Dutch estimate of female beauty is said to rest) what Horace calls the *columna*, and what we call *the trade*, would pronounce the latter to be the greater poet of the two by ever so many copies annually sold.

Some such incapacity, or disinclination at least, on the part of Mr. Browning, to adapt himself to the taste of the day, appears to intercept the natural effect of his genius upon the public mind. There are also, we think, certain defects of manner and taste in his compositions, which the indolent and luxurious readers of the nineteenth century will not tolerate. We doubt, therefore, whether the appearance of this little book will materially alter his position before the world, though, as we honestly appreciate his great and various merits, we shall be glad if we find ourselves mistaken. One of these faults of form, as it appears to us, is an ineradicable passion for every contorted and unimaginable rhyme which the English language, turned inside-out, can be coaxed or tortured into supplying. We readily concede that Mr. Browning dances in his self-imposed fetters with unusual lightness and ease; nevertheless, he is forced often to sacrifice conciseness and propriety of style, and sometimes the whole beauty of his image, to this somewhat mean exhibition of a merely mechanical skill.

110. From an unsigned article, 'A Poet Without a Public', *Chamber's Journal*

7 February 1863, xix. 91–5

This listing of the obstacles to Browning's popularity is concise and probably accurate. The chauvinistic tone which marks the end of the first paragraph seems somewhat amusing today, but it was hardly so in mid-Victorian England.

It is probable that no man of our times has written so much and so well without general acknowledgment as Robert Browning. The poet whom poets love best often lacks the favourable voice of the public; but although his more ambitious efforts may be unknown to them, some song, or graceful line, at least, of his, is usually familiar in many a mouth that cannot tell from whom they come. It very rarely happens that *everything* a writer of genius pens is '*caviare* to the multitude,' but it happens sometimes, and it has done so in the case of the author we have mentioned. Mr. Browning is the poetic idol of men who give laws to cliques and coteries. *The Athenæum* 'kotows' to him. Mr. Ruskin quotes from him at length in obvious admiration. Even at the university, where new poets find little acceptance, his exquisite verses are set by enthusiastic professors to be rendered into Greek by the candidates for the Classical Tripos. And yet we are afraid that not one in ten of the people who subscribe to *Mudie's*[1] have ever read a word of his writings. The reason of this is certainly not that they are not worth reading. They have great beauty, undoubted originality, and a dramatic vigour that is equalled by no poet living. The obstacles to his popularity are, on the other hand, manifold. He has chosen to make his dwelling in Italy, and to select from thence the subjects of his muse. His preference for that spot is undisguised, and, to Englishmen, almost repulsive. At all events, under such circumstances, a poet can scarcely expect to be accepted in his own country.

His topic being thus alien, to begin with, he takes pains to deprive

[1] The famous lending library, founded by Charles Edward Mudie in 1842.

it still more of interest by selecting the period of action two or three hundred years back or so, his favourite century being the sixteenth. Finally, he strains off his possible audience—select enough already—by writing in as involved a style as he can, with passing allusions to the most recondite matters—after the manner of Carlyle in his *French Revolution*—which he chooses to take for granted everybody must know all about.

111. Sir J. Skelton, *Fraser's Magazine*

February 1863, lxvii. 240–56

From his article 'Robert Browning'.

Sir John Skelton (1831–97), historian and essayist, was a regular contributor to *Fraser's* and *Blackwood's* under the pseudonym of Shirley.

It is about time that we began to do justice to Robert Browning. A nation should be able to make up its mind on the merits and demerits of its leaders in the course of thirty years. Thirty years have passed since Robert Browning's first volume of poems was published; and thirty years ago he was almost as widely known as he is to-day. He is like to share the fate of Milton, and of several other Englishmen,—and women too. . . . Browning's is, indeed, a curious fame. No one (except an unfrequent traveller, who remembers somewhat sadly now the kindly greetings which met him within that pleasant English household 'at Florence, on the hill of Bellosguardo') knows him personally: his works are read by an insignificant minority, few of whom profess to understand a tithe of what they read; only here and there do you meet vigorous and somewhat disagreeable people, addicted to sarcasm and other evil courses, who take him as a kind of tonic (he braces the nerves, they say, and rids them of mental effeminacy), and who fancy that an age which has Robert Browning and the Bible cannot be so very badly off after all.

I confess that this profound neglect and unpopularity has always rather surprised me. One who understands the people of England is of course prepared for many anomalous and inexplicable phenomena. Trial by jury is the palladium of our liberties; yet an English or Scotch jury (not to speak of an Irish) is the very last tribunal to which a wise man would be inclined to submit his cause. 'May God send thee a good deliverance' is not by any means the language of hope, when addressed to a friend who has to undergo this ordeal. The verdicts of the English public are often in like manner very incomprehensible; yet it is difficult to account for Browning's prolonged unpopularity. For he has many of the qualities which recommend a poet to the people. He is a master of the passions. His humour is bright and keen. He has a fine eye for colour. There is a rich and daring melody in his verse. He observes with minute and absolute fidelity. He is a philosophical poet; but the direct human element is always strong in his philosophy. Tennyson (our popular poet) is essentially an intellectual poet; but Browning is at once a more masculine, and a more intricate and subtle, thinker than the laureate.

Yet his unpopularity may be accounted for. He is not the poet to be perused with profit in the nursery or in a railway-carriage. He does not relish a platitude as Mr. Longfellow does, nor does his verse move with the same supple smoothness and graceful facility. He is not a rhetorician, like Lord Macaulay. Unlike Pope's, his couplet does not carry a sting in its tail. He does not care to be 'effective.' 'Point' is not his strong point. His meaning, besides, does not always lie on the surface. It has to be sought with diligence and close attention. Thus, to those who read while they run, he is commonly obscure, and often incomprehensible. He is never insipid, but—brusque, quaint, rugged, intricately ingenious, involved, ironical—he perplexes the dull and startles the timid. . . .

Yet these defects have been exaggerated, and are not wilful. The occasional obscurity of his language, and the irregularity of the poetic forms which he uses, cannot be attributed to affectation. They are the natural and appropriate garniture of a peculiar and complex genius. As a thinker, he is essentially original. *The Two Voices*—Tennyson's most directly philosophical poem—is composed of a series of rather commonplace reflections,—profusely adorned, no doubt. It is like a common water-jug, stuck all over with gems and precious stones. No very intricate speculations, no very keen doubts, find expression in that elaborately-polished verse. Mr. Browning does not only adorn,—he originates as well. His imagination flashes light into the dark places. The chasing is rich indeed,—but the pitcher has been designed by Cellini. *Paracelsus* and *Christmas Eve* deal with the weighty issues of the life— divine and human. *Paracelsus* (on which I would willingly linger, as in many respects the most remarkable of Mr. Browning's works, but time fails me) is the record of high hopes defeated, of lofty purposes thwarted, of pure aspirations and an unselfish ambition rendered fruitless. Carica- tures of religious fanaticism, coarse, but vigorous and vivacious as Hogarth's, pictures of material nature, pure as summer dawn, frescoes of judgment, heavy with the gloom and pomp of the Sistine, are grotesquely bound up together in *Christmas Eve*. Throughout that singular poem, in verse that halts, and stumbles, and aspires, the poet strives to read, honestly, patiently, courageously, humbly, 'the riddle of the painful earthy.'

To conclude. As the dramatic is the poetic form which Mr. Brown- ing prefers, we can seldom be sure that we meet the man himself in his poetry. It is, at nearest, one of his many moods—moods which cannot be safely identified with permanent character. On rare occasions, how- ever, we find him appearing in *propriâ personâ*. At these times—in the later years at least—a passion for Italian freedom, and a tender regard for that 'E. B. B.' to whom he offers his latest work, are most noticeable.

112. E. P. Hood,
The Eclectic and Congregational Review
May 1863, 6th Ser., iv. 436–64

Hood (1820–85) wrote popular biographies of Milton, Sweden-borg, Carlyle, and Wordsworth. This extract is from his article 'The Poetry of Robert Browning'.

Robert Browning is one of the least known of our great modern writers, although his name has been now so long before the world; yet it may perhaps be questioned whether, with all his native prodigality and munificent endowment of thought, scholarship, and genius, he is not better known as the husband of Mrs. Browning than by the productions of his own pen. He is now in about his fifty-third year, and far as his verses rise above the cockney school of literature, so much the subject of the sneers of the fine-gentlemen critics, he is a Londoner by birth; born in Camberwell, educated in the then especially pleasant little village of Dulwich. The broad and liberal tone of his mind, which never degener-ates into the cant of Church-of-Englandism, may perhaps be in some measure attributed to the fact, that as a scholar he graduated at the London University.[1] His first effort as a poet—*Pauline*—we suppose has passed from everybody's recollection. Its author does not seem desirous that it should be retained. We have never seen it. We suppose it gives no evidence of its author's powers. Nearly thirty years have passed by since the publication of *Paracelsus*, a most extraordinary poem to read now. It is not wonderful that it was received with chilling coldness then. At that time our country had no audience for that kind of literature. It is intensely subjective. Much has been done since: Wordsworth has been appreciated, and Tennyson has risen; teaching the cultivation of this poetry of thought. At the time of its publication there was neither school nor class; only here and there existed a solitary mind able to appreciate, and with one or two favourable notices, it fell powerless from the press. The audience would be a small one disposed to read or

[1] In fact, Browning attended London University for less than one term.

to listen to it now. Soon after *Paracelsus*, was published *Sordello*. Again we have to confess our ignorance. This poem is out of print, and it probably never will be reprinted. We are willing to accept the verdict which pronounces it to be the most utterly and completely unintelligible poem in the English language. Our readers have probably met with a good story of Douglas Jerrold. 'In those days he was recruiting himself at Brighton. A parcel of books was sent him down from London, among the rest *Sordello*. The health of the wit was shattered, and all books were forbidden excepting lighter fiction. But Mrs. Jerrold, or as one has expressed it, 'the domestic lifeguard', was out of the way. The parcel was opened, and *Sordello* plunged into. When Mrs. Jerrold returned, she found her husband, to her horror, a cold sweat breaking out over his face, exclaiming, "I am mad, I am mad! my mind is gone, I can make nothing of it." He put the book into her hand, and asked her to read, and as she read, he exclaimed, "Thank God, it's only gibberish, I am not mad after all!" ' This is a very well known and oft-repeated story [see No. 103 for one form of the anecdote.] We suspect that it is only the judgment of that clever and brilliant wag, Jerrold; but it shows the estimation in which the poem was held by contemporaries able to judge. On the contrary, Mr. Browning still insists to his friends that *Sordello* is amongst the simplest and clearest poems in the English language. It was in 1846 Robert Browning married Elizabeth Barrett, thus furnishing no doubt one of the rarest and most charming instances of the happy marriage of equal and congenial poets. . . . During the years of their married life they resided in Florence, and it is something of a drawback to our exceeding admiration of, and gratitude to both, that England and English scenes and English life never seem to enter into the texture either of their genius, their sympathies, or their writings.

And here we touch at once the most prominent of those obstacles interfering with the fame of Robert Browning. He writes for men—for men and women—but not for Englishmen. He unconditions himself from those circumstances which would attract English readers, lives in other ages, and other countries, and with a power we believe to be felicitously transparent and clear he seems to determine on making himself obscure. In this particular there is a contradiction between the essentially dramatic structure of his scenery and the magnificent dramatic grandeur of the passions he portrays and embodies, and the frequently involved tortuousness of his versification. A second thought shows us that this is indeed very natural to his peculiar genius. How he delights to work and worm and wind his way to the subtlest places of the soul, and to the mazy problems which the soul is perpetually seeking to solve! His knowledge is most recondite. Out-of-the-way magnificent scenes attract and claim and charm him—great historic incidents and historical characters, though great not by the rustle of the robe, or the clash or the armour along the chief streets of history, but by the exhibition they have made of the greatness of souls. He is a dramatist in all that we usually imply by that word, entering into the innermost arena of the being. His poems are, to quote the title of one of his dramas, *Soul tragedies*. We trust we shall not be misunderstood when we say they present an order of tragedy differing from Shakspeare's—the agony, the strife, the internal stress are more internalised. He transfers the circumstances of our being from the *without* to the *within*. In this way they all become noble pictures of the striving and the attaining soul.

113. Sir F. T. Marzials, *London Quarterly Review*

July 1863, xx. 527-32

Sir Frank Thomas Marzials (1840–1912) wrote biographies of Dickens, Thackeray, and Victor Hugo.

Mr. Browning is not a popular poet; his *Poems*, published in 1849, have only just reached a second edition; and his *Men and Women*, which appeared some eight years ago, has not yet arrived at the same dignity. There are many educated persons who have scarcely heard of him, and many more who have never read a line of his works. And yet, amidst this general neglect, he has a small band of very devoted admirers, and his name has for some years been mentioned with honour, whenever it has occurred in any of the leading literary journals. How is it that the general public has refused to ratify the verdict of the critics, and that Mr. Browning's poems remain unsold?

The reasons are, we think, obvious: his style is so obscure that it is often exceedingly difficult to determine his meaning. There are whole passages—nay, more, there are whole works, from which the reader turns with only a very indistinct and cloudy notion of what the poet was trying to say. Nor is this merely occasional obscurity, such as is to be found scattered here and there in the works of Shakespeare, Shelley, and Tennyson—the obscurity of some great and novel thought struggling for utterance. It is an habitual fault, running through everything Mr. Browning has written, marring the beauty of many of his finest passages, and making it a toil to read what might have been made a pleasure. It springs from the fact, that he either cannot or will not put his ideas into their simplest and most intelligible forms; but clothes them in a quaint and outlandish dress of words, and sends them forth into the world with much these sentiments: 'If people like your appearance and receive you, well—why, so much the better for them; but if not, let no one think that I shall ever change one gaudy ribbon in your bright attire to suit the taste of a race of men for whom I care nothing.' It is only by some such process that we can account for the impenetrable mistiness of such poems as 'Sordello,' which even we—admirers as we are of Mr. Browning's genius—have been unable to get through. It is, however, but just to say that this book, in which Herod out-Herods himself, was not reprinted with the collected edition of the *Poems* in 1849. Milton's description of poetry has been so often quoted and re-quoted, that one is half ashamed to make it do service again; and yet, after all the numberless essays which have been written to show what poetry is, and what it is not, his definition of it, as that which is 'simple, sensuous, passionate,' is one of the best, as it is unquestionably the shortest. Mr. Browning's works possess the two latter qualities in a very high degree: the first he has unfortunately neglected, and apparently despised.

Another defect which has also interfered, though by no means to the same extent, with his popularity, is a frequent hardness and want of music in the versification, and a habit of breaking a verse or a line at any point, no matter where, and beginning a new and totally different sentence. . . .

Another grave defect in all selections is, that probably no two admirers of any man's works would ever choose exactly the same passages. They would most likely agree on many of the pieces; but on many others they would be equally sure to differ. And thus every lover of Mr. Browning's poems, in going through this book, will probably miss many and many a verse which he can ill spare, and which he would rather have seen here than several that have been retained. Thus we confess that we find, with great regret, that the latter half of *Easter Day*, in which this earth is so grandly described as nothing more than the anteroom of heaven, has not been considered worthy of a place among its peers. We have been in the habit of considering it, not only as one of Mr. Browning's great pieces, but as one that will live when many of the popular works of the present time have gone to their abiding rest.

This brief notice of the produce of a life of artistic labour is necessarily incomplete. It will, however, have served its purpose, if it has induced the reader to turn to Robert Browning's pages and judge patiently for himself. They are a deep and often a dark and difficult mine; but there is gold to be found at the bottom: they are a casket the lock of which is hard to pick, but which contains rich treasures. Because a poet's works are obscure, they are not necessarily bad. Coleridge's poems, as we learn from his preface, were accused of the same fault, and the riddle of Shakespeare's sonnets is yet unread.

114. Algernon Charles Swinburne, Browning's Failure

c. 1863–4

From an unpublished essay, 'The Chaotic School', c. 1863–4, in *New Writings by Swinburne*, ed. Cecil Y. Lang (1964), pp. 40–60.

The circumstances which gave rise to this remarkable essay have been discussed by Professor Lang in *New Writings by Swinburne*, pp. 198ff.[1] This essay ought to be compared with Nos. 116 and 179.

There is a story current or adrift somewhere of a certain missionary who went among the savages and there inculcated divine or other truth to such a sensibly insufferable degree that the leading converts, discreetly tempering justice with indulgence, cut off exactly one half of his tongue and sent him back with the other half unextracted. The regrettable result of such untimely mercy was this; that being quite unable to hold the tongue which remained to him he went about talking in a dialect of which no mortal could make anything. Whether or not men in general suffered much loss or expressed much anguish in consequence of this privation, we cannot now say: but the missionary could by no means endure it for them. In the general interest of creation, he went to a surgeon who proved ingenious. This philanthropist, by judicious extirpation of what tongue was left, enabled (it is said) the patient to speak thenceforward in an audible intelligible manner, by a select use of gutturals and labials: to what purpose we can only conjecture.

It has long since been evident to the select and compassionate reader that a poet now living has for his auditor's sins and his own been judicially afflicted by the severe and inscrutable fates with the visitation which human barbarity inflicted on this missionary. With the relic of his tongue chafed perpetually from root to tip with a fruitless irritation or itch for impossible speech, this memorable though mournful example of strenuous human perseverance has now been uttering for the last

---

[1] © 1964 by Syracuse University Press, Syracuse, New York.

twenty or thirty years the inarticulate vocal appeal of a tongueless though verbose eloquence. The amount of pure noise produced is really, when one thinks of it, a praiseworthy thing. For a man with organs unimpaired it would indeed be unpardonable; in the case of Mr. Browning, it is more than pitiable—it is commendable. Occasionally too, in a manner interesting and instructive to philanthropic science, some articulate discord produces a qualified variety in the sad monotonous effect; and a sound that pierces and skirrs the agonized human ear becomes to a compassionate mind almost melodious when one reflects that to the tympanum of the afflictive but innocent being which produced it, it may carry the music of a sweet significance. Moreover, if for no cause that man can tell the singer of inarticulate discords takes pleasure in afflicting men, has not Providence for no cause visible to the sufferer taken pleasure in afflicting *it*? There is even a certain relief to reader as listener in coming upon these audible syllables which do hiss and grind, clash and shriek, in a consecutive manner and to some given tune of meaning. They are indeed too infrequent; and a scientific charity would fain hope that the invaluable surgeon may yet turn up with curative lancet to do all parties a good turn. For a good turn we believe it would be: however incalculably small may be the infinitesimal grain of a message worth delivering which lies presumably latent in the minstrel of Gigadibs and Bombastes,[1] it must be better worth hearing than mere inarticulations jerked up by painful fits out of the noisy verbal whirlpools of a clamorous chaos.

Or perhaps our first pitying illustration was not so applicable as charity yet suggests? and the infliction under which his audience labours is not due to any quite natural affliction on the lecturer's part? Inexcusable, unpardonable, in that case, are the hideous noises which issue, in many a windy gamut of inharmonious sound, from the platform of *Paracelsus:* shrieks of violated English, groans of grammar undergoing vivisection, gasps of expiring sense and moans of tormented metre. Never surely did any wretched inoffensive dialect of human speech endure such unnatural tortures as those time after time inflicted with diabolical versatility of violence on our patient mother-tongue by the inventive and unsparing author of *Sordello*. Historic illustration must again be invoked before we can find words to describe them. Either after the St. Bartholomew slaughter or in the time of the *dragonnades,*

---

[1] Gigadibs is the journalist-listener in *Bishop Blougram's Apology*; Bombaste refers to Theophrastus Bombastus von Hohenheim, who called himself Paracelsus and became the hero of Browning's *Paracelsus*.

history asserts, a party of the king's troops destroyed one family of Huguenots or quasi-Huguenots with quite exceptional cruelty; putting the mother in particular through all kind of agonies and brutalities before they made an end of her: hardly one soldier here and there interceding to have her 'killed quicker'. The simile is horrible; but more horrible is Mr. Browning's treatment of the Queen's innocent English. Read (if you must read to believe) six pages on end, say of *Sordello*; his biggest book, and accounted his best; which it may be if it please. Count the conjunctions torn out by the roots, the verbs impaled, the nouns crucified, the antecedents broken on the wheel, the relatives cut off by the neck or sawn through the middle, the entire sentences blundering, screaming, plunging, snorting, like harpooned whales or smashed locomotives, through whole horrible paragraphs of mutilation and confusion. . . .

To speak without metaphor: no reader could rationally deny that whatever other merit or demerit there may be in this man of letters, here beyond doubt, of all clever and cultivated men, is the one who does absolutely write the worst English. It is not the bad style of ignorance or hurry or patent stupidity. It is not the bad style which comes of bad training; it is not the bad style which comes from bad imitation of good or good imitation of bad models; it is not the bad style which comes of too intense an intricacy of thought or too original a fervour of speech. It is so execrable as to be past all such and all other explanation. The one reason producible or conjecturable for its existence at all is that it does exist. All these books, it is now superfluous to say, have enough of crude thought, of raw talent, of fruitless cunning, of sterile strength, of profitless learning, to furnish forth a whole school of verse. Such a poetic pack has indeed already begun to yelp more or less feebly about the lower slopes and looser fences of our too accessible Parnassus. Justice, long denied, is now at length accorded to what deserts this poet actually has: and there is therefore grave and sufficient reason for pointing out that beyond the limit of those deserts the praise of his adherents should not be permitted to stray. He is ingenious, learned, reflective, retentive, acquisitive, and self-reliant; he has a notable gift of confused and rapid jargon, of copious and chaotic fluency. He has an admirable capacity of compressing as with a vice or screw into the limit of some small monodrame or monologue the representative quality or spiritual essence of a period; such at least as he can conceive it to have been. He has some real humour, forcible and subtle in its way, and well under the command of his imaginative faculty. He has some fitful and erratic sense of violent or ignoble passion in its more obvious and theatrical forms. Being receptive and ruminative, he has matter usually at hand on which to exercise his natural vehemence of spirit. He retains, under an outside show of fresh and vigorous speculation and a manner which gives the idea of depth and subtlety to minds simpler and shallower than his own, a stock of spiritual commonplace, a rag-market of moral old-clothes, always on hand: most acceptable as fairings to the greasy-fingered chapman of intellectual wares. . . .

Having all these excellent gifts, and more which his sectaries may be left to discover and trusted to proclaim, what can he want that a poet or philosopher worth naming should have? Very little. He cannot write a play, he cannot sing a song, he cannot tell a story; contemptible things no doubt, and insignificant enough, but which happen as yet to be about the fairest means of testing the capacity of a dramatic, a lyrical, or a narrative writer. In the huge bulk of his lyrical baggage there is not one good song. In the tight and bulging knapsack of his close-packed dramatic outfit, there is not one good play. In his single attempt at sustained narrative he has erected the most monstrous monument of failure that ever was struck out by the blind concurrence of incongruous and hurtling verbal atoms. He has lavished his irrelevant and valueless praise on Keats, on Shelley, and on Landor; to what end? with what sincerity? under what influence? They are wholly good artists; melodious, spontaneous, perfect at their best; admirable workmen at their worst. A deaf man applauding good music, a blind man praising good colour, would be scarcely so capricious and inconceivable an anomaly as the author of *Sordello* praising the author of *Lamia*—the author of *Colombe's Birthday* praising the author of *The Cenci*—or the author of *Bells and Pomegranates* praising the author of *Hellenics*. It is not a question of different schools and all good in their way. It is not an evidence of liberal genius that can enjoy approving such good work as it cannot hope to enjoy performing. If any of the widely various ways of work pursued by these different poets is even approximately a right way, then are all the many barren tracks down which Mr. Browning gives tongue at every turn wholly and irretrievably wrong.

[Here follow nearly fourteen pages of specific examples, arguing that Browning fails as a lyricist, as a master of form; that whatever power of thought and imagination the poet may possess is ruined by his faulty execution. Having compared Browning unfavourably to a number of poets—Gautier and Baudelaire among them—Swinburne moves to his concluding paragraph.]

Let not therefore any sectary of his presume to say that we demand of him to do not his own work, but another man's; that we require at his hands not the gifts he has to give us, but the likeness of another man's gifts; that we, in a word, are among those who, as M. Vacquerie[1] has excellently expressed it, must be content that each tree should bear its own fruit but must needs go looking for grapes on peach-trees and cursing the figtree as barren because it will not grow pine-apples. We require of each man, first, that he should do his own work; then that the work should be really good of its kind. We desire the bird to sing well, the flower to smell sweet, the problem to come right, the poet to do good verse, the orator to speak, the moralist to be moral, the painter to paint, the musician to compose, the statesman to govern, the preacher to preach, the soldier to fight, the philosopher to observe, and the sailor to handle his ship well; we cannot afford to let one of these go wrong, though he were ever so able in some alien way, but so capable of managing another man's office. Let each man enlarge the field, expand the limits, heighten the aspirations, ennoble the day's work of his personal duty as much and as far as may be possible; but first let him see that it be done at all; let him look to that at his peril and its. This one possible and necessary thing we simply must and will have; and will be put off with nothing else whatever by way of exchange.

[1] Auguste Vacquerie, author of *Profils et grimaces* (1856).

DRAMATIS PERSONAE

May 1864

115. From an unsigned review, *The Athenæum*

4 June 1864, pp. 765–7

'Thou thoughtest that I was altogether such an one as thyself,' says the
quotation attached to Mr. Browning's 'Caliban', but most assuredly no
one ever thought Mr. Browning like unto any other poet! He could not
be if he would, and he would not be if he could. He pioneers his own
way, and follows no one's track for the sake of ease and smoothness. His
music is not as the music of other men. He frequently strikes out something nobly novel; but it is not to be quickly caught, for we have not
heard the like before, and at first the mind of the reader finds it difficult
to dance to the beat of the time. He has a horror of all that is hackneyed
in poetry, and so he goes to the antipodes to avoid it, and finds things
on the other side of the world with which we are not commonly
acquainted. The 'Golden' he thinks has been almost worn out in poetry;
it has become so familiar that 'gold' is no longer a precious metal. He
thinks it will be good to try 'brass' for a change; or iron might prove a
tonic, and steel give our poetry something of sterner stuff. 'Roses',
again, have run riot to such an extent, and been used for sole comparison
so long, that he thinks it were well if poppies had their turn. Crimson
has been your only red with the poets; but, like Turner[1] amongst the
painters, Mr. Browning tries the merits of scarlet. Cherries shall not
supply the only likeness for ruddy lips, whilst we have the wild berries
on every hedge, and the exquisite flesh-like flush of the sea-shells on
every shore. Then his poetry is as different from the sort that many
readers have been accustomed to as the pine-apple is to the summer
jenneting. But only pierce through the rough crust and you find subtle

---

[1] Joseph Mallord William Turner (1775–1851), best known for his water-colours and
landscapes.

secret qualities not found in the tamer fruit; genuine nectar gushing, and fragrance that comes from afar.

The new volume has much less of the old mannerism which so often pulled up the reader that there was always danger of his being thrown out of the saddle. . . .

Mr. Browning's art is chastened, his expression only rich now in the most precious plainness of speech. Rare, telling English language he speaks in. His imagination is cut down, so to speak, to bare poles, and the simplicity serves to show a greater majesty. There is much less play of fancy, fewer *purple* words, than in the earlier poems, but more royalty of thought and kinglier dignity of expression. Fine images are more scarce, but he can use a noble metaphor and give it magnificent setting.

[Quotes 'Rabbi ben Ezra', ll. 169–80.]

As usual, Mr. Browning shows his old predilection for doing things which no other writer has done, or could have done, and striking out a path where no human footprint is to be found. A good hard, knotty problem of human nature is as 'nuts' for him to crack. He reminds us somewhat of those Life Assurance Societies that only take up the rejected cases of all the rest. We should not be surprised if, on opening a new book of his, we found a full, true and particular account of 'The Man that Died on Wednesday'. Our wonder is never at where we find him, but where shall we meet with him next? Two or three striking illustrations of this occur in the *Dramatis Personae*. One in a poem called 'Caliban upon Setebos; or Natural Theology in the Island'. This revelation of what 'Caliban' 'thinketh' would have delighted Shakspeare himself, who would have been first to have acknowledged that it faithfully represented the inner man of his original creation. Only a great dramatic poet could have written this poem. We cannot quote it, and there is no need to emphasize its subtleties; these must be felt: and the reader will hardly fail to make out a good deal of the satire which Caliban's theology reflects upon ours. In another poem, and at another extreme of his very great range, the poet enters into the heart of a modern pretender to mediumship. Or rather he turns the poor wretch inside out, and in his reversed shape makes him go backward over his past history. On being found out by his patron he goes down on his knees and gradually makes as clean a breast as he can of so foul a business. The subject is not pleasant to dwell upon, but the way in which patronizing credulity leads into temptation those who have a love of tampering with human wonder, and opens its mouth and shuts its eyes so invitingly that it would be almost a sin not to deceive it, is exquisitely pictured. The dark eyes of Mr. Sludge's nature are not attractive to us, but the dramatic illumination of them is admirable. At a third extreme from the two poems last mentioned, is a 'Death in the Desert', perhaps, on the whole, the finest poem in the book. In manner it is somewhat like Mr. Browning's poem, the 'Epistle of Karshish'. It is massive and weighty thought, solemnly real and sagely fine. It embodies the death of St. John in the Desert, and has the piquancy of making the beloved apostle reply with last words, in far-off ghostly tones, which come, weirdly impressive, from that cave in the wilderness, to the Frenchman's 'Life of Jesus'. It is done simply and naturally; but could any sensation-novelist contrive anything half so striking?

Very startlingly does it put the fact that when St. John was speaking many in the world were asking each other about Christ's second coming, seeing signs of promise all around them; and now possibly there are as many asking, did Christ ever come at all?

The reader will pardon the length of our illustrations for the sake of the poetry, and hurry on eagerly to the book. Our remarks are intended to converge towards that end, for, with all faults admitted and all hindrances acknowledged, Mr. Browning is one of our very few living poets, and this book is a richer gift than we shall often receive at the hands of poetry in our time.

116. A. C. Swinburne, letter,

19 June 1864

From a letter to John Nichol, *The Swinburne Letters*, ed. by Cecil Y. Lang, I, 101–2.

Swinburne's appreciation of Browning fluctuated over the years: in 1875 he defended Browning against the charge of obscurity [No. 179], but he despised Browning's treatment of the *Agamemnon*, and in an essay he did not publish excoriated Browning as a member of the 'chaotic school' of poets [No. 114].

I have read all Browning's new book since we parted; and while quite holding to all I said and say about his work as a poet I must also say—I have even had the candour to say to Rossetti—that I fully recognize the unique and most admirable power of 'Sludge' and 'Caliban'. I want to send you my full acknowledgment of this: because we talked enough about the matter, and because I have really derived such rare and keen pleasure, in the teeth of all personal or artistic feelings of dislike, from these two poems (if poems they are to be called) that I don't want you to suppose me insensible to their delightful qualities. I class both these above Blougram—not as intellectual exercises, but as samples of good work done. They are as good as Swift—i.e. not so good here, and better there; incomparably above Thackeray—and I think only a little below Chamfort and Stendhal. This last with me is higher praise than all the rest. Not less noble is the opening of St. John ['A Death in the Desert']—but long before the end the poem is swamped in controversial shallows, and the finer features effaced under a mask of indurate theological mud. In all the rest of the book I see much that is clever and nothing that is good—much that is ingenious and nothing that is right.

117. Robert Bell, *The St. James's Magazine*

July 1864, x. 476–91

From his review.

Bell (1800–67), Irish journalist and man of letters, edited twenty-four annotated volumes of the English poets. Browning, of course, was not among them. Like many a later critic, Bell does not know quite what to think of Browning's optimism, is not certain whether, for Browning, evil is real or apparent.

. . . But whether Mr. Browning does or does not believe in Original Sin is a minor question! More than most men does he believe in the ever-present stimulation of divine agencies. Nor is he a mere torpid acceptor of the respectable, the orthodox; he has reasoned out the matter entirely to his own conviction.

This brings us to a point from which we wish to look at Browning's genius. Nothing, it seems to us, is more remarkable in his poetry than the steady determination shown by the writer to regard things from their best side, to look with lenience on human frailty and shortcoming, and to get as much good out of human character as possible. Browning is the 'Man of Feeling' without his stupidity and effeminacy. He does justice to everybody, even the most vicious, and discovers that even Mr. Sludge, the medium, has his good points; he won't be too hard even upon sophistry, so he shows glimpses of the divine even through the portly waistcoat of Bishop Blougram. He is not an optimist, but he is always trying, unsuccessfully, to be one. He seems grieved beyond measure when brought face to face with wickedness and humbug, so close that he must perforce see and recognize them; but he immediately sets to work to take them to pieces, not with a view to detecting the weak points, but solely in order to find out the good ones; and if the search prove unsatisfactory, he has always the grand resource of discovering the divine agency, whose marvellous workmanship brings him to his knees. He could see more fine points in the character of the Devil than any man that ever wrote, and solely for the reason he trusts so completely in the wisdom of the devil's master. In fact, he finds something to like everywhere, but he never likes without a reason; and his extraordinary sympathy with humanity in general makes him as much at his ease in Petticoat Lane as in Belgravia; as much at home at Stoke-in-Pogis, which is agitated by the squabbles of a vestry, as in Paris, which is softly stirred by the *on dits* of a *salon*. This is meant to be high praise, and it is praise which shows the distinction between Mr. Browning and the poets who, however exalted be their musings, are merely subjective. The merely subjective poet has very little sympathy with the world in general; he admires his own little circle, and he employs his faculties in inward contemplation. Intellectually speaking, he is as lonely as a St. Simeon Stylites. Like Wordsworth, he feels himself an exceptional creature in the world, or like Shelley, he endows all mankind with his own high-mindedness and generosity. It is pretty evident that such a man lacks the weapons to combat with materialistic reasoners; while he dreams, they work; they are not satisfied with his dreams, though they are facts to him; they ask proofs—he retreats in high dudgeon, and appeals to the invisible. But when the dramatist steps forward to do battle on the side of faith, the case is widely different; he is armed at all points, and is not to be laughed down. Like his opponents, he is content to confine his arguments to facts, and mighty are the facts that humanity affords him. He is content to allow the enemy to heap the Pelion of positive science upon the Ossa of scepticism, and to climb to the top, and to cry out that they can still behold no God, while he remains in the earth, and, entering into the psychology of motives, discovers the divine spark there. History aids him with her wondrous suggestions. While the other side has ascertained that the Pentateuch is a marvellous contradiction, the dramatist has held commune with the souls of Luther and St. Paul. If they cry 'Fate!' he answers 'Napoleon!' While they are raking the old red sandstone, he is standing at the death-bed of Voltaire.

And Mr. Browning is a dramatist of a very high, if not of the highest, order. He has not written a line which, however lyrical in form, is not essentially dramatic in expression. Even 'Evelyn Hope', that most exquisite of English *morceaux*, is the last sweet scene of a beautiful drama. His long plays are not successful, simply because the form they wear leads us to expect something more familiar in their character; but if they were divided into separate poems, they would rank among the noblest dramatic studies. It is in miniature pictures—such as 'My Last Duchess' and the 'Epistle of Karshish'—that Browning excels. Nothing could be nobler or truer than the description of Lazarus in the latter poem. The man lives before us—gentle, subdued, mysterious, after the spirit of Christ has passed over him:

> The man is witless of the size, the sum,
> The value in proportion of all things,
> Or whether it be little or be much.
> Discourse to him of prodigious armaments
> Assembled to besiege his city now,
> And of the passing of a mule with gourds—
> 'Tis one! Then take it on the other side,
> Speak of some trifling fact—he will gaze rapt
> With stupor at its very littleness
> (Far as I see),—as if in that indeed
> He caught prodigious import, whole results;
> And so will turn to us the bystanders
> In ever the same stupor (note this point)
> That we, too, see not with his open'd eyes.

> * * * * *

> And oft the man's soul springs into his face,
> As if he saw again and heard again
> His sage that bade him 'Rise', and he did rise.
> Something—a word, a tick of the blood within—
> Admonishes—then back he sinks at once
> To ashes, that was very fire before,
> In sedulous recurrence to his trade
> Whereby he earneth him the daily bread;
> And studiously the humbler for that pride,
> Professedly the faultier that he knows
> God's secret while he holds the thread of life.
> Indeed, the especial marking of the man
> Is prone submission to the heavenly will—
> Seeing it what is, and why it is.
> Sayeth, he will wait patient to the last
> For that same death which must restore his being
> To equilibrium, body loosening soul,
> Divorced even now by premature full growth.

This is a mere outline of the drawing, but it shows the subtilty of Mr. Browning's psychology. The result produced in Lazarus by the visible presence of Christ is such as now appears frequently in men when the invisible Spirit actuates. Mr. Browning seems to have gone about his work in a pre-Raphaelite spirit, and starting from the assumption that men are radically the same in all ages, he may have drawn Lazarus from a living model. As Browning paints him, Lazarus must doubtless have appeared to the learned men of his time—such as the Leech who tells the story; but the picture affords glimpses which are true to all time, and which will manifest themselves wherever there is great faith.

We have suggested that Mr. Browning's method is pre-Raphaelistic. Nothing could be more commonplace than this method, were it not raised above commonplace by the startling fidelity of its results. Like Millais,[1] Mr. Browning throws in the background by a few broad dashes of the brush, leaving a great deal to the imagination, and adopting a boldness of colour which sometimes startles one, as nature often does. Like Hunt, he is laboriously elaborate in the execution of his figures. His poetry, indeed, has the faults as well as the beauties of the pre-Raphaelites. These faults consist of a certain unpleasant look of the work at first sight, and a frequent smudginess of the tints on further examination; and they constitute what is known to a large portion of the public as Mr. Browning's *style*—a style so bold, rough-hewn, and withal so original, that it has never been imitated with any success. Those who call it careless don't know what they are talking about. It is the fine conscientious expression of clearly defined thought, startling one ever and again by unconscious effects; and if it be full of mannerisms, they are the mannerisms of a man who is so much in earnest that he has no time to fill his pictures with charmingly pretty bits of unnatural colour. . . . In more than one marked respect does Mr. Browning resemble the painters who preceded Raphael. He is so pre-eminently Christian that he sacrifices everything for the sake of truth, pure and simple. The central figure in his mind's eye is Christ, whose spirit breathes gently through all his poetry. We are inclined to think that those poems in which Mr. Browning deals with historical religious subjects are his masterpieces. The parsimony of their colouring results in one gentle and very lovely evenness of tone; for Christianity abhors tinsel.

[Summarizes 'A Death in the Desert' and 'Caliban upon Setebos'.]

But clever as 'Caliban' is, it is a mistake. The subject is exceedingly repulsive, and almost unfit for separate artistic treatment. As part of the strange machinery of a play brimful of characters, Caliban is invaluable; and while his character is abundantly conveyed in the strong touches of the great master, he is always kept studiously in the background. More

---

[1] John Everett Millais (1829–96) and, in the sentence which follows, Holman Hunt (1827–1910), were painters of the Pre-Raphaelite school.

than once Mr. Browning, in his desire to say the best he can of things, has affirmed that mere beauty is something; but what plea can he set up for mere ugliness—ugliness so extreme as to fill the gazer with instinctive detestation and loathing? What would Mr. Millais make of a gorilla? The poem is a mistake; yet we value it highly, as a true index to the character of the poet's mind. In the excess of his Christian love and sympathy, we have no doubt that he sees some points of sympathy between himself and the whelp of Sycorax. But his error lies here; though the point of sympathy is discernible, it is swamped in the solitary full-length figure of the monster. In Shakspere, Caliban is far more *likeable* than in Mr. Browning's poem.

One feels quite ashamed to find fault with so mighty a master of psychology as Mr. Browning, who is as far above mere fault-finding as it is possible for writer to be. Nothing is more remarkable in his career than the steady, determined manner in which, regardless of neglect and hostile censure, he has clung to what he considers the right principles of art, without deviating for a moment into unbelief or hesitation. Like the Christian painters before Raphael, he merges the means in the end, deeming fineness of workmanship of less importance than the plain representation of what is true. His Christian feeling guides him at every step, and gives force and meaning to his very roughest outlines. He is the Michael Angelo of poets, with the qualification that he has the advantage of modern progress, and perceives, instead of the Great Terror, the Great Charity. Even when raking the dregs of our contemporary life, and turning up that unmitigated humbug, 'Mr. Sludge, the Medium', Mr. Browning shows far more mercy than any one of his contemporary authors—Mr. Dickens, for instance—would have done under the same circumstances.

[Quotes 'Sludge', ll. 876–908.]

But the worst of this poem is that it proves nothing—lets in no new light upon the vexed question on which it touches. It proves that Sludge is a humbug—that is all, and of course it is gentler with humbug than it might have been; but we know that there are 'mediums' in the world, who, so far from being Sludges, are quite cultured enough to love and understand Mr. Browning. The intention of the writer, we guess, was merely to divert himself with a little psychological dissection. And the portrait, besides being grossly ill-favoured, becomes inconsistent with itself when it represents Sludge as talking tenderly about the spirits of infants, and quoting the 'Bridgewater Treatises.' It is very like Mr.

Browning to make his medium feel deeply conscious of the pathos which is woven in with the hypocrisy of his profession. But it is *not* like Sludge.

[Bell here goes on to discuss 'Abt Vogler' and 'Rabbi ben Ezra', interlacing his comments with quotations.]

Those who know the story of the one great loss of Mr. Browning's life feel *how* and *whence* has come to him the serene wisdom, the belief in things good, which is the best and most valuable characteristic of his poetry. Further, out of his great love for and belief in mankind, he takes his readers into his secret, though with a vague reticence that shows how profound and how sacred has been the man's agony. This is in the 'Epilogue', the spirit of which is, 'I believe *because* I have loved much.' How many men have learned this mystery, whereby belief is woven out of love? How many men know that when one loves wholly, he *must* believe? Yet this is the knowledge which it is the business of Mr. Browning, and all great modern poets, to teach.

118. E. P. Hood,
The Eclectic and Congregational Review
July 1864, 6th Ser., vii. 61–72

From his review.

For another view by Hood, see No. 112.

We suppose we are not alone in making the confession that, of the living masters of English poetry, Robert Browning gives us the greatest measure of delight . . . it is in the exploring of the profoundest recesses of human spirits—the loitering and the marvelling over, and seeking the solution of the most tough and knotty problems of human nature—it is in the making all this the disc on which a strange and most unusual imagination plays off its powers—it is in a pathos infinitely too deep for any but eclectic hearts, sufferers, doubters, and seers, to have much sympathy—it is in a reticence and reserve of verse which leaves you wondering, broken presently by a gush and sweep, and wing of verse which leaves you panting—it is by allusions and eruditions which mark the scholar but instruct the learner, set in words which make a carcanet of precious jewels over the pages that this author's superabundant power is made known.

119. From an unsigned review, *The Victoria Magazine*

1 July 1864, iii. 282–3

These, as much as any of Mr. Browning's previous works, except perhaps *Sordello*, demand faith and patience. The nut is undeniably hard to crack. Whether the kernel is worth the labour of getting at it, we shall not stay to argue . . . His poetry is not to be taken up to occupy an idle moment or to charm away an incipient headache. People who want poetry to serve such ends as these must go elsewhere . . . The present volume confirms the verdict which has already placed Mr. Browning in the foremost rank of modern poets.

120. William Stigand, *The Edinburgh Review*

October 1864, cxx. 537–65

Stigand (1825–1915) contributed political articles and literary reviews to a wide variety of periodicals. In this unsigned review, he treats the whole of Browning's literary career before coming to *Dramatis Personae*, a matter which irritated the poet. But having published three volumes of collected poems the year before, Browning was vulnerable. In a letter of 17 October 1864, Browning let his feelings be known to Julia Wedgwood:

And here am I spared to read the 'Edinburgh' this morning. The clever creature rummages over my wardrobe of thirty years' accumulation, strips every old coat of its queer button or odd tag and tassel, then holds them out, 'So Mr. Browning goes dressed now!'—of the cut of the coats, not a word. I had fancied that the bugholes of that crazy old bedstead were plugged-up at this time of the day,—but no, here is the nastiness on one again! or rather off already, for to smash it would make things worse. (*Robert Browning and Julia Wedgwood*, pp. 87–88.)

Although his opinion is hostile, Stigand is well informed, and this review, taken together with the *Saturday Review's* rebuttal (No. 122), presents a refreshing insight into mid-Victorian critisicm.

If the shades of Jeffrey and of Gifford were to appear among us and to survey the poetic literature of the present generation, they would feel a stern satisfaction and a self-gratulatory delight at the remembrance of the hard-handed castigations which they had inflicted on the young poets of the commencement of this century. For a style of poetry more at variance with the canons of criticism then recognised than that in which it is now the ambition of most of our poets to express themselves, is hardly conceivable. Even the chief offenders of those days would refuse to recognise their own offspring in many of the most belauded poetic flights of the present time, which frequently unite an affected simplicity with such tortured, artificial, and foppish vagueness of expression and fantastic flimsiness of ideas, that it is generally a labour of infinite pain to extract from them the little meaning they possess. Indeed, the age now appears to be ripe for some 'Theory of the Obscure,' which, like Pope's famous *Treatise on Bathos or the Art of sinking in Poetry*, might be copiously illustrated from the works of contemporary poets, and afford at least a warning to the young aspirant for the honours of verse. For such a book Mr. Browning's volumes would form an inexhaustible mine of examples, and the last volume which he has published is, perhaps, richer than any that have preceded it in materials for such a purpose. Yet much as we may lament the great defects of expression which enshroud his thoughts and distort his compositions, it were vain to deny that his steady perseverance in the course which he has chosen has won at length for himself an influence among readers of poetry second only to that of the Laureate, and no one pretending to be at all conversant with the literature of our time can forbear from making acquaintance with and forming some estimate of his labours. Every reader who glances at Mr. Browning's volumes however cursorily, must perceive that he is a man of rare accomplishments, with a singularly original mind capable of sympathising with a multiplicity of tastes and characters very far removed from every-day experience. We may regret that he has omitted to draw from those sources of the sublime, the tender, and the pathetic which will ever be the most potent means of touching and purifying the heart, refining the feelings, and elevating the imagination. We may regret also the habitual neglect of the ordinary canons of taste and judgment which lamentably diminishes the effectiveness of his poetry; but Mr. Browning now lays the work of thirty years before us, and we have but to take it to ourselves and to enjoy it and understand it as well as we can. For it is clear that he has so wedded himself to what is quaint and obscure in his forms of expression and choice of subject, that no change in these is to be hoped for from him; far different in this respect from Mr. Tennyson, whose last volume shows a power of adaptation and a pliability of invention which even his strongest admirers hardly anticipated. His two rustic sketches, 'The 'Grandmother' and 'The Northern Farmer' have enriched the language with two scenes of homely and rural life scarcely to be surpassed in truthfulness and simplicity of expression; while his two tales, 'Enoch Arden' and 'Aylmer's Field', although open to some objection as to the character and construction of the stories, are yet rare triumphs of poetic diction, and in their chastened strength form a very striking contrast with the highly-wrought and fastidious execution of 'Locksley Hall' and 'Œnone.' On the other hand, there is hardly a fault with which Mr.

Browning has ever been charged which is not, in the *Dramatis Personae*, intensified to an extravagant degree. It was said of an eminent lawyer that he wrote his opinions in three different kinds of handwriting—one which he and his clerk could read, another which only he himself could decypher, and a third which neither he or anybody could make out; and into similar categories we are compelled to parcel out the poems of the *Dramatis Personae*.

To form, however, a proper estimate of Mr. Browning as a poet, it would not be fair to dwell exclusively upon this volume, and we shall proceed therefore to pass in review the collected edition of his works as last given to the public. *Paracelsus*, published in 1835, was the first poem by which Mr. Browning became known to the world; its reception was not unfavourable, and this and one or two of Mr. Browning's tragedies may be regarded as the most perfect of his productions, besides being the most ambitious in conception. There is nothing particularly original in the scheme of *Paracelsus*; it depends for its interest, like Faust, René, Manfred, Jacopo Ortis, Oberman, *El mundo diablo*, Festus, and a crowd of lesser known productions, on psychological incidents and transformations—works which have their prototypes in the Book of Job and the Confessions of St. Augustine. The hero of the poem is a shadowy transfiguration of the notorious doctor, alchemist, and quack of the sixteenth century, who filled for a time the chair of physic and surgery at the University of Basle, and began his course by publicly burning in the amphitheatre the works of Galen and Avicenna, and informing his auditory that he was henceforth to hold the monarchy of science; one of his proper names was Bombastus, which from the inflated character of his discourse has passed into modern language, with a signification which will render it immortal. The *Paracelsus* of Mr. Browning is a very different character, however, from the vain and drunken Swiss empiric, as his drunkenness becomes converted into a sentimental attachment to the wine-cup, and his familiar demons, one of whom was said to reside in the handle of his sword, are kept for the most part unobstrusively behind the scenes. In the first division of the poem, Paracelsus, inspired by the conviction that he has been selected by God for a special mission, determines to go forth in search of knowledge,—having set before him *knowing* as the great end of achievement. He departs, contrary to the wishes of his friends, on a lonely pilgrimage to various countries to gather

> The sacred knowledge here and there dispersed
> About the world, long lost or never found.

In reply to the persuasions of his friend Festus to remain with him
and to avoid so perilous a career, he answers—

> What should I
> Do, kept among you all; your loves, your cares,
> Your life—all to be mine? Be sure that God
> Ne'er dooms to waste the strength He deigns impart!
> Ask the gier-eagle why she stoops at once
> Into the vast and unexplored abyss,
> What full-grown power informs her from the first,
> Why she not marvels, strenuously beating
> The silent boundless regions of the sky!
>   . . . . 'Tis time
> New hopes should animate the world, new light
> Should dawn from new revealings to a race
> Weighed down so long, forgotten so long; thus shall
> The heaven reserved for us, at last receive
> Creatures whom no unwonted splendours blind,
> But ardent to confront the unclouded blaze
> Whose beams not seldom blessed their pilgrimage,
> Not seldom glorified their life below.
>   . . . . I seemed to long
> At once to trample on, yet save mankind,
> To make some unexampled sacrifice
> In their behalf, to wring some wondrous good
> From heaven or earth for them, to perish, winning
> Eternal weal in the act: as who should dare
> Pluck out the angry thunder from its cloud,
> That, all its gathered flame discharged on him,
> No storm might threaten summer's azure sleep:
> Yet never to be mixed with men so much
> As to have part even in my own work, share
> In my own largess. Once the fact achieved,
> I would withdraw from their officious praise,
> Would gently put aside their profuse thanks.
>   . . . . I go to prove my soul!
> I see my way as birds their trackless way.
> I shall arrive! what time, what circuit first,
> I ask not: but unless God send His hail
> Or blinding fire-balls, sleet or stifling snow,
> In some time, His good time, I shall arrive:
> He guides me and the bird. In his good time!

In this sublime self-confidence, with this contempt of his kind and scorn of help from all his forerunners, Paracelsus sets forth in pursuit of knowledge—though what kind of knowledge he seeks is uncertain; apparently it consists of secrets, however, of some kind which are to lift the entire race up to a new heritage of glory. In the course of his travels he comes to Constantinople, and there pauses for awhile, partly wearied, and partly to sum up the results already attained. While at Constantinople, he falls in with Aprile, an Italian poet, who has failed in the search after love as the end of existence, and dies before Paracelsus of exhaustion and suffering. The seemingly invincible confidence of Paracelsus had already abandoned him before the meeting with Aprile, but a considerable portion of assurance still remains:

> At worst I have performed my share of the task;
> The rest is God's concern; mine, merely thus,
> To know that I have obstinately held
> By my own work. . . . .
> Crush not my mind, dear God, though I be crushed!
> Hold me before the frequence of Thy seraphs
> And say—"I crushed him, lest he should disturb
> My law. Men must not know their strength: behold,
> Weak and alone, how he had raised himself!"

This superb egotism melts away, however, before the presence of Aprile, whose desire of love has found vent in a passion for art, which is thus described by Mr. Browning in a passage not unworthy of Keats, though it is disfigured here and there by grotesque and extravagant conceits:

> I would love infinitely, and be loved.
> First: I would carve in stone, or cast in brass,
> The forms of earth. No ancient hunter lifted
> Up to the gods by his renown, no nymph
> Supposed the sweet soul of a woodland tree
> Or sapphirine spirit of a twilight star,
> Should be too hard for me; no shepherd-king
> Regal for his white locks; no youth who stands
> Silent and very calm amid the throng,
> The right hand ever hid beneath his robe,
> Until the tyrant pass; no lawgiver,
> No swan-soft woman rubbed with lucid oils,
> Given by a god for love of her—too hard!
> Every passion sprung from man, conceived by man,

Would I express and clothe it in its right form,
Or blend with others struggling in one form,
Or show repressed by an ungainly form. . . .
And, at the word, I would contrive and paint
Woods, valleys, rocks and plains, dells, sands, and wastes
Lakes which, when morn breaks on their quivering bed,
Blaze like a wyvern flying round the sun,
And ocean-isles so small, the dog-fish tracking
A dead whale, who should find them, would swim thrice
Around them, and fare onward—all to hold
The offspring of my brain. Nor these alone:
Bronze labyrinth, palace, pyramid and crypt,
Baths, galleries, courts, temples and terraces,
Marts, theatres, and wharfs—all filled with men!
Men everywhere! And this performed in turn,
When those who looked on, pined to hear the hopes
And fears and hates and loves which moved the crowd,
I would throw down the pencil as the chisel,
And I would speak; no thought, which ever stirred
A human breast should be untold; all passions,
All soft emotions, from the turbulent stir
Within a heart fed with desires like mine,
To the last comfort shutting the tired lids
Of him who sleeps the sultry noon away
Beneath the tent-tree by the wayside well:
And this in language as the need should be,
Now poured at once forth in a burning flow,
Now piled up in a grand array of words.
This done, to perfect and consummate all,
Even as a luminous haze links star to star,
I would supply all chasms with music, breathing
Mysterious motions of the soul, no way
To be defined save in strange melodies.
Last, having thus revealed all I could love,
Having received all love bestowed on it,
I would die: preserving so throughout my course
God full on me, as I was full on men:
He would approve my prayer, 'I have gone through
The loveliness of life; create for me
If not for men, or take me to Thyself,
Eternal, infinite Love!'

A new truth burst in upon Paracelsus from the ravings of Aprile, and
he says:

Love me henceforth, Aprile, while I learn
To love; and, merciful God, forgive us both!
We wake at length from weary dreams; but both
Have slept in fairy-land: though dark and drear
Appears the world before us, we no less
Wake with our wrists and ankles jewelled still.
I, too, have sought to KNOW as thou to LOVE—
Excluding love as thou refusedst knowledge.
Still thou hast beauty and I, power. We wake:
What penance canst devise for both of us?

Aprile, however, dies, but his example left on the mind of Paracelsus an ineffaceable influence:

Love's undoing
Taught me the worth of love in man's estate,
And what proportion love should hold with power
In its right constitution; love preceding
Power, and with much power, always much more love;
Love still too straitened in its present means,
And earnest for new power to set it free.

Paracelsus had yet, however, other lessons to learn, which are the subject of Third and Fourth Parts of the poem; he had to come to a due appreciation of the value of the praise and dispraise of his fellow-men, of both of which he had sufficient experience in his professorial chair; and the haughtiness of his nature led him of itself to despise men for the one and to hate them for the other, but in the final scene on his deathbed he sees his error:

In my own heart love had not been made wise
To trace love's faint beginnings in mankind,
To know even hate is but a mask of love's,
To see a good in evil, and a hope
In ill-success; to sympathise, be proud
Of their half-reasons, faint aspirings, dim
Struggles for truth, their poorest fallacies,
Their prejudice and fears and cares and doubts;
Which all touch upon nobleness, despite
Their error, all tend upwardly though weak,
Like plants in mines which never saw the sun,
But dream of him, and guess where he may be,
And do their best to climb and get to him.
All this I knew not, and I failed.

He dies in the conviction that men will ultimately recognise his worth:

> If I stoop
> Into a dark tremendous sea of cloud,
> It is but for a time; I press God's lamp
> Close to my breast; its splendour, soon or late,
> Will pierce the gloom: I shall emerge one day.
> You understand me? I have said enough?
> *Fest.* Now die, dear Aureole!
> *Par.*   Festus, let my hand—
> This hand, lie in your own, my own true friend!
> Aprile! Hand in hand with you, Aprile!
> *Fest.* And this was Paracelsus!

We have stayed somewhat long over *Paracelsus*, as it is, as we observed, the most complete of Mr. Browning's productions, and embodies a vital truth—although it costs an effort to extricate it from the obscurity of the text,—for Mr. Browning's diction, if not so obscure here as elsewhere, is still sufficiently so to render continuous perusal a laborious process. The moral of the fate of Paracelsus is expressed in his own words:

> Let men
> Regard me, and the poet dead long ago
> Who loved too rashly; and shape forth a third
> And better-tempered spirit, warned by both.

The prose rendering of which would appear to be that the culture of science must, in order to bear salutary and lasting benefits for humanity, be allied with the culture of beauty,—a truth which the present generation have especial need to lay to heart. We will not separate from this poem without quoting two or three of the beautiful passages which it contains:

> 'Tis only when they spring to heaven that angels
> Reveal themselves to you; they sit all day
> Beside you, and lie down at night by you,
> Who care not for their presence, muse or sleep,
> And all at once they leave you and you know them!

> 'Tis in the advance of individual minds
> That the slow crowd should ground their expectation
> Eventually to follow; as the sea

Waits ages in its bed, 'till some one wave
Out of the multitudinous mass, extends
The empire of the whole, some feet perhaps
Over the strip of sand which could confine
Its fellows so long time: thenceforth the rest,
Even to the meanest, hurry in at once,
And so much is clear gained.

My heart! they loose my heart! these simple words
Its darkness pierces which nought else could touch;
Like some dark snake that force may not expel
Which glideth out to music sweet and low.

Paracelsus was evidently written with some consideration for the public, and some fear of the critics before his eyes, which is more than can be asserted of Mr. Browning's next work, *Sordello*, published five years afterwards. This production alone would be amply sufficient to furnish all examples for the 'Theory of the Obscure,' which we suggested at the outset of our article. Singularly enough, too, this appears to be the only piece of the collection by the neglect of which Mr. Browning feels aggrieved. In a dedication to one of his French critics, who appears to have arrived at the singular felicity of understanding *Sordello*, Mr. Browning says that the poem was written only for a few, but he counted even on these few caring more for the subject than proved to be the case, and he is still sanguine enough to expect a wider public for *Sordello* than it has yet received.

Sordello is, like *Paracelsus*, a psychological study, the history of the growth of a soul; and the historical decoration is, as Mr. Browning informs us, put in merely by way of background; but, unfortunately, the decorative part is still more hard to comprehend than the crabbed metaphysics and aesthetics which are wrought up into the 'development of the soul.' The psychological revolutions and aims of Sordello's mind are so mixed and matted up with an inexplicable knot of tangled and indistinguishable incidents and personages in one of the darkest periods of Italian history, that nothing short of angelic patience is required to make them out at all, and even when the story of 'Sordello's soul' is unravelled from the weeds which adhere to it, there is little interest or novelty discoverable. Like many other poets, he doubts whether song or action should be his aim in life: in the first part of the poem he is constant to song—in the latter portion he forsakes song, takes to action and dies, it is not clear how, under the burden of it.

A single passage will suffice to show the nature of the narrative and the peculiar character of its obscurity, to which we confess that we are unable to give any meaning whatever:

> Heinrich, on this hand, Otho, Barbaross,
> Carrying the three Imperial crowns across,
> Aix' Iron, Milan's Silver, and Rome's Gold—
> While Alexander, Innocent uphold
> On that, each Papal key—but, link on link,
> Why is it neither chain betrays a chink?
> How coalesce the small and great? Alack,
> For one thrust forward, fifty such fall back!
> Do the popes coupled there help Gregory
> Alone? Hark—from the hermit Peter's cry
> At Claremont, down to the first serf that says
> Friedrich's no liege of his while he delays
> Getting the Pope's curse off him! The Crusade—
> Or trick of breeding strength by other aid
> Than strength, is safe. Hark—from the wild harangue
> Of Vimmercato, to the carroch's clang
> Yonder! The League—or trick of turning strength
> Against pernicious strength, is safe at length.

The psychological portions of the poem, in which *Sordello* exhibits a prophetic intimacy with Kantian metaphysics, are plain reading after such passages as the above, and come as a kind of relief; for though, in truth, equally unintelligible, the reader may be beguiled into thinking he understands them:

> He cast
> Himself quite through mere secondary states
> Of his soul's essence, little loves and hates,
> Into the mid deep yearnings overlaid
> By these; as who should pierce hill, plain, grove, glade,
> And on into the very nucleus probe
> That first determined there exist a globe.
> As that were easiest, half the globe dissolved,
> So seemed Sordello's closing-truth evolved
> By his flesh-half's break up—the sudden swell
> Of his expanding soul showed Ill and Well,
> Sorrow and Joy, Beauty and Ugliness,
> Virtue and Vice, the Larger and the Less,
> All qualities, in fine, recorded here,
> Might be but modes of Time and this one sphere,

Urgent on these, but not of force to bind
Eternity, as Time—as Matter—Mind,
If Mind, Eternity, should choose assert
Their attributes within a Life.

On the whole, however, this poem is, in our judgment, from its confused and tortuous style of expression, the most illegible production of any time or country. Every kind of obscurity is to be found in it. Infinitives without their particles—suppression of articles definite and indefinite—confusion and suppression of pronouns relative and personal —adjectives pining for their substantives—verbs in an eternal state of suspense for their subjects—elisions of every kind—sentences prematurely killed off by interjections, or cut short in their career by other sentences—parentheses within parentheses—prepositions sometimes entirely divorced from their nouns—*anacoloutha*, and all kinds of abnormal forms of speech for which grammarians have ever invented names—oblique narrations, instead of direct—and puzzling allusions to obscure persons and facts disinterred from Muratori or Tiraboschi, as though they were perfectly familiar to the reader. Indeed, to be compelled to look at a drama through a pair of horn spectacles would be a cheerful pastime compared with the *ennui* of tracing the course of *Sordello* through that veil of obscurity which Mr. Browning's style of composition places between us and his conception.

By a comparison of *Sordello* and *Paracelsus* it is easy to discover that the bent of Mr. Browning's genius has more of a dramatic than of an epic character. *Sordello* as a narrative is a signal failure, whereas the merits of *Paracelsus* had already encouraged its admirers to hope for something from Mr. Browning for the Drama. The stage had not yet become the thing which it now is—tragedies of a high order had not long before obtained distinguished success: Milman's 'Fazio', Shiel's 'Evadne', Miss Mitford's 'Rienzi', Barry Cornwall's 'Mirandola'; the plays of Sheridan Knowles and Talfourd had kept the tone and pathos of real tragic feeling alive in the hearts of the stage-going public. Great then was the expectation of those in the secret when it was known that Mr. Macready had undertaken to bring out at Drury Lane a play called *Strafford* by Mr. Browning—an expectation doomed to disappointment; for *Strafford* was as complete a failure as was the *Blot in the 'Scutcheon*, also produced some six years later at the same theatre. *King Victor and King Charles*, and *Colombe's Birthday*, were played subsequently at the Haymarket, but none of them succeeded in interesting the audience. Indeed, the faculty of narration—of easily unfolding the subject and clearly putting the circumstances and incidents of the subject before its hearers—is as necessary to a drama as to an epic, and in this lies Mr. Browning's most remarkable deficiency. Moreover, a stage writer is bound before all things to be pleasing; and this is an end which Mr. Browning never appears to have had in view. His manner of introducing his subject is so involved, fragmentary, and tortuous that it must have been utterly impossible to comprehend the story at a first sitting. Take, for example, the following passage from the *Return of the Druses,* where the verb is waiting for its subject over two parentheses and several lines of verse:

> Khalil. And did you call—(according to old laws
> Which bid us, lest the sacred grow profane,
> Assimilate ourselves in outward rites
> With strangers fortune makes our lords, and live
> As Christian with the Christian, Jew with Jew,
> Druse only with the Druses)—did you call
> Or no, to stand 'twixt you and Osman's rage,
> (Mad to pursue e'en hither thro' the sea
> The remnant of your tribe) a race self-vowed
> To endless warfare with his hordes and him,
> The White-cross Knights of the adjacent Isle?

It is to be observed that the obscurity here arises not from any depth of thought, not even from terseness or any intricacy of poetic expression, the facts to be told being simple, and the obscurity arising simply from clumsiness of diction. In reading the passage one may overcome the needless difficulty thus manufactured for the reader by looking back and finding out the governing verb. But for a hearer this is impossible. So also the dialogue is rendered unmercifully obscure, partly from carelessness and partly from a seeming impossibility to go straightforward with the work in hand. The personages of the drama have a most uncomfortable way of replying to one question by asking another; of giving entirely a different answer from what one would naturally expect; of breaking each other off in the middle of a sentence; and, above all, alluding to minute circumstances and objects they have been familiar with, as if the audience were equally familiar with them. For this latter purpose, the demonstrative pronouns *that* and *those* are unsparingly employed. Thus Berthold, in *Colombe's Birthday,* speaks incidentally of having wooed some girl called Priscilla under some convent-wall or other. Both Priscilla and the convent-wall are thrust upon us as old acquaintances, without any introduction:

And when I wooed Priscilla's rosy mouth
And failed so, under *that* grey convent-wall,
Was I more happy than I should be now
If failing of my Empire?

Failure in the wooing of a maiden, and failure in obtaining a kingdom, may, we suppose, admit of a comparison; but merely hinted at in
this obscure fashion, with the particular image of Priscilla and *that*
convent-wall flashed upon us like a momentary scene of a magic lantern,
we are simply dazzled and rendered quite unfit for the next sentence.
In the following opening of the scene between Ottima and her paramour
Sebald, the German music-teacher, in *Pippa Passes*, every line is a riddle.
It is morning, and the two lovers are alone in some building called a
'shrub-house,' closed with shutters apparently. Sebald opens the scene
by singing an extremely puzzling song in three jerking lines:

Sebald. [*sings*.] Let the watching lids wink!
　　　　　　　Day's a-blaze with eyes, think—
　　　　　　　Deep into the night, drink!
Ottima. Night?　Such may be your Rhine-land nights, perhaps;
　　　　　But this blood-red beam through the shutter's chink,
　　　　　—We call such light, the morning's: let us see!
　　　　　Mind how you grope your way, though!　How these tall
　　　　　Naked geraniums straggle!　Push the lattice
　　　　　Behind that frame!—Nay, do I bid you?—Sebald,
　　　　　It shakes the dust down on me!　Why, of course
　　　　　The slide-bolt catches.—Well, are you content,
　　　　　Or must I find you something else to spoil?
　　　　　Kiss and be friends, my Sebald!　Is it full morning?
　　　　　Oh, don't speak then!

If a critic should ever take it into his head to write a commentary on
the above passage, the explanatory *scholia* would require to be three
times as long as the original lines. No doubt Mr. Browning imagined
the interior of a shrub-house, and the relative position of flowers,
frames, and lattices, and the movements of Sebald and Ottima on
opening the lattice; but he has kept all these a secret from the reader,
and as the whole passage stands, it reads (Sebald's song included) as if
some drunken or fraudulent copyist had got hold of Mr. Browning's
MS., left out all the words necessary to the understanding of the piece,
and made a jumble of the remainder. It is to be observed that here, too,
none of the obscurity consists in the thought, nor is there anything
approaching to poetry in a single line, but that the obscurity is solely in

the description of the most trivial incidents. *Pippa Passes* was not, however, written for the stage; we turn, therefore, to 'Strafford,' to take a sample of such dialogue as Mr. Browning thinks adapted to stage purposes.

After Lady Carlisle has made a speech to which Strafford has not given the least attention, the latter says:

Strafford. When could it be? no! Yet . . was it the day
We waited in the anteroom, till Holland
Should leave the presence-chamber?
Lady Carlisle. What?
Strafford. —That I
Described to you my love for Charles?
Lady Car. (Ah, no—
One must not lure him from a love like that!
Oh, let him love the King and die! 'Tis past.
I shall not serve him worse for that one brief
And passionate hope, silent for ever now!)
And you are really bound for Scotland, then?
I wish you well: you must be very sure
Of the King's faith, for Pym and all his crew
Will not be idle—setting Vane aside!
Straf. If Pym is busy,—you may write of Pym.
Lady Car. What need, since there's your King to take your part?
He may endure Vane's counsel; but for Pym—
Think you he'll suffer Pym to . . .
Straf. Child, your hair
Is glossier than the Queen's!
Lady Car. Is that to ask
A curl of me?
Straf. Scotland——the weary way!
Lady Car. Stay, let me fasten it.
—A rival's, Strafford?
Straf. [*showing the George.*] He hung it there: twine *yours* around
it, child!

Even in the *Dramatic Lyrics* some of the best-known pieces are utterly spoiled by Mr. Browning's abhorrence of lucidity. The 'Ride to Aix,' for example, labours under this fatal defect. The poem is a spirited one, in spite of its quaintnesses, of which it has its full share. For example, if 'Dirck' is 'he' in the first line, why should he not be 'he' in the second? Then why did not Roland's rider put his riding-gear in good order before starting? and Roland must indeed have been a steady roadster if his bit could be chained slacker without interfering with his galloping. All these and other singularities do not hinder the poem from being a very spirited one. But what is fatal to its general success is the impossibility of knowing what all the galloping is about. Someone a few years ago, we observed, was so moved by Roland's achievements as to write to *Notes and Queries* to ask what was the news brought, but the inquiry still remains unanswered.

The incidents and actors represented are not, either in the case of his Tragedies or Dramatic Lyrics, such as to stir deeply the passions or touch the feelings; but are sometimes of an unpleasant character to dwell upon, and sometimes of that super-sublime or fantastic nature which excites no very deep sympathy. In *King Victor and King Charles*, father and son are scheming against each other for the possession of a crown, but the plot has none of the tragic awe of a great crime like that of Clytemnestra to subdue the natural repugnance produced by seeing son and parent in unnatural relations. In the *Blot on the 'Scutcheon*, a boy and girl of noble family are living in unchastity before marriage. The circumstances under which the seduction is described as innocently taking place are most improbable; and all sense of proportion of tragic crime and punishment is violated by its termination in a murder and two suicides. In the *Return of the Druses*, Djabal, the hero, is a mixture of the impostor and fanatic, for whom one has small concern, while the most interesting personage, Loys de Dreux, the Knight Novice—described as one of the noblest and most generous of men—thinks so lightly of the vows of his order and of his Christian faith, that he is quite ready to go off with the Druses and live with them as a renegade in Mount Lebanon.

Luria is the grandest character of all Mr. Browning's plays; but we cannot conceive the existence of such a character out of Mr. Browning's pages; and he certainly would be utterly unintelligible to any English audience. Luria, the Moor of Florence, is a sentimentally magnanimous Othello without his passions and without his Desdemona. He stands at the head of a devoted army—having often achieved a series of victories which has made Florence superior to all her rivals, and because he becomes aware that the ungrateful city is endeavouring, after the manner of Italian republics, to disembarrass herself of a successful general, he, notwithstanding that he has unlimited opportunities of revenge or of making his escape, forestalls her purpose and takes poison. It certainly required an immense deal of ingenuity to invent reasons for this act of self-immolation; Mr. Browning has, however, found some, though we apprehend that none but minds of his own subtle and ingenious turn can possibly appreciate them. Luria, a bold and passionate son of the East, having been converted by his irresistible yearning for European civilization into a blind and child-like reverence for the beauty and glory of Florence, yielded up himself and his irresistible military genius to be a passive instrument of her aggrandisement. The wrong done to himself he imagined must have been caused by prior wrong committed by himself. And rather than that he should run the risk of injuring the city whose inviolability and existence is the prime article of his faith, either by being estranged from her or by his judicial death, he determines to end his existence. He lives long enough, however, to know that his sacrifice was uncalled-for; since the Florentines, on receiving irrefragable evidence of his probity, had repented of their proceedings, and abandoned the evidence against him. The tragedy, nevertheless, in point of style is the best in the volume; it is true to the manners of Italy in the middle ages, and contains some good characters. Tiburzio, the commander of the Pisans, Puccio, Luria's chief officer, are both noble natures, and Braccio, the Commissary of the Republic of Florence, and Husain, the Moor, the friend of Luria, are truly conceived and developed.

The fantastic piece, however, with the fantastic title, *Pippa Passes*, is perhaps the best known of all Mr. Browning's dramatic efforts, and deservedly so, for it combines all his peculiar excellences at the same time that it omits some of his characteristic defects. The notion of 'Pippa,' the obscure girl of the silk-mills, exercising, unknown to herself, a good influence over the four little dramas of the piece is pretty enough, notwithstanding that the songs she sings seem little calculated to move the actors of each separate intrigue in the way they do. The verses overheard by Jules the sculptor are an ingenious and appropriate introduction to his story, which leaves him married and determined to be happy with his bride; although he had been befooled into espousing a girl he had never seen before. On the other hand, the criminal amour of Ottima and the German Sebald, which contains a description of a love-scene of questionable decency in a forest, has so uncertain an ending that we cannot tell whether simple suicide, or suicide and murder, or double suicide, or anything of the kind, happens—we only know that Luca Gaddi, the old husband, has been made away with, although he does not seem to have interfered with the happiness of the lovers more than enough to give zest to their illicit intercourse. Luigi goes off on some indefinite errand of assassination, but we are unable to determine whether the strange song which Pippa sings in his hearing had the effect of strengthening or making him waiver in his purpose; and we are quite left in the dark as to what the Monsignore—the most natural character in the piece—means to do after he has circumvented his Intendant and discovers that Pippa is his niece, and the heiress of his brother's property, of which he has arrived to take possession. It is to be regretted, too, that the conception of Pippa's character, which is simple and playful, should be marred by the grotesque rhymes and metaphors which are put into her mouth. Can any one imagine a simple village girl getting out of bed and saying?—

> Day!
> Faster and more fast,
> *O'er nights brim, day boils at last;*
> Boils, pure gold, o'er the cloud-cup's brim
> Where spurting and supprest it lay.

The idea of a 'boiling day' is not likely to be associated with the cool breath of a New Year's morn in the mind of any one but a writer straining a metaphor. The following playful prattle about the sunbeam is more natural, but the jingle of 'bits' and 'wits' spoils it altogether:

> Aha, you foolhardy sunbeam—caught
> With a single splash from my ewer!
> You that would mock the best pursuer,
> Was my basin over-deep?
> One splash of water ruins you asleep,
> And up, up, fleet your brilliant bits
> Wheeling and counterwheeling,
> Reeling, broken beyond healing—
> Now grow together on the ceiling!
> That will task your wits!

The strangest puzzle, however, occurs at the close of the day, where we are entirely at a loss to know what the lark is expected to do:

> Oh, Lark, be day's apostle
> To mavis, merle and throstle,
> Bid them their betters jostle
> From day and its delights!
> But at night, brother Howlet, far over the woods,
> Toll the world to thy chantry;
> Sing to the bats' sleek sisterhoods
> Full complines with gallantry:

> Then, owls and bats, cowls and twats,
> Monks and nuns, in a cloister's moods,
> *Adjourn to the oak-stump pantry* !

We are led by the concluding line to speak of Mr. Browning's passion for doggerel rhymes, which is one of his most striking peculiarities, and one which no estimate of his poetry can omit to take notice of. In a piece like that called the 'Pied Piper of Hamelin', a tale written expressly for children, and which, though of a quainter fashion than the 'Ingoldsby Legends', is a poem of the same order, we expect to find such rhymes as we meet with in the speech of the rat, the sole survivor of his legion, when describing the peculiar fascination in the tones of the piper's melody, which induced all his brethren to drown themselves in the Weser:

> At the first shrill notes of the pipe,
> I heard a sound as of scraping tripe,
> And putting apples, wondrous ripe,
> Into a cider-press's gripe:
> And a moving away of pickle-tub-boards,
> And a leaving ajar of conserve-cupboards,
> And a drawing the corks of train-oil-flasks,
> And a breaking the hoops of butter-casks;
> And it seemed as if a voice
> (Sweeter far than by harp or by psaltery
> Is breathed) called out, Oh rats, rejoice!
> The world is grown to one vast drysaltery!
> So, munch on, crunch on, take your nuncheon,
> Breakfast, supper, dinner, luncheon!

Here such rhymes may be in their place, but 'The Flight of 'the Duchess', who goes away so strangely to Gypsy-land—a tale intended to have something of the pathetic about it—has still stranger and much coarser rhymes. The mother of the Duke, the dowager Duchess, who was part of the torment of the young Duchess's life, painted, and the teller of the tale, with some pretence of squeamishness, describes it thus:

> And were I not, as a man may say, cautious
> How I trench, more than needs, on the nauseous,
> I could favour you with sundry touches
> Of the paint-smutches with which the Duchess
> Heightened the mellowness of her cheek's yellowness
> (To get on faster) until at last her
> Cheek grew to be one master-plaster

> Of mucus and fucus from mere use of ceruse:
> In short, she grew from scalp to udder
> Just the object to make you shudder.

Progressing from hence, we find doggerel in Mr. Browning's love verses, doggerel in his artistic poems, and even his professedly religious piece, *Christmas Eve and Easter Day*, is written, for a considerable portion, in Hudibrastic doggerel rhyme. Mr. Browning can apparently never resist the fascination of doggerel when it occurs to him. His most popular lyrics are probably the three 'Cavalier Tunes.' In the first of them the jingle of *'Charles'* and *'carles'* caught his ear, and he thought it so good that he has repeated it twice over in three short verses, united with the further rhymes of *parles* and *snarls—Charles, carles, parles, Charles, snarls, carles*. These ballads, however, are among Mr. Browning's best; they are very spirited, and have a certain smack of the times about them, although no one could fancy the Cavaliers singing them. No Cavalier ever called himself a 'great-hearted gentleman', or talked about the 'hot day brightening to blue from its silver gray.' The quaintest specimen, perhaps, of all Mr. Browning's success in doggerel is his description of Nelson:

> Leaning with one shoulder digging,
> Jigging, as it were, and zig-zag-zigging
> Up against the mizen-rigging.

In fact, there can hardly be brought a single complete poem from these volumes which would not prove that Mr. Browning has an ear and a taste incapable of distinguishing sufficiently the delicacies of rhyme and rhythm to become a lyric poet: his very best passages of rhyme have a creak in them which sets the teeth on edge. One of his best songs, for example, is in *Pippa Passes*; it is the song sung by Pippa in the hearing of Jules the sculptor; but pretty as the thought is, the rhymes in two instances hardly seem above doggerel; the expression is bad, and the fourth line of the second stanza is, we think, the harshest we ever read:

> Give her but a least excuse to love me!
> When—where—
> How—can this arm establish her above me,
> If fortune fixed her as my lady there,
> There already, to eternally reprove me?
> ('Hist'—said Kate the queen;
> But 'Oh'—cried the maiden, binding her tresses,

' 'Tis only a page that carols unseen
Crumbling your hounds their messes!')
Is she wronged?—To the rescue of her honour,
My heart!
Is she poor?—What costs it to be styled a donor?
Merely an earth's to cleave, a sea's to part!
But that fortune should have thrust all this upon her!
('Nay, list,'—bade Kate the queen;
And still cried the maiden, binding her tresses,
"'Tis only a page that carols unseen
Fitting your hawks their jesses!')

Mr. Browning's religious feelings and his daring ingenuity of thought and invention have found congenial application in subjects in which a foreknowledge of the Advent of Christ is introduced, as by David in the very fine poem called 'Saul'; or as dimly known to Karshish, the Arab physician, by hearsay report and by examination of Lazarus; or as just known to 'Cleon', the Greek poet and philosopher, who is not certain whether Paulus, 'the barbarian Jew,' 'is not one with him'; or as more fully known to John in the 'Death in the Desert.' All these four poems display a different and remarkable power; and it is to be observed that the daring of the poet has increased with each new attempt in handling the awful theme.

It was a bold undertaking to re-sing the song with which David chased away the evil spirit of Saul; to commence with the celebration of the joys of the shepherd and the reaper—to pass onward through the raptures of manhood and of strength—of the hunter and the warrior—through the praise of exaltation and kingly glory of royalty—finally, to describe the ineffable mercy of the coming of Christ; but the poem has fulfilled its promise more completely than any other of the volumes. It has something like real rhythm in it, and possesses a solemn, and at the same time an easy flow, and is, for Mr. Browning, remarkably clear in expression. The description of Saul, and of the effect of the various portions of David's song upon him, is extremely imposing, and remains upon the imagination. Less praise, however, can, in our opinion, be accorded to the 'Epistle containing the strange Medical Experience of Karshish, the Arab Physician.' The subject is treated with all Mr. Browning's usual subtlety, quaintness, and ingenuity; but it seems to us irreverent in the highest degree to attempt to describe, through his three days' experience of the mysterious realms of death. The piece is full of life-like touches—as where the learned leech becomes half ashamed from time to time to dwell much upon the 'case' of a resuscitated man, every quack professing to do as much in these days, and then, while he makes his report to his master in the science, he turns aside to give other more scientific information:

> Why write of trivial matters, things of price
> Calling at every moment for remark?
> I noticed on the margin of a pool
> Blue-flowering borage, the Aleppo sort,
> Aboundeth, very nitrous. It is strange!

But these familiar allusions in the person of the Arab physician present a strange contrast to the supernatural element in the poem. The description of Lazarus, and of his three days' experience of the world beyond the grave, is the reverse of natural, and we trace the far-fetched artifices of Mr. Browning's invention in every line. Much more, however, do we object to see St. John on his death-bed made a medium for a writer to philosophize upon the Gospel in Platonic strains, and to add an apocryphal chapter to the New Testament. This latter poem, however, is so obscurely written, that it would puzzle an inquisition of theologians to find any other heresy in it than that of its conception. 'Cleon', on the other hand, is kept strictly within the limits of the reverential, and is extremely happy in its invention. It was suggested apparently by the words of St. Paul's address to the Athenians: 'As certain also of your own poets have said',—indicating that some of these already had had a foretaste of some of the truths of Christianity. Mr. Browning, therefore, exhibits Cleon, the Greek poet and philosopher, writing to his friend Protos 'in his tyranny', discoursing on man, mind and its destination, the necessity of a future life, and the probability of a revelation; all this while St. Paul was preaching close at hand, whose doctrines, however, he refused to hear:

> I dare at times imagine to my need
> Some future state revealed to us by Zeus,
> Unlimited in capability
> For joy, as this is in desire for joy,
> —To seek which, the joy-hunger forces us:
> That, stung by straitness of our life, made strait
> On purpose to make sweet the life at large—
> Freed by the throbbing impulse we call death
> We burst there as the worm into the fly,
> Who, while a worm still, wants his wings. But, no!
> Zeus has not yet revealed it; and, alas,

> *He must have done so, were it possible!*
> Live long and happy, and in that thought die,
> Glad for what was. Farewell. And for the rest,
> I cannot tell thy messenger aright
> Where to deliver what he bears of thine
> To one called Paulus—we have heard his fame
> Indeed, if Christus be not one with him—
> I know not, nor am troubled much to know.
> Thou canst not think a mere barbarian Jew,
> As Paulus proves to be, one circumcised,
> Hath access to a secret shut from us?
> Thou wrongest our philosophy, O king,
> In stopping to inquire of such an one,
> As if his answer could impose at all.
> He writeth, doth he? well, and he may write.
> Oh, the Jew findeth scholars! certain slaves
> Who touched on this same isle, preached him and Christ;
> And (as I gathered from a bystander)
> Their doctrines could be held by no sane man.

The subtle reasoning in the course of the poem on the progressive nature of man's mental faculties is very characteristic of Mr. Browning, although there is of course much to be said against it, and of its applicability in the mouth of Cleon:

> We of these latter days, with greater mind
> Than our forerunners, since more composite,
> Look not so great, beside their simple way,
> To a judge who only sees one way at once,
> One mind-point, and no other at a time,—
> Compares the small part of a man of us
> With some whole man of the heroic age,
> Great in his way—not ours, nor meant for ours;
> And ours is greater, had we skill to know.

> The grapes which dye thy wine, are richer far
> Through culture, than the wild wealth of the rock;
> The suave plum than the savage-tasted drupe;
> The pastured honey-bee drops choicer sweet;
> The flowers turn double, and the leaves turn flowers;
> That young and tender crescent-moon, thy slave,
> Sleeping upon her robe as if on clouds,
> Refines upon the women of my youth.
> What, and the soul alone deteriorates?

I have not chanted verse like Homer's, no—
Nor swept string like Terpander, no—nor carved
And painted men like Phidias and his friend:
I am not great as they are, point by point:
But I have entered into sympathy
With these four, running these into one soul,
Who, separate, ignored each others' arts.

An equally characteristic class of poems with the above are those which deal with ancient and little-known artists of music and poetry; such as 'Old Pictures in Florence', 'Fra Lippo Lippi', 'A Toccata of Galuppi's', 'Master Hugues of Saxe-Gotha', and 'Abt Vogler'. The musical pieces, and that of 'Master Hugues of Saxe-Gotha' especially, show what an eccentric delight Mr. Browning finds in losing himself utterly in an obscure subject, and how entirely congenial to his own nature is the strange rhapsody of the organist who remains by himself in the old church with the lights expiring one by one, trying to wring out every crotchet of subtle meaning from the over-wrought *fugue* of Master Hugues, and has to grope his way from the loft to the foot of the 'rotten-runged rat-riddled stairs'. The piece called 'Fra Lippo Lippi' is also a very quaint mixture of strange humour, realistic treatment, and artistic theorising. No other writer could have conceived so strange a character as this wine-bibbing licentious monk and painter, dropping out of the convent-window by night, and caught by the watch while reeling back to his convent, to whom, with sundry snatches of song, he unburdens himself about his own life in particular, and art in general. In 'Andrea del Sarto', Mr. Browning has been less happy, and his piece contrasts unfavourably with the little drama of Alfred de Musset on the same subject—so finely, clearly, and delicately touched, as, indeed, all his pieces are, and full of action and interest. It is, however, in dramatic monologues of this kind that Mr. Browning has achieved the most complete success. He has the faculty of conceiving circumstantially, and sympathising with artist-natures of singular aims and secluded merit. Among such conceptions must also be classed the singular story, the 'Grammarian's Funeral', which, in spite of its extreme oddity of thought and imagination, is a noble elegy of one of the indefatigable seekers after learning such as lived shortly after the revival of learning.

To this curious sympathy with exceptional classes and persons we must attribute the excellence of portraiture of all his monks and ecclesiastics, from the monk of the 'Soliloquy of the Spanish Cloister' to the very confidential 'Bishop Blougram': the Monsignore in *Pippa Passes* and Ogniben, the Pontifical Legate, in the *Soul's Tragedy*, are also equally lifelike. For Mr. Browning's taste for human nature being something of the nature of a taste for rare china or odd old-fashioned weapons, he has, by dint of concentrating all the interest into one character and all the action into one incident, produced some very characteristic studies. It is, however, here not so much the poetry, as the very great condensation of a whole life or a drama into a few lines, which excites the reader's interest; and so artificial a production, where the whole of the speaker's life or character is to be derived from his own words, must always retain something of an air of improbability. In Mr. Tennyson's 'St. Simon Stylites', which, excepting, perhaps, the 'Ulysses' of the same writer, is the only analogous poem in the language, the monologue is natural from the very situation of the solitary fanatic; but in the piece called 'My Last Duchess', it is very unnatural that the Duke should betray himself so entirely to the envoy who comes to negotiate a new marriage as to let him have the same opportunity of knowing as we have ourselves that his cold austerity and pride had been the death of his late wife; and in the 'Bishop ordering his Tomb' on his death-bed we never lose the peculiar accents of Mr. Browning's quaintness for a moment. It is, for example, Mr. Browning who is speaking through the Bishop's mouth when he says—

> And then how I shall lie through centuries,
> And hear the blessed mutter of the mass,
> And see God made and eaten all day long,
> And feel the steady candle-flame, and taste
> Good strong thick stupifying incense smoke!

These lines have a characteristic aptness about them, but no bishop would describe Church ceremonies in this way. Nevertheless, the portrait of the old voluptuous antique-hunting, marble-purloining Roman ecclesiastic is one which cannot fail to strike and to please also to a certain extent; it is a rich example of Mr. Browning's humour in dealing with ecclesiastical subjects, which, however, finds its quaintest expression in the 'Heretic's Tragedy',—a Middle-Age Interlude, where the grotesque chuckle of triumph, of self-satisfied, undoubting mediaeval intolerance, over the burning of the Grand Master of the Templars at Paris, after two centuries have elapsed, is most characteristically but not pleasingly, rendered in the 'Conceit of Master Gysbrecht.'

The last passage we have quoted leads us to speak of Mr. Browning's descriptive power, which is remarkable. His faculty of word-painting, and of seeing quaint resemblances in dissimilar objects, by some happy touch often vividly calls up a scene before the imagination. In his two Italian sketches, the one called 'Up at a Villa—down in the City, as distinguished by an Italian person of quality', and 'The Englishman in Sorrento', Mr. Browning's descriptive faculty has produced some pleasant effects. In the following lines we are transplanted at once into the middle of some provincial Italian capital:

Ere opening your eyes in the city, the blessed church-bells begin:
No sooner the bells leave off, than the diligence rattles in:
You get the pick of the news, and it costs you never a pin.
By and by there's the travelling doctor gives pills, lets blood, draws teeth;
Or the Pulcinello-trumpet breaks up the market beneath.
At the post-office such a scene-picture—the new play, piping hot!
And a notice how, only this morning, three liberal thieves were shot.
Above it, behold the archbishop's most fatherly of rebukes,
And beneath, with his crown and his lion, some little new law of the Duke's!

. . . . .

BANG, *whang, whang* goes the drum, *tootle-te-tootle* the fife;
No keeping one's haunches still: it's the greatest pleasure in life.

The Sorrento poem is also a most vivid picture of Italian autumnal life, and has justly been cited by Mr. Ruskin as a choice example of this kind of painting.

Another peculiar class of poems forms no small portion of Mr. Browning's first volume, and this may be called the Sophistical,— embodying in rhyme the attempt to make the worse appear the better side. One of the most striking of these is the poem called 'The Glove.' Everybody knows Schiller's ballad on the same subject: how the Knight Delorges on being bidden by his lady to bring up her glove which she had wilfully thrown into the lion's den, leapt, brought it back, and threw it in her face. The ballad is not one of Schiller's best, but Schiller and the world in general have thought the knight to have been in the right. Mr. Browning, however, thinks there is something to be said for the lady, and he has written a poem on the subject. The poem is as ingenious as any of Mr. Browning's, but we doubt if the lady's defence of herself will make many converts, and it is suspicious, to say the least of it, that her excuse is pretty nearly as long as Schiller's whole poem. Perhaps the most successful as well as the most striking of all the poems of this class is that styled 'Holy Cross Day',—the day on which, before the present Pontificate, the Jews were compelled to attend on an annual

sermon at Rome. It does not, however, begin very promisingly. A Jew
is speaking:

> Fee, faw, fum! bubble and squeak!
> Blessedest Thursday's the fat of the week.
> Rumble and tumble, sleek and rough,
> Stinking and savoury, smug and gruff,
> Take the church-road, for the bell's due chime
> Gives us the summons—'t is sermon-time.
> Boh, here's Barnabas! Job, that's you?
> Up stumps Solomon—bustling too?
> Shame, man! greedy beyond your years
> To handsel the bishop's shaving shears?
> Fair play's a jewel! leave friends in the lurch?
> Stand on a line ere you start for the church.

The sermon is delivered, and its effect on the Jew audience and the
rascally converts, the black sheep of the tribe, is told in the same
grotesque but graphic fashion; but the most striking portion of the
poem is the Rabbi Ben Ezra's song of death which the unconverted sang
in church while obliged to sit there after the Bishop's sermon and
meditate on the truths he has been endeavouring to enforce upon them.

'Evelyn Hope' is one of the prettiest of Mr. Browning's love pieces,
because it is one of the simplest; though we by no means concur in the
exaggerated praises which have been heaped upon it. An elderly student,
of about fifty years of age, fell in love with Evelyn Hope, who died at
sixteen:

> For God's hand beckoned unawares,
> And the sweet white brow was all of her.

The lover speculates, in Mr. Browning's peculiar fashion, on what was
the use of his attachment:

> Is it too late then, Evelyn Hope?
>   What, your soul was pure and true,
> The good stars met in your horoscope,
>   Made you of spirit, fire and dew—
> And, just because I was thrice as old
>   And our paths in the world diverged so wide,
> Each was nought to each, must I be told?
>   We were fellow mortals, nought beside?
> No, indeed! for God above
>   Is great to grant, as mighty to make,
> And creates the love to reward the love:

I claim you still, for my own love's sake!
 Delayed it may be for more lives yet,
  Though worlds I shall traverse, not a few:
 Much is to learn and much to forget
  Ere the time be come for taking you.

This, an unjilted lover, consoles himself by placing a leaf in Evelyn Hope's dead hand and persuading himself she will understand all about it when she awakes:

I loved you, Evelyn, all the while!
 My heart seemed full as it could hold—
There was place and to spare for the frank young smile
 And the red young mouth and the hair's young gold.
So, hush—I will give you this leaf to keep—
 See, I shut it inside this sweet cold hand.
There, that is our secret! go to sleep;
 You will wake, and remember, and understand.

While on the subject of Mr. Browning's love poems, we must not omit to mention that his lovers are prepared to go lengths in the demonstration of their affection which we hardly like to contemplate. One lover concludes a love poem by exclaiming—

There you stand
Warm too, and white too; would this wine
Had washed all over that body of yours,
Ere I drunk it, and you down with it thus!

Another lover, we are informed by the lady, used to kiss her body 'all over till it burned.' Their playfulness is sometimes of an equally strange character. In a 'Lovers' Quarrel', two lovers are blocked up together for some time in a snow-storm; to wile the time away they devise games out of straws, draw each other's faces in the ashes of the grate, chatter like church daws, look in *The Times*, an old one we suppose, find there

A scold
At the Emperor deep and cold.

Practise table-turning, walk about the room with arms round each other's necks, while the lady teaches the gentleman

To flirt a fan
As the Spanish ladies can;

and the gentleman playfully takes the lady and

> Tints her lip
> With a burnt stick's tip,
> And she turns into such a man!
> Just the two spots that span
> Half the bill of the male swan.

In such endearments they pass away the time, until

> A shaft from the Devil's bow
> Pierced to their ingle-glow,
> And the friends were friend and foe!

Winter has fled, but the lover now that they are estranged wishes the spring away and November back.

> Could not November come,
> Were the noisy birds struck dumb
>   At the warning slash
>   Of the driver's lash—
> *I would laugh like the valiant Thumb*
>   *Facing the castle glum*
>   *And the giant's fee-faw-fum*!

In fact, he wishes the world to be stripped of all the adornments which make it easier for them to remain apart, then

> The world's hangings ripped,
> They were both in a bare-walled crypt!
> Each in the crypt would cry
> But one freezes here! and why?
>   When a heart as chill
>   At my own would thrill
> Back to life, and its fires out-fly?
>   Heart, shall we live or die?
> The rest, . . . settle it by and by!

The lover having concluded that each of them would cry out thus, in their hypothetical November, declares that it is twelve o'clock, and concludes with a meteorological prediction that a storm will come:

> In the worst of the storm's uproar,
>   I shall pull her through the door,
>   I shall have her for evermore!

Among, however, Mr. Browning's inexhaustible variety of poems about lovers—jilted lovers, deserted lovers, quarrelling lovers, forgiving lovers, fortunate lovers, unfortunate lovers, and lovers of every denomination, with their infinite perplexities of love, we come occasionally upon touches as delicate as the following in 'The Lost Mistress', where the lover considers how he shall behave towards the lady in future:

> Yes! I will say what mere friends say,
>   Or only a thought stronger;
> I will hold your hand but as long as all may,
>   *Or so very little longer!*

The self-questioning of a deserted mistress has some noticeable touches in spite of the lop-sided metre:

> Was it something said,
>   Something done,
> Vexed him? was it touch of hand,
>   Turn of head?
> Strange! that very way
>   Love began:
> I as little understand
>   Love's decay.

The peculiar humour of the 'Lovers' Quarrel', which we have just noticed, leads us to speak of Mr. Browning's humour generally, which is of as singular a character as his poetry—sometimes grim and grotesque as in the 'Heretic's Tragedy', 'Holy Cross Thursdays', 'Caliban upon Setebos'; sometimes refining, elaborate, like 'Bishop Blougram's Apology', or 'Mr. Sludge the Medium'; sometimes fantastic and trivial, like 'Nationality in Drinks', but always partaking of the same queer extravagance, such as we find in the strange poem called 'Sibrandus Schafnaburgensis.' Here some solitary joker reads an old pedantic volume in his garden:

> In the white of a matin-prime
> Just when the birds sang all together.

Having read the book through from beginning to end, for what reason, except mere whim, we are unable to divine, he proceeds to take his revenge on the volume by dropping it into the mossy hollow of an old plum-tree, in whose bottom there was a stagnant pool of rain water; he then goes into his home and brings out a loaf, half a cheese, and a bottle of Chablis, lays on the grass and forgets 'the oaf over a jolly chapter of Rabelais.' After awhile, when the spider had had time enough to spin his web over the buried volume, 'and *sat in the midst with arms akimbo,*' the ballad-maker took pity for learning's sake, and got a rake and fished up the 'delectable treatise', dried it and put it back on his book-shelf. The hero then proceeds to make merry over the past sufferings of his victim:

> How did he like it when the live creatures
>   Tickled and toused and browsed him all over,
> And worm, slug, elf, with serious features,
>   Came in, each one, for his right of trover?
> —When the water-beetle with great blind deaf face
>   Made of her eggs the stately deposit,
> And the newt borrowed just so much of the preface
>   As tiled in the top of his black wife's closet?

Cognate with Mr. Browning's strange sense of humour is his introduction of new interjections and combinations of letters into his poetry to express certain sounds. Thus we have *Gr—sh* and a variety of other new interjections, *Hy! Zy! Hine!* to represent the sound of a bell; *Bang-whang-whang* for a drum, *tootle-te-tootle* for a fife, *wheet-wheet* for a mouse, &c. The peculiar names of such personages as Bluphocks, Blougram, Gigadibs, &c., must be ascribed to the same quality.

But, whether in sport or in earnest, Mr. Browning has always chosen to adopt methods of execution, and to remain apart from the beaten track of the ordinary world; and we can imagine him sharing in the feelings of his own 'Pictor Ignotus' who refuses, though he possesses the power of painting 'pictures like that youth's you praise so,' to enter into competition with him, and thus expresses his contempt for the vulgar crowd—

> . . . Who summoned those cold faces that begun
> To press on me and judge me?   Though I stooped
>   Shrinking, as from the soldiery a nun,
> They drew me forth, and spite of me . . . enough!
>   These buy and sell our pictures, take and give,
> Count them for garniture and household-stuff,
>   And where they live our pictures needs must live
> And see their faces, listen to their prate,
>   Partakers of their daily pettiness,
> Discussed of—'This I love, or this I hate,
>   This likes me more, and this affects me less!'
> Wherefore I chose my portion.

So Mr. Browning has chosen his portion, and the popularity which he has despised will in all probability never be thrust upon him.

Having a sincere respect for what we know of Mr. Browning's character, and for his literary industry, we have not sought in the foregoing remarks to disparage or ridicule the efforts of his singular genius; but to enable our readers to form an impartial opinion of his merits or defects from the extracts we have made. Some of them will doubtless think that we have devoted too much of our space to these productions, and will ask, with alarm, whether these are specimens of the latest fashion of English poetry. We confess that it is to ourselves a subject of amazement that poems of so obscure and uninviting a character should find numerous readers, and that successive editions of them should be in demand. Yet this is undoubtedly the case; and far from having reason to complain of neglect, Mr. Browning has a considerable number of admirers in England, and more, we believe, in America. It would seem that in this practical and mechanical age, there is some attraction in wild and extravagant language—some mysterious fascination in obscure half-expressed thoughts. Mr. Browning in truth more nearly resembles the American writers Emerson, Wendell Holmes, and Bigelow, than any poet of our own country. Tried by the standards which have hitherto been supposed to uphold the force and beauty of the English tongue and of English literature, his works are deficient in the qualities we should desire to find them. We do not believe that they will survive, except as a curiosity and a puzzle. But they undoubtedly exercise a certain degree of influence over the taste of the present generation; and on this ground we think they deserve the notice we have bestowed upon them.

121. From an unsigned review, *The Dublin University Magazine*

November 1864, lxiv. 573-9

Several of the earlier poems in Browning's last volume, *Dramatis Personae* partake but too much of that obscurity, of which he gave so surpassing an example in *Sordello*. 'James Lee' is, we believe, a theme of unrequited love; and here and there, where the meaning is intelligible, the feeling is delicately touched, and the verses musical. 'Gold Hair', a legend of the Pornic, is a pretty story, and worked out with a little more definition than the other. 'The Worst of It' is very cloudy, as is also 'Dis Aliter Visum, or Le Byron de nos Jours', and 'Too Late'. The first theme in the volume, indeed, which possesses a clear poetic interest, is that entitled 'Abt Vogler', a monologue of the musician, after he had been extemporizing on a musical instrument of his invention. The dramatic soliloquy or monologue is a form which Browning much affects, and which is admirably chosen to body forth the peculiar turn of his mind. Many of the first pieces in his previous volumes are thrown into this shape, and, with the exception of three or four, all in his *Dramatis Personae. . . .*

There are many shorter poems in the volume, such as 'Confessions', 'May and Death', 'Youth and Art', &c., which are treated with Browning's characteristic dramatic power; and also a long soliloquy, 'Mr. Sludge, the Medium', in which he develops, with great power, though somewhat too much at length, the type of a complete scoundrel. So disagreeable a subject, and one admitting so little of any poetic faculty except the dramatic, was hardly worthy of such enlarged treatment; but, taking it as it is, rude and plain, in its prosaic language, it must be admitted to be drawn with great power of characterization, and knowledge of the basest springs of nature.

The power and beauty displayed in Browning's previous volumes—the striking delineation of character, dramatic interest, daring descriptive faculty, novelty of image therein exhibited, are sufficient to insure him a high place as a poet in the estimation of posterity, even despite the obscurity more than German, in which but too many of the productions of his genius are clouded, and their effect deteriorated. Upon the whole, his *Dramatis Personae*, in which a large amount of the mistiness referred to is displayed, must be regarded as inferior to his previous poetic essays, with the exception of its most characteristic poem, the Soliloquy of Caliban. The critical eye of succeeding ages will, doubtless, classify, both as regards originality and so far as style is concerned, the prose writer Carlyle with the poet Browning.

122. From an unsigned article, 'Mr. Browning and the *Edinburgh Review*', *The Saturday Review*

7 January 1865, xix. 15–17

This spirited rebuttal of No. 120 pleased Browning, who wrote to Julia Wedgwood in a postscript, 'Hasn't Perida [a fanciful name for Browning, derived from the legend of a Rabbi Perida who ground each lesson into his scholars by repeating it four hundred times] just got some nice tall fellow to take his part in this *Saturday Review!*' *Robert Browning and Julia Wedgwood*, p. 111.

Is the *Edinburgh*, our venerable and distinguished contemporary, behind or before the age? This obviously delicate question, although we hear it asked not less than four times every year, is one which we have, in general, forborne to meddle with. But in its number of last October the *Edinburgh* presented us with an article on Mr. Browning's poetry, and on Mr. Browning himself, which, both by the attitude throughout assumed by the writer, and by certain critical frailties that we shall have to point out in his performance, puts the above dilemma so forcibly before us that it is impossible, as a piece of our literary functions, not to bring the case under the eyes of our readers. Having done this, our part will have been fulfilled, and we shall leave to them the task of deciding.

We shall not, of course, attempt here any estimate of Mr. Browning's place in poetry. The opinion of this journal has been already more than once expressed on the subject, and, in common with the great majority of critics, we have recognised his keen intellectual insight, high moral purpose, depth and tenderness in delineating human passion, and singularly vivid faculty of painting in words—those qualities, we presume, which, to the 'amazement' of the *Edinburgh Reviewer*, have rendered it 'vain to deny that he has won for himself an influence among readers of poetry second only to the Laureate'. We have also endeavoured to do justice to the novelty and force of the themes selected by the most original of contemporary poets; whilst the fact has not been concealed that Mr. Browning anticipates much too often that his readers will be not only as cultivated, but as intelligent as himself, and has never aimed at a mass-popularity; nay, that, like all writers of a subtle cast of mind (Shakspeare and Shelley are examples), he is apt to entangle the reader in labyrinthine thoughts and verbal perplexities. We have recapitulated these points simply for the sake of clearness; for there is no reason why the most fervent of Mr. Browning's admirers should formally undertake his defence against a critic who appears totally incapable of understanding him. . . .

Leaving, however, this conjectural ground, we will try to give such an idea of the method of our Jeffrey Redivivus as shall explain why we think him worth examining. It is not to be understood that he altogether ignores Mr. Browning's merit. Here and there, indeed, he makes a vague attempt at grasping the subject of a piece, failing where it is not of the simplest character, but more often contenting himself with some indefinite word of compliment, and letting us carefully know that he 'by no means concurs in the exaggerated praises which have been heaped upon' such a poem as Evelyn Hope. Of an attempt to judge the poet's genius as a whole, of poetical discrimination, there is no trace. It is a sufficient proof of the last assertion, that he supposes Browning to resemble Emerson. The poet's works are submitted to a kind of bit-by-bit process, interspersing two or three lines of verse with a paragraph of prose, in which the writer perfectly accomplishes his purpose of making us feel the whole difference between the style of Mr. Browning and the style of an *Edinburgh* Reviewer. One is allowed to see throughout that he is half ashamed to have to review such an author at all, and that if he had not, as he is pleased to say—in both senses of the word, impertinently—'a sincere respect for what we know of Mr. Browning's character', he would, in fact, never have thought him deserving of the notice he has bestowed upon him. Everywhere we find him warning Mr. Browning that this or that is quite wrong, and informing him how (on pain of being told that 'his works are deficient in the qualities *we* should desire to find [in?] them'), he ought to have composed poems which are among the most finished and deeply conceived in our modern literature. Thus, in the Last Duchess—a page long since placed near Mr. Tennyson's Ulysses by the admirers of exquisite poetical characterization—Mr. Browning's main aim or idea was to set forth an historical fact, the security of insolence and lust reached by one of the Italian tyrants of the Sforza breed. That the Duke should speak in accordance with such a nature is precisely what the *Reviewer* picks out as 'very unnatural'. In his Kharshish, again, the poet describes how an Arabian physician, who has met with Lazarus after his restoration to life, speculates and wonders at the miracle. On this the comment is—

The description of Lazarus, and of his three days' experience of the world beyond the grave, is *the reverse of natural*;

which, we imagine, is precisely what readers who believe in the miraculous would expect to find it. . . .

A critic must assuredly be greatly before or greatly behind his age who now-a-days can venture to assume this style. We doubt whether, even in Jeffrey's time, it would have been quite admissible, and must rather look back to the golden period when the relations of literature to the public were expressed by the position of poet and patron. Generally, however, our critic's aim is to bring as much as he can venture of Browning's poems within the limits of that 'theory of the obscure' as illustrations of which his primary purpose is to treat them. A number of specimens are quoted to support the theory. The majority of these appear to us perfectly clear. We are sure they would not afford a moment's difficulty to any average schoolboy of poetical taste; and even in the entire absence of it, there is nothing which common power to understand English should fail to comprehend. In one case, the critic—who gives us his oracular decision about the drama, as about everything else in or out of his way—is staggered by a graceful but obvious bit of by-play between Strafford and Lady Carlisle. In another, he is unable to comprehend how a window can be opened from the outside. The Ride to Aix, again, is one of the author's most popular pieces. We have met with it in a child's collection. And it would be thought a conceited puppy of a child who should pretend that it was 'utterly spoiled by Mr. Browning's abhorrence of lucidity', find it 'fatal to its general success' that the poet has not mentioned the specific news which was carried, or proceed, in place of enjoying these brilliant verses, to put to his mother such questions as—

If 'Dirck' is 'he' in the first line, why should he not be 'he' in the second? Why did not Roland's rider put his riding-gear in good order before starting?

And then the critic goes on to complain that someone who asked in *Notes and Queries* 'what all the galloping is about', got no answer. Has this writer never heard of poetical invention? Does he confound a poem with a despatch-box, or think that Mr. Browning should have described the ride in the spirit of a Foreign Office messenger? But we are ashamed to weary the reader with such ineptitudes . . . .

Sordello, however, is the Reviewer's greatest perplexity. In finding this poem obscure, he is for once in complete agreement, we believe, with all the world, Mr. Browning included; who, when reprinting this vague though gorgeous youthful sketch, has acknowledged its many faults of expression, and explained why he thought it profitless to try to rectify them. The *Edinburgh Reviewer*, after giving an outline of the preface in which no trace of this acknowledgment appears, proceeds to quote a passage from the Fifth Book. And we at once admit, with him, that to this, as it stands, 'we are unable to give any meaning whatever.' Yet, difficult as the task may seem in the case of such a critic, we are not without hopes that we can here do a little to remove what he very properly calls 'the peculiar character of its obscurity.' For if he will turn again to the passage alluded to (page 404 of the edition which he professes to be using), by careful scrutiny he may discover that, before the first line of his quotation, come five lines and a half, separated from his first line by a comma, and containing the general proposition of which what he has quoted is the exemplification. If even this process fails in removing 'the peculiar character of its obscurity', we will aid him by furnishing an exact parallel. Should he find some brother critic complaining of the obscurity of Milton, and incapable of 'giving any meaning whatever' to the single passage—

> Of that forbidden tree, whose mortal taste
> Brought death into the world, and all our woe;

or vainly trying to paraphrase the isolated line,

> Of man's first disobedience, and the fruit;

we almost fancy that he may at last, for his own perplexity, find one plausible solution. And we hope no 'goodnatured friend' will ever be impertinent enough to supply him with another.

We have now given our readers materials enough to judge of this writer's capacity for poetical criticism. Accuracy in plain matter of fact is a much humbler portion of the critic's task, no doubt, than the compounding of epithets and the utterance of oracles. Yet the world has a habit of expecting correctness of statement, even from the most capable of poetical reviewers. We will test that of the writer before us by a single paragraph. Before proceeding to a final verdict against Mr. Browning's merits as a dramatist, he describes the theatre of thirty years ago, when the 'tone and pathos of real tragic feeling' (whatever the 'pathos of feeling' may be) were alive, and the stage 'had not yet become the thing which it now is':

> Great, then, was the expectation of those in the secret when it was known that Mr. Macready had undertaken to bring out *at Drury Lane* a play called *Strafford,* by Mr. Browning—an expectation doomed to disappointment; for *Strafford* was *as complete a failure* as was the *Blot in the 'Scutcheon. King Victor and King Charles,* and *Colombe's Birthday,* were played subsequently at the Haymarket, but none of them succeeded in interesting the audience.

Now here are at least four palpable blunders. 'The expectation of those in the secret' of *Strafford* was certainly 'doomed to disappointment', for it was at Covent Garden that the drama was performed. *King Victor* was not 'played at the Haymarket', nor did it fail 'in interesting the audience', for the best of all reasons—it was never played at all. And for the critic's most emphatic instance, the 'complete failure' of *Strafford,* let us respectfully direct his attention to the *Edinburgh Review* for July 1837, page 132, where he will find the following words, given in explanation why the article on *Strafford,* which they open, was written:

> This is a play which, aided by the exertions of Mr. Macready and one or two more of the most noted actors of the day, *has had a considerable success* on the London theatre this year. Low as the condition of our national stage at present is, *this favourable run of a simple historical play . . .* is a phenomenon to which we feel ourselves called upon to attend.

Were the 'shade of Jeffrey' to appear among us, we are almost afraid that the unlucky Reviewer of 1864 would be the first victim on whom he would long to bestow one of his 'hard-handed castigations.'

Now, leaving to the discrimination of our readers—those especially who may be induced by our brief sketch to turn to the great original— the answer to that inquiry with which we started, let us, in concluding, deprecate altogether the idea that our remarks have been inspired by anything except a spirit of the sincerest goodwill to our respected contemporary. Vexed and surprised as we are to find such a paper within the ancient blue and yellow covers, yet, considering the inevitable difficulties and accidents of conducting a review, we are gladly disposed to give the worthy editor the benefit of a conjecture that the offender may have slipped in by mere oversight. The fact that it appeared in the recess number of the *Edinburgh* may be thought perhaps to support this partial palliation of what, in all seriousness, we must take leave to call the most complete literary *fiasco* which any of our Quarterlies have perpetrated for very many years. No Review, it must be owned, can now hope to make or mar a poet's fortunes after the fashion of the *Edinburgh* and the *Quarterly* in the days of Jeffrey and of Gifford. Nor, amongst other causes, is it difficult to find the main reason of this. As poetical arbitrators, they died of Jeffreyism and of Giffordism.

> The oracles are dumb:
> No voice or hideous hum
> Runs through the arched roof in words deceiving:—

Yet at times, it would appear, some Pythoness 'shade of Jeffrey', puffed up with the dregs of the original *afflatus*, may be found 'humming' pompously about the shrine—her face, in Mr. Browning's phrase, wearing

> That hateful smirk of boundless self-conceit

which makes her take for oracles what to the world at large seem ravings. When this occurs, our leading question is pressed irresistibly upon all intelligent readers of the *Edinburgh*.

123. 'Modern Poets', *The Times*

11 January 1865, p. 12

Here, in this extract from an unsigned article, is an interesting expression of the insularity which so often cropped up in mid-Victorian England. Browning himself shared it, at least to the extent that, after Elizabeth's death, he brought his son back to England to get the stamp of character which, Browning felt, came only with an English education.

If banishment from England may be described as a misfortune for Mrs. Browning, who, it may be, in our trying English climate might never have been able to do any work at all, what was it for her husband? He, of all men, needed the English air, and he went away from it. His writings abound in faults which, perhaps, it never was in his power to get rid of; but his only chance of working himself free from them was in living among us, and learning to think more as we think, to feel as we feel, and to understand what language suits us best. How could he do so beside the Arno? We regret to say that the difficulties of his style are at present so great as to prevent him not only from being enjoyed, but even from being understood. Poetry is with him an occult science. All poetry has to do with occult associations, and meanings of words and thoughts which it is impossible to analyze, but on the surface it is generally simple and clear enough. Mr. Browning, however, having a strong sense of an occult power behind and within the language of the poet, is determined to be obviously occult, and by elliptical constructions, digressions, interpolations, dark hints and darker sayings, seems to talk riddles and to make poetry a game of hide and seek. . . .

. . . Mr. Browning asks too much of his readers. He has no right to expect that for the sake of the good things which he has to bestow he will find readers to encounter the difficulties of his style which he deliberately sets in their way. It is sometimes as difficult to follow out the line of his thought as to keep up with an argument conducted by Kant, or Schelling, or Hegel.

. . . After we have said the worst, however, about Mr. Browning's obscurities, there remain in his pages the materials of great poetry, there remains in him the semblance of a great poet. If his thought is difficult to reach, it is generally worth reaching. He may be described as a most learned poet whose learning oppresses him and makes him stagger, but his erudition, nevertheless, is very valuable, and gives a rich flavour to his sentiment. Nobody ever accused Robert Browning of having little to say. His fault is that he has too much to say, and that he compresses it into too small a compass. His style is full of jerks and wants continuity, but those who are willing to submit to a good deal of jolting will find themselves in company with a man of large mind and of deep thought. The true Browningites are so keenly impressed by his power that they place him above everybody else, and one of them has been heard to say in deprecation of his own liking—'I must confess that to read Browning is like dram drinking; it destroys the taste for everything else; every other liquor seems poor in comparison.' He will be found at his best in the first volume of his collected works, but also he shows extraordinary power in his last volume, published a few months ago under the title of *Dramatis Personae*. Here it is true that he defies us with his obscurities, as in the first poem of the volume, 'James Lee', which it will puzzle many a reader to follow out; but, on the other hand, no one can master the subtleties of such a poem as 'The Death in the Desert', in which the Apostle John discourses of the mysteries of the faith, or 'Caliban upon Setebos'.

124. Gerald Massey, *The Quarterly Review*

July 1865, cxviii. 77–105

From his unsigned review.

Massey (1828–1907), an active Christian Socialist, was a person of remarkably broad interests: he wrote poetry and theological speculations; he was a prominent Egyptologist and student of spiritualism. He is thought to have been the original of George Eliot's Felix Holt.

At a time like the present, when the tendency is for minds to grow more and more alike, all thinking the same thoughts with the regularity of Wordsworth's forty cattle feeding as one; when for a single original poet, like Mr. Tennyson, we have a hundred tuneful echoes, and one popular novelist has his scores of imitators, we think that a writer of Mr. Browning's powers ought to be better understood than he is, and the discrepancy lessened betwixt what is *known* of him by the few, and what is *thought* of him by the many. He has qualities such as should be cherished by the age we live in, for it needs them. His poetry ought to be taken as a tonic. He grinds no mere hand-organ or music-box of pretty tunes; he does not try to attract the multitude with the scarlet dazzle of poppies in his corn; he is not a poet of similes, who continually makes comparisons which are the mere play of fancy; he has nothing of the ordinary *technique* of poetry; he has felt himself driven, somewhat consciously, to the opposite course of using, as much as possible, the commonest forms of speech. The language of his verse is generally as sturdy as is the prose of Swift or De Foe. Certainly these homely words are to be found in singular places, saying strange things now and again,—many things not easily understood, and many which good taste must condemn,—but the poetry is full, nevertheless, of hearty English character. In his process of thinking, he is the exact reverse of those writers who are for making the most of their subject in expression. Mr. Browning can never concentrate sufficiently.

[Summarizes Browning's career and reputation, then turns to a discussion of 'A Grammarian's Funeral', quoting the last sixteen lines.]

Now, to our feeling, the movement of this verse is most dramatic, and answers admirably to the character of the poem. It conveys a great sense of going up-hill, and the weight of the burden,—together with the exultation of the bearers, which gives them strength to mount; it *toils* upward step by step—long line and short—best-foot forward,—and altogether carries out the idea of a spirit that climbed in life, and a burial that shall afford the dead rest at the effort's end, with his resting-place in the pathway of the Morning.

We must understand the principles of Mr. Browning's art, then, before we shall be on the way for interpreting his poems rightly. A good deal of the difficulty in getting at them lies here in the beginning. Next we must try to enter into the nature of his genius, and its peculiar predilections. He has 'strange far-flights' of imagination. He is fond of dwelling abroad, and of working widely apart from the life and circumstances of our time. He loves a gnarly character, or a knotty problem; a conflict that is mental rather than emotional; and he has given full scope to his choice at times in the strangest rhymes on record. He is not yet entirely free from the mannerisms of *Sordello*. Nor does he allow sufficiently for the difficulties of his own conditions, and for those of the reader in following him. Here, we think, is a grave fault in art. But, what strikes us as one of the greatest drawbacks of all, is this: that, whereas the subject selected, the character portrayed, is often of the remotest from the common apprehension, it is treated in a manner totally new to objective poetry. The objective poets of the past dealt with their subjects in a simpler way, and more in the mass.

[Massey turns, finally, to one character-portrait he particularly admires —that of St. John in 'A Death in the Desert'.]

The dying man rises and dilates, 'as on a wind of prophecy', whilst in solemn vision his spirit ranges forward into the far-off time, when in many lands men will be saying, 'Did John live at all? and did he say *he saw* the veritable Christ?' And, as he grows more and more inspired, and the energy of his spirit appears to rend itself almost free from the earthy conditions, the rigid strength of thought, the inexorable logic, the unerring force of will, have all the increased might that we sometimes see in the dying. We have no space left to touch the argument, but we should greatly regret if the poem failed to be made known far and wide. After M. Renan's 'Life of Jesus,'[1] and the prelections of the

[1] Renan's *Vie de Jésus,* published in 1863, emphasized Christ's humanity at the expense of his divinity, and so stirred up a furore. In the 'Epilogue' to *Dramatis Personae* Browning made Renan, of whom he disapproved, one of his three speakers.

Strasbourg school of theological thought, it should be welcome as it is worthy.

In the course of our explorations and explanations we have shown something of the poet's range, which is the result of peculiarity as well as of power. He carries along each line of the radius almost the same thoroughness of conception and surprising novelty of treatment. We have also shown that the obscurity is not always poetic incompleteness. It sometimes arises from the dramatic conditions. In support of this statement we may remind readers how much greater was the demand on their patience when Mr. Tennyson cast his poem 'Maud' in a dramatic mould, than with his previous poems. At other times it comes from the murky atmosphere in which the poet has had to take some of his portraits in mental photography; the mystery of the innermost life; the action of the invisible, which can only be apprehended dimly through the veil. His genius is flexible as it has been fertile. If he could have brought it to bear in a more ordinary way by illuminating the book of life with traits of our common human character, making the popular appeals to our home affections,—if he could have revealed to the many those rich colours in the common light of day, which have delighted the few in many a dark nook of nature and desert-place of the past, he would have been hailed long since as a true poet. His poetry is not to be dipped into or skimmed lightly with swallow-flights of attention. Its pearls must be dived for. It must be read, studied, and dwelt with for a while. The difficulties which arise from novelty must be encountered; the poetry must be thought over before its concentrated force is unfolded and its subtler qualities can be fully felt. Coming fresh from a great deal of our nineteenth-century poetry to that of Mr. Browning, we are in a new world altogether, and one of the first things we are apt to do is to regret the charms of the old. But the new land is well worth exploring; it possesses treasures that will repay us richly. The strangeness and its startling effects will gradually wear away, and there will be a growth of permanent beauty. With all its peculiarities, and all its faults, the poetry of Mr. Browning is thoroughly sanative, masculine, bracing in its fluence. It breathes into modern verse a breath of new life and more vigorous health, with its aroma of a newly turned and virgin soil.

125. A Verse Critique of *Sordello*

1864

Bayard Taylor, from a letter of 26 September 1864 to James T. Fields, *Life and Letters of Bayard Taylor*, ed. Marie-Hansen Taylor and H. E. Scudder (1884), i. 423–4.

An indefatigable parodist, Taylor (1825–78) tried his skill on Browning more than once, this attempt at *Sordello* and one on 'The Bishop Orders His Tomb' (called 'Angelo Orders His Dinner') being the most successful. Taylor knew the Brownings, having met them in 1851. For an account of their acquaintanceship, see Louise Greer, *Browning and America* (1952), *passim*.

> Who *wills* may hear Sordello's story told
> By Robert Browning; warm? (you ask) or cold?
> But just so much as seemeth to enhance—
> The start being granted, onward goes the dance
> To its own music—the poem's inward sense;
> So, by its verity . . . nay, no pretence
> Avails your self-created bards, and thus
> By just the chance of half a hair to us,
> If understood—but what's the odds to you,
> Who with no obligation to pursue
> Scant tracks of thought, if such, indeed, there be
> In this one poem . . . stay, my friend, and see
> Whether you note that creamy tint of flesh
> Softer than bivalve pink, impearled and fresh,
> Just where the small o' th' back goes curving down
> To the full buttock—ay, but that's the crown
> Protos, incumbered, cast before the feet
> Of Grecian women . . . ah! you hear me, sweet!

And so on, and so on. . . .

126. Walter Bagehot:
Browning and the Grotesque

1864

From his 'Wordsworth, Tennyson, and Browning; or Pure, Ornate, and Grotesque Art in English Poetry', *The National Review* (November 1864), xix. 27–67.

Bagehot's essay was reprinted frequently, both in England and in America.

Grotesque [art] shows you what ought to be by what ought not to be, when complete it reminds you of the perfect image, by showing you the distorted and imperfect image. Of this art we possess in the present generation one prolific master. Mr. Browning is an artist working by incongruity. Possibly hardly one of his most considerable efforts can be found which is not great because of its odd mixture. He puts together things which no one else would have put together, and produces on our minds a result which no one else would have produced, or tried to produce. He not only possesses superficial usable talents, but the strong something, the inner secret something which uses them and controls them; he is great, not in mere accomplishments, but in himself. He has applied a strong intellect to real life; he has applied the same intellect to the problems of his age. He has striven to know what *is*: he has endeavoured not to be cheated by counterfeits, not to be infatuated with illusions. His heart is in what he says. He has battered his brain against his creed till he believes it. He has accomplishments too, the more effective because they are mixed. He is at once a student of mysticism, and a citizen of the world. He brings to the club sofa distinct visions of old creeds, intense images of strange thoughts: he takes to the bookish student tidings of wild Bohemia, and little traces of the *demi-monde*. He puts down what is good for the naughty and what is naughty for the good. Over women his easier writings exercise that imperious power which belongs to the writings of a great man of the world upon such matters. He knows women, and therefore they wish to know him.

If we blame many of Browning's efforts, it is in the interest of art, and not from a wish to hurt or degrade him. Mr. Browning has undertaken to describe what may be called *mind in difficulties*—mind set to make out the universe under the worst and hardest circumstances. He takes 'Caliban', not perhaps exactly Shakespeare's Caliban, but an analogous and worse creature; a strong thinking power, but a nasty creature—a gross animal, uncontrolled and unelevated by any feeling of religion or duty. The delineation of him will show that Mr. Browning does not wish to take undue advantage of his readers by choice of nice subjects.

[Quotes 'Caliban Upon Setebos', lines 24–56.]

It may seem perhaps to most readers that these lines are very difficult, and that they are unpleasant. And so they are. We quote them to illustrate, not the *success* of grotesque art, but the *nature* of grotesque art. It shows the end at which this species of art aims, and if it fails it is from over-boldness in the choice of a subject by the artist, or from the defects of its execution. A thinking faculty more in difficulties—a great type,—an inquisitive, searching intellect under more disagreeable conditions, with worse helps, more likely to find falsehood, less likely to find truth, can scarcely be imagined. Nor is the mere description of the thought at all bad: on the contrary, if we closely examine it, it is very clever. Hardly anyone could have amassed so many ideas at once nasty and suitable. But scarcely any readers—any casual readers—who are not of the sect of Mr. Browning's admirers will be able to examine it enough to appreciate it. From a defect, partly of subject, and partly of style, many of Mr. Browning's works make a demand upon the reader's zeal and sense of duty to which the nature of most readers is unequal. They have on the turf the convenient expression 'staying power': some horses can hold on and others cannot. But hardly any reader not of special and peculiar nature can hold on through such composition. There is not enough of 'staying power' in human nature.

We are not judging Mr. Browning simply from a hasty recent production. All poets are liable to misconceptions, and if such a piece as 'Caliban Upon Setebos' were an isolated error, a venial and particular exception we should have given it no prominence. We have put it forward because it just elucidates both our subject and the characteristics of Mr. Browning. . . .

Mr. Browning possibly, and some of the worst of Mr. Browning's admirers certainly, will say that these grotesque objects exist in real life, and therefore they ought to be, at least may be, described in art. But though pleasure is not the end of poetry, pleasing is a condition of poetry. An exceptional monstrosity of horrid ugliness cannot be made pleasing, except it be made to suggest—to recall—the perfection, the beauty, from which it is a deviation. Perhaps in extreme cases no art is equal to this; but then such self-imposed problems should not be worked by the artist; these out-of-the-way and detestible subjects should be let alone by him. It is rather characteristic of Mr. Browning to neglect this rule. He is the most of a realist, and the least of an idealist of any poet we know.

127. *Sordello* Revisited

1867

Edward Dowden, from his review 'Mr. Browning's *Sordello*: First Paper', *Fraser's Magazine* (October 1867), lxxvi. 518–30.

Dowden (1843–1913) was Professor of English Literature at Trinity College, Dublin and became a distinguished Shakespearean critic. This article pleased Browning, but *Fraser's* declined to print a second paper on *Sordello*. *LRB*, pp. 122–3 and 354.

One word on the obscurity of *Sordello*. It arises not so much from peculiarities of style, and the involved structure of occasional sentences (too much has been said on this; as a rule the style of *Sordello* is vigorously straightforward), as from the unrelaxing demand which is made throughout upon the intellectual and imaginative energy and alertness of the reader. This constant demand exhausts the power of attention in a short time, and the mind is unable to sustain its watchfulness and sureness of action, so that if we read much at a sitting we often find the first few pages clear and admirable, while the last three or four over which the eye passes before we close the book leave us bewildered and jaded; and we say, '*Sordello* is so dreadfully obscure.' The truth is, Mr.

Browning has given too much in his couple of hundred pages; there is not a line of the poem which is not as full of matter as a line can be; so that if the ten syllables sometimes seem to start and give way under the strain, we need not wonder. We come to no places in *Sordello* where we can rest and dream or look up at the sky. Ideas, emotions, images, analyses, descriptions, still come crowding on. There is too much of everything; we cannot see the wood for the trees. Towards the end of the third book Mr. Browning interrupts the story that he may 'pause and breathe.' That is an apt expression; but Mr. Browning seems unable to slacken the motion of his mind, and during this breathing-space heart and brain, perceptive and reflective powers, are almost more busily at work than ever.

128. Solid or Merely Clever?

1868

William Allingham, from the diary entry 18 February 1868, *William Allingham: A Diary*, ed. H. Allingham and D. Radford (1907), pp. 174–5.

Mem.—Too often a want of solid basis for R. B.'s brilliant and astounding cleverness. *A Blot in the 'Scutcheon* is solid. How try to account for B.'s twists and turns? I cannot. He has been and still is very dear to me. But I can no longer commit myself to his hands in faith and trust. Neither can I allow the faintest shadow of a suspicion to dwell in my mind that his genius may have a leaven of quackery. Yet, alas! he is not solid—which is a very different thing from prosaic. *A Midsummer Night's Dream* is as solid as anything in literature; has imaginative coherency and consistency in perfection. Looking at forms of poetic expression, there is not a single utterance in Shakespeare, or of Dante as far as I know, enigmatic in the same sense as so many of Browning's are. If you suspect, and sometimes find out, that riddles presented to you with Sphinxian solemnity have *no* answers that really fit them, your curiosity is apt to fall towards freezing point, if not below it. Yet I always end by striking my breast in penitential mood and crying out, O rich mind! wonderful Poet! strange great man!'

129. Samuel Smiles:
Browning's Dramatic Merit

1868

From his *Brief Biographies* (1868), pp. 377–85.

Samuel Smiles (1812–1904) was an indefatigable writer of biographies and inspirational books aimed at the middle and lower classes. His *Self-Help* (1859) went into many editions and was translated into nearly a score of foreign languages. Browning's inclusion in *Brief Biographies* was a sure sign of growing popular interest. After tracing Browning's early career, Smiles comes to *Bells and Pomegranates*.

. . . If Mr. Browning had stopped here, the world would not have recognized him, as it now does, as one of the greatest dramatic poets since Shakespeare's day. He kept on writing, and between 1842 and 1846 produced, under the title of *Bells and Pomegranates*, a series of dramas and lyrics, or dramatic poems, for the lyrics are as dramatic, almost, as the dramas, upon which his fame thus far chiefly rests. The dramas are entitled *Pippa Passes*, *King Victor and King Charles*, *Colombe's Birthday*, *A Blot in the 'Scutcheon*, *The Return of the Druses*, *Luria*, and *A Soul's Tragedy*. In these poems, Mr. Browning displays that depth, clearness, minuteness, and universality of vision, that power of revealing the object of his thought without revealing himself, that force of imagination which 'turns the common dust of servile opportunity to gold', and the humour which sees remote and fanciful resemblances and develops their secret relationship to each other, which constitute the true poet and the great dramatist. The *Blot in the 'Scutcheon* is a piteous tragedy. It was produced at Drury Lane in 1843, but its success was moderate. This proves only that the applause of the pit is not the test of dramatic merit, for it is almost a perfect work. *Pippa Passes* is also a charming poem. In it occurs the following remarkable figure, startling as the lightning itself.

> OTTIMA (*to her paramour*)
> Buried in woods we lay, you recollect;
> Swift ran the searching tempest overhead;
> And ever and anon some bright white shaft
> Burnt through the pine-tree roof,—here burnt and there,
> As if God's messenger through the close wood screen
> Plunged and replunged his weapon at a venture,
> Feeling for guilty thee and me.

Some of the lyrics and romances included in this collection of poems have passed into the school-books and standard collections of poetry; for instance, 'The Pied Piper of Hamelin', 'How they brought the Good News from Ghent to Aix', and 'The Lost Leader', while others, among which may be mentioned the 'Soliloquy of the Spanish Cloister' and 'Sibrandus Schafnaburgensis', display a quaintness of humour which makes them exceedingly pleasant reading. . . .

[Turns to *Christmas Eve*.]

It deals with theological problems, and expresses some phase of the author's spiritual experience with great force and vividness. It also furnishes a remarkable instance of the ease with which Mr. Browning puts into melodious verse the elaborate niceties of a metaphysical argument, diversifying it with picturesque and humourous descriptions. Some of the pictures of country people and rural life are as faithful and minute as those of Crabbe.[1] . . . And we are confident that Mr. Browning's dramas and lyrics will long continue to find appreciative readers, and that, as culture and taste and love of pure art make progress, the number of his constant admirers will steadily increase. If we are mistaken, he must be consoled with the phrase from Milton which is expected to soothe all great and unpopular poets; for he may safely rely till the end of time upon his 'fit audience, though few.'

[1] George Crabbe (1754–1832), the realistic English poet more admired by critics than by the public of his time.

130. J. H. Stirling Exhorts Browning

1868

From his unsigned article, 'The Poetical Works of Robert Browning', *North British Review* (December 1868), xlix. 353–408.

James Hutchinson Stirling (1820–1909), Scottish philosopher, commentator on Hegel and Kant, and occasional literary critic.

. . . Like all original writers, Browning has a flavour of his own, of which, in the first taste, the newness repugns. He indeed whose standards of poetry have been successively acquired, as is most likely, so far at least as recent literature is concerned, from Scott and Byron, from Coleridge and Wordsworth, from Shelley and Keats and Tennyson, may rise from his first burst of reading into the sixty-two pieces that form this collection with a general sense of failure. He has read in a mood of censure, we will say, in which there have been but few breaks of applause. His dissatisfaction has been almost constant, and he cannot allow it to have been redeemed by what glimpses of success he is willing to acknowledge. Compared with the standards in his mind, this poetry, it may be, even surprises. It is so completely different, so wholly disparate, that it is at once felt to be foreign, and *must* be faulty. It is tame, too, he thinks; tame, insipid, colourless. It is something unaffecting, plainly; something uninteresting; something inconsiderable. It is prevailingly symbolical—that he thinks he sees; but he thinks, also, it is unhappy in its kind. Either the externality, he says, is so much an externality, or else the internality is so much an internality—that is, either the symbol itself is so hard and rude, or the meaning is so inextricably deep in it, that, while the concealment is perfect, the revealment is null. A weak, soft, plaintive, pleading thing, it is mostly—a breath conversationally low, he thinks; a small thin stream that runs by, almost uninfluenced by rhythm, almost unchecked by rhyme; broken only at times against single words like stones in mid-current, or losing itself and disappearing under the angle of an inversion. A descriptive touch, or a tone of tenderness, he cannot deny at intervals; but where, he asks, is the splendour of imagery, the rush of inspiration, the proud wave of exultant and transporting sound? There are no *passages*, he complains; nothing to strike. Rhyme, rhythm! why, in that low colloquial plaint, measure at all is hardly to be recognised. That is, whereas measure with us English usually consists of shorts and longs alternated to musical or passionate effect, here it seems all longs or all shorts, to no effect but that of prose. One can make music, he thinks, out of the usual calculated recurrence of iambuses, and passion out of breaks with spondees, etc., but one can make neither music nor passion where it is all spondees, or all pyrrhics, or at random either. What measure there is here, then, is to be pronounced mechanical merely; there is but the tact of time in it, the come and go of accent; tune there is none—we have line upon line, instead, that is flatly prose. No: music it cannot be called, that mere monotonous croon, that mere monotonous chime; croon or chime of such monotony that in so homogeneous an element even the unequal lengths of the lines look factitious somehow—the result, as it were, of an arbitrary clipping, and an arbitrary laying down. . . .

. . . He is a master crowned: he has but to speak. May we not expect him now, then, warmed into confidence, strung into strength, to smite, even with one light stroke, from the rock, such statue as, for power and majesty and glow of lineament, had been all-impossible in the past? Nor were, indeed, we may say, such statue unwelcome now— now that the element, indicated as having hitherto failed Browning, has been at length accorded him. Lusty with wine and oil, the mood of Tennyson has been for years assured and irresistible. Sound, colour, emotion, image—all have been mighty with him, and fused in a breath. With Browning hitherto, be his triumphs what they may, this, on the whole, has not been so. We cannot deny it: beside that full, flushed, victorious mood of Tennyson, as of one who has fed on nectar and ambrosia, the mood of Browning, in comparison, has looked, not seldom hitherto, dispirited and rebuked, as of one to whom fasting has been more familiar than abundance, blame than praise. We see, then, what is wanted for Browning, at least in larger presence, more apparent power. It is the pinion of assurance and security; the single flight in one full swoop, the one and ever-ascending gust of genius. And, for this, it may be, in these better days, we are warranted to look. Much as we glory, then, in *Luria* and 'Chiappino'—in 'Artemis', 'Caliban', 'Roland' —in 'Gismond' and the 'Balcony'—in 'Karshish', 'Cleon', 'Lippi', 'Sarto', 'Saul'—in the 'Soliloquy'—in 'St. Praxed's'—in the 'Duchess's Portrait' and the 'Duchess's Flight', we would fain still have, at the hands of Browning, one great and comprehensive work, which, adequate to his genius, we might set beside the 'Princess' and the *Idylls* and the 'In Memoriam.' Is it for Browning to be represented only by toygems and brilliants, however exquisite? Shall his be but scattered chambers and interrupted chapels? Shall he not raise a palace over many chambers, a minster over many chapels? Hitherto, indeed, Browning has probably despised colour. He mentions 'Naddo's staring nosegay's carrion bloom', and has avowedly no rivalry for 'flower-shows'. Not unaware, however, of what may wake music or stir emotion, and with even a wealth of imagery at will, he has his own other and higher gifts of analysis, thought, and vision. Browning, then, even should he be inferior from the first to Tennyson in all that splendour of imagery and richness of sound, and overpowering tenderness of emotion and absorbing gust of inspiration, which are Tennyson's, and so peculiarly and prodigally Tennyson's, is not yet under any necessity to quail. In colour, music, genius-gust, 'the garland and the singing robes', Milton, perhaps, is as superior to Shakespeare as Tennyson is to Browning; yet, in the end, the higher seat is not Milton's. As there, then, with Shakespeare and Milton, so it may be here with Browning and Tennyson. Yet great as is our love for Browning, we cannot allow ourselves to become unfaithful to an earlier and equal love conceived for Tennyson, and, in a dramatic reference, which is here the determining consideration, we would point to the vast passionate power in that kind which is present in 'Maud', and the 'Princess', and the *Idylls of the King*. Nay, even in psychological reference, and psychology is the bow of Browning, we would point to the 'Stylite', and the 'Farmer', and the 'Grandmother', and we would ask, Is it not true that these, in their own way, are unexcelled by anything of a like kind in Browning? But, be that as it may, it is still true that if Browning shall ever make good for himself a higher place than Tennyson's, he will be only able to accomplish this by superior excellence in an element dramatic. And so it is that we call to Browning—who has still in that direction steps to take, if he would occupy the height—for more, and again more, and always more in that kind. Does not the drama, indeed, seem but the natural consummation of psychology? and should not the latter be, at all hazards, perfected and matured into the former? Should not action come, in effect, as life to psychology, striking character into spontaneous evolution, as it were in the fire of trial? Already essentially dramatic, so far as the *personae* are concerned, Browning, then, has only to add this failing element to achieve, as at least seems likely, a place in the dramatic poetry of

England that shall be nearest Shakespeare's. Another *Tempest*, another *Midsummer Night's Dream*: in these there is stuff, perhaps, that we can never again expect from mortal. But Browning has already, in characters at least, given us a younger brother to the great *Moor of Venice*: are further triumphs in the kind impossible to him? Why should we or he despair of another *Winter's Tale*, or *Cymbeline*, or *Taming of the Shrew*, or *Merchant of Venice*? Nay, why should we or he despair of another *Lear*? That is it: let Browning give us—but whispering in his ear, Spare compositors that sweat of brow, and burn *Sordello*—another *Cymbeline*, another *Taming of the Shrew*, another *Lear*.

THE RING AND THE BOOK

November 1868–February 1869

---

131. 'Richelieu', *Vanity Fair*

28 November 1868, i. 46–7

From his review.

We have not been able to identify the critic who used this pseudonym in *Vanity Fair*.

In a few days Mr. Browning will publish another of those great and supposed enigmatical poems at which all Vanity Fair stands aghast—not exactly with terror, but with the half-amused, half-puzzled look of the honest country folk who hear for the first time in their lives a Frenchman or a German speaking in his own language. Once more the critics in plush will be heard echoing and re-echoing the verdict of the critics in kid gloves, and while the moustache is gracefully twirled, or the cigar held in suspense, *The Ring and the Book* will be turned over with a patronising air, and in all the sincerity of supercilious wonderment plaintively pronounced 'monstwously cwude in style, and altogether puzzling "to a fella", you know!' There is no help for this sort of thing. It is not Mr. Browning's fortune to stand on a level with the criticism of the present generation. His voice is 'the voice of one crying in the wilderness', and they who dwell in kings' houses will not go out to hear him, and are little likely to be influenced by his teaching.

By particular favour I have seen enough of Mr. Browning's new poem to be quite prepared for a repetition of the old verdict of *Vanity Fair* upon his choice of a subject and his treatment of it; yet I shall venture to speak of this book as one of the most striking lessons ever read by poet or philosopher in the ears of an evil generation. The story is a pitiful one—more pitiful than Hood's *Bridge of Sighs*, if that be possible. A young girl of Rome, in those old times which Mr. Browning loves to paint—yet not so remote from the present as his middle-aged dramas—is married to an Italian count, shortly after which she and her father and mother are found murdered by him—nay, he is taken red-handed almost in the very act of butchery, and is eventually executed for the crime. This is the substance of the story found by Mr. Browning in an old 'Book', How he treats it is to be gathered from his opening apologue of the *Ring*. Some alloy must be mingled with your virgin gold to make it workable, but the goldsmith having finished his design (the 'lilied loveliness' of the ring) the gold is set free from its baser companionship by the last touch of the workman's art. Once more it is pure gold, 'prime nature with an added artistry'. And so understood, the antique goldsmith's ring serves, in the fore-front of the poem, as a symbol or speaking emblem of the poet's method. Say he has a divine message. How shall he utter it? The story of Guido Franceschini and the babe-like woman he made his bride is the answer.

It is not, therefore, to relate this story with such embellishments as his poetic instinct and sense of artistic beauty might suggest, that Mr. Browning has written. There is a deeply-felt purpose in his work of art, and to accomplish that purpose he has mixed the gold with 'gold's alloy.' We are first told of the tragedy in all its naked ghastliness. Then what 'half Rome' said of it, and what the 'other half.' The motives of the different actors in the drama, and all the little incomplete incidents which go to make up its completeness, are thus vividly realised. We pass them all over, to remark on Mr. Browning's aim, or what may be called the gist of his message in the character of Seer. The handwriting on the wall seems to be this, 'Can evil be done and evil not come of it?' Or this, to vary the expression, 'Is the world ruled by man's cunning devices, or by God's laws?' Or, again, this, 'Can a lie be told, and not make itself manifest, sooner or later, as the work of him who is the father of lies?' Yet, *The Ring and the Book* is not a sermon. It is deeply, intensely, human. It is nevertheless, and for that very reason, a burning protest against the atheistic belief that men and women are the creatures of circumstances. It asserts a Presence in the world, before which every lie, spoken or acted, must wither up, and possibly—nay, most certainly —bring destruction upon those who trust in it.

We picture Dante walking, with sad wide-open eyes, through Purgatory and Hades before he reached the shore of the river across which the loving eyes of Beatrice beamed upon him, and he once more took comfort. So through Vanity Fair and its devious ways, crowded with spectres of men and women as mournful to seeing eyes as those which grieved the heart of the Mantuan bard, we follow the steps of the poet who has been entrusted with this message, and who has already given utterance to it in many like parables. All criticism of Mr. Browning's verse which does not recognise this central fact of his relationship to the age as a messenger of truth seems to me worthless. It is true the good folk in Vanity Fair do not like this sort of thing, and it may be there are times when none of us like it. Belshazzar at high festival has no relish for the mystical handwriting on the wall. It is not always pleasant to be in earnest, and, like Mr. Tennyson's 'Lotus Eaters', we rather enjoy floating down the stream; or like the crew in his glorious 'Voyage', we have aims of our own in which it is vexatious to be disturbed. The answer to this objection is that we are not troubled every day, or even every other day, with a great poet's earnest expression of feeling, or with his sense of the living truth of things. No fear that there will not always be space enough in the Fair for vain shows, or, let us say, for harmless mirth and pleasantry. Now and then we may surely pause a moment in the round of ambition or pleasure to hear the Voice of Truth, and to lay up a gracious remembrance for less festive occasions. This, at least, is the kind of appeal which Mr. Browning's new poem makes to the world, be it received how it may.

Were space available for the purpose, it would be easy to prove by quotations that I have not over-estimated the earnestness of Mr. Browning's purpose, or the reality of his Message. Passages of great force and poetic beauty might be cited to this effect. One such I must find room for. It is an invocation addressed to one whom only to name in the poet's hearing were to call up at once a great sorrow and a great sense of joy, both too sacred to be lightly evoked. Hats off, gentlemen! There are few strains of music so touchingly sweet and so deeply felt. The like may be found in Milton's sonnet to his 'late espoused saint', and in some of Mrs. Browning's own intense verse; not often, if at all, elsewhere—

[Quotes 'O lyric love'.]

While it is impossible to read a poem with such passages in it, without sharing in the solemnity of Mr. Browning's muse, it must not be overlooked that his genius is dramatic—not essentially didactic, any more than Shakespeare's is so. For force of drawing, for fire and strength, for passion reserved until it flashes like a sudden gleam of lightning in a dark sky, Mr. Browning is without his equal among the poets of this age. In a critique of sufficient scope I should be disposed to look for his parallel, if not for his master, in Keats. There is the same intensity in both, the same concentrated fire, the same whiteness of heat, sometimes hidden by a hard metallic crust, but always ready to burst in flame. There is, too, the same marvellous efflorescence of poetic beauty in occasional passages, breaking out like rose-blossoms, often in most unexpected places and on spiny stems. In a philosophical analysis of his genius it would be possible to show that these apparent contrarieties, and what some have weakly pronounced affectations, are simply a necessity of the poet's nature. In allowing the ruggedness of his verse to appear, and glorifying it with an occasional burst of loveliness, he is doing precisely that in his own way which the Poet Laureate confesses to in his—

> Behold, ye speak an idle thing:
> Ye never knew the sacred dust:
> I do but sing because I must,
> And pipe but as the linnets sing.[1]

Mr. Browning, however, should rather be classed with the wild beasts of creation than the birds—strong of limb and tawny of hue, with teeth like iron, and a roar like thunder. He is the spiritual athlete of poetry, descending into the arena as did the Roman gladiator of old, to grapple with terrible realities, and hold death itself in his strong grip. These are the thoughts which his new poem suggests. If people do not want the reality, with the occasional ruggedness of Nature, they had better not trouble themselves to open the book: *non cuivis*,[2] &c., milk for babes may be got elsewhere.

RICHELIEU.

[1] *In Memoriam*, XXI. 21–24.　　[2] 'It is not for them.'

132. From an unsigned review, *The Spectator*

12 December 1868, xli. 1464–6

As Mr. Browning issues his new poem in instalments, we may well suppose that he wishes it to be read, and studied, and conceived in instalments; indeed, that, with the help his prologue gives us, each of the subsequent parts (of which each volume, except the first, which contains two, will seemingly contain three) will form a whole in itself, organically complete, though suited, like each of the parts of the old Greek trilogies, to constitute, in conjunction with the other poetic facets or developments of the same story, a still more impressive and various whole. So far as we can judge from the quarter now presented to us, no one of Mr. Browning's works is likely to take a stronger hold on the public mind, if any so strong,—the only disadvantage being what the public may think its alarming length, though four small volumes about a tragedy so rich in picture and passion as this do not strike us as too much for any one who can really enter into Mr. Browning's works. Anyhow, the publication in instalments will do much to get over this difficulty. A public that has once tasted will not be satisfied to desist till it has drunk off all it can get of the draught, and this little volume is certainly in itself by no means alarming, offering as it does two separate pauses to the reader, and rising in fascination as it travels round each separate wind of the spiral in which the narrative mounts upwards towards a complete view of the tragedy on which it is based.

[Here follows a plot summary.]

Here is room enough for the free working of Mr. Browning's genius, and in this first volume, which is all we at present have, Mr. Browning's genius certainly has its fullest swing. He overflows, as he always overflows, in intellectual point, in acute comment, in quaint illustration. He is, as he always is, semi-dramatic, with the keenest of all eyes for every qualifying circumstance which alters the point of view of each age and each individual,—never quite dramatic, for we never lose sight of the critical eye of the poet himself, who discriminates all these different shades of thought, and tosses them off with a sharpness of outline, and sometimes an intellectual touch of caricature, often a sharp sarcasm, that could not have proceeded from the *inside* of the situation he is painting for us, that could only proceed from one outside it like himself, but who is looking (very keenly) *into* it. He paints, as he always paints, with wonderful swiftness and brilliance, but also with a certain wilful carelessness and singularity,—somewhat like the qualities shown in old David Cox's fine water-colour sketches,—and with a singular contempt for sweetness and finish of style. In fertility of intellectual resource there is no poetry anywhere like Mr. Browning's; in the brilliancy of his descriptions of character he has no rival; but for *beauty* of form he seems to us to have, as usual, almost a contempt. We do not mean that there are not here and there one or two lines of perfect loveliness,—not only in thought, but in expression,—but that even the very finest are marred by the close proximity of crabbed English, and grammar so condensed as to be either grating or excessively obscure, and that very frequently his narrative, though lucid enough in drift, is couched in almost carefully eccentric English,—singular nouns with no article, and used in the abstract sense; plural adjectives accumulated on one substantive as the Germans only pile them; new-coined combinations of nouns like 'ring-thing', the need for the coinage not being very clear; oddly interpolated ejaculations (quaint gestures of the narrator, as it were, interspersed in the narrative); and now and then a parenthesis, which is so long, striking, and interesting in itself as to break the current of the story in which it is imbedded, and give a grotesque effect to the whole, as if one gem were imbedded in the surface of another,—a curiosity, compounded of two beauties, but so compounded as to be itself not beautiful, only odd. Mr. Browning begins his story very characteristically. He says:

> Do you see this square old yellow Book, I toss
> I' the air, and catch again, and twirl about
> By the crumpled vellum covers,—pure crude fact,
> Secreted from man's life when hearts beat hard,
> And brains, high-blooded, ticked two centuries since?

That seems to us highly expressive even of the intellectual fashion in which Mr. Browning treats his subjects, tossing them in the air to catch them again, twirling them about by their crumpled outside surfaces, and generally displaying his sense of mastery, and the enjoyment which belongs to it, by acts not unfrequently something resembling caprice. Thus, the random, boyish, and almost freakish account of what Mr. Browning did with his intellectual prize when he had got it, seems to us as remarkable a piece of exuberance of intellectual spirits as ever an imaginative writer of the first order indulged in:—

[Quotes Book I, ll. 423–56.]

Characteristic of Mr. Browning though they be, these extremely bad puns[1] on Manning's, Newman's, and Wiseman's names do not seem to us fit elements for a prologue which is to introduce us to so great a theme, although boldly, freely, and buoyantly treated, as is usual with Mr. Browning. When overlooking the irregularities of style, the wilful caprices of the poet's immense and inexhaustible intellectual animation, we come to speak of the *power* with which the subject is treated, it is almost impossible to speak too highly. Always remembering that Mr. Browning's modes of thought never change as he passes from one point of sight to another; that, while rendering each new view,—individual or local, or it may be a class or party view,—with equal force and ability, the *style* of discourse, the springy, sharp definitions, the acute discriminations, the rapier-like thrusts of logic, are all the poet's own, and used by every one of his characters in succession,—it is impossible to speak too highly of the power with which he paints one 'facet' after another of the tragedy he has taken for his theme. His own argument of what he is going to give us is itself, barring the puns and such oddities, as brilliant a picture in miniature of the social and moral conditions affecting the public view of such a crime as Count Guido Franceschini's in 1698, as was ever drawn of the past. The sketch of the view taken by that half of Rome favourable to Count Guido's pardon begins perhaps in a strain of thought somewhat too plebeian for the admirably intellectual characterizations in which the supposed speaker afterwards indulges. It seems to us, for instance, scarcely the same critic who was so eloquent about the fine effect presented by the bodies of the poor old murdered pair when laid out in the Church of San Lorenzo with a profusion of wax-lights all round them, and who afterwards gives us this description of the Canon Caponsacchi,—but whether it be or not, the description is not the less vivid:

[Quotes Book II, ll. 780–95.]

Or take the description in the same division of the poem of how Count Guido's passion was excited on hearing of the birth of an heir whom he had supposed (or rather is by the speaker supposed to have supposed) to be illegitimate,—how

[1] In Book I, ll. 444–46.

[Quotes Book II, 11. 1389–91.]

Still more powerful is, we think, the third division of the poem, which gives the popular form of the view favourable to the victims and against the murderer. It is again, of course, Mr. Browning who speaks behind the mask; but the mask is good, and the voice behind tells as carefully what the supposed speaker might have felt, as if it did not give it in Mr. Browning's idiom. How fine is the sarcasm here:

> Though really it does seem as if she here,
> Pompilia, living so and dying thus,
> Has had undue experience how much crime
> A heart can hatch.   Why was she made to learn
> —Not you, not I, not even Molinos' self—
> What Guido Franceschini's heart could hold?
> Thus saintship is effected probably;
> No sparing saints the process!—which the more
> Tends to the reconciling us, no saints,
> To sinnership, immunity and all.

—how powerful the description of Count Guido driving his wife, 'hemmed in by her household bars', to destruction by chasing her 'about the coop of daily life'; how grand and touching the picture of the battered mind of the old confessor who was so sure of Pompilia's innocence!—

> Even that poor old bit of battered brass
> Beaten out of all shape by the world's sins,
> Common utensil of the lazar-house—
> Confessor Celestino groans, ' 'Tis truth,
> All truth, and only truth: there's something else,
> Some presence in the room beside us all,
> Something that every lie expires before:
> No question she was pure from first to last.'

In short, the little volume, as a whole, contains perhaps more of Mr. Browning's brilliant intellectual flashes of many-coloured light than almost any of his hitherto published works.

For pathos, and what comes near to lyric fire, there is no passage like that apostrophe which ends the prologue, the first couplet of which is the most truly inspired in all the range of his poems; but why has he ended such a passage with three lines so utterly obscure,—open to so many guesses and so little certainty,—as those which conclude it:

O lyric Love! half-angel and half-bird
And all a wonder and a wild desire,—
Boldest of hearts that ever braved the sun,
Took sanctuary within the holier blue,
And sang a kindred soul out to his face,— . . .
Thither where eyes, that cannot reach yet yearn
For all hope, all sustainment, all reward,
Their utmost up and on,—so blessing back
In those thy realms of help, that heaven thy home,
Some whiteness which, I judge, thy face makes proud,
Some wanness where, I think, thy foot may fall!

Mr. Browning describes 'the British public' in this poem as 'ye who like me not,' adding a grim 'God love you,'—somewhat as clergymen pray for their enemies,—but if it does not like him, it is only because while, with so great a power of lucidity, he will spoil his finest poetry by careless hieroglyphics such as these,—the mere shorthand of a poet, which to him, no doubt, recalls with sufficient precision what was in his own mind when he wrote it, but what certainly is not adapted to call it up for the first time in those who cannot know, from what is written, whether they have ever yet had it in their mind or not. But it is scarcely true that the British public love not Mr. Browning. They love him more and more, at all events. And the more they love him, the less they like the carelessness with which a poet of so much power of speech slurs over the great faults in his own style. Still, if the other three volumes of this poem are equal to the first, they will add greatly to the rich mines of intellectual wealth, full partly of gold ore, in less degree of sifted gold, to be found in Mr. Browning's writings.

133. R. W. Buchanan, *The Athenæum*

26 December 1868, pp. 875–6

From his unsigned review.

Buchanan's hopes for *The Ring and the Book* were fulfilled, apparently, for his review of the entire poem (No. 142) is probably the most enthusiastic one it received.

The Ring and the Book, if completed as successfully as it is begun, will certainly be an extraordinary achievement—a poem of some 20,000 lines on a great human subject, darkened too often by subtleties and wilful obscurities, but filled with the flashes of Mr. Browning's genius. We know nothing in the writer's former poems which so completely represents his peculiarities as this instalment of *The Ring and the Book*, which is so marked by picture and characterization, so rich in pleading and debating, so full of those verbal touches in which Browning has no equal, and of those verbal involutions in which he has fortunately no rival. Everything Browningish is found here,—the legal jauntiness, the knitted argumentation, the cunning prying into detail, the suppressed tenderness, the humanity,—the salt intellectual humour,—a humour not open and social, like that of Dickens, but with a similar tendency to caricature, differing from the Dickens tendency just in so far as the intellectual differs from the emotional, with the additional distinction of the *secretive* habit of all purely intellectual faculties. Secretiveness, indeed, must be at once admitted as a prominent quality of Mr. Browning's power. Indeed, it is this quality which so fascinates the few and so repels the many. It tempts the possessor, magpie-like, to play a constant game at hiding away precious and glittering things in obscure and mysterious corners, and—still magpie-like—to search for bright and glittering things in all sorts of unpleasant and unlikely places. It involves the secretive chuckle and the secretive leer. Mr. Browning's manner reminds us of the magpie's manner, when, having secretly stolen a spoon or swallowed a jewel, the bird swaggers jauntily up and down, peering rakishly up, and chuckling to itself over its last successful feat of knowingness and *diablerie*. However, let us not mislead our readers. We are not speaking now of Mr. Browning's style, but of his intellectual habit. The mere style of the volume before us is singularly free from the well-known faults—obscurity, involution, faulty construction; with certain exceptions, it flows on with perfect clearness and ease; and any occasional darkness is traceable less to faulty diction than to mental super-refining or reticent humour. The work as a whole is not obscure.

We are not called upon—it is scarcely our duty—to determine in what degree the inspiration and workmanship of *The Ring and the Book* are poetic as distinguished from intellectual: far less to guess what place the work promises to hold in relation to the poetry of our time. We scarcely dare hope that it will ever be esteemed a great poem in the sense that *Paradise Lost* is a great poem, or even in the sense that the *Cenci* is a great tragedy. The subject is tragic, but the treatment is not dramatic: the 'monologue', even when perfectly done, can never rival the 'scene'; and Mr. Browning's monologues are not perfectly done, having so far, in spite of the subtle distinction in the writer's mind, a very marked similarity in the *manner* of thought, even where the thought itself is most distinct. Having said so much, we may fairly pause. The rest must be only wonder and notes of admiration. In exchange for the drama, we get the monologue,—in exchange for a Shakspearean exhibition, we get Mr. Browning masquing under so many disguises, never quite hiding his identity, and generally most delicious, indeed, when the disguise is most transparent. The drama is glorious, we all know, but we want this thing as well;—we must have Browning as well as Shakspeare. Whatever else may be said of Mr. Browning and his work, by way of minor criticism, it will be admitted on all hands that nowhere in any literature can be found a man and a work more fascinating in their way. As for the man,—he was crowned long ago, and we are not of those who grumble because one king has a better seat than another—an easier cushion, a finer light—in the great Temple. A king is a king, and each will choose his place. . . .

[Summarizes the plot.]

Here, surely, is matter for a poem,—perhaps too much matter. The chief difficulty will of course be,—to avoid wearying the intellect by the constant reiteration of the same circumstances,—so to preserve the dramatic disguise as to lend a totally distinct colouring to each circumstance at each time of narration. So far as the work has gone, it is perfectly successful, within the limitations of Mr. Browning's genius. Though Mr. Browning's prologue, and 'Half Rome's' monologue, and

'Other Half Rome's' monologue, are somewhat similar in style,—in the sharp logic, in the keen ratiocination, in the strangely involved diction, —yet they are radically different. The distinction is subtle rather than broad. Yet nothing could well be finer than the graduation between the sharp, personally anxious, suspicious manner of the first Roman speaker, who is a *married man*, and the bright, disinterested emotion, excited mainly by the personal beauty of Pompilia, of the second speaker, who is a *bachelor*. With a fussy preamble, the first seizes the buttonhole of a friend,—whose cousin, he knows, has designs upon his (the speaker's) wife. How he rolls his eyes about, pushing through the crowd! How he revels in the spectacle of the corpses laid out in the church for public view, delighting in the long rows of wax candles, and the great taper at the head of each corpse! You recognize the fear of 'horns' in every line of his talk. Vulgar, conceited, suspicious, voluble, he tells his tale, gloating over every detail that relates in any degree to his own fear of cuckoldage. He is every inch for Guido;—father and mother deserved their fate,—having lured the Count into a vile match, and afterwards plotted for his dishonour; and as for Pompilia,—what was she but the daughter of a common prostitute, palmed off on old Pietro as her own by a vile and aged wife? Exquisite is the gossip's description of the Count's domestic *ménage*,—his strife with father-in-law and mother-in-law,—his treatment of the childish bride. Some of the most delicious touches occur after the description of how the old couple, wild and wrathful, fly from their son-in-law's house, and leave their miserable daughter behind.

Our description and extracts can give no idea of the value of the book as a whole. It is sown throughout with beauties,—particularly with exquisite *portraits*, clear and sharp-cut, like those on antique gems; such as the two exquisite little pictures, of poor battered old Celestine the Confessor and aged Luca Cini, the morbid haunter of hideous public spectacles. Everywhere there is life, sense, motion—the flash of real faces, the warmth of real breath. We have glimpses of all the strange elements which went to make up Roman society in those times. We see the citizens and hear their voices,—we catch the courtly periods of the rich gentlemen, the wily whispers of the priests,—we see the dull brainless clods at Arezzo, looking up to their impoverished master as life and light,—and we hear the pleading of lawyers deep in the learning of Cicero and Ovid. So far, only a few figures have stood out from the fine groups in the background. In future volumes, one after another figure will take up the tale; and when the work is finished, we shall have, in addition to the numberless group-studies, such a collection of finished single portraits as it will not be easy to match in any language for breadth of tone and vigour of characterization.

Anything further by way of censure would be ungracious. The great faults of the work have been Mr. Browning's faults all along, and it is too late to alter them now. It should be added, too, that we miss altogether the lyric light which saved 'Aurora Leigh' from mediocrity as a work of art. The power is strictly intellectual, without one flash of ecstasy, such as the matchless flashes in Mr. Browning's best lyrics. All this was the consequence of a gigantic and tentative subject. But if Mr. Browning impresses still more strongly on the world's heart the danger of overbearing judgment, he will be like a messenger from heaven, sent to teach the highest of all lessons to rashly-judging men.

134. From an unsigned review, *The Saturday Review*

26 December 1868, xxvi. 832–4

A new poem by Mr. Browning cannot fail to arouse interest in the readers of poetry. It is now some years since the keenness of his satire, and the subtlety of his appreciation of character, have forced themselves upon the notice, not merely of a few select adherents, but of all educated men. The slowness of the process by which this was accomplished is remarkable. Mr. Browning himself, to judge from a passage which occurs more than once in the present volume, appears to consider himself still as a comparatively unpopular writer. 'Such,' he writes,

> Such, British public, ye who like me not,
> (God love you!)—whom I yet have laboured for,
> Perchance more careful whoso runs may read
> Than erst when all, it seemed, could read who ran,—
> Perchance more careless whoso reads may praise
> Than late when he who praised and read and wrote
> Was apt to find himself the selfsame me,—
> Such labour had such issue. . . .

It is natural for Mr. Browning to write thus; but at present he certainly is not unhonoured; and though it is always a misfortune that a writer of high rank should fail of gaining what he ought to receive, there is something, we think, that may be said on behalf of the British public in this instance. In the first place, Mr. Browning is undeniably a very difficult writer to understand. Topics of great intellectual abstruseness have entered largely into the subjects on which he has written; and, so far from endeavouring to smooth the reader's way for their comprehension, he has dealt with them in a style even unnecessarily curt, rough, and full of unexplained allusions. Take *Paracelsus*; the whole theme is intellect, not action—the struggles of thought, not of nerve and physical resolution. And even at this day, when we know Mr. Browning to be a man of great eminence (always a material help in reading a book), it is nearly as hard work to get through *Paracelsus* as to get through Dr. Salmon's *Analytical Conics*.[1] Both of these excellent works are in the highest degree repaying; but we speak merely of the difficulty. There are, however, some lyrics in *Paracelsus* that are not merely extremely beautiful, but easy of comprehension. Even this is wanting in *Sordello*— a work which, we have been assured by some of Mr. Browning's admirers, is the poet's most admirable performance. Knowing our own ignorance, we accept this assertion in faith; but we must plainly say that it is pure unalloyed faith—with an absence of rationalism that might satisfy the Pope himself—by which we accept it.

But to come to the present poem. It is calculated to excite, not only interest, but astonishment. The volume before us contains four thousand six hundred and fifty-five lines. There are three volumes more to come; so that, if the remainder keep up the promise of the present one, the whole poem will contain somewhat over eighteen thousand six hundred lines, a length exceeding that of the Iliad by more than three thousand lines. We saw the other day, in a paper set at one of our public schools, this question asked—'Why are epic poems not written nowadays?' The questioner, if he had seen Mr. Browning's poem, would surely have thought his inquiry somewhat premature. For, though you may, if you please, restrict the term epic to such quasi-historical records as the Iliad and the Niebelungen-Lied, yet if *Paradise Lost* is to be termed an epic, why not the *Ring and the Book*? It at least professes to be a narration of pure fact, which cannot be said of a large part of *Paradise Lost*. However, perhaps a more accurate description of Mr. Browning's new poem would be to say that it is a report at great length of a criminal trial, the

[1] Not identified.

arguments of counsel on both sides being given *in extenso*, together with the remarks of the bystanders in the court, and copious annotations by a commentator. This is literally the character of it, as far as it has gone as yet. The volume is divided into three parts. . . .

It will possibly be thought, from the preceding account, that the *Ring and the Book* will not be so readable or poetical a poem as Mr. Browning's eminence would lead us to expect. However, we do not say this. It is never easy to judge Mr. Browning hastily; and we have not discerned in the present volume any token of falling-off of power, in the shape of a mannerism adopted purely as mannerism without a body of thought to sustain it. But as we have begun in rather a critical mood, we may as well go on to specify those points in the poem which appear to us open to objection, before proceeding to those that may justly claim admiration. To begin with the subject of the book; this is of a class which Mr. Browning frequently takes as his theme, but which from its intrinsic disagreeableness acts rather as a hindrance to the expression of lofty and noble sentiments. It is a history of fantastic, out-of-the-way, but low and mean, vice; of vice that twists and twirls itself through odd corners, and works by unexpected devices; but still vice pure, unadulterated, and unrelieved. If there is anything morally better to come in the succeeding volumes, there is small sign of it in the present; unless it be in the character of the Pope:—

[Quotes Book I, 325-40.]

This is in Mr. Browning's very best manner. But it is noticeable (and here we come to another, as it seems to us, fault in the poem) that this judgment, which is the final stroke and termination of the whole story, appears at the very beginning of the first volume, on the sixteenth and subsequent pages. In fact, there is no more consecutiveness in the narrative than in the story elicited from different witnesses in a court of justice. Many parts are repeated over and over again; the murder, the central point of the whole, is related at length three several times. Still, in spite of this prolongation and intricacy, the result is attained that the reader does in the end understand the plot; the sense of conflicting evidence, and of the different movements of the popular mind, is vividly given; and when we have come to the close of the volume, we are anxious to know how the real fact will develop itself out of the maze of conjecture and inconsistency.

[Summarizes the facts of the case.]

Such is the outline of the great criminal case that took place at Rome in the year 1698, which Mr. Browning presents to his readers. Up to this point the characters in the story are too undeveloped for it to be possible to criticize them with accuracy; and the main interest of the present volume lies in single passages and reflections of the poet. It need not be said that these are often most acute, and even brilliant. We think, indeed, that Mr. Browning often strains a metaphor or a simile too far. For example, the *Ring* that occurs in the title of the poem is only introduced for the sake of a simile, which is worked up in the first thirty lines, and alluded to continually afterwards. And again, in the second part, to find Mr. Browning saying, 'Where was I with that angler simile?' in reference to a simile that had been well finished three pages before, is a little annoying. It takes off one's attention from the subject.

[Quotes Book II, 465–84.]

In the above passage, as indeed not unfrequently, Mr. Browning reminds us of Persius.[1] There is the same brevity of expression, the same mode of allusion to common things. Moreover, Mr. Browning, like Persius, is a philosophic satirist; like Persius, he has a great power of feeling and enthusiasm, to which nevertheless he seldom gives the reins for long together, but breaks short in the midst of his most pathetic passages, as if ashamed of his pathos.

If any one thinks that we have not spoken with due praise of the present poem, let it be remembered that a great poet is judged by a higher standard than other people; nor can any one deny the originality, the compass, and the solidity of Mr. Browning's genius. We are disposed to think that nothing in the present volume equals some of his former pieces; but we may be mistaken; for he is not a writer whom it is easy to understand all at once, and he delights in regions novel and unexplored, which lie apart from the ordinary experience of men and the ordinary track of poets.

[1] Aulus Persius Flaccus (A.D. 34–62), Roman satirist, who also shared with Browning a taste for obscure allusions. See Lillian Feder, *Crowell's Handbook of Classical Literature* (1964), pp. 333–4.

135. Walter Bagehot, *Tinsley's Magazine*

January 1869, iii. 665-74

Bagehot (1826-77), historian, economist, literary critic, and businessman. This sensitive review is a fair sample of his critical mind.

The position of Robert Browning in the limited roll of contemporary poets is a very peculiar one. By his disciples and admirers—and they are a select, if not a numerous, body—Browning is considered to be, beyond all comparison, the master of modern English poetry; by the majority of intelligent book-readers—those who actually form their opinions from books, and not at second-hand, from the columns of weekly reviews—he is regarded as a man of vast intellectual power, who allows a certain capricious tendency towards mysticism or indirectness of phrase to run away with him; while by nearly all those who catch up the floating echoes of social literary judgment, he is held to be the leader of the *Festus* school,[1] a man intentionally obscure, a writer whom people who value easy literary digestion ought piously to avoid. Among men capable of forming an independent, unbiassed, and valuable opinion in such matters, the relative positions of Browning and Tennyson have for years been a vexed question, and the decision arrived at with regard to this question may generally be taken to be a pretty clear indication of the critic's personal idiosyncrasy. So clearly is this recognised to be the case, that one never thinks of weighing the arguments on both sides to discover upon which side the value of testimony hangs. If you deem Browning to be the first of living English poets, good. No one can gainsay you. Had Providence altered, by a hair's-breadth, the disposition of your intellectual sympathies, you would have been a worshipper of Tennyson. In either case, your judgment, being honestly in accordance with certain natural sympathies, is not to be controverted by argument. We have, thank goodness, no empirical or academical

---

[1] Philip James Baily's *Festus* underwent many enlargements after its initial publication in 1839. Its inflated style, often absurd, is characteristic of the 'Spasmodic School' of poetry.

rules by which any man's poetry may be tested or his position as a poet declared. The weakness of trying to measure the value of poetry by measuring the length of its lines, is confined to a few incapable critics; it is never shared by the public. It is true that if you confine the question to the music of poetry, you get the Browningites into a corner. Browning has an astonishing power both in versification and in the ring and clatter of words (witness his legend of the Piper of Hamelin), but he has none of the subtle modulation of Tennyson's sweet and gracious lines; in fact, the two men are not rivals; each is 'like a star, and dwells apart.' Whether you prefer the powerful intellectual vigour of Browning, or the calm, wise tenderness of Tennyson, does not much matter. In either case you have within you that receptive, reciprocative sympathy for which you ought to thank God.

We gather from some stray hints in this the first volume of *The Ring and the Book*, that Mr. Browning is well aware that he is not popular with the British public. Here are some lines (which at first sight look remarkably like a conundrum) referring to his relations with the public, and the reflex action of admitted public bewilderment:

> Such, British Public, ye who like me not
> (God love you!)—whom I yet have laboured for,
> Perchance more careful whoso runs may read
> Than erst when all, it seemed, could read who ran,—
> Perchance more careless whoso reads may praise
> Than late when he who praised and read and wrote
> Was apt to find himself the self-same me,—
> Such labour, &c.

But Mr. Browning's occasional obscurity—or shall we say carelessness of explanation?—is not the only reason why he lacks that popularity which so great a poet ought to have in his own country. Mr. Browning has lived the greater part of his literary life in Italy. The colouring of his mind and the colouring of his work are alike Italian. It is Italian life that he has so skilfully analysed; it is Italian scenery and accessories which form the background for his vivid dramatic pictures. If Mr. Browning had studied England and English character as faithfully and successfully as he has studied Italy and Italian character, his position as an English poet would have been other than it now is. So different is the material on which he has chosen to expend his poetical labour from all that we see around us, that we cannot regard the result otherwise than as a mere artistic product. Behind our admiration of such a poem as the *Morte d'Arthur, Maud,* or *In Memoriam,* there lies the distinct consciousness that the poet who speaks to us is one of ourselves, breathing the same atmosphere of inarticulate longing and tender hope, of unrest, and indignation, and wonder over the things that are. We are inclined to believe, however, that no poet ever lived who so accurately reflected the spirit of his time as Mr. Tennyson has done—it is his individual gift. And there is this further consideration, that genius has a wonderful selective faculty, a sort of divine instinct, which leads its possessor, in the face of prudential or other arguments, to select this or that material, this or that scene. Perhaps Mr. Browning has lived in Italy and written of things Italian because they best suited the bent of his dramatic, intense, colour-loving spirit. *Pippa Passes* could never have been written in England. It is easier to believe this than that Mr. Browning has paid the heavy price of a restricted audience for the merely personal pleasure of living in a more comprehensible climate, under brighter skies, and among more picturesque and less conventional people than England offered him.

The selective faculty of which we have spoken is almost invariably exercised unconsciously, and no doubt it was so in the choice Mr. Browning has made of a subject for his latest poem. It is impossible to think of one better fitted to draw out the special characteristics of his genius. *The Ring and the Book* is founded on the report of a trial for murder which took place at Rome in 1698. An Italian nobleman was accused of having, aided by four hired accomplices, murdered his wife (who had fled from his house) and the two old people with whom she was then living. The five were found guilty, and executed. But around and about the story hangs an atmosphere of mystery, which gives ample scope for the poet's imaginings. Who was the guilty one, the husband or the wife? What occult springs of human passion thus bubbled up through the crust of social quiet, and startled people with their colour of blood? Here, surely, is room for that play of psychical theory and suggestion which Browning loves. It is to be noted that nearly all the characterisation of Browning's most dramatic efforts is mental. There is little of the outside action with which most poets describe passion. He never deals in 'body-colour.' Even when glimpses of the glowing scenery of the South appear in his poems, they are only used in so far as they tint the mind of the speaker, colouring it transparently as the electric light colours a fountain. Browning's *dramatis personae* are disembodied souls that love, and quarrel, and fight in a spiritual world over which he, as master-magician, presides. True, they tell you of their solid appearance, and of the solid appearance of the world in which they move; they describe these coloured husks and shells in bright, vivacious touches; yet all the while you know that the action, and passion, and incidents coming before you are psychical, not physical. Hence Browning is at once intensely subjective and intensely dramatic—a curious combination. He does not display the acute emotional analysis of Tennyson, but he exhibits a wonderful intellectual analysis which produces as valuable results in another way. Put before him a psychological conundrum, and he will turn you off a dozen solutions in a minute. Nothing can equal his suggestiveness in accounting for mental phenomena. No one obvious explanation of anything ever occurs to him. There is a recurrent 'or' continually in his mind. He has always at command a dozen lines of rail tapering down to the same point on the horizon. When the young wife in the present poem is first struck by her husband, she prays that she may be allowed to live long enough to confess and be absolved; and lo! in spite of her grievous wounds, she still lingers on the margin of life. Whereupon the chronicler is ready with his divers theories of the miracle:

> Whether it was that, all her sad life long,
> Never before successful in a prayer,
> This prayer rose with authority too dread,—
> Or whether, because earth was hell to her,
> By compensation, when the blackness broke
> She got one glimpse of quiet and the cool blue,
> To show her for a moment such things were,—
> Or else—as the Augustinian Brother thinks,
> The friar who took confession from her lip—
> When a probationary soul that moves
> From nobleness to nobleness, as she,
> Over the rough way of the world, succumbs,
> Bloodies its last thorn with unflinching foot,
> The angels love to do their work betimes,
> Stanch some wounds here, nor leave so much for God.

This fertility of psychological explanation is the *raison d'être* of *The Ring and the Book*. The raw material of the original story is a profound problem, two solutions of which the poet here gives us, with a promise of others in the volumes to come. Out of these various theories, the product of various methods or capacities of observation, we are to extract the truth of the mystery. Perhaps the position of the poet and the aim of the poem will be more clearly understood by our having recourse to Mr. Browning's metaphor of the making of a ring:

> That trick is, the artificer melts up wax
> With honey, so to speak; he mingles gold
> With gold's alloy, and, duly tempering both,
> Effects a manageable mass, then works.
> But his work ended, once the thing a ring,
> O, there's repristination! Just a spirt
> O' the proper fiery acid o'er its face,
> And forth the alloy unfastened flies in fume;
> While, self-sufficient now, the shape remains,
> The rondure brave, the lilied loveliness,
> Gold as it was, is, shall be evermore.

As with the ring, so with the book—'this square old yellow book', which contains the legal history of the trial, the bare, outward facts of the case, the pleadings on both sides, the statements of witnesses. The poet takes up the pure gold of absolute fact, and mingles with it the gold's alloy of human interpretation, of human theories of causality, of his own dramatic readings of the possibilities of the case. He blends his imaginings with this hard mass of circumstance to make it pliable, and by and by you shall see a complete and perfect work of art evolved —a story intelligible and compact, with all the side-lights of human weakness and inconsistency bearing down upon and lessening the shadow of mystery which now hangs around it. . . .

[Summarizes the plot.]

Were *The Ring and the Book* to go no further than this first volume, we should be disposed to say that Mr. Browning had never written anything more powerful than the tragic story which is there conceived and developed. Doubtless its extreme severity will repel many readers. There is in it not a trace of that lyrical joyousness which runs through the varied scenes of *Pippa Passes* like a thread of silver. The air around Pompilia Comparini is too heavy for singing. Over the unhappy young wife's head there is no clear blue to which she may turn and listen for the song of a lark, but a lurid atmosphere of wrong, and hate, and suspicion. There is no room for music in the book. The harsh throats of 'Half-Rome' can only croak lies; the other half of Rome is struck with awe over the fate of the young wife, and wonders where the angels were to permit it. Here and there we find a touch of humour—it were not a poem of Browning's else—but it is that bitter humour which loves to gibe reflectively in a churchyard. There is not even in the poem the sad sweetness of unhappy love. There is no love in it. Pompilia had never a voice in her choice of a husband; and his regards were fixed upon her dowry. There was not even a young cavalier in the question, to suggest what *might* have been to the sad and weary wife. She accepted the services of the priest with gratitude, as she would have received the aid of a toothless peasant; and as for him—no hint of love is present to blot the white escutcheon of his noble self-sacrifice. So tragic is the tragedy that even the customary clown's scenes can find no place in it. But, on the other hand, no writer so carefully avoids *ad captandam* appeals to the emotions as Mr. Browning does. He does not pile up sorrow upon sorrow, and beseech you to weep. On the contrary, here, as elsewhere, the tragedy is related in an off-hand matter-of-fact way by men who do not perceive the drift of what they are saying. The narrators are too near, are too much taken up with minute points of detail, to see or comprehend the majesty of suffering they are unconsciously revealing. They are like the stone-cutters who, with augur, measure, and chisel, mechanically cut out of the block of marble the figure that the artist has modelled in clay. They are themselves only instruments, and are not supposed to have, like a Greek chorus, a divine knowledge of the emotional aspects of everything that is going on. They are never self-conscious. It is not their business to spin theories; they are too much alive and busy for that:

> 'Grau, theurer Freund, ist alle Theorie,
> Und grün des Lebens goldner Baum.'[1]

In the very process of narration they are unconsciously exhibiting their own little failings, their odd notions of things, the particular range of their sympathies; but they never appeal to the reader and bid him be sorrowful over the sad story. They are in Rome, not in England; and they live amid all the bustle, and wonder, and stir of the morning which announced the tragedy that had taken place in Pietro's house.

Nor can one fail to be struck by the manner in which the poet has kept himself in hand in this matter. We will say that in writing the section entitled 'Half-Rome' he was describing the views and opinions, directly opposed to his own, of a man or section of men whom he must hold in abhorrence or contempt. How great, therefore, was the temptation to exaggerate this or that mean interpretation so as to make the

---

[1] 'All theory, dear friend, is gray,
And the golden tree of life is green.'

speaker illogically at variance with himself and doubly contemptible! But the object of the book is not to point a moral of this obvious kind. It was necessary that, mean as were the suspicions and impressions of 'Half-Rome,' they should be reasonable, humanly possible of belief, with that appearance of truth which would commend them to a certain class. Mr. Browning has not permitted himself to take sides in the matter. In both cases he hints the presence of 'a hidden germ of failure' which shall baffle the honest feeling for truth:

> 'Some prepossession such as starts amiss,
> By but a hair's-breadth at the shoulder-blade,
> The arm o' the feeler, dip he ne'er so brave;
> And so leads waveringly, lets fall wide
> O' the mark his finger meant to find, and fix
> Truth at the bottom, that deceptive speck.'

Here, for the present, at least, we must leave *The Ring and the Book*. The advent of a fresh work of genius is not a thing to be passed over, in these times, with silence; and we have only done our duty to our readers in calling their attention to this powerful and elaborate work of art, written by one of the few strong men of our time.

136. Mortimer Collins,
The British Quarterly Review

January 1869, xlix. 248–9

From his unsigned review.

We hope very shortly to call the attention of our readers to Mr. Browning's poetry, and therefore do not now profess to attempt more than thanks for this instalment of what bids fair to be one of the most original, startling, and brilliant of all his poems. It is impossible to put the volume down until it is finished. This is some proof of its extraordinary power. When, added to this, we find the same weird, fearsome little story told, at least four, if not five times over in this first quarter of the poem, and that we are promised some six more repetitions of the wild romance from different points of view, and by different actors in the tragedy, we confess to something like awe at the prodigality of the force which is lavished on these pages. The '*gold*' of this 'ring' is the 'crude fact' which becomes present to the consciousness of the author, when he discovers an old book in Florence charged with the *proces verbal* of accusation, all the pleadings and the judgment, and the doom pronounced against an Italian Count who murdered his wife some two hundred years ago. Mr. Browning brings the fine 'alloy' of his 'fancy' to this crude fact, to the *ingot* of pure gold, and fashions his ring.

137. Unsigned review, *The Fortnightly Review*

1 January 1869, xi. 125–6

With only a fourth part of the complete work before us, there is as yet no adequate material for criticism. We see the subject, and have a glimpse of the manner in which it is to be treated. The theme is an Italian tragedy, and lies in that department to which English taste, narrow and rigid, usually expresses its repugnance by labelling it as morbid anatomy; persons with a less popular theory of art will find no objection in this, holding no subject morbid, but only treatment. That in his mode of handling a theme, at any rate, Mr. Browning is never morbid, needs not be said. Of all contemporary poets he is the most healthy, life-like, and human in his style and colour. In this, its first instalment, his new work abounds in ripe qualities, in variety of presentation, and in strength of fibre. Of course, it 'is not meant for little people or for fools'. Those who mark the construction of the poem will see a reason for its appearance in instalments, provided people read it as it is published; for it ensures that slow and prolonged absorption of the story which is essential to the success of the method in which it is composed.

138. John Addington Symonds,
Macmillan's Magazine
January 1869, xix. 258-62

From his review.

Symonds (1840-93), a disciple of John Ruskin, worked at biography criticism, and translation. His seven-volume *History of the Renaissance in Italy* (1875-6) is his crowning achievement.

After a silence of some years, Mr. Browning has again addressed the public in the book before us, which forms the fourth part of what, when it is completed, will be one of the longest poems in the world. The present volume contains 4,657 lines, which, upon the principle of *ex pede Herculem*,[1] may be taken as a fair basis for comparing the whole work with the *Iliad*, the *Divine Comedy*, or the *Orlando Furioso*. When we tell our readers that in the published sample of this gigantic poem we find but little of the obscurity which made a riddle of *Sordello*, and nearly all the power and subtlety of thought which went to the creation of *Paracelsus*, *Pippa Passes*, Karshish, and Cleon, they will understand that *The Ring and the Book* does not promise disappointment. Yet, no doubt, there will be some, even among Mr. Browning's warmest and most intelligent admirers, who will regret the choice of his subject and the style in which he has thought fit to develop it. The poem is written uniformly in blank verse. It contains but few of those "lyrical inter-breathings" which relieved the monotony of this metre in the works of our dramatists; and the frequent perplexities and involutions of language which impede the easy progress of the reader seem to have arisen from the constant effort to elude the prosiness into which narrative blank verse is apt to fall, rather than to have been forced upon the poet by the intricacy of his thoughts or the sublimity of his imagination. Mr. Browning has so amply proved his power of pouring forth the most exquisite strains of lyrical music, and of photographing subtle and ob-

[1] In effect, judging the size of the whole from the size of the first part seen, as one might estimate the size of Hercules from an examination of his foot or its print.

scure phases of mental activity and emotion in condensed and artistic pictures, that we cannot but regret the absence of short pieces from his volume. Still it is ungracious, with such a gift conferred upon us, to begin with a complaint. Let us rather take the poem as Mr. Browning has made it, and as it will remain to all time, the monument of a genius unique in its peculiar qualities of intellectual subtlety and imaginative force.

It may perhaps be wondered whether the majority of minds will find much pleasure in this piecemeal presentation of a bygone tragedy: this minute analysis of facts and motives,—this many-sided exhibition of a single problem. For those, however, who have the patience and the intellect to follow the elaborate and subtle working of the most profound of living artists, who are capable of delighting in the gradual unfolding of an intricate plot, and of weighing and comparing conflicting evidence, this poem offers attractions of the very highest order. As in a novel of Balzac's, their patience will be rewarded by the final effect of the accumulated details grouped together by the artist, and their intellect will be refreshed with the exhibition of prodigious power carefully exerted and marvellously sustained. It is certain that, as the chain of incident and comment gradually uncurls, each link will add some fresh sensation, until, when its huge length has been unwound, our minds will retain an ineffaceable and irresistible impression of the whole as conceived in the wonder-working brain of Mr. Browning. We are contented to peruse the facts and pleadings of a modern law-case; why should we not bring the same freshness of interest to bear upon this tragedy, not stripped, as happens in the newspapers, of its poetry, but invested with all the splendours of a powerful imagination, while retaining the reality of incidents and details that bear a crime of yesterday home to the hearts of every one?

It would scarcely be fair to Mr. Browning to take leave of his volume without some further quotation; and of the whole, no passage is, perhaps, so well worthy of being extracted as the following beautiful and touching invocation which concludes the first section of the poem:

[Quotes 'O Lyric Love'.]

139. From an unsigned review,
The Westminster Review

1 January 1869, xci (NS xxxv). 298–300

Mr. Browning's new poem promises to be the greatest of all his works. But before we proceed to criticize it, we have a word or two to say on a personal matter. Twice in the poem Mr. Browning breaks away from his subject to sneer at the

> British Public, ye who like me not,
> God love you.

Now, the real truth is, that the British Public do not know Mr. Browning. There is no question of liking or disliking in the matter. Ten years ago he was quite unknown except to a select few. We distinctly remember hearing in the winter of 1860 a well-known author, and editor of one of the most influential reviews of the day, declare, that he had never read a word of Mr. Browning's poetry. And the declaration struck nobody present as at all surprising. The exception, then, was to have read him. Such a declaration, however, in the year 1869 would be a confession of ignorance. But the British public at large still know no more about Mr. Browning than they did about Mill before he became member for Westminster. *The Ring and the Book* will, however, we venture to say, introduce Mr. Browning to the British public. Hitherto Mr. Browning's admirers have been few though fit. His present poem will do much to make him popular, no bad test, even remembering Mr. Martin Tupper's position, of the real worth of any poet.[1] In *The Ring and the Book* we so far meet fewer of those wilful extravagances, crabbedness verging to obscurity, and carelessness of expression, which looks like contempt for the reader. The blank verse, too, has a sustained roll and harmony. There is less of that ruggedness of expression which in Mr. Browning's earliest poems so marred the form of the thought. We are constantly arrested by lines of exquisite grace, full of that nameless beauty which, as Shakespeare says, 'makes

---

[1] Martin Tupper (1810–89), whose *Proverbial Philosophy* (1838) is filled with versified commonplaces. This is not the kind of popularity, of course, Browning would have wanted.

old rhyme beautiful.' Here, for instance, is a vision of Autumn in one line:—

> August's hair afloat in filmy fire—

which is as suggestive as Keats' picture of Autumn:

> Sitting careless on a granary floor,
> Thy hair soft-lifted by the winnowing wind.

Here, too, again, the seasons are painted by one swift stroke, so eminently characteristic of Mr. Browning's peculiar power, as—

> Each facet-flash of the revolving year.

But not in single lines is Mr. Browning's power shown. There are long passages of sustained beauty and pathos which win upon the reader the more that they are read. Here, for instance, is the close of the prologue. . . .

[Quotes 'O Lyric Love'.]

Such a passage as this, so passionate, so human, is in our opinion the highest tide-mark to which Mr. Browning's poetry has yet reached. It is unfortunate that *The Ring and the Book* is published in instalments. Author and critic both stand at a disadvantage. What the effect may be when seen as an organic whole we cannot say. Our criticism must for the present be confined to particular passages, without any regard to the scope of the poem. Some of the beauties we have already indicated. It is not difficult to see that Mr. Browning has sat at the feet of the Elizabethan poets. There are expressions and lines which recall Shakespeare's manner. Such words and phrases as 'sliver' (pp. 1, 169); 'mopping and mowing' (p. 30); 'ask that of any she' (p. 93), all proclaim their origin. Nor is that joyousness which so marks Shakespeare's poetry wanting. There is an overflow of spirits, a perfect exuberance of joy throughout certain passages in *The Ring and the Book*. The poet, describing himself, says, 'A spirit laughs and leaps through every limb'; just as Shakespeare says, 'The spring has put a spirit of youth in everything, that heavy Saturn laughed and leaped with him.' Mr. Browning, too, has been an evident student of words. Such old words, pregnant with meaning and full of antique grace, as 'scrannel' (Milton's word); the north country 'hull' (p. 52), for husk; 'handsel' (p. 85); and the expressive 'gruesome' (p. 99), all used with singular felicity, show what pains he has taken with the workmanship. Sometimes, however, we think that Mr. Browning carries his manufacture of words a little too far. A 'ring-thing' (p. 2) has a perilous resemblance to the vulgar 'thingumbob'. Lastly, we must ask Mr. Browning what is a 'peacock's egg'? (p. 160.)

140. Moncure D. Conway, *Atlantic Monthly*

February 1869, xxiii. 256–9

Conway (1832–1907), American Unitarian and abolitionist, was at the time of this review minister of South Place Chapel, Finsbury, London. His reviews and essays appeared in journals on both sides of the Atlantic, with the result that he became an instrument of Anglo-American culture.

Mr. Browning stands, with few rivals in the past and none in the present, at the head of what, in fault of a better phrase, may be called intellectual poetry. There are poets who rank him in imaginative lustre, there are more musical minstrels, there are—though these are few— warmer and more delicate colorists; but for clear, vigorous thinking, perfect sculpture of forms embodying thoughts (sculptures too tinted with the flush of life, with veins of blue and red), for the utterance of the right physiognomical word and phrase, he has no superior since Shakespeare. Yet intellectual as it is even to a Greek severity,—beyond even Landor[1] here,—it would by no means express the charm of his writings to style them philosophical. No theory can quote him, nor is he at all ethical. His religious fervor shows in points of white fire on every page, and yet no work aims at a moral lesson or object. He writes neither fable nor allegory. The world of men and women, with their actual passions, hopes, and loves, and the vast arenas for their play opened by these as rivers cut their channels,—these are enough for him.

[1] Walter Savage Landor, poet and friend of Browning. See the Introduction and the headnote to No. 59.

His worship is for man; his faith must find its joy in a divine Man. The world of forms, the city of bodies, represents to him the scattered rays of this mysterious humanity; and his art is not to change them into any moral monotony, but to cultivate and guard them in their various vitality and meaning, and report their dramatic interplay.

141. Frederick Greenwood, 'Browning in 1869'

From his unsigned article, *The Cornhill Magazine* (February 1869), xix. 249–56.

Journalist and man of letters, Greenwood (1830–1909) held a series of important editorial posts, including that of editor of *Cornhill* from 1862 to 1868. This review opens with a full description of the plot of Browning's poem.

No such description as this, no description at all, is capable of conveying an adequate idea of the intricacies of fact, argument, and character through which the poet moves with the light of his genius, startling one after the other into life, casting one after the other into a doubtful existence of shadow. That faculty of Shakspeare's which justifies the epithet 'divine' so freely applied to him—the faculty of looking all passions through and through with perfectly dispassionate eyes, and of dealing them here and there, each strictly after its kind, without an emotion—something of that supreme gift we discern in the intellectual candour displayed by Browning as he speaks with the mouth and mind of Guido, of Caponsacchi, of one half-Rome, the other half-Rome, and the gentleman of quality who expounds the *tertium quid*. It is noticeable, however, that we have a generally better *workmanship* when the poet speaks for those who are on the right side than when he speaks for those who are in the wrong. In mere ingenuity of reflection, inference, and argument he is splendidly impartial; but still there is enough of sympathy for one side to give a little extra warmth and colour to the verse whenever he is speaking for it. This, however, detracts but little from the poet's claims to a share of the Shaksperian quality aforesaid. First, we have the subtlety which out of the records of a trial creates half-a-dozen several and distinct characters, each consistent with every fact and suspicion brought out by the trial. But this is obscured by the finer subtlety which shows the play of these several minds over the same facts, the same doubts and suspicions, the different magnitude and significance of the same injuries, temptations, provocations, rights and wrongs. It is useless, however, to attempt any definition of such subtleties, or to appraise in criticism what the critic cannot possibly present to view. We can only say that whereas the scheme of the poem obviously demanded dramatic faculties of a high order, if it was to be a tolerable picture of life, what Browning has made of it is more than a picture: it is a brilliant demonstration of the human mind, seen under many varieties by one searching light. But that the poem is faultless we by no means say. Though its greatness is almost wholly dramatic, there is an error in its construction which the dramatist last of all should make. It is not that the poet's own sentiments about the story and his sympathy with certain of its personages are to be detected in the workmanship, whereas they should never show at all, but that he begins by an open declaration of them; says, to start with, that this is a villain and a liar whatever may appear in the course of the story, and that this other is at no moment to be mistaken for anything else than a suffering angel. She may run away with a young priest, and he may go off with her in the garb of a gay cavalier; but we shall find that it is all nothing. Surely this is not good art? The dramatist should have no more judgment about the character he displays and the passion he depicts than nature herself who first created them. He should never play the commentator; still less should he take sides and explain his reasons for doing so before the play begins. True it is that in this case the dramatic skill of the poet is so great that, even after we are told who really is right and who wrong, we follow every turn of the story with suspense—holding now with Pompilia, now inclining to Guido, and generally viewing the priest much as the 'finer sense of the city' did. Better testimony than this to the poet's genius and fidelity can scarcely be imagined; nevertheless, that which supplies a triumphant test of his skill is itself a fault. Altogether, the introduction, which explains the story, and how it originated, and how it is to be dealt with, is the least excellent part of the book. Though all the rest of the work might lead us to hope that Browning had abandoned the indulgence of the careless writing, the obscurity, the clipt prosaic lines which unquestionably do derogate from much of his work, this preface shows that he has not done so. Sentences twenty-five lines long, and every fifth line parenthetical, are to be found there. Such liberties as—

> A-smoke i' the sunshine Rome lies gold and glad,

for 'golden and glad', are frequent, intolerable as they are. What would be thought of the prose which set forth that a city lay gold and glad? that certain prints exposed for sale in the highway were 'saved by a stone from snowing broad the square'? We should call it unbearably bad English; and bad English in prose is worse in poetry. Haste or indifference leaves here, also, such torturing lines as—

> Turned wrong to right—proved wolves sheep, and sheep wolves.

Haste or indifference spoils such passages as this:

> There stands he,
> While the same grim black panelled chamber blinks,
> As though rubbed shiny with the sins of Rome,
> Told the same oak for ages.

In the same way (in page 57 of vol. i.), a lamp which is meant to light a dungeon, does, in grammatical truth, light the straw in it. Here, likewise, may be found too many instances of the fault of falling into superfluities, as in the description of the man of quality—

> Who breathing musk from lacework and brocade,
> His solitaire amid the flow of frill,
> Powdered peruke on nose, and bag on back,
> And cane dependent on the ruffled wrist,
> Harangues in silvery and selectest phrase,
> 'Neath sunlight in a glorified saloon,
> Where mirrors multiply the girandole;
> Courting the approbation of no mob,
> But Eminence This, and All-Illustrious That,— &c.

Here the last line but two is a fatal indulgence of the overmuch, spoiling a perfect little picture. Such faults as these are really serious faults, nor are they such as are sometimes pardoned as inseparable from a particular style. They are glaring and remediable errors, made in haste and permitted by negligence. Mr. Browning knows perfectly well that in blank verse a line like—

> An instance I find much insisted on

is not musical, and that

> . . . Rome lies gold and glad

is not grammatical; only he will not take the trouble to make that right which wrongs his verse. The wonder is that he should content himself with faulty writing whose mind has been cultivated as much by art as by literature, and for whom an antique gem or earthen cup has as much significance as a sonnet or a flower. The faculties by which he has delight in arts which, eloquent as they are, speak in no way but through exact proportion, grace of form, rhythm of colour and line, should have preserved him from the negligence which leaves his work marred in these very particulars of expression. This new book of itself shows that his workmanship can be as good as he chooses to make it. What flaws we have found are almost all in the prologue; they disappear before it ends in that most touching address to his wife in heaven. The four parts of the story itself, which is all we have read of it, are told in verse as clear and vigorous as any that ever came from the poet's pen; while, as for the subtlety, the insight, the light of genius which plays over the various incidents of the tragedy and the minds of those who were involved in it, they are the fullest and finest manifestations of Browning's power that have ever yet been made. In this poem we have a perfect survey of what was briefly though splendidly displayed in 'Caliban on Setebos'. What gives us additional pleasure in reading it is, that it is written so late. We share the poet's own pride in a genius which grows greater in his waning days, or shows more brightly as the fires of youth decline. This is not only his good fortune, but ours also; and it is a little remarkable that the same thing is true of both the great poets of our generation. Tennyson and Browning both face the downward slope—their backs are fairly turned to the hill now; and both have gained, in these later days, a greater power, while they display at least as fine and true a light. *Lucretius* is testimony for the one, *The Ring and the Book* is testimony for the other. Both men have many a year before them yet, in the natural course of life; and what each has done within these two years gives us the splendid promise of added honour to the age which they have already ennobled.

142. R. W. Buchanan, *The Athenæum*

20 March 1869, pp. 399–400

This extract from his unsigned review should be compared with No. 133, Buchanan's review of Books I–III alone.

At last, the *opus magnum* of our generation lies before the world—the 'ring is rounded'; and we are left in doubt which to admire most, the supremely precious gold of the material or the wondrous beauty of the workmanship. The fascination of the work is still so strong upon us, our eyes are still so spell-bound by the immortal features of Pompilia (which shine through the troubled mists of the story with almost insufferable beauty), that we feel it difficult to write calmly and without exaggeration; yet we must record at once our conviction, not merely that *The Ring and the Book* is beyond all parallel the supremest poetical achievement of our time, but that it is the most precious and profound spiritual treasure that England has produced since the days of Shakspeare. Its intellectual greatness is as nothing compared with its transcendent spiritual teaching. Day after day it grows into the soul of the reader, until all the outlines of thought are brightened and every mystery of the world becomes more and more softened into human emotion. Once and for ever must critics dismiss the old stale charge that Browning is a mere intellectual giant, difficult of comprehension, hard of assimilation. This great book *is* difficult of comprehension, *is* hard of assimilation; not because it is obscure—every fibre of the thought is clear as day; not because it is intellectual,—and it is intellectual in the highest sense,—but because the capacity to comprehend such a book must be spiritual; because, although a child's brain might grasp the general features of the picture, only a purified nature could absorb and feel its profoundest meanings. The man who tosses it aside because it is 'difficult' is simply adopting a subterfuge to hide his moral littleness, not his mental incapacity. It would be unsafe to predict anything concerning a production so many-sided; but we quite believe that its true public lies outside the literary circle, that men of inferior capacity will grow by the aid of it, and that feeble women, once fairly initiated into the

317

mystery, will cling to it as a succour passing all succour save that which is purely religious.

We should be grossly exaggerating if we were to aver that Mr. Browning is likely to take equal rank with the supreme genius of the world; only a gallery of pictures like the Shaksperean group could enable him to do that; and, moreover, his very position as an educated modern must necessarily limit his field of workmanship. What we wish to convey is, that Mr. Browning exhibits—to a great extent in all his writings, but particularly in this great work—a wealth of nature and a perfection of spiritual insight which we have been accustomed to find in the pages of Shakspeare, and in those pages only. His fantastic intel-lectual feats, his verbosity, his power of quaint versification, are quite other matters. The one great and patent fact is, that, with a faculty in our own time at least unparalleled, he manages to create beings of thoroughly human fibre; he is just without judgment, without pre-occupation, to every being so created; and he succeeds, without a single didactic note, in stirring the soul of the spectator with the concentrated emotion and spiritual exaltation which heighten the soul's stature in the finest moments of life itself.

As we have said above, the face which follows us through every path of the story is that of Pompilia, with its changeful and moon-like beauty, its intensely human pain, its heavenly purity and glamour. We have seen no such face elsewhere. It has something of Imogen, of Cordelia, of Juliet; it has something of Dante's Beatrice; but it is unlike all of those—not dearer, but more startling, from the newness of its beauty. From the first moment when the spokesman for the 'Other Half Rome' introduces her—

> Little Pompilia, with the patient brow
> And lamentable smile on those poor lips,
> And under the white hospital array
> A flower-like body—

to the moment when the good old Pope, revolving the whole history in his mind, calls her tenderly

> My rose, I gather for the gaze of God!

—from the first to the last, Pompilia haunts the poem with a look of ever-deepening light. Her wretched birth, her miserable life, her cruel murder, gather around her like clouds, only to disperse vapour-like, and reveal again the heavenly whiteness. There is not the slightest attempt to picture her as saintly; she is a poor child, whose saintliness comes of her suffering. So subtle is the spell she has upon us, that we quite forget the horrible pain of her story. Instead of suffering, we are full of exquisite pleasure—boundless in its amount, ineffable in its quality. When, on her sorry death-bed, she is prattling about her child, we weep indeed; not for sorrow—how should sorrow demand such tears?—but for 'the pity of it, the pity of it, Iago!'—

Extracts can do little for Pompilia: as well chip a hand or foot off a Greek statue. Very noticeable, in her monologue, is the way she touches on the most delicate subjects, fearlessly laying bare the strangest secrecies of matrimonial life, and with so perfect an unconsciousness, so delicate a purity, that these passages are among the sweetest in the poem. But we must leave her to her immortality. She is perfect every way; not a tint of the flesh, not a tone of the soul, escapes us as we read and see.

Only less fine—less fine because he is a man, less fine because his soul's probation is perhaps less perfect—is the priest, Giuseppe Caponsacchi. 'Ever with Caponsacchi!' cries Pompilia on her death-bed,

> O lover of my life, O soldier-saint!

And our hearts are with him too. He lives before us, with that strong face of his, noticeable for the proud upper lip and brilliant eyes, softened into grave melancholy and listening awe. What a man had he been, shining at ladies' feasts, and composing sonnets and 'pieces for music', all in the pale of the Church! In him, as we see him, the animal is somewhat strong, and, prisoned in, pricks the intellect with gall. Little recks he of Madonna until that night at the theatre,

> When I saw enter, stand, and seat herself,
> A lady, young, tall, beautiful, and sad.

Slowly and strangely the sad face grows upon his heart, until that moment when it turns to him appealingly for succour, and when, fearless of any criticism save that of God, he devotes his soul to its service.

> There at the window stood,
> Framed in its black square length, with lamp in hand,
> Pompilia: the same great, grave, grieffull air
> As stands i' the dusk, on altar that I know,
> Left alone with one moonbeam in her cell,
> Our Lady of all Sorrows.

The whole monologue of Caponsacchi is a piece of supreme poetry, steeped in lyrical light. The writer's emotion quite overpowers him, and here, as elsewhere, he must sing. In all literature, perhaps, there is nothing finer than the priest's description of his journey towards Rome with Pompilia, that night she flies from the horror of Guido's house. Every incident lives before us: the first part of the journey, when Pompilia sits spell-bound, and the priest's eyes are fascinated upon her,—

> At times she drew a soft sigh—music seemed
> Always to hover just above her lips,
> Not settle,—break a silence music too!—

the breaking dawn,—her first words,—then her sudden query—

> 'Have you a mother?" She died, I was born.'
> 'A sister then?' 'No sister.' 'Who was it—
> What woman were you used to serve this way,
> Be kind to, till I called you and you came?'

—every look, thought, is conjured up out of the great heart of the lover, until that dark moment when the cat-eyed Guido overtakes them. What we miss in the psychology Pompilia herself supplies. It is saying little to say that we have read nothing finer. We know nothing whatever of like quality.

All the monologues are good in their way, the only ones we could well spare being those of the two counsel, for and against Guido. These, of course, are extraordinarily clever; but cleverness is a poor quality for a man like Robert Browning to parade. The noblest portions of the book are 'Giuseppe Caponsacchi', 'Pompilia', and 'The Pope'. The last-named monologue is wonderfully grand—a fitting organ-peal to close such a book of mighty music; and it rather jars upon us, therefore, that we afterwards hear again, the guilty scream of Guido. It seems to us indeed, if we are bound to find fault at all, that we could have well dispensed with about a fourth of the whole work—the two legal speeches and Guido's last speech. To the two former we object on artistic grounds; to the latter, we object merely on account of its extreme and discordant pain. Yet in Guido's speech occurs one of the noblest touches in the whole work—where Guido, on the point of leaving his cell for the place of execution, exclaims—

> Abate,—Cardinal,—Christ,—Maria,—God . . .
> Pompilia, will you let them murder me?—

thus investing her at the last moment with almost God-like power and pity, in spite of the hatred which overcomes him,—hatred similar in kind, but different in degree, to that which Iscariot may be supposed to have felt for the Master. Nor let us forget to record that the poet, in his bright beneficence, has the lyric note even for Guido. We are made to feel that the 'damnable blot' on his soul is only temporary, that the sharp axe will be a rod of mercy, and that the poor, petulant, vicious little Count will brighten betimes, and be saved through the purification of the very passions which have doomed him on earth. No writer that we know, except Shakspeare, could, without clumsy art and sentimental psychology, have made us feel so subtly the divine light issuing at last out of the selfish and utterly ignoble nature of Guido Franceschini.

Fault-finders will discover plenty to carp at in a work so colossal. For ourselves, we are too much moved to think of trifles, and are content to bow in homage, again and again, to what seems to us the highest existing product of modern thought and culture. Before concluding, we should notice one point in which this book differs from the plays of Shakspeare,—*i.e.* it contains, even in some of its superbest passages, a certain infusion of what Mr. Matthew Arnold once called 'criticism'. So far from this 'criticism' being a blot upon the book, it is one of its finest qualities as a modern product. We cannot enlarge upon this point here, though it is one that is sure to be greatly enlarged upon in publications with more space at their command; but we should not conclude without explaining that the work is the more truly worthy to take Shakspearean rank because it contains certain qualities which are quite un-Shakspearean—which, in fact, reflect beautifully the latest reflections of a critical mind on mysterious modern phenomena.

143. John Rickards Mozley, 'Modern English Poets'

From his unsigned article, *The Quarterly Review* (April 1869), cxxvi. 328–59.

Not many reviewers had Mozley's perspicacity, and few indeed thought Browning in tune with his times.

The first thought which the *Ring and the Book* arouses, we do not say in the reader of it, but in any one who surveys only the outside of the four volumes in which it is contained, will be that it is one of the longest of poems. And after reading, on deliberate reflection, few can avoid the conclusion that it is decidedly too long. It is a weariness to the flesh to read so many arguments pro and con—so many varying shades of the same argument—on a critical case with so many ignoble elements in it, so little that is indisputably noble, as is that of Count Guido Franceschini. The subject is too slight for the mass of ability and thought that Mr. Browning has put into it; while this ability and thought have not in themselves been subjected long enough to the crucible; the pure golden ore is presented in crude entanglement with earth and common pebbles. The poem might have been a fifth part of the length, and have been improved by the omissions.

Yet we are far from wishing to undervalue it. Like all that Mr. Browning writes, it bears the stamp of a rare sincerity; nothing in it is put forward to take the popular ear, nothing without the manifest search after truth, and the conviction that the sentiments put forward are needful to be known and weighed. A distinct moral purpose runs through the poem; not a moral, not an obtrusive excrescence, not anything that can be expressed in a few neatly compacted sentences at the end; but a course of deep meditation on human action and the problems of life. Few poets have been so able to deliver arguments and judgments without being didactic. And with all Mr. Browning's carelessness of popularity, he feels deeply with the men of his own generation. A resolute keeping to the reality which he knows, a resolute abandonment of all the customary fictitious ornaments and appendages of poetry, everywhere mark his verse.

144. From an unsigned review, *The Saturday Review*

3 April 1869, xxvii. 460–1

After summarizing the plot, the reviewer gets to the heart of his matter: Browning's portrayal of Guido.

But Caponsacchi and Guido are Mr. Browning's most signal triumphs. We question if, since the great dramatists of the Elizabethan age, English poetry has ever produced characters so solid, so complex, so carefully thought out. How superior is Guido to Count Cenci, in Shelley's play! Cenci is a motiveless monster; he has a fiendish delight in cruelty and lust, but we recognise in him no community of nature with ourselves; the possibility of becoming like him does not occur to us in our wildest imaginations. But Guido is, every inch of him, a man of passions, reasonings, volitions, the like of which may be seen (though not in the same combination) in many of those whom we meet in our daily life. The union of his cold sceptical nature with the heat of his fierce revenge might have seemed contradictory if portrayed by an inferior master; but in Mr. Browning's hands the apparent inconsistency proves to be one of nature's contrasts, the more veritable because so unexpected. And again, it is true of him, what is true perhaps of every real human being, but what is not found in the exaggerated villains of novelists, that in spite of all his degradation we may admire somewhat in him—namely, the courage and coolness with which he conducts his defence. He has not indeed the physical courage to be able to face immediate death, and at the very last he breaks down in laments and supplications; but on no occasion on which forethought and prudence can be of any value to him does he flinch. Take his own account, in his first speech, of the murder he had committed; how plausible it is! How he had paused, in doubt as to the guilt or innocence of his wife; how he had determined to test her with the name of her lover; how he had pronounced outside the door the name 'Caponsacchi':

[Quotes Book V, ll. 1655ff.]

What follows is no whit inferior. But it is in his second speech that the genuine nature of Guido is most revealed; for here he is speaking privately, in prison, to the two ecclesiastics that are sent to prepare him for death, and consequently he gives much freer rein to his impulses than he had done in his public defence. On the surface, indeed, he seems to be laying aside all reserve, and uttering the very thoughts of his heart. Probably even he appeared to himself to be doing so, and it is not till the last moment, when the officers come to lead him to execution, that the deeper depth, the more vivid reality, is disclosed in his piercing cry for life. He tells his hearers that all he had hitherto said was vanity—the conceit of the head, not the truth of the heart—and he departs appealing to Pompilia for aid:

> Abate,—Cardinal,—Christ,—Maria,—God, . . .
> Pompilia, will you let them murder me?

So powerful a contrast between what a man deceives himself into thinking that he thinks, and what he really thinks when tried by the touchstone of reality, has rarely been described in poetry. It cannot be appreciated unless the whole of Guido's subtle shifting arguments are perused, arguments replete with a mocking cynicism, an affected carelessness, and a would-be heroism.

The fiery and open nature of Caponsacchi is a striking contrast to the character we have just been describing. His speech is of a kind which is a novelty in Mr. Browning's writings; there is in it so much of straightforward description, so little of argumentative subtlety. The poet is here deserting what has hitherto been his strongest ground; but few of his readers will regret the change.

145. John Doherty, *The Dublin Review*

July 1869, NS xxv. 48–62

From his unsigned review.

We do not affect to approach our present task with the perfect calmness and temper of judicial indifference. Catholics, it is true, especially in these islands, have become by long habit somewhat callous to calumny; yet it is pitiful to find a man of genius, such as Mr. Browning undoubtedly is, himself the dupe of most fantastic prejudices, and helping to perpetuate and multiply them in the minds of others. Whatever may be the grounds of his contempt for the British public and his conviction that they 'like him not', we are bound to say that he could not have taken a readier way of commending himself to their favour than by the construction of a tale in which, conformably to the venerable models of Mrs. Radcliffe's time, nearly all the scoundrels are priests; and though the hero is a priest too, he is so by an unhappy mistake; the author plainly indicating his opinion that being a priest is more of a hindrance than a help to being anything good. Perhaps it will be said that the character which he has drawn of the good Pope Innocent XII. is inconsistent with this view. We do not deny that Mr. Browning has meant to delineate him as, what he was, an eminently wise and holy Pontiff; but he has thought proper, in the execution of his design, to credit Innocent with sentiments and expressions which, however natural they would be in Mr. Browning, are highly improper, absurd, and ridiculous in the personage to whom they are attributed. We do not charge Mr. Browning with having entirely invented the anecdote given in vol. i., p. 17, but, as he tells it, it is not only incredible, but nonsensical. The Pope, we are told, was urged to condemn the errors of 'those Jansenists, re-nicknamed Molinists', which he refused to do, on the ground that the world would not hate them so much if there was not some good in them. We are satisfied that even an 'Honorary Fellow of Balliol'— by the way, what on earth is an 'honorary fellow'?—would feel rather ashamed of himself, if so many errors could be detected in his relation of any incident of secular history as are obvious and glaring in this very curious little story. . . .

[The reviewer lectures Browning on the Molinist heresy and on the differences in the numbering of the Catholic and Protestant versions of the Ten Commandments.]

Now, Mr. Browning seems to us to labour under either a great delusion or a great mistake. He is under a delusion if he thinks that every thought springs perfectly accoutred from his brain, like Pallas from the brain of Jove. He is under a mistake if he thinks it is of no consequence in what fashion his intellectual bantlings are presented to the world; whether washed or unwashed, dressed or undressed, with limbs decently composed or awkwardly sprawling. We are aware, and various examples indeed sufficiently show, that the highest functions of social or political life can be discharged, not discreditably, without the assistance of hands or feet. Mr. Browning seems to be of opinion that his lines get on equally well with or without the usual number of limbs, or with more than the usual number, and whether or not the limbs they have got are in the right places. What would be thought of the artist who should send a picture or statue to the Exhibition of the Royal Academy, in which picture the 'portrait of a gentleman', otherwise painted to perfection, had been left destitute of a nose, or which statue, chiselled in all else with the grace of a Chantrey, had been parsimoniously furnished with but one arm, or too liberally endowed with three? If such a work escaped the rigorous exclusion of the Hanging Committee, could the public, *spectatum admissi*, refrain from ridiculing and denouncing so preposterous a deformity? It may be that Mr. Browning would haughtily assert himself, like the Emperor Sigismund, superior to the paltry laws to which humbler poets are fain to yield. It may be that he would contend that for him who utters the burden of song with which the divine afflatus fills his soul, no voice is possible but that of the divinity speaking through him. If such were his explanation, it would only remain for us, while acknowledging the great and godlike presence of Apollo, to note with some wonder his sublime indifference to etymology, scorn of syntax, and persecution of prosody.

Seriously, it is to us a matter of surprise that, in whatever other respects Mr. Browning's last poem may be superior to those which have preceded it, many of them give proofs of much more care in composition, and contain passages, if not of greater power, certainly of greater finish. The faulty lines in *Paracelsus*, for instance, are few; though one does occur now and then to mar the effect of an otherwise fine passage. In such lines as

> You first collect how great a spirit he hid,

and

> To find the nature of the spirit they boast,

one has to make 'spirit' *spir't*, or read the whole as prose. Again, there are lines in which the phrases 'envy and hate', and 'early and late', must each be read as having only three syllables. It is hard to know what to do with such a line as

> Regard me and the poet dead long ago,

unless we make 'poet' *pote*; the only authority for which pronunciation, as far as we know, is an Irish ditty, in which it is averred that there was 'no one', not even

> Fitzjarald the pote,
> That ever yet wrote
> A fit rhyme for the Ram.

But these faults are accidental and venial in comparison with the deliberate offences, as we are compelled to regard them, against rhythm, good taste, and even the English language, committed in *The Ring and the Book*. The tale of the *Book*, as we shall explain more fully further on, is told in a great variety of ways. One of those is what the author calls the *Tertium Quid*, the way in which the story ran among the 'superior social section', supposed to be told by some 'man of quality' in 'silvery and selectest phrase'. Let us give a few samples of the distinguished Tertium Quid's exquisite phraseology:

> Go, brother, stand you rapt in the ante-room
> Of her Efficacy my Cardinal
> For an hour,—he likes to have lord-suitors lounge,—
> While I betake myself to the grey mare,
> The better horse,—how wise the people's word!—
> And wait on Madame Violante. (Vol. ii. p. 21.)

Another:

> Why not have taken the butcher's son, the boy
> O' the baker or candlestick-maker? In all the rest
> It was yourselves broke compact and played false,
> And made a life in common impossible. (p. 27.)

327

Another:

> So Guido rushed against Violante, first
> Author of all his wrongs, *fons et origo*
> *Malorum*—increasingly drunk,—which justice done,
> He finished with the rest. Do you blame a bull?
> In truth you look as puzzled as ere I preached. (p. 69.)

Very naturally. A few lines more:

> The Archbishop of the place knows and assists:
> Here he has Cardinal This to vouch for the past,
> Cardinal That to trust for the future,—match
> And marriage were a cardinal's making—in short
> What if a tragedy be acted here? (p. 70.)

Or a farce? Call'st thou this 'poetry', good 'Master' Browning? To us it reads far more like 'prose run mad'. It is absurd to defend such writing on the ground of its 'realism'. Realism, if it means anything, means conformity to reality, and to say that it is in conformity with reality to make an accomplished gentleman, or for that matter any rational person, express himself in dislocated doggerel, is an insult to common sense. Shakespeare and the other great dramatists of the Elizabethan age far better understood how to reproduce the real as well as how to give form to the ideal by their art, when they relieved the measured and poetic language of their principal *dramatis personae* by the homely but racy prose of the inferior characters.

Mr. Browning's genius is essentially dramatic, and many of his best efforts have naturally taken that form. The genuine and high inspiration of much of his poetry is indisputable. He has often great power of thought; generally great vigour, and sometimes great felicity, of expression. In 'insight and outsight', as he would say himself, the range and force of his imagination are transcendent. Properly disciplined and kept to his proper work, he might have been the Shakespeare of our century. As it is, he is not equal to Tennyson; whom, nevertheless, he as far surpasses in power of conception as he is surpassed by him in grace of execution. We doubt, indeed, if a more perfect 'artist in words' than Tennyson ever lived. If it could be true, as it cannot be, that a great poet is made, not born, it would be true of him. But Browning is a born poet, and only lacks the sense or the modesty to see that something else is wanting to him to be among the greatest. For want of artistic cutting, his diamonds often show but dully beside the paste of other men. For want of artistic development, the thought that should have been starry is often simply nebulous. . . .

The character of Pompilia is not only well contrasted with Guido's, but is itself an exquisite conception; for which also, perhaps, Mr. Browning is more indebted to his Italian experiences than he would care to own. It is a type of simplicity, innocence, and purity. She can scarcely understand why scandal couples her name with Caponsacchi's as it has done. To her he is not only a priest, but a hero and a saint. He is the angel and the help from God that delivered her from her hateful, yet not hated, husband's power, when the first promise of maternity impelled her to dare and suffer everything for a young life not yet come forth to the day, yet dearer than her own. Her love for him is not that of woman: there is something of the supernatural in it. Her deepest human love is for her child; but she has charity for all, even for her husband. Her excuse for him, however, that 'he did not make himself' is so evidently out of keeping with her character, that Mr. Browning is driven to the awkward necessity of making Guido envy her for having hit upon it. Considering, also, that it was rather an ideal than the real and imperfect Caponsacchi, whom she worshipped, it seems unnatural to make her excuse her admiration in this way:

> If I call 'saint' what saints call something else—
> The saints must bear with me, impute the fault
> To a soul i' the bud, so starved by ignorance,
> Stinted of warmth, it will not blow this year,
> Nor recognize the orb which spring-flowers know.
> But if meanwhile some insect with a heart
> Worth floods of lazy music, spendthrift joy—
> Some fire-fly renounced spring for my dwarfed cup,
> Crept close to me with lustre for the dark,
> Comfort against the cold,—what though excess
> Of comfort should miscall the creature—sun?
> What did the sun to hinder while harsh hands
> Petal by petal, crude and colourless,
> Tore me? This one heart brought me all the spring!
>
> (Vol. iii. pp. 73-4.)

Caponsacchi is a failure. If the author meant to make a hero of him, he ought to have been less like a young English parson. That is probably the highest type of the churchman—at least the young churchman—which Mr. Browning can conceive; but a good young priest, such as one can imagine in Caponsacchi's place, though not less than a brave, true, and honourable gentleman, would also be something more. Possibly, however, Mr. Browning recognises this, when he makes the

Pope speak of Caponsacchi, though with affection, as a 'scapegrace'.

Nothing strikes us more forcibly in this very remarkable poem than the judicial retribution which seems to fall on genius rendered self-forgetful by too much self-contemplation, and, like Narcissus, falling souse into the water. The fatuity of Narcissus, too, however ridiculous, had this excuse, that the image he bent to gaze upon was really beautiful. But a wrinkled, and puffy, and blotched Narcissus, grinning with delight at the reflection of a countenance which he fancies still 'as fair as Dian's visage', though to all but a set of silly sycophants it is simply hideous—that is a spectacle grotesque enough to tickle the very ribs of death with inextinguishable laughter. It is pitiful to see a great light of literature or art go out in a sputter and flare of noisome egotism. That was the end of Turner. It threatens to be the end of Dickens and Carlyle. It is very likely to be the end of Mr. Browning. Praise intoxicates them; vanity blinds them; the assurance of fame makes them heedless of how it should be legitimately retained. Then comes a reverse, if not a disillusion. Because King Nabucodonosor would inhale incense, therefore shall King Nebucodonosor eat grass. Just when the pedestal is raised so high that the statue towers above every surrounding fabric, down topples the rickety idol and 'shames its worshippers'. Of what immense value would that humility which is only another name for self-knowledge have been to such men, were it but to make them obedient to those laws of art which are, after all, the only sure basis of their fame!

We must not omit to say, in conclusion, that this is not a book for all hands. The milk of babes is not at all the sort of fare that Mr. Browning sets before his readers, but very strong meat, sometimes horse-flesh indeed, and that of the coarsest, with nothing of a Francatelli's art to disguise it in the cooking. So far, perhaps, it is all the better.

146. From an unsigned review, *Chamber's Journal*

24 July 1869, 4th Ser., xlvi. 473–6

If we except Scott, and still more Coleridge in England, and Goethe in Germany, we have since the beginning of the century been in the hands of the subjective school of poets. Poets, that is, who view the universe of men and things through a medium supplied by their own idiosyncrasies, and whose poetry comes to us savouring strongly of the mind and heart of the individual poet. Against this style of poetry Mr Browning's works supply a welcome and long desired reaction. More productive than Coleridge, and far surpassing Scott in delicacy of touch and finished treatment, we find him free from Mr Ruskin's 'pathetic fallacy', which attempts to depict external nature by investing it with human characters, and then painting it according to the tone of the artist's mind. In scenery, he gives us things as he sees them; and in dramatic poetry, which he chiefly loves, he thinks out his characters to the very heart's core, and then makes them speak for themselves, without coming forward like a chorus to explain the situation or scatter moral reflections over the drama. But it is in the work now before us that Mr Browning's genius reaches the culminating point. Henceforth, his place in the very first rank of English poets must be conceded without a murmur or a doubt. He has added a new lustre to English literature, and enriched our language with a possession for ever. . . . In Count Guido, Caponsacchi, and especially in Pompilia, we have distinct creations, characters which stand forth in clearness and completeness like Macbeth, Hamlet, or Cordelia. Pompilia is exquisite in her beauty, her unconscious grandeur and nobility of soul, her simplicity, and withal her dignity, maintained alike amid great sufferings and petty persecutions more lowering than sublime trials. We cannot point to a creation worthy of being compared with her in the whole range of English literature. For the choice of subject we have nothing but condemnation. It is Mr Browning's luck. But granting this, there is no mark of great and lofty poetry wanting in the elaboration of this noble masterpiece. There is no departure from the true concrete artistic treatment in any line of the whole poem; no putting aside the poet for the didactic teacher; no thrusting forward of the author's individuality to speak for the characters, or to interpret them to his readers.

Repulsive though it be, however, we must set some abstract of the story before our readers, or it will be impossible to convey to them by quotation any real idea of the beauty of the poem.

[Concludes with detailed summary and generally enthusiastic comment.]

147. J. H. C. Fane, *The Edinburgh Review*

July 1869, cxxx. 164–86

From his unsigned review.

Fane (1827–70), a member of the Cambridge Apostles at Trinity, was a diplomat, translator of *Heine*, and minor poet.

The occasional obscurity of Mr. Browning's style—although there is, we think, less of it in these four volumes than in any poem previously published by him—constitutes a defect of which we mitigate the purely literary importance in expressing our belief that it is avoidable. But we impugn the morality of the artist in presuming his potential skill. There are obscure passages in Mr. Browning's works where the difficulty resides, not in any complexity of thought, but in sheer slovenliness of ravelled expression; while, to prove such passages needlessly and therefore culpably obscure, the diction of the poet is often as remarkable for lucidity of exposition as the thought which it conveys is distinguished by subtlety of conception. With regard to these latter passages, dealing generally with the most important questions which can engage the attention of men, we hardly care to record our protest against the complaint that it requires a considerable effort of the mind to master them. Those who seek for shells may paddle at their ease in the fringe of the ocean 'that daily licks the shore'; those who seek for pearls must dive in deep water—and there is no diving without considerable effort.

We now pass to a fault in Mr. Browning arising from a combination of intellectual and moral audacity—a kind of temerity which finds its counterpart in M. Victor Hugo, and which particularly distinguishes both these writers when they assume (as they so frequently and success-fully assume) the character of mental pathologists .The study of morbid anatomy, whether moral or physical, is not to be prosecuted without contact with the unclean; but what we object to is that the processes of the dissecting-room should be conducted in the public street. It is quite possible to employ in art the valuable results of scientific mental analysis, without making the loathsome details of knowledge the vehicle of its communication. M. Hugo especially permits himself to handle ideas and words which were never meant for artistic manipulation. There is, for example, an incident, a word, connected with one of the decisive battles of the world which, however fit or unfit to be whispered by men in corners, and more or less appreciated as affording a fine example of passionate frankness, certainly does not form a proper object for a polite writer to present even on the tip of his pen to a polite public. You think not? You shall see M. Hugo take it up, pat it, pet it, grow maudlin over it, and show you with what dexterity a consummate artist can do what in your simplicity you deemed impossible. '*Cette bête de mot, impossible!*'[1] We confess that this manifestation of an intellectual capa-city to pirouette on a pin-head without falling into circumjacent filth, and the execution of similar literary gymnastics, betray a vanity alto-gether alien from Mr. Browning, but he rivals his illustrious con-temporary in the essentially French quality of 'audace.' In the present work he ventures with Pompilia upon ground of perilous lubricity— we freely admit without lapse; but there is both lapse and collapse of all that preserves the self-respect of art in the occasional outrages of thought and language—in one instance, the mental and verbal garbage —which he assigns to male characters in the drama. No reader who is familiar with Mr. Browning's works can for a moment doubt the essential purity of his mind. Indeed the whole conception of *The Ring and the Book* bears the impress of a mind pre-eminently pure, and we apprehend that Mr. Browning's temerity is inspired solely by the desire to be true to Nature. But to hold that, because human beings of a given temperament will, under given circumstances, say a given thing, there-fore the artist is justified in putting the same thing into the mouth of

[1] 'That beast of a word, impossible.'

corresponding personages in his drama, is to commit the radical mistake of assigning to art a reflective instead of a representative function.

With regard to another important fault of Mr. Browning's, the prevailing ruggedness of his versification, we have not much to say. When we consider it in connexion with the proofs which he occasionally gives of his mastery over rhythmical expression, we are as much perplexed by it as by the alternations of lucidity and nebulousness in his philosophical utterances. Here, again, the poet's skill is in conflict with his morals. Even the conventional respect due from a writer to his readers should restrain him from excoriating their ears by such lines as these—with decasyllabic pretensions:

> This a tough point, shrewd, redoubtable. . . .
>
> His wife, so putting, day by day and hour by hour. . . .
>
> Plainly, and need so be put aside. . . .
>
> Bids Law 'be damned!' adds Gospel 'nay'. . . .

But we cannot part thus from Mr. Browning. We have quoted some very discordant lines. We will let them be followed by a passage of verse which is 'musical as is Apollo's lute,' and which derives a sacred interest from the

> Bitter constraint and sad occasion dear

in which it originates. To those only who have passed, like Mr. Browning, through the darkest of the valleys of the shadow of death, identity of sorrow will reveal the full pathos and significance of his noble words. But they will be precious also to those who, without having experienced supreme calamity, may claim as lovers of English literature a community of sorrow with the poet, since the loss which he deplores has deprived them of one of the noblest and brightest of intellectual benefactors:

[Concludes with 'O Lyric Love'.]

148. H. B. Forman, 'Browning's Poetry'

In the *London Quarterly Review* (July 1869), xxxii. 325–57

Littérateur and collector, Harry Buxton Forman (1842–1917) was a Browning enthusiast. He purchased a MS. of *Colombe's Birthday* and edited various of Browning's poems and wrote frequently about him. See the Broughton index.

In naming the Psychological School of poetry, the issues opened up are much more complex, and therefore more vague. The term, as relating to followers of a leadership, is perhaps rather prophetic than now applicable. The great leader of the school, Browning, has followed a course so intensely original, that near imitations of him would be excessively difficult to effect: a course so unpopular hitherto that such imitations, even if practicable, have been uninduced by the market considerations which, of themselves, must have sufficed to furnish innumerable aspirants to Tennysonian imitation. At the same time there is scarcely a poet of mark now among us in whose works the influence of Browning may not be clearly discerned. . . .

This 'nobler stage the soul itself' is precisely the only stage made use of by Browning in the psychological monologue, whether Mrs. Browning had that idea in her mind or not; and it is the development and perfection of this monologue that yields the most important line of observation for the critic to take up in discussing Browning's labours. *Pauline* is the natural ancestor of *The Ring and the Book*: these two, his earliest and latest known poems, are the terminal vertebræ of of the spinal column of his works regarded as a body; and around that column are matters, by no means unimportant, but, still, *less* important —the dramas already referred to, some few pieces not strictly psychological monologues, one dramatic poem, one analytic narrative poem, and one prose piece.

Up to this stage in Browning's career, those who were inclined to slight his poetry had this point at which to make an advantageous attack—that, of his most perfectly finished and perfectly original works (works, that is, in which he had perfected a form peculiarly his own), none could be called important poems if measured by size. It has long been the fashion among the shallower 'critics' of the day to lose no available opportunity for a gird at the darknesses of *Sordello*, and the drynesses of *Paracelsus*, works which none the less will remain high in sight long after the world has let slip the remembrance that the nineteenth century boasted a school of 'critics' so blind as to think slightly of a profound contemporary poetic intellect. But now that it has become heterodox to sneer openly at even these works, the shortness of the poems by which Browning is best known serves as a stand-point for detractors; and it is to be hoped that *The Ring and the Book*, both as a work of size and as an intellectual effort—both as a contribution of new splendid matter, and as an elaboration of a new splendid manner—will set at rest this kind of criticism. Even since the publication of this work we have seen remarks on the 'awkwardness', 'ungainliness', and so on, of the form; presumably because the lesser critics had the book to 'do', and had not yet had their cue given them by more important brethren.

Whether *The Ring and the Book* is a 'success' in the ordinary sense, we have not to discuss; in the highest sense it certainly is. The poet himself seems not unhopeful when he says:

> British Public, who may like me yet,
> (Marry and amen!)—Vol. iv. p. 324.

Though he has certainly done no violence to his genius, by adopting aught from the popular style of the day, he has evidently laboured much to make his meaning perfectly clear in this last work. If popularity come in the poet's lifetime, well! 'If not, well also, but not so well.' Be it borne in mind that—

> What the poet writes,
> He writes: mankind accepts it if it suits,
> And that's success: if not, the poem's passed
> From hand to hand, and yet from hand to hand,
> Until the unborn snatch it, crying out
> In pity on their fathers' being so dull,
> And that's success too.

The idea that epics have 'died out with Agamemnon and the goat-nursed gods', is one which is obviously absurd, even without practical evidence to the contrary, and has arisen from the false notion that 'heroic' is a term applicable only to wars and large actions. Now that Walt Whitman has written the Epic of Democracy on the other side of the

Atlantic,[1] and Browning, on this side, has furnished what may be fitly termed the Epic of Psychology, the idea of the decease of the epic is more than ever a dead idea. The day has long gone by when heroism meant pugilism, and the might of man was measured by magnitude of muscle. Breadth of mind and width of heart come first now, and the largest action is not that which covers the greatest area and deploys the largest aggregate of physical powers, but that which involves most disinterestedness, philanthropy, purity of heart, power of thought—in short, the maximum of intellectual and moral force. For such a display, one set of modern men and women serves as well as another for types; and the Roman murder case of 150 years ago, which has so strongly taken hold of Browning, was the germ of what is more essentially modern than any great poetic production of these latter centuries.

That we have not done critical justice to *The Ring and the Book* we are sensible. The value of a work of this magnitude from a poet with the wide artistic powers, and the 'intellectual equipment' which we find in Browning, is not easy to estimate, when we take into consideration the range of a powerful poet's influence, not only on his contemporaries, but also on those to come in the long roll of the onward centuries.

149. Algernon Charles Swinburne, letter

1869

From a letter to Lord Houghton, *The Letters of Algernon Charles Swinburne*, ed. by Edmund Gosse and T. J. Wise, I (1919), 62–3.

What a wonderful work this is of Browning's. I tore through the first volume in a day of careful study, with a sense of absolute possession. I have not felt so strongly that delightful sense of being mastered— dominated—by another man's imaginative work since I was a small boy. I always except, of course, Victor Hugo's which has the same

[1] *Leaves of Grass.*

force and insight and variety of imagination together with that exquisite bloom and flavour of the highest poetry which Browning's has not: though it has perhaps a more wonderful subtlety at once and breadth of humourous invention and perception.

As for interest, it simply kills all other matters of thought for the time. This is his real work—big enough to give him breathing space, whereas in play or song he is alike cramped. It is of the mixed-political composite-dramatic order which alone suits him and serves him.

150. Sidney Lanier, letter

13 April 1870

From a letter to Paul Hamilton Hayne, in Edwin Mims, *Sidney Lanier* (1905), pp. 110–11.

These comments, sent by one American poet to another, take an added interest from the fact that Lanier greatly valued the music and the sound of poetry, qualities in which Browning has generally been thought to be lacking.

Have you seen Browning's *The Ring and the Book*? I am confident that, at the birth of this man, among all the good fairies who showered him with magnificent endowments, one bad one—as in the old tale—crept in by stealth and gave him a constitutional twist i' the neck, whereby his windpipe became, and has ever since remained, a marvellous tortuous passage. Out of this glottis-labyrinth his words won't, and can't, come straight. A hitch and a sharp crook in every sentence bring you up with a shock. But what a shock it is! Did you ever see a picture of a lasso, in the act of being flung? In a thousand coils and turns, inextricably crooked and involved and whirled, yet, if you mark the noose at the end, you see that it is directly in front of the bison's head, there, and is bound to catch him! That is the way Robert Browning catches

you. The first sixty or seventy pages of *The Ring and the Book* are altogether the most doleful reading, in point either of idea or of music, in
the English language; and yet the monologue of Giuseppe Caponsacchi, that of Pompilia Comparini, and the two of Guido Franceschini,
are unapproachable, in their kind, by any living or dead poet, *me
judice*. Here Browning's jerkiness come in with inevitable effect. You
get lightning glimpses—and, as one naturally expects from lightning,
zigzag glimpses—into the intense night of the passion of these souls.
It is entirely wonderful and without precedent. The fitful play of
Guido's lust, and scorn, and hate, and cowardice, closes with a master
stroke:

Christ! Maria! God! . . .
Pompilia, will you let them murder me?

151. A Negative View

1869

Alfred Austin, from his 'The Poetry of the Period', *Temple Bar*
(June 1869), xxvi. 316–33.

This famous article by Austin (1835–1913), critic, poetaster, and
—after 1896—Poet Laureate, brought Browning's anger to a
boil, with the results discussed in the Introduction, pp. 19–22.

Whether Mr. Browning keeps a Commonplace Book, we have no
means of knowing; but we have every means of knowing that he
thinks in prose, for the prose thoughts are there before us, gratuitously
turned by some arbitrary whim, which we confess completely puzzles
us, into metre. Mr. Browning is, as we have said, a profound thinker,
and nearly all his thoughts have the quality of depth. Now, probably
all thoughts to which this quality of depth can be ascribed, arrive at the
portals of the brain in this prose—their natural vesture; whilst, on the
contrary, lofty thoughts, their antitheses, usually enter it in the subtle

garb of music. Here we have clear difference in kind; prose thoughts, so to speak, from below—poetical thoughts, so to speak, from above. If we suppose a permeable plane dividing these two regions of thought, we can easily understand how there comes to be what we may call a sliding scale of poets, and a sliding scale of philosophical thinkers; some of the latter, to whom the faculty of philosophising cannot be denied, being rather shallow—some of the former, whose claims to poetical status cannot fairly be questioned, not being very soaring; and we can further understand how the natural denizens of one sphere may ever and anon cross the permeable plane, invade the other sphere, and seem to belong to it in the sense in which foreigners belong to a country they are constantly visiting. But for all that there ever remains a substantial difference between the two spheres and between their respective native inhabitants, between the country of poetry and the country of prose, between poetical power and instinct and philosophical power and proclivity. Accordingly, where a man talks the language of the sphere to which he properly belongs—in other words, when a philosophical thinker publishes his thoughts in prose, or a poetical thinker addresses us in verse—our task is comparatively simple. All we have got to do is to decide whether the former be profound or shallow, and whether the latter have a lofty or a lagging pinion. It is when a man affects to talk the language of the sphere to which he does not essentially belong, that he deceives some people, and puzzles us all. This is precisely what Mr. Browning has done. Hence most people scarcely know what to make of this poetico-philosophical hybrid, this claimant to the great inheritance of bardic fame, whose hands are the hands of Esau, but whose voice is the voice of Jacob. Several, whose eyes, like those of Isaac, are dim, and who therefore cannot see, admit the claim—hesitatingly, it is true, again like Isaac—of the hands, and accept him as a poet. But it is the true resonant voice, not the made-up delusive hand, which is the test of the singer; and to those whose sight is not dim, Mr. Browning is not a poet at all—save in the sense that all cultivated men and women of sensitive feelings are poets—but a deep thinker, a profound philosopher, a keen analyser, and a biting wit. With this key to what to most persons is a riddle—for, despite the importunate attempts of certain critics who, as we have already said, having placed Mr. Tennyson on a poetical pedestal considerably too high for him, are now beginning to waver in their extravagant creed, and are disposed to put him on one a trifle lower, placing Mr. Browning there instead, the general public has not yet become quite reconciled to the operation

—we think we shall be able to rid them of their perplexities. At any rate, we will keep applying it as we go along.

Let us revert to *Paracelsus* and take our start from it, as Mr. Browning himself did. His lyrical pieces apart—of which something anon—and the humouristic faculty which has since developed itself in him, Mr. Browning in *Paracelsus* is what Mr. Browning is in all the many so-called poetical works he has since given to the world. He is Mr. Browning, naturally not yet grown to his full size; not yet quite so deep, shrewd, obscure, fantastical, unmusical; but with the exceptions we have just made, what manner and matter of mental man he is may there be satisfactorily scrutinised. He is at his never-abandoned natural task of thinking deep thoughts in prose, and his artificial trick of turning them into verse. He is, as he imagines, working like a dramatist, just as he has since imagined himself to be working as a dramatist in such pieces as 'Bishop Blougram's Apology', 'Caliban on Setebos', &c. Indeed, he has let us into the secret of his method in *Sordello*, written very shortly after *Paracelsus*, in the following lines; which we quote, though at the risk perhaps of most of our readers declaring that they have not the faintest notion as to what they mean:

> How I rose,
> And how you have advanced! since evermore
> Yourselves effect what I was fain before
> Effect, what I supplied yourselves suggest,
> What I leave bare yourselves can now invest.
> How we attain to talk as brothers talk,
> In half-words, call things by half-names, no balk
> From discontinuing old aids. To-day
> Takes in account the work of Yesterday:
> Has not the world a Past now, its adept
> New aids? A single touch more may enhance,
> A touch less turn to insignificance,
> Those structures' symmetry the Past has strewed
> The world with, once so bare. Leave the mere rude
> Explicit details! 'tis but brother's speech
> We need, speech where an accent's change gives each
> The other's soul—no speech to understand
> By former audience: need was then to expand,
> Expatiate—hardly were we brothers! true—
> Nor I lament my small remove from you,
> Nor reconstruct what stands already. Ends
> Accomplished turn to means: my art intends
> New structure from the ancient.

It must not be supposed that we quote this passage with approbation. Not only do we think it not poetry, but we think it detestable gibberish, even if we look at it as prose. Had Mr. Browning been writing *bona-fide* prose, he would have put it very differently and much more intelligibly; but talking, to revert to our metaphor, in a foreign language over which he has not obtained due mastery, he is shockingly unintelligible, or at least painfully difficult to understand. By dint of great trouble we have arrived at understanding the above passage, and will endeavour briefly to explain its meaning. Our readers have no doubt heard the vulgar proverb, 'A nod is as good as a wink to a blind horse.' Mr. Browning wishes to intimate that a nod or a wink is really and seriously as good to an intelligent man of the nineteenth century as formal speech. Shakespeare and such unfortunate individuals, having had to deal with an inferior set of people, were compelled to use 'rude explicit details.' Mr. Browning's 'art intending new structure from the ancient,' has only to 'talk in half-words, call things by half-names,' and if they do not understand him, the fault is theirs of course, not his. They are not his brothers. In this same *Sordello*, from which we are quoting, over each page stands a prose heading, which is a continuation of the foregoing one. Over the passage from which we have made the above extract, the following headings occur: 'He asserts the poet's rank and right, Basing these on their proper ground, Recognizing true dignity in service, Whether successively that of Epoist, *Dramatist or, so to call him, analyst*, Who turns in due course synthesist.'

Now the last two headings are of great importance, just as is the passage in verse below them which we have quoted, because, however, false may be their matter, and however deplorable their manner, they contain Mr. Browning's own estimate of his office, and his own account of his method. As such, they are invaluable to us. Just one more brief confession on his part will complete for us the idea, as understood by himself, of his functions as a poet. In the Dedication of *Sordello* to Mr. Milsand, written in 1863, or twenty-three years after it was first published, Mr. Browning writes: 'The historical decoration was purposely of no more importance than a background requires; and my stress lay on the incidents in the development of a soul: *little else is worth study. I, at least, always thought so.*' Thus Mr. Browning's office, according to his own account, is that of an analyst who turns in due course synthesist and develops a soul by half-words; or, as we should put it, it is to get inside an imaginary or historical personage, and evolve him for the benefit of the intelligent public by nods and winks. This is how his 'new art intends new structure from the ancient.'

We hope our readers understand us; for, if they do not, they will certainly never understand Mr. Browning, and it is highly desirable that they should understand so much of him as the foregoing, both in order to be able to measure him as he asks to be measured, and to appreciate our account of him, which a very little reflection shows to be in perfect harmony with, and indeed substantially the same as, his own account of himself. What is his own account of himself? An analyst who turns in due course synthesist, whose subject matter is souls, and whose method of communication with the outer world is half-words arranged in metre. What is our account of him? A subtle, profound, conscious psychologist, who scientifically gets inside souls, and, having scrutinised their thoughts and motives in a prose and methodical fashion, then makes them give the result, as if they had been scrutinising themselves, in verse. This latter operation Mr. Browning evidently imagines is synthesis. There never was a more ludicrous mistake. It is, in reality, nothing more than the analysis completed and stated, and is no more synthesis than a lecture by Professor Huxley on the *vertebrata* is an animal. Mr. Browning labours under the greatest possible delusion when he imagines that he ever 'turns in due course synthesist.' That is precisely what he never does. He remains a mere analyst to the end of the chapter, pottering about among the brains and entrails of the souls he has dissected, and utterly unable to do anything with them, except to call attention to the component parts he has skillfuly laid bare with his knife. It would be wonderful if he could do anything more; just as wonderful as it would be if the anatomical professor could put together again the poor carcass of the dog he has reduced to so many inanimate members. He can galvanise them, it is true, for a moment, into simulating life. So can Mr. Browning. But that is the range of the synthesis of both of them. If Mr. Browning wants to know of a dramatist who is a real synthesist, we can easily tell him of one. His name is Shakespeare. But, then, Shakespeare was, luckily, not so great in analysis as Mr. Browning. Speaking properly, Shakespeare never analyses at all in our presence, and probably never did so even in the presence of his own consciousness, any more than millions of men who speak grammatically analyse the construction of their sentences before they utter them. Every real drama—indeed every real work of plastic (as opposed to mere technic) art—is an organism, a growth, a vitality, just as much as is a bird, a tree, or a mammal. Not only is it true that a poet is born, not made, but it is equally true that his poem is born, not made.[1] In his brain, heart, soul, whatever we like to call it—in his being would be, perhaps, the best word—exists the seed or germ of a poem or of many poems; and all that external conditions, sights, sounds, experiences, can do for this seed or germ is to foster or to check it. But the thing itself, the real living, poetic protoplasm, is not to be had or got *ab extra*. Going about seizing upon objects, and submitting them to analysis even though synthesis be then superadded, will by no means produce poetry, or any work of plastic art—using the word art properly, as opposed to craft. Otherwise a chemist, who finds out what a particular kind of gunpowder is made of, and then makes it, would be a poet. For to him is peculiarly applicable Mr. Browning's definition of 'dramatist'—terrible dramatist indeed! 'or, so to speak, analyst, who turns in due course synthesist.' But we assure Mr. Browning there is an impassable difference between dramas and detonating powder, and also between the process by which they are to be produced. We freely grant—indeed, we more than grant, we insist—that Mr. Browning, whatever may be said against his synthetical powers (and, as we have seen, even if he had them to perfection, he would not necessarily be a poet), is great as an analyst. But the analysed goose of the fable laid no more golden eggs; and analysed souls are just as little likely ever again to speak golden words. It is not the province of the poet to perform any such operation. It is the province of such men as Hartley, James Mill, and Professor Bain, and admirably do they perform their work. But we have not got any poems from them, nor is it likely that from the only living one of the illustrious trio we ever shall. Having a distinct comprehension of their office and its limits, they have accordingly kept within the sphere —the sphere of deep prose thoughts as opposed to that of lofty poetical thoughts, of which we have spoken—to which their talents and task naturally belonged. Hence their labours have been of inestimable service to the world. But Mr. Browning has perversely flitted from one sphere to the other, insisted on making himself at home where he is a perfect stranger, uttered profound thoughts in would-be poetic idiom, an idiom foreign to them and to him, and involved them accordingly in such abominable jargon that, when he and his affected admirers have passed away, they will be utterly lost to the world—for they *will* be a loss, on

---

[1] Hence the difficulty of defining poetry, just as there exists the well-known difficulty of defining life. But just as despite the latter difficulty we can always say in any particular instance what is *not* life, so despite the former one we can say in any particular instance what is not poetry.

account of their depth—and buried in permanent oblivion. Should he possibly be remembered at all, it will be because posterity, condensing this our judgment, will inscribe on his grave the words of Martial:

> Carmina . . . scribis et Apolline nullo
> Laudari debes.

Anglice:

> You kept on twanging at your lyre,
> Though no Apollo did inspire.

So much for Mr. Browning's *novum organum*, or new method of making poetry. Having considered the subject-matter of his work, and the process by which he labours on it, we have only to examine the form in which he presents it, when finished, to the public gaze. In other words, having scrutinised his matter and method, we have now to look at his manner, or, to speak still more plainly, his expression—those 'half-words,' as he himself called them, whereby he communicates with intelligent readers. Now, why does Mr. Browning communicate his thoughts in this fashion of half-words? The answer is exceedingly simple. Because, if he communicated them in full ones—*i.e.* explicitly and clearly—though still in verse, their prose nature would be seen at a glance by everybody; and everybody, the simplest person as well as the most pedantic, could not fail to perceive that the author was whimsically and gratuitously measuring them out into certain lengths, instead of unaffectedly not caring how many metrical feet there were in them, or whether they formed feet at all. For there is no difficulty in putting anything into verse, as may be seen in the versified rules of the *Gradus ad Parnassum*, or in the advertisements of Mr. Moses, the cheap outfitter. It would require very little ingenuity to turn *Euclid* into metre, and, for anything we know, it may already have been done. But, as in these instances the primary object is to be understood, the reader sees at once that he is not reading, or supposed to be reading, poetry, but only metre, so employed for mnemonic or for catchpenny purposes. In Mr. Browning's case the unsophisticated reader really does not know what it is he is reading. It is printed in arbitrary lengths, and therefore looks as if it cannot well be prose; yet it does not, as a rule, read like verse, and in nearly all cases its meaning is obscure, and in none very obvious. If it were, Mr. Browning would be found out without more ado. We do not mean to say that he consciously deceives his readers; he deceives his readers and himself too. He is the real M. Jourdain, who has been writing prose all his life without knowing it; very bad prose, it is true, as half-words arranged in lengths necessarily must be, but prose all the same. It would be idle to quote instances of this, for his works are one long almost uninterrupted instance of it. You may open any one of his volumes at any page you like for proof of the assertion. Surely the two passages we have already quoted from him though for a totally different purpose, will suffice as instances. If

> Since evermore
> Yourselves effect what I was fain before
> Effect, what I supplied yourselves suggest,
> What I leave bare yourselves can now invest.

does not strike everybody as very bad prose, consisting of half-words arranged in lengths, we own ourselves completely beaten, or at least baffled, in our demonstration. And what is true of these passages is true of Mr. Browning's compositions *passim*. For poetic thought has its natural utterance or expression, just as everything else has, and you cannot make it express itself differently save by travestying it. To put the case as extremely as possible, yet without travelling one hair's breadth beyond the limits of the strictest truth, a living tree expresses itself in foliage not more necessarily than does poetic thought express itself in a certain and inevitable kind and form of diction. But what is the diction of poetry? Is it half-words arranged in lengths? Is it obscure diction of any sort? Is the diction of poetry anything but diction that is at once clear—*that*, it shares with other diction—lofty, and musical? Who are the clearest and most musical poets? Unquestionably the great poets. Whose blank verse is fit to be mentioned, even for mere sound, after Shakespeare's? Only Milton's; and his, *longo intervallo*. Mr. Tennyson's, smooth as it is, is the poorest stuff compared with the blank verse of Shakespeare or Milton. It is melodious enough, no doubt (just as Moore, in rhyme, is the perfection of melody); but where is its harmony— where are the infinite harmonies in it? They are wanting. For melody is not the only thing in music. All the wonderful combinations that come of an innate familiarity with the use of fugue and counterpoint make something very different from mere melody. Shakespeare and Milton betray this innate familiarity in blank verse; Spenser and Byron betray it in rhyme; and so, whilst they are the greatest of our poets in other respects, they are, when one once knows what music really means and is, the most musical. Similarly they are the most clear. Poor Mr. Browning is both muddy and unmusical to the last degree. In fact, his style may fairly be described as the very incarnation of discordant obscurity. Is it wonderful? He has no voice, and yet he wants to sing. He is not a poet, and yet he would fain write poetry. We have no right to be surprised if he is inarticulate, and if we get only half-words cut into lengths. The wonder would be if we got anything else. In reading Mr. Browning, we are perpetually reminded of those lines in Mr. Bailey's *Festus*:

> The dress of words,
> Like to the Roman girl's enticing garb,
> Should let the play of limb be seen through it.
> . . . . *A mist of words,*
> *Like halos round the moon, though they enlarge*
> *The seeming size of thoughts, make the light less.*[1]

But, it will be urged, there is occasionally something else in Mr. Browning, which, if not poetry, is at least something very like poetry. Exactly: there is. But when? When Mr. Browning ceases to be Mr. Browning proper, when his *differentia* disappears, and he is no longer Mr. Browning 'the dramatist, or, so to call him, analyst,' but Mr. Browning the man pure and simple. It will be remembered that we have already incidentally said that Mr. Browning is not a poet save in the sense that all cultivated men and women of sensitive feelings are poets; and we made the statement deliberately and with the intention of reverting to it here. It would therefore be strange indeed if in the course of thirty-five years' obstinate practice of writing verse Mr. Browning had not once or twice deviated into penning something that resembled poetry, and was so much on the border-land of poetry or even across it that it ought to bear that name. Be it so. All that we are arguing for is that Mr. Browning is not specifically a poet, but is specifically something quite different. The poetic temperament and intellect are not the *proprium* of Mr. Browning, but only the *accidens*.

---

[1] Could we allow, which we cannot, that Mr. Browning is to be classed among poets, instead of among a totally different order of intellects, Mr. Bailey is the poet with whom we should be compelled to compare him; and were the comparison possible, it would certainly have to be pronounced that the author of *Festus* is, poetically speaking, immeasurably the superior of the author of *Paracelsus*, *Sordello*, &c., with which the former has occasionally many points in common. Mr. Bailey is unquestionably a poet. How is it he has for years persisted in silence? Is the following passage in *Festus* the explanation?—

> *Student.* Say, did thy friend
> Write aught beside the work thou tell'st of?
>
> *Festus.* Nothing.
> After that, like to the burning peak, he fell
> Into himself, and was missing ever after.

But let us see what is the highest result, when the latter has, so to speak, the upper hand, or the command of him.

> Oh! to be in England
> Now that April's there;
> And whosoever wakes in England
> Sees, some morning, unaware,
> That the lowest boughs and the brush-wood sheaf
> Round the elm-tree bole are in tiny leaf,
> While the chaffinch sings on the orchard bough
> In England—now!
>
> *Lyrics.*

> Love like mine must have return,
> I thought: no river starts but to some sea.
>
> *A Soul's Tragedy.*

Is this poetry? If it is, it is of a very commonplace sort, rather above than below average Magazine verse, and we could produce many examples of it from Mr. Browning if we had space, inasmuch as he perpetually, indeed invariably, lapses into commonplace when he allows himself to think, on the poetic side, naturally. Often, as though conscious that what poetic utterance he has in common with ordinary cultivated men and women of sensitive feelings is of this complexion, he will not allow himself to think naturally, but strains at being original whilst still wanting to remain poetical. Then the result is lamentable; is, in fact, spasmodic. For instance:

> Earth is a wintry clod:
> But spring-wind, like a dancing psaltress, passes
> Over its breast to waken it.
>
> *Paracelsus.*

> The sprinkled isles,
> Lily on lily, that o'erlace the sea,
> And laugh their pride when the light wave lisps, 'Greece'.
>
> *Cleon.*

> One wave,
> Feeling the foot of Him upon its neck,
> Gaped as a snake does, lolled out its large tongue,
> And licked the whole labour flat.
>
> *Dramatis Personae.*

> Is it better in May? I ask you. You've summer all at once;
> In a day he leaps complete with a few strong April suns!

'Mid the sharp short emerald wheat, scarce risen three fingers well,
The wild tulip, at end of its tube, blows out its great red bell,
Like a thin clear bubble of blood, for the children to pick and sell.
Up at a Villa—Down in the City.

These are pure spasms; specimens of the mental action of a man who is striving earnestly to be an original poet, and who for the life of him cannot be—since no striving will make a man such, any more than it will give him wings. Mr. John Stuart Mill has in one of his admirable *Dissertations and Discussions* made the unfortunate remark that probably any man of good abilities might by determination and persistence end by becoming as great a poet as Wordsworth—he himself thinking very highly of Wordsworth as a poet. In any philosophical question we should differ from Mr. Mill with great diffidence; but we have not a moment's hesitation in saying that such an assertion, save as applied to —say—one-half of Wordsworth's compositions, which, as we have already remarked, are perhaps not poetry at all, but only verse, must be described, despite the reverence we feel for Mr. Mill, as fundamentally erroneous. Accepted, however, to the limited extent we have prescribed to it, the assertion is true enough, and it is singularly applicable to Mr. Browning. Any ordinarily cultivated person of sensitive feelings who could write verse might have written the first two commonplace passages we have just quoted from Mr. Browning, and, being resolved to be original, might have strained himself till he concocted the last four. The former are examples of such natural versified speech as might be attained by almost anybody. The latter are instances of that artificial, acquired, laborious, *foreign* speech which is necessarily fallen into by people who are clumsily translating complex thoughts into an alien tongue. As for such pieces as 'Marching Along', and 'How they Brought the Good News from Ghent', they cannot be classed, at the very highest estimate, save with Macaulay's *Lays of Rome*, to which surely no impartial person can doubt they are very inferior—and yet no-one talks or thinks of Macaulay as specifically a poet—and ought more fairly to be classed with the Cavalier Songs of Mr. Walter Thornbury, whom no one has ever dreamt of alluding to save as a very spirited versifier.

Thus, as far as we have inquired, we find Mr. Browning, in his attempted *rôle* of poet, to be doing three things, and generally the first of them. Either playing the part of analyst, getting inside souls, and developing them to the reader by half-words, which is not writing poetry at all; or writing simple intelligible verse, which, if it is to be considered poetry, must honestly be described as commonplace poetry, both easy and by no means infrequent of production; or, in dread and dislike of being commonplace, writing what has so happily been termed spasmodic poetry, poetry that comes of violent straining after effect, and which ought, on no account, to be written by anybody, since it sins against that eternal truth, so well put in the same passage in *Festus* from which we have already quoted:

> Simplicity
> Is nature's first step, and the last of art.

Which quotation we may supplement, for the benefit of Mr. Browning and his admirers, by another from a still higher authority, and in itself still more suggestive and instructive:

> This is an art
> Which doth mend nature, change it rather, but
> The art itself is nature.
>
> *Winter's Tale,* iv. 3.

That is just the art which Mr. Browning has not got.

But how about 'Andrea del Sarto', 'Fra Lippo Lippi', 'A Death in the Desert', 'Caliban on Setebos', and 'Bishop Blougram's Apology'? What have we to say about these? This much. That, with the exception of 'Caliban on Sebetos'—which, on account of its rendering certain prevailing modes of thought on theological questions, has been very much over-estimated—they are productions betraying the possession of peculiar imagination, of mordant wit of almost the highest kind, of a delicious sense of humour, and, in 'Andrea del Sarto', of deep tenderness. But neither tenderness, nor humour, nor wit, nor even imagination, nor indeed all these together, will constitute a man a poet. Laplace, Bacon,[1] Copernicus, Newton, Mr. Darwin, all have immense imagination; and we might, of course, extend the list indefinitely. We think we have allowed it to be seen that we regard Mr. Browning's intellectual powers as very considerable indeed. 'Bishop Blougram's Apology'

[1] A brief extract from Mr. Bain upon the nature of Bacon's genius will throw some light on this subject. 'Although Bacon's imagery,' says that profound and accurate writer, 'sometimes rises to poetry, this is not its usual character; his was not a poetic sense of Nature, but a broad general susceptibility, partaking more of the natural historian than of the poet, by which all the objects coming before his view or presented to his imagination took a deep hold, and, by the help of his intense attraction of similarity, were recalled on the slightest similitude. Many great writers in English literature have had this strong susceptibility to the sensible world at large without a special poetic sense, while some have had the poetic sense super-added. These last are our greatest poets.' This is nearly as good an account of Mr. Browning's 'sense of Nature' as it is of Bacon's.

is an astonishing production, which we invariably read almost throughout with unflagging zest. But it is not poetry. There is not a line of
poetry in it from first to last, and we confess we prefer it to all Mr.
Browning's compositions. Suppose he had never written anything else,
would it have occurred to anybody that he was a poet, or even aspiring
to be a poet? In order still further to illustrate our meaning, suppose
Mr. Tennyson had never written anything but 'The Northern Farmer'
—a piece we chuckle over with inexpressible delight—again, would it
have occurred to anybody that Mr. Tennyson was a poet, or was
pretending to be such? Of course not; no more than it would have
occurred to his contemporaries to have regarded Cowper as a poet if
he had never written anything but 'John Gilpin,' whose pre-eminent
success positively annoyed its author? So with 'Bishop Blougram's
Apology', and all of Mr. Browning's compositions, or passages in his
compositions, which are *ejusdem generis* with it. They are witty, wise,
shrewd, deep, true, wonderful—anything or everything but poetry. It
is the greatest, though apparently the commonest, mistake in the world
to suppose that the quality of verse, provided the thoughts it expresses
are excellent thoughts, involves for those thoughts and their expression
the quality of poetry. This has been Mr. Browning's *ignis fatuus* through
life; and the absurd chase it has led him he in turn has led those who
have not found out what it is he has all along been following. In a word,
Mr. Browning's so-called Muse is a *lusus naturæ*, a sport, to use gar-
deners' language; but certain sapient critics have been exulting over it,
as though it were a new and finer specimen of the old true poetic stock.
Moreover, Mr. Browning's undoubted faculty of depth has bewitched
and bewrayed them. Despite their protestations of being perfectly
content with Mr. Tennyson as the great poet who justifies the period,
they are not content with him. They have all along more or less consciously felt what we insisted on in our article last month—his want of
loftiness. Now, in Mr. Browning they have found something that
unquestionably is not in Mr. Tennyson, and they have begun to fancy
that that something may possibly supply Mr. Tennyson's shortcomings.
That comes of not having thought the matter out with regard to either
of these authors. They know Mr. Tennyson wants something or other:
they know Mr. Browning has something or other. But from lack of
patient reflection and investigation they fail to perceive for themselves
that what Mr. Tennyson wants is height, and what Mr. Browning has
is depth. This once clearly perceived, it is obvious that the latter characteristic cannot mend the imperfection of the former characteristic. You

might just as well try to make a mountain higher by excavating round it, or make swallows fly more soaringly by yourself descending a coal-pit. We have already very explicitly given our estimate of Mr. Tennyson as a poet; and though it is such as thousands of men who have fancied themselves beloved of the Muses would have given anything to have honestly formed of them, it is far removed from that in which his more ardent admirers at times affect to indulge. One thing, however, is certain. They need be in no fear lest Mr. Tennyson should be displaced by any critic in his sound senses to make way for Mr. Browning. When men desire to behold the flight of an eagle, and cannot get it, they do not usually regard the tramp of an elephant as a substitute.

We therefore beg of the general public to return to the bent of its own original judgment, and, unbewildered by those who would fain be its guides, to treat Mr. Browning's *Poetical Works* as it treated *Paracelsus*, &c., on its first appearance—as though they were non-existent. We know it has now much to contend against. When the academy and the drawing-room, when pedantry and folly, combine to set a fashion, it requires more self-confidence than the meek public commonly possess to laugh the silly innovation down. To Mr. Tennyson's credit be it spoken, he has never gone looking for fame. The ground we tread on is delicate; and we will, therefore, only add that we should have been better pleased if the author, who is now so ridiculously obtruded as his rival, had imitated him in that particular. Small London literary coteries, and large fashionable London salons, cannot crown a man with the bays of Apollo. They may stick their trumpery tinsel wreaths upon him, but these will last no longer than the locks they encircle. They may confer notoriety, but fame is not in their gift. All they can bestow is as transitory as themselves. Let the same general public, therefore, we say, take heart, and bluntly forswear Mr. Browning and all his works. It is bad enough that there should be people, pretending to authority among us, who call a man a great poet when, though unquestionably a poet, he has no marks of greatness about him. But that is a venial error, and a trifling misfortune, compared to what would be the misery of living in an age which gibbetted itself beforehand for the pity of posterity, by deliberately calling a man a poet who—however remarkable his mental attributes and powers—is not specifically a poet at all. We hope we shall be spared this humiliation. At any rate, we must protest against being supposed willingly to participate in it.

P.S.—It will be observed that we have abstained from all mention of *The Ring and the Book*. Our readers must not, however, suppose that the foregoing paper was written before that work appeared. Not at all. But *The Ring and the Book* throws no new light on the subject; and what we have said of Mr. Browning's aim, method, and manner, whilst examining his other compositions, holds equally good of his latest, wonderful but unpoetical, production. We have refrained from scrutinising it, only because conscientious criticism of art, like art itself, is long, and Magazine articles are short.

152. Deep, But Seldom Clear

1870

J. Hain Friswell from his *Modern Men of Letters Honestly Criticised* (1870), pp. 119–31.

Friswell's honesty proved rather too blunt and, as the result of a suit for libel, the book was suppressed.

Half the English speaking-world could not understand Browning; let us say two-thirds, or three-fourths; or what do you say to nine-tenths? Take all the people who really can read Shakespeare with pleasure, and comprehend that clear, deep, intense writer; not one-half of these could understand Browning. And yet he is a great poet, deep, intense, but seldom quite clear.

BALAUSTION'S ADVENTURE, INCLUDING A TRANSCRIPT FROM EURIPIDES

August 1871

153. Thomas Carlyle, diary entry

28 June 1871

From *William Allingham: A Diary*, ed. H. Allingham and D. Radford (1907), p. 205.

I read it all twice through, and found out the meaning of it. Browning most ingeniously twists up the English language into riddles—'There! there is some meaning in this—can you make it out?' I wish he had taken to prose. Browning has far more ideas than Tennyson, but is not so truthful. Tennyson means what he says, poor fellow! Browning has a meaning in his twisted sentences, but he does not really go into anything, or believe much about it. He accepts conventional values.

154. From an unsigned review, *The Athenæum*

12 August 1871, pp. 199–200

It would be an insult to the one honorary fellow of Baliol to congratulate him upon a good translation of Euripides. And yet it is not too much to say that the translation reads as if the Master of Baliol had bent upon it his provokingly microscopic care,

> Crimine ab uno
> Disce.[1]

Let any one compare the following lines with the original:—

> Why look'st so solemn and so thought-absorbed?
> To guests, a servant should not sour-faced be,
> But do the honours with a mind urbane.
> While thou, contrariwise, beholding here
> Arrive thy master's comrade, hast for him
> A churlish visage, all one beetle-brow—
> Having regard to grief that's out-of-door!
> Come hither, and so get to grow more wise!

He will probably own that the words

> στυγνῷ προσώπῳ καὶ συνωφρυωμένῳ[2]

are translated almost as well as he could translate them himself; and more than this no critic could be expected to admit. There are, fortunately, no *Agamemnoniæ cruces*[3] in the *Alcestis*; and Mr. Browning is, consequently, under no temptation to allow his personality to overpower his scholarship.

There is a *Nova Alcestis* of Mr. Browning's own, tacked on by Balaustion to her song. On this the reader must form his own judgment, or allow Mr. Nettleship[4] to form it for him. Ἐξ ὠτὸς ὔϊκοῦ πῶς

---

1 'From one crime learn (of) all.' *Aeneid*, II, 65–6.

2 'With a countenance sullen and frowning.' *Alcestis*, 1, 777.

3 'Textual problems like those of the Agamemnon.'

4 John. T. Nettleship, whose *Essays on Robert Browning's Poetry* (1868) had given him a reputation as an interpreter.

355

βαλάντιον[1]; Admetus was hardly meant to be a hero; and, however gilded, he will always remain a sneak. But even Mr. Tennyson has allowed his own King Arthur to lead him into all kinds of strange speculations; and of Admetus, it must at least be admitted that he is a most respectable and decorous consort, of whom the most that can *not* be said is that

> ——nothing in his life
> Became him like the leaving it.

But Balaustion herself is too welcome to allow an old friend—or, rather, old foe—with a new face to disconnect us. Mr. Browning excels in short, sharp, vivid, dramatic sketches of character; and, little as we see of Balaustion, she yet has as distinct and well-defined a personality of her own as ever had even Waring himself.

For the rest, it remains to ask, where this new poem leaves Mr. Browning? Confessedly a May-month amusement, it may be said of it, that it is worthy of Mr. Leighton's picture,[2] and of its own dedication, but that—for those who reverence Mr. Browning, and there are such —it has been written in May to be read in August. It is high praise of a great poet to say that such a poem will add nothing to Mr. Browning's fame. Equally certain it is that it will take nothing from it, and that it will be read with satisfaction, if not with keen enjoyment. A comparison of its merits with those of the *Atalanta* is inevitable[3]—as critics go; and absolutely impertinent. There is no one common point in the two by which they can be measured.

It is to be hoped that in a second edition we shall see a less pedantic spelling. 'Olumpian'—the *u* pronounced as in 'lump,' or even as in 'lŏŏmp'—does not look pleasant to the eye. Besides, Σίσυρος became *Tityrus*; and it is perfectly probable that 'Olympian' (without the *u*) more correctly represents Hellenic pronunciation. Such spellings are out of place, except in critical editions, as of the Twelve Tables or of the Salian hymns. We need not call Heracles Hercules—which (as Mommsen has taught schoolboys) he never was, having but little to do with ἕρκος; but, on the other hand, we need not give him a *k* for which he never craved.

---

[1] 'How (does one) make a purse out of a sow's ear?'

[2] Frederick Leighton, friend of Browning, whose painting of the dead Alcestis was famous in its time. The poem was dedicated to another friend, the Countess Cowper.

[3] Swinburne's *Atalanta in Calydon* was published in 1865. Most critics would agree that he was more successful than Browning in capturing the spirit of the original.

155. From an unsigned review, *The Examiner*

12 August 1871, pp. 804-5

Having undertaken to tell in modern English verse one of the stories of old Greek tragedy, it is not strange that Mr Browning should have made his selection from Euripides. In Æschylus there is an intense belief in the supernatural: men are the sport of the gods; the gods themselves are the creatures of destiny. In Sophocles this view of things is much toned down and softened; but belief in the supernatural realities is almost as vividly portrayed: Æschylus is almost as strictly religious a poet as Sophocles. In Euripides, however, religion passes into philosophy. Vivid and impressive as are his tragedies, he shows in them that he hardly believes in the great powers which he describes, or rather that he partly believes them to be forces under human control and partly uses them as convenient phrases for expressing the operation of that general law of nature to which men are forced to submit and which is uniform in its method, one and absolute by whatever various names it may be known. That, clearly, is the view of life, and its secrets, with which Mr. Browning is most in accord, and he shows it very notably in the beautiful 'transcript', as he calls it, which he has here made of the tragedy of *Alcestis*.

It would be an interesting study to compare the old and the new poems, to see in detail what Mr Browning has taken from Euripides, where he has varied the meaning, and where he has introduced thoughts altogether fresh. We shall not here attempt that work, however; and we advise no reader of *Balaustion's Adventure* to attempt it until he has thoroughly enjoyed the poem as it stands. Most of the dialogue parts are accurate translations, but the story has so filtered through Mr Browning's mind that it is a thoroughly original poem, and as such it claims to be read and mastered before classical criticism is allowed to have play. . . .

357

156. Matthew Browne, *Contemporary Review*

September 1871, xviii. 284–96

From his review.

Matthew Browne was the pseudonym used by W. B. Rands (1823–82), who also wrote popular books for children.

The story, in its essence, seems to us unmanageable from any modern point of view. Once get rid of the vague presence of Destiny—which, if you retain it, makes the moral unities impossible, while it shrouds everything in a vapour of *must-have-been* which half-stifles criticism and blurs all dividing-lines—once get rid of that, we say, and Admetos becomes a person to kick, and the tragedy something rather like a farce. Our readers know in what other ways than this the same idea has found expression, or half-expression. Hence, Mr. Browning has to go about to make Admetos presentable, and Balaustion informs us that Heracles discerned that he was, after all, 'weak, not bad.' If that is not a false note, there never was one in this world.

Still more strongly do we hear the voice of Mr. Browning through the mask, and feel the incongruity of the story and the 'moral' when we come to the beautiful rendering of the former at the close of the work—'the new Admetos, new Alkestis' as the girl calls her version. This version we shall not do the book the injustice of quoting, and indeed it is too long for quotation; but, except for the unnecessary and far too lengthy illustration of the two athletes, it is one entire and perfect chrysolite. True, it is a good deal more like Fouqué than like anything Greek; but it is so exquisitely beautiful that we rise from the volume in a mood of warm thankfulness to the poet, and more than forgive for its sake whatever has not pleased us.

157. G. A. Simcox, *The Academy*

1 September 1871, ii. 409–10

From his review.

Simcox reviewed a number of Browning's later poems in *The Academy*; see Nos. 165 and 171.

This book is a problem in more ways than one; perhaps all the other problems depend upon one, viz. what the author meant his book to be. Is the 'transcription' from Euripides intended to be more or less than a translation? Is the adventure of Balaustion the subject of the volume, or only the setting of the real subject? The title-page suggests one answer, and the text suggests another. After the first one-and-twenty pages, we have nothing of Balaustion, for the comments upon the play and the legend are unmistakably Mr. Browning's, and hardly profess to be hers although they are put into her mouth. On the other hand, the title runs, *Balaustion's Adventure, including a Transcript*, as if the adventure were the greater, and the transcript were the less. If we might think that Mr. Browning was asked to translate the *Alcestis*, and had devised this framework for the translation without attaching much importance to it, we should be at liberty to admire the strength which is so strong when it unbends, without raising the premature and thankless question whether Mr. Browning is not ceasing to be subtle since he has ceased to be perplexed. Certainly the translation and comment are good enough to stand alone. No Greek tragedy has been better translated, and the commentary will bear comparison with Bishop Thirwall's famous essay upon the *Ajax* of Sophocles.[1] If the poet has less learning than the scholar, he makes amends by even keener insight, if not into the mind of Euripides, into what is almost more important, the turning points of a poem which has a life and meaning of its own apart from the intentions of the person who was privileged to usher it into the world.

[1] Connop Thirlwall (1797–1875) was Bishop of St. David's and a Greek scholar.

359

30 September 1871, xliv. 1179–81

The loquacity and dexterity of the Athenians and their 'extraordinary fondness for arguing' could not exceed the loquacity and dexterity of Mr. Browning's 'men and women', or their fondness for presenting their own individual view of life in the best argumentative form. The keenness of Mr. Browning's vigilance for small circumstances giving a local colour to a scene is certainly even greater than that of Euripides; like Euripides, again, his style of dialogue, if not essentially spruce,—it is too careless and wayward for that,—is extremely keen and adroit, and can be, when he pleases, terse to the last degree, while he is even fonder of the language of the market-place than the poet from whom he adapts and translates. Finally, he is mindful of Euripides' fancy for putting a woman in the front of the battle in this recast of the *Alcestis*, which he has put into the mouth of a girl of Rhodes; and in the selection of Alcestis,—a woman with whose self-sacrifice and whose slight scorn for the man for whom she laid down her life, 'modern thought' is thoroughly well disposed to sympathize,—he has got a character which is peculiarly well adapted for his shrewd, sharp touch. On the whole, while to our mind modern *réchauffés* of antique subjects are seldom great successes, yet Euripides was, in the keen unsettled sharpness of his moral criticism, so like a modern, and in this particular case treated the old myth with so hesitating a hand, that Mr. Browning has been able to recast it with far less loss to the original, and far less of jarring effect from the accessions which his abrupt and irregular genius gives it, than would have been possible with any other Greek dramatist, and perhaps with any other of even this dramatist's plays.

159. From an unsigned review, *The St. James's Magazine*

October 1871, xxviii. (NS viii) 83–91

Balaustion's Adventure is as rich in descriptive passion, in dramatic sensation, in sharply defined, strongly individualized characters as we could desire. Over the misty horizon of the past, Mr. Browning has thrown the magnetic light of his genius, and has shown us the clear keen features of some of the dwellers in that region. Take Balaustion herself, for instance. She *was* a legend, a pretty old tradition, that was all. Now she *is*, she exists, she has an individuality, a personality, that can never be obliterated, or taken away from her. . . .

160. From an unsigned review, *The Times*

6 October 1871, p. 8

. . . Mr. Browning's ideas are not incompatible with simple expression—no idea which is worth words ever is, and a reader of average ability would not find the slightest difficulty, when once he has fathomed them, in putting them into plain language. Mr. Browning may say that his language is plain enough to himself; so it may be, and also to the admirers who are bound hand and foot to him and choose to make a study of his works. To leave such persons out of the question, all writers understand their own writing, for this good reason—that their understanding works by a process the reverse to that by which their readers' works. They have to put words on paper to represent a meaning already in their heads, their readers have nothing but the words on the paper to go upon, and have to get the meaning into their heads as best they can. Unless it flash there at the first sight, nine people out of ten will not trouble themselves to look again, and their laziness is justice in disguise, just as very often, though not in Mr. Browning's case, obscurity is weakness in disguise. There never was a more pernicious piece of false criticism—pernicious because understood as praise and not as the blame it really is—than that in vogue of Mr. Browning. 'His beauties lie beneath the surface.' Such a burial is the burial of a writer's own genius and his own fame. This poem of *Balaustion's Adventure*, uncongenial and effete though its theme be, would have been read by thousands of Englishmen and women, who, as it is, will never look at it, had it been written in language as translucent as that of the verse we quoted just now from *Childe Harold*. By common consent, it is less obscure than most of Mr. Browning's poetry, yet we have had to read many passages four or five times over before we could unravel the thread of their entangled sense and beauty. A devotee may do this for his idol, and a reviewer must do it for his author, but the general public would not do it for Shakespeare himself.

161. H. B. Forman, *London Quarterly Review*

January 1872, xxxvii. 346–68

From his review.

For Forman, see the headnote to No. 148.

Balaustion's Adventure is a new evidence at once of Mr. Browning's great and emphatically poetical gift, and of his marked divergence from the precedents of subject, method, and form. The very title-page of the book, to begin at the beginning, is characteristic in its suggestiveness. Balaustion, 'Flower-of-the-wild-pomegranate-tree,'—how the word brings into the mind ideas of colour and fragrance, of wild beauty and freshness! And, again, *a transcript from Euripides* clearly tells those who know the poet what they are to expect. We cannot readily fancy

Mr. Browning bringing himself into such close training as to *translate* a poem from an alien tongue, any more than we can imagine him sitting down to give us a dull reproduction of the 'Old Square Yellow Book', the account of the Roman murder-case, on which he founded his master-piece, *The Ring and the Book*; but just as that old book's crabbed Latin and Italian prose was dissolved in the crucible of his imagination and re-integrated into a noble poem, so the Euripidean drama of Alkestis and her perfect love has entered into his imagination and come out again quite a different thing. In building up his poem of that beautiful legend, Mr. Browning has *transcribed* from Euripides the greater part of the original play; but he has not done this with the formal aim of translation: he has built it in, bit by bit (in proper order), to the fabric of his work, and has reduced the exquisite harmony of various form found in the original to a harmony of another kind: so that the poem as it now stands, though un-Hellenic, is as far removed from patchiness as anything can well be.

162. Margaret Oliphant, *The Edinburgh Review*

January 1872, cxxxv. 221–49

In a letter of January 1872, Browning wrongly attributed the opening paragraph of this unsigned review to Henry Reeve, editor of the *Edinburgh* and complained that, as usual, his poem had been stupidly misinterpreted. (*DI*, p. 372). The passage certainly seems out of place in a review of *Balaustion's Adventure*. For Mrs. Oliphant, see No. 100.

The *Prince Hohenstiel-Schwangau, Saviour of Society*,—for that is the title of Mr. Browning's latest production—is a rhapsody, without much metre or meaning, for the glorification of Napoleon III.—the 'one wise man'—and the Second Empire. We regret that Mr. Browning should entertain and express such false and unworthy sentiments and opinions on modern politics; and we prefer to see him in the classical garb of antiquity.

Of all ages in the world this is the one which has taken most deeply into its consideration the force of idiosyncrasy, the power of circumstances, the complications of thought and feeling which lend to human nature a constantly varying interest, and fill it with those picturesque uncertainties and contradictions which are peculiar to itself and distinguish it from all the rest of creation. Into the constantly arising problems of a life thus conscious that scarcely one of its sentiments or emotions possesses perfect unity and singleness, the distinctive intellectual development of our age delights to enter; and of all the writers who have given expression to this general tendency Mr. Browning is perhaps the most subtle. He is the embodiment of the intellectual instinct of his generation—its curiosity, its power of patient examination, and, above all, of its imaginative sympathy. In this last expression, indeed, we may sum up in a breath the character which we desire to indicate. It is its nature and ambition to look at everything, not from without but from within. It is not content to accept only what it sees, but has set its heart upon learning what are the secret springs from which any visible result proceeds. This, in its strength and weakness, is Mr. Browning's chief characteristic. His sympathetic imagination throws itself into the nature even of the very villain whom he detests, with an attempt to enter into the working of his thoughts, and say the best that is to be said for him. We need not say how this principle reigns, and indeed luxuriates and runs to riot, in the *Ring and the Book*, and may even explain the *Prince Hohenstiel-Schwangau*. It is this which gives its chief value also to the poem before us.

Here he has taken up a labour greater than that of Hercules, and worked at it like a man. He has done all for the heroine of Euripides that mortal can do. He has made an almost passionate effort to drag her husband up to her level and make her and the reader forget his ignoble weakness. He has put him through a process of reformation elaborate and anxious, letting slip no chance of improvement for him. He has brought all possible influences to work—the sudden reality of loss which stuns him, the sharp fire of anger which burns away the veil over his eyes, the sense of void and vacancy in his life, the 'hateful entry, hateful countenance, of the widowed walls.' All these he masses together with subtle touches of description and accumulation, labouring to work us up into a belief that the slight soul of the man had grown deep and true, and that his own meanness and misery had become in-

tolerable to him. But with all this great strain and effort, we are compelled to admit that Mr. Browning has not been successful. Admetus
remains Admetus still. It is not easy to change nature; and the vehement
desire which the poet has to do so is often attended with very little
result. Admetus finds out that the price he has paid for his life is a very
heavy price indeed, and that the existence he has thus secured is full of
drawbacks as well as advantages. He is sorry and he is ashamed, and has
a certain consciousness that he has not come through the transaction
with much credit to himself. But this is not reformation. Even his
contrast between the fate of Alcestis and his own, which Mr. Browning
accepts as showing a real sense of her virtue and his own shame, might
bear a much less amiable interpretation:

> Her, indeed, no grief will ever touch,
> And she from many a labour pauses now,
> Renowned one! Whereas I, who ought not live,
> But do live, by evading destiny,
> Sad life am I to lead, I learn at last!
> For how shall I bear going indoors here?
> Accosting whom? By whom saluted back,
> Shall I have joyous entry?

Mr. Browning accepts these words, we say, in his anxiety, as proof
of the change that has taken place in Admetus; but we cannot agree
with him. To us it seems evident that at the best it is his own suffering
which is the only thing that has moved him. Somehow or other (he
seems to feel) it is his wife who always has the advantage of him. Even
when the world supposes she has been made a sacrifice of, is it not he
who is the worse sufferer still—left to bear grief, while she is past all
grieving? This is not repentance; it is rather the last stronghold of
selfishness, and shows that the man is really unchanged. But Mr.
Browning at least has the satisfaction of feeling that he has reformed him
and made him fit to stand once more by Alcestis' side, and be her closest
companion. We do not share this charitable opinion, but the conversion
is as good, no doubt, as many a one which an anxious wife has trusted
to, and which has passed muster with the world.

But this is all that can be said. The modern poet, with his subtler
reasoning, has not succeeded in bridging over that gulf between Admetus and Alcestis. And the ancient poet has not attempted to bridge it
over. He has left it as human problems have to be left so often, without
explanation, a revelation of the dread gaps and breaks that come into

life, without any suggestion of a cure or even any strong sense of its necessity. He goes off into the easier arbitrary world of gods and miracles with a light heart, ignoring all the difficulties. But not so Mr. Browning. To him, as to his age, it has become the chief of wonders, the greatest of griefs, that such a mystery should be left unsolved. But the mystery exists and baffles the observer, notwithstanding his anxiety. It is a difficulty which with all his intimate and universal knowledge of humanity he has not been able either to harmonise or to explain.

PRINCE
HOHENSTIEL - SCHWANGAU,
SAVIOUR OF SOCIETY

December 1871

163. From an unsigned review, *The Examiner*

23 December 1871, pp. 1267–8

. . . The subject is one admirably suited to the poet's favourite mode
of treatment, and he has treated it admirably. If *Prince Hohenstiel-
Schwangau* is not superior to some other of the splendid monologues in
which Mr Browning allows various individualities to express themselves with marvellous force and clearness, it is, perhaps, as good as any;
and the immediate interest of its theme, combining some important
contributions to great and perplexing political questions of the day with
a very subtle dissection of the character of the hero of the poem, makes
it of especial value. And, though finer passages may be found elsewhere,
Mr Browning has never, we are inclined to think, exhibited more
pungent wit and caustic humour than in some portions of this latest of
his works.

The method of its construction is that which Mr Browning has
invented and brought to something like perfection, as the method best
adapted for such dramatic writing as he excels in. Prince Hohenstiel-
Schwangau—whom there is no difficulty in identifying with Napoleon
III., as he may have seemed to himself some year and a-half ago, just
before his empire collapsed—fancies himself an exile again in Leicester-
square, puffing his cigar, while a lady of the *demi-monde* sips her tea
beside him, and opening his thoughts to her without restraint and with
notable completeness. In the choice of that situation, and its description
in the first few lines of the poem, there is a concentration of satire such
as no living poet but Mr Browning could thus develope. And satire is
not wanting in the pages that follow. . . .

[Further summary, interspersed with quotations, has been omitted.]

This poem, like most of his others, ends abruptly; and we are left to assume that he has been revealing to us, with all the skill of a practised soul-anatomist, the temper of hearty self-approval—yet clouded ever by a vague consciousness that the self-approval was self-deception, and that the confidence in his own future was ill-grounded—with which Napoleon III. entered on the war that overthrew his Empire. Whether Mr Browning is himself somewhat deceived as to the character of the man whom he paints under the thinnest possible cloak of fiction, it is hardly worth while to inquire. They who most condemn the bearing of the late Emperor during the twenty years of his rule, and who refer to it many of the ills from which France is now suffering, should be most willing to admit that all can be admitted in extenuation of his offences. And that, as we apprehend, is what Mr Browning wishes us to do. That is Mr Browning's way as a poet.

And that constitutes Mr Browning's especial merit as a poet. He can do other things well. He is a master of his craft in so far as the poetical craft consists in powers of expression and other technical appliances. But his speciality as a poet of our own day, and for all days, is that, just as others have used their poetry for working upon the sentiments of their hearers concerning patriotism or religion, sexual passion and the like, his function is to make poetry the handmaid of philosophy, and to analyse the minds of men as deftly as a surgeon can dissect their bodies. Therein he has no peer.

164. From an unsigned review, *The Spectator*

30 December 1871, xliv. 1606–7

Browning, of course, had no intention of making 'an exhaustive discussion' of the Napoleonic problem. He would have to suffer even worse misinterpretations of *Prince Hohenstiel*; for example, see No. 165.

On the whole, this poem of Mr. Browning's, with all its mixture of harsh and grand, of rude and glowing, of intricate parenthetical explanations and terse pictorial images, must be regarded as a mere fragment, not as exhausting even the apology which such a ruler as he is describing could make for the policy he had aimed at,—for there would be much selfish, and of its kind vigorous, argument of which Mr. Browning has taken no notice at all,—still less as even attempting to paint this ruler's own estimate of his own character and capacity,—but as simply discussing, and discussing finely, the controversy likely to have taken place in his own mind between that view of government which makes the physical comfort of the masses its main object, and that which aims at encouraging the development of a higher culture and a more refined freedom. As a fragment it is powerful. As an exhaustive discussion, even of this question in relation to the genius of any one nation, it would be obviously very incomplete.

15 January 1872, iii. 24–6

The last paragraph of this review is not untypical of the critical
obtuseness about which Browning so often complained.

Mr. Browning has always had a predilection for the type of characters
which the moralist finds it convenient to class as hypocrites. An artist
who begins to analyse character quite disinterestedly is met very soon
by the difficulty which character he is to analyse, the character which
the man indulges or the character which he assumes; nor is it allowable
to cut the knot and say that a man is what he allows himself to be, and
is not what he assumes himself to be. The assumption seriously influences his conduct, and it is quite as essential to his comfort that the
assumption should impose upon himself as that it should impose upon
others; if it come to the point, he would even prefer to allow himself
in less rather than give up the assumption altogether. In fact, the study
of human character, in general, might almost be resolved into an attempt
to ascertain the true relations between what we claim to be and what we
tend to be; and this problem is obviously best approached in the individuals in whom the contrast assumes the most piquant form. In the
same way the ethical distinction between honest men and rogues is
replaced by the aesthetical distinction between those who recognise and
accept and those who rebel against the inevitable contrast between the
ideal and the natural self. On the one side we have Mr. Sludge and
Bishop Blougram, and the bishop who orders his tomb in St. Praxede,
and the other bishops who display their successful or unsuccessful
diplomacy in the *Return of the Druses* and *The Soul's Tragedy*; on the
other side, there is the noble Djebal, one of the loftiest of all tragic
characters, and the pitiful Chiappino and poor Mr. Gigadibs. It is
worth noticing that Djebal comes nearest to the common conception
of a common imposter, just because his enthusiasm is too deep not to
be practical, too sustained not to become unscrupulous, while the
worthless Gigadibs is too shallow to be unsincere.

Of course the Saviour of Society belongs to the more intelligent if not to the more estimable class. The machinery of the poem is intricate, and it is difficult to believe that the whole of it was written upon a single plan. For 142 pages out of 148 the Saviour of Society, in exile, is explaining his career to a young lady; nearly 60 pages of the explanation are a history of his reign as it ought to have been, which is carried down to the end of the Italian war. Here the speaker discovers that it is five o'clock in the morning, opines that the young lady is asleep, moralises on the impossibility of a really sincere *apologia pro vita suâ*. In the last half-page we learn that he has not yet begun his second exile, has no young lady to talk to; but the whole reverie has arisen out of the possible consequences of an ultimatum, which he has still to decide upon sending. On the other hand, he says early in the poem:

> I could then, last July, bid courier take
> Message for me, post-haste, a thousand miles.

These lines and the whole context prove that the speaker was intended to be actually in exile, not merely anticipating what he would say when he was. It seems as if the poet had felt the ideal history of Prince Hohenstiel-Schwangaus' reign was getting too long, and had altered his plan in order to cut it short with effect; in a way the effect is gained, but it is at the price of an inconsistency which makes the last six pages very obscure. Another matter for regret is that the history of Hohenstiel-Schwangau should be simply identical with the history of France. One can understand the author's motive for choosing to write of Hohenstiel-Schwangau; but the choice entailed obvious obligations. It would have been very indecorous for Johnson to make the senate of Lilliput debate an expedition to Canada, and it is little better to make Thiers an historian, and Victor Hugo, a poet of Hohenstiel-Schwangau.

166. Browning's Portrayal of Character

1871

Richard Henry Stoddard, from his 'Robert Browning', *Appleton's Journal* (11 November 1871), vi. 533–6.

Stoddard (1825–1903) was an American critic and minor poet.

Mr. Browning has never been a popular poet, and never can be. Perhaps he does not desire to be. Ceratinly, it is not much to desire just now. There is one thing to be said for Mr. Browning, and that is that if when we have finished one of his dramas, or dramatic soliloquies, we have leisure—I will not say to think it over, for that does not help the matter, but leisure to let his work explain and justify itself, some things that were obscure in reading become tangible in memory—taking, or making shapes out of the clouds in which they were diffused; in short, orbing themselves into stars of greater or lesser brilliancy and distinctness.

To be a little more explicit, I must return to Shakespeare, if his scholars will pardon my momentary invasion of their province. Shakespeare's characters are all actualities, and the passions they exhibit and develop are such as we find in the men and women we know. We understand them when they speak, and when they act. Mr. Browning's characters are possibilities, perhaps, but we have never met with them. We cannot follow them in their talk, and their actions puzzle us. They are too subtle, too metaphysical, too remote, from mankind. It is wise for a poet to work 'from within outward,' but he should not work from so far within as never to come to the surface. There is a world of surface-work in Shakespeare, as in Homer, but how delightful it is! Mr. Browning disdains it, except in his *Dramatic Lyrics*, which will live when his dramas are forgotten. He excels Shakespeare, I think, in the art—if it be art—with which he makes his characters betray what they really are. They may deceive themselves, but they cannot deceive us. 'My Last Duchess' is a fine instance of this art, and 'Andrea Del Sarto' another. Nothing in literature is more masterly than the faultless painter's unconscious betrayal of his unknown shame. I know of nothing like this in Shakespeare—nothing so profound in any poet.

167. C. S. Calverley, A Parody

1872

From his 'The Cock and the Bull', *Fly Leaves* (1872), pp. 113–20.
Probably the most popular of Browning parodies. 'The Cock and
the Bull' was reprinted many times. The poem runs to 133 lines.

THE COCK AND THE BULL

You see this pebble-stone? It's a thing I bought
Of a bit of a chit of a boy i' the mid o' the day—
I like to dock the smaller parts-o'-speech,
As we curtail the already cur-tailed cur
(You catch the paronomasia, play o' words?)
Did, rather, i' the pre-Landseerian days.
Well, to my muttons. I purchased the concern,
And clapt it i' my poke, and gave for same
By way, to-wit, of barter or exchange—
'Chop' was my snickering dandiprat's own term—
One shilling and fourpence, current coin o' the realm.
O-n-e and f-o-u-r four
Pence, one and fourpence—you are with me, Sir?—
What hour it skills not: ten or eleven o' the clock,
One day (and what a roaring day it was!)
In February, eighteen sixty nine,
Alexandrina Victoria, Fidei
Hm—hm—how runs the jargon? being on throne.

Such, sir, are all the facts, succinctly put,
The basis or substratum—what you will—
Of the impending eighty thousand lines.
'Not much in 'em either,' quoth perhaps simple Hodge.
But there's a superstructure. Wait a bit.

FIFINE AT THE FAIR

June 1872

168. From an unsigned review, *The Spectator*

6 July 1872, xlv. 853–5

Divine truth is known not by looking outside the soul, but by watching the permanent residuum left beneath all its own changes. Mr Browning preaches that what men believe only because they desire it, is all human,—the falsehood through which Truth at last manifest itself,—but that the Truth which manifests itself through these falsehoods is that which forces itself back again upon the mind after all its efforts to believe otherwise, and which we could not know to be true till after the falsehoods had tried and failed to supersede it. That which endures in spite of not redounding to men's vanity and dignity, that which after every effort to magnify humanity forces us into submission to its will, being quite other than our will,—this is divine will. Yet the true is gained through the false,—just as the air was breathed by the swimmer through the help of the water which taken alone would have drowned him,—and could not have been gained without its aid. It is the experience of human dreams which alone enables us to see that that which disappoints and breaks human dreams, and which forces us to mould ourselves into keeping with it, instead of indulging them any longer, is above and beyond all human dreams, and is indeed the permanent to which their transience leads us:

> Each lie
> Redounded to the praise of man, was victory
> Man's nature had both right to get, and might to gain,
> And by no means implied submission to the reign
> Of other quite as real a nature, that saw fit
> To have its way with man, not man his way with it.
> This time, acknowledgment and acquiescence quell
> Their contrary in man; promotion proves as well

Defeat: and Truth, unlike the False with Truth's outside,
Neither plumes up his will nor puffs him out with pride.
I fancy, there must lurk some cogency i' the claim,
Man, such abatement made, submits to, all the same.

But, if time's pressure, light's
Or rather, dark's approach, wrest thoroughly the rights
Of rule away, and bid the soul submissive bear
Another soul than it play master everywhere
In great and small,—this time, I fancy, none disputes
There's something in the fact that such conclusion suits
Nowise the pride of man, nor yet chimes in with attributes.
Conspicuous in the lord of nature. He receives
And not demands—not first likes faith and then believes.

Such is the general tenor of this curious philosophical poem,—a poem which is connected in the slightest possible way with its title, *Fifine at the Fair*. Fifine is only a gipsy acrobat, who appears with her husband at the Breton fair of Pornic, and whose habits, tastes, and loves, and unwomanly type of beauty, serve as graphic texts from which to start on these long dissertations as to the true philosophy of art and love and faith. The deeply-rooted gipsy lawlessness which hates civilised order, while yet it is attracted to it, hovers round it, and lives upon what it can snatch from it, starts Mr. Browning on his first vein of thought, that it is through experience of what is false and temporary that we alone earn any knowledge of what is true, even though it is the spark of truth in us which enables us to live in the false and temporary. But Fifine's share in the poem, though graphic as far as it goes, and not wanting in picturesque elements, is extremely slight.

We have taken some pains to give a sort of *résumé* of Mr. Browning's teaching in this poem, because the style is abrupt, not always very easy to construe, and full of sharp digressions. As a poem, though it has much that is very vigorous and striking in it, we cannot think it one of his best. The philosophy is questionable, but always, when it is clear, ingenious and brilliantly illustrated. But the movement is harsh, and the treatment is far too intellectual,—far too little harmonised by art. We cannot endure what we have termed his short-hand style. In a poem, to leave out the little connecting links for the sake of brevity, is like stripping a rose-tree of its leaves for the sake of gaining space. Take the briefest of specimens:

What sound out-warbles brook, while, at the source, it wins
That moss and stone dispart, allow its bubblings breathe?

Just conceive speaking of 'a brook' as 'brook'! It is as jarring to us as the bourgeois custom of some wives of calling their husbands Mr. B. or Mr. C. And then the compression of 'that moss and stone allow its bubblings *to* breathe', 'or let its bubblings breathe', into 'allow its bubblings breathe.' That is not only not poetry; it is hardly prose. And why need Mr. Browning make his certainly very unpleasant-mannered husband say, when he gives a sharp hit at his wife's weaknesses, '*pouch that*'? He might almost as well let him give her a blow in the stomach. This is the kind of fault which makes a poet full of intellectual resource and ability,—indeed one whom one sometimes is tempted to think too intellectual by half for poetry, because he thinks so much more of the substance than the form of what he says,—so often repulsive as to offend his warmest admirers, and almost always 'caviare to the million.' *Fifine at the Fair* is one of his most thoughtful,—almost morbidly thoughtful,—poems. But no one will compare it with the volume containing *Men and Women* or with *The Ring and the Book*, for elements of true beauty. It is, indeed, on the whole, difficult, and more than usually abrupt and violent in the turns of its thought.

169. From an unsigned review, *The Westminster Review*

1 October 1872, NS xlii. 545–6

The complaint against Browning's crabbed constructions did not diminish with the years.

What, we should like to know, is Mr. Browning but the Fifine of poets? Does he not alternately charm, plague, and flirt with us wretched critics, till we are perfectly bewildered? Is he not always piping before us, shredding grammar, prosody, sense, and all such toys? Don't the Elvires of the world constantly say to us 'What is it you can possibly see to admire in this Mr. Browning, with his pink and impudence? Why

don't you like Tennyson, who is always musical? Or if you don't like
Tennyson, why can't you read the good Tupper?[1] But Browning!'—
and Elvire clasps her hands, and looks more than she has brains to utter.
The truth is, if we are to attack the Fifines, Mr. Browning must be the
first to suffer. And this we take to be the meaning of his poem—it is an
apology for himself and his poetry. Now we are going no further into
the matter. It is not Fifine, but Fifine's dancing which we admire. And
after this distinction, we proceed with a clear conscience. So far we have
laughed. But it is a subject for the deepest regret that Mr. Browning
should have cast his poem, dealing as it does with some of the most
perplexing problems of human nature, those terrible difficulties, which
in proportion—and this is the saddest part—as a man is endowed with
a spiritual nature, beset him and hinder him and even altogether stop
him, into such a form. The subject-matter of *Fifine at the Fair*, would
undoubtedly, treated as Browning could treat it, and as he has treated
it here in many passages, have made the epic of the present day. We
believe that he has put more substance into *Fifine at the Fair* than into
any other poem. But for the ordinary reader it might just as well have
been written in Sanscrit. There are such breaks, digressions, involutions,
crabbed constructions, metaphysical hair-splitting, that reading becomes
a positive fatigue. On the other hand, a perfect anthology of beauties
might be culled. If the duty of poetry has ever been fulfilled, it is by the
prologue. Here the muse assumes her true office—to comfort us with
hope, and to suggest that there may be possibilities which lie beyond
the range of our philosophy. The epilogue is utterly unworthy of
Browning. There is to our mind something akin to profanation about
it. As to the main scope of the poem—the necessity of individual life
and independent personality, for this course is the moral, if we may use
the hackneyed term—we need say nothing. We think, however, that
the lesson might have been taught by a far better example than poor
battered Fifine.

[1] Martin Tupper (1810–89), whose numbers ran as trippingly as his maxims in
Proverbial Philosophy.

RED COTTON NIGHT-CAP COUNTRY

May 1873

170. A Disagreeable Story

From an unsigned review, *The Spectator* (10 May 1873), xlvi. 606–7.

The charge of tastelessness, as will be seen in other reviews, was a common one.

As to style, we must add that there is far less of obscurity, but also far less of fitful eloquence, than usual with Mr. Browning. There is the same faulty, short-hand, article-eliminating hurry of style, as if the poet had to get his story told within a certain number of minutes, and every superfluous word, and many words by no means superfluous, must therefore be left to the reader to guess at. But there are very few passages the meaning of which is not quite clear at the second reading, and as our extracts will have shown, there are some of great subtlety and intellectual vivacity. Still Mr. Browning has not succeeded in giving any true poetic excuse for telling a story so full of disagreeable elements. When told, it fails to purify, as tragedy should, 'by pity and by fear'.

171. G. A. Simcox, from his review, *The Academy*

2 June 1873, iv. 201–3

When Mr. Browning published *Dramatis Personae* in 1864 it seemed permissible to suppose that his reputation was in some sense fixed. It was generally admitted that his poetry had certain faults; it was coming to be generally admitted that it had also certain merits whose value might be open to discussion but in any case deserved to be rated high. It seemed too that criticism might be spared the sterile labour of balancing the faults against the merits when one grew visibly out of the other, and might settle down at leisure to the fruitful work of analysing the sources of the author's undeniable power, if it was too early to hope to ascertain his literary rank. Since then Mr. Browning has resolved to make the British public like him; he has set to work with a will to get rid of the faults which went naturally with the merits that he had; perhaps it was hardly surprising that in spite of his stupendous cleverness he has fallen into other faults which naturally go with merits which he will never have. We do not mean that his work is falling off, or that his own public have a right to be disappointed, but they have a right to feel disconcerted. Every new book is a surprise to them, they never know what to expect of him; not because he is always putting forth new powers, but because he is always inventing fresh uses for old powers. The mere astonishing bulk and completeness of the *Ring and the Book* extorted too unlimited admiration for it to be obvious at once that clearness was purchased at the expense of prolixity, and even if it had been obvious it might have been retorted that *Sordello* was prolix without being clear. But *Balaustion's Adventure* and *Prince Hohenstiel-Schwangau* suggested a more alarming suspicion: it almost looked as if in rubbing off his roughness Mr. Browning would rub off his distinction too—as if he would file away asperities till nothing was left except an ingeniously intricate arrangement of too sterling common sense. Such fears were happily set at rest by the appearance of *Fifine*: the profane might object that the old harshness and obscurity were if possible exaggerated, but the faithful easily overlooked those familiar blemishes (and after all the meaning had more room in the Alexandrine couplets than in the rhyming heroics of *Sordello*); it was enough for them to recover the old shifting subtlety of suggestion, the rapid depth of insight, which were not to be found elsewhere. Even in *Fifine* however it was possible to trace new aims which mingled themselves with the familiar charm: the dramatic power was unimpaired, but it was less disinterested, less impersonal than in most of the earlier work: the author seemed resolved to get out of the ideal medium altogether into the actual workaday world, and, though this was not altogether a novelty, he was preoccupied with some didactic purpose. Both the last characteristics come out very strongly in *Turf and Towers*; but, like everything else that Mr. Browning has published since *Dramatis Personae*, it compels us to revise our estimate of him. Certainly there is no lack of clearness here, there is no excess of rapidity to create confusion, but the distinctive feature of the book is a resolute pursuit of purely artistic graces. Talleyrand used to say that the Duke of Wellington spoke French with a great deal of courage: Mr. Browning has practised elegance and irony and other refinements of a Platonic dialogue with a vehement uncompromising energy which cannot but deepen our admiration of his prodigious intellectual force.

172. William Dean Howells,
The Atlantic Monthly

July 1873, xxxii. 114-15

From his review.

This hostile review, appearing in one of America's most influential literary magazines, and coming from the pen of an important critic and novelist, is a fair sample of the significant shift in American opinion of Browning after *The Ring and the Book*.

The *Red Cotton Night-Cap Country* is the antic name of that strange last performance of Mr. Browning's, to which, for reasons of his own, he has given the outward form and typographical mask of poetry; but why he should have called it *Red Cotton Night-Cap Country*, sooner than 'The Man in the Moon', or 'Ding-Dong Bell', does not finally appear to the distracted reader of the work. . . . [The plot is] horrible and revolting in itself; and it is so told as to bring out its worst with a far-reaching insinuation, and an occasional frantic rush at expression of its unseemliness for which the manure-heap affords the proper imagery of 'dung', and 'devil's dung'. We suppose we shall be told of power in the story; and power there undeniably is, else no one could be dragged through the book by it. The obscurity of three fourths of it—of nearly all one might say, except the merely narrative passages—becomes almost amusing. It seems as if Mr. Browning lay in wait, and, lest any small twinkling or glimmer of meaning should reach his reader, sprang out and popped a fresh parenthesis on the offending chink that let it through. Fifty-six mortal pages explain, why the story is called *Red Cotton Night-Cap Country*, but without making the reader understand why, and he is left dancing upon nothing for many pages more, till his aching foot is glad to rest even on the uncleanly history of M. Miranda's intrigue and lunacy. The poem—if it is a poem—is as unhandsome as it is unwholesome; it is both bad art and bad taste, and is to be defended, it seems to us, neither as a lesson from a miserable fact, nor as a successful bit of literary realism.

173. Edith J. Simcox, *Fortnightly Review*

July 1873, xx. 137–8

From her review.

Edith Simcox was later to write *Natural Law: An Essay in Ethics* (1877).

> If we have souls, know how to see and use,
> One place performs, like any other place,
> The proper service every place on earth
> Was framed to furnish man with: serves alike
> To give him note that, through the place he sees,
> A place is signified he never saw;
> But, if he lack not soul, may learn to know.

In those lines Mr. Browning half explains the secret of the power which he and all great dramatists possess of making the same story bear a different meaning, or a different story produce the same effect, according to the mood of the poet or his reader. Nearly all our impressions are interchangeable, because in all the thing signified is distinct from the thing seen, and it rests with the mind to attach what meaning it pleases to the sign. Dramatic art is triumphant when it has given a vivid impression, while at the same time disclosing all the possibilities of significance concealed within it; and it is the constant exercise of this power that makes Mr. Browning's works, whatever their outer form, so essentially dramatic in effect. His use of the power is sometimes tyrannical, but it is almost irresistible, and if he insists on making nightcaps the object of candid contemplation, we are constrained to admit that—

> Night's notice, life is respited from day—

is worth contemplating. There is a little harshness, however, in the transition from the playful moralizing addressed to Miss Thackeray[1] about the 'dubious life, half sleep,' of Norman villagers, to the tragedy which is the proper subject of the volume.

[1] Anne Thackeray (1837–1919), later Lady Ritchie, gave Browning the idea for the title of this poem, which he dedicated to her. In 1892 she published her reminiscence of the circumstances and the place which gave rise to the poem, in her *Records of Tennyson, Ruskin, and Browning*.

174. From an unsigned review,
The British Quarterly Review

1 July 1873, lviii. 240–1

Mr. Browning's is a style which is beset with temptations. It is confessedly analytical and apologetic. Now, the passion for analysis tends to grow by what it feeds on, and needs—greatly needs—the corrective of frank presentation of healthy human interests; whilst the experiment of apology, as we all know, sometimes even overbalances self respect in the determination to justify itself in justifying its object. Mr. Browning has very nearly passed the legitimate line in this new work, which may be designated as an endeavour, 'dramatically,' to deal with purely morbid elements in human life, and to find relief or justification in nothing else than the mode of treatment. Any other writer of our day would have hopelessly failed in the effort. Mr. Tennyson would have too plainly shown a personal shrinking from some points raised here, as from *proud* flesh—for some such shrinking is perceptible in his dealing with the 'Arthurian Legends'. Mr. Swinburne, we fear, would have now and again displayed too much *warmth* of sympathy. Mr. Browning saves himself by the curious, self-removed, half-quizzical habit of analysis, which sometimes becomes almost grotesque, but never wholly so. *Fifine* is the proper passage-way from *The Ring and the Book*, with its sweet Pompilia, to this French law-tragedy wrought up with its adventuress of a heroine, who has been mistress to several men before meeting the hero. Our interest in this story is maintained by our being led perforce to trace the process by which the poet finds in what seem the most perverted elements the dim reflex of high possibilities, ruined by admixture of incompatible qualities of temperament; and, as a tinge of that *fatefulness* which somehow will intrude into the dramatic art, and move especially into every form of it which is obviously apologetic, thus communicates itself, in spite of the grotesquerie of manner, something of tragic 'pity and terror' returns to the work, if we only try to view it faithfully *as a whole*. But only so; and in this lies a fair criticism, inasmuch as few readers seek, or can be expected to dwell on such works till the underlying idea of the whole reveals itself completely.

175. J. R. Dennett, *Nation*

14 August 1873, xvii. 116–18

From his unsigned review.

Dennett also reviewed *The Ring and the Book* and *Balaustion's Adventure* for this American periodical, in both instances emphasizing—as he does here—Browning's psychological manner.

Mr. Browning's latest poem tells with rather less than his usual convolutions a story which has to the full the quality of psychological subtlety in which he so much delights. The introduction, too, is fine-drawn to a degree that corresponds with the structure to which it is the porch. It is, perhaps, indefensibly whimsical, and wraps up in as many wrappings as Mr. Browning used to allow to a mummified princess, a body of little or no value. Still it is read with pleasure as well as curiosity, though one smiles to think of what would be made of it all by a reader who had not been broken to Browning before he wrote *The Red Cotton Night-Cap Country*.

On the whole, the admirer of Browning will find in this poem, or this story in blank verse, a pleasant production of the *musa pedestris* of its author; and an occasional touch reveals the master—as where the poet meets his fair friend as if their meeting-place

> . . . Were just that Rome
> Out in the champaign, say, o'er-rioted
> By verdure, ravage, and gay winds that war
> Against strong sunshine settled to his sleep.

But no new admirers will it give him; and some backsliders it will confirm in their fallen state.

176. Unsigned notice, *Harper's Magazine*

August 1873, xlii. 461

Red Cotton Night-Cap Country is the somewhat enigmatical title of Mr. Browning's last very enigmatical poem. It is a volume of over two hundred pages, and is quite as mystical in its pseudo-philosophy and quite as obscure and perplexing in its twisted and tortured sentences as any thing he has ever written; nor does it contain in any large measure the flashes of his peculiar genius. It is, or to the great majority will be, an intolerably wearisome book, and we venture the assertion that even of the critics who write glowing eulogies upon it only a very small minority will ever read it through. There are some books which are condemned by the critics, but read by the people; there are others which are applauded by the critics, but read by nobody. *Red Cotton Night-Cap Country* belongs to the latter category. It may be readily imagined that we have not read it through; nor have we: it is not necessary to traverse every square mile of the Great Desert to know that its scenery is tame. We have read enough to know both the story and the manner in which it is told, and to enter our strong protest against the endeavour to glorify an illicit love with one who had been in succession a profligate woman and an unfaithful wife. The very abstruse and scarcely comprehensible moral which is tacked on at the close does not save the story from its essential spirit of immorality. Neither does the pseudo-satire on Romanism relieve it in any wise. It can only be characterized as harmless because the class of people who would be liable to be harmed by it will not understand nor even read it.

177. Mrs. Sutherland Orr:
Browning's Casuistry

1874

From her article 'Mr. Browning's Place in Literature', *Contemporary Review* (May 1874), xxiii. 934–65.

Alexandra Sutherland Leighton Orr (1828–1903), sister of Frederick Leighton the painter, became a close friend of Browning. In an unpublished letter of 28 November 1885, he called her 'the dearest woman friend I can boast of in the world.' (Quoted in *Learned Lady: Letters from Robert Browning to Mrs. Thomas Fitzgerald, 1876–1889*, ed. by Edward C. McAleer [1966], p. 22.) Her biography of the poet and her handbook to his works are important (see the bibliography), but not always accurate, sources of information for students of Browning.

The one quality of Mr. Browning's intellectual nature which is at present most universally recognized is its casuistry—his disposition to allow an excessive weight to the incidental conditions of human action, and consequently to employ sliding scales in the measurement of it. The most remarkable evidence of this quality, supplied by his later works, is to be found in *Prince Hohenstiel-Schwangau*. It is displayed with more audacity in *Fifine at the Fair*, with larger and more sustained effect in *The Ring and the Book*. But *Fifine at the Fair*, though very subjective in treatment, verges too much on the grotesque to be accepted as a genuine reflection of the author's mind; and *The Ring and the Book* represents him as a pleader, but at the same time as a judge. It describes the case under discussion from every possible point of view, but does not describe it as subject to any possible moral doubt. *Prince Hohenstiel-Schwangau* is a deliberate attempt on the author's part to defend a cause which he knows to be weak, and as such is a typical specimen, as it is also a favourable one, of his genius for special pleading. It places in full relief the love of opposition which impels him to defend the weaker side, and the love of fairness which always makes him subsume in the defence every argument that may be justly advanced against it; and it also exhibits that double-refracting quality of his mind which can convert a final concession to the one side into an irresistible last word in favour of the other. . . .

We should naturally infer, from the temper of Mr. Browning's mind, that the warmth of its affectations would belie the indifferentism of its ideas, and we constantly find it to be so. An innate veneration for moral beauty, of which we find scarcely any trace in his philosophizing poems, asserts itself in all those of a more emotional character, and so various is his mode of self-manifestation that the evidence contained in his collective works of his belief in the necessary relativity of judgment is not a whit stronger than their indirect advocacy of courage, devotion, singleness of heart—in short, of all the virtues which are born of conviction. His imagination is keenly alive to every condition of love; but its deepest and most passionate response is always yielded to that form of tenderness which by its disinterested nature most approaches to the received ideal of the Divine. This feeling attains its highest expression in 'Saul,' where the anthropomorphism so often apparent in the author's conception of God is justified by historic truth and ennobled by a sustained intensity of lyric emotion which has been rarely equalled and probably never surpassed. It is the outpouring of a passionate human friendship gradually raised by its own strength to the presentiment of a divine love manifest in the flesh, and to which in its final ecstasy the very life of nature becomes the throbbing of a mysterious and expectant joy. The love of love is the prevailing inspiration of all such of Mr. Browning's poems as even trench on religious subjects, and it often resolves itself into so earnest a plea for the divine nature and atoning mission of Christ, that we can scarcely retain the conviction that it is his heart, and not his mind, which accepts it.

The one peculiarity of Mr. Browning's verse through which his character of poet is most generally impugned is its frequent want of melody, and his known contempt for melody as distinct from meaning would be sufficient to account for the occasional choice of subjects that excluded it. But he thus admits the more fully the essential unity of matter and form; and the unmusical character of so much of his poetry is in some degree justified by the fact, that its subjects are in themselves unmusical.

> So I will sing on fast as fancies come;
> Rudely, the verse being as the mood it paints.[1]

[1] *Pauline,* II. 258–9.

His actual ruggedness lies far more in the organic conception of his ideas than in the manner of rendering them, whilst his rapid alternations and successions of thought often give the appearance of ruggedness where none is. In beauty or the reverse his style is essentially expressive, and when, as in *Pauline, Paracelsus*, almost all the Dramas, and most of the minor poems, there is an inward harmony to be expressed, it is expressed the more completely for the rejection of all such assistance as mere sound could afford. He has even given to so satirical a poem as 'The Bishop orders his Tomb in St. Praxed's Church', a completely melodious rythm, its satire being borrowed from the simple misapplication of an earnest and pathetic emotion. If he ever appears gratuitously to rebel against the laws of sound it is in his rhymed and not in his blank verse; and there might be truth in the idea that his contempt for the music of mere iteration is excited by the very act of employing it, but that so many of his grandest and sweetest inspirations have been appropriately clothed in rhyme.

178. Browning's Originality

1875

From his *Victorian Poets* (1875), pp. 293–341.

Edmund Clarence Stedman (1833–1908), minor American poet and stockbroker, compiled anthologies which were widely read in their time.

Has the lapse of years made Browning any more attractive to the masses, or even to the judicious few? He is said to have 'succeeded by a series of failures,' and so has, as far as notoriety means success, and despite the recent increase of his faults. But what is the fact which strikes the admiring and sympathetic student of his poetry and career? Distrusting my own judgment, I asked a clear and impartial thinker,—'How does Browning's work impress you?' His reply, after a moment's consideration, was: 'Now that I try to formulate the sensation which it always has given me, his work seems that of a grand intellect painfully striving for adequate use and expression, and never quite attaining either.' This was, and is, precisely my own feeling. The question arises, What is at fault? Browning's genius, his chosen mode of expression, his period, or one and all of these? After the flush of youth is over, a poet must have a wise method, if he would move ahead. He must improve upon instinct by experience and common-sense. There is something amiss in one who has to grope for his theme and cannot adjust himself to his period; especially in one who cannot agreeably handle such themes as he arrives at. More than this, however, is the difficulty in Browning's case. Expression is the flower of thought; a fine imagination is wont to be rhythmical and creative, and many passages, scattered throughout Browning's works, show that his is no exception. It is a certain caprice or perverseness of method, that, by long practice, has injured his gift of expression; while an abnormal power of ratiocination, and a prosaic regard for details, have handicapped him from beginning. Besides, in mental arrogance and scorn of authority, he has insulted Beauty herself, and furnished too much excuse for small offenders. What may be condoned in one of his breed is intolerable when mimicked by every jackanapes and self-appointed reformer.

A group of evils, then, has interfered with the greatness of his poetry. His style is that of a man caught in a morass of ideas through which he has to travel,—wearily floundering, grasping here and there, and often sinking deeper until there seems no prospect of getting through. His latest works have been more involved and excursive, less beautiful and elevating, than most of those which preceded them. Possibly his theory is that which was his wife's instinct,—a man being more apt than a woman with some reason for what he does,—that poetry is valuable *only* for the statement which it makes, and must always be subordinate thereto.

Still, he has dramatic insight, and a minute power of reading other men's hearts. His moral sentiment has a potent and subtile quality:— through his early poems he really founded a school, and had imitators, and, although of his later method there are none, the younger poets whom he has most affected very naturally began work by carrying his philosophy to a startling yet perfectly logical extreme.

Much of his poetry is either very great or very poor. It has been compared to Wagner's music, and entitled the 'poetry of the future'; but if this be just, then we must revise our conception of what poetry really is. The doubter incurs the contemptuous enmity of two classes of the dramatist's admirers: first, of the metaphysical, who disregard considerations of passion, melody, and form; secondly, of those who are sensitive to their master's failings, but, in view of his greatness, make it a point of honor to defend them. That greatness lies in his originality; his error, arising from perverseness or congenital defect, is the violation of natural and beautiful laws. This renders his longer poems of less worth than his lyrical studies, while, through avoidance of it, productions, differing as widely as *The Eve of St. Agnes* and *In Memoriam*, will outlive *The Ring and the Book*.

179. Swinburne Defends Browning

Algernon Charles Swinburne, from his introduction to *The Works of George Chapman* (1875), pp. xiv–xix.

In a letter of 31 January 1875, Swinburne expressed his pride in this passage on Browning, calling it 'the truest criticism . . . that has appeared on the subject'. See *The Letters of Algernon Charles Swinburne*, ed. by Edmund Gosse and Thomas J. Wise (1919), I, 172–5. Browning expressed his gratitude in a letter of 23 February 1875, printed in *LRB*, p. 166.

The charge of obscurity is perhaps of all charges the likeliest to impair the fame or to imperil the success of a rising or an established poet. It is as often misapplied by hasty or ignorant criticism as any other on the roll of accusations; and was never misapplied more persistently and perversely than to an eminent writer of our own time. The difficulty found by many in certain of Mr. Browning's works arises from a quality the very reverse of that which produces obscurity properly so called. Obscurity is the natural product of turbid forces and confused ideas; of a feeble and clouded or of a vigorous but unfixed and chaotic intellect. . . . Now if there is any great quality more perceptible than another in

Mr. Browning's intellect it is his decisive and incisive faculty of thought, his sureness and intensity of perception, his rapid and trenchant resolution of aim. . . . He is something too much the reverse of obscure; he is too brilliant and subtle for the ready reader of a ready writer to follow with any certainty the track of an intelligence which moves with such incessant rapidity, or even to realize with what spider-like swiftness and sagacity his building spirit leaps and lightens to and fro and backward and forward as it lives along the animated line of its labour, springs from thread to thread and darts from centre to circumference of the glittering and quivering web of living thought woven from the inexhaustible stores of his perception and kindled from the inexhaustible fire of his imagination. He never thinks but at full speed; and the rate of his thought is to that of another man's as the speed of a railway to that of a waggon or the speed of a telegraph to that of a railway. It is hopeless to enjoy the charm or to apprehend the gist of his writings except with a mind thoroughly alert, an attention awake at all points, a spirit open and ready to be kindled by the contact of the writer's. To do justice to any book which deserves any other sort of justice than that of the fire or the waste-paper basket, it is necessary to read it in the fit frame of mind; and the proper mood in which to study for the first time a book of Mr. Browning's is the freshest, clearest, most active mood of the mind in its brightest and keenest hours of work. Read at such a time, and not 'with half-shut eyes falling asleep in a half-dream', it will be found (in Chapman's phrase) 'pervial' enough to any but a sluggish or a sandblind eye; but at no time and in no mood will a really obscure writer be found other than obscure. The difference between the two is the difference between smoke and lightning; and it is far more difficult to pitch the tone of your thought in harmony with that of a foggy thinker than with that of one whose thought is electric in its motion. To the latter we have but to come with an open and pliant spirit, untired and undisturbed by the work or the idleness of the day, and we cannot but receive a vivid and active pleasure in following the swift and fine radiations, the subtle play and keen vibration of its sleepless fires; and the more steadily we trace their course the more surely do we see that all these forked flashes of fancy and changing lights of thought move unerringly around one centre and strike straight in the end to one point. Only random thinking and random writing produce obscurity; and these are the radical faults of Chapman's style of poetry. We find no obscurity in the lightning, whether it play about the heights of metaphysical speculation or the depths of character and motive; the mind derives as much of vigorous enjoyment from the study by such light of the one as of the other. The action of so bright and swift a spirit gives insight as it were to the eyes and wings to the feet of our own; the reader's apprehension takes fire from the writer's, and he catches from a subtler and more active mind the infection of spiritual interest; so that any candid and clear-headed student finds himself able to follow for the time in fancy the lead of such a thinker with equal satisfaction on any course of thought or argument; when he sets himself to refute Renan through the dying lips of St. John or to try conclusions with Strauss in his own person, and when he flashes at once the whole force of his illumination full upon the inmost thought and mind of the most infamous criminal, a Guido Franceschini or a Louis Bonaparte, compelling the black and obscene abyss of such a spirit to yield up at last the secret of its profoundest sophistries, and let forth the serpent of a soul that lies coiled under all the most intricate and supple reasonings of self-justified and self-conscious crime. And thanks to this very quality of vivid spiritual illumination we are able to see by the light of the author's mind without being compelled to see with his eyes, or with the eyes of the living mask which he assumes for his momentary impersonation of saint or sophist, philosopher or male-factor; without accepting one conclusion, conceding one point, or condoning one crime. It is evident that to produce any such effect re-quires above all things brightness and decision as well as subtlety and pliancy of genius; and this is the supreme gift and distinctive faculty of Mr. Browning's mind. If indeed there be ever any likelihood of error in his exquisite analysis, he will doubtless be found to err rather through excess of light than through any touch of darkness; we may doubt, not without a sense that the fittest mood of criticism might be that of a self-distrustful confidence in the deeper intuition of his finer and more per-fect knowledge, whether the perception of good or evil would actually be so acute in the mind of the supposed reasoner; whether for instance a veritable household assassin, a veritable saviour of society or other incarnation of moral pestilence, would in effect see so clearly and so far, with whatever perversion or distortion of view, into the recesses of the pit of hell wherein he lives and moves and has his being; recognising with quick and delicate apprehension what points of vantage he must strive to gain, what outposts of self-defence he may hope to guard, in the explanation and vindication of the motive forces of his nature and the latent mainspring of his deeds. This fineness of intellect and dramatic sympathy which is ever on the watch to anticipate and answer the unspoken imputations and prepossessions of his hearer, the very movements of his mind, the very action of his instincts, is perhaps a quality hardly compatible with a nature which we might rather suppose, judging from public evidence and historic indication, to be sluggish and short-sighted, 'a sly slow thing with circumspective eye' that can see but a little way immediately around it, but neither before it nor behind, above it nor beneath; and whose introspection, if ever that eye were turned inward, would probably be turbid, vacillating, cloudy and uncertain as the action of a spirit incapable of self-knowledge but not incapable of self-distrust, timid and impenitent, abased and unabashed, remorseless but not resolute, shameless but not fearless. If such be in reality the public traitor and murderer of a nation, we may fairly infer that his humbler but not viler counterpart in private life will be unlikely to exhibit a finer quality of mind or a clearer faculty of reason. But this is a question of realism which in no wise affects the spiritual value and interest of such work as Mr. Browning's. What is important for our present purpose is to observe that this work of exposition by soliloquy and apology by analysis can only be accomplished or undertaken by the genius of a great special pleader, able to fling himself with all his heart and all his brain, with all the force of his intellect and all the strength of his imagination, into the assumed part of his client; to concentrate on the cause in hand his whole power of illustration and illumination, and bring to bear upon one point at once all the rays of his thought in one focus.

Apart from his gift of moral imagination, Mr. Browning has in the supreme degree the qualities of a great debater or an eminent leading counsel; his finest reasoning has in its expression and development something of the ardour of personal energy and active interest which inflames the argument of a public speaker; we feel, without the reverse regret of Pope, how many a firstrate barrister or parliamentary tactician has been lost in this poet. The enjoyment that his best and most characteristic work affords us is doubtless far other than the delight we derive from the purest and highest forms of the lyric or dramatic art; there is a radical difference between the analyst and the dramatist, the pleader and the prophet; it would be clearly impossible for the subtle tongue which can undertake at once the apology and the anatomy of such motives as may be assumed to impel or to support a 'Prince Hohenstiel-Schwangau' on his ways of thought and action, ever to be touched with the fire which turns to a sword or to a scourge the tongue of a poet to whom it is given to utter as from Patmos or from Sinai the word that fills all the heaven of song with the lightnings and thunders of chastisement. But in place of lyric rapture or dramatic action we may profitably enjoy the unique and incomparable genius of analysis which gives to these special pleadings such marvellous life and interest as no other workman in that kind was ever or will ever again be able to give: we may pursue with the same sense of strenuous delight in a new exercise of intellect and interest the slender and luminous threads of speculation wound up into a clue with so fine a skill and such happy sleight of hand in *Fifine at the Fair* or the sixth book of *Sordello*, where the subtle secret of spiritual weakness in a soul of too various powers and too restless refinement is laid bare with such cunning strength of touch, condemned and consoled with such far-sighted compassion and regret. This last-named poem has been held especially liable to the charge which we have seen to be especially inapplicable to the general work of its author; but although the manner of its construction should not seem defensible, as to me I may confess that it does not, it would be an utter misuse of terms to find in obscurity of thought or language the cause of this perceptible defect. The point of difference was accurately touched by the exquisite critical genius of Coleridge when he defined the style of Persius as 'hard—not obscure:' for this is equally true in the main of the style of *Sordello*; only the hard metal is of a different quality and temper, as the intellect of the English thinker is far wider in its reach, far subtler in its action and its aim, than that of the Roman stoic. The error, if I may take on myself to indicate what I conceive to be the error, of style in *Sordello* is twofold; it is a composite style, an amalgam of irreconcilable materials that naturally refuse to coalesce; and, like a few of the author's minor poems, it is written at least partially in shorthand, which a casual reader is likely to mistake for cipher, and to complain accordingly that the key should be withheld from him. A curious light is thrown on the method of its composition by the avowal put forth in the dedication of a reissue of this poem, that since its first adventure on publicity the writer had added and had cancelled a notable amount of illustrative or explanatory matter, preferring ultimately to leave his work such a poem as the few must like, rather than such as the many might. Against this decision no one has a right to appeal; and there is doubtless much in the work as it stands that all imaginative thinkers and capable students of poetry most assuredly must regard with much more than mere liking; but when the reader is further invited to observe that the sole aim kept in sight, the sole object of interest pursued by the author was the inner study of an individual mind, the occult psychology of a single soul, the personal pathology of a special intelligence, he has a right to suggest that in that

394

case there is too much, and in any other case there is not enough, of external illustration and the byplay of alien actions and passions which now serve only to perplex the scheme they ought to explain. If it was the author's purpose to give to his philosophic poem a background of historic action, to relieve against the broad mass and movement of outer life the solitary process of that inward and spiritual tragedy which was the main occupation of his mind and art, to set the picture of a human spirit in the frame of circumstances within which it may actually have been environed and beset with offers of help, with threats and temptations, doubts and prospects and chances of the day it had on earth,—if this were his purpose, then surely there is not here enough of such relief to illustrate a design which there is more than enough of it to confuse. But if, as we are now obliged to assume, the author's purpose was studiously and strenuously to restrict within the limits of inner spiritual study the interest and the motive of his work, to concentrate our attention with his own upon the growth and the fortune, the triumph and the failure, the light and the darkness of this one human spirit, the soul of a man of genius fallen upon evil days and elect for great occasions and begirt with strange perplexities, then surely there is here far too much of external distraction and diversion for the reader's mind even to apprehend the issue, much less to comprehend the process, of this inner tragic action. The poem, in short, is like a picture in which the background runs into the foreground, the figures and the landscape confound each other for want of space and keeping, and there is no middle distance discernible at all. It is but a natural corollary to this general error that the body like the spirit of the poem, its form not less than its thought, should halt between two or three diverse ways, and that the style should too often come to the ground between two stools or more; being as it is neither a dramatic nor a narrative style, neither personal nor impersonal, neither lyric nor historic, but at once too much of all these and not enough of any. The result may be to the hasty reader no less repellent than the result of obscurity in thought or in style; but from identity of effect we are not to infer an identity of cause. The best parts of this poem also belong in substance always and sometimes in form to the class of monodramas or soliloquies of the spirit; a form to which the analytic genius of Mr. Browning leads him ever as by instinct to return, and in which alone it finds play for its especial faculties and security against its especial liabilities to error and confusion of styles; a security for want of which his lyric and dramatic writing is apt to be neither dramatic nor lyrical, simply because of the writer's natural and inevitable tendency to analysis, which, by the nature of things as well as by the laws of art, can only explain and express itself either through the method of direct exposition or in the form of elaborate mental monologue. The whole argument of the sixth book is monodramatic; and its counterpart is to be sought in the most dramatic and to me the most delightful passage of equal length in the poem, the magnificent soliloquy of Salinguerra in the fourth book, full of the subtle life and reality and pathos which the author, to speak truth as it seems to me, too generally fails to transfer from monologue into dialogue, to translate into the sensible action and passion of tragedy, or adequately to express in fullness and fitness of lyric form. The finest and most memorable parts of his plays not less than of his poems are almost always reducible in their essence to what I have called monodrama; and if cast into the monodramatic form common to all his later writings would have found a better if not a keener expression and left a clearer if not a deeper impression on the mind. For one example, the communing of old King Victor with himself on his return to the palace he has resigned is surely far more impressive and memorable to any reader than the rest of the play where his character is exhibited in the mutual action and reaction of dialogue among characters who seem unable to say rightly what they should say except when alone or secure from interruption. Even Chapman, from whom I may be thought to have wandered somewhat far in this inquiry as to what is or is not properly definable as obscurity, has in my judgment a sounder instinct of dramatic dialogue and movement than the illustrious writer who has carved out for himself in the second period of his career a new and better way to the end appointed by nature for the exercise of his highest powers: and Chapman was certainly not remarkable among the great men of his day for the specially dramatic bent of his genius.

I have dwelt thus long on a seemingly irrelevant and discursive inquiry because I could discover no method so fit to explain the nature of the fault I cannot but find in the poet of whom I have to speak, as by contrast of his work with the work of another, upon whom this fault has been wrongly charged by the inaccurate verdict of hasty judges. In answer to these I have shown that the very essence of Mr. Browning's aim and method, as exhibited in the ripest fruits of his intelligence, is such as implies above all other things the possession of a quality the very opposite of obscurity—a faculty of spiritual illumination rapid and intense and subtle as lightning, which brings to bear upon its central object by way of direct and vivid illustration every symbol and every detail on which its light is flashed in passing. Thus in *Fifine* the illustration derived from a visionary retrospect of Venice, and in *Sordello* the superb and wonderful comparison of the mental action of a man who puts by for a season the memories in which he has indulged for a moment before turning again to the day's work, with that of a fugitive slave who thinks over in a pause of his flight and puts aside for more practical means of revenge the thought of enchantments 'sovereign to plague his enemies', as he buckles himself again to the grim business of escape—these and other such illustrative passages are not more remarkable for the splendour of their imaginative quality than for the aptness of their cunning application and the direct light reflected from them on the immediate argument which is penetrated and vivified throughout by the insinuation and exploration of its radiance.

ARISTOPHANES' APOLOGY

April 1870

180. John Addington Symonds, *Academy*

17 April 1875, vii. 389–90

A lengthy and admiring summary precedes this excerpt from his review. For information on Symonds, see the headnote to No. 138.

This miserable outline indicates the general drift of *Aristophanes*. A score of quotations had been marked to illustrate the poet's style of treatment. But these I, the reviewer, have omitted: for not a sentence in this poem is superfluous; and, wrenched from its context, each passage seems an insult to its author. What praise is greater than this? Mr. Browning is unrivalled in the art of following thought through all its windings, tracing and retracing labyrinths of sophistry and prejudice, blending the specious and the true as he conceives them, the coarse and the refined, spinning with words a closely-fitting veil of gossamer for the spirit he imprisons in his verse. Therefore no poet suffers more from the process of such villainous abbreviation as a taster for the public in a first review is bound to venture on.

181. From an unsigned review, *The Athenæum*

17 April 1875, pp. 513-14

Browning was irritated by the suggestion that he might have received assistance from Jowett, 'with whom' [he wrote] 'I never had a conversation about Aristophanes in my life.' *LRB*, p. 171. Jowett, who had no very high opinion of Browning's Greek scholarship, likewise would not have been flattered.

The vignette to the *Symposium* is the key-note of Mr. Browning's poem, and he has in his own manner worked it into a fugue, as puzzling, as full of subtleties and ironies, as capricious, and as iridescent as his *Sordello*. The world has had warnings of late that critics must never be personal. And yet it is—we venture to think—impossible to understand or even to dimly sympathize with *The Last Adventure of Balaustion* without knowing a few simple facts—facts that are matter of notoriety—about its author. Mr. Jowett is Master of Baliol, Mr. Browning is the one Honorary Fellow whom Baliol has elected, and the two are friends. Mr. Jowett, no old Oxford man need be reminded, is especially fond of the *Symposium*, for its own sake as a work of art, and still more for the sake of the subtle problem which its last few sentences throw down, and to which we know but one solution—that the dialogue itself is the answer. This being so, it is to be hoped we in no way exceed our province in suggesting that the Master of Baliol and its Honorary Fellow must have talked over the conclusion of the *Symposium* more than once, and possibly even until cock-crow, and that in some way the poem has grown out of the discussion.

182. Margaret Oliphant,
Blackwood's Edinburgh Magazine
July 1875, cxviii. 91–4

From her unsigned review.

Mrs. Oliphant (1828–97) was a popular novelist, critic, and biographer. Her view, in this case at least, no doubt was widely shared.

Mr Browning's last poem is, we think, very little worthy of him. What has come to him in these latter days? What bewildering spirit has carried him round the fatal circle and landed him once more in those wilds of confused wordiness which made *Sordello* the wonder and the fear of all readers? The noble interval between which he has peopled with the *Men and Women* of his most perfect poetical effort, and with the three great figures which, amid much indifferent matter, we find in the *Ring and the Book*, has given absolute proof that he is not compelled by any mystery of nature to entangle himself in those uncouth shrouds of diction, the complicated parentheses and inharmonious syllables, which, by some perverted operation of taste, he chose to begin with, and which he has come back to with such fatal effect. Here is another terrible result of Greek, as appalling as any which Mr Symonds[1] has put before us in the history of the Renaissance. A profligate prince is a very horrible and dangerous thing; but he affects us less in this well-protected island than does a wasted poet. Alexander VI. at this long interval we can ignore or forget; he has served a great many purposes since, and pointed the moral against the Papacy to the utter obliteration of all good Popes and the perfect satisfaction of every good Protestant for generations, so that even his depravity may have had its uses; but what is there to console us when we make our moan over our poet wasted, our anticipations deceived? Mr Browning threw himself into this perilous path of Greek with a fervour which we pardoned in that first adventure of *Balaustion*, which embodied the drama of *Alcestis*, one of those efforts of the great

1 See the headnote to No. 138.

muse of Greece which is most in harmony with later tenets of art and the workings of the modern mind. A translation of one poet by another, though we may demur to it as a waste of power, has, doubtless, great recommendations; and the English poet in this case rendered the Greek with as much truth and fidelity as poetic force. But, alas! it had been better if the first experiment had not succeeded, when its success leads us to nothing better than a poetical argument, nearly four hundred pages long, between a half-tipsy Greek, half buffoon, half philosopher, and an enthusiastic poetess as long-winded as himself. There can be no doubt, however much it is to be deplored (if it is to be deplored), that three-fourths of the readers of English poetry are absolutely indifferent to the question why Aristophanes attacked Euripides in his comedies, which is exactly one of those details which the *dilettante* critic delights in, but which convey neither information nor edification to any one else. A good translation of a great poem is a totally different matter. We have our own opinion as to the difficulty of such an effort, and the almost impossibility of conveying any high conception of the poetry (as poetry, distinct from the character or story conveyed in it) of one language into another; but it is the very foolishness of scholarship to suppose that the world of today can be excited by an explanation of the motives which led the comic to assail the tragic poet with such broad sarcasm and pointed jest as delighted the vulgar crowd of Athenian spectators. The fact is not pleasant in the first place; though it may be so far instructive as to the unchanged tenor of human nature, that it shows how Wit gibed at Wisdom a thousand years ago, and how the meaner and grosser public enjoyed the sport when a real poet, unworthily occupied, poked fun at Socrates and Plato.

Mr Browning, however, attempts to show the English reader, to whom the whole matter is absolutely indifferent, and who probably never heard of the quarrel, that Aristophanes was partially ashamed of himself all the while; and to explain how he was beguiled into it, by motives which certainly have not ceased to tell upon critics, by the dogmatism of the philosophers' followers, and the exaggerated commendation of the poet's admirers. We have seen parodies of Mr Browning himself, which a little crowd of University-men, closest and narrowest of all clique-audiences, chuckled and exulted over, as infinitely cleverer and better than the original; a decision which very probably these young heroes would have been ashamed of, had any indignant young Balaustion flashed down upon them the lightning of her enthusiasm. But it is the very extravagance of faith to believe that any fame of any poet would carry into the popular heart a long discussion—however mixed with digressions into general human sentiment —of the excellence of Euripides, and the reasons why a contemporary should have gibed and laughed at him in works almost as notable as his own. We should be disposed to laugh too, if the question were not so serious; but, unfortunately, it is very serious. Let us allow that Greek is sublime, that even its jokes—though a shallow modern intellect, destitute of the pure classic flavour, may find them coarse or even stupid, like other buffoonery—are of more value than jokes are nowadays. Yet the fact remains that Englishmen are not Greeks, and that no poem nor other work plentifully besprinkled with classic vocables, and made up of classic allusions, ever will or can be anything but caviare to the multitude, and never can or will be anything original or great. This fact being fully granted, Mr Browning, or any one else, may play what pranks he pleases for the gratification of a small and select audience, and throw his genius into a parrot monologue if he likes. Thought is free, and we have no right to interfere with his fantasy; but the penalty is certain, and can no more be escaped than any other natural punishment.

183. From an unsigned review, *The Spectator*

3 July 1875, xlviii. 853–4

It is an obvious criticism on Mr. Browning's last poem to say that it is the work of a poet, but by no means a poem. It is not that the subject is unsuitable; verse is the best, it may even be said, from one point of view, the only way of treating it. But Mr. Browning permits the passion for analysing character so to dominate him, that he becomes careless of things essential to his art. Sweetness, brightness, grace, melody, eloquence are either absent, or present at but the rarest intervals. Here and there he condescends to give us a glimpse of them. Once in some twenty pages or so comes a beautiful line, even a beautiful passage, though seldom this latter without some harshness to blot it. The reader will catch at it, read it aloud, dwell on it with a delight all the greater,

because there is so little in the main course of the argument, full of vigour
and thought as it is, to call it forth. The first few pages are richer in such
promise than what follow. When Balaustion, flying from conquered
Athens, wishes that some noble and tragical end had overtaken the city,
the thought is finely put:

> Doomed to die,
> Fire should have flung a passion of embrace
> About thee till, resplendently inarmed,
> (Temple by temple folded to his breast,
> All thy white wonder fainting out in ash),
> Some vaporous sigh of soul had lightly 'scaped,
> And so the immortals bade Athenai back!

Elsewhere they are rare, but they are worth looking for. Such is
Euripides' description of the occasional glimpses of nobility in his great
assailant's work:

> Murk the marsh,
> Yet where a solitary marble block
> Blanches the gloom, there let the eagle perch.

But there is no need to prove that Mr. Browning can write beautiful
verse. We can only regret that he does not care to write it more
frequently.

THE INN ALBUM

November 1875

---

184. John Addington Symonds, *The Academy*

27 November 1875, viii. 543-4

For Symonds, see No. 138. A brief plot-summary leads to this excerpt from his unsigned review.

The passionate anguish of *King Lear* needs no relief: its awful beauty is enough. But the raw material of a 'penny dreadful', such as the theme here is, requires more artistic manipulation than Mr. Browning has given it before it can be called a poem. Beauty of any kind is what he has carefully excluded. Vulgarity, therefore, is stamped upon *The Inn Album*, in spite of the ingenuity with which, by suppressing name and place and superfluous circumstance, the writer succeeds in presenting only the spiritual action and reaction of his characters upon each other, in spite of the marvellous scalpel-exercise of analysis which bares the most recondite motives, in spite of the intellectual brilliancy which gives a value to everything he has to say.

185. Greater than *The Ring and the Book*
1875

From an unsigned review, *The Athenæum* (27 November 1875), pp. 701–2.

This is among the most favourable reviews *The Inn Album* received, and the general opinion was otherwise.

A great artist chooses his subjects. All we could wish is that there had been more in the scoundrel[1]—that he had been less of the common card-sharper and rook, who is the peculiar product of Regent Street and its disreputable clubs. We could have wished this, not for the sake of the poem merely, but for the sake of the lady. The villain is good enough to take in the boy—perhaps, though even the boy sees through him:

> Oh, no airs!
> Because you happen to be twice my age
> And twenty times my master, must perforce
> No blink of daylight struggle through the web
> There's no unwinding? You entoil my legs,
> And welcome, for I like it: blind me,—no!

But he is, surely, too commonplace a villain to be the first actor or, at any rate, the first mover in such a tragedy. Nor is it the least intelligible part in the woman that such a second-rate rogue should have marred her life. Her after-history is strange—not strange for a woman perhaps; many women have done the same—but strange for her. We can only remember the little foot-note under 'Marching Along,' at the commencement of the *Dramatic Lyrics*: 'Such poems as the majority in this volume might also come properly enough, I suppose, under the head of 'Dramatic Pieces,' being, though often lyric in expression, always dramatic in principle, and *so many utterances of so many imaginary persons, not mine.*' People will say, in a word, that the subject is painful, the story horrible; perhaps Mr. Austin,[2] who can never be brought to see that

---

[1] 'The Elder Man', villain of *The Inn Album*.
[2] Alfred Austin, for whom see the Introduction.

Browning has now and then written poetry, will call it 'melo-dramatic', by way of 'question-begging appellative.' Painful the tale is—as always is fit subject for a tragedy. But it is powerfully told. Once admit that such subjects are to be handled at all, and who is there but Mr. Browning able to handle them? For ourselves, if we may express a personal opinion, we rank *The Inn Album* far beyond *Hohenstiel-Schwangau*, beyond *Fifine at the Fair*, beyond *The Ring and the Book*—beyond anything Mr. Browning has written of late. To us it seems it would be, if we knew it equally well. Mr. Browning is reverting to his original simplicity, and with it his old strength is, not coming back, but once more fully showing itself.

186. Bayard Taylor, *New York Daily Tribune*

4 December 1875, p. 8

From his parody.

Taylor, who had met Browning in London in 1851, liked both the man and the poet; but Browning's poetic manner after *The Ring and the Book*, coupled with some unkind words Browning was purported to have said about Taylor's translation of Goethe's *Faust*, led Taylor to a severer view. See Louise Greer, *Browning and America* (1952), pp. 105-7 and *passim*.

What's this? a book? 16 mo.—Osgood's page,[1]
Fair, clear, Olympian-typed, and save a scant
O' the margin, stiff i' the hurried binding, good!
Intituled how? '*The Inn Album*, Robert Brown
ing, Author.' Why should he not say, as well,
The Hotel Register?—cis-Atlantic term!
Nay, and he should, the action might purvey
To lower comprehensions: so not he!

[1] J. R. Osgood and Co. published the poem in America.

Reflect, 'tis Browning!—he neglects, prepense,
All forms of form: what *he* gives must we take,
Sweet, bitter, sour, absinthean, adipose,
Conglomerate, jellied, potted, salt, or dried,
As the mood holds him—ours is not to choose!
Well (here huge sighs be heard!) commending us
To Heaven's high mercy, let us read!
        —Three hours:
The end is reached; but who begins review,
Forgetful o' beginning, with the end?
Turn back!—why, here's a line supplies us with
Curt comment on the whole, though travesty,—
Hail, calm obliquity, lugubrious plot![1]

   .   .   .   .   .

This bard's a Browning!—there's no doubt of that:[2]
But, ah, ye gods, *the sense!* Are we so sure
If sense be sense unto our common-sense,
Low sense to higher, high to low, no sense,
All sense to those, all sense no sense to these?
That's where your poet tells!—and you've no right
(Insensate sense with sensuous thought being mixed)
To ask analysis!

   .   .   .   .   .

The meaning ask you, O ingenuous soul?
Why, were there such for you, what then were left
To puzzle brain with, pump conjecture dry,
And prove you little where the poet's great?
Great must he be, you therefore little:—go!
The curtain falls, the candles are snuffed out:
End, damned obliquity, lugubrious plot!

[1] A parody of line 11 of *The Inn Album,* which reads 'Hail, calm acclivity, salubrious spot'.

[2] A travesty of lines 17–18:

      That bard's a Browning; he neglects the form:
      But ah, the sense, ye gods, the weighty sense!

Mr. Browning, the greater part of whose poetry shows strong tragic instincts, has never chosen a more dramatic, or, it may be added, a more terrible, subject than he has done in *The Inn Album*. In this he has displayed more than anywhere else the essentially dramatic power of concentration which he possesses in a marked degree. On some occasions he has been apt to disregard the value of this faculty; his imagination has seemed to be so full that it could not resist the various suggestions offered by things which should be merely episodical; and in letting it dwell at length upon these, he has thrown away the penetrating vigour which he might have gained by keeping closer to the telling of his story. The force of his new poem, which is appalling in the swift convergence of three histories of tragic passion, is little marred by any wandering into the realms of the speculative reflection that takes a reader's attention away from the characters put before him. The four chief personages of the narrative, and even 'the obsequious landlord', are brought into distinct life, and with but few exceptions retain their individuality clearly throughout. The masterly way in which the situation that Mr. Browning has invented is grasped and handled recalls the works of another poet, Alfred de Musset,[1] between whom and Mr. Browning there is in other respects no resemblance. But the vague presentiment of a coming terror, suggested in some indefinable manner from the first, the suddenness and completeness of its descent upon its victims, and the compression of a vast extent of passion into the speech and action of a few hours, are common to *The Inn Album*, and, to take one striking instance from the French poet's productions, *Les Caprices de Marianne*.[2]

In Mr. Browning's work these qualities are the more remarkable from the presence of certain difficulties which he has himself thrown in the way. One of these lies in the form, neither properly narrative nor

---

[1] Musset (1810–75) was a French poet and dramatist of the Romantic school.

[2] Musset's prose comedy (1833), which deals with a husband's discovery of his young wife's affairs.

dramatic, which he has constantly affected, and which we cannot think him wise in adopting. The habit of omitting any indication from the writer as to which of his characters is speaking cannot but tend to confusion; and the very force of the poet's dramatic perception, constantly suggesting that his conception could be more happily carried out in the form of drama than in narration, can hardly fail to produce some sense of incompleteness. Again, Mr. Browning has been careful not to assign a name to any of the persons in his poem; by doing which he has gained for himself the credit of triumphing over a somewhat needless difficulty, and has thrown considerable difficulties in the way of any who may wish to repeat his story after him.

To say that the writer's meaning is occasionally obscure, and the metre frequently rugged, is only to say what might safely have been predicted. There is, however, far less of obscurity in *The Inn Album* than in *Red Cotton Nightcap Country* or *Fifine at the Fair*, and it may be said that in the case of a poet of signal worth one can afford to be at some trouble in arriving at his intention. Of the ruggedness of his metre the poet is evidently as conscious as any one else. One of his characters, turning the pages of the Inn Album, comes upon this metrical effort—

> If a fellow can dine On rumpsteaks and port wine,
> He needs not despair Of dining well here—

and observes:

> '*Here!*' I myself could find a better rhyme!
> That bard's a Browning; he neglects the form:
> But ah, the sense, ye gods, the weighty sense!

It is matter of speculation whether Mr. Browning's neglect of form is entirely deliberate. He has shown in many of his shorter pieces a full command of an easy swing of metre; and this suggests that he may think his powerful thought is better conveyed in the 'springless and uncushioned vehicles' which he is apt to choose for it than in some more gracious fashion. If so, we venture to conceive that he is wrong, and that his works will live, not in any way by reason of the gnarled form which snatches rather than attracts attention, but by the strong imagination and thought which overcome their uncouth clothing.

188. Robert Louis Stevenson, *Vanity Fair*

11 December 1875, clxxx, 332

From his unsigned notice.

Mr. Browning intends apparently to finish a laborious life in an access
or paroxysm of indiscriminate production. He floods acres of paper with
brackets and inverted commas. He showers octavos on the public with
a facility and grace like that of a conjuror scattering shoulder-knots and
comfits out of a confederate's hat. What! we exclaim, all this monstrous
quantity of verse out of no more of a poet than can be buttoned into
one single-breasted waistcoat!

And yet the prodigy is not really so marvellous as it seems at first,
and the problem resolves itself somewhat after the same fashion as the
old school question of the lever—what you gain in power you lose in
time. The more octavos the looser stuff. It smacks of a paradox, but is
none the less true, that all this incredible effusion of writing-ink is not a
sign of passionate industry, as you might suppose, but a phase of sheer
and incurable idleness. Even this notice, slight as it is, would give us a
deal less trouble if we let it run to twice the length. Compression is the
mark of careful workmanship, and it takes less real power out of a man
and gives fewer headaches to write a folio full of scimble-scamble,
skirmishing literature than to fashion a dozen sonnets into perfect shape.

The Press is utterly silent nowadays about Mr. Browning's ragged,
renegade versification, for the good reason that they have said their say
even unto satiety, and Wisdom cannot be always crying at the street
corner. If Mr. Browning will not hearken to her accents, he must just
go his own way until a dart strikes through his liver. And yet it is not
without a considerable pang that we leave a brilliant spirit like his to
'take directly up the way to destruction'; that we see a man who has
now and again written fine and shapely verses pour out before us year
after year—nay, we had almost said month after month—his periodic
quantity of devilled prose. It is a pity to let the public into literary
secrets; but a word in their ear is due to them. Mr. Browning's verse is a
thing infinitely more easy to write than anything like careful prose. It is

simply the result of a clever man 'giving way.' And he has a trick of his own when he wishes to cloak and dissemble the ill-success of his own lines before his heavenly Father and his earthly brethren, which we here denounce with the delight of all virtuous men in virtuous actions.

Suppose you were conducting an orchestra, and had arrived at a particular juncture in the piece where you knew, from previous rehearsals, a false note was on the cards; and suppose, with an ingenuity worthy of the Evil One, you calculated your time to a nicety, and, just at the moment when the ear-piercing discord was to be expected, you upset your music-stand with a prodigious crash? Well, it could not be said that you had really spared the sensibilities of the audience, and yet you would have saved your orchestra some disgrace. Nay, there would not be wanting persons to describe you as a specially dashing conductor, all passion and eccentricity, and burning in a white heat for art.

Now this is purely and simply what is done by Mr. Browning. When he finds a line shambling out from underneath him in a loose mass of unaccented syllables; when he finds it, like an ill-made blancmange, subside into a squash or quagmire instead of standing on its own basis with a certain sort of dignity or strength—quick, says Mr. B., break it up into an unexpected parenthesis, choke off the reader with a dash, leave him clinging at the verse's end to a projecting conjunction, cut a somersault before him, flick off his hat with your toe in true Mabille fashion; in short, do what you will so you bewilder him and the limping verse will get away to cover undetected.

So it will, for a while; and for a while sheer idleness may pass itself off under the *alias* of eccentricity. But at last the public will begin to put their heads together and wag their solemn beards. 'This man,' they will say, 'gives himself out for more than ordinarily handsome. It may be so; but why does he always come before us in an Indian war-paint and cutting fantastic capers? Let him wash the red off his nose and the green off his ears; let him uncurl his legs from about his neck, and sit down quietly for a moment in this easy-chair, and then we shall see what he is, and tell him candidly whether he is Apollo or Quasimodo.'

Only Mr. Browning is such a wag and so volatile that you will require to get up very early in the morning to find him sitting honestly on a chair. He is always upside down or outside in. . . .

The young millionaire, with his sheepish admiration of vice and his tigerish return to a sort of undergraduate virtue, is one of the best creations in Mr. Browning's long gallery.

As for the heroine, she is perhaps better conceived than executed.

For all that, the new book is as clever as any that went before it, and has the strange merit of being interesting. It bears a remarkable resemblance to some of Balzac's shorter tales, and might very well have been a transcript in verse from the author of *Le Colonel Chabert* or *La Duchesse de Langeais*. It has the same purely human import and the same fundamental cruelty that we find in the great world of the *Comédie humaine*. Only, alas! it is done so much more carelessly! Old Balzac, wrestling with obdurate language, honestly determined to tell his tale as well as lay in him, would steam like a tea-urn on cold nights in an agony of intellectual effort. And perhaps if Mr. Browning had had one or two such vigils over the "Inn Album," it would have happened to him to re-write the better part of it in some form more worthy of an admirable conception; and it would not have occurred to us, when his heroine dies towards the end, to lose five minutes of our brief life ere we could find out the how or the why of this deplorable catastrophe. It was only after a close examination of what went before, a sort of coroner's inquest in our own mind, that we were enabled to give in a verdict of *felo-de-se*. And this at the climax of the story! O fie, Mr. Browning!

We are weary of finding fault with one who is perhaps too old to improve, and is certainly far too strong and caustic to be lightly quarrelled with. It goes against the grain to cavil at a man to whom we owe so many happy hours and so much occasion for intellectual gymnastic. We really do not like to play the little critic snarling at the heels of a great poet.

And, indeed, there is no more fault to find. Three out of the four characters who take part in this little tragedy (and the fourth is a mere outline) are firmly conceived and brilliantly drawn. Mr. Browning's power of ventriloquism—for he is more of a mimic than a dramatist—has rarely been seen to more advantage.

Most men will own some kinship to the wicked lord, as he indulges in useless repentance in the bright summer morning. These bright summer mornings, with their birds and their dew-drops, and their confounded affectation of innocence, are certainly the very moment for remorse; and all the worse, if, like his lordship in *The Inn Album*, you have not been to bed the night before. Not less natural in its own way is his shameful conduct in the parlour, when he grows more and more Satanic as he finds those around him more virtuous. To have been really repentant half an hour before, is so bad for the moral tone half an hour after!

189. From an unsigned review, *The Spectator*

11 December 1875, xlviii. 1555-7

It is always with hesitation and pain that we speak unfavourably of the work of any writer to whom the world owes as much as it does to Mr. Browning. And we have felt this so keenly on the present occasion, that the fear of missing something great in what superficially appeared poor, has kept us silent till there seemed no danger of misapprehension. It is, however, impossible to say that we find anything really admirable in this repulsive and very roughly versified story. It is not tragedy, for tragedy should 'purify', if not 'by pity and by fear', still somehow by mingled sympathy for human weakness and reverence for human greatness, and Mr. Browning does not manage either to touch our sympathy for the erring, nor to thrill us with the high passion of a great mind. We dislike the victim almost as keenly as we dislike the betrayer of his story, and find in the delineation neither of the one nor of the other that vividness and truthfulness of conception which convince us that we are dealing with real life, though it be only the real life of a true poet's imagination. The story has all the faults of a melodrama, that is, of a sensational situation in which the tragic effect of the circumstances narrated, rises in agony far above the tragic effect of the feeling portrayed; and the lines of true poetry contained in the two hundred pages are quite too few to relieve the heavy atmosphere by gleams of that undefinable light 'that never was on sea or land.' Our objection to the *Inn Album* is briefly this,—that it tells a tale of a wrecked life and dwells on the grimmest caprices of the irony of fate, without either touching the reader's heart or filling his imagination with the mystery of the mutilated hopes and broken purposes he finds portrayed. . . .

[A detailed account of the characters and plot follows.]

Assuredly, as a whole, this poem is not worthy of Mr. Browning. His immoral lord is simply pert, and often vulgar; his injured lady is hard, without a trace of humility, or anything of that large store of love which would fain win back to better ways him who had ruined her life. Then there is not a trace of Mr. Browning's acute and often most instructive thoughtfulness in the poem. From the beginning to the end

413

of it, we have found not one of those rare bits of wisdom of which his earlier poems were full. The grating character of his style is exaggerated; the reflective light has disappeared from it; and the action of the characters on each other resembles rather the clirr of cog-wheels, than the influence of mind on mind. The *Inn Album* will not live.

190. From an unsigned review, *The British Quarterly Review*

1 January 1876, lxiii. 236–40

A very full account of the story precedes this excerpt, whose interest lies in the charge of vulgarity.

. . . Such is *The Inn Album*; such our impression of it. It is full of rare and penetrating power, which flows out here and there into passages instinct with genius of the highest order. But separate passages do not make a dramatic poem. It is vicious in conception, and exaggerates to excess many of the author's former errors; it is now rugged and now so unnecessarily coarse, and even vulgar, that to all save students of literature, whose duty it is to read and to study morbid developments and their relations to literature, we say, pass *The Inn Album* by, and devote yourself to what is purer, or, at any rate, broader and healthier in its mode of dealing with the vice and folly of real life and their issues.

191. Henry James, *The Nation*

20 January 1876, xxii. 49–50

This unsigned review is a typically Jamesian production, both in style and in content. For another view of James's opinion, however, see No. 248 and his short story, *The Private Life*, in which James modelled his principal character after Browning.

This is a decidedly irritating and displeasing performance. It is growing more difficult every year for Mr. Browning's old friends to fight his battles for him, and many of them will feel that on this occasion the cause is really too hopeless, and the great poet must himself be answerable for his indiscretions. Nothing that Mr. Browning writes, of course, can be vapid; if this were possible, it would be a much simpler affair. If it were a case of a writer 'running thin', as the phrase is, there would be no need for criticism; there would be nothing in the way of matter to criticise, and old readers would have no heart to reproach. But it may be said of Mr. Browning that he runs thick rather than thin, and he need claim none of the tenderness granted to those who have used themselves up in the service of their admirers. He is robust and vigorous; more so now, even, than heretofore, and he is more prolific than in the earlier part of his career. But his wantonness, his wilfulness, his crudity, his inexplicable want of secondary thought, as we may call it, of the stage of reflection that follows upon the first outburst of the idea, and smooths, shapes, and adjusts it—all this alloy of his great genius is more sensible now than ever. *The Inn Album* reads like a series of rough notes for a poem—of hasty hieroglyphics and symbols, decipherable only to the author himself. A great poem might perhaps have been made of it, but assuredly it is not a great poem, nor any poem whatsoever. It is hard to say very coherently what it is. Up to a certain point, like everything of Mr. Browning's, it is highly dramatic and vivid, and beyond that point, like all its companions, it is as little dramatic as possible. It is not narrative, for there is not a line of comprehensible, consecutive statement in the two hundred and eleven pages of the volume. It is not lyrical, for there is not a phrase which in any degree does the office of the poetry

415

that comes lawfully into the world—chants itself, images itself, or lingers in the memory. 'That bard's a Browning; he neglects the form!' one of the characters exclaims with irresponsible frankness. That Mr. Browning knows he 'neglects the form', and does not particularly care, does not very much help matters; it only deepens the reader's sense of the graceless and thankless and altogether unavailable character of the poem. And when we say unavailable, we make the only reproach which is worth addressing to a writer of Mr. Browning's intellectual power. A poem with so many presumptions in its favor as such an authorship carries with it is a thing to make some intellectual use of, to care for, to remember, to return to, to linger over, to become intimate with. But we can as little imagine a reader (who has not the misfortune to be a reviewer) addressing himself more than once to the perusal of *The Inn Album*, as we can fancy cultivating for conversational purposes the society of a person afflicted with a grievous impediment of speech.

[A 500-word plot-summary follows.]

The whole picture indefinably appeals to the imagination. There is something very curious about it and even rather arbitrary, and the reader wonders how it came, in the poet's mind, to take exactly that shape. It is very much as if he had worked backwards, had seen his dénouement first, as a mere picture—the two corpses in the inn-parlor, and the young man and his cousin confronted above them—and then had traced back the possible motives and sources. In looking for these Mr. Browning has of course encountered a vast number of deep discriminations and powerful touches of portraitures. He deals with human character as a chemist with his acids and alkalies, and while he mixes his colored fluids in a way that surprises the profane, knows perfectly well what he is about. But there is too apt to be in his style that hiss and sputter and evil aroma which characterize the proceedings of the laboratory. The idea, with Mr. Browning, always tumbles out into the world in some grotesque hind-foremost manner; it is like an unruly horse backing out of his stall, and stamping and plunging as he comes. His thought knows no simple stage—at the very moment of its birth it is a terribly complicated affair. We frankly confess, at the risk of being accused of deplorable levity of mind, that we have found this want of clearness of explanation, of continuity, of at least superficial verisimilitude, of the smooth, the easy, the agreeable, quite fatal to our enjoyment of *The Inn Album*. It is all too argumentative, too curious and recondite. The people talk too much in long set speeches, at a moment's notice, and the anomaly so common in Browning, that the talk of the women is even more rugged and insoluble than that of the men, is here greatly exaggerated. We are reading neither prose nor poetry; it is too real for the ideal, and too ideal for the real. The author of *The Inn Album* is not a writer to whom we care to pay trivial compliments, and it is not a trivial complaint to say that his book is only barely comprehensible. Of a successful dramatic poem one ought to be able to say more.

192. Browning's Affectations

1876

From an unsigned article 'Affectations', *The Saturday Review* (12 February 1876), cxxix. 248–51.

Nobody, for instance, can doubt that some of the later uncouthnesses of Mr. Carlyle and Mr. Browning are correctly styled affectations. It is absurd to suppose that a writer can be wholly unconscious of mannerisms which have frequently been thrust as it were under his very eyes; and when one sees an author persevering in such eccentricities after these criticisms with rather more energy than before, and in cases where no other eye than his own, however kindly, can discover any advantage in their employment, it seems a fairly safe inference that the writer is obstinately affected. Yet it is no less clear that it is always more or less hazardous to predicate this quality of any man's style.

193. William Michael Rossetti, *Macmillan's Magazine*

March 1876, xxxiii. 418–29

From his 'William Bell Scott and Modern British Poetry'.

See the Introduction for the influence of the Rossetti circle upon Browning's reputation.

One of the first things that you appreciate in Browning is his many-sidedness; passion, imagination, mental and moral analysis, knowledge of life, pictorial and picturesque *couleur locale*, the devious preferences of a scholar and a student of all sorts of things past and present, make up a most extraordinary personality, whether individual or literary. Perhaps the mainspring of his whole performance is intellectual keenness; the insight to discern and discriminate, the equally patient, tenacious, and eager energy in scrutinizing. His mind flows into every cranny of his subject; and he presents it to the reader, concrete in itself, and informed besides with new vitality from the mental processes which replenish its forms. It might be compared to one of those anatomical or microscopi-cal preparations into which some colouring-matter has been poured, so as to exhibit all its otherwise undefined veining. One can easily under-stand that the great danger of such a poet lies in his very subtlety. In manipulating his subject-matter, he teases and tangles it; in addressing the reader, he plies him confusingly—not perhaps confusedly—with thought upon thought, suggestion after suggestion, and side-light traversing side-light.

PACCHIAROTTO, AND HOW HE WORKED IN DISTEMPER

July 1876

194. From an unsigned review, *The Athenæum*

22 July 1876, pp. 101–2

Mr. Browning is, and always has been, an etcher, and (we imply no disrespect by using short words) he by no means increased his popularity when he took to writing long poems. Mr. Nettleship[1] may say what he likes—and he has a good deal to say—but *Sordello* always was, and always will be, a failure; while, in his smaller pieces, such as those collected in *Men and Women*, or *Dramatic Lyrics*, or *Dramatic Romances*, Mr. Browning appeals at once to any one who is sufficiently intelligent to attempt to read him. His mistake all through has been to suppose that people will take the trouble to wrestle with difficulties; that because his longer poems are worth understanding, the public would try to understand them. Amongst mathematicians it is recognized that certain men, not always eminent in other respects, have what is known as 'a knack for problems.' Mr. Browning's poetry is to all ordinary forms of art what a problem is to a mathematical demonstration. You have to read it three or four, or it may be even a dozen times, until suddenly—as with those fantastic pictures which, according to the position of the axes of the eye, represent two or more things at once—you focus the whole piece. Of late years Mr. Browning has been vehemently accused of a tendency to write at unpardonable length, and life, it is urged, even for those who have nothing to do but to devote themselves to culture, is too short to allow the requisite attention being paid to a somewhat crabbed narrative spread over 300 pages, simply because it is written by the poet who wrote *Porphyria's Lover*, and who might, if he pleased, write at any moment something equally short and equally good.

[1] John T. Nettleship, whose *Essays on Robert Browning's Poetry* (1868) was the first book about Browning.

In the present volume Mr. Browning returns to his more popular method of working. It is an ungrateful task to compare the later productions of a great man with his earlier efforts, and it is needless to inquire whether 'Pacchiarotto' is or is not equal to those shorter poems by which Mr. Browning is best known. There are, however, pieces in this volume which those who know Mr. Browning well, and like him, will not be slow to prize.

195. Edward Dowden, *The Academy*

29 July 1876, pp. 99–100

From his review of Pacchiarotto.

Dowden (1843–1913), critic, biographer, and Shakespearean scholar, published *The Life of Robert Browning* in 1904.

The present volume is no such gift as was *Dramatis Personae*. It contains several interesting poems, and one—'Numpholeptos'—in Mr. Browning's best manner. There is, of course, throughout the whole, the presence of a vigorous personality; we can tumble and toss even in the rough verse of *Pacchiarotto* as we do in a choppy sea on which the sun is a-shine, and which invigorates while it—not always agreeably—bobs our head, and dashes down our throat. But of the highest qualities of Mr. Browning's genius obtaining adequate expression—such as they obtained in *Men and Women*, and in *Dramatis Personae*—there is less than we had looked for in this volume of miscellaneous pieces. Its speciality, as compared with preceding volumes, is that it contains not a little running comment by Mr. Browning upon himself and his own work, together with a jocular-savage reply to his unfriendly critics. In the *Epilogue* the poet informs us that those who expect from him, or from any poet, strong wine of verse which is also sweet demand the impossible. Sweet the strong wine *shall* be; but not until it has lain mellowing till the century's close:

> Mighty and mellow are never mixed,
> Though mighty and mellow be born at once.
> Sweet for the future—strong for the nonce.

The experience of Mr. Browning's readers contradicts this statement. Some who drank the good wine of 1855 and that of 1864 in the years of the vintages found that they were strong and needed no keeping to be sweet. Wine-tasters must make distinctions, and one of them who expected to find 1876 an extraordinary year must in his report describe the quality of its yield as 'average.'

196. Mr. Browning and his Critics

1876

Unsigned article, *The Examiner* (12 August 1876), pp. 904–5.

Given the nature of the Browning-Austin quarrel (for which, see the Introduction), it was inevitable that some journal would adopt a holier-than-thou position.

We have spoken very highly of the literary merits of Mr. Browning's *Pacchiarotto*, and we see no cause to alter our opinion that it is the wittiest and most successful poem of its kind since *Hudibras*. But the language which Mr. Browning incidentally applies to such of his critics as are also writers of verse, raises a moral question as to the limits of fair retort. We do not think it is for the public entertainment, or even for the public good, that those limits should be unduly confined; but Mr. Browning has at one point stepped so flagrantly beyond the limits commonly accepted that it becomes necessary to make some attempt to rectify the frontier. For much of the abuse which Mr. Browning heaps upon his critics he can plead the established practice of poets in all ages. No man

likes to be criticised, and no poet likes to take criticism silently. What is
the good of having all language as one's province, if one cannot use it to
vex and confound one's enemies? and a poet's enemies are all who venture to dispute the intuitions of his genius. It is perfectly natural that
Mr. Browning should try to place his critics in the most contemptuous
light that he possibly can, more particularly when those critics aspire
to teach him by example. In *Pacchiarotto* he imagines them as chimney-
sweeps, whose work it is to 'sweep out his chimbly.' That is their proper
function, but they came, he says, one May morning under his window
with drums, fifes, triangles, tongs and bellows, blown with Saturnalian
insolence, to show him how to make music. This was very different
from the salutation which poets in old time were accustomed to receive
from rival songsters on May morning; but Mr. Browning did not, he
tells us, lose his temper. He thanked God that he was not as his critics
were—dingy, dirty wretches, who did not sing all the year round like
himself, but could only allow themselves one holiday, and misspent that
in insulting their betters. He did not kick them out of his grounds, but
chucked them some halfpence, told them that they were ignorant, im-
pudent, envious, and malicious, and bade them be off, because his
housemaid had her eye upon them, and suspected them of bringing
more filth into the house than they took away. A terrible person is this
housemaid of Mr. Browning's. 'Quick march!' he cries to the chimney-
sweeps,

> for Xanthippe my housemaid,
> If once on your pates she a souse made
> With what, pan or pot, bowl or *skoramis*,
> First comes to her hand,—things were more amiss!
> I would not for world be your place in—
> Recipient of slops from her basin!

There is not much to be said against this. There is little sweetness and
light in it, certainly; but there is a rude primeval humour, and if Mr.
Browning chooses thus to express his view of the relations between
himself and his poet-critics, there must be some of his readers who will
be more amused than disgusted. It is an attribute of poetic greatness to
be childlike; the great poet deals with primeval feelings; and there is
probably no conception which would appeal more cordially to children
and savages than that of emptying a *skoramis*—even Mr. Browning does
not venture to translate the word—on the head of an enemy. 'Poetry
hath in it,' Bacon says, 'some participation of the divine,' but it hath also
in it some participation of the vulgar; and in these self-distrustful days it

is well that the sentiment of personal elation and inflation should be kept alive. Then, too, it is to be noted that Mr. Browning does make some concession to modern refinement. It is his housemaid, not himself, whom he glories in imagining as the active instrument in inflicting the indignity. He would not touch a *skoramis* himself with a pair of tongs; he gathers his 'garland and singing robes about him', and points at the means of revenge with a jewelled finger.

We should be sorry to deny Mr. Browning the imaginary use of the *skoramis*, with these delicate refinements, if it gives him any satisfaction. But in the vindication of his high rank as a poet, Mr. Browning goes farther, and has recourse to more questionable weapons of offence. He singles out one of his critics in particular, the ringleader on this May morning intrusion, and addresses him thus:

> While as for Quilp-Hop-o'-my-thumb there,
> Banjo-Byron that twangs the strum strum there—
> He'll think as the pickle he curses,
> I've discharged on his pate his own verses!
> 'Dwarfs are saucy,' says Dickens; so, sauced in
> Your own sauce * * *

Mr. Browning does not complete the last verse, at the request he says of the printer's devil, who pleads with his royal highness of song not to be 'satirical on a thing so very small'; but the missing rhyme may be found without the use of a dictionary. Now what has Mr. Alfred Austin done to provoke this gross assault? Has he ever hurled any personality of the same sort at Mr. Browning? If he had, Mr. Browning would best have consulted his own dignity by making no reply. But the assault, which passes all the limits which good breeding has imposed on literary squabbles, is utterly unprovoked. Some years ago Mr. Austin wrote some criticisms, which made a good deal of noise at the time, on contemporary poets, and on Mr. Browning among the rest. But he confined himself strictly to Mr. Browning's books, and their history. No doubt doubt he said much which could not be pleasing to Mr. Browning, and some things which a strict taste would have forced him to cancel. He imagined that there was a conspiracy in 'the academy and the drawing-room' to obtrude Mr. Browning as the rival of Mr. Tennyson, as the 'next King' of song, the worthy recipient of the homage which the world was growing weary of paying to Mr. Tennyson. Mr. Austin stated his reasons for refusing to join in this conspiracy. He did not regard Mr. Browning as being 'specifically a poet at all.' He was only 'a man who was striving earnestly to be an original poet, and who for the life of him could not be.' He admitted Mr. Browning's intellectual power, but declared that it was analytic and not poetic in its natural manifestations. His verse was 'muddy and unmusical,' 'the very incarnation of discordant obscurity,' and so forth. Mr. Browning could not have liked to be told this. But it would have been much more dignified to leave the defence of his poems to other hands than his own. And if he was to undertake his own defence, if he was to empty an imaginary *skoramis* on the aggressor, if he considered this kind of raillery worthy of his position, at least he should have had sufficient self-respect not to taunt Mr. Austin with personal deformity. 'Mr. Browning is an analyst rather than a poet', says Mr. Austin. 'Hold your tongue, Quilp,' retorts the angry bard, 'you are a saucy dwarf.'

How these poets love one another! And what privilege of strong language they enjoy! We who are cabined, cribbed, and confined within the prose paddock of language, as Mr. Browning triumphantly puts it, with a clog at our fetlocks, cannot help envying those who are free of all its four corners. But the line must be drawn somewhere, and common feeling for several generations has discountenanced attacks upon a rival's natural defects of body as being brutal and unmanly. In the good old days such attacks were common enough. If a man had bandy legs, or a club foot, or a cock eye, or a wart on his nose, it was considered quite fair to publicly jeer him on his deformity. But even in those days it was considered equally fair to retort by hiring a bully to give the satirist a good thrashing with a cudgel or a rope's end. The general sense of justice recognized this as the only fitting remedy for such an offence. Even in the days of duelling, the man who descended to such inexcusable brutality of attack could not expect to be called upon to give the satisfaction of a gentleman. At the beginning of this century, Southey made some grossly personal allusions to Byron's private life, and Byron sent him a challenge. But if Southey had jeered at him because he had a club foot, we may be sure that he would have left the insult to the public contempt which its vulgar brutality deserved. We do not object to hard hitting among poets. Perhaps in view of the enormous territorial expansion and aggressive ambition of Science, it would be wise for them not to weaken their empire by internal dissension. But they delight to bark and bite, and poet-baiting is still numbered among the legitimate forms of public entertainment. Only they should remember that there are certain blows which the laws of the game declare to be foul. Poets seem to be constantly tempted to forget this. They seem never to have altogether recovered the triumph of Archilochus.[1] We are not sure that it would not have been for the advantage of poetry if the daughters of Lycambes had hanged Archilochus instead of hanging themselves.

197. From an unsigned review, *The Saturday Review*

12 August 1876, xlii. 205-6

Mr. Browning's unparalleled and increasing rapidity of production is, as might be expected, attended by an additional redundance of the peculiarities which appear admirable only to himself. The present volume abounds in proofs of the sensitiveness with which he repels the imputation of that obscurity and harshness which might seem to be natural results of excessive volubility. If the immunity from criticism which Mr. Browning claims were conceded in personal deference to his genius, it would still be a legitimate cause for regret that he should of late seldom have taken time to embody in intelligible forms the conclusions of a subtle and imaginative intellect. In the present volume he challenges all who presume to form and express an independent judgment of his poems in language so unprovoked, so unreasonable, and so coarse that it would be almost an act of cowardice not to answer his defiance. Like some other men of genius, and like a multitude of writers who have no pretence to genius, Mr. Browning, while he professes to denounce criticism, really objects only to censure. He may perhaps be indifferent to praise, but it is improbable that he should dislike it. The plea to the jurisdiction is only filed as a precaution against an adverse judgment. There are competent and incompetent critics; but it is a monstrous pretension to deny the right of criticism to students who have perhaps proved the accuracy of their taste by a keen enjoyment of the best poetry of all countries, and even by their appreciation of Mr.

1 Archilochus, a Greek poet of the seventh century B.C., was refused the hand of Neobule, daughter of Lycambes, upon which turn of events the poet produced so vicious a satire that Lycambes and his daughters committed suicide.

Browning's works before he wrote the *Inn Album* and *Pacchiarotto*. The claim of a poet to live in regions inaccessible to ordinary men is a fantastic and modern affectation suggested rather by suspected weakness than by conscious strength. It would not have occurred to Chaucer or to Shakespeare that he was a demi-god, and still less that it was not his business to deal with mankind. A speaker who is too much above his audience is not a master of his business; and he stands self-condemned if he boasts of being unintelligible to the most competent judges of his subject and his art. A thoughtful and scholarly critic would regret that involuntary contempt for a feeble and passionate protest should even seem to apply to a great writer who would on other occasions command his respect. Unsavoury topics, and careless or perverse treatment, cannot be justified by vehement and exaggerated boasts. Murders, criminal trials, and the hanging, beheading, and torturing of murderers, may advantageously be excluded from literature. . . .

[The reviewer goes on to summarize the title poem.]

Mr. Browning, in his dreary and laboured jocosity, has apparently confounded geese with ducks; but it is a graver mistake to suppose that clearness is inseparable from malignity, frivolity, and baseness. If poets wish to put into a line not so vulgar a meaning as 'a big and bouncing thought,' but a pregnant condensation of wisdom, such as Dante, and, in his happier moods, Mr. Browning himself, has sometimes included in a verse, they must put it in so that it can be found there; and not leave it out, while they mistake their own uncommunicated reflections for products of creative art. Mr. Browning's frequent and growing obscurity resembles a cypher of which the key is withheld. The poet is evidently thinking of something casually associated in his mind with expressions that convey no meaning to the most intelligent reader, unless he by accident finds the clue. Sometimes the reference is to a curious fragment of knowledge which rests in the poet's memory; but more often he has grudged the labour, or has been wanting in the skill, to give expression to a complicated thought. The indolence which is inseparable from habitual rapidity of composition is the most frequent cause of a flagrant and undeniable defect. The puerile vanity of professing to live in an upper chamber where critics cannot clamber would be more pardonable in an inferior writer. The rough vituperation addressed to critics by no means indicates the transcendent superiority which it is intended to assert. Mr. Browning may be well assured that in *Pacchiarotto* there is as little wisdom as poetry.

198. The Militant Transcendentalist

1877

Edward Dowden, from his 'The Transcendental Movement and Literature', *Contemporary Review* (July 1877), xxx. 297–318.

For Dowden, see No. 195. Here Dowden puts his finger upon a point which irritated such philosopher-critics as Henry Jones and George Santayana. The subject is treated in Boyd Litzinger's *Time's Revenges: Robert Browning's Reputation as a Thinker, 1890–1955* (1962), *passim*.

Two particulars in his work assign to Mr. Browning his place in the literary history of our century. First, he attempts to re-establish a harmony between what is infinite and what is finite in man's nature. In the early years of the century, infinite passion, infinite desire had found unsatisfying all the materials provided for them by our earthly life, and a cry of despair had gone up from earth. Mr. Browning, throughout the entire series of his writings, regards this world as a school or gymnasium, and also a place of test and trial for other lives to come. Therefore all the means of education in our school are precious —knowledge, beauty, passion, power—all are precious, not absolutely, but with reference to the higher existence for which they are to prepare us. In proportion to the ardour with which we pursue these, and finding them insufficient, pass through them and beyond them, have we made them yield to us their worthiest service. Hence infinite desire, infinite aspiration, is the glory and virtue of our manhood; and through art, through science, through human love, we ascend unsatisfied to God. If, on the other hand, we rest in any attainment of knowledge, or love, or creation of beauty by art, accepting it for its own sake and as final, we have forfeited our high distinction as men, we have become beasts which graze in the paddock and do not look up. Thus Mr. Browning not counselling moderation, nor attempting to restrain the emotional ardour, the dilated passion, of the early nineteenth-century literature of imagination, yet endeavours to convert this from a source of disease and

427

despair into an educational instrument, a source of courage and hope, a pledge of futurity. Worldliness, a low content, a base prudence, the supine heart—these are the signs of fatal disaster to man's higher nature; to succeed perfectly on earth is to fail in heaven; to fail here, even as Paracelsus failed, is less piteous than to prosper and be at ease as Blougram prospered, extinguishing the light that was in him.

Secondly, what determines Mr. Browning's place in the history of our literature is that he represents militant transcendentalism, the transcendental movement at odds with the scientific. His acceptance of the Christian revelation, say rather his acceptance of the man Christ Jesus, lies at the very heart of Mr. Browning's poetry; and in the mode of his accepting the Christ of history he approaches close to the spirit of Mr. Maurice's theology.[1] With an energy of intellect such as few poets have possessed he unites a spiritual ardour which if not associated on the one hand with an eager and combative intellect, on the other with strong human passions and affections, might have made Mr. Browning a religious mystic; and he sets his intellect to defend the suggestions or intuitions of the spirit. In his 'Caliban upon Setebos' the poet has, with singular and almost terrible force, represented what must be the natural theology of one who is merely an intellectual animal, devoid of spiritual cravings, sensibilities, and checks. It is these which discover to us not only the power of God but the love of God everywhere around us, and which enable us to perceive that there is a supreme instance or manifestation of God's love, which is very Christ. But what of the historical Jesus of Nazareth? Is He not disappearing from the world, criticized away and dissolved into a Christ-myth?

> We gazed our fill
> With upturned faces on as real a Face
> That, stooping from grave music and mild fire,
> Took in our homage, made a visible place
> Through many a depth of glory, gyre on gyre,
> For the dim human tribute. Was this true?

And is that divine face recoiling out of reach of our prayers and praise into the darkness, until at last we shall lose it altogether? Mr. Browning's answer implies some such creed as, if we were required to seek a label for it, we should name 'Christian Pantheism.' He looks at the spectacle of the world and life as it plays, ocean-like, around each of us, and show itself all alive and spiritual. The fishermen of Galilee told of a

[1] F. D. Maurice (1805–72), leading Broad Church theologian, and one of the founders of Christian Socialism.

love of God which eighteen hundred years ago became flesh and dwelt with men; but here we behold an omnipresent and eternal love of God:

> Why, where's the need of Temple when the walls
> O' the world are that? What use of swells and falls
> From Levites' choir, priests' cries, and trumpet calls?

> That one Face, far from vanish, rather grows,
> Or decomposes but to recompose,
> Become my universe that feels and knows![1]

Since Mr. Browning, transcendentalism has fared ill in English poetry.

199. Browning's Public in 1877

T. Bayne, from his 'Our Modern Poets, No. ix—Robert Browning', *St. James' Magazine* (August 1877), xli. 153–64.

The place held by Mr. Browning among English poets is altogether unique. There is no other that can fairly be compared with him. He needs to fear no rival, and he can afford to despise imitators. The author of *Paradise Lost* dwelt not more apart from his fellows than the author of *The Ring and the Book*. It is no doubt possible to parody Mr. Browning's style, and even to reproduce some of his apparent mannerisms of thought, but all such attempts—that, for example, of Mr. Bayard Taylor,[2] in his amusing *Diversions*,—invariably suggest little more than quick perception and clever mechanical achievement. Mr. Browning may influence individuals, but will hardly affect classes. There is certainly little probability that he will found a school of poetry. His subjects are not those the crowd will take delight in; his trains of thought are not instantly and directly evident; and his method is hardly calculated to attract the ordinary reader of poetry. Altogether, Mr. Browning's single-handed fight, at once against the powers of evil and the

---

[1] The closing stanzas of the 'Epilogue' to *Dramatis Personae*.
[2] The parodist, for whom see No. 186.

prejudices of his fellow-citizens, has in it much that is heroic. The poet is an earnest searcher after truth, if only the British Public could be brought to believe it, and to recognise the fact that all knowledge lies not on the surface. His links of association are apt to be abrupt and sudden, and his mode of expression corresponds in apparent harshness and want of symmetry. The whole question, indeed, as between Mr. Browning and readers of poetry, resolves itself into this,—that poetry, to be read with interest, should not form a series of puzzles wantonly fitted together. It is questionable, for example, whether those addressed as follows, in *The Ring and the Book*, where the author gives an account of his plan, will be either reconciled or edified by the apostrophe and the explanation:

> Such, British Public, ye who like me not,
> (God love you!)—whom I yet have laboured for,
> Perchance more careful whoso runs may read
> Than erst when all, it seemed, could read who ran,—
> Perchance more careless whoso reads may praise
> Than late when he who praised and read and wrote
> Was apt to find himself the self-same me,—
> Such labour had such issue, so I wrought
> This arc, by furtherance of such alloy,
> And so, by one spirit, take away its trace
> Till, justifiably golden, rounds my ring.

It were certainly hard upon the British Public to blame them for failing to see a compliment in this: and it would be a reflection on their collective intuitions to calculate how much of a rebuke they infer in it. The first two lines are fairly intelligible, and it is possible that a majority of the poet's readers will never go beyond them. They will find a carefully balanced antithesis, with a parenthetical exclamation of infinite 'promise and potency.' Mr. Browning clearly takes his stand as a labourer hitherto unrewarded: he has piped, and the British Public have not danced. But, then, they have so much else to dance to, prepared for them by pipers whose sense of their terpischorean possibilities is so much finer than Mr. Browning's, that, after all, the musician should strive to see the matter as they do, and be a little more reasonable. What, however, may not lurk in that parenthetical 'God love you!' Is it not possible, all this time, that the British Public are being exquisitely trifled with, and that the poet has the laugh all to himself? Thus the majority read and discuss, and close the book with an air charged with final decision.

If, then, the greatest happiness of the greatest number be the sublime object of virtuous conduct, it is clear that Mr. Browning is sadly wasting his strength. The greatest number have no faith whatever in his virtue; indeed, it is probable they give him little credit, when they do think of him, for any such sum of qualities as is implied in the word. Shakspeare they know, and Milton, and Cowper, and Burns; some of them know a little of Byron and Wordsworth, and most of them profess familiarity with Scott; they even quote Mr. Tennyson sometimes, and they are interested in youthful exuberances like those of Mr. A. C. Swinburne and Mr. Robert Buchanan[1] (learned mainly from the newspapers), but the claims of this Mr. Robert Browning they decline to allow. Now what does this imply? It cannot be doubted that a man may read Shakspeare, and even fancy he understands him, and yet miss his meaning altogether. Some of the fun in *The Tempest*, made at the expense of that odd fish Caliban, may be fairly interpreted as expressive of Shakspeare's own estimate of the value of English popular applause. 'Any strange fish there will make a man!' is at once a pleasantry and a criticism: it shews the speaker's good nature, and leaves a decided impress on those in whose power the making of the man is vested. It is one of the most common experiences to hear poets misquoted altogether, or quoted to wrong purpose. A passage is ruthlessly severed from the context, and turned to uses the author never dreamt of when he inserted it in its only fitting place. Or a famous quotation will be continually in the mouths of the majority, who will neither know nor care whence it is taken. Popularity is not always the sign of intelligent appreciation; 'an audience fit, though few', is the appropriate prayer for the poet. At the same time, there might be an audience fit enough for Mr. Browning, and yet not quite so few as he has had to complain of, were he to comply with some prosaic conditions in matters of detail. It might be possible, for example, to construct sentences according to the generally accepted rules of English syntax; and condensation need not always imply confusion of the parts of speech. Profound thought is not necessarily enigmatic, and Platonic intuition should bear to be parsed. If Mr. Browning will insist upon an exclusively oracular attitude, the bewildered British Public may fairly be excused if they ignore him, or look on at his performances from a respectful distance.

[1] Buchanan (1841–1901), poet, novelist, and critic whose attack on Swinburne and the Pre-Raphaelites ('The Fleshly School of English Poetry') became famous.

THE AGAMEMNON OF
ÆSCHYLUS

October 1877

200. Carlyle: Browning as Translator

1877

From the diary entry 27 October 1877, *William Allingham: A Diary*, ed. H. Allingham and D. Radford (1907), pp. 257–8.

Though somewhat less generous than most of the published reviews, these private comments of Carlyle's strike the common chord: in attempting to be literal, Browning failed to make his translation either readable or artistic.

'Oh yes, he called down some months ago to ask if he might dedicate it to me. I told him I should feel highly honoured. But—O bless me! *Can you understand it, at all?* I went carefully into some parts of it and for my soul's salvation (laughs) couldn't make out the meaning. If any one tells me this is because the thing is so remote from us—I say things far remoter from our minds and experiences have been well translated into English. The book of Job, for instance. It's bad Hebrew, I understand, the original of it, and a very strange thing to us. But the translator said to himself, "the first thing I have to do is to make this as intelligible as possible to the English reader; if I do not this I shall be—h'm—I shall be—in fact *damned*." But he succeeded most admirably, and there are very few books so well worth reading as our Book of Job.

'Yes, Browning says I ordered him to do this translation—he winds up his preface (highly to his own satisfaction, in a neat epigrammatic manner) by saying so,—summing it all up in a last word; and I did often enough tell him he might do a most excellent book, by far the best he had ever done, by translating the Greek Dramatists—but O dear! he's a very foolish fellow. He picks you out the English for the Greek word by word, and now and again sticks two or three words together with hyphens; then again he snips up the sense and jingles it into rhyme! I could have told him he could do no good whatever under such conditions.'

201. Frederick Apthorp Paley, *The Athenæum*

27 October 1877, pp. 525–7

From his review.

Paley (1815–88), professor and classical scholar, edited and translated many Greek and Roman authors. Few professional scholars, however, were as generous as Paley in his estimate of Browning's *Agamemnon*.

'I should require a translator to be literal at every cost save that of absolute violence to our language.' Thus writes Mr. Browning in a characteristic Preface, and any reader comparing his transcript with the original will concede that Mr. Browning has unswervingly adhered to this excellent but most shackling basis of procedure. All embellishments of the translator's own brain are strenuously reprobated, as no better than the restorations of 'old Muytens', a Stockholm picture-cleaner, who took upon himself to widen the eyes and enlarge the mouths of certain nymphs painted by Rubens. What we want are the ideas of Æschylus, his metaphors, and the turn of his phrases 'in as Greek a fashion as English will bear'. Æschylus and Æschylus only before all things. The rendering may under these restrictions be clumsy, it must often be bald and unsonorous. Never mind. 'There is abundant musicality elsewhere', observes Mr. Browning with a gentle spice of sarcasm. Adhere to Æschylus, and if the best English equivalents only convert into harshness and commonplace, why harsh and commonplace let us be. But one concession our translator does claim, and insists that he has to this a thorough right: he is not forced to turn Æschylus into the dialect of modern London. Should an old-fashioned construction, or phrase now out of favour, best fit a special passage, it shall be utilized without scruple. Its very obsoleteness, its neglected antiquity render it surely 'all the more appropriate to archaic workmanship'. One more maxim for the translator's behoof: Do as you would be done by. As he would wish, say, the *Return of the Druses* to be rendered into Japanese centuries hence, so does Mr. Browning now propose to deal with the Greek tragedian's masterpiece. The maxim is Mr. Browning's, the instance ours; for instances, however hypothetical, help to realize a precept and define its scope. Thus much, condensed and roughly paraphrased, does Mr. Browning's suggestive Preface come to.

For in atmosphere, in phrase, even in *naïveté*, this version is faithfully and rigidly true to its prototype. This said, it of necessity follows that we have here a transcript, which cannot be expected to present a perfectly unbroken uniformity of fine passages and flowing periods. Yet what a man of genius could do has been done. Some modicum of the blame may, in all humility, be laid at the feet of the King of Tragedy. There are marks of Shakspearean-like haste even in Æschylus. The spider's web simile, for instance, is twice repeated in the same con- nexion by two consecutive choruses. There are endless repetitions of the same word in neighbouring lines; sometimes the effect produced is pathetic or sonorous, but in most cases such echoes are utterly pointless and flat. Indeed, in those days bards had no canons of self-criticism; they wrote to be recited, not to be read. The ear is more lenient to repetitions than is the eye. There was then less rule and more spontaneity, and most poetry of the impulsive and impassioned order abounds in iterations. But the poets of to-day submit their more spontaneous out- bursts to sedulous revision; hence, these little samenesses seldom reach the printing-press. But over and beyond some slight apparent inequality in the Greek original, we must bear well in mind the severe restrictions under which Mr. Browning has worked. He proposed to himself, a *poetical* translation of the most rigid literality, and manfully has he kept his word. In the choruses alone does he allow himself some very slight latitude, expanding the actual, but never engrafting an alien, meaning. These choruses are rhymed, and some percentage of their rhymes are double ones, which increases the lyrical effect and trebles the difficulty. They have evidently taxed the resources of the best English rhymist since the author of *Hudibras* to the utmost. The trochaic and anapæstic measures of the original are approximately rendered.

The speeches and dialogues follow the ordinary trimeter iambics of Greek tragedy. They reproduce word for word, and line for line, the sense of the original. None of the prose versions which we have seen is, choruses excepted, so literal as Mr. Browning. And this for several reasons. One, these prose versions as a rule insist on being sadly too genteel, and, indeed, it may be conceded to them that in the fervid impulse of poetry literalisms may be introduced intolerable in the cold blood of prose. We shall give instances of this presently. Another reason: the better the poet, the better the translator. If he will only deny himself, and, putting aside all the personal touches and tantalizing embellishments which occur to him in the recasting of nearly every sentence, employ that vast structural power over language, which he alone of men possesses, to one end. How can I turn, let him say, what this Greek sang above two thousand years ago into exactly correlative English, giving my version a metrical drapery, and *when possible* beauty of English phrase? And because Mr. Browning has nobly and unfalteringly acted up to these precepts, his transcript is most unequal in its excellence. Had he been less conscientious, he could, no man better, have given us not one bald or common-place line from the exordium of the watchman, sleeping the wakeful sleep of a house-dog, to the final strut of Ægistheus beside Clytemnestra. But Mr. Browning *has* splendidly denied himself, and is unflinchingly crude, pointless, even clumsy, where the Greek pushes and compels him. Yet in the most rugged passages he never once flings his literality over board. To such crisis and ἀπορία[1] Mr. Browning is happily not reduced above some half-dozen times within the compass of the present transcript. His verbal resource is amazing. But, here and again, when, under his masterly touch, the Greek has rendered itself for a page without to us apparent effort, word for word, and phrase by phrase, into English, eloquent and sonorous, all at once, some single line crops up, which cannot be rendered both beautifully and exactly; so Mr. Browning leaves it unbeautiful and bald, and careers on as finely as before; seeing all the time, far better than his critics, how the impracticable passage lies a blot and blur across the very ὀμφαλός[2] of a brilliant description. Yet has Mr. Browning his compensative reward: some of his most charming touches in this play arise from the fearless audacity with which he will track out a word's root-meaning; which grasped, down he sets it, homely or not, so only that Æschylus so meant and spoke it.

Nothing stamps the poetaster so irretrievably as his perpetual fear

---

[1] straits   [2] centre

of using a vulgar word. If he cannot avoid vulgarity save by forethought and introspective solicitude, he will never avoid it at all. Here is the text to our comment, being part of the famous lion-cub simile, as Mr. Browning has it:

> And thus a man, by no milk's help,
> Within his household reared a lion's whelp
> That loved the teat
> In life's first festal stage:
> Gentle as yet.
> A true child-lover, and, to men of age,
> A thing whereat pride warms;
> And oft he had it in his arms
> Like any new-born babe, bright-faced, to hand
> Wagging its tail, at belly's strict command.

Now this, although rhymed, is perfectly literal. The squeamish may, if they please, read the last line 'sporting playfully through the needs of its appetite', as a good prose version has it; but Æschylus spake in Greek as Mr. Browning speaks in English. We might, however, wish to omit the comma after 'bright-faced' and introduce it after 'hand', but Mr. Browning may, of course, prefer his own punctuation of the sentence. Here is an instance of how effective a bold literalism can be. Of Artemis it is said:

> Thus ready is the beauteous one with help
> To those small *dew-drop things* fierce lions whelp,
> And udder-loving litter of each brute
> That roams the mead.

An irresistible reminiscence of Blake. It required a poet-translator here to dare to be exact. So, again,

> To my heart has run
> *A drop of the crocus-dye:*
> Which makes for those
> On earth by the spear that lie,
> A common close
> With life's descending sun.
> Swift is the curse begun.

How much better than 'ruddy life-blood' and parallel inanities, to which the dictionaries would here assist us. Here is, perhaps, the most Æschylean line in the whole transcript. Cassandra, most pathetic

character in the *Agamemnon*, tells the chorus how Apollo became enamoured of her:

> KASSANDRA.
> Prophet Apollon put me in this office.
> CHOROS.
> What, even though a god, with longing smitten?
> KASSANDRA.
> At first, indeed, shame was to me to say this.
> CHOROS.
> For, more relaxed grows every one who fares well.
> KASSANDRA.
> *But he was athlete to me—huge grace breathing!*

This is tremendous. Æschylus surely to the very echo.

Note, also, how Mr. Browning's fine instinct has enabled him to
imply rather than convey that peculiar Greek use of πνεῖν in the erotic
sense, for which there is absolutely no English equivalent. Observe, also,
how awkwardly the last line but one renders itself. Here, too, is a fine
description with four lines of stubborn untranslatable Greek perforce
left in to spoil it. It is the sacrifice of Iphigenia at Aulis:

> His ministrants, vows done, the father bade—
> Kid-like, above the altar, swathed in pall,
> Take her—lift high, and have no fear at all,
> Head-downward, and the fair mouth's guard
> And frontage hold,—press hard
> From utterance a curse against the House
> By dint of bit—violence bridling speech.
> And as to ground her saffron-vest she shed,
> She smote the sacrificers all and each
> With arrow sweet and piteous,
> From the eye only sped,—
> Significant of will to use a word,
> Just as in pictures: since, full many a time,
> In her sire's guest-hall, by the well-heaped board
> Had she made music,—lovingly with chime
> Of her chaste voice, that unpolluted thing,
> Honoured the third libation,—paian that should bring
> Good fortune to the sire she loved so well.

This is most touchingly given. It will be seen that the 'gagging' lines
are hopeless, from a crabbed periphrastic redundancy. The passage is
given *in extenso*, inasmuch as the completeness of the scenic effect required no suppression of detail. Moreover, from a choric extract of this

kind both the powers and the difficulties of Mr. Browning can be best appreciated.

For, as we need scarcely premise, it is, of course, in the translation of the choruses that the chief *crux* of this transcript has rested. Here Mr. Browning's difficulties have culminated; here mainly it is that any one perusing this version in the light of an original poem is sensible now and again of slight hitch and jar in his author's work. How could this in the exigencies of the case be otherwise? Mr. Browning has decided that a Greek chorus in English must be rhymed. Mr. Swinburne, in his *Atalanta*, convinced us all of that. We shall hardly get nearer the Greek chorus in English than in the magnificent lyrical outbursts which the *Atalanta* and *Erechtheus* contain. The best unrhymed choruses are Mr. Matthew Arnold's, but they lag far behind: the genius of our language seems to require rhyme in articulating such mental emotions as the higher functions of the Greek chorus presuppose. But it would be in the present instance wholly preposterous to expect from Mr. Browning's nearly literal renderings the fervour and lilt of a poet who can mould his chorus at his own lyrical will: who is neither translating nor clogged with a text in many places corrupt, in some places defective; whose choruses are made in certain passages of prepense trimming, oracular, ambiguous even to the intelligence of a Greek audience.

Once for all, let us distinctly say that Mr. Browning is never obscure in the compass of the present translation. When he seems so, turn to the original, and *there* the obscurity will be found. Indeed, so anxious is he to set forth his author clearly that he manages to make very plausible-looking sense out of many a dubious periphrasis, as in—

> Whence hast thou limits to the oracular road,
> That evils bode?

In the more terrible passages of the *Agamemnon*, Mr. Browning rises with the ease of master to the emergency of the situation. In scenic representation it seems to us that the horror of anticipation is always keener than horror realized. When the stage is littered with abundant death the feelings of the audience are in comparison blunted. Hence, to our minds, the tragic terror of the *Agamemnon* reaches its climax in the child-vision of Cassandra. Then it is that the murderess, unseen with her skulking paramour, is preparing the net and poniard. The haze of a vast gloom is beginning to deepen the marble shadows of the devoted palace. The wings of Atè seem to winnow and clash in weird silences beyond; the trailing robes of Furies seem to hiss along the threshold of incest. The chorus, livid with terror, is chirping futilities about Zeus and Duty, and hoping with trembling hands that all will be for the best. We can almost hear the grinding of the knife-edge for the King of Men. Then it is that Cassandra sees her grand and fearful vision. Ghost-like, yet lovely as infancy can make them, the murdered children of Thyestes rise; they bear—most piteous burden—in their once rosy hands the symbols of their martyrdom; too innocent to know or hunger after vengeance, they symbolize the vengeance at the doors. One line of the transcript is supremely beautiful, like the bird-note voice of one of these very children, heard clear among the shambles and the furnaces of these halls of Acheron:

> Behold ye those there, in the threshold seated,—
> Young ones,—of dreams approaching to the figures?
> *Children, as if they died by their beloveds—*
> Hands they have filled with flesh, the meal domestic—
> Entrails and vitals both, most piteous burthen,
> Plain they are holding!—which their father tasted!

To conclude. In the sublime and eagle-like passages of this greatest tragedy of the greatest Greek tragedian, Mr. Browning has succeeded —well. In passages where the terrible almost trenches on the grotesque, as in the description of the household dæmon of the Atridæ, he is almost the only one of our poets who is thoroughly at home in this perplexing borderland of beauty and deformity. In the few tender passages—they are not many,—one where the nightingale has leave to sing us a few notes in resemblance to Cassandra,—he has here, as else-where, shown himself a master of love and tears. As Mr. Swinburne translates to us the harmonies of Greece in the Lydian, so does Mr. Browning render them in the Dorian mode; and this couplet from his brother poet might well stand on Mr. Browning's title-page:

> With wind-notes as of eagles. Æschylean,
> And Sappho singing in the nightingale.

202. John Addington Symonds, *The Academy*

3 November 1877, xii. 419–20

We might have expected after studying his Preface that Mr. Browning would have chosen the prose alternative; for it is clearly not his purpose to reproduce the impression made upon his aesthetic sense by the Greek in an English poem, but to represent as faithfully as possible the ideas of Aeschylus, and to use the English language as a castmaker uses plaster of Paris. His translation is, however, in verse. In the choric passages he even uses rhyme, with that characteristic mastery for which he is famous: and here it may be parenthetically observed that in the rhymed structure, whether of the Choruses or of the Kommos in which Cassandra plays so terrific a part, his version is noblest, purest, and clearest, and is also, I think, really closest to the Greek. This choice of verse shows that Mr. Browning aimed, not only at representing the ideas of Aeschylus, but also at reproducing his form. The *gesso* of the English language was to take the very mould and pressure of the Greek outline in his hand. But language, unlike plaster, will not simply take a mould. It cannot be used as a mere vehicle, because it has its own vitality, its own independent suggestiveness, its own inevitable form. And here, in my humble opinion, the compromise adopted by Mr. Browning in his method of translation reveals its weak point. The result, as regards both language and form, is neither English nor Greek. It does not convey to the English reader either the pleasure of a poem in his own tongue, or the impression which the original makes on a scholar's mind. Nor can its archaisms and quaint turns of phrase, suggesting as they do a thousand English reminiscences, convey the same aroma as the antiquated Aeschylean diction did to an Athenian of the age of Alexander.

203. From an unsigned review, *The Spectator*

10 November 1877, i. 1402–3

We expected great things from this translation, and we have been bitterly disappointed. In the irritation caused by that disappointment we may have said what we should be sorry for, but we feel keenly that the language which De Quincey used, and by his own admission unfairly, about Keats might not unfairly be applied to Mr. Browning. He has trampled upon his mother-tongue as with the hoofs of a buffalo, and played such fantastic tricks with its syntax, prosody, and idiom that it requires all the noble poems with which he has enriched and adorned the English language 'to weigh against the deep treason of these unparalleled offences'. If he should ever think of writing more 'transcriptions', we hope that before doing so he will read and mark and inwardly digest the warning given by a far more 'topping critic' than ourselves:

> Nec verbum verbo curabis reddere fidus
> Interpres; nec desilies imitator in arctum,
> Unde pedem proferre pudor vetet, aut operis lex.[1]

[1] 'Neither shall you take the trouble to render word for word as a slavish translator, nor as an imitator shall you leap down into a tight place, whence shame or the law of your work prevents you from freeing yourself.' Horace, in *Ars Poetica.*

204. From an unsigned review, *The Saturday Review*

17 November 1877, xliv. 617–19

It was conceivable that Mr. Browning would give us a work that should stand above question as the one true image of Æschylus for Englishmen. The greater is our disappointment at the result. Mr. Browning, taking an extreme view of a translator's duty, has sought to be literal 'at every cost save that of absolute violence to our language'; he has carried out his theory only too well, and his version, by dint of straining to be impossibly faithful to Æschylus in every point, does—the translator's intended caution notwithstanding—constant violence to English, and, after all, is not like Æschylus in the whole.

Whether the workman in this kind is called a translator or a transcriber, he cannot transcribe in facsimile; he is bound by the conditions of a character different from that of his original. Surely his true duty is not to kick against this necessity, but to accept it as a law which, if rightly studied, may give harmony to his work. He should be on the watch to seize analogies in the genius of the two languages where crude reproduction fails, and should look to large effects rather than to the brilliancy of particular touches. Even the laxity of the old school of translators may be more tolerable to the unlearned reader, for whose sake translations are supposed to exist, than photograph-like sharpness and severity. That where Æschylus is obscure Mr. Browning has left him so can be no just matter of complaint. It is no less right that where Æschylus is abrupt, or strange, or grotesque his translator should be so likewise. But of this we may and do complain, that the excrescences and irregularities are not only preserved but exaggerated and multiplied. Æschylus is often strange, often abrupt, at times even grotesque; but Mr. Browning was not therefore bound to give all these qualities to his English in places where the phrase of Æschylus was to Greek ears simply Greek and natural.

205. Torturing the English Tongue
1878

From an unsigned review, *The London Quarterly Review* (April 1878), i. 232–4.

A young Oxford B.A., speaking lately of Mr. Browning's 'transcription,' said: 'at almost every page I had to turn to the Greek to see what the English meant.' This is severe, but it is not unmerited. Mr. Browning, so delightfully clear when he pleases, as in *The Ride to Ghent, The Pied Piper of Hamelin,* &c., usually affects obscurity; *Rednightcap Country* is in parts obscure enough; long passages in that terribly long poem *The Ring and the Book,* are very tough reading. But in this 'transcription' he outdoes himself, and certainly rivals his original. Now a translation (for we do not profess to say anything about the transcription) proposes to itself one of two objects, either it is to help the unclassical reader to some understanding of the original, or it is to please the scholar, by showing him how gracefully and yet adequately the thought with which he is familiar may be rendered in English words. The danger for the first class of translations is lest they run into paraphrase. Pope's *Homer* has given thousands an interest in the 'tale of Troy divine', but it is not a translation. Even Dryden's *Virgil* does not altogether deserve the name. Translations of the other class are sometimes apt to become stiff and pedantic,—word-puzzles rather than natural arrangements of words. But, at any rate, their general aim is to please in some way or other. Mr. Browning is far above such an unworthy aim; his object is simply to reproduce his author 'with all the artistic expression of tenses, moods, and persons with which the original teems', and also, we must add, with all the picturesque incomprehensibility which the very corrupt state of the text gives to that original. Æschylus, no doubt, is not an easy poet; yet we will not believe that he who in his *Prometheus* writes what ordinary men can, with more or less thought, get a fair meaning out of, would in the *Agamemnon* have become as obscure as Mr. Browning makes him. The fault, in this play, and in the *Supplices,*[1] is in the exceed-

---

[1] *The Suppliants,* an Aeschylean tragedy, was the first part of a trilogy, the other parts of which are not extant.

ingly corrupt state of the text, as to which even Mr. Browning remarks: 'I keep to the earlier readings, so long as sense can be made out of them.' And, so keeping, he strives to be 'literal at every cost, save that of absolute violence to our language.' It is, of course, a question how much wrestling of the ordinary forms and introduction of inversions, and archaism, and strange juxta-positions may be indulged in, short of actual violence. If you twist a lad's arm round till the muscles crack, you may say you are using no actual violence, but the sufferer will think differently. We wonder what this poor English tongue of ours thinks of the way in which Mr. Browning has tortured it of old, and now tortures it even more fiercely. Our readers must judge whether the few extracts which we shall give are 'turned in as Greek a fashion as the English will bear,' or are not rather barbarous nonsense. We don't want 'to gape for Æschylus and get Theognis;' but we do not think we get Æschylus, or if anything of him only his skeleton, in the book before us.

Any attempt to reproduce 'the reputed magniloquence and sonorosity of the Greek' Mr. Browning wholly disclaims; he will give us 'the ideas of the poet—a strict bald version of word pregnant with thing.' But we contend that in such a form the ideas (supposing them there) are worthless. To the unlearned they say little or nothing; to the scholar they suggest a painful reminiscence of school-boy flounderings through passages at most a quarter understood.

LA SAISIAZ AND THE TWO POETS OF CROISIC

May 1878

206. Walter Theodore Watts, A Protest Against Scientific Materialism

1878

From his unsigned review, *The Athenæum* (25 May 1878), pp. 661–4.

Watts (1832–1914), later Watts-Dunton, is best remembered for his solicitude in caring for the ailing Swinburne. He contributed regularly to *The Athenæum*, and reviewed a number of Browning's later volumes. See No. 226.

No poet since Burns—none, perhaps, since Shakspeare—has known and felt so deeply as Mr. Browning the pathos of human life. Other poets can feel as deeply as he its mystery and its wonderfulness. Other poets can feel as deeply as he—more deeply, perhaps—the fire of personal passion; at least, they can thrill us more intensely than he with the cries of an individual soul in its supreme ecstasy of joy or pain.

But none save the two we have mentioned and Mr. Tennyson in 'Tears, Idle Tears', realizes as he does the unutterable pathos of the tangled web as a whole; none sees so clearly what a pathetic thing it is to live and die, and to be surrounded by myriads of others who live and die—'to be here,' as Corporal Trim says, 'to-day and gone to-morrow'—to come we know not whence, fluttering for a day or two 'in the sunshine and the rain'; to leave it and go we know not whither; to feel that our affections, however deep, our loves, however passionate, are twined around beings whose passage is more evanescent than 'the flight of the swift bird across the sky.'—nay, more fleeting (as the Talmud says) than 'the shadow along the grass of the bird as it flies,'—beings dearer to us nevertheless than our hearts' blood; and dearer still for this, that when they leave us we know we shall never see them any more as they now are, and half dread that we may never see them any more at all.

Mr. Browning tells us, in *The Two Poets of Croisic*, that

> ——a bard's enthusiasm
> Comports with what should counterbalance it—
> Some knowledge of the world!

But how rare it is that 'a bard's enthusiasm' is so 'counterbalanced'! Yet, in order to feel that deep pathetic meaning of human life that we have been speaking of, a poet must have done something more than feel his own joys and woes; and he must have done something more than sit in his chamber weaving the high fancies of his soul, as the pageantry of life goes by. He must be able to say, as Voltaire said, with pardonable boastfulness—'At least, I have *lived*.' If he has been 'cradled into poetry by wrong' he must have learned therefrom something more than the trick of bemoaning it; if he has suffered more than other men, he must also have enjoyed more; if he has wept more than other men, he must also have laughed more. He must not only have 'loved his beautiful lady'; he must also, like the Knight of Beauvais, have 'loved much to listen to the music of beauteous ladies.' He must not only have 'greatly loved his friend,' he must also have had his 'sweet enemies,' and

> Drunk delight of battle with his peers.

Above all, he must have had the rare faculty of enjoying, through sympathy, the perennial freshness of human youth.

Every-day life, which rhymesters call prosaic and flee from, is not prosaic to him, but a romance; and his love of man becomes intensified by the very thought of the evanescence of man's life; as the preciousness of a vase, says Pliny, is intensified by the thought of its fragility. And, as we have said,—since Burns certainly—perhaps since Shakspeare— no one has expressed this feeling so deeply and so continually as Mr. Browning.

It is not merely in such opposite poems as 'Evelyn Hope', 'The Flight of the Duchess', &c., but even in such lyrical outbursts as 'Meeting at

Night' and 'Parting at Morning' the 'still, sad music of humanity' floats over all the passion. But, in giving us this music, in showing how 'sweet it is to live'—'how straight God writes in crooked lines'—how rich in every kind of compensation is life, if we will only wait and hope, —in showing all this, Mr. Browning has never written anything so lovely as the following lines. They are so playful, and yet so deep, and tender, and true, that in reading them the struggle between the smile and the tear, commencing at the first stanza, goes on and on till at the end the reader feels that the divinest of lyrics has been written:

[Quotes the eighteen stanzas of 'What a Pretty Tale You Told Me'.]

La Saisiaz has the same *motif,* but unluckily the action of the poem is merely used as an occasion for ratiocinative writing, such as, as Charles Lamb would say, is 'proper for a sermon'.

The story is simple enough, and touching enough, and deserved the telling. Last autumn Mr. Browning was staying with two ladies at a Swiss village. One night, after having made an excursion in the neighbourhood, they planned to ascend next day the mountain at the base of which they were staying. The poet rose early next morning, took his accustomed bath and his accustomed walk,—did everything according to his custom. On returning home, he went to call upon the ladies, and found one of them dead on the floor. . . . Five days after the lady's death, the poet—urged by that instinct for self-torture which, in the very healthiest minds, will sometimes reveal itself (like the asp which had lain for twenty years in Hasan's bazaar)—ascends alone the heights which he and she were to have climbed together; and the poem is a record of the thoughts and arguments upon life and death which came to him on that occasion.

The artistic form in which these thoughts and arguments are embodied cannot, we think, be the *raison d'être* of the poem. If it is,—there has been in poetic art no such striking failure for a long time. To have attempted ratiocinative work such as this in blank verse would have been a mistake; to have attempted it in the iambic couplets of the heroic metre would have been a still greater mistake; but to attempt it in trochaics,—especially in the most sprightly of all trochaics, the form called 'trochaicum tetrametrum catalecticum,' implies wilfulness rather than mistake—perversity rather than obtuseness to the meaning and function of metre. For, although seven-syllabled trochaic verse may, by clever intermingling of iambic lines, lose its so-called 'Anacreontic' effect, and acquire an almost solemn march, as it does in *Il Penseroso*, yet the verse in question—which, in English, is indeed only a variety of the 'eight and six' ballad metre—must always retain that brisk and business-like quality which is its chief characteristic. . . . As the *raison d'être*, then, of the poem is not the form, and (seeing how soon the emotive treatment of the subject is left for the ratiocinative) it is not the outpouring of emotion,—it must be the expression of those thoughts and arguments of which most of the lines are composed. It seems necessary, therefore, to examine these, and see what they are worth as thoughts and arguments; to treat the poem as though it were not a poem but an essay; for what any literary work pretends to do it should do, whether it be verse or prose. If it fails to do that, the failure must be pointed out.

The gist of *La Saisiaz*, then, is contained in the concluding line of the poet's soliloquy on the mountains. It is that Mr. Browning,—as the result of the reasonings presented in the poem,—

> Believes in soul—is very sure of God.

Baron d'Holbach, on being told by a certain French abbé that he was 'very sure of God', made answer, 'I congratulate you, sir. I wish I was sure of only *half* as much. But, may I ask you, *What* God?' Certainly, it is in no irreverent mood that we record the infidel's retort; but Mr. Browning sets out to answer infidels; and his answer if weak is worse than worthless; for, as Bacon has told us, the worst enemies of truth are its weak defenders.

When a man writes a poem to say that he is 'very sure of God', the question is not at all impertinent, 'What God?' For there are 'gods and gods'. There is the God of Jacob, for instance; there is the God of Calvin, of Bismarck and the German Emperor; and there is the god of Timbuctoo. The fact is, as some one has hinted, that no sooner had God created 'man in his own image', than man returned the compliment and created God in his; and, from the very first, man has always been 'sure' of his handiwork,—as history tells us only too sadly. Here is Mr. Browning's definition:

Is it fancy I but cherish, when I take upon my lips
Phrase the solemn Tuscan fashioned, and declare the soul's eclipse
Not the soul's extinction? take his 'I believe and I declare—
Certain am I—from this life I pass into a better, there
Where that lady lives of whom enamoured was my soul'—where this
Other lady, my companion dear and true, she also is?
I have questioned and am answered. Question, answer presuppose
Two points: that the thing itself which questions, answers,—is, it knows;

As it also knows the thing perceived outside itself,—a force
Actual ere its own beginning, operative through its course,
Unaffected by its end,—that this thing likewise needs must be;
Call this—God, then, call that—soul, and both—the only facts for me.
Prove them facts? that they o'erpass my power of proving, proves them such:
Fact it is I know I know not something which is fact as much.
What before caused all the causes, what effect of all effects
Haply follows,—these are fancy.

In other words, there is in the universe Mr. Browning, who, with pardonable egotism, calls himself 'Me,'—the famous cogitating 'Ego,' in short,—and there is also the *not* Mr. Browning, *i.e.*, the something outside the reasoner,—

————A force
Actual ere its own beginning, operative through its course,
Unaffected by its end, that this thing needs must be.

Now, no one will deny all this; for, people do not commonly deny truisms. The poet is, of course, at liberty to call the *not* Mr. Browning God, if he likes; but in doing so he is doing neither more nor less than indulging in a *petitio principii*. The Yagur Veda escapes all such difficulties by calling the *non ego* 'That':

Fire is *That*, the sun is *That*;
The air, the moon—so also the pure Brahm;
Waters, and the lord of all creatures.

And this, perhaps, is why children, unsophisticated as yet by teleology on the one hand and science on the other, say sometimes, when asking for a doll, or the moon, or some other portion of the *non ego*, 'Give me my "That".' Mr. Browning is at liberty to call 'That' God, but in doing so he is talking pure Pantheism—he ranges himself with Hermes Trismegistus, who calls all things 'parts and members of God', and Mr. Swinburne in *Hertha*. And, without the smallest disrespect to Hermes and Mr. Swinburne, their mere Theism has never been considered of much account among Theists. We dwell upon this in no spirit of unkindness, and certainly in no spirit of disrespect to Mr. Browning, who is, on the whole, the strongest man that has expressed himself in English verse since the death of Milton; but we do so in order to reiterate what we have often said, that ratiocinative poetry is a mistake. Not by syllogism, but *per saltum*, does, and should, the poet reach his conclusions. We listen to him—we allow him to address us in rhyme instead of reason,—we allow him to sing to us while other men are only allowed to talk,—not because he reasons more logically, more truly, but because he feels more truly. It is for his readers to be knowing and ratiocinative —it is for him to be gnomic and 'divinely wise'. . . .

La Saisiaz, indeed, is nothing more nor less than a vigorous and eloquent protest against the scientific materialism of the day. It seems, indeed, becoming the fashion now, among poets and others in the world of *belles lettres*, to rail against scientific materialism and the psychology of the scalpel. But, in truth, there is no little confusion of thought upon the subject. 'The age is sunk into gross materialism,' say poets like Mr. Tennyson and Mr. Browning: 'the *savants* have done it,' say the clergy. But is the age really so sunk? We doubt it, and a word may be said on behalf of the *savants*. . . . Indeed the flood of scientific talk nowadays—from Royal Institution lectures down to the penny-a-liners—is more incessant than religious talk used to be. And this is why externally it appears as if materialism were universal. Still, whatever may be said of German inquirers, English *savants* have endeavoured to read the facts as they must be read. For instance, they refuse to burk the fact that biogenesis is the law; and, this being so, evolution has placed materialism further back than ever; for organism is the result of 'life', not 'life' of organism; and, this being established, the immaterialist may rest perfectly content as to what will be the accepted cosmogony in a few years; and Mr. Browning may leave ratiocination alone—or at least leave it alone in verse—and go on 'believing in soul', and being 'very sure of God'—though not, perhaps, for the reasons given here. . . .

The poem is full of beautiful thoughts, beautifully expressed. What Mr. Browning says about 'the first life claiming a second' and about the doctrine of compensation strikes us as being especially beautiful and just. If it is true that there is a future life—if it is true that the law of that life is moral progression—if is true that

> Our broken hopes are threaded into stars—

then assuredly the game of life is that of 'who loses wins'.

207. From an unsigned review, *The Saturday Review*

15 June 1878, xlv. 759–60

The poem which takes its name from the hamlet of La Saisiaz is founded on personal experience of the sudden death of a near friend. The poet tells how he climbed to the top of Salève because he had arranged a few days before to make the ascent in the company of two others, one of whom, a lady staying at Saisiaz, died on the morning appointed for the expedition. From a touching expression of feelings natural on the occasion, Mr. Browning passes into a long and subtle course of reasoning on the probability of a future life. As in many other poems, he rather indicates than expresses thoughts which have probably in his own mind both a logical and an imaginative sequence. The attempt to decipher the full meaning is not unattractive, and sometimes it may be partially successful; but the argument is written in a shorthand of crabbed and condensed phrases, which seem designed rather to remind the poet of his own process of reflection than to communicate his conclusions to others. No poet would excel Mr. Browning in the faculty of reasoning in verse if he could but condescend to be lucid. Even fragments of instruction collected by diligent attention sustain a curiosity which finds no complete satisfaction. Long metaphysical discussions are agreeably relieved by the introduction of things so concrete as proper names. Looking across the lake from a spot near Rousseau's birthplace to Geneva and Lausanne, the poet is naturally reminded of Voltaire, of Gibbon, and of Byron. The pessimism of Rousseau and the affected misanthropy of Byron are noticed with humorous terseness; and the poet, if his meaning is rightly conjectured, fancies himself for the moment and for a special purpose possessed of the fame of all four, though he is careful to intimate his contempt for the supposed distinction. First he has the learning of Gibbon:

This the trunk, the central solid Knowledge, kindled core, began
Tugging earth-deeps, trying heaven-heights, rooted yonder at Lausanne.

A tree with a serpent coiled round it symbolizes Voltaire:

> Laughter so bejewels Learning—What but Ferney nourished it?

Rousseau contributes his eloquence, and Byron his poetry:

> As Rousseau then, eloquent, as Byron prime in poet's power,
> Detonations, fulgurations, smiles—the rainbow, tears, the shower—
> Lo! I lift the coruscating marvel, Fame! and famed declare
> Learned for the nonce as Gibbon, witty as wit's self Voltaire,
> O the sorriest of conclusions to whatever man of sense
> Mid the millions stands the unit, takes no flare for evidence,
> Yet the millions have their portion, live their calm or troublous day,
> Find significance in fireworks; so, by help of mine, they may
> Confidently lay to heart and lock in head their lifetime—this:
> 'He there with the brand flamboyant, broad o'er night's forlorn abyss,
> Crowned by prose and verse, and wielding, with Wit's bauble, Learning's
>   rod—
> Well? Why he at least believed in Soul, was very sure of God!'

Mr. Browning apparently means to say that, if he had the learning of Gibbon, the wit of Voltaire, the eloquence of Rousseau, the poetic power of Byron, and the collective fame of them all, although it is foolish and contemptible to pay respect to fame, he would nevertheless use his opportunity by proclaiming to the world that the most accomplished and famous of men believe in a soul and in God. It would scarcely be allowable to deduce conclusions so definite from the preceding labyrinth of ingenious ratiocination; but the actual province of authority in matters of opinion is far wider than the range of argument. The distinct proposition which ends the inquiry furnishes a comment on its previous course. To himself at least Mr. Browning's speculations seem not to end in a puzzle.

The poet and his lost friend had discussed, or are, for the purposes of the poem, supposed to have discussed, a recent well-known Essay on a Soul and Future Life, written to prove that, except in a figurative sense, there is neither the one nor the other. He might, he says, have trifled with the question if they had still been talking at leisure, but he has no heart

> to palter, when the matter to decide
> Now becomes 'Was ending ending once and always, when you died?'
> Did the face, the form I lifted as it lay, reveal the loss
> Not alone of life but soul?

The survivor will himself in turn furnish the same matter for thought;

and the essayist who may comment on his death will only provide his friends with the consolation that others, though not himself, will live after he is dead.

> So both memories dwindle, yours and mine together linked,
> Till there is but left for comfort, when the last spark proves extinct,
> This, that somewhere new existence led by men and women new
> Possibly attains perfection coveted by me and you.
> Why repine? There's ever some one lives although ourselves be dead.

Time spent during youth in learning to construe the hardest choruses of the Greek tragedians will not have been wasted if it enables the maturer mind to understand Mr. Browning's trochaic tetrameter-catalectics—of which it may be well to take a comparatively easy specimen:

> I have questioned, I am answered. Question, answer presuppose
> Two points: that the thing itself which questions, answers—is, it knows;
> As it also knows the thing perceived outside itself—a force
> Actual ere its own beginning, operative through its course,
> Unaffected by its end—that this thing likewise needs must be;
> Call this—God, then, call that—soul, and both—the only facts for me.
> Prove them facts? that they o'erpass my power of proving, proves them
>   such.
> Fact it is I know I know not something which is fact as much.

The last line has scarcely been excelled in obscurity by Hegel in prose or by Mr. Browning in verse. The meaning seems to be—It is a fact that I know that I am ignorant of something which is also a fact. The rugged versification is not ill suited to the laborious evolution of argument. The passage is the beginning, and not the end, of an elaborate comparison of reasons on both sides, which are superseded rather than summed up in the profession of faith which has already been quoted.

Mr. Browning has often expressed his contempt for criticisms on the almost impenetrable obscurity which to himself, looking from the other side, is perfectly transparent. A master of caligraphy might, if he thought it worth while, assert with equal reason the privilege of writing illegibly at his pleasure. Much may be borne at the hands of a true artist which would not be pardonable in a mere pretender. The abstruse reasoning of *La Saisiaz* affords a favourable example of Mr. Browning's less easy style. The key to the cipher is in this instance contained in the text, consisting, not in some odd and recondite fragment of knowledge, but in a complicated process of thought which might perhaps be approximately understood by an equally subtle intellect. Some parts of the argument may be followed with the aid of ordinary acuteness and close attention.

The whole is evidently the unaffected result of a train of natural associations. The riddle is pardonable because it has been constructed for the intellectual amusement of its author, and not for the vulgar purpose of perplexing simple readers. The transition of feelings with which all can sympathize into abstruse and complicated meditation affords a not uninteresting study. Painful emotion, not so intense as to absorb for the time all other faculties, readily connects itself with the gravest problems which habitually occupy reflective minds. When the man of genius in fiction was oppressed with a sudden misfortune, he neither suppressed his grief nor indulged it to excess, but he talked it off. In the management of his sorrow, as in other passages of his life, Mr. Shandy's proceeding, though slightly caricatured for artistic purposes, was natural, typical, and wise. The reflections on the fall of cities and empires which he quotes from Cicero serve as well as Mr. Browning's dialogue between Fancy and Reason the purpose of diverting attention from unprofitable pain. To all but the most morbid dispositions, whatever is common to humanity becomes comparatively tolerable. The philosophic speculations and fancies which occupy the later pages of *In Memoriam* are the proper correctives of the personal suffering which was the original subject of the poem. The ascent of the Salève suggests at every step recollections of a recent loss; but from the summit the poet is at leisure to observe the spots which have become historical by the birth or residence of famous French and English writers. Very few students will trouble themselves to understand the metaphysical portion of the poem. The short and plain description of a lonely burying-place will be more generally appreciated:

> Therefore, paying piteous duty, what seemed you have we consigned
> Peacefully to—what I think were, of all earth-beds, to your mind
> Most the choice for quiet, yonder; low walls stop the vine's approach;
> Lovingly Salève protects you; village sports will ne'er encroach.
> On the stranger lady's silence, whom friends bore so kind and well
> Thither 'just for love's sake'—such their own word was, and who can tell?

It is useless to regret, and perhaps it would be presumptuous to blame, the careless workmanship which all but spoils a graceful and touching passage. Mr. Browning has always taken pleasure in irritating admiring readers by harsh constructions in grammar and in prosody, by stress laid on the weakest syllables, such as in one line 'what', 'of', and 'to'. The caprices of irresponsible power resting on unquestioned rank are not confined to hereditary sovereigns; yet both poets and kings do well to remember that they have duties as well as rights.

DRAMATIC IDYLS

Published in two series, the first April 1879,
the second June 1880

208. Mrs. Sutherland Orr, *Contemporary Review*

May 1879, xxxv. 289–302

From her review.

For another opinion by Mrs. Orr, see No. 177.

Mr. Browning's *Dramatic Idylls* contain all that the terms properly imply; very little of that which popular association connects with them; and though the graceful unrealities suggested by the word Idyllic could never be looked for in any work of his, he has exceeded forecast in the opposite direction. The concentrated vigour of his latest volume may startle even those who have learnt by long experience that his genius is incapable of attenuation, and that writing six short poems, instead of one long one, means with him, not the suspension of constructive effort, but a constructive effort multiplied so many times. It justifies the stereotyped opinion concerning him by dealing chiefly with the unusual in character and circumstance, and with emotions more startling than sympathetic. It belies it in so far that the unusual in its pictures adds often not only to their impressiveness, but to their truth, recalling, as they do, forgotten, rather than improbable aspects of human life; and rough-hewn possibilities, rather than over-specialized forms of human feeling. That the result is on the whole somewhat stern and sad will be approved or disapproved according to the temperament of the reader. It seems superfluous to say, what is implied by the shortness of these poems, that they are free from all tedious elaboration; or to add that the intellectual matter which they contain is strictly subordinate to their dramatic form.

209. From an unsigned review, *The Spectator*

31 May 1879, lii. 692–3

This is by far the best book which Mr. Browning has published for many years. Though not reaching the level of his *Men and Women*, or of the finest portions of *The Ring and the Book*, it has many passages full of his characteristic power, and except where a rough style gives dramatic force to the sketch, as in the picture of John Bunyan's penitents, Ned Bratts and his wife, nothing at all of the truculent ugliness, the ostentatious broken-windedness of his latest gasping style of English verse. Of course, his subjects are, as usual with Mr. Browning, startling subjects. He not only loves to flash his weird figures upon the imagination with all the suddenness and abruptness of a magic lanthorn, but to present you with a subject that takes your breath away as much by the singularity of its attitude as by the suddenness of its appearance. He rejects purposely the shading and the moral atmosphere which make the grimmest subjects seem natural when they are given in connection with all the conditions of their history and origin, for his object is to make you see the wonder of the world, rather than its harmony, or the context which, partly at least, explains it. But assuming, as the critic always must assume, the poet's special bent and genius, there is nothing specially harsh in this volume, and much that is really powerful, while the harshest pictures in it are lent a touch of grandeur by the purpose which penetrates the life portrayed. . . .

The Russian idyl, Ivàn Ivànovitch, on the old subject of the mother who threw three of her babies to the pursuing wolves in order to save her own life, is also very grim and powerful, especially in its ending,—. . . This is, on the whole, decidedly the finest of these idyls. It paints a grandeur of unhesitating, calm self-reliance in the village hero, such as is hardly conceivable in our world of doubts and scruples, and paints, too, the clearness and coldness and freedom from all liability to agitation, which would be the only possible conditions of such Draconic rigour of purpose.

210. G. Allen, *Fortnightly Review*

July 1879, xxxii. 149–53

From his review.

Probably Grant Allen (1848–99), author of *Physiological Aesthetics* and some thirty works of fiction.

Those who admire Mr. Browning will admire the present idyls: those who find him incomprehensible will find the latest addition to his incomprehensibles more incomprehensible than ever. Probably no poem which he has ever written will prove a sorer stumbling-block to bewildered spellers-out of his meaning than the all but inarticulate story of *Ned Bratts*.

The *Dramatic Idyls* comprise one truly noble Hellenic poem, *Pheidippides*; one transcendently horrible English nightmare, *Ned Bratts*; and three or four less striking pieces of similar character to the latter.

Martin Relph, with which the little volume opens, is a powerful dramatic monologue of the kind in which Mr. Browning delights, rendered in a formless stanza with even less of music than Mr. Browning usually condescends to bestow upon us. But neither the stumbling and halting versification, the inveterate objection to the definite article where other Englishmen find it indispensable, nor the jerky and dislocated run of the narrative, can prevent us from seeing that *Martin Relph* is genuine poetry. The incident is sensational, as are almost all the others in the present collection; indeed, Mr. Browning seems to have been indulging in a prolonged course of horrible stories; but it is powerfully told, and the horror is well kept back for a few stanzas at the end of the piece. The two opening verses will give an idea of its general ring and tone:

> If I last as long as Methuselah, I shall never forgive myself:
> But—God forgive me, that I pray, unhappy Martin Relph,
> As coward, coward I call him—him, yes, him! away from me!
> Get you behind the man I am now, you man that I used to be!

> What can have sewed my mouth up, set me a-stare, all eyes, no tongue?

People have urged, 'You visit a scare too hard on a lad so young!
You were taken aback, poor boy,' they urge, 'no time to regain your wits:
Besides it had maybe cost you your life.' Ay, there is the cap which fits!

If, when English has become a dead language, the ingenuous youth
of coming races should ever be given the *Dramatic Idyls* as a classic, I
must express my sincere commiseration for the unhappy lads who are
requested to *scan* the third and fifth lines of this passage. . . .

[The reviewer turns to 'Pheidippides', which he summarizes briefly.]

One or two minor matters, however, ask for criticism. Even the
most determined purist might truly shrink from the spelling 'Olumpos'.
It is well that we should dress up the grand old Hellenic words as near as
possible in their native guise: but this rendering does not come half so
close to the true pronunciation as 'Olympos', while it is sure to be read
by the English reader as though it were a compound of the English
word 'lump'. And why does Mr. Browning, who is so anxious for
correctness in these small points, throw the accent upon the short vowel
in Miltĭadês?

The two other principal poems, *Ivàn Ivànovitch* and *Ned Bratts*, though
of course powerful—one is tired of forever repeating that word about
Mr. Browning's work, yet one has no choice—are very painful. The
first is a piece of wild Russian folk-lore, wildly rendered in verse of
quite appropriate rudeness; the second is a terrible story of English
justice in the worst hanging days. A Bedford publican and his wife,
temp. Charles II.—a pair of murderers, thieves, perjurers, and common
informers—in a fit of spasmodic conversion, induced hysterically by
reading the 'Pilgrim's Progress', burst into the court-house during full
assize and, confessing their crimes with a horrid glibness, ask leave to be
hanged before the effects of grace have time to pass away.

So, happily hanged were they,—why lengthen out my tale?
Where Bunyan's statue stands facing where stood his jail.

It is on the whole, in spite of intense dramatic skill, perhaps the most
disjointed piece of workmanship which even Mr. Browning has ever
produced. Take as a specimen, but a comparatively gentle one, these
lines:

Well, things at jolly high-tide, amusement steeped in fire,
While noon smote fierce the roof's red tiles to heart's desire,
The Court a-simmer with smoke, one ferment of oozy flesh,
One spirituous humming musk mount-mounting until its mesh

Entoiled all heads in a fluster, and Serjeant Postlethwayte—
Dashing his wig oblique as he mopped his oily pate—
Cried, 'Silence, or I grow grease! No loophole lets in air!
Jurymen,—Guilty, Death! Gainsay me if you dare!'
—Things at this pitch, I say—what hubbub without the doors?
What laughs, shrieks, hoots, and yells, what rudest of uproars?

On the other hand, as a piece of character thoroughly realised in the concrete, look at the peroration of the newly-converted publican's speech, with its wonderful glimpses of the coarse, frank, brutal nature, frankly and brutally accepting its selfish salvation, prepared to believe that a Moody-and-Sankey[1] penitence will make amends for its unpardonable gross self:

                              So hang us out of hand!
Make haste, for pity's sake! A single moment's loss
Means—Satan's lord once more: his whisper shoots across
All singing in my heart, all praying in my brain.
'It comes of heat and beer'! hark how he guffaws plain!
'To-morrow you'll wake bright, and, in a safe skin, hug
Your sound selves, Tab and you, over a foaming jug!
You've had such qualms before, time out of mind.' He's right. . . .

                    ★ ★ ★ ★ ★

Oh, waves increase around—I feel them mount and mount!
Hang us! To-morrow brings Tom Bearward with his bears:
One new black-muzzled brute beats Sackerson, he swears;
(Sackerson for my money!) and, baiting o'er, the Brawl
They lead on Turner's Patch,—lads, lasses, up tails all,—
I'm i' the thick o' the throng! That means the Iron Cage,
—Means the Lost Man inside! Where's hope for such as wage
War against light? Light's left, light's here, I hold light still,
So does Tab—make but haste to hang us both! You will?

---

[1] Dwight Moody (1837–99) and Ira Sankey (1840–1908), the noted American evangelists, had made a successful tour of Great Britain in 1873–5.

211. From an unsigned article, 'Three Small Books: By Great Writers', *Fraser's Magazine*

July 1879, NS xx. 103–24

The 'Three Small Books' are George Eliot's *Impressions of Theophrastus Such*, Tennyson's *The Lover's Tale*, and Browning's *Dramatic Idyls*. Browning, unfortunately, comes off third-best. Preceeding this excerpt is an account of Tennyson's popularity.

. . . Mr. Browning has not by any means been received with the same acquiescence in his claims. He has had the more natural fate of the poet for whom a vehement band of disciples contend on one side almost with violence, while on the other the world resists with all the more vigour that it cannot by any means shake off a disagreeable consciousness that posterity will not uphold its opinion. This is a much more usual, and we are disposed to think natural, position for a writer of genius in face of his generation than the other. At the same time the fact must not be overlooked that Mr. Browning himself is very greatly to blame. He has never so much as attempted to please the public, which on its side desired nothing better than to be pleased. He has teased it by perverse convolutions of language—by broken rhymes, contracted words, ellipsis, parenthesis, every confusing twist of which style is capable; and by a still more perverse choice of subject—until he has made his very name an exasperation to many good people, who cannot quite consent to give him up though he has been so unkind to them. When he jeers at the British public who 'love me not', it is with an air more jaunty than bitter, as of a man not half-displeased to be above his audience, nor quite unproud of that distinction—sentiments which no audience is likely to approve of. But indeed the public has always shown itself very well disposed to do him justice when he could persuade himself to put aside those tricks of style which form no part of any passport to immortality, and to let the simple reader perceive the noble manliness of his conceptions, the penetrating keenness of his insight, the passion of sympathy

461

Dramatic Idyls

—tender, indignant, and tuned to all lofty things—that is in him. But if a poet prefers to play such pranks before high heaven as make the vulgar jeer, and his friends and lovers retire confused from the lists where they have been ready to defend him against all comers, he has only himself to blame. . . .

Mr. Browning has fortunately afforded us the means of a remarkable contrast [with Tennyson].

No one will say that his heroes are of this visionary sort, or that he is wanting in vigour or passion. Unluckily he has so strange an idea on the other side of poetical language, and so little sympathy with the smooth and sweet, that he has, with a perverseness most exasperating to his admirers, got himself at enmity with the public rather than taken the place to which his genius entitles him as one of its leading influences. He has not acted the part of Orpheus with his lute as Mr. Tennyson has done: and the trumpet notes which he has sounded forth have always had more or less a jar in them. He has seemed to take a malicious satisfaction in disconcerting us with a flood of dislocated syllables after his finest outbursts. He has interrupted himself in his most exciting narratives to catch at the tail of a stray metaphor, in parenthesis within parenthesis. To read one of his poems aloud requires as much care and study as if it were written in an imperfectly known foreign language. His disciples have to suffer for their devotion to him, and according to all appearance he likes to have it so. We are not sure that there is not a certain attraction in the mere fact that we have thus something to pay for our delight: it binds Mr. Browning's poetical following together, and gives them a warmth of partisanship scarcely to be found among the adherents of other and easier poets. Indeed such was the charm of this, that up to a recent date the Browningites were almost as strenuous in their defiance of the world and maintenance of their leader's standard, as are the Burne-Jonesites now. At the period of *The Ring and the Book* this bold and fearless band were ready to strike upon any man's shield in proof of their devotion. That wonderful poem was perhaps too long, we were willing to allow; but even the unconverted newspapers, even those critics who know so little about it, though they prate so much, were obliged to acknowledge the subtle force with which old Guido was made to paint himself upon the glowing canvas, the pathetic sweetness of Pompilia, the heroic manhood of Caponsacchi. But since that day the party has grown timorous. Mr. Browning, moved by some will and pleasure of his own, unfathomable by the meaner intelligence, has chosen to become more dislocated, more elliptical, more parenthetic

462

than ever. He has picked out of the mud the most disagreeable subjects he has been able to find, and he has sung his songs in the most creaking voice and with the most disjointed eccentricity. One by one his partisans have fallen silent; the unconverted papers have crowed aloud, the critics have been rampant, and we, who love Mr. Browning, have held our tongues, unable to make any way against the tide in favour of the Red Cotton Night-cap or the Inn Album, or the ear-rending versification of Pacchiorotto. We have been silent, not knowing what to say for our poet—we have gone into corners and read the *Men and Women*, and said to ourselves, what Galileo did not say, 'E pur si muove:' still he is a poet. Yes, still he is a poet, and a great one—and we hasten to proclaim to all the brotherhood, if discouraged by previous failure, they may not have had the hardihood to take up this last volume, that, after long wading in these dismal marshes, our minstrel has got to shore again. Praisèd be heaven! This time he comes with no basket of mud, no screech-owl's cry. His imagination has got fitter food; he brings us a few of those heroic rhymes in which no one has surpassed him, embodying incidents which are worth his telling, and inspired by that profound acquaintance with human feeling at its highest strain, which few writers possess in the same superlative degree. . . .

We think that, notwithstanding a few harsh rhymes and awkward words (the above astonishing line about 'the bell therein to hitch' among others), which will we, nill we, we are obliged to accept from Mr. Browning—his wayward toll and tribute, to be paid by all whom he carries along the great and nobly flowing river of song—we have read few things finer than this grand ballad, if so it may be called. The peasant's rude, primitive, but noble sense of justice, unreflecting, unhesitating, contrasts in the most forcible way with the fluttering frenzy of the woman, her brain sharpened by need to every subterfuge of casuistry, the desperate skill of self-defence. The poet knows better than to leave in us any emotions of pity for the ignoble creature who can anticipate the sweetness of life's after years after the tragedy she has lived through; and the calm of the executioner is noble, not cruel, as it might so easily have been made to appear. Thus once more the foundation of story, not original, and something too horrible for ordinary treatment, is ennobled by the new element in it, the new setting and moral. Any possible reproach as to the absence of invention shown in the choice of these old tales is thus met and extinguished in the most noble way.

We cannot conclude, however, without an energetic protest against

'Ned Bratts'. Some foolish worshippers in the press have, we see, been persuading Mr. Browning that it is a fine poem. We wonder that his own fingers were not pulled from the joints as he wrote those dislocated and dislocating pages. Ned Bratts and his wife Tab, odious criminals of the very worst class, get suddenly converted by Bunyan in prison, and rush wildly into the court at 'Bedford Special Assize', when the bench and the jury and all the audience are sweltering with heat (of which Mr. Browning spares us not one detail), and in great want of an excitement —and suddenly confessing a mass of undiscovered crimes, demand with much earnestness to be hanged, making which prayer—

> the mass of man sank meek upon his knees,
> While Tab, alongside, wheezed a hoarse 'Do hang us, please!'

Mr. Browning informs us that there was 'no eye but ran with tears at this moment;' but for our part we have much ado to believe that he can mean us to do anything but laugh. The ridiculous here is certainly much too close to the sublime; and we fear we shall have still a losing battle to fight for him so long as he will mistake the grotesque for the great—so strange a mistake for one who is capable of the noblest work, and whose mind can give originality and novel form, by touching them, to the oldest fables! Let us at least take comfort that after so many eccentricities he has consented to let us have so fine a poem as 'Ivàn Ivànovitch'. It is enough to cover a multitude of sins.

212. *A Perverse Musician*

1880

From an unsigned review, *The Times* (23 August 1880), p. 3.

We do not go to the extent of asserting that in the present volume Mr. Browning is smooth and facile. His lines are commonly, as formerly, broken-backed. No better test of an instinct for rhythm could be proposed to a lad aspiring after the vocation of a poet than to set him the task of reading aloud, for instance, 'Pietro of Abano', so as to keep the flow of a tune. Mr. Browning's rhymes continue to be perpetual *tours de force*. 'Jews' age' is coupled with 'usage', 'Ipse dixi' with 'fix eye', 'mortar' with 'sort are', 'somewhat' with 'come what', 'exact eight' with 'tractate'. Not rarely he leaps upon a rhyme, and it crumbles under his feet, as when, to take obliges 'aether' to do duty with 'together', 'martyrs' with 'quarters', 'dullard' with 'coloured', 'discernment' with 'adjournment'. But, at all events, there is a ring in the air, though the musician perversely sweeps his fingers over the keys and jangles the melody.

213. From an unsigned review, *The British Quarterly Review*

1 October 1880, 2nd Ser. lxxii. 506–7

This little volume would suggest a whole article indicative of the peculiarities of Mr. Browning's genius. For years past we have noticed his
volumes as they have appeared, signalizing any special features that they
presented, and we find ourselves in face of this one with a yet keen
desire to attempt a full and satisfactory analysis. That, however, must in
the meantime wait; because no mere general statements could have
effect apart from illustrative extracts, and too much space would be
demanded for that in such a notice as this. Suffice it to say that Mr.
Browning exhibits all his old art in the use of quasi-dramatic mediums
through which he may reflect his own moods. It is evident that he has
seriously endeavoured to impart variety by the choice of such themes as
would, in the hands of an objective writer like Sir Walter Scott, become mere ballads of action; but Mr. Browning's *demon* is too much for
him, and he expresses his prevailing tendencies most completely when
he is resolved, if he can, to escape from them. The unnamed, who came
to the aid of the Greeks against the Persians—the man who—

> Kept no rank, and his sole arm plied no spear
> As a flashing came and went, and a form i' the van, the rear,
> Brightened the battle up, for he blazed now there, now here,
> Nor helmed nor shielded, he! but a goat-skin all his wear,
> Like a tiller of the soil, with a clown's limbs broad and bare,
> Went ploughing on and on; he pushed with a ploughman's share—

is here all too Browningesque in its traits; and the story of Kiri glimmers
with the reflections of Mr. Browning's curious and daring imagination,
that will permit none of the ordinary links of association to be patent,
and actually obtrudes his own countenance continually in the lapses.
Muléykeh is a remarkable study in every respect, setting forth some
traits of Arab character well, though under Mr. Browning's hand some
thread or other of grotesque intrudes into the pathos. Pietro of Abano
is full of this character. Best of all, however, we like the last idyl, which
is but an idyl, and the only poem that fully justifies the name—'Pan

and Luna'—an old Greek legend of the moon, which is fresh, and lucid, and living, a thing Mr. Browning has made his own as by his indelible seal set upon it. Lovers of Mr. Browning will hardly exhaust the signifi- cance of this volume; to any other than lovers and students of Mr. Browning it must often bear too much the aspect of a psychological puzzle.

214. Tennyson and Browning in 1880

Justin McCarthy, from his *A History of Our Own Times* (1880), I. 540–4.

In surveying the literary achievement of Victorian England, McCarthy comes to the inevitable comparison of Tennyson with Browning.

The paths of the two poets who first sprang into fame in the present reign are strangely remote from each other. Mr. Tennyson and Mr. Browning are as unlike in style and choice of subject, and indeed in the whole spirit of their poetry, as Wordsworth and Byron. Mr. Tennyson deals with incident and picturesque form, and graceful legend, and with so much of doubt and thought and yearning melancholy as would belong to a refined and cultured intellect under no greater stress or strain than the ordinary chances of life among educated Englishmen might be expected to impose. He has revived with great success the old Arthurian legends, and made them a part of the living literature of England. But the knights and ladies whom he paints are refined, grace- ful, noble, without roughness, without wild or, at all events, complex and distracting passions. It may perhaps be said that Tennyson has taken for his province all the beauty, all the nobleness, all the feeling that lie near to or on the surface of life and of nature. His object might seem to be that which Lessing declared the true object of all art, 'to delight'; but it is to delight in a somewhat narrower sense than was the meaning of

Lessing. Beauty, melancholy, and repose are the elements of Tennyson's poetry. There is no storm, no conflict, no complication. Mr. Browning, on the other hand, delights in perplexed problems of character and life—in studying the effects of strange contrasting forces of passion coming into play under peculiar and distracting conditions. All that lies beneath the surface; all that is out of the common track of emotion; all that is possible, that is poetically conceivable, but that the outer air and the daily walks of life never see, this is what specially attracts Mr. Browning. In Tennyson a knight of King Arthur's mythical court has the emotions of a polished English gentleman of our day, and nothing more. Mr. Browning would prefer, in treating of a polished English gentleman of our day, to exhibit him under some conditions which should draw out in him all the strange elementary passions and complications of emotion that lie far down in deeps below the surface of the best ordered civilization. The tendency of the one poet is naturally to fall now and then into the sweetly insipid; of the other, to wander away into the tangled regions of the grotesque. It is, perhaps, only natural that under such conditions the one poet should be profoundly concerned for beauty of form, and the latter almost absolutely indifferent to it. No poet has more finished beauty of style and exquisite charm of melody than Tennyson. None certainly can be more often wanting in grace of form and delight of soft sound than Mr. Browning. There are many passages and even many poems of Browning which show that the poet could be melodious if he would; but he seems sometimes as if he took a positive delight in perplexing the reader's ear with harsh, untuneful sounds. Mr. Browning commonly allows the study of the purely psychological to absorb too much of his moods and of his genius. It has a fascination for him which he is seemingly unable to resist. He makes of his poems too often mere searchings into strange deeps of human character and human error. He seldom abandons himself altogether to the inspiration of the poet; he hardly ever deserves the definition of the minstrel given in Goethe's ballad who 'sings but as the song-bird sings'. Moreover, Mr. Browning has an almost morbid taste for the grotesque; he is not unfrequently a sort of poetic Callot. It has to be added that Mr. Browning is seldom easy to understand, and that there are times when he is only to be understood at the expense of as much thought and study as one might give to a controverted passage in an ancient author. This is a defect of art, and a very serious defect. The more devoted of Mr. Browning's admirers will tell us, no doubt, that the poet is not bound to supply us with brains as well as poetry, and that if we cannot understand what he says it is the fault simply of our stupidity. But an ordinary man who finds that he can understand Shakespeare and Milton, Dryden and Wordsworth, Byron and Keats without any trouble, may surely be excused if he does not set down his difficulty about some of Browning's poems wholly to the account of his own dullness. It may well be doubted whether there is any idea so subtle that if the poet can actually realize it in his own mind clearly for himself, the English language will not be found capable of expressing it with sufficient clearness. The language has been made to do this for the most refined reasonings of philosophical schools, for transcendentalists and utilitarians, for psychologists and metaphysicians. No intelligent person feels any difficulty in understanding what Mill, or Herbert Spencer, or Huxley means; and it can hardly be said that the ideas Mr. Browning desires to convey to his readers are more difficult of exposition than some of those which the authors we name have contrived to set out with a white light of clearness all round them. The plain truth is that Mr. Browning is a great poet, in spite of some of the worst defects that ever stood between a poet and popularity. He is a great poet by virtue of his commanding genius, his fearless imagination, his penetrating pathos. He strikes an iron harp-string. In certain of his moods his poetry is like that of the terrible lyre in the weird old Scottish ballad, the lyre that was made of the murdered maiden's breastbone, and which told its fearful story in tones 'that would melt a heart of stone'. In strength and depth of passion and pathos, in wild humor, in emotion of every kind, Mr. Browning is much superior to Mr. Tennyson. The poet-laureate is the completer man. Mr. Tennyson is, beyond doubt, the most complete of the poets of Queen Victoria's time. No one else has the same combination of melody, beauty of description, culture, and intellectual power. He has sweetness and strength in exquisite combination. If a just balance of poetic powers were to be the crown of a poet, then undoubtedly Mr. Tennyson must be proclaimed the greatest English poet of our time. The reader's estimate of Browning and Tennyson will probably be decided by his predilection for the higher effort or for the more perfect art. Browning's is surely the higher aim in poetic art; but of the art which he essays Tennyson is by far the completer master. Tennyson has, undoubtedly, thrown away much of his sweetness and his exquisite grace of form on mere triflings and pretty conceits; and perhaps as a retribution those poems of his which are most familiar in the popular mouth are just those which least do justice to his genuine strength and intellect. The cheap sentiment of 'Lady Clara Vere de Vere', the yet cheaper pathos of

'The May Queen', are in the minds of thousands the choicest representation of the genius of the poet who wrote *In Memoriam* and the *Morte d'Arthur*. Mr. Browning, on the other hand, has chosen to court the approval of his time on terms of such disadvantage as an orator might who insisted in addressing an assemblage in some tongue which they but imperfectly understood. It is the fault of Mr. Browning himself if he has for his only audience and admirers men and women of culture, and misses altogether that broad public audience to which most poets have chosen to sing, and which all true poets, one would think, must desire to reach with their song. It is, on the other hand, assuredly Mr. Tennyson's fault if he has by his too frequent condescension to the drawing-room, and even the young ladies' school, made men and women of culture forget for the moment his best things, and credit him with no higher gift that that of singing *virginibus puerisque*. One quality ought to be mentioned as common to these two poets who have so little else in common. They are both absolutely faithful to nature and truth in their pictures of the earth and its scenes and seasons. Almost all the great poets of the past age, even including Wordsworth himself, were now and then content to generalize nature; to take some things for granted; to use their memory, or the eyes of others, rather than their own eyes, when they had to describe changes on leaf, or sky, or water. It is the characteristic of Tennyson and Browning that they deal with nature in a spirit of the most faithful loyalty. Not the branch of a tree, nor the cry of a bird, nor the shifting colors on sea or sky will be found described on their pages otherwise than as the eye sees for itself at the season of which the poet tells. In reading Tennyson's description of woodland and forest scenes one might almost fancy that he can catch the exact peculiarities of sound in the rustling and moaning of each separate tree. In some of Mr. Browning's pictures of Italian scenery every detail is so perfect that many a one journeying along an Italian road and watching the little mouse-colored cattle as they drink at the stream, may for the moment almost feel uncertain whether he is looking on a page of living reality or recalling to memory a page from the author of *The Ring and the Book*. The poets seem to have returned to the fresh simplicity of a far-distant age of poetry, when a man described exactly what he saw, and was put to describing it because he saw it.

SELECTIONS FROM
THE POETICAL WORKS OF
ROBERT BROWNING

1880

215. From an unsigned review,
The British Quarterly Review

1 July 1880, 2nd Ser. lxxii. 235–6

Mr. Browning, as every one knows, is not seldom abstruse; more concerned to make manifest the hidden and recondite and unexpected relations of his subject than to deal with the more general and apparent aspects of it. It may be that he has thus sacrificed popularity; but he has maintained individuality, and made it necessary that every student of literature should study him. This volume will have the good affect of showing that he can deal effectively with common things; and that his peculiar style is due as much to choice as to necessity. The very first poem, 'The Flower's Name', may stand as a companion to 'Evelyn Hope', included in the first series; and 'The Garden Fancies' are full of character. 'St. Martin's Sermons'[1] and 'James Lee's Wife' are, in their different ways, exquisite. We are not quite sure if 'Numphaleptos', 'Sludge the Medium', and 'Bishop Blougram's Apology', are quite so suitable for such a collection; but here they are. We vastly prefer 'May and Death', and some of the simpler lyrics.

[1] The correct title, of course, is 'St. Martin's Summer'.

216. Gerard Manley Hopkins on Browning

1881

Gerard Manley Hopkins, from a letter of 12 October 1881, *The Correspondence of Gerard Manley Hopkins and Richard Watson Dixon*, ed. C. C. Abbott (1955), pp. 74–5.

This variation of the common theme that Browning exercised too little care in the poetic art is the more interesting because it comes from a poet whose work is marked by, and in part valued for, an almost obsessive attention to poetic detail.

I read some, not much, of *The Ring and the Book*, but as the tale was not edifying and one of our people, who had been reviewing it, said that further on it was coarser, I did not see, without a particular object, sufficient reason for going on with it. So far as I read I was greatly struck with the skill in which he displayed the facts from different points of view: this is masterly, and to do it through three volumes more shews a great body of genius. I remember a good case of 'the impotent collection of particulars' of which you speak in the description of the market place at Florence where he found the book of the trial: it is a pointless photograph of still life, such as I remember in Balzac, minute upholstery description; only that in Balzac, who besides is writing prose, all tells and is given with a reserve and simplicity of style which Browning has not got. Indeed I hold with the oldfashioned criticism that Browning is not really a poet, that he has all the gifts but the one needful and the pearls without the string; rather one should say raw nuggets and rough diamonds. I suppose him to resemble Ben Jonson, only that Ben Jonson has more real poetry.

217. An Address to the Browning Society

1881

J. Kirkman, from his 'Introductory Address to the Browning Society' (28 October 1881), *Browning Studies*, ed. Edward Berdoe (1895), pp. 1–20.

Kirkman's address, despite his opening disclaimer, set the tone for most of the Society's efforts to spread the fame of their poet, with the result that an inevitable reaction followed (see No. 225, for example).

Although we cannot and would not shoulder Browning up into a factitious popularity that would be sure to become extinct like fireworks, we may be instrumental in organizing, developing, and cultivating, the recognition, which is the first element in our *raison d'être*, that Browning is undoubtedly the profoundest intellect, with widest range of sympathies, and with universal knowledge of men and things, that has arisen as a poet since Shakespeare. In knowledge of many things he is necessarily superior to Shakespeare, as being the all-receptive child of the century of science and travel. In carefulness of construction, and especially in the genius of constructing drama, he claims not comparison with Shakespeare. But his truly Shakespearian genius pre-eminently shines in his power to throw his whole intellect and sympathies into the most diverse individualities; to think and feel as one of them would, although undoubtedly glorified by Browning's genius within.

218. The Browning Society at Cambridge

1881

Unsigned notice, *The Academy* (5 November 1881), xx. 345.

The preliminary meeting of the Cambridge Browning Society is to be held at Mr. Bradshaw's rooms, at King's, on the evening of Friday, November 11. The chair will be taken by the Rev. Prof. Westcott; a paper will be read on 'Browning as a Poet', by Dr. Charles Waldstein; and the society will then be formally organized. The intention is to develop the society into one for the more thorough study and deeper appreciation of modern literature, making Browning, as *the* representative modern English poet, the centre of the society's work.

219. The Imperial Genius

1881

James (B.V.) Thomson, from his article 'The Ring and the Book', *Gentleman's Magazine* (December 1881), ccli (NS xxvii). 682–95.

Thomson (1834–82) is best known for his powerful but despairing poem, *The City of Dreadful Night*. His empathy with Meredith and with the Browning of *The Ring and the Book* can probably be attributed to their 'realism'.

Certain rare works of literature, like others of art and philosophy, appear too gigantic to have been wholly wrought out each by the one man who we yet know did accomplish it unaided. Such a work reminds us of a great cathedral, which, even if ultimately finished in accordance with the plans of the supreme architect who designed it, could not be completed under his own supervision or during his own lifetime, being too vast and elaborate for fulfilment in a single generation. And as such a colossal work *The Ring and the Book* has always impressed me. And, indeed, without straining comparison, one may pursue with regard to it the suggestion of a great Gothic cathedral. For here truly we find the analogues of the soaring towers and pinnacles, the multitudinous niches with their statues, the innumerable intricate traceries, the gargoyles wildly grotesque; and, within, the many-coloured light through the stained windows with the red and purple of blood predominant, the long pillared echoing aisles, the altar with its piteous crucifix and altarpiece of the Last Judgment, the organ and the choir pealing their *Miserere* and *De Profundis* and *In Excelsis Deo*, the side chapels, the confessionals, the phantastic wood-carvings, the tombs with their effigies sculptured supine; and beneath, yet another chapel, as of death, and the solemn sepulchral crypts. The counterparts of all this and all these, I dare affirm, may veritably be found in this immense and complicate structure, whose foundations are so deep and whose crests are so lofty.

[Here Thomson summarizes the twelve books intelligently and sympathetically.]

As I have said already, these iterations and reiterations of the same terrible story, told by so many typical and historical personages as beheld from so many standpoints, are the very reverse of monotonous; each new relation tends to deepen and expand the impression left by all that preceded it. The persistent repetition is as that of the smith's hammer-strokes welding the red-hot iron into shape; or rather as that of the principal theme in a great Beethoven fugue, growing ever more and more potent and predominant as its vast capabilities are more and more developed through countless intricate variations and transmutations of time and key and structure and accompaniment. Only, to adequately evolve these capabilities, we must have the consummate master; an imperial genius wielding unlimited resources; an insuppressible irresistible fire fed with inexhaustible fuel. I know of but one other living English poet to whom we can turn for the like supreme analytical synthesis, the patient analysis of a most subtle and unappeasable intellect, the organic synthesis of a most vivid and dramatic imagination; which the better critics at length publicly recognised in *The Egoist*, after almost ignoring or wholly underrating them in the *Modern Love*, *The Ordeal of Richard Feverel*, the *Emilia in England*, *The Adventures of Harry Richmond*, and other great original works of George Meredith.

JOCOSERIA

March 1883

220. Richard Holt Hutton, *The Spectator*

17 March 1883, lvi. 351–3

Hutton (1826–97), principal of University Hall, London, was active as an editor (*The Spectator*, *The Economist*, *National Review*) and wrote much literary and theological criticism. The following is from his unsigned review.

Mr. Browning might have taken as a motto for his work as a poet one of Cardinal Newman's striking verses:

> Can Science bear us
> To the hid springs
> Of human things?
> Why may not dream,
> Or thought's day-gleam,
> Startle, yet cheer us?[1]

He never publishes a volume in which there is not some protest against the notion that Science can bear us to the hid springs of human things. He never publishes a volume without pressing and even urging on us that dreams and thought's day-gleams *may* startle, yet cheer us. And almost all he does for us is done by the startling method. He loves to awaken the sleep of the intellect, the sleep of the affections, the sleep of the spirit, by some sudden shock to which we respond by a sort of jump. His very rhymes are often carefully designed to electrify, as we shall soon see; but his constructions are still more so,—indeed, he may be said to have anticipated Wagner in the use of discords, if that were really the secret in the art of the great musician who has lately left us,—

[1] From Newman's 1833 poem, 'Wanderings'.

a matter on which the present writer is profoundly incompetent to pass any judgment. Abruptness is Mr. Browning's secret. Take the prefatory poem to his new volume of *Jocoseria*, just published by Smith and Elder, a poem which is the nearest thing to a lyric that the book contains, and nevertheless, though a lyric, is a succession of slight shocks:

> Wanting is—what?
> Summer redundant,
> Blueness abundant,
> —Where is the spot?
> Beamy the world, yet a blank all the same,
> —Framework which waits for a picture to frame:
> What of the leafage, what of the flower?
> Roses embowering with nought they embower!
> Come then, complete incompletion, O comer,
> Pant through the blueness, perfect the summer!
> Breathe but one breath
> Rose beauty above,
> And all that was death
> Grows life, grows love,
> Grows love!

How abruptly the opening interrogation breaks upon us. How enigmatic the reply;—we do not mean that its drift is not soon enough apprehended, but that on the first blush the reply seems to be explaining not the essence of the state of want, but the essence of those conditions which ought most to satisfy want. And then, how curiously elliptic is the question,—'Where is the spot?' Of course, what Mr. Browning means is something of this sort,—'Where is the spot where the redundant summer and the abundant blueness find their way into the soul so as to satisfy it?' But that is carrying ellipsis to the point of an electric shock, for it is startling merely to feel how much of the poet's meaning we are expected to gather from his hints, and supply in part from our own resources. Then the adjective 'beamy', which is chosen to describe the world, is unquestionably an odd one for the purpose, and chosen, as we should say, for the jerk it administers to the imagination. Nothing, on the whole, could express the sense of a blank somewhere, which the poet wants to express, better than these sudden little tugs and jerks at the reader's mind. But then, again, when he wants to indicate what would best fill in the blank, and give a rounded completion to the desolate framework, one is startled afresh to find that the new power which is to give us this, and which is 'to complete incompletion', is expected to 'pant through the blueness', and so to 'perfect the summer'. Could anything that 'panted' really 'complete incompletion'? The phrase suggests a locomotive rather than a divine presence. That which breathes a breath of rose-beauty, surely ought *not* to pant. But Mr. Browning loves spasm, loves successive shocks of thought or feeling, and can hardly deny himself the satisfaction of thinking that even the spirit of perfect love and harmony is perpetually starting this dull world by galvanising it with vivid spasms of thought and feeling, such as he himself has the skill to administer.

So it is with almost every remarkable poem in Mr. Browning's new volume. The rhythm, the rhyme, the thought, the feeling are all chosen to strike sparks out of the reader's mind, as the steel strikes sparks out of a flint; and the result naturally is that the reader feels towards Mr. Browning somewhat as a bit of flint might feel which has served this purpose to a fragment of steel,—a little sore and a little fractured. . . . It is Mr. Browning's method of startle as often and as smartly as he can the imagination he appeals to, and to indicate rather than state, the directions he wishes their minds to follow. It is this which makes Mr. Browning at his best and vividest the most awakening of writers, the one who most signally arrests the attention, and most successfully insists on his reader's lending him the whole force of his own mind. But for that very reason, his work is almost always defective as poetry. The part of it which he does for us is too incisive, too short, sharp, and sudden, for anything like harmony; and the part which he obliges us to do for him in order to enter into his drift, is too imperfectly done to succeed in connecting the isolated points which he has jotted down for us into the flowing curve of true beauty. Mr. Browning touches life, especially the life of the intellect and the spirit, at as many points as any poet who ever wrote; but he does not blend these touches into the true poetic vision. He awakens and educates the highest imaginative powers, but he does not attempt to satisfy their cravings.

221. Browning's Originality

1883

From an unsigned review, *The Saturday Review* (24 March 1883), lv. 376–7.

Some of the poems in Mr. Browning's last volumes are open to criticism; but, like all his writings, they are thoroughly original in choice of subjects, in treatment, and in style. It may be thought an ambiguous form of praise to say that there is not a line which could have been written by any one but himself. It is highly satisfactory to find that after a poetical career which extends over nearly fifty years Mr. Browning's characteristic vigour is in no degree abated. Some part of his deep, if not wide, popularity is undoubtedly owing to the enigmatic method which is closely connected with his habitual study of moral or intellectual complications and paradoxes. Complacency in the successful solution of a riddle facilitates appreciation of the imaginative skill with which it has been constructed. A careful and experienced student of Mr. Browning's poetry can almost always ascertain his meaning, feeling meanwhile a just confidence that the result will be well worth the labour which it has cost. It is not known whether the odd Society which was formed to interpret Mr. Browning still maintains its existence. It may perhaps, notwithstanding the whimsical nature of the project, have served as a symbol of the special attraction which he exercises over minds in which the receptive faculty bears a certain relation to his genius. Possibly some of his admirers may find pleasure in gratuitous deviation into familiarity or doggerel. If the word *Jocoseria* were legitimately formed, it would express with some degree of accuracy the gravely playful element which is to be found in all Mr. Browning's poems, and especially in those of the last ten years. It may be added, at the risk of provoking contempt on the part of the author, that there is no humour in putting into the mouth of the Queen of Sheba such a phrase as, Construe, or *vulgo conster*. He might even have omitted the address to Solomon which invites an absurd rhyme, as 'World's marvel, and well-nigh monster.' If it was expedient to retain for the subject of a long and abstruse poem the uncouth name of Jochanan Hakkadosh, the final syllable need not have been placed at the end of a line. The inevitable consequence is the insertion of the inelegant ejaculation. 'Scoffer, spare thy bosh!' The word may possibly be admissible in Persian literature; but it is neither graceful nor English. Fortunately there are not many instances of similarly barbarous jingle. A little skit at the profanity of critics receives the title of 'Pambo', that it may rhyme with one Latin and one French word:

> Brother, brother, I share the blame,
> *Arcades sumus ambo!*
> Darkling I keep my sunrise-aim,
> Lack not the critic's flambeau,
> And *look to my ways*, yet, much the same,
> *Offend with my tongue*—like Pambo!

Little slips of the tongue, especially when they are intentional, are not worth defending. The critic's *flambeau* does no disservice to the poet in throwing occasional light on passages which are not absolutely transparent. In one instance Mr. Browning himself has thought that the poem on Jochanan requires an illustrative note; but, as he has thought fit to use the Hebrew language and character, it is possible that some of his readers may be little the better for his considerate assistance.

222. John Addington Symonds, *The Academy*

31 March 1883, xxiii. 213–14

This book displays Mr. Browning's well-known qualities, not at the prime, indeed, and height of his achievement, but nowhere markedly below its average. Some critics have already gone far afield in quest of the title—so far even as to a Dutch or German Swertzius, whose name Sterne might have placed beside that of Slawkenbergius in *Tristram Shandy*. *Jocoseria*, however, as a title, needs no commentary; it only invites the casual remark that, when we have exhausted the rather middling humour of two title pieces upon Adam and the Queen of Sheba, the remaining poems in this volume, with the further exception of an apologetic Envoy, are serious. 'Ixion', indeed, is grimly, powerfully tragic. After a lyrical introduction, a dim but graceful invocation to love considered as the final bloom on life, Mr. Browning opens with a vigorous, humane, dramatic tale of the Scotch Highlands called 'Donald.' Sharp and keen, he here thrusts the blade of a true story, more trenchant than satire or than sermon, into the sophistries whereby sportsmen are wont to palliate the brutalities and cruelties of their amusements. This poem—the best, I think, as it certainly is the clearest, in the book—ought not to be spoiled by description or quotation. It should be read with glowing cheek and a beating heart.

223. Browning and Carlyle Compared

1883

From an unsigned review, *The Athenæum* (24 May 1883), i. 367–8.

Just as the originality of the ornithorhynchus does not make that interesting creature a higher organism than a horse, so the originality of Carlyle does not make him a greater prose writer than Swift, and the originality of Mr. Browning does not make him a greater poet than Shakspeare. Between Mr. Browning and Carlyle there is, perhaps, some kind of affinity, as we have before hinted; but there is this fundamental difference between them, that while Carlyle's originality is mostly, if not always, an originality *voulue*, Mr. Browning's originality is, beyond all doubt, a genuine and inevitable expression of idiosyncrasy, a fact which this volume shows as clearly as does any of its predecessors. . . .

Though *Jocoseria* is not rich nor so full as Mr. Browning's last volume, our extracts will show how far it is from indicating any decline in his dazzling and unique powers. There is the same alertness, the same exuberance of vitality, the same unrivalled intellectual subtlety, the same brilliant wit and searching humour, with which he has been familiarizing us for many years.

224. George Parsons Lathrop, *Atlantic Monthly*

June 1883, li. 840–3

From his review.

Lathrop (1851–98), literary critic and Nathaniel Hawthorne's son-in-law, was an editor of the *Atlantic Monthly* (1875–77) and a frequent contributor to its pages.

An author's influence upon other authors may be expressed in terms of either attraction or repulsion; and the one who repels is often found to be the one whose influence is deepest although it be more tardily acknowledged. Today Robert Browning exhibits the most sharply accented personality among writers of English poetry; and his latest publication proves that he is not likely to lose the distinction with advancing age. . . .

Beauty and ugliness, the lovely and the grotesque, must according to his practice be treated with a commanding impartiality, which shall leave chiefly with the reader the task of striking the balance. Hence proceed his many deficiencies of form; and the same cause may be assigned for the result that his eminence as a dramatist (not for the modern stage) is hardly surpassed by his power as a writer of lyrical and meditative verse. Such a man must be equally capable in the management of several dissimilar modes of imparting thought. It is not surprising, either that his impartiality should issue in something allied to a buoyant indifference, which might be said fitly to terminate with a collection like *Jocoseria*; because we find in its contents a mingling of sober and even tragic elements with others of a facetious or half-cynical cast, and there runs through the whole a vein of mildly contemptuous pity for the lot of mankind, their illusions, their meannesses, aspirations, and self-deceits.

'Darkling, I keep my sunrise-aim,'

he reminds us, in the closing lines of *Jocoseria*. He keeps on asserting his personality, too, with spontaneous vehemence. He is more various, though lyrically less great and in art less well-balanced, than Tennyson. The most masculine nature and the most subtile perception of character owned by any contemporary English poet are admitted to be his. And yet he is not the leader of the younger school, which—for instance through one of its most skilled and winning representatives, Mr. Edmund Gosse—shows a decided affinity with Rossetti. On the other hand we know that Rossetti himself, in the earlier part of his career, felt deeply the influence of Browning. Is there not some plausibility in the speculation that the younger men, by following Rossetti, will turn out to have been paying tribute indirectly to the genius which at first commanded Rossetti's own? The fact that their work moves in a direction so opposed to Browning's ought perhaps to be regarded as merely one swing of the pendulum, which will be followed by an action precisely reverse. But, whatever the case may be as to that point, one will very naturally look to this latest volume by the author of *Sordello* and *The Ring and the Book* for some further clue as to what the 'sunrise-aim' really has been, to which he alludes. Without entering into any lengthy analysis, we may say that it has consisted apparently in a resolve to depict through the medium of verse, regardless of technical tradition, every possible phase of life just as it chanced to impress the writer. All the jagged prominences, the deep abysses of crime or imperfection, the strange sinuosities of passion eating its way into the heart of man, the dewy valleys in which pure love rests, the sudden bursts of feeling, the stretches of barrenness not without meaning, which present themselves on a general view of human nature, were to be reproduced as if upon a raised map; or we might say by means of an orrery, having suitable apparatus to demonstrate the movements of bodies terrestrial and celestial. Mr. Browning's own comment was to supply a sort of poetic anthropology. There had always been a somewhat scientific bias in his view of life; but it was empirical, wanting in method, and continually swayed this way or that by a desire for purely poetic expression. The very essence of his aim, however, seems to have been to avoid bringing observation within the bounds of any symmetrical or classically moulded design. . . .

225. A Rebute to Officious Supporters

1884

From an unsigned article, 'The Browning Society', *The Saturday Review* (6 December 1884), lviii. 721–2.

Whenever the Browning Society gives token of its existence, it is impossible to avoid wondering what the more intelligent of the members think of one poem in particular, that entitled *At the "Mermaid."* This work was written several years before a number of well-meaning but unnecessarily officious persons decided upon taking up and patronizing a poet who must surely feel a sense of grim amusement at such patronage. Many writers have claimed for poets the power of prophecy since Cicero approved what Ennius said of those whose gifts were from the gods.[1] Does it not appear as if Mr. Browning had foreseen the establishment of the Browning Society, and had with prophetic accuracy estimated the company of its members when he asked—

> Which of you did I enable
>   Once to slip inside my breast,
> There to catalogue and label
>   What I like least, what love best,
> Hope and fear, believe and doubt of,
>   Seek and shun, respect—deride?
> Who has right to make a rout of
>   Rarities he found inside?

Does not this fit to a nicety? Mr. Browning is the most independent of poets. He appeals to his own audience, take him or leave him. ' 'Tis said I brew stiff drink,' he remarks in one of his poems—'Epilogue.' It pleases him to supply 'stuff for strength', instead of the 'sheer sweet' which it is the desire of many poets to pour forth; and he does what he pleases. If he chose he could provide prime wine 'of potable strength, with sweet to match'; but he in no way seeks popularity for his own peculiar vintage, and if he does not seek it himself, still less does he need

[1] *De Divinatione*, I. lviii. 132.

485

a Society to seek popularity for him. The strength and the weakness of Mr. Browning are perfectly perceived by intelligent students of English literature. 'Tous les grands hommes ont toujours du caprice, quelque petit grain de folie mêlé à leur science,' Molière says, and of this truth Mr. Browning is an example. His fatal facility for rhyming leads him— as in *Pacchiarotto* especially— into excesses which are often only irritating; beyond all doubt he is frequently obscure: if readers 'cough and blink' they have reason; at times he passes from the fanciful to the fantastic, and on to the grotesque. Nevertheless, Mr. Browning is a great writer, a true poet, and those who perceive this most strongly are those who most resent the tone of the Society. A number of very little men hang on to the tails of a very big man, endeavour thus to acquire a little easy reputation for themselves, and assume meantime an air as though they were helping the big man forward.

FERISHTAH'S FANCIES

November 1884

226. Walter Theodore Watts-Dunton, A Poet Without Dignity

1884

From his unsigned review, *The Athenæum* (6 December 1884), pp. 725–7.

For Watts-Dunton's opinion of *La Saisiaz*, see No. 206.

Here, as elsewhere, that which gives the special flavour to his work is his unequalled faculty of keeping his eye fixed firm and straight upon human life and of telling what he sees—telling it always in his own bright, lively, if too mannered and fantastic way, for it must always be remembered that, notwithstanding his love of displaying his learning and his miscellaneous knowledge of books, no man is less of a book-poet than he. The charm of Landor's poetry is, as we have said on a previous occasion, that of 'subtle reminders of the great poets of old'; the charm of Mr. Browning's poetry is that it reminds us of nothing but Mr. Browning. That which gives vitality to his work is not book-lore, we say, but the lore that can be only learnt by deep and sympathetic study of man and woman—men and women. Between the outer world and the eyes of most modern poets of a high order there floats an artistic atmosphere through which the poet must needs gaze if he gaze at all. This atmosphere, while it transfigures and enobles human life, gives it also a certain quality which may perhaps be called a dignified remoteness. What the artistic poet gains in dignity, however, he loses in other ways. As a witness of the human drama, for instance, he loses in apparent trustworthiness and apparent authority. 'The light that never was on sea or land' is apt to fall with a somewhat chilling effect

487

upon this our real land where men and women live and love and hate and strive. Mr. Browning's muse knows no such light, gazes at the world through no atmosphere of the golden clime, but confronts life with the frank familiar eyes with which the actors in the real drama gaze at each other. This lends his work a freshness peculiar to itself, but gives it also that air of familiarity which is the proper quest of the prose delineator of human life rather than that of the poet. It is no wonder, then, that of all high-class poets he is the most entirely without dignity. There is no turn of phrase so familiar that he will shrink from it. There is no ingenuity of rhythm or rhyme that is too common and too cheap for him. It is difficult to understand the mood into which a poet of high genius and culture could have passed when he considered such rhymes as the following suited to any kind of verse save that of the cockney burlesque:

> Pray, Reader, have you eaten ortolans
>   Ever in Italy?
> Recall how cooks there cook them: for my plan's
>   To—Lyre with Spit ally.
> They pluck the birds,—some dozen luscious lumps,
>   Or more or fewer,—
> Then roast them, heads by heads and rumps by rumps,
>   Stuck on a skewer.

Nothing is easier than such ingenuity as this if a writer will give his mind to it. What, then, could have induced Mr. Browning to begin so fine a book of poetry with such verses? Spite, however, of a few blemishes such as these, Mr. Browning's admirers will welcome this volume.

227. As Wilful as Ever

1884

From an unsigned review, *The Saturday Review* (6 December 1884), lviii. 727–8.

The idea that Browning had a special appeal to those who liked to solve literary puzzles gained currency during the 1880s. See also No. 221.

Every new volume of Mr. Browning's affords fresh proof that he is as vigorous, as fertile, and as wilful as ever. His late poems have for the most part had a narrative form, and therefore they have not placed an extraordinary strain on the faculties of the reader. On the present occasion he has reverted to the didactic and enigmatic style. Ferishtah, a dervish who is a kind of Persian Socrates, propounds to successive disciples mysterious doctrines, sometimes expressed in parables, and for the most part tending to the refutation of their supposed errors. It is not surprising that the oracular response should, until its full import has been mastered, appear perplexing and ambiguous. Profundity is, as Mr. Browning explained in a satirical poem published a few years ago, mistaken for obscurity merely because it is intrinsically difficult of expression. A great thought requires a corresponding phrase, whereas the geese to whom Mr. Browning unkindly compared his critics had no difficulty in finding a vehicle for their simple conceptions. 'Plain quack, quack,' said the poet, 'is easily uttered.' The victims of his sarcasm reminded him in vain that 'quack' is the note of the duck and not of the goose. His contempt would not be modified by the substitution of cackling for quacking. It is perhaps presumptuous to wish that Ferishtah or the author of his being could bring hard sayings within the reach of the ordinary understanding; but genius must be accepted in the shape which it condescends to assume, and the student well knows that Mr. Browning's riddles are worth solving, both on account of the meaning which may be eventually disclosed, and for the pleasure of observing the elaborate art with which the puzzles have been constructed. One of the reasons of Mr. Browning's popularity is the activity of mind which he stimulates by insisting on laborious efforts to appreciate his imaginative wisdom. The successful interpreter feels proud of his collaboration with the poet, and he would be ill pleased to learn that his labour and ingenuity have been wasted. On two or three occasions, as if distrustful of the resources of English in disguising thought, Mr. Browning quotes passages from the Old Testament in the Hebrew language and character. In one of these instances he adds the authorized version of the passage, 'Does Job serve God for nought?' Hebrew scholars will probably find the other quotations equally appropriate. It is to be hoped that Mr. Browning, who began the same practice in a former publication, will be merciful in his future employment of unknown or out-of-the-way tongues. *Ferishtah's Fancies* are not, like one or two of Mr. Browning's poems, dependent for comprehension on an external cipher.

228. Browning and Shakespeare Compared

1886

From an unsigned review, *The London Quarterly Review* (January 1886), lxv. 238–50.

This view is typical of many late nineteenth- and early twentieth-century commentators who admired Browning so much as a philosopher-poet that they provoked an inevitable reaction in the period 1910–30, a reaction from which Browning has not yet fully recovered.

The poetry of Browning, far more than that of Tennyson or Swinburne, is a growth. His career, while seeming at each point of its progress to be defiantly stationary, has been in reality one continuous march; a march in the course of which he has resolutely thrown aside, one by one, everything hampering to a direct passage. The progress, being gradual and continuous, and extending from 1833 to 1884, has naturally led a long way. To read in the *Pauline* of 1833, say, the lines commencing—

> Night, and one single ridge of narrow path
> Between the sullen river and the woods;

and on laying down the book to turn to the *Ferishtah's Fancies* of 1884, and read—

> 'Look, I strew beans,' resumed Ferishtah, 'beans
> Blackish and whitish,'

is to experience the sensation of one who should step from Italy to Iceland. But, let it be remembered, this is only in matters of style, of technique. In tone and intention there is no body of poetry known to us more consistent in its unity than that of Browning. The thing he wishes to say is the same now as it was long ago; it is only the manner of saying it that has changed.

And what is the thing that he wishes to say? This is a light question to ask, but it needs a long answer. Browning is not one of those who may be dismissed when you have complimented them on their pretty tunes. His aim has never been to please our ears by the tinkle and jingle of rhyme, or even, primarily, by the music of rhythm, but to sing such songs as should not slip easily into our minds, nor easily slip out of them. To be accounted a poet, is to him to be held that which the Greeks meant when they said, not singer, but maker—Ποιητής. The poetry of most of our modern masters is directed to other ends than that of *making*. They sing with Shelley, meditate with Wordsworth, dream with Keats, declaim with Byron. But the poetry of Browning is neither an attempt to sing, nor to meditate, nor to dream, nor to declaim. It may be all of these, in measure, at times; but in aim it is none of them. It is rather an endeavour to create. It is concerned with live men and women, with their thoughts and loves and hates, with their creeds, their whims, their passions, their hopes, fears, struggles, conquests, defeats; with these as an object, not as a means; in their entirety and nakedness, as they subsist in the soul, not so much in a cunning adjustment of them to the require-ments of the modern theatre.

Browning's art is essentially dramatic, but essentially untheatrical. Elsewhere we have tried to show that his informal drama of the soul may be claimed as the nineteenth century equivalent—equivalent, observe, not imitation—of the formal drama of action which flourished gloriously in the right sixteenth-century soil. His drama has all the life of action, but it is not action. It is as if one caught a wave at its poise, and held it for a moment, motionless with all its suspended thrill and fury of movement. In an eloquent pause and silence, when life lived to the fullest culminates in one crisis of joy, pain, passion, or disgust, Browning seizes and possesses his opportunity. Into that one moment he crowds the thought, action and emotion of a lifetime; the poem will be a little drama, perhaps only fifty lines, but yet *multum in parvo*, instinct with vitality and suggestion.

It is this aim of dramatic picturing that Browning has always had before him—an aim, as we have shown, at expressing, with the utmost delicacy of perfection, in a word, with the utmost *truth*, every phase and feature of the human mind. Co-existent with this primary aim, there is another and secondary. Browning is not merely a great dramatist but a great thinker. 'Browning is the greatest thinker in poetry since Shakespeare', we have heard it said; and the remark appears to us no exaggeration. Like Shakespeare, too, he has that universality, that range of philosophic insight, that profound and subtle sympathy with every form of individual belief, which can seem to embrace opposites. Shakespeare, as we know, has been proved everything, from devout Christian to blasphemous Atheist. Papers have been read before the Browning Society in which the modern poet has been credited with almost as many creeds as his predecessor. And in the case of Browning at least, whatever may be the fact as to Shakespeare, this is not to be attributed to any vagueness or indifference on the part of the poet, but wholly to the breadth of his grasp on many-sided truth, and the sureness of his dramatic method. Unlike Shakespeare, however, our ultimate pattern and guide in all things, Browning has not possessed the art of always clothing his thought in the garb of grace which should belong to poetry.

A BLOT REVIVED

1885

229. An unsigned review, *The Athenæum*

9 May 1885, p. 610

This review ought to be compared with those published in 1843. See Nos. 47–52.

Since it was given, February 11th, 1843, at Drury Lane Theatre, with Mr. Phelps as Tresham, *The Blot in the 'Scutcheon* of Mr. Robert Browning has, we believe, been a stranger to the stage. A revival attempted under the patronage of the Browning Society at St. George's Hall, though carried out by amateurs, has, accordingly some interest. The general representation, though justice was not done to the strongest situations, was creditable. The impression conveyed is that which naturally presents itself on perusal, that the piece is a dramatic sketch rather than a drama. When once the stronger passages are reached the interest is sufficient to hold the public in a firm grip. Many passages are, however, too purely psychological for dramatic effect, and the period of their introduction is not seldom inopportune. It is pleasant to hear the more nervous passages, just as it is pleasant to read them. The work gains, however, comparatively little from representation, and will always be more of a favourite in the closet than on the boards. In giving it at the St. George's Hall the action, with the consent of the author, was carried back a century to the early Stuart period. Under these circumstances one or two trifling alterations of text were called for. The reference to periwigs becomes an anachronism, and should be omitted.

493

PARLEYINGS WITH CERTAIN PEOPLE OF IMPORTANCE IN THEIR DAY

January 1887

230. Richard Holt Hutton, *The Spectator*

5 February 1887, lx. 181-2

Hutton wrote elsewhere of Browning. See Nos. 220 and 238.

Mr. Browning does not condescend more generously to the minds of his readers in age than he did in youth. The Dean of St. Paul's, in the gracious and exquisitely written interpretation of *Sordello* which he has just put forth in *Macmillan's Magazine*, says very justly that the readers of that enigmatic poem feel that they are 'in strong hands, and with eyes that have really seen,—seen, with keenness, with truth, with thought,— only their owner is not disposed to save us any trouble in making us see what he has seen.'[1] Say rather that Mr. Browning, in such works as *Sordello* and the present volume, is determined to give his readers more trouble than ninety-nine out of a hundred readers of poetry will take, in catching even a glimpse of what he means to say; that he appears to wish to sift out the keen-sighted and painstaking readers from among the dull-sighted and careless readers, and to spare himself the indignity of receiving either admiration or so much as misunderstanding on the part of the latter,—for we will venture to say that without considerable effort, the greater number of these pages cannot even be *mis*understood; they will simply present to the superficial reader a face of perfect inscrutability. In the first place, the 'persons of importance in their day'

[1] Dean Richard William Church (1815-90) published his article in *Macmillan's Magazine* (February 1887), lv. 241-53. The essay was reprinted in his *Dante and Other Essays* (1888), which in turn was reprinted a number of times.

494

with whom Mr. Browning converses, are not, on the whole, remembered at all in our day. The present writer knew that Bernard de Mandeville had written *A Fable of the Bees*; that Christopher Smart had translated Horace into very poor prose; and that George Bubb Dodington was a corrupt politician. But of the other 'persons of importance in their day' he had never heard. Bartoli, Furini, De Lairesse, and Charles Avison were not even names to him. That, however, does not add much to the difficulty; for Mr. Browning gives us enough hints as to the character of the persons with whom he holds discourse, to apprehend his meaning if he would but expound his meaning with more care and continuity of thought. But this is just what he will not do. He frequentlyd ashes off, suddenly and without warning, at at angent to his previous train of thought; he is habitually highly elliptical; he often leaves it a matter of guesswork to whom his various pronouns refer. All this makes the mastery of Mr. Browning's drift an effort of no mean kind; and though he constantly gives one a brilliant glimpse of landscape, or a quaint touch of humour, to reward one's progress, it is with the sense of walking down a long and dark passage, with here and there, in an embrasure, a window commanding a fine view, that we toil through his volume,—which has hardly, indeed, enough unity of subject to make the whole, when read, a very lucid commentary on the more obscure parts.

In general, we should say,—judging by the discussion in the Prologue between Apollo and the Fates, and by the Epilogue on the inventor of printing, as well as by the drift of several of the separate poems,—that it has been Mr. Browning's chief object to show that life is an exceedingly complex matter, in which evil and good are so indissolubly interwoven that the very thread which seems evil in one light seems good in another, and the tares seem as necessary to the wheat as the ground from which it grows. . . .

231. From an unsigned review, *The Athenæum*

19 February 1887, pp. 247-9

The people parleyed with are Bernard de Mandeville, Daniel Bartoli, Christopher Smart, George Bubb Dodington, Francis Furini, Gerard de Lairesse, and Charles Avison—a heterogeneous group, some members of it not very familiar to us! The 'parleying' that will, we think, best please the mere exoteric reader is the one with Gerard de Lairesse, the painter and critic who in the plenitude of his powers was struck blind. In it are descriptive passages of extraordinary excellence—passages which Mr. Browning alone, perhaps, could have written. . . .

We are by no means sure that poets in creating imaginary characters will in future times continue to think it worth their while to christen them after the characters of history, calling them Thomas à Becket, Mary Stuart, Paracelsus, Sordello, Bernard de Mandeville, and what not. We are by no means sure that they will always consider themselves justified in doing so. They have, no doubt, the highest authority for this kind of dramatic art—the very highest; but then as regards Mr. Browning, he sets himself to spurning authority in art. As Carlyle has said, the mere facts of history have a special and peculiar preciousness of their own just because they are facts and not poetic fancies about facts. However, this is too large a question to be discussed here. And after all Mr. Browning has again given us a book which will add to the wealth of English poetry, and if in the above remarks we have glanced with any excess of severity at what seem to us defects in his style, it is we who have cause to regret it; for assuredly, whatever may be his exact place in the poetry of the world, it is a high place somewhere among the immortals.

232. Margaret Oliphant,
Blackwood's Edinburgh Magazine

March 1887, cxli. 417–23

Mrs. Oliphant (1828–97), in addition to plying the critic's trade for *Blackwood's*, wrote an enormous number of novels, of which probably the best was *Salem Chapel* (1863). Her comment that Browning is 'too careless of popularity' is interesting in light of the great popularity her now-forgotten novels once enjoyed. The following is extracted from her unsigned feature, 'The Old Saloon'.

This volume will not, we fear, secure many more followers to the poet, too careless of popularity, who has injured his own acceptance by an indifference to the capacity and capabilities of the reader, which, perhaps, he has an abstract right to entertain if he so pleases, but for which he must pay, as all eccentrics have to do. But it will repay those who will make the effort of studying it; and amid the many lawless voices which disturb the harmony of nature it is well to find one so peculiar, so profoundly intellectual, in which there is no failure in respect to the fundamental principles of human life, the God above, the future before us. Mr. Browning is perhaps not very orthodox, but he is better than orthodox: and his manly and reasonable determination to accept 'Man's portion,' the 'truth in part, before entrusted with the whole,' is one with which all our sympathies go.

233. An unsigned notice,
The Westminster Review

April 1887, cxxviii. 132

In his last volume, *Parleyings with Certain People*, it must be admitted that Mr. Browning is harder and darker than ever. We are reminded of the intolerable puzzlement of *Fifine at the Fair*, rather than of the comparative perspicuity of *Jocoseria* and *Ferishtah's Fancies*. In the first place, the 'certain people who were of importance in their day' have died out of the remembrance of the world at large. Special, and perhaps accidental, study has revealed their existence to Mr. Browning, but to most of us they are names to be searched for in a biographical dictionary. And, secondly, the style is more than usually involved, and the drift harder to be discovered. The Prologue, which takes the form of a dialogue between Apollo and the Fates, appears to be a balancing of arguments for and against the possibility of happiness to man. The Fates maintain that all joy is an illusion, wrought by the bright beams of the Sun God. Apollo, with the help of a bowl of wine, strives to convince them that pleasure is real. It would appear from the issue that 'the Fates have it.' At best, man's life is a riddle. Sunshine and shade cross and re-cross, and at last—how else were life possible?—comes Death. The dramatic contrast of Apollo and the Moirai, and the marvellous way in which Mr. Browning has invested the 'night born hags' with a living personality, atones for much that is harsh and obscure. Of the Parleyings we prefer that with Francis Furini. A disquisition on the Nude resolves itself into a defence of the existence of a Cause. The picture of Joan of Arc bathing in the lake is in Mr. Browning's happiest manner. But what shall we say of 'Instigator Spasm' as a paraphrase for the 'Great First Cause?' Positivity of Negation, as certain Hegelians used to have it, is comparatively intelligible.

234. Edward Dowden, Browning's Poetry
A Galvanic Battery

1887

From his article, 'Victorian Literature', *Fortnightly Review* (June 1887), xlvii. 833–67.

For other of Dowden's opinions see Nos. 127 and 195. This sort of adulation, in the long run, did the poet's reputation little good.

If Mr. Arnold is the poet of our times who as poet could least resist *la maladie du siècle* in its subtler forms, he whose energy of heart and soul most absolutely rejects and repels its influence is Mr. Browning. To him this world appears to be a palæstra in which we are trained and tested for other lives to come; it is a gymnasium for athletes. Action, passion, knowledge, beauty, science, art—these are names of some of the means and instruments of our training and education. The vice of vices, according to his ethical creed, is languor of heart, lethargy or faintness of spirit, with the dimness of vision and feebleness of hand attending such moral enervation. Which of us does not suffer now and again from a touch of spiritual paralysis? Mr. Browning's poetry, to describe it in a word, is a galvanic battery for the use of spiritual paralytics. At first the shock and the tingling frightened patients away; now they crowd to the physician and celebrate the cure. Which of us does not need at times that virtue should pass into him from a stronger human soul? To touch the singing robes of the author of *Rabbi Ben Ezra* and *Prospice* and *The Grammarian's Funeral*, is to feel an influx of new strength. We gain from Mr. Browning, each in his degree, some of that moral ardour and spiritual faith and vigour of human sympathy which make interesting to him all the commonplace, confused, and ugly portions of life, those portions of life which, grating too harshly on Mr. Matthew Arnold's sensitiveness, disturb his self-possession and trouble his lucidity, causing him often, in his verse, to turn away from this vulgar, distracting world to quietism and solitude, or a refined self-culture that lacks the most masculine qualities of discipline. To preserve those spiritual truths which are most precious to him Mr. Browning does not retreat, like the singer of *In Memoriam*, into the citadel of the heart; rather, an armed combatant, he makes a sortie into the world of worldlings and unbelievers, and from among errors and falsehoods and basenesses and crimes, he captures new truths for the soul. It is not in calm meditation or a mystical quiet that the clearest perception of divine things comes to him; it is rather through the struggle of the will, through the strife of passion, and as much through foiled desire and defeated endeavour as through attainment and success. For asceticism, in the sense of that word which signifies a maiming and marring of our complete humanity, Mr. Browning's doctrine of life leaves no place; but if asceticism mean heroic exercise, the *askesis* of the athlete, the whole of human existence, as he conceives, is designed as a school of strenuous and joyous asceticism. 'Our human impulses towards knowledge, towards beauty, towards love,' it has been well said, 'are reverenced by him as the signs and tokens of a world not included in that which meets the senses.' Therefore, he must needs welcome the whole fulness of earthly beauty, as in itself good, but chiefly precious because it is a pledge and promise of beauty not partial and earthly, but in its heavenly plenitude. And how dare he seek to narrow or enfeeble the affections, when in all their errors and their never-satisfied aspirations, he discovers evidence of an infinite love, from which they proceed and towards which they tend? Nor would he stifle any high ambition, for it is a wing to the spirit lifting man towards heights of knowledge or passion or power which rise unseen beyond the things of sense, heights on which man hereafter may attain the true fulfilment of his destiny.

235. Edgar Fawcett, Adulation Rebuked

1888

From his article, 'The Browning Craze', *Lippincott's Monthly Magazine* (January 1888), xli. 81–96.

Fawcett (1847–1904) wrote satiric dramas centering on the old Dutch families in New York. His acid comments make a nice contrast with those of Edward Dowden (No. 234).

Critical surprise has been more than once expressed, of late, that in an age so militant against the development of the poetic spirit, a single man should find himself (and that, too, at an advanced period of his life) surrounded, not to say besieged, by hosts of ardent admirers. Everybody has now heard of the 'Browning Craze', and it is quite probable that many had heard of it while Mr. Robert Browning himself was hardly more to them than a meaningless name. And yet to the majority of literary men and women in England and America this cult has long been a familiar one. Not until perhaps a decade ago did it begin to assume its present spacious proportions. I remember meeting devout Browningites at least twenty years ago, when almost a boy. And as boys will, when their thoughts turn toward the letters of their time and land, I soon felt an ambitious craving to graduate into a Browningite myself.

Such a worship then possessed so fascinating an element of rarity! It was so attractive a role for one to give a compassionate lifting of the brows and say, 'No, really?' when somebody declared himself quite unable to understand the obscure author of *Sordello*. You knew perfectly well that any number of his lines were Hindostanee to you, and yet you made use of your patronizing pity and your 'No, really?' all the same. There is safety in the assertion that Mr. Browning has driven more pedantic youngsters to unblushing falsehood than any other writer in the language. . . .

One of the most distressing features about Mr. Browning's existent reputation—distressing, I mean, to those who discern and measure its basis of humbug—is the way in which his admirers are never tired of saying that it wholly outshines the renown of Lord Tennyson and that its possessor has touched, thus far in our century, the high-tide mark of English poetry. So, until not very long since, fanatics cried that Carlyle, with his barbarisms, loomed above that most masterly and dignified of writers, Macaulay; but now the brief prejudice of the hour has passed, and the morrows have begun to dole out equity, as they generally do, with no matter how tardy a service.

Never was a greater literary injustice perpetrated than the placing of Mr. Browning above Lord Tennyson. The Laureate has indeed served his art with a profound and lovely fidelity, while it is no exaggeration to state of Mr. Browning that he has not seldom insulted his as though it were a pickpocket.

236. 'The Easy Chair' on Browning in 1888

George William Curtis, from his unsigned column, 'The Editor's Easy Chair' (October 1888), lxxvii. 798–9.

Curtis, who by this time had been writing the 'Easy Chair' for thirty years, was a sensitive observer of the literary scene in America.

'The Easy Chair' heard the other day of a Browning club in a Western State which for some mysterious reason preferred not to be known as such, but which was betrayed by its own zeal and devotion. It decided to hold a reception at which everything should be brown. A brown tablecloth was covered with brown china. Brown bread and brown sugar held places of honor. The hosts appeared in brown dresses. Brown curtains were hung over the windows. Brown was universal, and when one of the guests, looking around the room, at last exclaimed, 'Well, I declare I really believe you are a Browning club,' there was no member in brown hardy enough to deny it. Matthew Arnold was in a remote and small village among the New England hills, which reminded him, he said, in some way of a solitary hamlet in the Tyrol. 'And what,' he asked, 'do the good people do for amusement?' 'Well,' said his companion, 'they had a lecture on Browning last week.' Arnold lifted up his hands in amazement and laughed, as he replied, 'I am evidently not in the Tyrol.'

The interest in Browning is a very striking and significant fact. He has never been a popular poet in England, although for nearly half a century he has been regarded as the only real competitor of Tennyson for the highest place in contemporary English poetry. Like Carlyle, he was first recognized in America as a literary figure of the first importance. He is too obscure a poet for the general reader. Very few of his poems are popular in the sense of the word as applied to Scott or Byron or Tennyson or Longfellow, and he has contributed few lines or phrases or characters to current and familiar speech. But no poet of the time seems to have taken stronger hold upon the enthusiasm of the readers of poetry in this country.

This is perhaps especially true of the West, where literary culture is sought by many young people with an ardor and earnestness which are remarkable. To such a class, the very fact of the obscurity of Browning's verse is an allurement, because it gives them a reason for devoted study and comparative interpretation. A Longfellow or Tennyson club would be constituted for the pleasure of reading the works of those poets, and perhaps of tracing their development from earlier literary influences and sources. But the meaning and purpose of their poetry and its general scope would not be a subject of investigation or discussion.

There is indeed the feeling in regard to the Browning club that the members are attracted by the god because he is unknown—*omne ignotum pro magnifico*. Yet it is not his obscurity alone which attracts, but the evident conviction that the mystery is but the cloud enveloping an Alp, on which the edelweiss blooms and the chamois leaps. Thackeray one day came in upon a friend reading Browning, and after expressing his surprise, asked him if he understood what he read. When his friend said that he thought he did, Thackeray answered, with rueful humor, 'I wish I could, but I have no head above my eyes.' He evidently had the feeling that there was something to be understood, and not that it was all 'rubbish'. It is this conviction which animates the clubs. Doubtless the peering commentators often see what is not to be seen, and Browning has himself accepted certain interpretations as probably correct. Hawthorne said that a painter is entitled to the credit of everything that anybody sees in his picture, and a poet is not likely to disclaim the diamond which is found in his mine.

The philosophic systems and spiritual meaning which the hierophants often discover are perhaps not unlike the cloud-capped towers and gorgeous palaces which rise and multiply and fill with stately splendor the sunset west. Yet 'The Easy Chair' holds with Hawthorne that that is legitimate. If you find something there, it is there, whether the poet meant to place it there or not. But we must not dogmatize and insist that others shall see it, and own that it only is the key to the poem.

In the literary taste and earnestness, the diligence of study and ingenuity of interpretation, which show themselves in this way amid all the material prosperity and development of the great West, there are interesting signs of the spirit which will enrich and elevate its life. That these signs appear so largely among the young women is most promising for the future. The tastes of the girls of to-day will affect the training of the children of to-morrow, of whom those girls will be the mothers. The Browning clubs will have their influence not less than the grain elevators. Literary and intellectual culture must begin and must long be imperfect. But what is called half-culture and superficial and smattering knowledge are the germination of the seed. It will be whole culture and fuller knowledge presently.

237. Andrew Lang, His Magic and Art

1888

From his article, 'Esoteric Browningism', *Forum* (November 1888), vi. 300–10.

Lang (1844–1912) was a man of letters with many interests; he wrote poetry, criticism, history, and delved into the origins of religious beliefs. He saw clearly that Browning's fame would rest upon poems of the kind that made up *Men and Women* and, only a decade later, he was able to write that 'the rude, audacious vigour of romance, passion, and adventure in Browning's *Men and Women* has already outlived the ponderous blank verse treatises of his later volumes'. ('Victorian Literature', *Good Words* [February 1897], xxxviii. 91–5.)

. . . It may not need all this quoting of passages and numbering of names to remind readers that Mr. Browning is something other than a scientific analyst of souls, using a jargon worse than scientific. It should be superfluous to repeat that he is as full of magic, of charm, of art; that he has raised and can raise as many phantoms, fair or terrible, as ever Faust beheld in the magic mirror. He has interpreted every one of our emotions from divine love to human friendship, from the despair of the soul to the depths of personal hatred. He has unravelled with delicate fingers the words of Andrea del Sarto, and has not disdained beauty, but has made

A common greyness silver everything.

He has piped to children, like his own Pied Piper, and they have followed him as willingly as they of Hamelin. All these poems, and scores of others, need no interpreter, no commentator; any boy of sixteen who cares for verse can read them as easily as he can read Longfellow.

This later generation is in danger of forgetting the real poet in the multitude of dissertations about poems which need explaining. It is for this reason that one has attempted, however weakly, to praise that in

Mr. Browning's work which is divine and imperishable. It is not that one undervalues *The Ring and the Book*, or *Balaustion's Adventure*, or *Pippa Passes*. But time, that sifts poets like wheat, will almost certainly treat much that Mr. Browning has written as time has treated the dark pieces of George Chapman or the *Cassandra* of Lycophron.[1] They will survive, indeed, but rather because a poet wrote them than because they are poetry. They can hardly survive, as Theocritus hoped one of his idyls would do, 'on the lips of all, and chiefly on those of the young.' There is, however, no reason why the central and perfect poems of Mr. Browning should not survive thus, in men's pockets, not only on their shelves; in men's hands, not only in scholar's libraries. But there is at present this danger, that young readers, just waking to poetry, may be lost in *Red Cotton Night-Cap Country*, and may emerge with difficulty, as from a Sleepy Hollow haunted by nightmares—may emerge and may never again choose to enter even that demesne which is peopled by *Men and Women*. In that event great would be their loss, nor less great if, by way of approving themselves clever and 'cultured,' they try to heat themselves into an enthusiasm for the poems commended by commentators, and for the riddles which are their despair and delight.

[1] Greek poet and grammarian of third century B.C. whose 'Cassandra'—a soliloquy in which Cassandra predicts the fall of Troy—is all that now remains of his work.

238. R. H. Hutton, Browning and Tennyson Contrasted

1889

From his unsigned article 'Browning and Tennyson', *Spectator* (21 December 1889), lxiii. 879–80.

The first part of Hutton's analysis presents the typical Victorian view of the two poets. But in the second part of this excerpt, Hutton notes some similarities his contemporaries often overlooked. For Hutton's opinion of *Parleyings*, see No. 230.

In some respects the two greatest imaginative poets of our day are striking contrasts. Browning is careless and impatient in execution; Tennyson careful and elaborate. Browning is rough and ungainly; Tennyson smooth and stately. Browning trots or gallops; Tennyson walks or canters. Browning almost gasps out his meaning, omitting half the articles and particles which weave speech into a flexible texture; Tennyson touches and retouches the form till it is no less perfect, or even more perfect, than the thought or emotion to be expressed, so that the artistic workmanship sometimes attracts even more attention than the imaginative substance on which it is expended. Again, Tennyson studies either beauty or grace or majesty of form in almost all his poems; Browning, we might almost say, studies the neglect of these qualities, or, if that be exaggeration, at least ignores them altogether, and hews away right and left, like a pioneer in a jungle, instead of shaping anxiously and lovingly as a sculptor shapes his marble. Tennyson treats words and all their associations with the utmost sympathy and reverence; Browning tumbles them about and rolls them over almost as a tempest does the rocks of an Alpine valley, sometimes producing very weird effects with them, but effects which have a great deal of the appearance of rough play about them, like the casts in some giant's game at bowls. Tennyson not unfrequently wears the graceful negligence of manner appropriate to one who is on easy terms with the Muses; Browning is apt to play them tricks, and indulge in familiarities with them which suggest that he does not revere them as Muses at all.

Yet, in spite of all these marked contrasts, there are points of resemblance which are due partly to the common interests of the social world in which both these poets have lived, partly to the intellectual tendencies of the time. Both are at heart idealists with a strong desire not to ignore the realities with which idealists must deal. Both are possessed by Christian convictions; both are eager students of the philosophy of faith. Both have made elaborate studies of ecclesiastical eccentricities,— Tennyson of St. Simeon Stylites; Browning of the Bishop who orders his tomb at St. Praxed's Church. Both have given the most anxious attention to provincial and vernacular peculiarities,—Tennyson in his two 'Northern Farmers', his 'Grandmother', and just now in his 'Owd Roä'; Browning in his Yorkshire Halbert and Hob, and his study of Bunyan's coarse converts, Ned Bratts and his wife. And both, with a very strong desire to master the religious attitude of a world far removed from our own,—Tennyson the mysticism of the age of chivalry, Browning the peculiarities of mediæval or modern superstition,—have been intensely modern; modern in their faith and in their sympathies, in their confidence that they are 'heirs of all the ages,' and that they stand on a summit of knowledge and experience higher than that of even the greatest of their predecessors.

ASOLANDO: FANCIES
AND FACTS

December 1889

Because *Asolando* was published on the day of Browning's death (12 December), the reviews inevitably took on an obituary tone, and the reviewers tended toward summary estimates.

239. A Typical Obituary Notice

1889

From an unsigned notice, *The Nation* (19 December 1889), xlix. 492–4.

When a great man full of years and honour passes from us, the memorial words of regret and sorrow are as often as not conventional. The more outspoken even of his admirers will say with truth: His work was done, he was tired of life, it was a happy release. But in the hearts of the many persons of all classes who knew Robert Browning there must awake at this moment a kindling regret which needs no words to fan it. Death has come between us and his spirit like a sudden cloud; and though we know that the radiance is behind it, we feel and see the darkness. It is no question now whether or no his mind had laid by its labour of love in this life, or whether greater work was in store. While he lived, his brain lived and burned; and his personality, had he never written another line, would, till however remote an end, have been a vivifying fact for all who had the privilege of seeing him face to face. And the spiritual effect of it had for some years gone on increasing, as though a new youth and a fresh outlook were growing into being through the visible fading of the flesh.

240 Joseph Jacobs, 'Mr. Robert Browning',
Athenæum

21 December 1889, pp. 858-60

In 1891, Jacobs reprinted this unsigned essay, with others on
George Eliot, Newman, and Arnold, in book-form. This empha-
sis upon the moral value of Browning's poetry was a staple of
Browningism.

No English poet has felt like Browning the pathos of the battle of life.
Yet keenly as he felt it, he did not despair nor bid the world despair.
'We bid ye be of good hope' was his message to the seeming failures in
life, a class of ever-growing importance in this self-conscious age. His
philosophy of life was eminently manly, and has brought cheer to many
a despairing soul. If we could condense it into a formula, the maxim
would run 'Aspiration is achievement'. Herein his philosophy approached closely one of the implicit assumptions of the wordly life.
The man of the world regards every experience as such as a gain, apart
from its moral implications. It is better to have sinned and lived than
never to have lived at all—never, that is, to have developed one's own
personality. Much of Browning's thought comes perilously near this,
and is only redeemed from it by his acute sense of the mordant poign-
ancy of the conscience-pang. On the whole, his influence is of the very
highest kind in this part of his work. It acts as a moral tonic to be brought
in contact with such a manly, cheery soul, that does not faintly trust the
larger hope, but is confidently sure that in aiming at the highest we are
doing the best for our best selves.

Nowhere is his influence higher in this regard than in his love poems,
the highest test of a poet's powers. The world is right in thinking that
the chief business of the poet is to express love and to teach how to love.
Browning's love poems are equally remarkable for their range and for
their intensity. Nowhere in English literature does this passion of love
burn higher or burn purer. The passion that pulsates through 'In a
Balcony' or 'In a Gondola' is as intense as anything in Heine, and yet it
is purged of all fleshly dross. Not by any sacrifice of body to spirit, nor

by any lapse into sickly sentimentalism, does Browning reach this result. The claims of the whole being, body and spirit, are admitted to the utmost, and as a consequence those of the former die away in the serener glow of the spiritual passion. As Browning regarding the struggle of life—the contest of soul with soul or against all souls—is eminently a man, so in his depicting of love—the union of soul with soul—he is pre-eminently the gentleman. Refinement is of the very soul of him, and that without, as so often happens, any loss of virile strength. Here more than anywhere we trace the influence of his marriage, that ideal union of two equally gifted souls which is unique in the world's history.

241. From an unsigned review, *The Saturday Review*

21 December 1889, pp. 711–12

This review and the next are typical of the reception given *Asolando*. Reviewers were uniformly surprised at the musicality, the vigour, and the lightness of these last lyrics—as students of Browning continue to be surprised today.

To those who watch, with a humorous and yet reverent sympathy, the turns of human life, it will be a strangely interesting task to note how Mr. Browning's swan-song of *Asolando* reverts to his better style. There is here so little as to be almost nothing of the small mannerisms which have gained him the plaudits of fools, so much as to be almost everything of the large manner which has gained him the admiration of wise men—and women. No volume of his for a whole quarter of a century has contained so many poems, and hardly any, except *Jocoseria*, has contained even one such poem, of the kind which we indicated here last week as his masterpiece. Here we have at least half a dozen such, any one of which would make the fortune of an ordinary book of verse. Such are 'Now', 'Humility', 'Summum Bonum', 'A Pearl, a Girl', 'Speculative', part of 'Bad Dreams', and not a few more. . . .

[Brief quotations from several poems have been omitted here.]

We must leave to readers 'Imperante Augusto natus est', 'Development' (an excellent morality), and two singularly beautiful poems—'Rephan' and 'Reverie'—in the most 'thoughtful' style of the author, but not in that style in which 'thoughtfulness' induces verbiage and mannerism. Indeed, the whole volume gives a very curious and delightful example of reversion late in life and work to the best characteristics of each. In hardly any one of his books—certainly in none for nearly a generation—has Mr. Browning put so many of his different qualities at his best as here.

Let us hope, in conclusion, that *Asolando* (*asolare*, to disport oneself in the sun, a neologism attributed to Cardinal Bembo) will soon be united to the rest of the author's works in an edition at once complete and compact. From the lowest point of view, it is certain that such an edition, parallel to that which now for more than ten years has been attainable with successive enlargements of Lord Tennyson's poems, would be successful—from the highest it is equally certain that it ought to be given.

242. Margaret Oliphant,
Blackwood's Edinburgh Magazine

January 1890, cxlvii. 131–51

From her unsigned feature, 'The Old Saloon'.

For Mrs. Oliphant in an earlier, less receptive, mood, see No. 182.

Mr Browning's little volume takes its name from a pleasant conceit, never absolutely recorded in literature, but handed down by fond tradition, which makes of the name, Asolo, of a certain village in the old Veneto, once famous, a verb, 'Asolare; to disport in the open air, amuse one's self at random.' It is accordingly *asolando* in the way of sport and rural pastoral pastime such as went on at that famous palace-hamlet, that our poet, one of the Italianissimi, loving his Venice as he had loved his Florence, and as the poets love, now presents himself before us. . . . It is not to be expected after this that Mr Browning will put many of the graver productions of his genius into this basket of dainties, among the soft songs of the love which is half a merry masquing, and verses that seem to swing with the swaying of the fine processions all linked together with chains of flowers. Here is one snatch of melody which might very well have been sung as the line wound in over the garden path and along the marble pavement, Bembo with a careful brow supervising every careless couple, as they went to pay their homage to the Queen—once of Cyprus, now of society and poetry and prettiness, and all the pageants which the old Venetians loved:

> What girl but, having gathered flowers,
> Stript the beds and spoilt the bowers,
> From the lapful light she carries
> Drops a careless bud?—nor tarries
> To regain the waif and stray:
> 'Store enough for home'—she'll say.
> So say I too: give your lover
> Heaps of loving—under, over,
> Whelm him—make the one the wealthy!

> Am I all so poor who—stealthy
> Work it was!—picked up what fell:
> Not the worst bud—who can tell?

Or here is another, where the masquing, and the ornate words, and the antiquated elaborate compliments are otherwise treated, and reduced to the truer and more wholesome level of honest life:

> 'So say the foolish!'   Say the foolish so, Love?
> 'Flower she is, my rose,'—or else 'My very swan is she'—
> Or perhaps 'Yon maid-moon, blessing earth below, Love,
>   That art thou!'—to them, belike: no such vain words from me.

> 'Hush, rose, blush! no balm like breath,' I chide it:
> 'Bend thy neck its best, swan,—hers the whiter curve!'
> Be the moon the moon: my Love I place beside it:
>   What is she?   Her human self,—no lower word will serve.

This is the true last word of genuine poetry: the poet pauses in the midst of all the conceits, and breaks the fantastic procession, and throws away the garlands to recognise true life and love and nature, the modest truth which is above all. It is needful to the very grace of the old pageant that there should be some one standing by to humour and indulge the revellers, yet point the better way. But next page he is rhyming again, *asolando*, about pearls and girls and blossoms and sunshine.

243. A Review of the *Complete Works*

1890

Unsigned review, *The London Quarterly Review* (January 1890), lxxiii. 205–25.

It is now five-and-fifty years since Robert Browning came before the world with his surprising youthful poem, *Paracelsus*; it is full fifty years since he put forth to his countrymen that rare poetic riddle which he called *Sordello*, and which remains yet an unsolved riddle for the multitude. To-day his publishers give us their Uniform Edition of his Complete Works, and show us in its sixteen compact volumes how productive have been all these long years, how full of a restless, fruitful energy; how little this poet lies open to the charge of having buried his golden talent in the earth. At least, it is not as a slothful servant that he can be condemned.

Nor, among the select company of his readers, will any be found to deny the splendour of the gift so liberally put to use for the world's service. It is not our own time that will show us a poet more royally equipped for his work. Alive to all the rich harmonies of form and colour in the poet's sphere of working, he has the word-painter's faculty of flashing on you what picture he will from the great gallery of his imagination. He has also, when he lists to use it patiently and with loving intensity of care and consciousness, the highly educated musical sensibility that can teach how to make verse tread with the airy foot of a dancer, swing lightly as a bird upon a bough, or move with the massive march of an army, the solemn sweep of a procession. More and better than even these, he has the quick-divining observation, the large intuitive sympathy that, looking under the human mask, discerns the truth about his fellows in their sorrow, their joy, even their guilt, and, comprehending much, scorns little; while a certain robust and sturdy common-sense, a saving salt of manliness, never allows this sympathetic tolerance to sicken into sentimentalism. The seeing eye, the hearing ear, the understanding heart, are his in sovereign measure, not less than the poet's special dower, 'the hate of hate, the scorn of scorn, the love of love.' To those friendly fortune has added a large and liberal culture, artistic as well as literary, comprehending alike classic lore and modern thought; and, to aid in the attaining of all needful accomplishment, there has been added to these greater things a wordly position so well assured that this poet may write and publish as seems him good, never needing either to sell great thoughts for bread, or to toil at uncongenial work because it brings the better price.

To one so excellently gifted, and so favoured by fortune, we look rightly for good and lasting work. Nor are we disappointed. Marvellous as are the mutations of earthly fame, large as are the poetic treasures which the world's weary memory is ever letting slip, there is much of Robert Browning which will hardly perish while men continue to speak the language in which he has written, much which the world should not and scarcely can let die. Yet, strange as it might seem, it is true that to a large majority of the English-reading public, including not a few gifted and accomplished persons, this kingly poet remains a name only, and for certain of them not even that, being actually known to some eager thinkers and readers solely through the parodist's sneer at him in the clever piece of mockery, where he figures as one who

> Loves to dock the smaller parts of speech,
> As men curtail the already curtailed cur—

the imitation being ridiculously good enough to prove effective in deterring from the study of the original.

Nor does the half-adoring enthusiasm of the poet's sworn admirers avail very greatly against the vague distaste of a public, much out of love with depth and difficulty in the works it reads for delight. The ardent devotees of Browning are too apt to speak in the style of the elect, to whom alone out of a wicked world it has been granted to penetrate into certain holy mysteries, which, nevertheless, they are willing to expound to the outside crowd, if they will humbly listen; but the wicked world resents their tone of superiority, and inclines to go on its way heedless of their lore.

That this should be so cannot but at times irritate some, themselves admirers of Browning, who are concerned that no good influence should be wasted, and wishful that as many as are worthy should share in the heritage of delight of which this true poet can make them free. For hardly is there a living writer to whose pages the understanding reader may turn with such a certainty of finding in many of them the keen and stimulating pleasure that arises from high and deep thoughts arrayed in splendid imagery, while his message for the world, when the world can understand it, is full often one well worthy to be heard.

To be angry, however, that the immediate circle of Browning's influence is but narrow, is idle enough. Indirectly that influence is widely diffused, filtering through many a receptive writer who has the art of re-imparting it to the average reader in such measure and in such guise as are fitting. This must content us perforce, since the master-singer has not cared to learn that humble art himself. Even the brief survey of his life-work that we are about to make will show us that he has in full measure *les défauts de ses qualités*, subtlety degenerating sometimes into obscurity, strength becoming mere ruggedness, and both tending to produce peculiarities of form and of diction the reverse of attractive.

There is nothing necessarily unpopular in the predominatingly impersonal character which Browning has chosen to confer on his poems —poems, to a very great extent, 'dramatic in principle'—as their writer has said 'so many utterances of so many imaginery persons, *not me*.' He has willed rather to project himself into the minds of others, and to express *their* thoughts, than to give language to his own; avoiding the error of Byron, most undramatic because least sympathetic of writers, whose personages, one and all, are mere hollow masks and brazen mouthpieces for sending forth to the world the magnified echoes of their creator's single soul, his special personal hopes and fears and despairs, loves and hates, his hates more particularly.

This Byron-method finds small favour with Browning, who refuses very definitely to take the world so deep into his confidence, who will not be lured into 'sonnet-writing about himself,' even by Shakspeare's example.

> With this same key
> Shakspeare unlocked his heart, once more?
> Did Shakspeare?   If so, the less Shakspeare he!

is his blunt answer to the plea that he, too, would so unfold himself, 'unlock his heart with a sonnet-key.' An earthquake, indeed, may shake your house, shiver it from top to bottom, leave it gaping so that the malign curiosity of the mob may explore all its domestic secrets; that you cannot help; but why throw your house open with your own hand? Such over-frankness our poet abjures, preferring to speak in parables and enforce his beliefs and convictions by life-like examples, not his own. And, certainly, if infinite variety in his list of *dramatis personæ* could defend him against overmuch self-revelation, that safety would be his. Here in his pageant you see moving the figures of not a few historic men and women, mingling with a cloud of fictitious personages, typical of many classes: Paracelsus, the charlatan of genius; Sordello, Dante's precursor, amid his Guelf and Ghilbellin contemporaries; Strafford, the great earl, and the master who betrayed him, and the men of the Long Parliament, greater than both; kings, bishops, popes; musician, painter, Dervish, spiritualist; Arab physician, Jewish rabbi, Christian martyr, and hero-king of Israel, womanhood, beautiful, forlorn, innocent, or guilty; manhood, noble, debased, sceptical, or believing; Caliban, half-human brute, exponent of the devil-worshipping tendency of the savage; Rabbi Ben Ezra, exemplifying the divinest aspiration of the Hebrew. Has not our poet acted well up to the saying of that Latin playwright who was also an African freedman—*Homo sum; humani nihil a me alienum puto?*[1]

But how has he succeeded in his chosen work? Many are the poems in which he has aimed deliberately—as in *Sordello*—at setting forth 'incidents in the development of a soul', considering, as he avows, that 'little else is worth study'. Therefore we find him bringing his mind to bear on the doings of men and women, trying to 'uncombine motive from motive', and to show what forces may be at work on the human spirit, determining belief, influencing conduct, moulding character, deciding whether this or that immortal soul shall rise heavenward or sink towards the abyss. Has he seen clearly and judged rightly in these matters?—and has he, led by a happy intuition, chosen always the best vehicle for his thought, that mode of expression which most certainly would impress other minds with his opinion, compel them to see and judge as he does? In endeavouring to deal with such questions, relating to the effort and achievement of a master-poet, it behoves us to walk modestly and warily.

Wishful, therefore, to avoid such oracular decisiveness of tone as might befit those inner-court worshippers, the illuminati of the Browning Society, and desirous above all to speak with the humility befitting mere outsiders, we yet do not fear to say that Browning has often succeeded magnificently in his difficult self-imposed task, while sometimes, so far as the mass of his readers is concerned, he has attained only an amazing failure. A failure it assuredly is, when the sacred *Vates*, the appointed messenger of Heaven's truth to men, is all but unintelligible to his hearers. The secret of this disparity in the poet's work is not to

[1] Terence is credited with saying 'I am a man, and nothing human can be alien to me.'

be found in the nature of the themes he has handled, in their varying degrees of grandeur or difficulty. Some of his most daring *tours de force* are just those which conquer admiration most thoroughly, which compel us to say, 'This is how it really was; this was the true meaning of the life; this was the innermost secret of the man's thought and action; thus the event must have appeared to such an observer; and thus, to such another one'.

244. Browning not Among the Supreme Poets

1890

From an unsigned review, *The Atlantic Monthly* (February 1890), lxv. 243–8.

This reviewer's concluding comment—that Browning and Tennyson represent a second stage of Romanticism—is rather perceptive for the times.

The prevalent opinion even now is that Browning, notwithstanding the rare intellectual power which enriches much of his inferior work, will suffer very seriously from his defective art. Nevertheless, he must rank as the most powerful realist in the representation of human life who has appeared in England since Shakespeare. He also possessed a lyrical gift which, in its best expression, entitles him to a place only below the first. He had, too, a peculiar felicity in rendering mysticism, in giving form to vague feeling, and in expressing the moods of indefinite suggestion that music awakens. He had an estate in the borderland of thought and feeling, on the confines of our knowledge, in the places that look to the promised land. This faculty yielded to him a few characteristic and original poems, in which there is a kind of exaltation at times, and at times of sorcery. The fascination in these, together with his dramatic realism and his lyrical movement, constitute his power as a poet, apart from all consideration of what he said. They do not place him among the few supreme poets of his country.

It was fortunate that long life was given him, so that he made the most of his gifts. The romantic movement thus found in him one of its most original and striking products, and gained by his strong sense of reality and his wide-ranging intellect. It completes in him and in Tennyson its second stage of development.

245. R. E. Prothero, General Characteristics

1890

Rowland Edward Prothero, 1st Baron Ernle, from his unsigned article 'On Robert Browning', *Quarterly Review* (April 1890), clxx. 476–502.

Prothero (1851–1937), who became editor of the *Quarterly* in 1894, later edited the *Letters and Journals of Lord Byron*.

If Browning's poetic force were allied with a corresponding feeling for poetic form,—if his poetic susceptibility were paired with an equal endowment of poetic sense,—he would have been beyond dispute the greatest poet England has possessed for many generations. Whether his work is classed as prose or poetry, it towers above the low level of ordinary literature. Those who have traversed the rocks which are confusedly hurled together like fragments of an earlier world, and climbed the rugged heights which sentinel the road, bring back glowing reports of an enchanted land. The wind blows hard in their teeth; the path is uphill all the way; but the summit is a shining table-land of ideal beauty, commanding a wide survey of human life, and breathing a bracing and invigorating atmosphere.

No poet has enjoyed more ardent admirers; no poet has had fewer casual acquaintances. Defects of manner and of form—so real that they cannot be explained away, so patent that they cannot be ignored—repel the advances of would-be readers. Yet these superficial obstacles have perhaps militated less against his popularity than his matter. And here the fault lies at least as much with the reader as with the poet. Browning's poetry is peculiarly needed by the present generation. It is a counter-irritant to that poison of subjectivity which impels poets to shut themselves up in the maze of their own personal experiences, and to humanize Nature because they cannot dramatise Man. When, day by day, originality grows more rare, when eccentricity masquerades as independence, when men's minds are more and more cast in uniform moulds, and when forty poets write like one, it is something that Browning reversed the conventional value of expression above substance, refused to turn the handle of a music-box, disdained the shower of similes which displayed the ingenious fancy of the pyrotechnic artist. His very ruggedness is a protest against that creamy smoothness which emasculates religion, enervates literature, and robs character of its virility. The poet is popular who expresses the sentiments of the age with the most graceful tenderness. But Browning never, or rarely, echoes the thoughts of others. He constrains them to think with him. His poetry cannot be read by the man who runs. It demands study; it cannot be skimmed. And here again he opposed the tendency of the day. Modern education and modern haste encourage snatchy habits of thought and reading. Our minds are built to resemble modern houses in which all is imitation and show, and in which stucco does duty for stone and veneer for oak. We resent continuous effort. We refuse pearls, if we ourselves have to dive for them.

Yet, in spite of these and other obstacles to popularity, the opinion is gaining ground that Browning is our greatest modern seer. It is a less debatable position to say that in bulk his work has never been surpassed, and that his seventeen volumes are crammed to congestion with condensed thought, imagination, suggestion, characterization, and dramatic situation. His themes are not more varied than his treatment. In both his versatility is phenomenal. He appeals to his readers by the catholicity of his poetic gifts, by intellectual strength, refinement, swiftness and sustained energy of thought, imaginative power, broad realistic humour, spiritual passion, the capacity to conceive, and express, the subtlest complexities of the human mind. He accepts and enjoys the world without losing sight of its unseen realities. He possesses a profound knowledge of human nature in all its infinite graduations; yet he confronts with steady courage the problems of life and destiny. He is a valiant soldier of humanity, chanting his *sursum corda* to the world, not in ecstatic hope but in calm conviction, indulging in no humanitarian extravagances, never lapsing into despondency or philosophical morbidity. He presents life to us as at once serious and joyous—a boon to be enjoyed, a means to be used. He explores its mazes, feeling where he cannot see. Keenly alive to the questions of doubt, he yet says his say on the side of faith with emphatic earnestness, and urges with unrivalled force the moral arguments for the working idea of Christianity. His spiritual influence has been as wide as it has also proved stimulating. . . .

In numerous cases no plea of dramatic propriety can be pleaded in defence of Browning's violations of the self-respect of art. But a distinction should be maintained between those defects which are meaningless, and those irregularities which serve a definite, if mistaken, purpose. No excuse can be urged for the former. The justification of his intentional breaches of the laws of poetic composition, like the defence of obscurities which arise from the complexity, rapidity, or dramatic presentation of his thought, depends upon considerations involved in the third group of charges.

Browning did not subordinate his intellectual powers to the purposes of his art. If he possessed the artistic conscience, he often suffered its supremacy to be usurped. He allowed the exercise of the intellect to become an independent object of interest, and gratified to excess, and out of reason, his casuistry, metaphysical subtlety, and analytical skill. The use of these powers gave freshness, breadth, originality, to his many-sided assertion of human individuality. Their abuse betrayed him into his cardinal defects. It undermined his moral sense, so that he is rather a religious, than a moral, poet. It lured him to select subjects in which failure was inevitable. Such compositions as 'Mr. Sludge the Medium' display intellectual gifts of the highest order; but no stretch of the term can class them as poetic. They are thought out in prose and then translated into verse. They miss the essence though they possess the form of poetry. They offer no scope for the transfusion of the intellect with feeling. Though they inspire admiration of the poet's cleverness, they produce no thrill of sympathy. The same preponderance of intellect over heart led Browning to ignore the difficulties, under which he himself worked, or which hindered others in pursuit of his meaning. Exulting in his power of tracing the devious workings of the human mind, he delighted in abnormal subjects, and lost in the pursuit of their complications his sense of the point where artistic sufficiency is attained. Not content to explore, he must also exhaust, the mysteries of human nature. Stimulated by the desire to be true to the personality which he sought to present, he assigned to his characters a mass of mental or verbal gabble and garbage without considering whether poetic artists are justified in such crudities. The same abuse of intellectual strength led him to forget that Art is essentially representative, not reflective. Instead of selecting the class of feelings or thoughts which most power-fully illustrated his subject, he dissipated his force by endeavouring to crowd into his lines the whole mass of impressions to which his keenly susceptible nature was alive.

It is an ungrateful task to dwell upon the faults which mar the work of one of the greatest minds of the century. His poetic gifts, though they were, in our opinion, unduly stunted by his speculative interests, were many and great. His satire was keen, but never cynical; his humour could touch the whole range from pathos to the pure grotesque; his irony could sting as well as smile. Seen at his best, passion, ardour, impulse, burn in his lines, and kindle into flame the pregnant reflections, acute comments, and concentrated wisdom which give substance to his verse. When the poetic fire has laid firm hold upon him, it becomes, from the mass on which it feeds, no mere crackling of the thorns, but a mighty conflagration radiating far and wide its vital warmth. His imaginative power transfigures his realism. His colour is broad and strong, his wealth of imagery copious; he scatters similes with the prodigality of one who thinks in images, and whose vocabulary is hieroglyphic. He had a power of observation at once wide and micro-scopical, an intense enjoyment of life combined with remarkable gifts of rich illustration and graphic presentment, dramatic qualities which in their own direction have never been rivalled, faculties of thought that were at once rapid, penetrating, and trenchant. But as the essence of his philosophical teaching is an insistence upon individuality, so the strongest impression left by his poetry is an abiding, everpresent sense of the robust, substantial, personality of the poet. There is a mind con-scious of its strength and rejoicing in the swiftness of its movement,—a temper full of courage, manly, sincere, and resolute,—a sympathy frank, impartial, comprehensive,—a tenderness which is passionate, yet tranquil in the repose of strength,—a speech direct, animated, forcible, coming straight from the man. The whole work leaves behind it the sense of health, reality, and greatness. Had he illuminated his book of life with more common traits of human character, had he chosen his examples from more ordinary types, or eschewed the dark nooks of nature and the desert places of the past for the broad frequented highways of life, he would have doubled and trebled his influence. He can never become a popular poet with the simple as well as the learned. His lines will not pass into household words, for his strength lies not in single stanzas but in totality of impression. Yet the value of his influence can never be destroyed. His hopefulness and spiritual energy were alike indomitable. His optimism was not facile. Without closing his eyes to the reality of evil, he still could say:

> God's in His heaven,
> All's right with the world.

246. Oscar Wilde on Browning

1890

From 'The True Function and Value of Criticism', *Nineteenth Century* (July 1890), xxviii. 123–47.
This passage, from a critique in the form of a Platonic dialogue, contains a fair number of the subtleties and paradoxes which mark most of Wilde's work.

The members of the Browning Society, like the theologians of the Broad Church Party, or the authors of Mr. Walter Scott's Great Writer's Series, seem to me to spend their time in trying to explain their divinity away. Where one had hoped that Browning was a mystic, they have sought to show that he was simply inarticulate. Where one had fancied that he had something to conceal, they have proved that he had but little to reveal. But I speak merely of his incoherent work. Taken as a whole, the man was great. He did not belong to the Olympians, and had all the incompleteness of the Titan. He did not survey, and it was but rarely that he could sing. His work is marred by struggle, violence, and effort, and he passed not from emotion to form, but from thought to chaos. Still, he was great. He has been called a thinker, and was certainly a man who was always thinking, and always thinking aloud;

but it was not thought that fascinated him, but rather the processes by which thought moves. It was the machine he loved, not what the machine makes. The method by which the fool arrives at his folly was so dear to him as the ultimate wisdom of the wise. So much, indeed, did the subtle mechanism of mind fascinate him that he despised language, or looked upon it as an incomplete instrument of expression. Rhyme, that exquisite echo which in the Muse's hollow hill creates and answers its own voice; rhyme, which in the hands of a real artist becomes not merely a material element of metrical beauty, but a spiritual element of thought and passion also, waking a new mood, it may be, or stirring a fresh train of ideas, or opening by mere sweetness and suggestion of sound some golden door at which the Imagination itself had knocked in vain; rhyme, which can turn man's utterance to the speech of gods; rhyme, the one chord we have added to the Greek lyre, became in Robert Browning's hands a grotesque, misshapen thing, which made him at times masquerade in poetry as a low comedian, and ride Pegasus too often with his tongue in his cheek. There are moments when he wounds us by monstrous music. Nay, if he can only get his music by breaking the strings of his lute, he breaks them, and they snap in discord, and no Athenian tettix, making melody from tremulous wings, lights on the ivory horn to make the movement perfect or the interval less harsh. Yet, he was great: and though he turned language into ignoble clay, he made from it men and women that live. He is the most Shakespearian creature since Shakespeare. If Shakespeare could sing with myriad lips, Browning could stammer through a thousand months. Even now, as I am speaking, and speaking not against him but for him, there glides through the room the pageant of his persons. There, creeps Fra Lippo Lippi with his cheeks still burning from some girl's hot kiss. There, stands dread Saul with the lordly male-sapphires gleaming in his turban. Mildred Tresham is there, and the Spanish monk, yellow with hatred, and Blougram, and the Rabbi Ben Ezra, and the Bishop of St. Praxed's. The spawn of Setebos gibbers in the corner, and Sebald, hearing Pippa pass by, looks on Ottima's haggard face, and loathes her and his own sin and himself. Pale as the white satin of his doublet, the melancholy king watches with dreamy treacherous eyes too loyal Strafford pass to his doom, and Andrea shudders as he hears the cousin's whistle in the garden, and bids his perfect wife go down. Yes, Browning was great. And as what will he be remembered? As a poet? Ah, not as a poet! He will be remembered as a writer of fiction, as the most supreme writer of fiction, it may be, that we have ever had. His sense of dramatic situation was unrivalled, and, if he could not answer his own problems, he could at least put problems forth. Considered from the point of view of a creator of character he ranks next to him who made Hamlet. Had he been articulate he might have sat beside him. The only man living who can touch the hem of his garment is George Meredith. Meredith is a prose-Browning, and so is Browning. He used poetry as a medium for writing in prose.

247. Henry Reeve, Tennyson and Browning as Artists

1890

From his unsigned article 'Tennyson and Browning', *Edinburgh Review* (October 1890), clxxii. 301–16.

Henry Reeve (1813–95) was the editor of *The Greville Memoirs*, from which Browning had derived the basic story for *The Inn Album*. The distinctions Reeve makes between Tennyson and Browning as stylists are fair, but the view is typically late-Victorian and would not meet with complete agreement among critics today.

In point of style and mastery of poetical language, Tennyson reached, by infinite labour, the very highest pitch of literary art. Nothing is careless, nothing out of place; and those hidden laws of prosody, which are felt more than they are known, rule the choice of every word and its position in every line. His earlier lyrics have a melodious tone that lingers on the ear like notes of music, and no modern poet has given to the language so many touching and graceful expressions which have passed unconsciously into the familiar speech of our people. The greatest test of a supreme poetical power in an English poet is the mastery of blank verse, which derives its strength and beauty from metrical structure without the aid of rhyme, and in this respect resembles the great measures of antiquity. To that art Shakespeare owes his most admirable passages, Milton his superlative grandeur, Wordsworth the long-drawn charm of his greatest works, not, however, unmingled with chasms and breaks of prosaic dulness. But no greater master of blank verse has ever used it than Alfred Tennyson. It flows in the *Idylls* with the even pace of a large stream—always full, never overflowing, clear, correct, and musical throughout.

It seems never to have occurred to Mr. Browning that there was any mystery or art in the matter. His lines run on in so many syllables as the fancy takes him, without a thought whether they scan at all. Prosody and grammar are, no doubt, very humble slaves to great poets, but they cannot be treated with absolute indifference. It would be easy to quote passages in some of his narratives which would, with here and there the addition of a preposition or an article, become at once in-different prose. They are broken and interspersed with a thousand metaphors, ellipses, and allusions, which distract the attention and des-troy the current of the work; but this entire failure of scientific skill is disguised, for the most part, by a rare ingenuity of rhyme. In rhyme nothing daunts him. There are rhymes for every imaginable word, not natural, not self-sought, but often grotesque and wild. The rhyme being found in some improbable place, carries off the poet to a new order of ideas, and leads, instead of following, the course of thought. The result is crude, vague, and diffuse; for, as all Tennyson's writings are marked by an intense concentration of thought, and convey within a very few lines—sometimes within a single line—all he wishes to say, Browning dilutes and inundates his subject with an incontinence of words, want-ing, sometimes, in symmetry and sense. The one makes a lasting impres-sion on the memory, and is quoted evermore; the other is read with a sort of amazed curiosity, which leaves no permanent mark upon the mind.

The tendency and the spirit of Tennyson's poetry is to ennoble every subject he touches. Most of those subjects were taken from English homely life; they are drawn from the heart of England in all its ranks, from the simplicity of 'Dora' and 'The Miller's Daughter', the sturdy independence of the 'Northern Farmer', the joy of a 'May Morning', the plaint of 'Locksley Hall', looking beyond the times—

> For I doubt not thro' the ages one increasing purpose runs,
> And the thoughts of men are widened with the process of the suns:—

up to the real language of afflicted love, torn by the early death of one we knew, and who lives in everlasting memory with Lycidas and Adonais. In these poems all is serene and pure. And when the poet aimed at greater things, he chose for his epic theme the visionary realm of British chivalry; he drew in Arthur the ideal knight 'who reverenced his conscience as his king', surrounded him with noble comrades, fought against all that was barbarous, vicious, and vile without and within the camp, and remained unspotted by the wiles of Vivien and the frailty of Guinevere. The spirit of duty and self-sacrifice, the spirit of honour and truth, breathe throughout these pages. The poet disdains to touch the vulgar, the guilty, the false. He breathes no vain complaints, he seeks to fling abroad the winged shafts of truth, for, to use his own language—

> The poet in a golden clime was born,
>   With golden stars above,
> Dowered with the hate of hate, the scorn of scorn,
>   The love of love.

Not such was the influence of Italy on Mr. Browning and on his works. His was not the Italy of the fourteenth century, when the great luminaries of faith and philosophy rose on the horizon; not the Italy of the magnificent court of Lorenzo, surrounded by the splendour of renovated art; nor the Italy of Tasso and Ariosto, with the passion and chivalry of a gallant age. Unhappily it was the Italy of the seventeenth century, when the land had sunk in hideous profligacy and corruption to the lowest depths of crime, and when the annals of the public tribunals record a series of abominable examples of treachery, impurity, and guilt, unparalleled in any other country. . . .

To sum up these few remarks on two men who have interested the present century, and will interest posterity, it may be said that the poetry of Tennyson is essentially ideal; it aspires to the glory of a pure and noble life, somewhat above the range of ordinary mortality, and it contains not a line or a personage animated by any low or guilty passion. Even the love passages of Queen Guinevere and Sir Lancelot are faintly touched upon and left to the imagination of the reader, though they form the dark background of the Arthurian romance. Browning, on the other hand, is above all things analytical and a realist; he seizes and depicts details with photographic minuteness, and, like the modern school of French novelists, he recoils from no scene of depravity and crime; and, even in his language, he descends to eccentricity and sometimes to doggerel. In the one, all is sustained at the highest pitch of thought and feeling; in the other, the poet ranges from the lofty mysteries of philosophy, in which he loses himself and his reader, to the vulgar familiarity of common life, and to a still lower level. The reputation of Mr. Browning would stand far higher if a considerable portion of his random verses had never been written, and if it rested on a few of his highly finished works, into which he undoubtedly threw a large amount of power and feeling. His own careless facility was his worst enemy. Of Lord Tennyson we scarcely know a line that could be abandoned without regret.

A volume might be written on the fallacies of critics, to show how often they have misjudged their contemporaries and misconceived the future fate of authors. There are fashions in poetry, as in the sister arts, and it is rash to predict what may be the taste of future generations. Few, indeed, are the poets who have reached that inaccessible height of fame, from which they look down, changeless on the changes of the world. In our time the lustre of Scott, Byron, and Moore has considerably waned; the influence and admiration of Wordsworth, Coleridge, Keats, and Shelley have increased. Lord Tennyson and Mr. Browning have been exposed to the rare test of the criticism of three generations in their lifetime, and they have gained by it, year by year, a higher position. No one has yet appeared to rival or contest their fame. But it is premature to speculate on the future. The qualities which are most essential to the performance of poetic fame are, first, the perfection of form, for without beauty and grace of expression no poet can live; and, secondly, the power of expressing, in words that strike their mark, sentiments which are not ephemeral but perennial. The works of Homer, Virgil, Dante, and Shakespeare are immortal, because, although they speak of ages and races long gone by, they utter, in language that does not pass away, the common sentiments of mankind. It is scarcely a paradox to say that the more closely a poet touches his own generation, the less likely he is to command the sympathy of future ages. If there be any truth in these remarks, we are led to the conclusion that Lord Tennyson, from the exquisite finish and melody of his style, and from the breadth and elevation of his thoughts, not only stands upon a far higher pinnacle than Mr. Browning ever reached, but also will take a more permanent place hereafter amongst the greatest of English poets.

248. Henry James, 'Browning in Westminster Abbey'

1891

From *The Speaker* (4 January 1891), pp. 11–12.

This summary estimate of Browning by a sensitive reader who was himself a great writer is important enough to be given in its entirety. For an earlier opinion of Henry James, see No. 191.

The lovers of a great poet are the people in the world who are most to be forgiven a little wanton fancy about him, for they have before them, in his genius and work, an irresistible example of the application of the imaginative method to a thousand subjects. Certainly, therefore, there are many confirmed admirers of Robert Browning to whom it will not have failed to occur that the consignment of his ashes to the great temple of fame of the English race was exactly one of those occasions in which his own analytic spirit would have rejoiced and his irrepressible faculty for looking at human events in all sorts of slanting coloured lights have found a signal opportunity. If he had been taken with it as a subject, if it had moved him to the confused yet comprehensive utterance of which he was the great professor, we can immediately guess at some of the sparks he would have scraped from it, guess how splendidly, in the case, the pictorial sense would have intertwined itself with the metaphysical. For such an occasion would have lacked, for the author of *The Ring and the Book*, none of the complexity and convertibility that were dear to him. Passion and ingenuity, irony and solemnity, the impressive and the unexpected, would each have forced their way through; in a word the author would have been sure to take the special, circumstantial view (the inveterate mark of all his speculation) even of so foregone a conclusion as that England should pay her greatest honour to one of her greatest poets. At any rate, as they stood in the Abbey on Tuesday last those of his admirers and mourners who were disposed to profit by his warrant for inquiring curiously, may well have let their fancy range, with its muffled step, in the direction which *his* fancy would probably not have shrunk from following, even perhaps to the dim corners where humour and the whimsical lurk. Only, we hasten to add, it would have taken Robert Browning himself to render the multi-fold impression.

One part of it on such an occasion is of course irresistible—the sense that these honours are the greatest that a generous nation has to confer and that the emotion that accompanies them is one of the high moments of a nation's life. The attitude of the public, of the multitude, at such hours, is a great expansion, a great openness to ideas of aspiration and achievement; the pride of possession and of bestowal, especially in the case of a career so complete as Mr. Browning's, is so present as to make regret a minor matter. We possess a great man most when we begin to look at him through the glass plate of death; and it is a simple truth, though containing an apparent contradiction, that the Abbey never strikes us so benignantly as when we have a valued voice to commit to silence there. For the silence is articulate after all, and in worthy instances the preservation great. It is the other side of the question that would pull most the strings of irresponsible reflection—all those conceivable postulates and hypotheses of the poetic and satiric mind to which we owe the picture of how the Bishop ordered his tomb in St. Praxed's. Macaulay's 'temple of silence and reconciliation'—and none the less perhaps because he himself is now a presence there—strikes us, as we stand in it, not only as local but as social—a sort of corporate company; so thick, under its high arches, its dim transepts and chapels, is the population of its historic names and figures. They are a company in possession, with a high standard of distinction, of immortality, as it were; for there is something serenely inexpugnable even in the position of the interlopers. As they look out, in the rich dusk, from the cold eyes of statues and the careful identity of tablets, they seem, with their converging faces, to scrutinise decorously the claims of each new recumbent glory, to ask each other how he is to be judged as an accession. How difficult to banish the idea that Robert Browning would have enjoyed prefiguring and disintegrating the mystifications, the reservations, even perhaps the slight buzz of scandal in the Poets' Corner, to which his own obsequies might give rise! Would not his great relish, in so characteristic an interview with his crucible, have been his perception of the bewildering modernness, to much of the society, of the new candidate for a niche? That is the interest and the fascination, from what may be termed the inside point of view, of Mr. Browning's having received, in this direction of becoming a classic, the only official assistance that is ever conferred upon English writers.

It is as classics on one ground and another—some members of it perhaps on that of not being anything else—that the numerous assembly in the Abbey holds together, and it is as a tremendous and incomparable modern that the author of *Men and Women* takes his place in it. He introduces to his predecessors a kind of contemporary individualism which surely for many a year they had not been reminded of with any such force. The tradition of the poetic character as something high, detached and simple, which may be assumed to have prevailed among them for a good while, is one that Browning has broken at every turn; so that we can imagine his new associates to stand about him, till they have got used to him, with rather a sense of failing measures. A good many oddities and a good many great writers have been entombed in the Abbey; but none of the odd ones have been so great and none of the great ones so odd. There are plenty of poets whose right to the title may be contested, but there is no poetic head of equal power—crowned and recrowned by almost importunate hands—from which so many people would withhold the distinctive wreath. All this will give the marble phantoms at the base of the great pillars and the definite personalities of the honorary slabs something to puzzle out until, by the quick operation of time, the mere fact of his lying there among the classified and protected makes even Robert Browning lose a portion of the bristling surface of his actuality.

For the rest, judging from the outside and with his contemporaries, we of the public can only feel that his very modernness—by which we mean the all-touching, all-trying spirit of his work, permeated with accumulations and playing with knowledge—achieves a kind of conquest, or at least of extension, of the rigid pale. We cannot enter here upon any account either of that or of any other element of his genius, though surely no literary figure of our day seems to sit more unconsciously for the painter. The very imperfections of this original are fascinating, for they never present themselves as weaknesses—they are boldness and overgrowths, rich roughnesses and humours—and the patient critic need not despair of digging to the primary soil from which so many disparities and contradictions spring. He may finally even put his finger on some explanation of the great mystery, the imperfect conquest of the poetic form by a genius in which the poetic passion had such volume and range. He may successfully say how it was that a poet without a lyre—for that is practically Browning's deficiency: he had the scroll, but not often the sounding strings—was nevertheless, in his best hours, wonderfully rich in the magic of his art, a magnificent master of poetic emotion. He will justify on behalf of a multitude of devotees the great position assigned to a writer of verse of which the nature or the fortune has been (in proportion to its value and quantity) to be treated rarely as quotable. He will do all this and a great deal more beside; but we need not wait for it to feel that something of our latest sympathies, our latest and most restless selves, passed the other day into the high part—the show-part, to speak vulgarly—of our literature. To speak of Mr. Browning only as he was in the last twenty years of his life, how quick such an imagination as his would have been to recognise all the latent or mystical suitabilities that, in the last resort, might link to the great Valhalla by the Thames a figure that had become so conspicuously a figure of London! He had grown to be intimately and inveterately of the London world; he was so familiar and recurrent, so responsive to all its solicitations, that, given the endless incarnations he stands for to-day, he would have been missed from the congregation of worthies whose memorials are the special pride of the Londoner. Just as his great sign to those who knew him was that he was a force of health, of temperament, of tone, so what he takes into the Abbey is an immense expression of life—of life rendered with large liberty and free experiment, with an unprejudiced intellectual eagerness to put himself in other people's place, to participate in complications and consequences—a restlessness of psychological research that might well alarm any pale company for their formal orthodoxies.

But the illustrious whom he rejoins may be reassured, as they will not fail to discover: in so far as they are representative it will clear itself up that, in spite of a surface unsuggestive of marble and a reckless individualism of form, he is quite as representative as any of them. For the great value of Browning is that at bottom, in all the deep spiritual and human essentials, he is unmistakably in the great tradition—is, with all his Italianisms and cosmopolitanisms, all his victimisation by societies organised to talk about him, a magnificent example of the best and least dilettantish English spirit. That constitutes indeed the main chance for his eventual critic, who will have to solve the refreshing problem of how, if subtleties be not what the English spirit most delights in, the author of, for instance, *Any Wife to any Husband* made them his perpetual pasture and yet remained typically of his race. He was indeed a wonderful mixture of the universal and the alembicated. But he played with the curious and the special, they never submerged him, and it was a sign of his robustness that he could play to the end. His voice sounds loudest, and also clearest, for the things that, as a race, we like best—the fascination of faith, the acceptance of life, the respect for its mysteries, the endurance of its charges, the vitality of the will, the validity of character, the beauty of action, the seriousness, above all, of the great human passion. If Browning had spoken for us in no other way he ought to have been made sure of, tamed and chained as a classic, on account of the extraordinary beauty of his treatment of the special relation between man and woman. It is a complete and splendid picture of the matter, which somehow places it at the same time in the region of conduct and responsibility. But when we talk of Robert Browning's speaking 'for us' we go to the end of our privilege, we say all. With a sense of security, perhaps even a certain complacency, we leave our sophisticated modern conscience, and perhaps even our heterogeneous modern vocabulary, in his charge among the illustrious. There will possibly be moments in which these things will seem to us to have widened the allowance, made the high abode more comfortable for some of those who are yet to enter it.

1812   May 7, born at Camberwell, suburb of London, to Robert and Sara Wiedemann Browning.

1828   Attended University of London for a short while.

1833   Published *Pauline*.

1835   Published *Paracelsus*.

1837   *Strafford*, first of Browning's dramas, acted.

1838   Travelled to Italy for research on *Sordello*.

1840   Published *Sordello*.

1841–6 Published *Pippa Passes*, first of *Bells and Pomegranates*, a series to include *King Victor and King Charles* (1842), *Dramatic Lyrics* (1843), *The Return of the Druses* (1843), *A Blot in the 'Scutcheon* (1843), *Colombe's Birthday* (1844), *Dramatic Romances and Lyrics* (1845), *Luria* (1846), and *A Soul's Tragedy* (1846).

1846   Married Elizabeth Barrett.

1846–61 Resided in Italy, with occasional visits to England and France.

1848   Robert W. B. Browning ('Pen'), the poet's only child, born.

1850   Published *Christmas-Eve and Easter-Day*.

1855   Published *Men and Women*.

1861   Death of Mrs. Browning; Browning returned to live in England.

1864   Published *Dramatis Personae*.

1867   Received honorary M.A. from Oxford.

1868–9 Published *The Ring and the Book*.

1872   Published *Fifine at the Fair*.

1876   Published *Pacchiarotto*.

1879   Published *Dramatic Idyls, First Series*.

1880   Published *Dramatic Idyls, Second Series*.

1881   Browning Society established in London.

1883   Published *Jocoseria*.

1884   Published *Ferishtah's Fancies*.

1889   Published *Asolando*; died 12 December while visiting his son in Venice; buried 31 December in Poet's Corner, Westminster Abbey.

The favour of the reading public in any era is a fickle thing, given here, withdrawn there, for reasons which the literary historian often finds incomprehensible. Even so, the student of Browning and his poetry must find it especially difficult to believe that, in terms of printing orders and sales, Browning was relatively a failure.[1] Exact figures are not always available, but it seems certain that no original English edition of any of Browning's volumes before *The Ring and the Book* exceeded 2,000 copies. The early titles—from *Pauline* through *Bells and Pomegranates*—were probably printed in editions of 500, and even these did not move well. For example, of the 500 copies of *Sordello* printed in 1840, 257 still remained in the publisher's hands in 1855. Until *Dramatis Personae*, of which 2,000 copies were printed in 1864 by Chapman and Hall, no book of Browning's had achieved even a second edition. Copies of *Men and Women* (1855), containing Browning's best poems, were still available from the publisher in the late 1860s.

With *The Ring and the Book* (1869) matters improved somewhat. 3,000 copies of the first two volumes, and 2,000 of the last two, were originally printed, and by 1872 a second edition was needed. After this point, most of Browning's poems were first issued in printings of 2,500, a number—but not all—of these later titles going into second or third editions. Browning's most successful book, *Ferishtah's Fancies*, reached a third edition within a year of its publication in 1884 (probably, as Browning assumed, because of the enthusiasm of the Browning Society), but these printings probably totalled fewer than 7,500 copies.

When one compares these figures with those compiled for Browning's contemporaries—Mrs. Browning and Tennyson, for instance—one wonders at Browning's generally maintained equanimity. Elizabeth Barrett Browning's verse-novel, *Aurora Leigh* (1857), sold out within two weeks, and by mid-1860 had reached a fifth edition. Tennyson's *In Memoriam* (1850) sold 25,000 copies within eighteen months;

---

[1] For much of the following information I have drawn upon a number of helpful sources, especially Louise Greer's *Browning and America*, Richard D. Altick's *The English Common Reader: A Social History of the Mass Reading Public, 1800–1900*, and the Broughton *Bibliography*.

his most popular poem, *Enoch Arden*, had a first edition of 60,000, of which 40,000 copies were sold within a few weeks. Longfellow's poems sold more than a million copies in nineteenth-century England. Finally, when one contemplates the fact that Martin Tupper's *Proverbial Philosophy* reached a 50th edition, and that John Keble's *The Christian Year* sold more than a third of a million copies from the day of its publication in 1827 to the expiration of its copyright in 1873, one can only be appalled at Browning's fate.

In America, ironically, Browning's situation was better. In the early 1840s, the group centering around Ralph Waldo Emerson and Margaret Fuller was acquainted with Browning through various of the *Bells and Pomegranates* series, and in 1849 the firm of Ticknor, Reed, and Fields printed an unauthorized edition of Browning's *Poems*. In 1855, Fields made the then-rare and generous step of offering Browning £60 for the right to print *Men and Women* (a gesture for which Browning was grateful), and from that time on the firm became the authorized American publishers of Browning's poems. The American printings were larger, on the whole, than the British ones, and sales were consistently higher, until the publication of *Balaustion's Adventure* in 1871. After that point, while Browning's popularity at home rose, his American audience declined. Considering the after-history of Browning criticism, it is probable that modern readers share the taste of the nineteenth-century Americans who prized what Browning wrote before 1870 over what he wrote thereafter.

In France, the case was different. The number of French readers of English poetry was not large, and men like Browning's friend Milsand were a distinct minority. As early as 1840 readers of *Revue des deux mondes* were made aware of Browning (through a brief mention of *Paracelsus*), and in 1855 Elizabeth wrote to her sister Henrietta that 'They are making translations of nearly half of them [the poems in *Men and Women*] for the *Revue des deux mondes*'; but, as far as can be determined, no edition of his poems in French was published during Browning's lifetime. The situation in Germany was no better, and Europeans therefore had to read their Browning 'in the original', through the English editions which made their way across the channel and, after 1872, in the selections published in the Tauchnitz series at Leipzig.

Select Bibliography

ARMSTRONG, A. J., 'A Bibliography of Foreign Browniana', *Baylor Bulletin* (1933), xxxvi. 97–187.

BROUGHTON, L. N., C. S. NORTHUP, and ROBERT PEARSALL, *Robert Browning: A Bibliography, 1830–1950*. Ithaca, New York: Cornell University Press, 1953. The best of Browning bibliographies, with bibliographical descriptions, useful annotation, and excerpts from some reviews.

CRAMER, M. B., 'Browning's Friendships and Fame before Marriage (1833–46)', *PMLA* (1940), lv. 207–30.

—— 'Browning's Literary Reputation at Oxford, 1855–1859', *PMLA* (1942), lvii. 232–40.

—— 'What Browning's Literary Reputation Owed to the Pre-Raphaelites, 1847–1856', *English Literary History* (1941), viii. 305–21.

DREW, PHILIP (ed.), *Robert Browning: A Collection of Critical Essays*. London: Methuen and Co., 1966.

FORSTER, META, and W. M. ZAPPE, *Robert Browning Bibliographie*. Halle: Max Niemeyer Verlag, 1939.

GREER, LOUISE, *Browning and America*. Chapel Hill: University of North Carolina Press, 1952. The best study of the growth of Browning's reputation in America.

LITZINGER, BOYD, *Time's Revenges: Browning's Reputation as a Thinker, 1889–1962*. Knoxville: University of Tennessee Press, 1963.

—— and K. L. Knickerbocker (eds.), *The Browning Critics*. Lexington: University of Kentucky Press, 1965. Contains a supplement to the Broughton bibliography, an unannotated listing of articles and books published between 1951 and 1963.

LOUNSBURY, T. R., *The Early Literary Career of Robert Browning*. New York: Charles Scribner's Sons, 1911.

MCELDERRY, B. R., Jr., 'Browning and the Victorian Public, 1868–69', *Research Studies of the State College of Washington* (1937), v. 193–203.

PHELPS, W. L., 'Browning in France', *Modern Language Notes* (January 1916), xxxi. 24–32.

—— 'Browning in Germany', *Modern Language Notes* (January 1913), xxviii. 10–14.

Select Index

Heraud, J., 48
Hickey, Emily, 24
Hogarth, William, 208
Holmes, Wendell, 260
Home, D. D., 201
Homer, 372
Hood, E. P., 209, 228, 284
Hood, Thomas, 159n.
Hopkins, Gerard Manley, 472
Horne, Richard Hengist, 9, 67, 91, 144n.
Houghton, Esther Rhoades, 185
Houghton, Walter E. 185, 337
Howells, William, 381
Huddart, Miss, 131
Hugo, Victor, 211, 333, 371
Hunt, Leigh, 2, 4, 7, 14, 43, 129
Hutton, Richard Holt, 477, 494, 507
Huxley, Professor, 343, 469

Ingoldsby, Thomas, see Barham, Richard Harris, 159n.
Innocent XII, Pope, 325

Jacobs, Joseph, 510
James, Henry, 415, 530
Jameson, Mrs, 11
Jeffrey, Francis, 230, 266, 267
Jerrold, Douglas, 6, 194, 210
Jones, Henry, 27, 427
Jonson, Benjamin, 472
Jowett, Benjamin, 18, 399

Kant, Immanuel, 268, 280
Kean, Charles, 8
Keats, John, 1, 68, 217, 280, 287, 311, 441, 469, 491, 529
Kelsall, Thomas, 55
Kenyon, John, 8
Kingsley, Charles, 146
Kirkman, J., 473
Knowles, James Sheridan, 91n, 240

Lairesse, Gerard de, 495, 496

Landor, Walter Savage, 4, 7, 9, 17, 58n., 108, 153, 217, 312n.
Lang, Andrew, 505
Lang, Cecil Y., 214, 222
Lanier, Sydney, 338
Lathrop, George Parsons, 483
Lechy, James, 24
Leighton, Frederick, 336n., 386
Lewes, George Henry, 119
Lippincott, Sara Jane Clarke, 148
Litzinger, Boyd, 185, 427
Longfellow, Henry Wadsworth, 204, 207, 503
Lowell, James Russell, 123
Lyell, Sir Charles, 19
Lytton, Robert, 17

McAleer, Edward C., 386
Macaulay, Lord, 207, 349, 502, 531
McCarthy, Justin, 467
McNicoll, T., 190
Macready, William Charles, 4, 8, 41, 50, 52, 53, 56, 130, 133, 240, 266
Maginn, William, 38
Mandeville, Bernard de, 495, 496
Marston, John Westland, 91n.
Martin, Theodore, 52n.
Martineau, Harriet, 4, 6
Marx, Eleanor, 24
Marzials, F. T., 211
Massey, Gerald, 270
Masson, David, 178, 183
Maurice, F. D., 428n.
Meredith, George, 475, 526
Merivale, Herman, 58
Milton, John, 178, 206, 209, 265, 286, 311, 346, 431, 469, 527
Millais, John Everett, 226n., 227
Mill, James, 344, 469
Mill, John Stuart, 3, 37, 349
Milman, 240
Milsand, Joseph, 2, 12, 13, 14, 343
Mims, Edwin, 338
Mitchell, Donald, 194

II INDEX OF POEMS

III INDEX OF PERIODICALS

IV CHARACTERISTICS OF BROWNING AND ASPECTS OF HIS CAREER